Mexican American Literature
A Portable Anthology

Edited by

DAGOBERTO GILB

CentroVictoria: Center for Mexican American Literature and Culture
University of Houston-Victoria

RICARDO ANGEL GILB

bedford/st.martin's
Macmillan Learning
Boston | New York

For Bedford/St. Martin's

Vice President, Editorial, Macmillan Higher Education
 Humanities: Edwin Hill
Editorial Director, English and Music: Karen S. Henry
Executive Editors: Ellen Thibault and Vivian Garcia
Editorial Assistant: Eliza Kritz
Senior Production Editor: Rosemary Jaffe
Senior Production Supervisor: Lisa McDowell
Marketing Manager: Joy Fisher Williams
Copy Editor: Steven Patterson
Director of Rights and Permissions: Hilary Newman
Senior Art Director: Anna Palchik
Text Design: Janis Owens
Cover Design: John Callahan
Cover Art: © Patssi Valdez
Composition: Jouve
Printing and Binding: Edwards Brothers Malloy, Inc.

Manufactured in the United States of America.

0   9   8   7   6   5

f   e   d   c   b   a

For information, write: Bedford/St. Martin's, 75 Arlington Street,
Boston, MA 02116   (617-399-4000)

ISBN 978-1-319-02108-5

Acknowledgments

Text acknowledgments and copyrights appear at the back of the book on pages 501–4, which
constitute an extension of the copyright page. Art acknowledgments and copyrights appear on
the same page as the art selections they cover. It is a violation of the law to reproduce these
selections by any means whatsoever without the written permission of the copyright holder.

About the Authors

Dagoberto Gilb is the author of *Before the End, After the Beginning, The Flowers, Woodcuts of Women, Gritos, The Last Known Residence of Mickey Acuña*, and *The Magic of Blood*. He also edited the canonical *Hecho en Tejas: An Anthology of Texas Mexican Literature*. He was a union, high-rise carpenter for over a decade. His fiction and nonfiction have appeared in a range of magazines regional and national, including *The New Yorker* and *Harper's*, and anthologies such as *The Best American Essays* and *The O. Henry Prize Stories*, and are reprinted widely. Among his honors are a Guggenheim Fellowship and the PEN/Hemingway Award, and he has been a finalist for both the PEN/Faulkner and National Book Critics Circle Awards. Gilb makes his home in Austin, and he is the executive director of CentroVictoria, a center for Mexican American literature and culture at the University of Houston-Victoria.

Ricardo Angel Gilb grew up in El Paso, Texas, and graduated from Stanford University. His writing has appeared in *The Texas Observer* and *The San Francisco Chronicle*. His graduate work is in American history and culture at the University of Rochester.

Contents

Introduction

If you're from Texas, or the American Southwest for that matter, and a fan of its music, your ears surely perked up when the popular National Public Radio program *Fresh Air* focused an episode on the accordion. Many would say that the "squeeze box" is the region's sound and, thus, its most original contribution to America's musical heritage. Yet that's not what *Fresh Air*'s host had heard or knew anything about. Instead, she'd thought the instrument was about as exciting as the 1950s TV show with Lawrence Welk—which was for an already dated, slow waltz crowd in the years it was being produced. She considered accordions, therefore, corny and annoying, valuable only, maybe, for bar mitzvahs. But times changed, her ears were re-tuned, and with her show's guest, we were to learn that the accordion was a surprisingly not dull instrument, loved in Cajun, avant-garde, folk, indie pop, even something called klezmer, and that its sound's reach was not just Eastern Europe, but Argentina, Madagascar, and especially in a new French Musette "explosion."

Out in the boonies of America's West, where these national shows are well-heard, there lives a loud, boisterous tradition of music that dates from the turn of the last century that goes by the name "conjunto." It is true that it belongs to a native people of the West, a people whose history can be traced back at least two centuries to what is American soil—born and raised within the geographical and historical boundaries of the United States—and this music, which at its big stage center is the accordion, has been its magnetic draw. Not only in the legendary sound of South Texas's Narciso Martínez, or San Antonio's don Santiago Jiménez, but especially through his two sons, Santiago Jr. and Leonardo, better known as "skinny": Flaco Jiménez's fame, in particular, is so grand and wide that in 2015 he received a Lifetime Achievement Grammy Award for his accordion virtuosity and preeminence. And it was for the Mexican American music—not South American, African, or European—that didn't get a mention on *Fresh Air*'s one-hour episode.

Really there is nothing surprising or new about most of the country being unaware of the culture and community of MexAmerica. On the other hand, it is such a strange form of ignorance—let me hyphenate to adjust the connotation, make it *ignore-ance*—that one might want to call it utterly fascinating in that unique quality. It requires omitting consciousness that so much of the western landmass of the continental United States has rivers, valleys, mountain ranges, states, cities, streets,

1

and people with Spanish-language names. Over the years (and by years I mean at least fifty) historians and scholars are inclined to attribute that unawareness to an "invisibility" of the community. But the implication of this becomes that it must be something of a quaint, natural character inside the MexAm people, and not the effect of poverty or consequence of a lack of political power. I'd suggest that it's more a visual degeneration in the center of the dominant culture's eyes. No faces, only hands serving enchilada plates and then busing away what's left of the spicy yum yum. Beds are made after a fun vacation day, floors swept and waxed for the bright, bustling morning in the office, lawns mowed and edged, healthy veggies simply appear in the grocery store: people are not seen, neighborhoods go unknown, songs unheard, deaths not mourned . . . no cries of birth, sighs of first love, screams of sports joy; no bandages for knees, catechisms for church, homework for teacher, pink socks or baseballs or first cars or skateboards or bad boyfriends or off to war or diplomas or retirement dinners or college or family potlucks or buelita turned 99. And though I believe most of the ignorance about MexAms is not conscious or willful, it is equally true that enough is, be it forced by racist politicians in Arizona or an ongoing blow of American history that began with President James K. Polk's want of the land by any means necessary. Even now, too many media stories that do attach are about immigration from the border, inferring that the entire community is recent and, worse, invasive—which, ironically, would be more appropriately descriptive of the Anglo migration from the South in Texas and the Midwest in California. More ironic—bizarre?—is how much it loves, besides the food, everything about the region's Mexican culture, art, and architecture, yet is shocked that these "other" people live here. "Invisible" is not the best word, that is certain. The culture is everywhere, is highly accepted, as mainstream American as the taco has become. But just as the Spanish rejected the corn tortilla of the conquered *indios*, the essence of the MexAm culture is regarded as too "lesser" to be taken seriously.

Accustomed as its own nation is to treating Mexican Americans as negligible or dismissible, times are changing as demographics do. It is said that this century will be about the power of the Latino. Latino? Take away the 66 percent of this population, the MexAm proportion, that one so hidden away in its western homeland, and what national power then? With the other third divided into several single percentage groups, MexAms ought to receive a landslide of attention. Yet, already and again, the raw facts haven't created any gain, let alone advantage. Money and political pull are on the East Coast, and the national media's stories are about those who are there; Puerto Ricans, Cubans, and Dominicans are more the voice of The Latino, following the last century's big city paradigm of Italian, Irish, and Jewish immigrants. MexAms don't fly from New York to Mexico City, Los Angeles to Chihuahua. Instead, they are home in a poor city like El Paso or Ysleta or Eagle Pass, McAllen, San Antonio, Santa Ana, Riverside, Fresno, Chula Vista, Tucson, Nogales, Albuquerque, Denver, or Boyle Heights, El Monte, La Puente, Lynwood, South Gate. Though everybody's house has family *allá*, most have never been farther across—*across*, meaning the "other side," Mexico—than Matamoros, Juárez, or Tijuana to look for cheaper prescription drugs or dentistry.

And so it goes with literature. The "national" scene knows the very least about Mexican American literature, historically or currently. Though it may not always be as clear as an Arizona school board banning material for ambitious, college-bound young Mexican American students who notice their culture's absence in their curriculum, the offense, sadly, is the same, only larger in scale, when written voices and stories are passively ignored by all school districts, even when their student body is predominantly of Mexican American descent. Or even more: why aren't we going past wanting to educate MexAm children, in their own neighborhoods, to have ordinary pride in who they are and where they've come from, and asking how long *all* of our country can ignore a huge American region and heritage? How can it not want to understand or appreciate its people beyond enchiladas or child care talents, but as craftsmen, business owners, artisans and artists, thinkers, as purposeful voters, as the country's future leaders? Too much to say as *friends*? As those who work alongside so many and have children who are in the same classes as their own? Is it possible to ignore and dismiss, to undervalue, an entire people without consequence? How should we educate *all* our own to each other?

Two hundred years in the region that was once upon a time mapped as the north in New Spain, which became México, and then what we now call Texas and California and the American Southwest, annexed with a much-abused Treaty of Guadalupe Hidalgo, a people lived on the land, and though no one could possibly call their existence "thriving," it was constant and consistent. There began stories that came as poetry. With more time, their stories of love and pride, bravery, heritage, God, family, loss and fight and skill and home, became songs known as *corridos*. It's where this literature truly began.

The people here have gone by many names. They have been Mexicans forever, though pronounced with Anglicized inflections, drawls, often in two syllables. Called Tejanos, Hispanos, Californios. In the 1960s, a young activist movement made Americans of Mexican descent Chicanos. In the seventies, the women wanted their own, Chicana, while the Nixon administration created the Hispanic. That the word emphasized Spain's hegemony generated a counterword, Latino. By the 1990s, adding a slash—as in Chicana/o—was the academic solution for conjoining both Chicanas and Chicanos, and a larger group, too, became Latina/o. It will be said that Mexican American is an older nomenclature. The choice here was for simplicity. Even within the region itself now, usage is confused and mixed, and the solution isn't. MexAm is a neutral shorthand.

What this book attempts to do, in fifty selections, is offer the variety of Mexican American experience as it has passed through the decades and cardinal points of its large region. The want is to highlight topics and style in a range from hardcore serious to the straight-up funny. It begins with the first naturalized Tejano whose religious skills are a model of cultural *mestizaje*, and closes with a writer from that shipwreck's coast who ran to the country's other northernmost coast to blend away from his birth home. The group gets lumped together imperfectly as "writers" or "authors"; they are really explorers, politicians, novelists, columnists, poets, teachers, activists, journalists, pachucos, cartoonistas. They are chronicling a culture, in distinctive particularity, its strengths and weaknesses, its beauty and not so much. Their engagement is what makes their words worth reading and studying.

This anthology most clearly is not all there is. Only a restricted fifty of writers and poets who, for reasons of popularity or renown, have stood out. So many more names! In randomized order, here are others who were closely considered, who have been in anthologies of the past or will be in those of the future: Yxta Maya Murray, Manuel Muñoz, Diana López, Victor Villaseñor, Sheryl Luna, Miguel Mendez, Eduardo C. Corral, Reyna Grande, José Antonio Burciaga, Fermina Guerra, Josefina Niggli, Aristeo Brito, Alejandro Murguía, Estela Portillo Trambley, José Antonio Villarreal, Alejandro Morales, Daniel Hernández, ire'ne lara silva, Maria Amparo Ruiz de Burton, Luis Omar Salinas, Marisela Norte, Max Martinez, Bernice Zamora, Rigoberto González, Richard Vasquez.

My thanks, quiet and huge: to Ellen Thibault, who insisted on this, and to Ricardo Angel Gilb and Rebeca Gilb.

—DAGOBERTO GILB
AUSTIN, TEXAS

1

ÁLVAR NÚÑEZ CABEZA DE VACA [c. 1490–1557]

How the Following Day They Brought Other Sick People

From Chronicle of the Narváez Expedition [1536]

GENRE: HISTORICAL NARRATIVE

The Spanish explorer Álvar Núñez Cabeza de Vaca was born around the year 1490 in Extremadura, a region where many conquistadores were born, including Hernán Cortés and Francisco Pizarro. Unlike his more famous contemporaries, Cabeza de Vaca earned his renown not through conquest but through failure. In 1527, he joined a disastrous expedition headed by Pánfilo de Narváez to the northern coast of the Gulf of Mexico. While at sea the explorers were struck by a hurricane, and on land the journey became even more treacherous. Out of an original six hundred men, only Cabeza de Vaca and three others survived long enough to meet up with rescuers in 1532 near what is now Sinaloa. In the Chronicle of the Narváez Expedition, *his history of the journey, Cabeza de Vaca shows himself to be a good observer of his surroundings, recording details about the geography, culture, and peoples of present-day Texas and Mexico. For Cabeza de Vaca's contemporaries, such details helped make his incredible stories about survival in this recently reached and still mysterious region seem real, even though they were full of "many new things that many people will find hard to believe."**

The following excerpt from Chronicle of the Narváez Expedition *tells of one adventure of Cabeza de Vaca and his three companions, who are named Dorantes, Castillo, and Estevanico, after they are shipwrecked on the coast of Texas, probably in present-day Galveston. They become known as healers, proudly trumpeting their Catholicism to the Indians, making them the first evangelists of the New World.*

---

*From Ilan Stavans, "Álvar Núñez Cabeza de Vaca," in *A New Literary History of America*, ed. Greil Marcus and Werner Sollors.

As you read, think of this text not only as a fantastic survival tale, but as one of the earliest, and most vivid, descriptions of the complexity of life in the Southwest and of the mix of Spanish and indigenous beliefs that became the religion of the New World.

Early the next day many Indians came and brought five people who were paralyzed and very ill and who had come for Castillo to cure them. Each patient offered him his bow and arrows, which Castillo accepted, and by sunset he had made the sign of the cross over each of the sick people, commending them to God, our Lord. We all prayed to him as well as we could to restore them to health and he, seeing there was no other way of getting those people to help us so that we might be saved from our miserable existence, had mercy on us. In the morning they all woke up well and hearty and went away in such good health that it was as if they never had had any ailment at all. This created great admiration among them and moved us to thank our Lord and to greater faith in his goodness and the hope that he would save us, guiding us to where we could serve him. For myself I may say that I always had full faith in his mercy and that he would liberate me from captivity, and I always told my companions so.

When the Indians had gone with their now healthy Indians, we moved on to others called Cultalchulches and Maliacones, who speak a different language and who were eating prickly pears as well. With them were still others, called Coayos and Susolas, and in another area were the Atayos, who were at war with the Susolas and exchanged arrow shots with them every day.

In this whole country, nothing was spoken of but the wonderful mysteries that God, our Lord, performed through us. They came from far and wide to be cured, and after having been with us two days, some of the Susolas begged Castillo to go and attend to a man who had been wounded, as well as to others that were sick and among whom, they said, was one who was on the verge of death. Castillo was very fearful, especially in frightening and dangerous cases, always afraid that his sins might interfere and prevent the cures from being effective. Therefore the Indians told me to go and perform the cure. They liked me. They remembered that I had cured them while they were out gathering walnuts, for which they had given us walnuts and hides, which had taken place at the time I was on my way to join the Christians. So I had to go, and Dorantes and Estevanico went with me.

When I got close to their huts I saw that the sick man we had been called to cure was dead, for there were many people around him weeping and his lodge was torn down, which is a sign that the owner has died. I found the Indian with his eyes rolled back, without pulse and with all the marks of death, at least it seemed so to me, and Dorantes said the same thing. I removed the mat with which he was covered, and as best I could I prayed to our Lord to restore him to health as well as any others in need. After I had made the sign of the cross and breathed on him many times, they brought his bow and presented it to me, as well as a basket of ground prickly pears, and then they took me to many others who were suffering from sleeping sickness. They gave me two more baskets of prickly pears, which I left for the Indians that had come with us. Then we returned to our living quarters.

Our Indians, to whom I had given the prickly pears, remained. At night 5 they returned, saying that the dead man whom I attended to in their presence had resuscitated, risen from his bed, walked about, eaten, and talked to them, and that everyone I had treated was well and in very good spirits. This caused great surprise and awe, and all over the land nothing else was spoken of. Everyone who heard about it came to us so that we might cure them and bless their children. When the Cultalchulches, who were in the company of our Indians, had to return to their country, before parting they offered us all the prickly pears they had for their journey, not keeping a single one. They gave us flint stones as long as one and a half palms, which are greatly prized among them and with which they cut. They begged us to remember them and pray to God to keep them healthy always, which we promised to do. Then they left, the happiest people on earth, having given us the very best of what they owned.

We remained with the Avavares for eight months, according to our reckoning of the moons. During that time people came to us from far and wide and said that we were truly the children of the sun. Until then Dorantes and the Negro had not cured anyone, but we found ourselves so pressed by the Indians coming from all sides that all of us had to become medicine men. I was the most daring and reckless of all in undertaking cures. We never treated anyone that did not afterward say he was well, and they had such confidence in our skill that they believed that none of them would die as long as we were among them.

These Indians and the ones we left behind told us a very strange tale. From their account it may have occurred fifteen or sixteen years ago. They said that at that time there wandered about the country a man whom they called "Bad Thing," who was short and bearded. Although they could never see his features clearly, whenever he would approach their dwellings their hair would stand on end and they would begin to tremble. In the doorway of the lodge a firebrand would then appear. The man would come in and take hold of anyone he chose. With a sharp knife made of flint, as broad as a hand and two palms in length, he would then make a cut in that person's flank, thrust his hand through the gash, and take out the person's entrails. Then he would cut off a piece one palm long, which he would throw into the fire. Afterward he would make three cuts in one of the person's arms, the second one at a place where people are usually bled, and twist the arm, but would reset it soon afterward. Then he would place his hands on the wounds, which, they told us, would close up at once. Many times he appeared among them while they were dancing, sometimes in the dress of a woman and other times as a man, and whenever he took a notion to do it he would seize a hut or lodge, take it up into the air, and come down with it again with a great crash. They also told us how, many a time, they set food before him, but he would never partake of it. When they asked him where he came from and where he had his home, he pointed to a rent in the earth and said his house was down below.

We laughed a great deal at those stories and made fun of them. Seeing our disbelief they brought us many of those he had taken, they said, and we saw the scars from his slashes in the places they had said. We told them he was a demon and explained as best we could that if they would believe in God, our Lord, and be Christians like ourselves, they would not have to fear that man, nor would he come and do these things to them, and they might be sure that as long as we were in this country he would not dare to appear again. This pleased them greatly and they lost much of their apprehension.

The same Indians told us they had seen the Asturian and Figueroa with other Indians from further along the coast whom we had named the People of the Figs. None of them know how to reckon the seasons by either sun or moon, nor do they count by months and years; they judge the seasons by the ripening of fruit, by the time that fish die, and by the appearance of the stars, and in all of this they are very clever and expert. While with them we were always well treated, although our food was never too plentiful, and we had to carry our own water and wood. Their dwellings and their food are like those of the others we had known, but they are much more prone to hunger, having neither corn nor acorns or walnuts. We always went naked like them and at night covered ourselves with deerskins.

During six of the eight months we were with them we suffered greatly 10 from hunger, because they do not have fish either. At the end of that time the prickly pears began to ripen. Without their noticing it the Negro and I left and went to other Indians further ahead, called Maliacones, at a distance of one day's travel. Three days after we arrived I sent him back to get Castillo and Dorantes, and after they rejoined me we all departed in company of the Indians, who went to eat a small fruit of a certain type of tree, on which they subsist for ten or twelve days, until the prickly pears are fully ripe. There they joined other Indians called Arbadaos, whom we found to be so sick, emaciated, and bloated that we were greatly astonished. The Indians with whom we had come went back on the same trail, and we told them that we wished to remain with the others, which made them sad. So we remained with the others in a field near their dwellings.

When the Indians saw us, they gathered together and, after having talked among themselves, each one took the one of us he had claimed by the hand and led us to their homes. While we were with them we suffered more from hunger than we had with any of the others. In the course of a whole day we did not eat more than two handfuls of the fruit, which was green and contained so much milky juice that it burned our mouths. Since water was very scarce, whoever ate them became very thirsty. Finally we grew so hungry that we purchased two dogs in exchange for nets and other things and a hide that I used to cover myself.

I have said already that we went naked in that land, and not being accustomed to it, we shed our skin twice a year, like snakes. Exposure to the sun and air covered our chests and backs with great sores that made it very painful to carry big and heavy loads, the ropes of which cut into the flesh on our arms.

The country is so rough and overgrown that often after we had gathered firewood in the forest and dragged it out, we would bleed freely from the thorns and spines that cut and slashed us wherever they touched us. Sometimes it happened that I was unable to carry or drag out the firewood after I had gathered it with great loss of blood. In all that trouble my only relief or consolation was to remember the passion of our Savior, Jesus Christ, and the blood he shed for me, and to consider how much greater his sufferings had been from those thorns than I from the ones I was then enduring.

I made a contract with the Indians to make combs, arrows, bows, and nets for them. We also made the matting from which their lodges are constructed and which they greatly need, for, although they know how to make it, they do not like to do any work, in order to be able to go in search of food. Whenever they work they suffer greatly from hunger.

At other times, they would make me scrape skins and tan them, and the greatest luxury I enjoyed was on the day they would give me a skin to scrape, because I scraped it very deeply in order to eat the parings, which would last me two or three days. It also happened that, while we were with these Indians and those mentioned before, we would eat a piece of meat they gave us raw, because if we broiled it the first Indian who came along would snatch it away and eat it. It seemed useless to take any pains, in view of what we might expect, nor did we care to go to any trouble in order to have it broiled and might just as well eat it raw. Such was the life we led there, and we had to earn even that scant sustenance by bartering the objects we made with our own hands.

Reading

1. How do Cabeza de Vaca and his companions become known as healers? How do they heal people?

2. What is Cabeza de Vaca doing when he says he would "bleed freely from the thorns and spines that cut and slashed us" (par. 13)? How does he find consolation from the pain?

Thinking Critically

1. Does Cabeza de Vaca believe that he has special powers as a healer? How do you know?

2. How do you think the indigenous people feel about Cabeza de Vaca and his companions? Use evidence from the text to support your perspective.

Connecting

1. Read "The Country" (p. 32), by Américo Paredes, a selection from his nonfiction book *With His Pistol in His Hand*. In "The Country," Paredes tries to describe the interaction between people with different histories and beliefs. Are there aspects of Cabeza de Vaca's writing that remind you of Paredes? How do their approaches differ from each other?

Writing

1. What is Cabeza de Vaca's attitude toward the indigenous people he meets? Is he respectful? Frightened? Dismissive? Using specific examples from the text to support your answer, write an essay exploring this aspect of Cabeza de Vaca's writing.

Creating

1. **Illustrate the text.** In this excerpt from *Chronicle of the Narváez Expedition*, Cabeza de Vaca describes many different people, jobs, foods, ailments, and even demonic creatures. Choose any of these and draw a picture of it, basing it as closely as you can on the description you find in the text. When you present your picture, explain what Cabeza de Vaca's description does and doesn't include.

2

JOVITA GONZÁLEZ [1899–1983]

The Bullet-Swallower

From The Woman Who Lost Her Soul and Other Stories
[1935]

GENRE: FICTION / FOLKLORE

Mexican culture in the Southwest has a long history. Jovita González, descended from the earliest settlers of the region, found in that history the sources for her work, which included academic research and fiction. González was born in the Texas border town of Roma and attended college in nearby San Antonio. Graduate work at the University of Texas at Austin introduced her to J. Frank Dobie, one of the most significant figures in Texas literary history. Dobie encouraged her studies of the "folklore" of South Texas — the customs, stories, and traditions — that grew out of the unique cultural and racial mixture of South Texas. She completed her master's thesis, Social Life in Cameron, Starr, and Zapata Counties, *in 1930 and, for the next decade, presented studies of the region to both the Texas Folk-Lore Society and the League of United Latin American Citizens (LULAC), one of the oldest Mexican American advocacy groups in the country. The knowledge she gained from her research was transformed into several sets of stories and two unpublished novels, including* Caballero, *a historical novel set in the aftermath of the Mexican American War.*

Because González wrote for a predominantly white audience, the Mexican American culture in her work can seem exotic and quaint. It is not presented as the basis for a strong political identity as it would be by Chicano writers of later decades. Still, in stories like "The Bullet-Swallower," originally published in 1935 by the Folk-Lore Society, the dispassionate tone of the folklorist doesn't hide the signs of persistent political and racial tensions, such as the Texas Rangers' frequently violent actions against Mexicans.

As you read, think about the ways the story reflects the history of early twentieth-century Texas, as well as how it provides a background for other writers collected in this anthology.

He was a wiry little man, a bundle of nerves in perpetual motion. Quicksilver might have run through his veins instead of blood. His right arm, partly paralyzed as a result of a *machete* cut he had received in a saloon brawl, terminated in stiff, claw-like, dirty-nailed fingers. One eye was partly closed—a knife cut had done that—but the other, amber in color, had the alertness and the quickness of a hawk's. Chairs were not made for him. Squatting on the floor or sitting on one heel, he told interminable stories of border feuds, bandit raids and smuggler fights as he fingered a curved, murderous knife which ended in three inches of zigzag, jagged steel. "No one has ever escaped this," he would say, caressing it. "Sticking it into a man might not have finished him, but getting it out—ah, my friend, that did the work. It's a very old one, brought from Spain, I guess," he would add in an unconcerned voice. "Here is the date, 1630."

A landowner by inheritance, a trail driver by necessity, and a smuggler and gambler by choice, he had given up the traditions of his family to be and do that which pleased him most. Through some freakish mistake, he had been born three centuries too late. He might have been a fearless *conquistador*, or he might have been a chivalrous knight of the Rodrigo de Narváez type, fighting the infidels along the Moorish frontier. A tireless horseman, a man of *pelo en pecho* (hair on the chest), as he braggingly called himself, he was afraid of nothing.

"The men of my time were not lily-livered, white-gizzarded creatures," he would boast. "We fought for the thrill of it, and the sight of blood maddened us as it does a bull. Did we receive a gash on the stomach? Did the guts come out? What of it. We tightened our sash and continued the fray. See this arm? Ah, could it but talk, it would tell you how many men it sent to the other world. To Hell, perhaps to Purgatory, but none I am sure to Heaven. The men I associated with were neither sissies nor saints. Often at night when I can not sleep because of the pain in these cursed wounds, I say a prayer, in my way, for their souls, in case my prayers should reach the good God.

"People call me *Traga-Balas*, Bullet-Swallower—Antonio Traga-Balas, to be more exact. *Ay*, were I as young as I was when the incident that gave me this name happened!

"We were bringing several cartloads of smuggled goods to be delivered 5 at once and in safety to the owner. Oh, no, the freight was not ours but we would have fought for it with our life's blood. We had dodged the Mexican officials, and now we had to deal with the Texas Rangers. They must have been tipped, because they knew the exact hour we were to cross the river. We swam in safety. The pack mules, loaded with packages wrapped in tanned hides, we led by the bridle. We hid the mules in a clump of *tules* and were just beginning to dress when the Rangers fell upon us. Of course, we did not have a stitch of clothes on; did you think we swam fully dressed? Had we but had our guns in readiness, there have might been a different story to tell. We would have fought like wildcats to keep the smuggled goods from falling into their hands. It was not ethical among smugglers to lose the property of a Mexican to Americans, and as to falling ourselves into their hands, we preferred death a thousand times. It's no disgrace and dishonor to die like a man, but it is to die like a rat. Only canaries sing; men never tell, however tortured they may be. I have seen the Rangers pumping water into the mouth of an innocent man because he would not confess to something he had not done. But that is another story.

"I ran to where the pack mules were to get my gun. Like a fool that I was, I kept yelling at the top of my voice, 'You so, so and so gringo cowards, why don't you attack men like men? Why do you wait until they are undressed and unarmed?' I must have said some very insulting things, for one of them shot at me right in the mouth. The bullet knocked all of my front teeth out, grazed my tongue and went right through the back of my neck. Didn't kill me though. It takes more than bullets to kill Antonio Traga-Balas. The next thing I knew I found myself in a shepherd's hut. I had been left for dead, no doubt, and I had been found by the goatherd. The others were sent to the penitentiary. After I recovered, I remained in hiding for a year or so; and when I showed myself all thought it a miracle that I had lived through. That's how I was rechristened Traga-Balas. That confounded bullet did leave my neck a little stiff; I can't turn around as easily as I should, but outside of that I am as fit as though the accident—I like to call it that—had never happened. It takes a lot to kill a man, at least one who can swallow bullets.

"I've seen and done many strange things in my life and I can truthfully say that I have never been afraid but once. What are bullets and knife thrusts to seeing a corpse arise from its coffin? Bullets can be dodged and dagger cuts are harmless unless they hit a vital spot. But a dead man staring with lifeless, open eyes and gaping mouth is enough to make a man tremble in his boots. And, mind you, I am not a coward, never have been. Is there any one among you who thinks Antonio Traga-Balas is a coward?"

At a question like this, Traga-Balas would take the knife from its cover and finger it in a way that gave one a queer, empty spot in the stomach. Now he was launched upon a story.

"This thing happened," he went on, "years ago at Roma beside the Río Bravo.° I was at home alone; my wife and children were visiting in another town. I remember it was a windy night in November. The evening was cool, and, not knowing what else to do, I decided to go to bed early. I was not asleep yet when someone began pounding at my door.

Río Bravo: The Río Grande, as it is called in Mexico.

"'Open the door, Don Antonio; please let me in,' said a woman's   10
voice. I got up and recognized in the woman before me one of our new
neighbors. They had just moved into a deserted *jacal*° in the alley back of
our house.

"'My husband is very sick,' she explained. 'He is dying and wants to see
you. He says he must speak to you before he dies.'

"I dressed and went out with her, wondering all the time what this
unknown man wanted to see me about. I found him in a miserable hovel,
on a more miserable pallet on the floor, and I could see by his sunken
cheeks and the fire that burned in his eyes that he was really dying, and
of consumption, too. With mumbled words he dismissed the woman
from the room and, once she had gone, he asked me to help him sit up. I
propped him on the pillows the best I could. He was seized with a fit of
coughing followed by a hemorrhage and I was almost sure that he would
die before he could say anything. I brought him some water and poured
a little *tequila* from a half empty bottle that was at the head of the pallet.
After drinking it, he gave a sigh of relief.

"'I am much better now,' he whispered. His voice was already failing.
'My friend,' he went on, 'excuse my calling you, an utter stranger, but I
have heard you are a man of courage and of honor and you will understand what I have to say to you. That woman you saw here is really not
my wife; but I have lived with her in sin for the last twenty years. It weighs
upon my conscience and I want to right the wrong I did her once.'

"As the man ended this confession, I could not help thinking what
changes are brought about in the soul by the mere thought of facing
eternity. I thought it very strange that after so long a time he should have
qualms of conscience now. Yet I imagine death is a fearful thing, and,
never having died myself nor been afraid to die, I could not judge what
the dying man before me was feeling. So I decided to do what I would
have expected others to do for me, and asked him if there was anything
I might do for him.

"'Call a priest. I want to marry her,' he whispered.   15

"I did as he commanded me and went to the rectory. Father José María
was still saying his prayers, and when I told him that I had come to get
him to marry a dying man, he looked at me in a way he had of doing
whenever he doubted anyone, with one eye half closed and out of the
corner of the other. As I had played him many pranks in the past, no
doubt he thought I was now playing another. He hesitated at first but
then got up somewhat convinced.

"'I'll take my chance with you again, you son of Barabbas,' he said. 'I'll
go. Some poor soul may want to reconcile himself with his Creator.' He
put on his black cape and took the little bag he always carried on such

jacal: Shack.

occasions. The night was as black as the mouth of a wolf and the wind was getting colder and stronger.

"'A bad time for anyone to want a priest, eh, Father?' I said in an effort to make conversation, not knowing what else to say.

"'The hour of repentance is a blessed moment at whatever time it comes,' he replied in a tone that I thought was reprimanding.

"On entering the house, we found the man alone. The woman was in the kitchen, he told us. I joined her there, and what do you suppose the shameless creature was doing? Drinking *tequila*, getting courage, she told me, for the ordeal ahead of her. After about an hour, we were called into the sick room. The man looked much better. Unburdening his soul had given him that peaceful look you sometimes see in the face of the dead who die while smiling. I was told that I was to be witness to the Holy Sacrament of Matrimony. The woman was so drunk by now that she could hardly stand up; and between hiccoughs she promised to honor and love the man who was more fit to be food for worms than for life in this valley of tears. I'd never seen a man so strong for receiving sacraments as that one was. He had received the Sacrament of Penance, then that of Matrimony—and I could see no greater penance than marrying such a woman—and now he was to receive Extreme Unction, the Sacrament for the Dying.

"The drunken woman and I held candles as Father José María anointed him with holy oil; and when we had to join him in prayer, I was ashamed that I could not repeat even the Lord's Prayer with him. That scene will always live in my mind, and when I die may I have as holy a man as Father José María to pray for me! He lingered a few moments; then, seeing there was nothing else to do, he said he would go back. I went with him under the pretext of getting something or other for the dying man, but in reality, I wanted to see him safe at home. On the way back to the dying man I stopped at the saloon for another bottle of *tequila*. The dying man might need a few drops to give him courage to start on his journey to the Unknown, although from what I had seen I judged that Father José María had given him all he needed.

"When I returned, the death agony was upon him. The drunken woman was snoring in the kitchen. It was my responsibility to see that the man did not die like a dog. I wet his cracked lips with a piece of cloth moistured in *tequila*. I watched all night. The howling of the wind and the death rattle of the consumptive made the place the devil's kingdom. With the coming of dawn, the man's soul, now pure from sin, left the miserable carcass that had given it lodging during life. I folded his arms over his chest and covered his face with a cloth. There was no use in calling the woman; she lay on the dirt floor of the kitchen snoring like a trumpet. I closed the door and went to see what could be done about arrangements for the funeral. I went home and got a little money—I did not have much—to buy some boards for the coffin, black calico for the covering and for a mourning dress for the bride, now a widow—although I felt she did not deserve it—and candles.

"I made the coffin, and when all was done and finished went back to the house. The woman was still snoring, her half-opened mouth filled with buzzing flies. The corpse was as I had left it. I called some of the neighbors to help me dress the dead man in my one black suit, but he was stiff already and we had to lay him in the coffin as he was, unwashed and dirty. If it is true that we wear white raiments in Heaven, I hope the good San Pedro gave him one at the entrance before the other blessed spirits got to see the pitiful things he wore. I watched the body all day; he was to be buried early the following morning. Father José María had told me he would say Mass for him. The old woman, curse her, had gotten hold of the other bottle of *tequila* and continued bottling up courage for the ordeal that she said she had to go through.

"The wind that had started the night before did not let down, in fact, it was getting stronger. Several times the candles had blown out, and the corpse and I had been left in utter darkness. To avoid the repetition of such a thing, I went to the kitchen and got some empty fruit cans very much prized by the old woman. In truth she did not want to let me use them at first, because, she said, the food on the paper wrapping looked so natural and was the only fruit she had ever owned. I got them anyway, filled them with corn, and stuck the candles there.

"Early in the evening about nine, or thereabouts, I decided to get out   25 again and ask some people to come and watch with me part of the night. Not that I was afraid of staying alone with the corpse. One might fear the spirits of those who die in sin, but certainly not this one who had left the world the way a Christian should leave it. I left somewhat regretfully, for I was beginning to have a kindly feeling towards the dead man. I felt towards that body as I would feel towards a friend, no doubt because I had helped it to transform itself from a human being to a nice Christian corpse.

"As I went from house to house asking people to watch with me that night, I was reminded of a story that the priest had told us once, and by the time I had gone half through the town I knew very well how the man who was inviting guests to the wedding feast must have felt. All had some good excuse to give but no one could come. To make a long story short, I returned alone, to spend the last watch with my friend the corpse.

"As I neared the house, I saw it very well lighted, and I thought perhaps some people had finally taken pity upon the poor unfortunate and had gone there with more candles to light the place. But soon I realized what was really happening. The *jacal* was on fire.

"I ran inside. The sight that met my eyes was one I shall ever see. I was nailed to the floor with terror. The corpse, its hair a flaming mass, was sitting up in the coffin where it had so peacefully lain all day. Its glassy, opaque eyes stared into space with a look that saw nothing and its mouth was convulsed into the most horrible grin. I stood there paralyzed by the horror of the scene. To make matters worse the drunken woman reeled into the room, yelling, 'He is burning before he gets to Hell!'

"Two thoughts ran simultaneously through my mind: to get her out of the room and to extinguish the fire. I pushed the screaming woman out into the darkness and, arming myself with courage, reentered the room. I was wearing cowboy boots and my feet were the only part of my body well protected. Closing my eyes, I kicked the table, and I heard the thud of the burning body as it hit the floor. I became crazy then. With my booted feet I tramped upon and kicked the corpse until I thought the fire was extinguished. I dared not open my eyes for fear of what I might see, and with my eyes still closed I ran out of the house. I did not stop until I reached the rectory. Like mad, I pounded upon the door, and when the priest opened it and saw me standing there looking more like a ghost than a living person, he could but cross himself. It was only after I had taken a drink or two—may God forgive me for having done so in his presence—that I could tell him what had happened.

"He went back with me and, with eyes still closed, I helped him place the poor dead man in his coffin. Father José María prayed all night. As for me, I sat staring at the wall, not daring once to look at the coffin, much less upon the charred corpse. That was the longest watch I ever kept.

"At five o'clock, with no one to help us, we carried the coffin to the church, where the promised Mass was said. We hired a burro cart to take the dead man to the cemetery, and, as the sun was coming up, Father José María, that man of God, and I, an unpenitent sinner, laid him in his final resting place."

Reading

1. How does Antonio "Traga-Balas" get his nickname?

2. In the story Don Antonio recounts, why is Father José María needed in the middle of the night?

Thinking Critically

1. What is "folklore"? What features of the story of the Bullet-Swallower make it folklore?

2. "The Bullet-Swallower" is focused on just one man, but it also provides insight into the culture around that one man. What can you learn from this story about the culture that Don Antonio is a part of?

Connecting

1. As Jovita González does in "The Bullet-Swallower," José Montoya, in his poem "El Louie" (p. 103), presents the story of a proud, strong man. What similarities or differences do you find in the characters of Don Antonio and Louie? How do the approaches and goals of the two writers differ?

Writing

1. Don Antonio is proud of his reputation for fearlessness. However, one can find signs of other qualities, positive and negative, in the story. Using evidence from the text, write about the many aspects of Don Antonio's character, paying close attention to the ways that González communicates them.

Creating

1. **Record a storyteller.** As a folklorist, Jovita González collected stories that people told her and used them to understand the culture and customs of South Texas. Her writing reflects the influence of these storytellers. Make a recording of someone you know telling a story, and write briefly about how the story reflects the cultural surroundings of your storyteller.

3

SABINE ULIBARRÍ [1919–2003]

My Grandma Smoked Cigars

From Mi Abuela Fumaba Puros, y Otros Cuentos de Tierra Amarilla [1977]

GENRE: FICTION

The deep connection to the land that marks Sabine Ulibarrí's writing began early in his life. He was born a few miles south of Albuquerque, New Mexico, in Las Nutrias, a string of ranches that his grandfather helped establish. At eight years old, he moved to the town of Tierra Amarilla, which became the setting for many of his later writings. He stayed in New Mexico through high school and

*into college. His school career was temporarily interrupted by
World War II, in which he served as a gunner, flying thirty-five
missions and receiving a Distinguished Flying Cross. After the
war, Ulibarrí resumed his studies and earned bachelor's and master's degrees from the University of New Mexico, followed by a
Ph.D. from the University of California, Los Angeles. He returned
to his native state to teach at the University of New Mexico for
three decades, during which time he published several collections
of poems and short stories, including his first book of poems,*
Al cielo se sube a pie, *in 1961, and his best-known book of stories, named for the city he grew up in,* Tierra Amarilla: Cuentos de
Nuevo Mexico, *in 1964. "No one can take from me the pathways
of memory and nostalgia to my Tierra Amarilla," he wrote in a
poem. There he could hear "the voices of the old ones that survive
in the wind."*

*Mi Abuela Fumaba Puros, the collection from which this story
is drawn, was published in 1977 and has Tierra Amarilla as its setting. Though the story can be read as a simple tribute to a grandmother, it is, like much of Ulibarrí's writing, also a tribute to what
a grandmother can represent: the landscape, history, and traditions
of New Mexico that long predate the Americanization of the area.
"The Spanish-speaking peoples are known for the tenacity with
which they hold on to their traditions," Ulibarrí has written. "Our
roots run deep and sinuous in the land of our forefathers."*

As you read, notice the ways that Ulibarrí's stories and characters symbolize old traditions.

The way I've heard it, my grandfather was quite a guy. There are many
stories about him. Some respectable, others not quite. One of the latter
goes as follows. That returning from Tierra Amarilla to Las Nutrias, after
cups and cards, sometimes on his buggy with its spirited trotters, sometimes on his *criollo°* horse, he would take off his hat, hang it on a fence
post, pull out his six-gun and address himself to the stiff gentleman of his
own invention.

"Tell me, who is the richest man in all these parts?"

Silence.

"Well then, take this."

A shot. Splinters flew out of the post or a hole appeared in the hat.   5

criollo: Highly admired breed of horse native to the Americas.

"Who's the toughest man around here?"

Silence.

"Well then, take this."

The same thing happened. He was a good shot. More questions of the same kind, punctuated with shots. When the sassy post learned his lesson and gave my grandfather the answers he wanted to hear, the ritual ended, and he went on his way, singing or humming some sentimental song of the period. The shooting was heard back in the town without it bothering anyone. Someone was sure to say with a smile, "There's don Prudencio doing his thing."

Of course my grandfather had other sides (the plural is intended) that   10 are not relevant to this narrative. He was a civic, social and political figure and a family man twice over. What I want to do now is stress the fact that my relative was a real character: quarrelsome, daring and prankish.

He died in a mysterious way, or perhaps even shameful. I've never been able to find out exactly what streetcar my distinguished antecedent took to the other world. Maybe that wooden gentleman with his hat pulled over his eyes, the one who suffered the insults of the hidalgo° of Las Nutrias, gave him a woody and mortal whack. An hidalgo he was—and a father of more than four.

I never knew him. When I showed up in this world to present my Turriaga credentials, he had already turned his in. I imagine that wherever he is he's making violent and passionate love to the ladies who went to heaven—or hell, depending . . . That is if my grandmother hasn't caught up with him in those worlds beyond the grave.

I don't think he and my grandmother had an idyllic marriage in the manner of sentimental novels where everything is sweetness, softness and tenderness. Those are luxuries, perhaps decadences, that didn't belong in that violent world, frequently hostile, of Río Arriba County at the end of the past century. Furthermore, the strong personalities of both would have prevented it. I do believe they were very happy. Their love was a passion that didn't have time to become a habit or just friendship. They loved each other with mutual respect and fear, something between admiration and fury, something between tenderness and toughness. Both were children of their land and their times. There was so much to do. Carve a life from an unfriendly frontier. Raise their rebellious and ferocious cubs. Their life was an affectionate and passionate sentimental war.

I say all of this as a preamble in order to enter into my subject: my grandmother. I have so many and so gratifying memories of her. But the first one of all is a portrait that hangs in a place of honor in the parlor of my memory.

hidalgo: Nobleman.

She had her moments in which she caressed her solitude. She would   15
go off by herself, and everyone knew it was best to leave her alone.

She always dressed in black. A blouse of lace and batiste up front. A skirt down to her ankles. All silk. A cotton apron. High shoes. Her hair parted in the middle and combed straight back, smooth and tight, with a round and hard bun in the back. I never saw her with her hair loose.

She was strong. As strong as only she could be. Through the years, in so many situations, small and big tragedies, accidents and problems, I never saw her bend or fold. Fundamentally, she was serious and formal. So a smile, a compliment or a caress from her were coins of gold that were appreciated and saved as souvenirs forever. Coins she never wasted.

The ranch was big business. The family was large and problematic. She ran her empire with a sure and firm hand. Never was there any doubt about where her affairs were going nor who held the reins.

That first memory: the portrait. I can see her at this moment as if she were before my eyes. A black silhouette on a blue background. Straight, tall and slender. The wind of the hill cleaving her clothes to her body up front, outlining her forms, one by one. Her skirt and her shawl flapping in the wind behind her. Her eyes fixed I don't know where. Her thoughts fixed on I don't know what. An animated statue. A petrified soul.

My grandfather smoked cigars. The cigar was the symbol and the   20
badge of the feudal lord, the *patrón*. When on occasion he would give a cigar to the foreman or to one of the hands on impulse or as a reward for a task well done, the transfiguration of those fellows was something to see. To suck on that tobacco was to drink from the fountains of power. The cigar gave you class.

They say that when my grandfather died my grandmother would light cigars and place them on ashtrays all over the house. The aroma of the tobacco filled the house. This gave the widow the illusion that her husband was still around. A sentimentalism and romanticism difficult to imagine before.

As time went on, and after lighting many a cigar, a liking for the cigars seemed to sneak up on her. She began to smoke the cigars. At nightfall, every day, after dinner, when the tasks of the day were done, she would lock herself in her room, sit in her rocker and light her cigar.

She would spend a long time there. The rest of us remained in the living room playing the family role as if nothing were amiss. No one ever dared interrupt her arbitrary and sacred solitude. No one ever mentioned her unusual custom.

The cigar that had once been a symbol of authority had now become an instrument of love. I am convinced that in the solitude and in the silence, with the smell and the taste of the tobacco, there in the smoke, my grandmother established some kind of mystical communication with my grandfather. I think that there, all alone, that idyllic marriage, full of tenderness, softness and sweetness was attained, not possible while he lived. It was enough to see the soft and transfigured face of the grandmother when she returned to us from her strange communion, to see the affection and gentleness with which she treated us kids.

Right there, and in those conditions, the decisions were made, the posi-   25 tions were taken that ran the business, that directed the family. There in the light or in the shade of an old love, now an eternal love, the spiritual strength was forged that kept my grandmother straight, tall and slender, a throbbing woman of stone, facing the winds and storms of her full life.

When my parents married they built their home next to the old family house. I grew up on the windy hill in the center of the valley of Las Nutrias, with pine trees on all the horizons, with the stream full of beaver, trout and suckers, the sagebrush full of rabbits and coyotes, stock everywhere, squirrels and owls in the barns.

I grew up alongside my grandmother and far away from her, between tender love and reverent fear.

When I was eight years old, it was decided in the family that we should move to Tierra Amarilla so that my brothers and I could attend school. The furrows the tears left on my face still burn, and I still remember their salty taste the day we left my straight, tall and slender grandmother, waving her handkerchief, with the wind on her face on the hill in the center of the valley.

In Tierra Amarilla I was antisocial. Having grown up alone, I didn't know how to play with other children. I played with my dogs instead. In spite of this I did all right in school, and one day I was fifteen years old, more or less adapted to my circumstances.

One winter day we got ready to go to Las Nutrias. All with a great deal   30 of anticipation. To visit my grandmother was always an event. The family would go with me in the car. My father with the sleigh and the hired hands. It was a matter of cutting fence posts.

We sang all the way. That is until we had to leave the highway. There was a lot of snow. The highway had been cleared, but the little road to Las Nutrias hadn't.

I put chains on the car, and we set out across the white sea. Now we were quiet and apprehensive. We soon got stuck. After a lot of shoveling and much pushing we continued, only to get stuck again farther on, again and again.

We were all exhausted and cold, and the day was drifting away. Finally we climbed the hill and came out of the pine grove from where we could see my grandmother's house. We got stuck again. This time there was no way of pulling the car out. My mother and the children continued on foot, opening their way through two and a half feet of soft snow. My brother Roberto pulled my sister Carmen on a small sled. It was getting dark. A trip of nine miles had taken us all day.

Juan Maes, the foreman, quickly came with a team of horses and pulled me home.

I had barely come in and was warming up. My mother had brought me   35 dry clothes, when we saw the lights of a car in the pine grove. We saw it approach slowly, hesitating from time to time. It was easier now; the road was now open.

It was my uncle Juan Antonio. The moment he came in we all knew he had bad news. There was a frightening silence. No one said a word. Everyone silent and stiff like wooden figures in a grotesque scene.

My mother broke the silence with a heartbreaking "Alejandro!"

My uncle nodded.

"What happened?" It was my grandmother.

"Alejandro. An accident."   40

"What happened?"

"An accidental shot. He was cleaning a rifle. The gun went off."

"How is he?"

"Not good, but he'll pull through."

We all knew he was lying, that my father was dead. We could see it in   45 his face. My mother was crying desperately, on the verge of becoming hysterical. We put our arms around her, crying. My uncle with his hat in his hands not knowing what to do. Another man had come with him. No one had noticed him.

That is when my grandmother went into action. Not a single tear. Her voice steady. Her eyes two flashing spears. She took complete control of the situation.

She went into a holy fury against my father. She called him ungrateful, shameless, unworthy. An inexhaustible torrent of insults. A royal rage. In the meantime she took my mother in her arms and rocked her and caressed her like a baby. My mother submitted and settled down slowly. We did too. My grandmother who always spoke so little did not stop talking that night.

I didn't understand then. I felt a violent resentment. I wanted to defend my father. I didn't because no one ever dared to talk back to my grandmother. Much less me. The truth is that she understood many things.

My mother was on the verge of madness. Something had to be done.

My grandmother created a situation, so violent and dramatic, that it   50 forced us all, my mother especially, to fix our attention on her and shift it away from the other situation until we could get used to the tragedy little by little. She didn't stop talking in order not to allow a single aperture through which despair might slip in. Talking, talking, between abuse and lullaby, she managed that my mother, in her vulnerable state, fall asleep in the wee hours of the morning. As she had done so many times in the past, my grandmother had dominated the harsh reality in which she lived.

She understood something else. That my father didn't fire a rifle accidentally. The trouble we had to bury him on sacred ground confirmed the infallible instinct of the lady and mistress of Las Nutrias. Everything confirmed the talent and substance of the mother of the Turriaga clan.

The years went by. I was now a professor. One day we returned to visit the grandmother. We were very happy. I've said it before, visiting her was an event. Things had changed a great deal. With the death of my father, my grandmother got rid of all the stock. The ranch hands disappeared with the stock. Rubel and his family were the only ones who remained to look after her.

When we left the highway and took the little used and much abused road full of the accustomed ruts, the old memories took possession of us. Suddenly we saw a column of black smoke rising beyond the hill. My sister shouted.

"Grandma's house!"

"Don't be silly. They must be burning weeds, or sage brush, or trash." I 55 said this but apprehension gripped me. I stepped hard on the gas.

When we came out of the pine grove, we saw that only ruins remained of the house of the grandmother. I drove like a madman. We found her surrounded by the few things that were saved. Surrounded also by the neighbors of all the ranches in the region who rushed to help when they saw the smoke.

I don't know what I expected but it did not surprise me to find her directing all the activities, giving orders. No tears, no whimpers, no laments.

"God gives and God takes away, my son. Blessed be His Holy Name."

I did lament. The crystal chandeliers, wrecked. The magnificent sets of tables and washstands with marble tops. The big basins and water jars in every bedroom, destroyed. The furniture brought from Kansas, turned to ashes. The bedspreads of lace, crochet, embroidery. The portraits, the pictures, the memories of a family.

Irony of ironies. There was a jar of holy water on the window sill in the 60 attic. The rays of the sun, shining through the water, converted into a magnifying glass. The heat and the fire concentrated on a single spot and set on fire some old papers there. And all of the saints, the relics, the shrines, the altar to the Santo Niño de Atocha,° the palms of Palm Sunday, all burned up. All of the celestial security went up in smoke.

Santo Niño de Atocha: The Holy Child of Atocha.

That night we gathered in what had been our old home. My grandmother seemed smaller to me, a little subdued, even a little docile: "Whatever you say, my son." This saddened me.

After supper my grandmother disappeared. I looked for her apprehensively. I found her where I could very well have suspected. At the top of the hill. Profiled by the moon. The wind in her face. Her skirt flapping in the wind. I saw her grow. And she was what she had always been: straight, tall and slender.

I saw the ash of her cigar light up. She was with my grandfather, the wicked one, the bold one, the quarrelsome one. Now the decisions would be made, the positions would be taken. She was regaining her spiritual strength. Tomorrow would be another day, but my grandmother would continue being the same one. And I was happy.

Reading

1. Why does the narrator's grandmother begin smoking cigars? Does this change the symbolism of the cigar?

2. What incidents does the author use to show the character of the grandmother?

Thinking Critically

1. Why do you think the story's narrator admires his grandmother so much? What does she represent for him?

2. Why does the grandmother react to the death of her son in the way she does? Do you think it is admirable? Why or why not?

Connecting

1. Like Ulibarrí's story "My Grandma Smoked Cigars," Carmen Tafolla's poems "Tía Sofía" and "Curandera" (p. 188) pay tribute to women of earlier generations. Read Tafolla's poems. Do Tafolla and Ulibarrí find the same qualities admirable? Do they express their admiration in different ways?

Writing

1. The narrator of Ulibarrí's story says of his grandmother, "She was strong. As strong as only she could be" (par. 17). But there are other ways one could describe the somewhat reserved, mysterious, authoritative figure that appears in this story. Why do you think the author describes her in

the way he does? Using examples from the text, write an essay about what qualities she represents.

Creating

1. **Create a presentation on symbols.** In this story, Sabine Ulibarrí presents cigar smoking as a symbol of strength and the keeping up of tradition. Make a slide show of several objects that you think can also function as powerful symbols, whether for an individual or for a large group. When you present your slides, discuss what each object symbolizes and why you think it functions as a symbol.

4

MARIO SUÁREZ [1923–1998]

Maestría

From Arizona Quarterly 4 [1948]

GENRE: FICTION

Mario Suárez is one of the earliest writers to transform his personal experiences as a Mexican American into literary fiction. He grew up in Tucson, Arizona, in the barrio called "El Hoyo" that he described in one of his first published stories. Like many men of his generation, Suárez had his education delayed by service in World War II. After being stationed in Brazil and New Jersey, Suárez attended the University of Arizona. In 1947, with the encouragement of two professors who enjoyed his portraits of the people and places he'd grown up around, he successfully submitted his early work to the Arizona Quarterly. *He continued to write stories, publishing several more in the same journal over the next several years. Suárez later became a teacher in California and completed four novels that he left unpublished, feeling they were not adequately polished. After his death, his stories were collected and published as* Chicano Sketches *in 2004.*

Suárez, in "El Hoyo," compared Chicano life to capirotada: *"Its origin is uncertain. But, according to the time and the circumstance, it is made of old, new, or hard bread. . . . And so it is with El Hoyo's chicanos. While being divided from within and without, like the* capirotada, *they remain chicanos." As this quotation suggests, Suárez tried to take an honest look at the diversity and complexity of life in the barrio, rather than trying to find its essence. As a result, he became one of the first to realistically describe modern Chicano life in postwar America. In the story below, "Maestría," which was first published in 1948, Suárez describes, with sympathy and a light touch, one of the fading practices of the older generation of Mexicans in the barrio.*

As you read, notice how Suárez is able to combine a quirky story with a look at a whole community.

Whenever a man is referred to as a *maestro* it means that he is master of whatever trade, art, or folly he practices. If he is a shoemaker, for example, he can design, cut, and finish any kind of shoe he is asked for. If he is a musician he knows composition, direction, execution, and thereby plays Viennese waltzes as well as the *bolero*. If he is a thief he steals thousands, for he would not damn his soul by taking dimes. That is *maestría*. It is applied with equal honor to a painter, tailor, barber, printer, carpenter, mechanic, bricklayer, window washer, ditchdigger, or bootblack if his ability merits it. Of course, when a man is greying and has no apparent trade or usefulness, out of courtesy people may forget he is a loafer and will call him a *maestro*. Whether he is or not is of no importance. Calling him a *maestro* hurts no one.

During the hard times of Mexico's last revolution many *maestros* left Mexico with their families with the idea of temporarily making a living north of the Rio Grande. But the revolution lasted for such a long time that when it finally came to an end the *maestros*, now with larger families, remained here in spite of it. During the hard times of the last depression they opened little establishments on West Broad Street and North Pike where they miraculously made a dollar on some days and as many as two or three on others—always putting on, because they were used to hard times, a good face. When good times returned, most of the *maestros* closed up their little establishments and went to work for the larger concerns which came back in business. Some left for the increasing number of factory jobs in California. But some, enjoying their long independence and believing that it is better to be a poor lord than a rich servant, kept their little establishments open.

Gonzalo Pereda, for example, was a *maestro* who kept a little saddle shop open on West Broad Street. Being a great conversationalist he was not against having company at all hours. Being easy with his money he was always prey for those that told him of need in their homes. And easier prey still for those that often talked him into closing up his establishment, so that they might gossip of old times over a bottle of beer. Being a good craftsman, therefore, had never helped to give the *maestro* more than enough with which to provide for his family.

But if there were men in the world who worried about their work after being through for the day, as far as the *maestro* was concerned they deserved to die young. It certainly was not so with Gonzalo Pereda. Life, he figured, was too short anyway. When he closed up in the afternoon he rid his mind completely of jobs pending and overhead unpaid. He simply hurried home to feed his stable of fighting roosters and to eat supper with his family. Even before taking off his hat he made his way to the back yard to see that his roosters had fresh water and that their cages were clean. That the *maestro* did all of this before going in to greet his family does not mean that he liked the roosters better. But the family, now grown up and with its own affairs, could wait. The roosters, dependent on his arrival for their care, could and should not.

One day when the *maestro* came home, he found a little cage in his   5
back yard. Attached to the top of it was a tag which read, "A present from your friend Bernabé Lerda. Chihuahua, México." In the cage was a red rooster. The *maestro* stuck his finger through an opening and had to jerk it out immediately when the rooster picked at it with a bill which seemed to be made of steel. The *maestro* took a thin leather strip from his pocket, opened the cage, and tied it to the rooster's leg. Then he took the rooster out in order to examine him carefully. The *maestro* looked closely at the rooster's long thick legs, at his tail, which by its length might have belonged to a peacock, at the murder in both of his eager eyes; and the *maestro* knew that this rooster would assassinate any unfortunate fowl pitted against him.

After gazing around a bit the little rooster stretched and strutted. He flapped his wings a few times and then he crowed. The *maestro* was amazed. How could it be, he asked himself, that an animal could possess such pomp? How was it that he knew he was a better rooster than any other that had ever emerged from a hen's egg and therefore strutted about like a race horse confident of winning the Kentucky Derby? How did he know he was such a handsome example of chicken-hood that he, without doubt, could be the Valentino of any chicken yard? Well, it was unbelievable, but it was so. And the *maestro* was sure that this rooster, being from Mexico no less, would slash his way to thirty victories once they put him in the pit. A few minutes later, when one of the *maestro*'s sons saw the rooster, both decided that he must have a worthy name: they decided to call him *Killer.*

So great a stir did Killer cause that the *maestro* forgot all about eating supper that night. While he watched admiringly, Killer took his time about eating his grain and drinking his cool water. One would have thought that the *maestro* could aliment himself by merely gazing at the conceited rooster as he strutted about. The *maestro* said, "The minute he goes into the pit the other rooster will drop dead from fright. Just look at the beautiful creature."

And so it was. The following Sunday afternoon the *maestro* burst in through the front door with Killer. Killer was still hot under the wings from having chased the other rooster and then having slashed it to ribbons. He was still kicking inside the cage as if asking for all the roosters who ever sported a gaff to take him on. "You should have seen him," said the *maestro* to his wife. "Killer is the greatest rooster that ever lived." Then he took Killer to the back yard to cool off.

During the night there was big commotion in the yard. Killer had gotten out of his cage and was attacking the other rooster through the wire fronts of their cages. Already, in a minute or so, there was blood in front of the cage belonging to a rooster named General, who had retreated to the back of his cage for safety. Killer was squaring off, with his neck feathers ruffled, at another cage, in an effort to pick out the eyes of a rooster named Diablo. "He is really cute, isn't he?" asked the *maestro*. Then he took Killer and holding him said, "Well, I guess it is only natural for him to want to fight. He had no competition this afternoon." When Killer was put in another cage, the *maestro* and his son went back to bed.

After the Killer's second fight, the following Sunday, the *maestro* once again came in through the front door with Killer. This time Killer had disposed of his adversary in less than two minutes. The *maestro* was happy. "I am convinced," he said, "that Killer is a butcher if there ever was one." And in victory the *maestro* brought Killer through the front door after the third, fourth, and fifth fight. Now, of course, Killer traveled to and from the pit in style. His was a big cage, made and designed to give him a lot of comfort, with letters reading, "Killer." 10

On the Sunday that Killer won his sixth fight the *maestro* was so happy when he brought Killer through the front door for his wife to admire that tears came from his eyes as he said, "Every rooster that sees this champion can say that the Devil has taken him." And on that day Killer established himself firmly as the best rooster that had ever come to fall in the *maestro*'s possession. This Sunday, after all, had been a great one for the *maestro*, financially speaking and otherwise.

The following Sunday the *maestro* got up very early. Before his daughter left for church he had her take out the camera in order to photograph

Killer. The picture that came out best would be sent away to *Hook and Gaff*, a magazine dedicated to cockfights and poultry. They photographed Killer from various angles. In the arms of the *maestro*. Perched on top of a pole. Looking into a hen roost.

But that afternoon, after the fight, the *maestro* did not storm through the front door to tell how Killer had all but peeled and removed the entrails from the opposing rooster. The *maestro* hurried around the side of the house to the back yard with Killer in his hands. Killer, the invincible one, had met its match. After six battles had come his Waterloo. The reason that Killer was not dead was because the *maestro* had stopped the fight and forfeited his bet. But Killer seemed more dead than alive. His bill was open as if to force breath into his lungs. One of his wings was almost torn off. His back was deeply gashed. One of his eyes was closed. The *maestro* worked frantically to keep Killer alive. He put flour under the torn wing. He took a damp rag and wiped the blood off Killer's head. The *maestro* looked as though he had lost his best friend.

For many days the Killer did not eat. He only stood, and weakly, on his long, thick legs. The *maestro* came home many times to take care of him. He brought Killer some baby-chicken feed in order that he might eat something when he recuperated enough to open his eyes. But to no avail. The *maestro*'s gladiator still seemed close to death.

Then, of a sudden, Killer got better. He began to pick at the baby-chicken feed. And the *maestro* was overwhelmed with joy. Killer did not strut as before, or crow, or flap his wings, but he would, in time. Many things, the *maestro* often said, were fixed by time alone. **15**

Toward the end of Killer's convalescence the *maestro* felt proud of the job he had done in rescuing the Killer from death. As a finishing touch he decided to give the rooster, who was beginning to act somewhat like the Killer of old, some little pieces of liver. These would give him more blood. So, while the *maestro*'s son opened Killer's bill, the *maestro* pushed a little piece of liver down Killer's throat. But the second piece caused Killer to gurgle, to kick momentarily, and then suddenly to die in the *maestro*'s hands. With tears in his eyes the *maestro* stroked his beloved Killer, bit his lip as he wrapped the limp body of his Spartan in a newspaper, and tenderly put it in the garbage can. Then, without supper, the *maestro* went to bed. His beloved Killer was gone.

Like Killer's plight, it might be added, is the plight of many things the *maestros* cherish. Each year they hear their sons talk English with a rapidly disappearing accent, that accent which one early accustomed only to Spanish never fails to have. Each year the *maestros* notice that their sons' Spanish loses fluency. But perhaps it is natural. The *maestros* themselves seem to forget about bulls and bullfighters, about guitars and other things so much a part of the world that years ago circumstance forced them to leave behind. They hear instead more about the difference between one baseball swing and another. Yes, perhaps it is only natural.

Ofttimes when *maestros* get together they point out the fact that each year there are less and less of their little establishments around. They proudly say that the old generation was best; that the new generation knows nothing. They point out, for example, that there are no shoemakers any more. They say that the new generation of so-called shoemakers are nothing but repairers of cheap shoes in need of half soles. They say that the musicians are but accompanists who learned to play an instrument in ten lessons and thus take money under false pretenses. Even the thieves, they tell you, are nothing but two-bit clips. The less said about other phases of *maestría*, they will add, the better.

When one of the *maestros* dies, all the other *maestros* can be counted upon to mourn him. They dust off the dark suits they seldom wear, and offer him, with their calloused hands folded in prayer, a Rosary or two. They carry his coffin to and from the church. And they help fill his grave with the earth that will cover him thereafter. Then they silently know the reason why there are not so many of the little establishments as before. Perhaps it is natural. There are not so many *maestros* any more.

Reading

1. How does Killer die?

2. What signs in the story suggest the decline of *maestría*?

Thinking Critically

1. Why do you think that Gonzalo Pereda develops such an attachment to Killer?

2. What is Pereda's attitude toward the *maestros*? Do you think he is unhappy about their decline? Why or why not?

Connecting

1. Read the excerpt from Rolando Hinojosa's novel *Estampas del Valle* (p. 152). Like Suárez, Hinojosa attempts to capture the wide range of experience found in Mexican American life. What similarities and differences do you find in their styles? Which author's writing seems more realistic? Why do you think so?

Writing

1. Suárez writes, "Like Killer's plight . . . is the plight of many things the *maestros* cherish" (par. 17). Using examples from the text, write a brief essay about what you think the story of the rooster suggests about the *maestros* generally, and about Gonzalo Pereda in particular.

Creating

1. **Photograph a neighborhood.** Mario Suárez was interested in describing the many different kinds of characters that he saw living around him. Pick a neighborhood near you and take some photos of the different people there, and briefly describe how you think they fit into the neighborhood. Is there anything that obviously unites them, or are they more like Suárez's *capirotada* — differing but unified by being part of the same community?

5

AMÉRICO PAREDES [1915–1999]

The Country

From With His Pistol in His Hand: A Border Ballad and Its Hero [1958]

GENRE: NONFICTION

Américo Paredes was one of the most successful Mexican American scholars of the twentieth century, combining talents as a writer, researcher, and academic organizer. He spent the early part of his life in Brownsville, Texas, leaving after his first years of junior college. He showed his interest in and talent for literature with the 1937 publication of Cantos de adolescencia, *a book of poetry. With the onset of World War II, Paredes left the country, first as an employee of Pan American Airlines, then as an army draftee, and then after the war as a public relations officer for the Red Cross. Upon his return, he earned his bachelor's, master's, and doctoral degrees from the University of Texas at Austin, where he spent the rest of his professional career teaching English and anthropology. His doctoral study of Gregorio Cortez, the hero of a* corrido—*a*

Mexican form of folk song—was published in 1958 as With His
Pistol in His Hand: A Border Ballad and Its Hero. *The book's bit-
ing wit and well-researched attack on the entrenched myths about
Texas history showed his abilities as a scholar and a writer, earning him a wide readership and creating a foundation for the work
of later Chicano writers and activists. Paredes also became the
first director of the university's Center for Mexican American Studies in 1970 and is often called the father of Chicano studies. In
addition to his many academic studies of Mexican American culture, near the end of his life he published a book of short stories
called* The Hammon and the Beans *and* George Washington Gó-
mez, *a novel he had written decades earlier.*

*Like Jovita González (p. 11) before him, Paredes called himself a
folklorist. Unlike González, however, Paredes put Texas's cultural
conflicts, along with their economic and social consequences, at the
center of his studies.* With His Pistol in His Hand, *excerpted here,
is a study of the long background of the shootout between the Texas
Rangers and folk hero Gregorio Cortez. This section, titled "The
Country," discusses the culture of the Lower Río Grande people and
the origins of the hostile attitudes of Anglo-Texans toward it.*

As you read, notice the ways that Paredes shows that culture of
the Lower Río Grande people to be stable and complete and, for
many readers and future writers, a source of pride.

NUEVO SANTANDER

The Lower Rio Grande Border is the area lying along the river, from its
mouth to the two Laredos. A map, especially one made some thirty or
forty years ago, would show a clustering of towns and villages along both
river banks, with lonely gaps to the north and to the south. This was the
heart of the old Spanish province of Nuevo Santander, colonized in 1749
by José de Escandón.

In the days before upriver irrigation projects, the Lower Rio Grande
was a green, fertile belt, bounded on the north and south by arid plains,
situated along a river which, like the Nile, irrigated and fertilized the
lands close to its banks and periodically filled countless little lakes,
known as resacas and esteros. Isolated by natural barriers, the country
was still unexplored long after the initial wave of Spanish conquest had
spent itself and Spain was struggling with the problems created by her
earlier successes. Spanish colonization had gone as far north as New

Mexico on the west, and to the east it had jumped overseas to Texas. The Lower Rio Grande, known as the Seno Mexicano (the Mexican Hollow or Recess), was a refuge for rebellious Indians from the Spanish presidios,° who preferred outlawry to life under Spanish rule. Thus, at its earliest period in history the Lower Rio Grande was inhabited by outlaws, whose principal offense was an independent spirit.

Toward the middle of the eighteenth century Spanish officialdom decided that better communications were needed between Texas and Mexico City, routes which would cross the Seno Mexicano. José de Escandón was ordered to colonize the Lower Rio Grande. Four months after his appointment, Escandón was already on his way with parties of exploration.

Escandón was a wise and far-sighted administrator, and his methods were different from those of most Spanish colonizers. The *presidio*, symbol of military authority over settlers and Indians alike, was not part of his plans. The soldiers assigned to each settlement of Nuevo Santander were settlers too, and their captain was the colony's most prominent citizen.

The colonists came from the settled Spanish families of surrounding   5
regions and were induced to settle on the Rio Grande by promises of free land and other government concessions. One of these concessions was freedom from interference by officialdom in the faraway centers of population. The colony of Nuevo Santander was settled much like the lands occupied by westward-pushing American pioneers, by men and their families who came overland, with their household goods and their herds.

The Indians seem to have given little trouble. They were neither exterminated in the English manner, nor enslaved according to the usual Spanish way. They lived in the same small towns as the Spanish settlers, under much the same conditions, and were given a measure of self-government.

By 1755, a bare six years after the founding of Nuevo Santander, there were only 146 soldiers still on duty among 8,993 settlers. There were 3,413 Indians in the towns, not counting those that still remained in a wild state.[1] In succeeding generations the Indians, who began as vaqueros and sheepherders for the colonists, were absorbed into the blood and the culture of the Spanish settlers. Also absorbed into the basically Spanish culture were many non-Spanish Europeans, so that on the Border one finds men who prefer Spanish to English, who sometimes talk scornfully about the "Gringos," and who bear English, Scottish, Irish, or other non-Spanish names.

By 1755 towns had been founded near the present site of Laredo—the only north-bank settlement of the time—and at Guerrero, Mier, Camargo, and Reynosa on the south bank. The colonists were pushing into the

presidio: Military fort.

Nueces–Rio Grande area in search of pasturage for their rapidly increasing herds. Don Blas María Falcón, the founder of Camargo, established a ranch called La Petronila at the mouth of the Nueces at about this time.

By 1835 there were three million head of livestock in the Rio Grande–Nueces area, according to the assessments of the towns along the Rio Grande.[2] Matamoros, founded near the river mouth in 1765 by people from Reynosa, had grown into the metropolis of the colony with 15,000 inhabitants. The other riverbank towns, though not so large, were correspondingly prosperous. The old province of Nuevo Santander was about to emerge from almost a century of isolation and growth, when war in Texas opened the period of border strife.

THE RIO GRANDE PEOPLE

Most of the Border people did not live in the towns. The typical community was the ranch or the ranching village. Here lived small, tightly knit groups whose basic social structure was the family or the clan. The early settlements had begun as great ranches, but succeeding generations multiplied the number of owners of each of the original land grants. The earliest practice was to divide the grant among the original owner's children. Later many descendants simply held the land in common, grouping their houses in small villages around what had been the ancestral home. In time almost everyone in any given area came to be related to everyone else.

The cohesiveness of the Border communities owed a great deal to geography. Nuevo Santander was settled comparatively late because of its isolated location. In 1846 it took Taylor a month to move his troops the 160 miles from Corpus Christi to Brownsville. In 1900 communications had improved but little, and it was not until 1904 that a railroad connected Brownsville with trans-Nueces areas, while a paved highway did not join Matamoros with the interior of Mexico until the 1940's.

The brush around Brownsville in the 1870's was so heavy that herds of stolen beef or horses could be hidden a few miles from town in perfect secrecy.[3] Even in the late 1920's the thick chaparral isolated many parts of the Border. Ranches and farms that are now within sight of each other across a flat, dusty cotton land were remote in those days of winding trails through the brush. The nearest neighbors were across the river, and most north-bank communities were in fact extensions of those on the south bank.

The simple pastoral life led by most Border people fostered a natural equality among men. Much has been written about the democratizing influence of a horse culture. More important was the fact that on the Border the landowner lived and worked upon his land. There was almost no gap between the owner and his cowhand, who often was related to him anyway. The simplicity of the life led by both employer and employee also helped make them feel that they were not different kinds of men, even if one was richer than the other.

Border economy was largely self-sufficient. Corn, beans, melons, and vegetables were planted on the fertile, easily irrigated lands at the river's edge. Sheep and goats were also raised in quantity. For these more menial, pedestrian tasks the peon was employed in earlier days. The peon was usually a *fuereño*, an "outsider" from central Mexico, but on the Border he was not a serf. Peón in Nuevo Santander had preserved much of its old meaning of "man on foot." The gap between the peon and the vaquero was not extreme, though the man on horseback had a job with more prestige, one which was considered to involve more danger and more skill.

The peon, however, could and did rise in the social scale. People along the Border who like to remember genealogies and study family trees can tell of instances in which a man came to the Border as a peon (today he would be called a *bracero*) and ended his life as a vaquero, while his son began life as a vaquero and ended it as a small landowner, and the grandson married into the old family that had employed his grandfather—the whole process taking place before the Madero Revolution. In few parts of Greater Mexico before 1910 could people of all degrees—including landowners—have circulated and obviously enjoyed the story of Juan, the peon who knew his right, and who not only outwitted his landowning employer but gave him a good beating besides, so that the landowner afterward would never hire a peon who "walked like Juan."

This is not to say that there was democracy on the Border as Americans recognize it or that the average Borderer had been influenced by eighteenth-century ideas about the rights of man. Social conduct was regulated and formal, and men lived under a patriarchal system that made them conscious of degree. The original settlements had been made on a patriarchal basis, with the "captain" of each community playing the part of father to his people. . . .

The patriarchal system not only made the Border community more cohesive, by emphasizing its clanlike characteristics, but it also minimized outside interference, because it allowed the community to govern itself to a great extent. If officials saw fit to appoint an *encargado°* to represent the state, they usually chose the patriarch, merely giving official recognition to a choice already made by custom.

Thus the Rio Grande people lived in tight little groups—usually straddling the river—surrounded by an alien world. From the north came the

encargado: One in charge of a specific task.

gringo, which term meant "foreigner." From the south came the *fuereño*, or outsider, as the Mexican of the interior was called. Nuevo Santander had been settled as a way station to Texas, but there was no heavy traffic over these routes, except during wartime. Even in the larger towns the inhabitants ignored strangers for the most part, while the people of the remoter communities were oblivious of them altogether. The era of border conflict was to bring greater numbers of outsiders to the Border, but most Borderers treated them either as transients or as social excrescences. During the American Civil War and the Mexican Empire, Matamoros became a cosmopolitan city without affecting appreciably the life of the villages and ranches around it. On the north bank it took several generations for the new English-speaking owners of the country to make an impression on the old mores. The Border Mexican simply ignored strangers, except when disturbed by violence or some other transgression of what he believed was "the right." In the wildest years of the Border, the swirl of events and the coming and going of strange faces was but froth on the surface of life.

In such closely knit groups most tasks and amusements were engaged in communally. Roundups and brandings were community projects, undertaken according to the advice of the old men. When the river was in flood, the patriarchal council decided whether the levees should be opened to irrigate the fields or whether they should be reinforced to keep the water out, and the work of levee-building or irrigation was carried out by the community as a whole. Planting and harvesting were individual for the most part, but the exchange of the best fruits of the harvest (though all raised the same things) was a usual practice. In the 1920's, when I used to spend my summers in one of the south-bank ranch communities, the communal provision of fresh beef was still a standard practice. Each family slaughtered in turn and distributed the meat among the rest, ensuring a supply of fresh beef every week.

Amusement were also communal, though the statement in no way should suggest the "dancing, singing throng" creating as a group. Group singing, in fact, was rare. The community got together, usually at the patriarch's house, to enjoy the performance of individuals, though sometimes all the individuals in a group might participate in turn.

The dance played but little part in Border folkways, though in the twentieth century the Mexicanized polka has become something very close to a native folk form. Native folk dances were not produced, nor were they imported from fringe areas like southern Tamaulipas, where the *huapango* was danced. Polkas, mazurkas, waltzes, lancers, *contradanzas*, and other forms then in vogue were preferred. Many Border families had prejudices against dancing. It brought the sexes too close together and gave rise to quarrels and bloody fights among the men.

There were community dances at public spots and some private dances in the homes, usually to celebrate weddings, but the dance on the Border was a modern importation, reflecting European vogues.

Horse racing was, of course, a favorite sport among the men. In the home, amusements usually took the form of singing, the presentation of religious plays at Christmas, tableaux, and the like. This material came from oral tradition. Literacy among the old Border families was relatively high, but the reading habit of the Protestant Anglo-Saxon, fostered on a veneration of the written words in the Bible, was foreign to the Borderer. His religion was oral and traditional.

On most occasions the common amusement was singing to the accompaniment of the guitar: in the informal community gatherings, where the song alternated with the tale; at weddings, which had their own special songs, the *golondrinas*; at Christmastime, with its *pastorelas* and *aguinaldos*; and even at some kinds of funerals, those of infants, at which special songs were sung to the guitar.

The Nuevo Santander people also sang ballads. Some were songs remembered from their Spanish origins, and perhaps an occasional ballad came to them from the older frontier colony of Nuevo Mexico. But chiefly they made their own. They committed their daily affairs and their history to the ballad form: the fights against the Indians, the horse races, and the domestic triumphs and tragedies—and later the border conflicts and the civil wars. The ballads, and the tradition of ballad-making as well, were handed down from father to son, and thus the people of the Lower Rio Grande developed a truly native balladry.

It was the Treaty of Guadalupe that added the final element to Rio   25
Grande society, a border. The river, which had been a focal point, became a dividing line. Men were expected to consider their relatives and closest neighbors, the people just across the river, as foreigners in a foreign land. A restless and acquisitive people, exercising the rights of conquest, disturbed the old ways.

Out of the conflict that arose on the new border came men like Gregorio Cortez. Legends were told about these men, and ballads were sung in their memory. And this state of affairs persisted for one hundred years after Santa Anna stormed the Alamo.

MIER, THE ALAMO, AND GOLIAD

In the conflict along the Rio Grande, the English-speaking Texan (whom we shall call the Anglo-Texan for short) disappoints us in a folkloristic sense. He produces no border balladry. His contribution to the literature of border conflict is a set of attitudes and beliefs about the Mexican which form a legend of their own and are the complement to the *corrido*, the Border Mexican ballad of border conflict. The Anglo-Texan legend may be summarized under half a dozen points.

1. The Mexican is cruel by nature. The Texan must in self-defense treat the Mexican cruelly, since that is the only treatment the Mexican understands.

2. The Mexican is cowardly and treacherous, and no match for the Texan. He can get the better of the Texan only by stabbing him in the back or by ganging up on him with a crowd of accomplices.

3. Thievery is second nature in the Mexican, especially horse and cattle rustling, and on the whole he is about as degenerate a specimen of humanity as may be found anywhere.

4. The degeneracy of the Mexican is due to his mixed blood, though the elements in the mixture were inferior to begin with. He is descended from the Spaniard, a second-rate type of European, and from the equally substandard Indian of Mexico, who must not be confused with the noble savages of North America.

5. The Mexican has always recognized the Texan as his superior and thinks of him as belonging to a race separate from other Americans.

6. The Texan has no equal anywhere, but within Texas itself there developed a special breed of men, the Texas Rangers, in whom the Texan's qualities reached their culmination.

This legend is not found in the cowboy ballads, the play-party songs, or the folk tales of the people of Texas. Orally one finds it in the anecdote and in some sentimental verse of nonfolk origin. It is in print — in newspapers, magazines, and books — that it has been circulated most. In books it has had its greatest influence and its longest life. The earliest were the war propaganda works of the 1830's and 1840's about Mexican "atrocities" in Texas, a principal aim of which was to overcome Northern antipathy toward the approaching war with Mexico.[4] After 1848, the same attitudes were perpetuated in the works, many of them autobiographical, about the adventurers and other men of action who took part in the border conflict on the American side. A good and an early example is the following passage from *Sketches of the Campaign in Northern Mexico*, by an officer of Ohio volunteers.

> The inhabitants of the valley of the Rio Grande are chiefly occupied in raising stock. . . . But a pastoral life, generally so propitious to purity of morals and strength of constitution, does not appear to have produced its usually

happy effect upon that people . . . vile rancheros; the majority of whom are so vicious and degraded that one can hardly believe that the light of Christianity has ever dawned upon them.[5]

In more recent years it has often been the writer of history textbooks and the author of scholarly works who have lent their prestige to the legend. This is what the most distinguished historian Texas has produced had to say about the Mexican in 1935.

Without disparagement, it may be said that there is a cruel streak in the Mexican nature, or so the history of Texas would lead one to believe. This cruelty may be a heritage from the Spanish of the Inquisition; it may, and doubtless should, be attributed partly to the Indian blood. . . . The Mexican warrior . . . was, on the whole, inferior to the Comanche and wholly un-equal to the Texan. The whine of the leaden slugs stirred in him an irresistible impulse to travel with rather than against the music. He won more victories over the Texans by parley than by force of arms. For making promises—and for breaking them—he had no peer.[6]

Professor Webb does not mean to be disparaging. One wonders what his opinion might have been when he was in a less scholarly mood and not looking at the Mexican from the objective point of view of the historian. In another distinguished work, *The Great Plains*, Dr. Webb develops sim-ilar aspects of the legend. The Spanish "failure" on the Great Plains is blamed partly on the Spanish character. More damaging still was misce-genation with the Mexican Indian, "whose blood, when compared with that of the Plains Indian, was as ditch water."[7] On the other hand, Amer-ican success on the Great Plains was due to the "pure American stock," the "foreign element" having settled elsewhere.[8]

How can one classify the Texas legend—as fact, as folklore, or as still something else? The records of frontier life after 1848 are full of instances of cruelty and inhumanity. But by far the majority of the acts of cruelty are ascribed by American writers themselves to men of their own race. The victims, on the other hand, were very often Mexicans. There is always the implication that it was "defensive cruelty," or that the Mexicans were being punished for their inhumanity to Texans at the Alamo, Mier, and Goliad.

There probably is not an army (not excepting those of the United States) that has not been accused of "atrocities" during wartime. It is remarkable, then, that those atrocities said to have occurred in connec-tion with the Alamo, Goliad, and the Mier expedition are universally attributed not to the Mexican army as a whole but to their commander, Santa Anna. Even more noteworthy is the fact that Santa Anna's orders were protested by his officers, who incurred the dictator's wrath by

30

pleading for the prisoners in their charge. In at least two other cases (not celebrated in Texas history) Santa Anna's officers were successful in their pleading, and Texan lives were spared. Both Texan and Mexican accounts agree that the executions evoked horror among many Mexicans witnessing them—officers, civilians, and common soldiers.[9]

Had Santa Anna lived in the twentieth century, he would have called the atrocities with which he is charged "war crimes trials." There is a fundamental difference, though, between his executions of Texan prisoners and the hangings of Japanese army officers like General Yamashita at the end of the Pacific War. Santa Anna usually was in a rage when he ordered his victims shot. The Japanese were never hanged without the ceremony of a trial—a refinement, one must conclude, belonging to a more civilized age and a more enlightened people.

Meanwhile, Texas-Mexicans died at the Alamo and fought at San Jacinto on the Texan side. The Rio Grande people, because of their Federalist and autonomist views, were sympathetic to the Texas republic until Texans began to invade their properties south of the Nueces. The truth seems to be that the old war propaganda concerning the Alamo, Goliad, and Mier later provided a convenient justification for outrages committed on the Border by Texans of certain types, so convenient an excuse that it was artificially prolonged for almost a century. And had the Alamo, Goliad, and Mier not existed, they would have been invented, as indeed they seem to have been in part.

The Texan had an undeniable superiority over the Mexican in the matter of weapons. The Texan was armed with the rifle and the revolver. The ranchero fought with the implements of his cowherding trade, the rope and the knife, counting himself lucky if he owned a rusty old musket and a charge of powder. Lead was scarce, old pieces of iron being used for bullets. Possession of even a weapon of this kind was illegal after 1835, when Santa Anna disarmed the militia, leaving the frontier at the mercy of Indians and Texans. Against them the ranchero had to depend on surprise and superior horsemanship. Until the Mexican acquired the revolver and learned how to use it, a revolver-armed Texan could indeed be worth a half-dozen Mexicans; but one may wonder whether cowards will fight under such handicaps as did the Borderers. The Rio Grande people not only defended themselves with inadequate armament; they often made incursions into hostile territory armed with lances, knives, and old swords.[10]

The belief in the Mexican's treachery was related to that of his cowardice. As with the Mexican's supposed cruelty, one finds the belief perpetuated as a justification for outrage. Long after Mexicans acquired the revolver, "peace officers" in the Nueces–Rio Grande territory continued to believe (or pretended to do so) that no Mexican unaided could best a Texan in a fair fight. The killing of innocent Mexicans as "accomplices" became standard procedure—especially with the Texas Rangers—whenever a Border Mexican shot an American. The practice had an important influence on Border balladry and on the lives of men such as Gregorio Cortez.

The picture of the Mexican as an inveterate thief, especially of horses and cattle, is of interest to the psychologist as well as to the folklorist. The cattle industry of the Southwest had its origin in the Nueces–Rio Grande area, with the stock and the ranches of the Rio Grande rancheros. The "cattle barons" built up their fortunes at the expense of the Border Mexican by means which were far from ethical. One notes that the white Southerner took his slave women as concubines and then created an image of the male Negro as a sex fiend. In the same way he appears to have taken the Mexican's property and then made him out a thief.

The story that the Mexican thought of the Texan as a being apart and distinguished him from other Americans belongs with the postcards depicting the United States as an appendage of Texas. To the Border Mexican at least, Texans are indistinguishable from other Americans, and *tejano* is used for the Texas-Mexican, except perhaps among the more sophisticated. The story that the Mexican believes he could lick the United States if it were not for Texas also must be classed as pure fiction. The Border Mexican does distinguish the Ranger from other Americans, but his belief is that if it were not for the United States Army he would have run the Rangers out of the country a long time ago.

Theories of racial purity have fallen somewhat into disrepute since the end of World War II. So has the romantic idea that Li Po and Einstein were inferior to Genghis Khan and Hitler because the latter two were bloodier and therefore manlier. There is interest from a folkloristic point of view, however, in the glorification of the Plains savage at the expense of the semicivilized, sedentary Indian of Mexico. The noble savage very early crept into American folklore in the form of tales and songs about eloquent Indian chiefs and beautiful Indian princesses. Such stories appear to have had their origin in areas where Indians had completely disappeared.[11] On the frontier the legend seems to have been dichotomized. After the 1870's, when the Indian danger was past, it was possible to idealize the Plains savage. But the "Mexican problem" remained. A distinction was drawn between the noble Plains Indian and the degenerate ancestor of the Mexican.

The legend has taken a firm grip on the American imagination. In the Southwest one finds Americans of Mexican descent attempting to hide their Indian blood by calling themselves Spanish, while Americans of other origins often boast of having Comanche, Cherokee, or other wild Indian blood, all royal of course. The belief also had its practical aspects in reaffirming Mexican racial inferiority. The Comanche did not consider

Mexican blood inferior. Mexican captives were often adopted into the tribe, as were captives of other races. But the Comanche had never read the Bible or John Locke. He could rob, kill, or enslave without feeling the need of racial prejudices to justify his actions.

Even a cursory analysis shows the justification value of the Texas legend and gives us a clue to one of the reasons for its survival. Goldfinch puts most Americans coming into the Brownsville-Matamoros area after the Mexican War into two categories: those who had no personal feeling against the Mexicans but who were ruthless in their efforts to acquire a fortune quickly, and those who, inclined to be brutal to everyone, found in the Mexican's defenseless state after the war an easy and safe outlet for their brutality.[12] It was to the interest of these two types that the legend about the Mexican be perpetuated. As long as the majority of the population accepted it as fact, men of this kind could rob, cheat, or kill the Border Mexican without suffering sanctions either from the law or from public opinion. And if the Mexican retaliated, the law stepped in to defend or to avenge his persecutors.

In 1838 Texas "cowboys" were making expeditions down to the Rio Grande to help the Rio Grande people fight Santa Anna. In between alliances they stole their allies' cattle. McArthur states that their stealing was "condemned by some" but that it was "justified by the majority on the ground that the Mexicans belonged to a hostile nation, from whom the Texans had received and were still receiving many injuries; and that they would treat the Texans worse if it were in their power to do so."[13] In the 1850's and 1860's when the filibuster William Walker—a Tennessean—operated in Central America, he did so to the cry of "Remember the Alamo!"[14] Al Capone in the 1920's, sending his men off to take care of some German shopkeeper who had failed to kick in, might just as well have cried, "Remember Caporetto, boys! Remember the Piave!" But perhaps Scarface Al lacked a sense of history.

This does not explain why the legend finds support among the literate and the educated. The explanation may lie in the paucity of Texas literature until very recent times. Other peoples have been stirred up by skillfully written war propaganda, but after the war they have usually turned to other reading, if they have a rich literature from which to draw. J. Frank Dobie has said that if he "were asked what theme of Texas life has been most movingly and dramatically recorded . . . I should name the experiences of Texans as prisoners to the Mexicans."[15] If it is true that the best writing done about Texas until recent times was ancient war propaganda directed against the Mexicans, it is not strange that the prejudices of those early days should have been preserved among the literate. The relative lack of perspective and of maturity of mind that Mr. Dobie himself deplored as late as 1952 in writers about the Southwest also played its part.[16]

Is the Texas legend folklore? The elements of folklore are there. One catches glimpses of the "false Scot" and the "cruel Moor," half-hidden among the local color. Behind the superhuman Ranger are Beowulf, Roland, and the Cid, slaying hundreds.[17] The idea that one's own clan or tribe is unique is probably inherent in certain stages of human development. Sometimes the enemy is forced to recognize the excellence of the hero. Achilles' armor and the Cid's corpse win battles; the Spanish hosts admit the valor of Brave Lord Willoughby, the Englishman; and the Rangers recognize the worth of Jacinto Treviño, the Mexican.

The difference, and a fundamental one, between folklore and the Texas 45 legend is that the latter is not usually found in the oral traditions of those groups of Texas people that one might consider folk. It appears in two widely dissimilar places: in the written works of the literary and the educated and orally among a class of rootless adventurers who have used the legend for very practical purposes. One must classify the Texas legend as pseudo folklore. Disguised as fact, it still plays a major role in Texas history. Under the guise of local pride, it appears in its most blatant forms in the "professional" Texan.

NOTES

1. William Curry Holden, *Fray Vicente Santa María: Historical Account of the Colony of Nuevo Santander*, Master's thesis, University of Texas, 1924, p. xi.

2. Cecil Bernard Smith, *Diplomatic Relations between the United States and Mexico*, Master's thesis, University of Texas, 1928, p. 5.

3. *Informe de la Comisión Pesquisidora de la Frontera del Norte*, Mexico, 1877, p. 32.

4. See J. Frank Dobie, *The Flavor of Texas*, Dallas, 1936, pp. 125ff., for some of the aims and the effects of this type of work.

5. [Luther Giddings], *Sketches of the Campaign in Northern Mexico*, New York, 1853, p. 54.

6. Walter Prescott Webb, *The Texas Rangers*, Cambridge, 1935, p. 14.

7. Walter Prescott Webb, *The Great Plains*, Boston, 1931, pp. 125–26.

8. *Ibid.*, p. 509.

9. For a Mexican condemnation of the Alamo and Goliad, see Ramón Martínez Caro, *Verdadera idea de la primera campaña en Tejas*, Mexico, 1837, published one year after the events.

10. J. Frank Dobie in *The Mustangs*, New York, 1954, pp. 195 and 261, makes some interesting observations about the Mexican armament of the time.

11. See Austin E. Fife and Francesca Redden, "The Pseudo-Indian Folksongs of the Anglo-American and French-Canadian," *Journal of American Folklore*, Vol. 67, No. 265, pp. 239–51; No. 266, pp. 379–94.

12. Charles W. Goldfinch, *Juan N. Cortina 1824–1892, a Re-Appraisal*, Brownsville (Texas) 1950, p. 40.

13. Daniel Evander McArthur, *The Cattle Industry of Texas, 1685–1918*, Master's thesis, University of Texas, 1915, p. 50.

14. Dobie, *The Flavor of Texas*, p. 5.

15. *Ibid.*, p. 125.

16. J. Frank Dobie, *Guide to Life and Literature of the Southwest*, Dallas, 1952, pp. 90–91.

17. In epic story, however, the enemy is rarely cowardly. Very often it is one of the hero's own side who is the least admirable character—Thersites among the Greeks, the Counts of Carrión among the Castilians, the weeping coward among the Border raiders.

Reading

1. How does Paredes describe the economic situation of the "Rio Grande people"?

2. What are the elements of the "Texas legend"? In what sources does Paredes say the legend can be found?

Thinking Critically

1. What is Paredes's attitude toward the "Texas legend"? Do you think he tries to hide his own feelings? In what ways is his opinion revealed in this excerpt?

2. Because Paredes writes as a folklorist, he analyzes events and people as reflective of their cultures — in this case, of Anglo and Mexican cultures. What do you think are the strengths and weaknesses of this approach?

Connecting

1. Read Tino Villanueva's poem, "Scene from the Movie *GIANT*" (p. 183), which celebrates a movie scene showing a Texas Anglo standing up for Mexicans. How do you think Paredes would respond to the poem? Does it fit with Paredes's description of the cultures of Texas, or does it show something that Paredes left out?

Writing

1. Américo Paredes believed that a careful study of history and culture was a part of combatting racial intolerance. In an essay, explore the ways you think that "The Country" might help do this. Support your arguments with examples from the text.

Creating

1. **Compose a *corrido*.** Gregorio Cortez, the hero of the *corrido* at the heart of *With His Pistol in His Hand*, is caught up in a cultural conflict. Songs about heroic rebels and their exploits are common in many genres of music. Write a song or poem about a hero who you think represents a culture in conflict with another, and include a brief description of the conflict's historical and cultural background.

6

RUBÉN SALAZAR [1928–1970]

La Nacha Sells Dirty Dope . . .

From El Paso Herald Post [1955]

GENRE: JOURNALISM / NEWS ARTICLE

The death of Rubén Salazar in 1970 at the hands of a Los Angeles policeman made him the most famous martyr of the Chicano Movement—a journalist in his prime killed while bringing national attention to the growing movimiento. *He was born in Juárez, Mexico, and grew up just across the Río Grande in El Paso, Texas. After serving in the army during the Korean War, he attended the University of Texas at El Paso, studying journalism. He soon began writing stories for the* El Paso Herald Post, *once even posing as a drunk and getting arrested so that he could report on the terrible conditions in the city's jail. A few years later he began work for the* Los Angeles Times, *covering the Mexican American community and then becoming a foreign correspondent in the Dominican Republic, Vietnam, and Mexico City, where he became bureau chief. He returned to Los Angeles in 1968 to cover the city's growing Mexican American community and its politics. On August 29, 1970, when thousands joined a Chicano Moratorium march to protest the disproportionate fatalities of Mexican Americans in the Vietnam War, Salazar came as a reporter. Fights between marchers and the police broke out, and when an officer fired a tear gas canister into a crowded bar, Salazar was hit in the head and died. Though now most famous as a martyr, whose death has remained clouded by suspicion, Salazar is*

*significant for his success as a journalist and for his coverage of a
pivotal time in the history of Mexican Americans.*

*The newspaper article "La Nacha Sells Dirty Dope . . ." originally
ran in the* El Paso Herald Post *on August 17, 1955, and shows the
lengths to which Salazar would go for a story. It is a work of journalism, but in both its subject matter and its style, it has clear similarities with other stories that explore barrio life, providing
interested readers with their first glimpse of another world.*

As you read, notice the way that Salazar uses his skill at description to make a news piece evoke a place and a culture.

LA NACHA SELLS DIRTY DOPE AT $5 A "PAPEL"
HERALD-POST REPORTER MAKES PURCHASE FROM
BORDER "QUEEN"

August 17, 1955

EL PASO, Texas—La Nacha° is the Dope Queen of the Border. She is big
stuff. But she will sell you one "papel" (paper) of heroin just like any
"pusher" on a street corner.

If you aren't too far gone, the dirty-looking stuff in the folded paper is
good for two shots. But that's true only for those who are beginning.

A dope addict, whom I will call "Hypo," buys the $10 size. It has more
than the two of the $5 papers, Hypo said. One lasts him a day—most days.

He Met the Queen

La Nacha—right name Ignacia Jasso—lives in a good house in a bad
neighborhood. She's fat, dark, cynical and around 60. She deals out misery from her comfortable home.

She sells usually what is called a "dirty load," which is one that is not   5
white as heroin should be, but a dirty, dusty color.

Her prices are in American money. She does business with many
American addicts. She's as casual about it as if she were selling tortillas.

Hypo took me to La Nacha's home and introduced me to the dope
queen.

I visited her twice. The first time Hypo and I bought a $5 paper of
heroin. The second time we bought the large economy $10 size.

Nacha: Nickname for Ignacia.

The papers contained dope all right. I saw Hypo, an El Paso married man of 24 whose 19-year-old wife has a three-month-old baby, inject himself with the "carga" (load).

He's Got to Have It

Hypo, who says he wants to be cured, cannot live without heroin. It costs 10 him about $10 a day—or hours of excruciating pain. Hypo prefers heroin to pain and gets the $10 a day any way he can. He sold all his furniture for heroin. He was evicted from his apartment for not paying rent. He has stolen, borrowed and now has given me his story for $15 which he spent on heroin.

Hypo and I went to visit La Nacha in the afternoon. We parked the car a few blocks from her house. She lives in Bellavista district, which means "Beautiful View." It is far from beautiful. The streets are unpaved and most of the houses are adobe. Naked kids were running about the streets.

We turned on Mercuro alley and walked toward La Nacha's house, which is on the corner of the alley and Violetas (Violets) Street. Hers is the only decent-looking house in the neighborhood. It is yellow and has fancy iron grillwork on the windows.

She Has a TV Set

Hypo and I walked through the nicely kept green patio.

Inside, the house has all the conveniences of a modern home: gas, stove, nice living room furniture, TV and a saint's statue on the wall.

I had been to Hypo's El Paso apartment and couldn't help thinking 15 about his bare rooms after he had sold the furniture for heroin. The last time I had been at Hypo's apartment, I had seen the baby on the floor on a blanket and Hypo's wife sitting in a corner watching the baby. There was a sad, vacant look in her eyes.

Once inside the house, which Hypo knows so well that he doesn't even bother to knock, we met Nacha's daughter. She was sitting on a bed talking to another woman. Hypo told her he was going away and wanted to introduce me so I could buy the stuff myself.

"You'll have to ask Mother," Nacha's daughter said.

Then I was introduced to Nacha's son. He is heavyset, wears a mustache and had on an expensive watch.

I noticed a stool nearby which had white strips of paper neatly arranged on top.

She Looked Him Over

Then La Nacha came in. I remembered Hypo's advice that I should be   20
polite to her. She gave me the once-over, I was introduced. She sat in front
of the stool and started working the strips. They were the heroin papers.

Hypo told La Nacha that I was a musician working in a dance hall in
El Paso and wanted to start buying "loads."

La Nacha glanced at my arms. Hypo explained that I wasn't a "mainliner." That I just liked to "jornear" — breathe the heroin. A "mainliner" is
one who injects himself with a hypodermic needle.

La Nacha said, "All right, any time."

"At night we sell it across the street," La Nacha's daughter said,

Hypo asked La Nacha for "a nickel's worth." She handed me a paper of   25
heroin. (She wanted to know if I would handle the stuff, Hypo told me
later.) Hypo gave her $5 and we left.

Quicker and Better

After we bought the load we went to a cheap hotel in Juarez. There I saw
Hypo, who is a "mainliner," inject himself with heroin.

"You feel better quicker that way," Hypo said.

"Mainliners" need a cup of water, a syringe with a needle, an eye dropper, a bottle cap and the expensive heroin to make them feel, in Hypo's
word, "normal."

"A man who is hooked (that is, one who has the habit bad) never feels
normal unless he's had at least two shots a day," Hypo said.

I watched Hypo go through the process of injecting himself with her-   30
oin. First he carefully placed half a paper of heroin in the bottle cap with
a knife. Then with an eye dropper he placed a few drops of water in the
cap. He took a match and placed it underneath the cap while holding it
with the other hand. After it was heated Hypo dropped a tiny ball of cotton in the cap. "This is so the hypodermic can suck all the heroin out the
cap," Hypo explained. The cotton works like a filter.

Wild Eyes Gleam

Hypo then placed the hypodermic syringe in the cap and the brownish
substance could be seen running up into the syringe.

Hypo's wild eyes gleamed with excitement.

Hypo crouched on the floor balanced on the front of his shoes.
He injected the heroin in his vein. His vein was swollen from so many
punctures.

Almost as soon as the heroin had gone into his vein he started rocking back and forth. I asked him how he felt.

"Muy suave, ese," he said. "Real good."   35

Before long he passed out. His stomach sounded like a washing machine. He snored loudly and uncomfortably. I tried to wake him. I couldn't. So I went home.

Took an Overdose

Later he explained that he had taken an overdose.

"The load was real clean and I misjudged the amount I should have taken," Hypo said. "I could have died."

The second time I saw Hypo we must have bought a load not as clean or he judged the right amount. For the reaction was much different. Before he injected himself he looked worse than I had ever seen him. His eyes looked like two huge buttons. He complained of pains all over his body. Hypo couldn't even hold a cigarette because of his shaking hands.

We went to La Nacha's and bought some heroin. We only stayed a min-   40 ute. Hypo needed to be "cured" quick.

After he injected himself this time he actually looked better than before, talked better and acted better. He was only half dead—instead of three quarters.

He stopped shaking. He smoked almost calmly and was talkative. "I've got to quit this habit," he said. "For my little daughter's sake. I love her very much. God, I wish I could stop it."

I, too, hope he can.

Reading

1. Who is "La Nacha"?

2. Where does the nickname "Hypo" come from?

Thinking Critically

1. What is Salazar's attitude toward La Nacha and Hypo? Is he sympathetic? Hostile? Why do you think so?

2. Why do you think Salazar wrote this story?

Connecting

1. About a decade after this article was written, Oscar Acosta, author of *The Revolt of the Cockroach People* (p. 131), helped invent "gonzo" journalism, in which reporters become part of the story they describe.

Read the selection from Acosta's *The Revolt of the Cockroach People* and compare his writing to Salazar's. Do you find any similarities? Do you find one writer more trustworthy than the other? Why or why not?

Writing

1. As a reporter, Rubén Salazar tried to give a reliable, objective account of what he witnessed. Still, his personality comes through in his writing. In a brief essay, using examples from the text, write about Salazar's style and what you can learn about him from this article.

Creating

1. **Write a news article.** Newspapers and news sites are among the most important sources of information about the world we live in. Reporters must learn to communicate information as accurately and concisely as possible while keeping their own opinions silent. Write a news article about a person or an event that you think others ought to know more about.

7

JOHN RECHY [b. 1934]

From *City of Night* [1963]

GENRE: FICTION

With the publication in 1963 of City of Night, *John Rechy became the first Mexican American to achieve a national reputation as a writer. Like the narrator of that novel, Rechy was born and raised in El Paso, Texas. After college he traveled the country, moving through the hidden urban worlds of prostitution, drug use, and homosexuality. After some of his writing was published in the* Evergreen Review, *Rechy began working on a novel based on his experiences, and* City of Night *was released in 1963. Its publisher, the New York–based Grove Press, was known for its proud promotion of the countercultural movement of the 1950s and 1960s that also included the figures of Jack Kerouac, Allen Ginsberg, and Oscar "Zeta" Acosta (p. 131). Critics were divided over Rechy's*

novel, but it became a bestseller and made Rechy famous as a pio-
neering gay writer. In several later books, he continued the explora-
tion of the underworld begun in City of Night. *Rechy was never*
shy about being Mexican American or putting Mexican American
characters into his books, yet, having been labeled as a "gay writer,"
his heritage was often unacknowledged. "I'm Mexican-American,
but for a long time I was pushed out of any references to Mexican-
American writers," he said in an interview. "It was easier to come
out as a gay man than it was to come out as a Mexican-American."
He examines that heritage most directly in This Day's Death, *a*
1970 novel about a Mexican American woman trying to deal with
her son's homosexuality. Rechy's life is recounted in his 2008 auto-
biography, About My Life and the Kept Woman.

Though City of Night *is based on Rechy's personal experience,*
it is best viewed as a novel. In this selection from the beginning of
City of Night, *which describes the childhood of the narrator, one*
finds the descriptive skill, directness, and pacing that made Rechy's
book so powerful.

As you read, think about how Rechy's writing style helps readers understand the world his book explores.

Later I would think of America as one vast City of Night stretching gaud-
ily from Times Square to Hollywood Boulevard—jukebox-winking,
rock-n-roll-moaning: America at night fusing its darkcities into the unmistakable shape of loneliness.

Remember Pershing Square and the apathetic palmtrees. Central Park
and the frantic shadows. Movie theaters in the angry morning-hours.
And wounded Chicago streets. . . . Horrormovie courtyards in the
French Quarter—tawdry Mardi Gras floats with clowns tossing out glass
beads, passing dumbly like life itself. . . . Remember rock-n-roll sexmu-
sic blasting from jukeboxes leering obscenely, blinking manycolored
along the streets of America strung like a cheap necklace from 42nd
Street to Market Street, San Francisco. . . .

One-night sex and cigarette smoke and rooms squashed in by
loneliness. . . .

And I would remember lives lived out darkly in that vast City of Night,
from all-night movies to Beverly Hills mansions.

*From an interview with *Slate*: slate.com/blogs/outward/2013/12/09/city_of
_night_a_hustler_s_story_an_interview_with_john_rechy.html.

But it should begin in El Paso, that journey through the cities of night.   5
Should begin in El Paso, in Texas. And it begins in the Wind. . . . In a
Southwest windstorm with the gray clouds like steel doors locking you in
the world from Heaven.

I cant remember now how long that windstorm lasted—it might have
been days—but perhaps it was only hours—because it was in that timeless time of my boyhood, ages six through eight.

My dog Winnie was dying. I would bring her water and food and place
them near her, stand watching intently—but she doesnt move. The saliva
kept coming from the edges of her mouth. She had always been fat, and
she had a crazy crooked grin—but she was usually sick: Once her eyes
turned over, so that they were almost completely white and she couldnt
see—just lay down, and didnt try to get up for a day. Then she was well,
briefly, smiling again, wobbling lopsidedly.

Now she was lying out there dying.

At first the day was beautiful, with the sky blue as it gets only in memories of Texas childhood. Nowhere else in the world, I will think later, is
there a sky as clear, as blue, as Deep as that. I will remember other skies:
like inverted cups, this shade of blue or gray or black, with limits, like
painted rooms. But in the Southwest, the sky was millions and millions
of miles deep of blue—clear, magic, electric blue. (I would stare at it
sometimes, inexplicably racked with excitement, thinking: If I get a stick
miles long and stand on a mountain, I'll puncture Heaven—which I
thought of then as an island somewhere in the vast sky—and then
Heaven will come tumbling down to earth. . . .) Then, that day, standing
watching Winnie, I see the gray clouds massing and rolling in the horizon, sweeping suddenly terrifyingly across the sky as if to battle, giant
mushrooms exploding, blending into that steely blanket. *Now youre
locked down here so Lonesome suddenly youre cold.* The wind sweeps up
the dust, tumbleweeds claw their way across the dirt. . . .

I moved Winnie against the wall of the house, to shelter her from the   10
needlepointed dust. The clouds have shut out the sky completely, the
wind is howling violently, and it is Awesomely dark. My mother keeps
calling me to come in. . . . From the porch, I look back at my dog. The
water in the bowl beside her has turned into mud. . . . Inside now, I
rushed to the window. And the wind is shrieking into the house—the
curtains thrashing at the furniture like giant lost birds, flapping against
the walls, and my two brothers and two sisters are running about the
beat-up house closing the windows, removing the sticks we propped
them open with. I hear my father banging on the frames with a hammer,
patching the broken panes with cardboard.

Inside, the house was suddenly serene, safe from the wind; but staring
out the window in cold terror, I see boxes and weeds crashing against the

walls outside, almost tumbling over my sick dog. I long for something miraculous to draw across the sky to stop the wind. . . . I squeezed against the pane as close as I could get to Winnie: *If I keep looking at her, she cant possibly die!* A tumbleweed rolled over her.

I ran out. I stood over Winnie, shielding my eyes from the slashing wind, knelt over her to see if her stomach was still moving, breathing. And her eyes open looking at me. I listen to her heart (as I used to listen to my mother's heart when she was sick so often and I would think she had died, leaving me Alone—because my father for me then existed only as someone who was around somehow; taking furious shape later, fiercely).

Winnie is dead.

It seemed the windstorm lasted for days, weeks. But it must have been over, as usual, the next day, when Im standing next to my mother in the kitchen. (Strangely, I loved to sit and look at her as she fixed the food—or did the laundry: She washed our clothes outside in an aluminum tub, and I would watch her hanging up the clean sheets flapping in the wind. Later I would empty the water for her, and I stared intrigued as it made unpredictable patterns on the dirt. . . .) I said: "If Winnie dies—" (She had of course already died, but I didnt want to say it; her body was still outside, and I kept going to see if miraculously she is breathing again.) "—if she dies, I wont be sad because she'll go to Heaven and I'll see her there." My mother said: "Dogs dont go to Heaven, they havent got souls." She didnt say that brutally. There is nothing brutal about my mother: only a crushing tenderness, as powerful as the hatred I would discover later in my father. "What will happen to Winnie, then?" I asked. "Shes dead, thats all," my mother answers, "the body just disappears, becomes dirt."

I stand by the window, thinking: It isn't fair. . . .   15

Then my brother, the younger of the two—I am the youngest in the family—had to bury Winnie.

I was very religious then. I went to Mass regularly, to Confession. I prayed nightly. And I prayed now for my dead dog: God would make an exception. He would let her into Heaven.

I stand watching my brother dig that hole in the backyard. He put the dead dog in and covered it. I made a cross and brought flowers. Knelt. Made the sign of the cross: "Let her into Heaven. . . ."

In the days that followed—I dont know exactly how much later—we could smell the body rotting. . . . The day was a ferocious Texas summerday with the threat of rain: thunder—but no rain. The sky lit up through the cracked clouds, and lightning snapped at the world like a whip. My older brother said we hadnt buried Winnie deep enough.

So he dug up the body, and I stand by him as he shovels the dirt in our   20 backyard (littered with papers and bottles covering the weeds which occasionally we pulled, trying several times to grow grass—but it never grew). Finally the body appeared. I turned away quickly. I had seen the decaying face of death. My mother was right. Soon Winnie will blend into the dirt. There was no soul, the body would rot, and there would be Nothing left of Winnie.

That is the incident of my early childhood that I remember most often. And that is why I say it begins in the wind. Because somewhere in that plain of childhood time must have been planted the seeds of the restlessness.

Before the death of Winnie, there are other memories of loss.

We were going to plant flowers in the front yard of the house we lived in before we moved to the house where Winnie died. I was digging a ledge along the sidewalk, and my mother was at the store getting the seeds. A man came and asked for my father, but my father isnt home. "Youre going to have to move very soon," he tells me. I had heard the house was being sold, and we couldnt buy it, but it hadnt meant much to me. I continue shoveling the dirt. After my mother came and spoke to the man, she told me to stop making the holes. Almost snatching the seeds from her—and understanding now—I began burying them frantically as if that way we will have to stay to see them grow.

And so we moved. We moved from that clean house with the white walls and into the house where Winnie will die.

I stand looking at the house in child panic. It was the other half of a 25 duplex, the wooden porch decayed, almost on the verge of toppling down; it slanted like a slide. A dried-up vine, dead from lack of water, still clung to the base of the porch like a skeleton, and the bricks were disintegrating in places into thin streaks of orangy powder. The sun was brazenly bright; it elongates each splinter on the wood, each broken twig on the skeleton vine. . . . I rushed inside. Huge brown cockroaches scurried into the crevices. One fell from the wall, spreading its wings—almost two inches wide—as if to lunge at me—and it splashes like a miniature plane on the floor—*splut!* The paper was peeling off the walls over at least four more layers, all different graycolors. (We would put up the sixth, or begin to—and then stop, leaving the house even more patched as that layer peeled too: an unfinished jigsaw puzzle which would fascinate me at night: its ragged patterns making angryfaces, angry animalshapes—but I could quickly alter them into less angry figures by ripping off the jagged edges. . . .) Where the ceiling had leaked, there are spidery brown outlines.

I flick the cockroaches off the walls, stamping angrily on them.

The house smells of Rot. I went to the bathroom. The tub was full of dirty water, and it had stagnated. It was brown, bubbly. In wild dreadful panic, I thrust my hand into the rancid water, found the stopper, pulled it out holding my breath, and looked at my arm, which is covered with the filthy brown crud.

Winters in El Paso for me later would never again seem as bitter cold as they were then. Then I thought of El Paso as the coldest place in the world. We had an old iron stove with a round belly which heated up the whole house; and when we opened the small door to feed it more coal or wood, the glowing pieces inside created a miniature of Hell: the cinders crushed against the edges, smoking. . . . The metal flues that carried the smoke from the stove to the chimney collapsed occasionally and filled the house with soot. This happened especially during the windy days, and the wind would whoosh grimespecked down the chimney. At night my mother piled coats on us to keep us warm.

Later, I would be sent out to ask one of our neighbors for a dime — "until my father comes home from work." Being the youngest and most soulful looking in the family, then, I was the one who went. . . .

Around that time my father plunged into my life with a vengeance.   30

To expiate some guilt now for what I'll tell you about him later, I'll say that that strange, moody, angry man — my father — had once experienced a flashy grandeur in music. At the age of eight he had played a piano concert before the President of Mexico. Years later, still a youngman, he directed a symphony orchestra. Unaccountably, since I never really knew that man, he sank quickly lower and lower, and when I came along, when he was almost 50 years old, he found himself Trapped in the memories of that grandeur and in the reality of a series of jobs teaching music to sadly untalented children; selling pianos, sheet music — and soon even that bastard relationship to the world of music he loved was gone, and he became a caretaker for public parks. Then he worked in a hospital cleaning out trash. *(I remember him, already a defeated old man, getting up before dawn to face the unmusical reality of soiled bloody dressings.)* He would cling to stacks and stacks of symphonic music which he had played, orchestrated — still working on them at night, drumming his fingers on the table feverishly: stacks of music now piled in the narrow hallway in that house, completely unwanted by anyone but himself, gathering dust which annoyed us, so that we wanted to put them outside in the leaky aluminum garage: but he clung to those precious dust-piling manuscripts — and to newspaper clippings of his once-glory — clung to them like a dream, now a nightmare. . . . And somehow I became the reluctant inheritor of his hatred for the world that had coldly knocked him down without even glancing back.

Once, yes, there had been a warmth toward that strange red-faced man — and there were still the sudden flashes of tenderness which I will tell you about later: that man who alternately claimed French, English, Scottish descent — depending on his imaginative moods — that strange man who had traveled from Mexico to California spreading his seed—that turbulent man, married and divorced, who then married my Mother, a beautiful Mexican woman who loves me fiercely and never once understood about the terror between me and my father.

Even now in my mother's living room there is a glasscase which has been with us as long as I can remember. It is full of glass objects: figurines of angels, Virgins of Guadalupe, dolls; tissuethin imitation flowers, swans; and a small glass, reverently covered with a rotting piece of silk, tied tightly with a fadedpink ribbon, containing some mysterious memento of one of my father's dead children. . . . When I think of that glasscase, I think of my Mother . . . a ghost image that will haunt me—Always.

When I was about eight years old, my father taught me this:

He would say to me: "Give me a thousand," and I knew this meant I 35 should hop on his lap and then he would fondle me—intimately—and he'd give me a penny, sometimes a nickel. At times when his friends—old gray men—came to our house, they would ask for "a thousand." And I would jump on their laps too. And I would get nickel after nickel, going around the table.

And later, a gift from my father would become a token of a truce from the soon-to-blaze hatred between us.

I loathed Christmas.

Each year, my father put up a Nacimiento—an elaborate Christmas scene, with houses, the wisemen on their way to the manger, angels on angelhair clouds. (On Christmas Eve, after my mother said a rosary while we knelt before the Nacimiento, we placed the Christchild in the crib.) Weeks before Christmas my father began constructing it, and each day, when I came home from school, he would have me stand by him while he worked building the boxlike structure, the miniature houses, the artificial lake; hanging the angels from the elaborate simulated sky, replete with moon, clouds, stars. Sometimes hours passed before he would ask me to help him, but I had to remain there, not talking. Sometimes my mother would have to stand there too, sometimes my younger sister. When anything went wrong—if anything fell—he was in a rage, hurling hammers, cursing.

My father's violence erupted unpredictably over anything. In an instant he overturns the table—food and plates thrust to the floor. He would smash bottles, menacing us with the sharpfanged edges. He had an old sword which he kept hidden threateningly about the house.

And even so there were those moments of tenderness—even more bru- 40 tal because they didnt last: times in which, when he got paid, he would fill the house with presents—flowers for my mother (incongruous in that patched-up house, until they withered and blended with the drab-ness), toys for us. Even during the poorest Christmas we went through when we were kids—and after the fearful times of putting up the Nacimiento—he would make sure we all had presents—not clothes, which we needed but didnt want, but toys, which we wanted but didnt need. And Sundays he would take us to Juarez to dinner, leaving an exor-bitant tip for the suddenly attentive waiter. . . . But in the ocean of his hatred, those times of kindness were mere islands. He burned with an anger at life, which had chewed him up callously: an anger which blazed more fiercely as he sank further beneath the surface of his once almost-realized dream of musical glory.

One of the last touches on the Nacimiento was two pieces of craggy wood, which looked very heavy, like rocks (very much like the piece of petrified wood which my father kept on his desk, to warn us that once it had been the hand of a child who had struck his father, and God had turned the child's hand into stone). The pieces of rocklike wood were located on either side of the manager, like hills. On top of one, my father placed a small statue of a red-tailed, horned Devil, drinking out of a bottle.

Around that time I had a dream which still recurs (and later, in New Orleans, I will experience it awake). We would get colds often in that drafty house, and fever, and during such times I dreamt this: Those pieces of rocklike wood on the sides of the manger are descending on me, to crush me. When I brace for the smashing terrible impact, they become soft, and instead of crushing me they envelop me like melted wax. Sometimes I will dream theyre draped with something like cheese-cloth, a tenebrous, thin tissue touching my face like spiderwebs, gluing itself to me although I struggle to tear it away. . . .

When my brothers and sisters all got married and left home—to Escape, I would think—I remained, and my father's anger was aimed even more savagely at me.

He sat playing solitaire for hours. He calls me over, begins to talk in a very low, deceptively friendly tone. When my mother and I fell asleep, he told me, he would set fire to the house and we would burn inside while he looked on. Then he would change that story: Instead of setting fire to the house, he will kill my mother in bed, and in the morning, when I go wake her, she'll be dead, and I'll be left alone with him.

Some nights I would change beds with my mother after he went to sleep—they didnt sleep in the same room—and I surrounded the bed with sticks, chairs. The slightest noise, and I would reach for a stick to beat him away. In the early morning, before he woke, my mother would change beds with me again.

Once—without him, because he was working on his music—we were going to take a trip to Carlsbad Caverns, in New Mexico: my mother, my

45

sister and her husband my older brother and his wife, and I. My mother prepared food that night.

In the morning, before dawn, I woke my mother and went to my sister's house to wake her. When I returned, I saw my mother in our backyard (under the paradoxically serene starsplashed sky). "Dont go in!" she yells at me. I ran inside, and my father is standing menacingly over the table where the food we were taking is. Swiftly I reached for the food, and he lunges at me with a knife, slicing past me only inches short of my stomach. By then, my sister's husband was there holding him back. . . .

There was a wine-red ring my father wore. As a tie-pin, before being set into the gold ring-frame, it had belonged to his father, and before that to his father's father—and it was a ruby, my father told me—a ruby so precious that it was his most treasured possession, which he clung to. As he sat moodily staring at his music one particularly poor day, he called me over. Quickly, he gave me the ring. The red stone in the gold frame glowed for me more brilliantly than anything has ever since. A few days later he took it back.

During one of those rare, rare times when there was a kind of determined truce between us—an unspoken, smoldering hatred—I was crossing the street with him. He was quite old then, and he carried a cane. As we crossed, he stumbled on the cane, fell to the street. Without waiting an instant, I run to the opposite side, and I stand hoping for some miraculous avenging car to plunge over him.

But it didnt come.   50

I went back to him, helped him up, and we walked the rest of the way in thundering silence.

And then, when I was older, possibly 13 or 14, I was sitting one afternoon on the porch loathing him. My hatred for him by then had become a thing which overwhelmed me, which obsessed me the length of the day. He stood behind me, and he put his hand on me, softly, and said—gently: "Youre my son, and I love you." But those longed-for words, delayed until the waves of my hatred for him had smothered their meaning, made me pull away from him: "I hate you!—youre a failure—as a man, as a father!" And later those words would ring painfully in my mind when I remembered him as a slouched old man getting up before dawn to face the hospital trash. . . .

Soon, I stopped going to Mass. I stopped praying. The God that would allow this vast unhappiness was a God I would rebel against. The seeds of that rebellion—planted that ugly afternoon when I saw my dog's body beginning to decay, the soul shut out by Heaven—were beginning to germinate.

When my brother was a kid and I wasnt even born (but I'll hear the story often), he would stand moodily looking out the window; and when, once, my grandmother asked him, "Little boy, what are you doing by the window staring at so hard?"—he answered, "I am occupied with life." Im convinced that if my brother hadnt said that—or if I hadnt been told about it—I would have said it.

I liked to sit inside the house and look out the hall-window—beyond   55
the cactus garden in the vacant lot next door. I would sit by that window looking at the people that passed. I felt miraculously separated from the world outside: separated by the pane, the screen, through which, nevertheless—uninvolved—I could see that world.

I read many books, I saw many, many movies.

I watched other lives, only through a window.

Sundays during summer especially I would hike outside the city, along the usually waterless strait of sand called the Rio Grande, up the mountain of Cristo Rey, dominated at the top by the coarse, weed-surrounded statue of a primitive-faced Christ. I would lie on the dirt of that mountain staring at the breathtaking Texas sky.

I was usually alone. I had only one friend: a wild-eyed girl who sometimes would climb the mountain with me. We were both 17, and I felt in her the same wordless unhappiness I felt within myself. We would walk and climb for hours without speaking. For a brief time I liked her intensely—without ever telling her. Yet I was beginning to feel, too, a remoteness toward people—more and more a craving for attention which I could not reciprocate: one-sided, as if the need in me was so hungry that it couldnt share or give back in kind. Perhaps sensing this—one afternoon in a boarded-up cabin at the base of the mountain—she maneuvered, successfully, to make me. But the discovery of sex with her, releasing as it had been merely turned me strangely further within myself.

Mutually, we withdrew from each other.   60

And it was somewhere about that time that the narcissistic pattern of my life began.

From my father's inexplicable hatred of me and my mother's blind carnivorous love, I fled to the Mirror. I would stand before it, thinking: I have only Me! . . . I became obsessed with age. At 17, I dreaded growing old. Old age is something that must never happen to me. The image of myself in the mirror must never fade into someone I cant look at.

And even after a series of after-school jobs, my feeling of isolation from others only increased.

Then the army came, and for months I hadnt spoken to my father. (We would sit at the table eating silently, ignoring each other.) And when I left, that terrible morning, I kissed my mother. And briefly I looked at my father. His eyes were watering. Mutely he held out the ruby-ring which once, long ago, he had given me and then taken back. And I took it wordlessly. And in that instant I wanted to hold him—*because he was crying*, because he did feel something for me, because, I was sure, he was overwhelmed at that moment by the Loss I felt too. I wanted to hold him then as I had wanted to so many, many times as a child, and if I could have spoken, I know I would have said at last: "I love you." But that sense of loss choked me—and I walked out without speaking to him. . . . Only a few weeks later, in Camp Breckenridge, Kentucky, I received a telegram that he was very sick.

And I came back to El Paso.   65

I felt certain that this time it would be different.

I reached our house, in the government projects we had moved into from that house with the winged cockroaches, and I got in with the key I had kept. There is no one home. I called my brother. My father was dead.

I hang up the telephone and I know that now Forever I will have no father, that he had been unfound, that as long as he had been alive there was a chance, and that we would be, Always now, strangers, and that is when I knew what Death really is—not in the physical discovery of the Nothingness which the death of my dog Winnie had brought me (in the decayed body which would turn into dirt, rejected by Heaven) but in the knowledge that *my Father* was gone, *for me*—that there was no way to reach him now—that his Death would exist only for me, who am living.

And throughout the days that followed—and will follow forever—I will discover him in my memories, and hopelessly—through the infinite miles that separate life from death—try to understand his torture: in searching out the shape of my own.

The army passed like something unreal, and I returned to my Mother and   70
her hungry love. And left her, standing that morning by the kitchen door crying, as she always would be in my mind, and I was on my way now to Chicago, briefly—from where I would go to freedom: New York!— embarking on that journey through nightcities and nightlives—looking for I dont know what—perhaps some substitute for salvation.

Reading

1. What childhood event does the narrator remember best?

2. What does the narrator think is the reason his brothers and sisters left home?

Thinking Critically

1. Why do you think that Winnie is so important to the narrator?

2. Does the narrator's relationship with his father change during his childhood? How does that relationship affect the narrator?

Connecting

1. The narrator of Benjamín Alire Sáenz's story "Sometimes the Rain" (p. 342) feels a similar need to leave the stifling environment of his childhood home. What similarities do the two characters have? What differences do they have that suggest they will have very different lives in the future?

Writing

1. In the chapter of *City of Night* printed in this anthology, we read mostly descriptions of the narrator's family: his father, his mother, his brothers, and even his dog. By examining those descriptions, however, we can learn something about the narrator himself. Write a brief essay describing the narrator, supporting your description with examples from the text and with analysis of the style of the piece. Is he passionate? Cold? Sarcastic?

Creating

1. **Write a story or poem about home.** In the first chapter of John Rechy's *City of Night*, we are introduced to the narrator and his family partly through contrasting descriptions of the Texas landscape and of his childhood home. Write a story or a poem about your own home, or a home you used to live in, in such a way that it introduces readers to people who are important in your life.

8

RODOLFO "CORKY" GONZALES [1928–2005]

I Am Joaquín [1967*]

GENRE: POETRY

For Rodolfo "Corky" Gonzales, poetry was an integral part of a life's work of creating a unified, strong Chicano community. Gonzales came to activism poetry by an indirect route. After high school in Denver, Colorado, he became a top-ranked professional boxer and then used his fame to propel himself into a career as a political activist. Gonzales led the ¡Viva Kennedy! clubs in Colorado, which helped elect John F. Kennedy to the presidency in 1960. Within a few years he left Democratic Party politics and founded the Crusade for Justice, which focused on cultural and educational issues within the Chicano community. In 1969, the Crusade, with the charismatic Gonzales at its head, sponsored the National Chicano Youth Liberation Conference, out of which came the famous Plan Espiritual de Aztlán, *a declaration of Chicano nationalism with the words of the poet Alurista (p. 78) as its preface. Gonzales was also one of the chief architects—along with the Texas activist and scholar José Ángel Gutiérrez—of the national political party La Raza Unida, which held its first convention in 1972 in El Paso.*

The epic poem "I Am Joaquín" was first published in 1967 and was widely reprinted and distributed, with a staged version even being performed by Luis Valdez (p. 82) and his Teatro Campesino in 1969. Its fusion of artistic expression and political declaration helped define the Chicano Renaissance of the following decade, and it remains a central text for any study of Chicano literature. Gonzales referred to it as "a journey back through history, a painful self-evaluation, a wandering search for my peoples, and most of all, for my own identity." The poem is a huge gathering of symbols and figures from several centuries, including that of Joaquín Murrieta, who, after the war between Mexico and the United States that ended with the 1848 Treaty of Guadalupe Hidalgo, resisted the takeover of lands formerly belonging to Mexico.

*The poem was originally self-published in 1967.

As you read, ask yourself what unites the images and symbols in the poem, and try to understand just what identity Gonzales has found after his "wandering search."

I am Joaquín,
lost in a world of confusion,
caught up in the whirl of a
        gringo° society,
confused by the rules,   5
scorned by attitudes,
suppressed by manipulation,
and destroyed by modern society.
My fathers
        have lost the economic battle   10
and won
        the struggle of cultural survival.

And now!
        I must choose
                between   15
        the paradox of
victory of the spirit,
despite physical hunger,
                or
        to exist in the grasp   20
of American social neurosis,
sterilization of the soul
        and a full stomach.

Yes,
I have come a long way to nowhere,   25
unwillingly dragged by that
        monstrous, technical,
        industrial giant called
                Progress
and Anglo success . . .   30
        I look at myself.
        I watch my brothers.
        I shed tears of sorrow.
        I sow seeds of hate.

gringo: Derisive word used for white Americans.

I withdraw to the safety within the   35
circle of life—
          MY OWN PEOPLE

I am Cuauhtémoc,
proud and noble,
      leader of men,   40
king of an empire
civilized beyond the dreams
      of the gachupín° Cortés,
who also is the blood,
      the image of myself.   45
I am the Maya prince.
I am Nezahualcóyotl,
great leader of the Chichimecas.
I am the sword and flame of Cortés
             the despot   50
           And
I am the eagle and serpent of
         the Aztec civilization.

I owned the land as far as the eye
could see under the Crown of Spain,   55
and I toiled on my Earth
and gave my Indian sweat and blood
         for the Spanish master
who ruled with tyranny over man and
beast and all that he could trample   60
           But . . .
      THE GROUND WAS MINE.
I was both tyrant and slave.

As the Christian church took its place
      in God's name,   65
to take and use my virgin strength and
            trusting faith,
the priests,
      both good and bad,
              took—   70
but
      gave a lasting truth that

gachupín: Spaniard established in the Americas.

                Spaniard
                Indian
                    Mestizo°   75
were all God's children.
And
        from these words grew men
                who prayed and fought
                            for   80
        their own worth as human beings,
                for
                    that
                GOLDEN MOMENT
                    of   85
                FREEDOM.
I was part in blood and spirit
        of that
                courageous village priest
                            Hidalgo   90
who in the year eighteen hundred and ten
rang the bell of independence
and gave out that lasting cry—
        el grito de Dolores:°
        "Que mueran los gachupines y que viva   95
la Virgen de Guadalupe° . . ."

I sentenced him
        who was me
I excommunicated him, my blood.
I drove him from the pulpit to lead   100
        a bloody revolution for him and me . . .
                    I killed him.
His head,
        which is mine and of all those
        who have come this way,   105
I placed on that fortress wall
        to wait for independence.
Morelos!
        Matamoros
                Guerrero!   110

Mestizo: Person of mixed Spanish and indigenous heritage.   **el grito de Dolores:** The Cry of Dolores.   **"Que mueran los gachupines . . .":** "May the Spaniards die and may the Virgin of Guadalupe live."

all compañeros° in the act,
STOOD AGAINST THAT WALL OF
                    INFAMY
    to feel the hot gouge of lead
        which my hands made.   115
I died with them . . .
    I lived with them . . .
        I lived to see our country free.
Free
    from Spanish rule in   120
        eighteen-hundred-twenty-one.
            Mexico was free??

The crown was gone
            but
all its parasites remained,   125
                and ruled,
                and taught,
        with gun and flame and mystic power.
I worked,
I sweated,   130
I bled,
I prayed,
        and waited silently for life
                    to begin again.
I fought and died   135
            for
                Don Benito Juarez,
guardian of the Constitution.
I was he
        on dusty roads   140
                on barren land
as he protected his archives
    as Moses did his sacraments.
He held his Mexico
        in his hand   145
            on
                the most desolate
                    and remote ground
                    which was his country.

compañeros: Comrades, like "brothers."

And this giant   150
        little Zapotec
                gave
    not one palm's breadth
of his country's land to
        kings or monarchs or presidents   155
of foreign powers.

I am Joaquín.
I rode with Pancho Villa,
        crude and warm,
a tornado at full strength,   160
nourished and inspired
        by the passion and the fire
        of all his earthy people.
I am Emiliano Zapata.
        "This land,   165
                this earth
                        is
                        OURS."

The villages,
        the mountains,   170
                the streams
                belong to Zapatistas.
                        Our life
                        or yours
is the only trade for soft brown earth   175
and maize.
All of which is our reward,
        a creed that formed a constitution
                for all who dare live free!
"This land is ours . . .   180
        Father, I give it back to you.
                Mexico must be free. . . ."

I ride with revolutionists
                against myself.
I am the Rurales,   185
                coarse and brutal,
I am the mountain Indian,
                superior over all.
The thundering hoof beats are my horses.

The chattering machine guns   190
   are death to all of me:
      Yaqui
        Tarahumara
          Chamala
            Zapotec   195
              Mestizo
                Español.

I have been the bloody revolution,
The victor,
The vanquished.   200
I have killed
   and been killed.
        I am the despots Díaz
        and Huerta
and the apostle of democracy,   205
        Francisco Madero.
I am
the black-shawled
faithful women
who die with me   210
or live
depending on the time and place.
I am
   faithful,
      humble   215
        Juan Diego,
        the Virgin of Guadalupe,
        Tonantzín, Aztec goddess, too.
I rode the mountains of San Joaquín.
I rode east and north   220
      as far as the Rocky Mountains,
        and
all men feared the guns of
        Joaquín Murrieta.
I killed those men who dared   225
   to steal my mine,
   who raped and killed
          my love
          my wife.
Then   230
I killed to stay alive.

I was Elfego Baca,
     living my nine lives fully.
I was the Espinoza brothers
     of the Valle de San Luis.   235
All
were added to the number of heads
that
     in the name of civilization
were placed on the wall of independence,   240
heads of brave men
who died for cause or principle,
good or bad.

                    Hidalgo! Zapata!
                         Murrieta! Espinozas!   245
are but a few.
They
dared to face
the force of tyranny
                         of men   250
                    who rule
               by deception and hypocrisy.
I stand here looking back,
and now I see
                    the present,   255
and still
     I am the campesino,°
     I am the fat political coyote—
                              I,
of the same name,   260
                    Joaquín,
in a country that has wiped out
all my history,
               stifled all my pride,
in a country that has placed a   265
different weight of indignity upon
          my
               age-
                    old
                         burdened back.   270
          Inferiority
is the new load . . .

campesino: Farmworker.

The Indian has endured and still
emerged the winner,
    the Mestizo must yet overcome,   275
        and the gachupín will just ignore.
I look at myself
and see part of me
who rejects my father and my mother
and dissolves into the melting pot   280
    to disappear in shame.
        I sometimes
        sell my brother out
    and reclaim him
for my own when society gives me   285
    token leadership
        in society's own name.

I am Joaquín,
who bleeds in many ways.
The altars of Moctezuma   290
        I stained a bloody red.
    My back of Indian slavery
        was stripped crimson
    from the whips of masters
    who would lose their blood so pure   295
        when revolution made them pay,
standing against the walls of
    retribution.

        Blood
        has flowed from   300
        me
on every battlefield
        between
campesino, hacendado,°
    slave and master   305
    and
    revolution.
I jumped from the tower of Chapultepec
    into the sea of fame—
my country's flag   310
    my burial shroud—

hacendado: Wealthy landowner.

with Los Niños,
      whose pride and courage
could not surrender
        with indignity   315
          their country's flag
to strangers . . . in their land.
Now
    I bleed in some smelly cell
    from club   320
    or gun
    or tyranny.

I bleed as the vicious gloves of hunger
    cut my face and eyes,
as I fight my way from stinking barrios°   325
    to the glamour of the ring
      and lights of fame
        or mutilated sorrow.

My blood runs pure on the ice-caked
hills of the Alaskan isles,   330
on the corpse-strewn beach of Normandy,
the foreign land of Korea
        and now
          Vietnam.
Here I stand   335
      before the court of justice,
        guilty
for all the glory of my Raza°
      to be sentenced to despair.
Here I stand,   340
    poor in money,
    arrogant with pride,
      bold with machismo,
      rich in courage
      and   345
    wealthy in spirit and faith.

My knees are caked with mud.
My hands calloused from the hoe.

barrios: Mexican American neighborhoods.   **Raza:** Term used for all people of
Mexican descent.

I have made the Anglo rich,
          yet   350
    equality is but a word—
        the Treaty of Hidalgo has been broken
    and is but another treacherous promise.
My land is lost
          and stolen,   355
My culture has been raped.
        I lengthen
        the line at the welfare door
and fill the jails with crime.

    These then   360
are the rewards
        this society has
for sons of chiefs
    and kings
    and bloody revolutionists,   365
who
gave a foreign people
    all their skills and ingenuity
to pave the way with brains and blood
for   370
those hordes of gold-starved
                   strangers,
who
changed our language
and plagiarized our deeds   375
          as feats of valor
          of their own.

They frowned upon our way of life
    and took what they could use.
        Our art,   380
        our literature,
        our music, they ignored—
so they left the real things of value
and grabbed at their own destruction
        by their greed and avarice.   385
They overlooked that cleansing fountain of
        nature and brotherhood
    which is Joaquín.

The art of our great señores,°
                    Diego Rivera,   390
                    Siqueiros,
                    Orozco, is but
another act of revolution for
        the salvation of mankind.
        Mariachi music, the   395
                heart and soul
                of the people of the earth,
                the life of the child,
                and the happiness of love.

The corridos° tell the tales   400
        of life and death,
                of tradition,
        legends old and new,
        of joy
                of passion and sorrow   405
        of the people—who I am.
I am in the eyes of woman,
                sheltered beneath
her shawl of black,
                deep and sorrowful   410
                eyes
that bear the pain of sons long buried
                or dying,
                dead
on the battlefield or on the barbed wire   415
                of social strife.

Her rosary she prays and fingers
endlessly
        like the family
working down a row of beets   420
                to turn around
                and work
                and work.
                There is no end.
Her eyes a mirror of all the warmth   425
        and all the love for me,

señores: Plural of **señor**, meaning *sir*.   **corridos:** Musical ballads sung to
tell stories.

and I am her
and she is me.
    We face life together in sorrow,
    anger, joy, faith and wishful   430
    thoughts.

I shed the tears of anguish
as I see my children disappear
behind the shroud of mediocrity,
never to look back to remember me.   435
I am Joaquín.
        I must fight
            and win this struggle
            for my sons, and they
            must know from me   440
            who I am.
Part of the blood that runs deep in me
could not be vanquished by the Moors.
I defeated them after five hundred years,
and I have endured.   445
        Part of the blood that is mine
        has labored endlessly four hundred
        years under the heel of lustful
            Europeans.
            I am still here!   450

I have endured in the rugged mountains
    of our country
I have survived the toils and slavery
    of the fields.
            I have existed   455
in the barrios of the city
in the suburbs of bigotry
in the mines of social snobbery
in the prisons of dejection
in the muck of exploitation   460
and
in the fierce heat of racial hatred.

And now the trumpet sounds,
the music of the people stirs the
            revolution.   465
Like a sleeping giant it slowly

rears its head
to the sound of
                    tramping feet
                    clamoring voices   470
                    mariachi strains
                    fiery tequila explosions
              the smell of chile verde° and
        soft brown eyes of expectation for a
                              better life.   475

And in all the fertile farmlands,
                    the barren plains,
the mountain villages,
smoke-smeared cities,
              we start to MOVE.   480
     La Raza!
Mejicano!
     Español!
          Latino!
               Hispano!   485
                    Chicano!
or whatever I call myself,
                    I look the same
                    I feel the same
                    I cry   490
                         and
                    sing the same.

I am the masses of my people and
I refuse to be absorbed.
          I am Joaquín.   495
The odds are great
but my spirit is strong,
              my faith unbreakable,
              my blood is pure.
I am Aztec prince and Christian Christ.   500
          I SHALL ENDURE!
          I WILL ENDURE!

chile verde: Green chile.

Reading

1. What is the central issue faced by the speaker of the poem?

2. Is the speaker of the poem optimistic about the future? How do you know?

Thinking Critically

1. What unites the historical figures that Gonzales writes about in the poem?

2. Do you think the effect of Gonzales's poem on a listener is different than on a reader? Explain.

Connecting

1. How do the historical figures found in "I Am Joaquín" compare to the figure of Louie Rodríguez, the hero of José Montoya's poem "El Louie" (p. 102)? Do you think that the two poems share any characteristics that you think made them significant for the Chicano Movement?

Writing

1. "I Am Joaquín" is a declaration of pride and identification with a tradition. Using examples from the poem, write an essay in which you analyze the sources of pride found in the poem, and write about what they suggest about identity.

Creating

1. **Create a timeline for "I Am Joaquín."** In this poem, Gonzales brings up a number of historical figures and events. Using clues from the text and from outside research, identify as many of them as you can. Then, working in groups, use your information to create an annotated timeline that can accompany the poem.

9

ALURISTA [b. 1947]

fértil polvo •
What Now . . . Corn

From Timespace huracán: Poems 1972–1975 [1975] AND
Tunaluna [2010]

GENRE: POETRY

*By skillfully mixing the rhythms of English and Spanish and by
introducing the concept of Aztlán, Alurista (the adopted name of
Alberto Baltazar Urista) became one of the pioneering poets of the
Chicano Movement. Alurista was born in Mexico and came to
San Diego at thirteen. He began getting involved with the Chicano
Movement while attending San Diego State University. In 1969,
while still a student, he attended the National Chicano Youth Liberation Conference, led by Rodolfo Gonzales (p. 63). One of his
poems was adopted as the preface to* El Plan Espiritual de Aztlán
*issued by the conference. To identify Aztlán, the mythical northern
homeland of the Aztec people, with the present-day southwestern
United States was to claim it as a physical and cultural home for
Mexican Americans. For artists, it gave the movement an artistic,
symbolic, and linguistic heritage that gave dignity and nobility to
the lives of Chicanos. Alurista has said of his relationship to this
heritage that "the people are the authors of the language; the people
are the authors of the imagery, of the symbols. All I do is weave
them together in such a way that our people can reflect themselves
in them." Alurista's first collection of poetry,* Floricanto en Aztlán,
*was published in 1971, soon after he earned his bachelor's degree.
He has authored several other books of poetry, including* Nation-
child Plumaroja *in 1972 and* Timespace huracán *in 1975, and
later earned a Ph.D. from the University of California, San Diego.*

*Both "fértil polvo" and "What Now . . . Corn" highlight im-
portant characteristics of Alurista's work. In "fértil polvo," written
in the 1970s, he mixes English with Spanish and suggests a
pre-Columbian sense of unity between humans and the earth.
"What Now . . . Corn" is from his 2010 collection* Tunaluna *and is
a criticism of the actions of President George W. Bush in a mix of
languages and American dialects.*

As you read both poems, think about how the author's frequent switching back and forth between languages affects the rhythm and spirit of his writing.

FÉRTIL POLVO°

la vida o la muerte°
no existen°
  life hastens its pace
    on to death
      death waits for the wheel   5
      to begin revolution
        again
          in the carcass of
          all matter
            the worms of life   10
            are born
              to turn gusanos°
              into butterflies
                de colores brillantes°
                  hijas del sol°   15
                salen de la tierra°
              y en polvo
              convierten
                fértil tierra°
                  dust turns with time   20
                and space remains
                occupied
                flesh merely passes
                and huesos° waited
                  to pulverize   25
                and be the wind
                  to caress mariposas°
                  into papaloteadas°
                  across the fleeting
                  light of dusk   30

fértil polvo: Fertile dust.   **la vida o la muerte:** Life or death.   **no existen:** They do not exist.   **gusanos:** Worms.   **de colores brillantes:** Of brilliant colors. **hijas del sol:** Daughters of the sun.   **salen de la tierra:** They come out of the earth.   **y en polvo / convierten / fértil tierra:** And into dust they transform fertile earth.   **huesos:** Bones.   **mariposas:** Butterflies.   **papaloteadas:** Flutterings.

WHAT NOW . . . CORN

what now dog, bush barking hot
  pos orale pues gato° 'n' howl hoot
    lo que es,° olive, busca°
it b. yes! it b oil, black gold!
        petroleum   5
what it b about . . . a boot?
zorri for all of them flying, falling
        metal birds . . .
  no, really the aeroplanos
      the bombs 'r' now directed   10
at rak 'n' ran . . . or the ganis . . . why I ask?
the answer b clear . . . money 'n' oil pumps
    ¿cuál es tu santa verdad, jorgito?°
      nosotros nos damos cuenta
  de las tarugadas   15
        que ya has cometido°
        Senior
señor?   . . . que gran explotador!°
the earth disagrees with u, your family
        'n' your economic plans   20
$$4$$
    let alone the estamos undidos
de angloamérica . . . . . perdonen la palabra . . . pendejo . . . °
    get a clue 'n' balance
      our budget . . . baboso°   25
quit beating 'round your own   . . mr pres
    act like one for all
  else there b none . . . . zonzo°
cats abound midst gringolandia°

pos orale pues gato: Well all right now, cat. **lo que es:** What it is.
busca: Look for it. **¿cuál es tu santa verdad, jorgito?:** What is your sacred
truth, little Jorge (George)? **nosotros nos damos cuenta / de las tarugadas /
que ya has cometido:** We are well aware of the stupid blunders you have
already committed. **señor? . . . que gran explotador!:** Sir? what a great
exploiter! **the estamos undidos / de angloamérica . . . . . perdonen la
palabra . . . pendejo . . . :** The "we are sunk" of Anglo-America [this is a play on
Estados Unidos de América, Spanish for the *United States of America*] . . .
pardon the word . . . asshole. **baboso:** Imbecile. **zonzo:** Stupid.
gringolandia: Gringoland.

Reading

1. ("fértil polvo") What natural process does the poem describe?
2. ("What Now . . . Corn") What actions of President George W. Bush does the poem criticize?

Thinking Critically

1. How does the form of the poem "fértil polvo" contribute to its meaning or its mood? Does it change the way you read it? Explain.
2. What languages and dialects can you detect in "What Now . . . Corn"? Why do you think Alurista includes them in the poem?
3. What do you think is the meaning of the title "What Now . . . Corn"?

Connecting

1. Compare the intimate relationship between humans and the earth suggested by Alurista in "fértil polvo" to that suggested by Gary Soto's "The Elements of San Joaquin" (p. 195). Is the relationship the same? Do the two poets write about it for different reasons?

Writing

1. Alurista was a pioneer in writing bilingual and even multilingual poetry. Write a line-by-line paraphrase in one language of one of the two poems, and write briefly about what you think the use of multiple languages adds to the poem.

Creating

1. **Create a collage of symbols.** Alurista thought that much of his work as a poet consisted in finding important symbols in order to "weave them together." Make a collage of the images and symbols that are important in your own culture or that help to unify a group you are familiar with. Describe what each image or symbol represents, and briefly explain what you think makes it so important. Alternatively, you could make a collage of the images and symbols in Alurista's poems.

10

LUIS VALDEZ [b. 1940]

Las Dos Caras del Patroncito
[1965*] • Los Vendidos [1967*]

GENRE: DRAMA

In a long and successful career in theater and film, Luis Valdez has brought Chicano art to wide audiences and shown that artistic expression can change lives. Valdez's career in the theater began with studies at San Jose State and a brief membership in the San Francisco Mime Troupe. Valdez then took his talents to southern California to work closely with César Chávez and the farmworkers' movement, and in 1965 created Teatro Campesino, which would became the most influential theatrical group of the Chicano Movement, to help spread the word about the union. Valdez's early plays featured highly symbolic and stylized characters drawn from Chicano culture, and they used humor and satire to criticize the racism and the unfair practices of the bosses. Valdez successfully adapted this style for professional theater and film, and a year after his 1978 play Zoot Suit *achieved success in Los Angeles, it became the first Chicano play to reach Broadway. Like José Montoya (p. 102), Valdez transformed the story of a pachuco into a representative story for Chicano audiences. In 1981,* Zoot Suit *was also made into a film, making a star out of actor Edward James Olmos. Valdez reached his highest levels of mainstream success with his screenplay for the 1987 film* La Bamba, *dramatizing the life of Mexican American rock and roll star Richie Valens.*

The one-act plays below date from Valdez's Teatro Campesino period. The first of these actos, Las Dos Caras del Patroncito, *was often performed by farmworkers while on strike in 1965 and had a profound impact on them: "I found out that one of the hardest things for me to do was to get campesinos to act like growers,"* Valdez *said later. "But the moment that they did the boss, they changed. They became better organizers. They became confident*

Las Dos Caras del Patroncito was performed in 1965. *Los Vendidos* was performed in 1967. The plays appear in *Luiz Valdez: Early Works*.

and in control of themselves."* *Like* Las Dos Caras, Los Vendidos *makes use of clear character types known to his audiences, in this case satirizing them as roles played for others. As was fitting for a first performance among Brown Berets, a group of radical Chicanos who often wore military attire, the play ends by celebrating the role of the* revolucionario.

As you read, think not only of the message of Valdez's plays in their entirety, but also about the meaning of each individual role and the effect it might have had on individual performers.

LAS DOS CARAS DEL PATRONCITO°

First Performance: The Grape Strike, Delano, California on the Picket line

Characters
ESQUIROL°
PATRONCITO
CHARLIE, *Armed Guard*

In September, 1965 six thousand farmworkers went on strike in the grape fields of Delano. During the first months of the ensuing Huelga,° the growers tried to intimidate the struggling workers to return to the vineyards. They mounted shotguns in their pickups, prominently displayed in the rear windows of the cab; they hired armed guards; they roared by in their huge caruchas,° etc. It seemed that they were trying to destroy the spirit of the strikers with mere materialistic evidence of their power. Too poor to afford la causa,° many of the huelguistas° left Delano to work in other areas; most of them stayed behind the picket through the winter; and a few returned to the fields to scab, pruning vines. The growers started trucking in more esquiroles from Texas and Mexico.

In response to this situation, especially the phoney "scary" front of the ranchers, we created "Dos Caras." It grew out of an improvisation in the old pink house behind the huelga office in Delano. It was intended to show the "two faces of the boss."

A FARMWORKER enters, carrying a pair of pruning shears.

From "The Struggle in the Fields," part 3 of the PBS documentary series Chicano! A History of the Mexican American Civil Rights Movement.

Las Dos Caras del Patroncito: *The Two Faces of the Boss* (the diminutive ending *-cito* is ironically affectionate).   **Esquirol:** Strike breaker, scab.   **Huelga:** Strike. **caruchas:** Cars.   **la causa:** The cause.   **huelgistas:** Strikers.

FARMWORKER: (*To audience.*) ¡Buenos días!° This is the ranch of my
patroncito, and I come here to prune grape vines. My patrón bring
me all the way from Mexico here to California, the land of sun and
money! More sun than money. But I better get to jalar now because
my patroncito he don't like to see me talking to strangers. (*There is a*   5
roar backstage.) Ay, here he comes in his big car! I better get to work.
(*He prunes. The* PATRONCITO *enters, wearing a yellow pig face mask.*
He is driving an imaginary limousine, making the roaring sound of
the motor.)
PATRONCITO: Good morning, boy!   10
FARMWORKER: Buenos días, patroncito. (*His hat in his hands.*)
PATRONCITO: You working hard, boy?
FARMWORKER: Oh, sí patrón. Muy° hard. (*He starts working furiously.*)
PATRONCITO: Oh, you can work harder than that, boy. (*He works harder.*)
Harder! (*He works harder.*) Harder! (*He works still harder.*) Harder!   15
FARMWORKER: Ay, that's too hard, patrón! (*The* PATRONCITO *looks*
downstage then upstage along the imaginary row of vines, with the
farmworker's head alongside his, following his movement.)
PATRONCITO: How come you cutting all the wires instead of the vines,
boy? (*The* FARMWORKER *shrugs helplessly frightened and defense-*   20
less.) Look, lemme show you something. Cut this vine here. (*Points to*
a vine.) Now this one. (FARMWORKER *cuts.*) Now this one. (FARM-
WORKER *cuts.*) Now this one. (*The* FARMWORKER *almost cuts the*
PATRONCITO's *extended finger.*) Heh!
FARMWORKER: (*Jumps back.*) Ah!   25
PATRONCITO: Aint' you scared of me, boy? (FARMWORKER *nods.*) Huh,
boy? (FARMWORKER *nods and makes a grunt signifying yes.*) What,
boy? You don't have to be scared of me! I love my Mexicans. You're
one of the new ones, huh? Come in from . . .
FARMWORKER: México, señor.°   30
PATRONCITO: Did you like the truck ride, boy? (FARMWORKER *shakes*
head indicating no.) What?!
FARMWORKER: I loved it, señor!
PATRONCITO: Of course, you did. All my Mexicans love to ride in trucks!
Just the sight of them barreling down the freeway makes my heart feel   35
good; hands on their sombreros, hair flying in the wind, bouncing along
happy as babies. Yes, sirree, I sure love my Mexicans, boy!
FARMWORKER: (*Puts his arm around* PATRONCITO.) Oh, patrón.
PATRONCITO: (*Pushing him away.*) I love 'em about ten feet away from
me, boy. Why, there ain't another grower in this whole damn valley   40
that treats you like I do. Some growers got Filipinos, others got

¡Buenos días!: Good morning.   **Muy:** Very.   **señor:** Sir.

Arabs, me I prefer Mexicans. That's why I come down here to visit
you, here in the field. I'm an important man, boy! Bank of America,
University of California, Safeway stores, I got a hand in all of 'em.
But look, I don't even have my shoes shined.   45
FARMWORKER: Oh, patrón, I'll shine your shoes! (*He gets down to shine*
PATRONCITO's *shoes.*)
PATRONCITO: Never mind, get back to work. Up, boy, up I say! (*The*
FARMWORKER *keeps trying to shine his shoes.*) Come on, stop it.
Stop it! (CHARLIE *"la jura°" or "rent-a-fuzz" enters like an ape. He*   50
immediately lunges for the FARMWORKER.) Charlie! Charlie, no! It's
okay, boy. This is one of my mexicans! He was only trying to shine
my shoes.
CHARLIE: You sure?
PATRONCITO: Of course! Now you go back to the road and watch for   55
union organizers.
CHARLIE: Okay. (CHARLIE *exits like an ape. The* FARMWORKER *is off*
to one side, trembling with fear.)
PATRONCITO: (*To* FARMWORKER.) Scared you, huh boy? Well lemme
tell you, you don't have to be afraid of him, as long as you're with me,   60
comprende? I got him around to keep an eye on them huelguistas.
You ever heard of them, son? Ever heard of huelga? or César Chávez?
FARMWORKER: ¡Oh, sí, patrón!
PATRONCITO: What?
FARMWORKER: ¡Oh, no, señor! ¡Es comunista! Y la huelga es puro pedo.   65
¡Bola de colorados, arrastrados, huevones! ¡No trabajan porque no
quieren!°
PATRONCITO: That's right, son. Sic'em! Sic'em, boy!
FARMWORKER: (*Really getting into it.*) ¡Comunistas! ¡Desgraciados!°
PATRONCITO: Good boy! (FARMWORKER *falls to his knees hands in*   70
front of his chest like a docile dog; his tongue hangs out. PATRONCITO
pats him on the head.) Good boy. (*The* PATRONCITO *steps to one side*
and leans over. FARMWORKER *kisses his ass.* PATRONCITO *snaps*
up triumphantly.) 'At's a baby! You're okay, Pancho.
FARMWORKER: (*Smiling.*) Pedro.   75
PATRONCITO: Of course you are. Hell, you got it good here!
FARMWORKER: Me?
PATRONCITO: Damn right! You sure as hell ain't got my problems, I'll tell
you that. Taxes, insurance, supporting all them bums on welfare. You

---

la jura: Police.   **¡Es comunista! Y la huelga . . . :** He's a communist! And the
strike is a bunch of bullshit! A bunch of reds, low-lifes, lazy-asses! They don't
work because they don't want to!   **¡Desgraciados!:** Worthless bastards.

don't have to worry about none of that. Like housing, don't I let you   80
live in my labor camp, nice, rent-free cabins, air-conditioned?
FARMWORKER: Sí, señor, ayer se cayó la puerta.
PATROCINTO: What was that? English.
FARMWORKER: Yesterday the door fell off, señor. And there's rats también.
Y los escusados, the restrooms, ay, señor, fuchi! (*Holds fingers to his*   85
nose.)
PATRONCITO: Awright! (FARMWORKER *shuts up.*) So you gotta rough it
a little. I do that every time I go hunting in the mountains. Why, it's
almost like camping out, boy. A free vacation!
FARMWORKER: Vacation?   90
PATRONCITO: Free!
FARMWORKER: Qué bueno. Thank you, patrón!
PATRONCITO: Don't mention it. So what do you pay for housing, boy?
FARMWORKER: Nothing! (*Pronounced naw-thing.*)
PATRONCITO: Nothing, right! Now what about transportation? Don't I let   95
you ride free in my trucks? To and from the fields?
FARMWORKER: Sí, señor.
PATRONCITO: What do you pay for transportation, boy?
FARMWORKER: Nothing!
PATRONCITO: (*With* FARMWORKER.) Nothing! What about food? What   100
do you eat, boy?
FARMWORKER: Tortillas y frijoles con chile.
PATRONCITO: Beans and tortillas. What's beans and tortillas cost, boy?
FARMWORKER: (*Together with* PATRON.) Nothing!
PATRONCITO: Okay! So what you got to complain about?   105
FARMWORKER: Nothing!
PATRONCITO: Exactly. You got it good! Now look at me, they say I'm
greedy, that I'm rich. Well, let me tell you, boy, I got problems. No
free housing for me, Pancho. I gotta pay for what I got. You see that
car? How much you think a Lincoln Continental like that costs?   110
Cash! $12,000! Ever write out a check for $12,000, boy?
FARMWORKER: No, señor.
PATRONCITO: Well, lemme tell you, it hurts. It hurts right here! (*Slaps his*
wallet in his hind pocket.) And what for? I don't need a car like that. I
could throw it away!   115
FARMWORKER: (*Quickly.*) I'll take it, patrón.
PATRONCITO: Get you greasy hands off it! (*Pause.*) Now, let's take a look
at my housing. No free air conditioned mountain cabin for me. No
sir! You see that LBJ ranch style house up there, boy? How much you
think a house like that costs? Together with the hill, which I built?   120
$350,000!

FARMWORKER: (*Whistles.*) That's a lot of frijoles, patrón!

PATRONCITO: You're telling me! (*Stops, looks toward house.*) Oh yeah, and look at that, boy! You see her coming out of the house, onto the patio by the pool? The blonde with the mink bikini?   125

FARMWORKER: What bikini?

PATRONCITO: Well, it's small, but it's there. I oughta know, it cost me $5,000! And every weekend she wants to take trips. Trips to L.A., San Francisco, Chicago, New York. That woman hurts. It all costs money! You don't have problems like that, muchacho,° that's why you're so   130
lucky. Me, all I got is the woman, the house, the hill, the land. (*Starts to get emotional.*) Those commie bastards say I don't know what hard work is, that I exploit my workers. But look at all them vines, boy! (*Waves an arm toward the audience.*) Who the hell do they think planted all them vines with his own bare hands? Working from sun up   135
to sunset! Shoving vine shoots into the ground! With blood pouring out of his fingernails. Working in the heat, the frost, the fog, the sleet! (FARMWORKER *has been jumping up and down trying to answer him.*)

FARMWORKER: You, patrón, you!

PATRONCITO: (*Matter of factly.*) Naw, my grandfather, he worked his ass   140
off out here. But, I inherited it, and it's all mine!

FARMWORKER: You sure work hard, boss.

PATRONCITO: Juan . . . ?

FARMWORKER: Pedro.

PATRONCITO: I'm going to let you in on a little secret. Sometimes I sit up   145
there in my office and think to myself: I wish I was a Mexican.

FARMWORKER: You?

PATRONCITO: Just one of my own boys. Riding in the trucks, hair flying in the wind, feeling all that freedom, coming out here to the fields, working under the green vines, smoking a cigarette, my hands in the   150
cool soft earth, underneath the blue skies, with white clouds drifting by, looking at the mountains, listening to the birdies sing.

FARMWORKER: (*Entranced.*) I got it good.

PATRONCITO: What you want a union for, boy?

FARMWORKER: I don't want no union, patrón.   155

PATRONCITO: What you want more money for?

FARMWORKER: I don't want . . . I want more money!

PATRONCITO: Shut up! You want my problems, is that it? After all I explained to you? Listen to me, son, if I had the power, if I had the power . . . wait a minute, I got the power! (*Turns toward* FARM-   160
WORKER, *frightening him.*) Boy!

muchacho: Boy.

FARMWORKER: I didn't do it, patrón.
PATRONCITO: How would you like to be a rancher for a day?
FARMWORKER: Who me? Oh no, señor. I can't do that.
PATRONCITO: Shut up. Gimme that. (*Takes his hat, shears, sign.*)   165
FARMWORKER: ¡No, patrón, por favor, señor! ¡Patroncito!
PATRONCITO: (*Takes off his own sign and puts it on farmworker.*) Here!
FARMWORKER: Patron . . . cito. (*He looks down at the "Patrón" sign.*)
PATRONCITO: All right, now take the cigar. (FARMWORKER *takes cigar.*)
And the whip. (FARMWORKER *takes whip.*) Now look tough, boy.   170
Act like you're the boss.
FARMWORKER: Sí, señor. (*He cracks the whip and almost hits his foot.*)
PATRONCITO: Come on, boy! Head up, chin out! Look tough, look mean.
(FARMWORKER *looks tough and mean.*) Act like you can walk into
the governor's office and tell him off!   175
FARMWORKER: (*With unexpected force and power.*) Now, look here,
Ronnie! (FARMWORKER *scares himself.*)
PATRONCITO: That's good. But it's still not good enough. Let's see. Here
take my coat.
FARMWORKER: Oh, no, patrón. I can't.   180
PATRONCITO: Take it!
FARMWORKER: No, señor.
PATRONCITO: Come on!
FARMWORKER: Chale. (PATRONCITO *backs away from* FARMWORKER.
He takes his coat and holds it out like a bullfighter's cape, assuming the   185
bullfighting position.)
PATRONCITO: Uh-huh, toro.°
FARMWORKER: ¡Ay! (*He turns toward the coat and snags it with an ex-*
tended arm like a horn.)
PATRONCITO: Ole!° Okay, now let's have a look at you. (FARM-   190
WORKER *puts on coat.*) Naw, you're still missing something! You
need something!
FARMWORKER: Maybe a new pair of pants?
PATRONCITO: (*A sudden flash.*) Wait a minute! (*He touches his pig mask.*)
FARMWORKER: Oh, no! Patrón, not that! (*He hides his face.* PATRON-   195
CITO *removes his mask with a big grunt.* FARMWORKER *looks up*
cautiously, sees the PATRON's *real face and cracks up laughing.*)
Patrón, you look like me!
PATRONCITO: You mean . . . I . . . look like a Mexican?
FARMWORKER: ¡Sí, señor! (FARMWORKER *turns to put on the mask,*   200
and PATRONCITO *starts picking up* FARMWORKER's *hat, sign, etc.*
and putting them on.)

toro: Bull.   **Ole!:** A shout of approval in a bullfight.

PATRONCITO: I'm going to be one of my own boys. (FARMWORKER, *who has his back to the audience, jerks suddenly as he puts on* PATRONCITO's *mask. He stands tall and turns slowly, now looking*   205 *very much like a patrón. Suddenly fearful, but playing along.*) Oh, that's good! That's . . . great.

FARMWORKER: (*Booming, brusque, patrón-like.*) Shut up and get to work, boy!

PATRONCITO: Heh, now that's more like it!   210

FARMWORKER: I said get to work! (*He kicks* PATRONCITO.)

PATRONCITO: Heh, why did you do that for?

FARMWORKER: Because I felt like it, boy! You hear me, boy? I like your name, boy! I think I'll call you boy, boy!

PATRONCITO: You sure learn fast, boy.   215

FARMWORKER: I said shut up!

PATRONCITO: What an act. (*To audience.*) He's good, isn't he?

FARMWORKER: Come here boy.

PATRONCITO: (*His idea of a Mexican.*) Sí, señor, I theeenk.

FARMWORKER: I don't pay you to think, son. I pay you to work. Now   220 look here, see that car? It's mine.

PATRONCITO: My Lincoln Conti . . . oh, you're acting. Sure.

FARMWORKER: And that LBJ ranch style house, with hill? That's mine too.

PATRONCITO: The house too?   225

FARMWORKER: All mine.

PATRONCITO: (*More and more uneasy.*) What a joker.

FARMWORKER: Oh, wait a minute. Respect, boy! (*He pulls off* PATRONCITO's *farmworker hat.*) Do you see her coming out of my house, onto my patio by my pool? The blonde in the bikini? Well,   230 she's mine too!

PATRONCITO: But that's my wife!

FARMWORKER: Tough luck, son. You see this land, all these vines? They're mine.

PATRONCITO: Just a damn minute here. The land, the car, the house, hill,   235 and the cherry on top too? You're crazy! Where am I going to live?

FARMWORKER: I got a nice, air conditioned cabin down in the labor camp. Free housing, free transportation . . .

PATRONCITO: You're nuts! I can't live in those shacks! They got rats, cockroaches. And those trucks are unsafe. You want me to get killed?   240

FARMWORKER: Then buy a car.

PATRONCITO: With what? How much you paying me here, anyway?

FARMWORKER: Eighty-five cents an hour.

PATRONCITO: I was paying you a buck twenty-five!

FARMWORKER: I got problems, boy! Go on welfare!   245

PATRONCITO: Oh no, this is too much. You've gone too far, boy. I think
you better give me back my things. (*He takes off* FARMWORKER'*s
sign and hat, throws down shears and tells the audience.*) You know
that damn César Chávez is right? You can't do this work for less than
two dollars an hour. No, boy, I think we've played enough. Give me   250
back . . .
FARMWORKER: Get your hands off me, spic!
PATRONCITO: Now stop it, boy!
FARMWORKER: Get away from me, greaseball! (PATRONCITO *tries to
grab mask.*) Charlie! Charlie! (CHARLIE *the rent-a-fuzz comes bounc-*   255
ing in. PATRONCITO *tries to talk to him.*)
PATRONCITO: Now listen, Charlie, I . . .
CHARLIE: (*Pushes him aside.*) Out of my way, Mex! (*He goes over to*
FARMWORKER.) Yeah, boss?
PATRONCITO: This union commie bastard is giving me trouble. He's   260
trying to steal my car, my land, my ranch, and he even tried to rape
my wife!
CHARLIE: (*Turns around, an infuriated ape.*) You touched a white
woman, boy?
PATRONCITO: Charlie, you idiot, it's me! Your boss!   265
CHARLIE: Shut up!
PATRONCITO: Charlie! It's me!
CHARLIE: I'm gonna whup you good, boy! (*He grabs him.*)
PATRONCITO: (CHARLIE *starts dragging him out.*) Charlie! Stop it!
Somebody help me! Where's those damn union organizers? Where's   270
César Chávez? Help! Huelga! Huelgaaaaa! (CHARLIE *drags out the*
PATRONCITO. *The* FARMWORKER *takes off the pig mask and turns
toward the audience.*)
FARMWORKER: Bueno,° so much for the patrón. I got his house, his land,
his car. Only I'm not going to keep 'em. He can have them. But I'm   275
taking the cigar. Ay los watcho.° (*Exit.*)

Bueno: Well then.   **Ay los watcho:** Chicano slang for "See you guys later."

LOS VENDIDOS°

First Performance: Brown Beret junta, Elysian Park, East Los Angeles.

Characters
HONEST SANCHO
SECRETARY
FARMWORKER
PACHUCO°
REVOLUCIONARIO°
MEXICAN-AMERICAN

Scene: HONEST SANCHO's *Used Mexican Lot and Mexican Curio Shop. Three models are on display in* HONEST SANCHO's *shop. To the right, there is a* REVOLUCIONARIO, *complete with sombrero, carrilleras and carabina 30-30.° At center, on the floor, there is the* FARMWORKER, *under a broad straw sombrero. At stage left is the* PACHUCO, *filero° in hand.* HONEST SANCHO *is moving among his models, dusting them off and preparing for another day of business.*

SANCHO: Bueno, bueno, mis monos, vamos a ver a quién vendemos ahora, ¿no?° (*To audience.*) ¡Quihubo!° I'm Honest Sancho and this is my shop. Antes fui contratista, pero ahora logré tener mi negocio.° All I need now is a customer. (*A bell rings offstage.*) Ay, a customer!
SECRETARY: (*Entering.*) Good morning, I'm Miss Jimenez from . . .   5
SANCHO: Ah, una chicana! Welcome, welcome Señorita Jiménez.°
SECRETARY: (*Anglo pronunciation.*) JIM-enez.
SANCHO: ¿Qué?°
SECRETARY: My name is Miss JIM-enez. Don't you speak English? What's wrong with you?   10
SANCHO: Oh, nothing, Señorita JIM-enez. I'm here to help you.
SECRETARY: That's better. As I was starting to say, I'm a secretary from Governor Reagan's office, and we're looking for a Mexican type for the administration.

Los Vendidos: The Sellouts. **Pachuco:** A Mexican American who hung out in the streets and became known for a distinctive way of dressing and speaking. (For example, see the introduction to José Montoya's poem "El Louie" on p. 103.) **Revolucionario:** Revolutionary. **sombrero, carrilleras and carabina 30-30:** A hat, a bandolier (straps worn across the chest to hold bullets), and a type of rifle. **filero:** Chicano slang for *knife*. **Bueno, bueno, mis monos, . . . :** Well, well, my monkeys, let's see who we sell today. **¡Quihubo!:** What's up? **Antes fui contratista, pero . . . :** Before, I was a contractor, but now I'm able to have my own little business. **Señorita Jiménez:** Miss Jimenez (usually pronounced with the accent on the second syllable). **¿Qué?:** What?

SANCHO: Well, you come to the right place, lady. This is Honest   15
Sancho's Used Mexican Lot, and we got all types here. Any particular
type you want?

SECRETARY: Yes, we were looking for somebody suave°. . .

SANCHO: Suave.

SECRETARY: Debonaire.   20

SANCHO: De buen aire.°

SECRETARY: Dark.

SANCHO: Prieto.°

SECRETARY: But of course, not too dark.

SANCHO: No muy prieto.   25

SECRETARY: Perhaps, beige.

SANCHO: Beige, just the tone. Así como cafecito con leche, ¿no?°

SECRETARY: One more thing. He must be hard-working.

SANCHO: That could only be one model. Step right over here to the
center of the shop, lady. (*They cross to the* FARMWORKER.) This is   30
our standard farmworker model. As you can see, in the words of our
beloved Senator George Murphy, he is "built close to the ground."
Also, take special notice of his 4-ply Goodyear huaraches,° made
from the rain tire. This wide-brimmed sombrero is an extra added
feature; keeps off the sun, rain and dust.   35

SECRETARY: Yes, it does look durable.

SANCHO: And our farmworker model is friendly. Muy amable.° Watch.
(*Snaps his fingers.*)

FARMWORKER: (*Lifts up head.*) Buenos días, señorita.° (*His head drops.*)

SECRETARY: My, he is friendly.   40

SANCHO: Didn't I tell you? Loves his patrones! But his most attractive
feature is that he's hard-working. Let me show you. (*Snaps fingers.*
FARMWORKER *stands.*)

FARMWORKER: ¡El jale!° (*He begins to work.*)

SANCHO: As you can see he is cutting grapes.   45

SECRETARY: Oh, I wouldn't know.

SANCHO: He also picks cotton. (*Snaps.* FARMWORKER *begins to pick
cotton.*)

SECRETARY: Versatile, isn't he?

SANCHO: He also picks melons. (*Snaps.* FARMWORKER *picks melons.*)   50
That's his slow speed for late in the season. Here's his fast speed.
(*Snap.* FARMWORKER *picks faster.*)

Suave: Soft.   **De buen aire:** Having a good manner.   **Prieto:** Very dark.
Así como cafecito con leche, ¿no?: Like coffee with milk, no?   **huaraches:**
Sandals.   **Muy amable:** Very friendly.   **Buenos días, señorita:** Good morning,
young lady.   **¡El jale!:** Work!

SECRETARY: Chihuahua . . . I mean, goodness, he sure is a hardworker.

SANCHO: (*Pulls the* FARMWORKER *to his feet.*) And that isn't the half of
it. Do you see these little holes on his arms that appear to be pores?   55
During those hot sluggish days in the field when the vines or the
branches get so entangled, it's almost impossible to move, these holes
emit a certain grease that allows our model to slip and slide right
through the crop with no trouble at all.

SECRETARY: Wonderful. But is he economical?   60

SANCHO: Economical? Señorita, you are looking at the Volkswagen of
Mexicans. Pennies a day is all it takes. One plate of beans and tortillas
will keep him going all day. That, and chile. Plenty of chile. Chile jalapeños, chile verde, chile colorado.° But, of course, if you do give him
chile, (*Snap.* FARMWORKER *turns left face. Snap.* FARMWORKER   65
bends over.) then you have to change his oil filter once a week.

SECRETARY: What about storage?

SANCHO: No problem. You know these new farm labor camps our Hon-
orable Governor Reagan has built out by Parlier or Raisin City? They
were designed with our model in mind. Five, six, seven, even ten in   70
one of those shacks will give you no trouble at all. You can also put
him in old barns, old cars, riverbanks. You can even leave him out in
the field over night with no worry!

SECRETARY: Remarkable.

SANCHO: And here's an added feature: every year at the end of the sea-   75
son, this model goes back to Mexico and doesn't return, automatically, until next Spring.

SECRETARY: How about that. But tell me, does he speak English?

SANCHO: Another outstanding feature is that last year this model was
programmed to go out on STRIKE! (*Snap.*)   80

FARMWORKER: ¡Huelga! ¡Huelga! Hermanos, sálganse de esos files.°
(*Snap. He stops.*)

SECRETARY: No! Oh no, we can't strike in the State Capitol.

SANCHO: Well, he also scabs. (*Snap.*)

FARMWORKER: Me vendo barato, ¿y qué?° (*Snap.*)   85

SECRETARY: That's much better, but you didn't answer my question.
Does he speak English?

SANCHO: Bueno . . . no, pero° he has other . . .

SECRETARY: No.

SANCHO: Other features.   90

Chile jalapeños, chile verde, chile colorado: Jalapeño chile, green chile, red
chile.   **Hermanos, sálganse de esos files:** Brothers, get out of those fields.
Me vendo barato, ¿y qué?: I sell myself cheap, and what about it?   **Bueno . . .
no, pero:** Well . . . no, but.

SECRETARY: No! He just won't do!
SANCHO: Okay, okay, pues.° We have other models.
SECRETARY: I hope so. What we need is something a little more
sophisticated.
SANCHO: Sophisti-qué?   95
SECRETARY: An urban model.
SANCHO: Ah, from the city! Step right back. Over here in this corner of
the shop is exactly what you're looking for. Introducing our new 1969
JOHNNY PACHUCO model! This is our fast-back model. Stream-
lined. Built for speed, low-riding, city life. Take a look at some of   100
these features. Mag shoes, dual exhausts, green chartreuse paint-job,
dark-tint windshield, a little poof on top. Let me just turn him on.
(*Snap.* JOHNNY *walks to stage center with a* PACHUCO *bounce.*)
SECRETARY: What was that?
SANCHO: That, señorita, was the Chicano shuffle.   105
SECRETARY: Okay, what does he do?
SANCHO: Anything and everything necessary for city life. For instance,
survival: he knife fights. (*Snaps.* JOHNNY *pulls out a switchblade and
swings at* SECRETARY. SECRETARY *screams.*) He dances. (*Snap.*)
JOHNNY: (*Singing.*) "Angel Baby, my Angel Baby . . ." (*Snap.*)   110
SANCHO: And here's a feature no city model can be without. He gets
arrested, but not without resisting, of course. (*Snap.*)
JOHNNY: En la madre, la placa.° I didn't do it! I didn't do it! (JOHNNY
*turns and stands up against an imaginary wall, legs spread out, arms
behind his back.*)   115
SECRETARY: Oh no, we can't have arrests! We must maintain law and
order.
SANCHO: But he's bilingual.
SECRETARY: Bilingual?
SANCHO: Simón que yes.° He speaks English! Johnny, give us some   120
English. (*Snap.*)
JOHNNY: (*Comes downstage.*) Fuck-you!
SECRETARY: (*Gasps.*) Oh! I've never been so insulted in my whole life!
SANCHO: Well, he learned it in your school.
SECRETARY: I don't care where he learned it.   125
SANCHO: But he's economical.
SECRETARY: Economical?
SANCHO: Nickels and dimes. You can keep Johnny running on
hamburgers, Taco Bell tacos, Lucky Lager beer, Thunderbird wine,
yesca . . .   130

pues: Then.   **en la madre, la placa:** Fuck it, the cops.
Simón que yes: For sure he is.

SECRETARY: Yesca?

SANCHO: Mota.

SECRETARY: Mota?

SANCHO: Leños . . . marijuana. (*Snap.* JOHNNY *inhales on an imaginary joint.*) 135

SECRETARY: That's against the law!

JOHNNY: (*Big smile, holding his breath.*) Yeah.

SANCHO: He also sniffs glue. (*Snap.* JOHNNY *inhales glue, big smile.*)

JOHNNY: Tha's too much man, ese.°

SECRETARY: No, Mr. Sancho, I don't think this . . . 140

SANCHO: Wait a minute, he has other qualities I know you'll love. For example, an inferiority complex. (*Snap.*)

JOHNNY: (*To* SANCHO.) You think you're better than me, huh, ese? (*Swings switchblade.*)

SANCHO: He can also be beaten and he bruises. Cut him and he bleeds, 145
kick him and he . . . (*He beats, bruises and kicks* PACHUCO.) Would you like to try it?

SECRETARY: Oh, I couldn't.

SANCHO: Be my guest. He's a great scape goat.

SECRETARY: No really. 150

SANCHO: Please.

SECRETARY: Well, all right. Just once. (*She kicks* PACHUCO.) Oh, he's so soft.

SANCHO: Wasn't that good? Try again.

SECRETARY: (*Kicks* PACHUCO.) Oh, he's so wonderful! (*She kicks him* 155
again.)

SANCHO: Okay, that's enough, lady. You'll ruin the merchandise. Yes, our Johnny Pachuco model can give you many hours of pleasure. Why, the LAPD just bought 20 of these to train their rookie cops on. And talk about maintenance. Señorita, you are looking at an entirely self- 160
supporting machine. You're never going to find our Johnny Pachuco model on the relief rolls. No, sir, this model knows how to liberate.

SECRETARY: Liberate?

SANCHO: He steals. (*Snap.* JOHNNY *rushes to* SECRETARY *and steals her purse.*) 165

JOHNNY: ¡Dame esa bolsa, vieja!° (*He grabs the purse and runs. Snap by* SANCHO, *he stops.* SECRETARY *runs after* JOHNNY *and grabs purse away from him, kicking him as she goes.*)

SECRETARY: No, no, no! We can't have any more thieves in the State Administration. Put him back. 170

---

ese: Dude.   **¡Dame esa bolsa, vieja!:** Give me that purse, old lady!

SANCHO: Okay, we still got other models. Come on, Johnny, we'll sell
you to some old lady. (SANCHO *takes* JOHNNY *back to his place.*)
SECRETARY: Mr. Sancho, I don't think you quite understand what we
need. What we need is something that will attract the women voters.
Something more traditional, more romantic.   175
SANCHO: Ah, a lover. (*He smiles meaningfully.*) Step right over here,
señorita. Introducing our standard Revolucionario and/or Early
California Bandit type. As you can see, he is well-built, sturdy,
durable. This is the International Harvester of Mexicans.
SECRETARY: What does he do?   180
SANCHO: You name it, he does it. He rides horses, stays in the moun-
tains, crosses deserts, plains, rivers, leads revolutions, follows revolu-
tions, kills, can be killed, serves as a martyr, hero, movie star. Did I
say movie star? Did you ever see *Viva Zapata? Viva Villa, Villa Rides,
Pancho Villa Returns, Pancho Villa Goes Back, Pancho Villa Meets*   185
Abbott and Costello?
SECRETARY: I've never seen any of those.
SANCHO: Well, he was in all of them. Listen to this. (*Snap.*)
REVOLUCIONARIO: (*Scream.*) ¡Viva Villaaaaa!
SECRETARY: That's awfully loud.   190
SANCHO: He has a volume control. (*He adjusts volume. Snap.*)
REVOLUCIONARIO: (*Mousey voice.*) Viva Villa.
SECRETARY: That's better.
SANCHO: And even if you didn't see him in the movies, perhaps you saw
him on TV. He makes commercials. (*Snap.*)   195
REVOLUCIONARIO: Is there a Frito Bandito in your house?
SECRETARY: Oh yes, I've seen that one!
SANCHO: Another feature about this one is that he is economical. He
runs on raw horsemeat and tequila!
SECRETARY: Isn't that rather savage?   200
SANCHO: Al contrario,° it makes him a lover. (*Snap.*)
REVOLUCIONARIO: (*To* SECRETARY.) Ay, mamasota, cochota, ven pa 'ca!°
(*He grabs* SECRETARY *and folds her back, Latin-lover style.*)
SANCHO: (*Snap.* REVOLUCIONARIO *goes back upright.*) Now wasn't
that nice?   205
SECRETARY: Well, it was rather nice.
SANCHO: And finally, there is one outstanding feature about this model I
know the ladies are going to love: he's a genuine antique! He was
made in Mexico in 1910!
SECRETARY: Made in Mexico?   210

Al contrario: On the contrary.   **mamasota, cochota, ven pa 'ca:** Sweet mama,
pretty thing, come here.

SANCHO: That's right. Once in Tijuana, twice in Guadalajara, three times in Cuernavaca.

SECRETARY: Mr. Sancho, I thought he was an American product.

SANCHO: No, but . . .

SECRETARY: No, I'm sorry. We can't buy anything but American made   215
products. He just won't do.

SANCHO: But he's an antique!

SECRETARY: I don't care. You still don't understand what we need. It's true we need Mexican models, such as these, but it's more important that he be American.   220

SANCHO: American?

SECRETARY: That's right, and judging from what you've shown me, I don't think you have what we want. Well, my lunch hour's almost over, I better . . .

SANCHO: Wait a minute! Mexican but American?   225

SECRETARY: That's correct.

SANCHO: Mexican but . . . (*A sudden flash.*) American! Yeah, I think we've got exactly what you want. He just came in today! Give me a minute. (*He exits. Talks from backstage.*) Here he is in the shop. Let me just get some papers off. There. Introducing our new 1970   230
Mexican-American! Ta-ra-ra-raaaa! (SANCHO *brings out the* MEXICAN-AMERICAN *model, a clean-shaven middle class type in a business suit, with glasses.*)

SECRETARY: (*Impressed.*) Where have you been hiding this one?

SANCHO: He just came in this morning. Ain't he a beauty? Feast your eyes   235
on him! Sturdy U.S. Steel frame, streamlined, modern. As a matter of fact, he is built exactly like our Anglo models, except that he comes in a variety of darker shades: naugahide, leather or leatherette.

SECRETARY: Naugahide.

SANCHO: Well, we'll just write that down. Yes, señorita, this model rep-   240
resents the apex of American engineering! He is bilingual, college educated, ambitious! Say the word "acculturate" and he accelerates. He is intelligent, well-mannered, clean. Did I say clean? (*Snap.* MEXICAN-AMERICAN *raises his arm.*) Smell.

SECRETARY: (*Smells.*) Old Sobaco,° my favorite.   245

SANCHO: (*Snap.* MEXICAN-AMERICAN *turns toward* SANCHO.) Eric? (*To* SECRETARY.) We call him Eric García. (*To* ERIC.) I want you to meet Miss JIM-enez, Eric.

MEXICAN-AMERICAN: Miss JIM-enez, I am delighted to make your acquaintance. (*He kisses her hand.*)   250

SECRETARY: Oh, my, how charming!

Sobaco: Armpit.

SANCHO: Did you feel the suction? He has seven especially engineered
suction cups right behind his lips. He's a charmer all right!
SECRETARY: How about boards, does he function on boards?
SANCHO: You name them, he is on them. Parole boards, draft boards,   255
school boards, taco quality control boards, surf boards, two by fours.
SECRETARY: Does he function in politics?
SANCHO: Señorita, you are looking at a political machine. Have you ever
heard of the OEO, EOC, COD, WAR ON POVERTY? That's our
model! Not only that, he makes political speeches.   260
SECRETARY: May I hear one?
SANCHO: With pleasure. (*Snap*.) Eric, give us a speech.
MEXICAN-AMERICAN: Mr. Congressman, Mr. Chairman, members of
the board, honored guests, ladies and gentlemen. (SANCHO *and*
SECRETARY *applaud*.) Please, please. I come before you as a   265
Mexican-American to tell you about the problems of the Mexican.
The problems of the Mexican stem from one thing and one thing
only: he's stupid. He's uneducated. He needs to stay in school. He
needs to be ambitious, forward-looking, harder-working. He needs to
think American, American, American, American, American! God   270
bless America! God bless America! God bless America! (*He goes out of
control.* SANCHO *snaps frantically and the* MEXICAN-AMERICAN
finally slumps forward, bending at the waist.)
SECRETARY: Oh my, he's patriotic too!
SANCHO: Sí, señorita, he loves his country. Let me just make a little   275
adjustment here. (*Stands* MEXICAN-AMERICAN *up*.)
SECRETARY: What about upkeep? Is he economical?
SANCHO: Well, no, I won't lie to you. The Mexican-American costs a
little bit more, but you get what you pay for. He's worth every extra
cent. You can keep him running on dry Martinis, Langendorf   280
bread . . .
SECRETARY: Apple pie?
SANCHO: Only Mom's. Of course, he's also programmed to eat Mexican
food at ceremonial functions, but I must warn you, an overdose of
beans will plug up his exhaust.   285
SECRETARY: Fine! There's just one more question. How much do you
want for him?
SANCHO: Well, I tell you what I'm gonna do. Today and today only, because you've been so sweet, I'm gonna let you steal this model from
me! I'm gonna let you drive him off the lot for the simple price of,   290
let's see, taxes and license included, $15,000.
SECRETARY: Fifteen thousand dollars? For a Mexican!!!!
SANCHO: Mexican? What are you talking about? This is a Mexican-
American! We had to melt down two pachucos, a farmworker and

three gabachos° to make this model! You want quality, but you gotta   295
pay for it! This is no cheap run-about. He's got class!
SECRETARY: Okay, I'll take him.
SANCHO: You will?
SECRETARY: Here's your money.
SANCHO: You mind if I count it?   300
SECRETARY: Go right ahead.
SANCHO: Well, you'll get your pink slip in the mail. Oh, do you want me
to wrap him up for you? We have a box in the back.
SECRETARY: No, thank you. The Governor is having a luncheon this after-
noon, and we need a brown face in the crowd. How do I drive him?   305
SANCHO: Just snap your fingers. He'll do anything you want. (SECRE-
TARY *snaps.* MEXICAN-AMERICAN *steps forward.*)
MEXICAN-AMERICAN: ¡Raza querida, vamos levantando armas para libe-
rarnos de estos desgraciados gabachos que nos explotan! Vamos . . .°
SECRETARY: What did he say?   310
SANCHO: Something about taking up arms, killing white people, etc.
SECRETARY: But he's not supposed to say that!
SANCHO: Look, lady, don't blame me for bugs from the factory. He's your
Mexican-American, you bought him, now drive him off the lot!
SECRETARY: But he's broken!   315
SANCHO: Try snapping another finger. (SECRETARY *snaps.* MEXICAN-
AMERICAN *comes to life again.*)
MEXICAN-AMERICAN: ¡Esta gran humanidad ha dicho basta! ¡Y se ha
puesto en marcha! ¡Basta! ¡Basta! ¡Viva la raza! ¡Viva la causa! ¡Viva
la huelga! ¡Vivan los brown berets! ¡Vivan los estudiantes! ¡Chicano   320
power!° (*The* MEXICAN-AMERICAN *turns toward the* SECRETARY,
who gasps and backs up. He keeps turning toward the PACHUCO,
FARMWORKER *and* REVOLUCIONARIO, *snapping his fingers and
turning each of them on, one by one.*)
PACHUCO: (*Snap. To* SECRETARY.) I'm going to get you, baby! ¡Viva   325
la raza!
FARMWORKER: (*Snap. To* SECRETARY.) ¡Viva la huelga! ¡Viva la huelga!
¡Viva la huelga!
REVOLUCIONARIO: (*Snap. To* SECRETARY.) ¡Viva la revolución! (*The three
models join together and advance toward the* SECRETARY, *who backs*   330

gabachos: Derogatory term for white people.   **¡Raza querida, vamos levantando . . . :** Cherished raza, let's take up arms to free ourselves from these
worthless white people who exploit us! Let's go.   **¡Esta gran humanidad . . . :**
This great humanity has said enough! It is on the march! Enough! Enough! Long
live la Raza! Long live the cause! Long live the strike! Long live the Brown Berets!
Long live the students! Chicano power!

up and runs out of the shop screaming. SANCHO *is at the other end of the shop holding his money in his hand. All freeze. After a few seconds of silence, the* PACHUCO *moves and stretches, shaking his arms and loosening up. The* FARMWORKER *and* REVOLUCIONARIO *do the same.* SANCHO *stays where he is, frozen to his spot.*)   335
JOHNNY: Man, that was a long one, ese. (*Others agree with him.*)
FARMWORKER: How did we do?
JOHNNY: Pretty good, look at all that lana,° man! (*He goes over to* SANCHO *and removes the money from his hand.* SANCHO *stays where he is.*)   340
REVOLUCIONARIO: En la madre,° look at all the money.
JOHNNY: We keep this up, we're going to be rich.
FARMWORKER: They think we're machines.
REVOLUCIONARIO: Burros.°
JOHNNY: Puppets.   345
MEXICAN-AMERICAN: The only thing I don't like is how come I always get to play the goddamn Mexican-American?
JOHNNY: That's what you get for finishing high school.
FARMWORKER: How about our wages, ese?
JOHNNY: Here it comes right now. $3,000 for you, $3,000 for you, $3,000 350
for you and $3,000 for me. The rest we put back into the business.
MEXICAN-AMERICAN: Too much, man. Heh, where you vatos going tonight?
FARMWORKER: I'm going over to Concha's. There's a party.
JOHNNY: Wait a minute, vatos. What about our salesman? I think he 355
needs an oil job.
REVOLUCIONARIO: Leave him to me. (*The* PACHUCO, FARMWORKER *and* MEXICAN-AMERICAN *exit, talking loudly about their plans for the night. The* REVOLUCIONARIO *goes over to* SANCHO, *removes his derby hat and cigar, lifts him up and throws him over his shoulder.* 360
SANCHO *hangs loose, lifeless. To audience.*) He's the best model we got! ¡Ajúa!° (*Exit.*)

Reading

1. In *Las Dos Caras del Patroncito*, how does the Patroncito's perspective change when he is no longer in charge?

2. In *Los Vendidos*, which of the characters does the Secretary decide to purchase from Honest Sancho?

---

lana: Slang for *money* (literally, *wool*).   **En la madre:** An exclamation, equivalent to "Fuck!"   **Burros:** Donkeys.   **¡Ajúa!:** Shout of approval.

Thinking Critically

1. (*Las Dos Caras del Patroncito* and *Los Vendidos*) What effect do you think these roles might have on a performer? Why?

2. Who are "the sellouts" referred to in the title of *Los Vendidos*? What makes them sellouts?

Connecting

1. Luis Valdez creates characters in both plays that are based on types known to his audiences, much the same way a cartoonist would. In what ways are the characters in the Valdez plays similar to the characters in Lalo Alcaraz's cartoon strip *La Cucaracha* (p. 418)? Do some of the same characters appear? Do Valdez and Alcaraz use their characters to make similar points? If so, identify the characters and the points made.

Writing

1. In the plays he wrote for Teatro Campesino, Luis Valdez was very concerned with communicating with his audiences. What message is he trying to send in *Los Vendidos* and *Las Dos Caras del Patroncito*? Write an essay exploring the themes and the lessons of the two plays above, supporting your arguments with specific examples from the texts.

Creating

1. **Draw one of Valdez's characters.** *Los Vendidos* is full of character types. Draw a cartoon version of one of the characters in the plays. Create six cartoon frames that present action and dialogue or monologue that are in keeping with the character Valdez presents.

11

JOSÉ MONTOYA [1932–2013]

El Louie

From Rascatripas [1970]

GENRE: POETRY

José Montoya has been called the godfather of Chicano public art for his work as a painter. In his poetry as well, Montoya—along with Alurista (p. 78) and Corky Gonzales (p. 63)—helped to create the imagery of the early Chicano Movement. Where the other two had found inspiration by turning to the distant past, Montoya found it in the pachuco of the 1940s, dressed in his distinctive zoot suit and viewed, before Montoya made him a hero, as a disreputable character only slightly better than a criminal.

Montoya was born in Albuquerque, New Mexico, but grew up, like El Louie, in California as a barrio vato. *After serving in the Korean War he earned a bachelor's degree from California College of Arts and Crafts in Oakland and then began a career as an artist and teacher in Sacramento. In 1971, he founded the Royal Chicano Air Force, which, in spite of a militaristic name that briefly aroused suspicion from the FBI, was an art collective that would become famous within the Chicano Movement for its public art projects, including murals and staged events. "The reason for doing art was to take forward the notion of Aztlán, the notion of the Movimiento, the notion of La Causa," Montoya recalled of the era.* In 1972 Montoya published his first book,* El sol y los de abajo and Other R.C.A.F. Poems, *and though his next collection,* In Formation: 20 Years of Joda, *was not published until 1992, he never stopped writing and reading his poetry. Montoya was also a professor at Sacramento State University for nearly three decades.*

The poem "El Louie" achieved its popularity as much through performance as through publication. In it, Montoya made the pachuco's nonconformist attitude and willingness to create a style an inspiration for Chicanos of a new generation. The pachuco would later reach a huge audience when it was taken up by Luis Valdez (p. 82) in his play and film Zoot Suit, *for which Montoya acted as advisor and graphic artist.*

---

*Quote from an interview with Montoya on Latinopia.com.

As you read the poem, listening carefully to its sounds and rhythms, think about how Louie Rodríguez embodies a struggle against hardship, resistance to the dominant culture, and all the tragedy and nobility of Chicano existence.

Hoy enterraron al Louie°

And San Pedro o sanpinche°
are in for it. And those
times of the forties
and the early fifties   5
lost un vato de atolle.°

Kind of slim and drawn,
there toward the end,
aging fast from too much
booze y la vida dura.° But   10
class to the end.

En Sanjo° you'd see him
sporting a dark topcoat
playing in his fantasy
the role of Bogart, Cagney   15
or Raft.

Era de Fowler el vato,°
carnal del Candi y el
Ponchi°—Los Rodríguez—
The Westside knew 'em,   20
and Selma, even Gilroy.

'48 Fleetline, two-tone—
buenas garras° and always
rucas—como la Mary y
la Helen° . . . siempre con   25
liras bien afinadas
cantando La Palma, la
que andaba en el florero.°

Hoy enterraron al Louie: Today they buried "the Louie." (Using *el* and *la* before a person's name is slang and implies singularity or uniqueness.) **San Pedro o sanpinche:** Saint Peter or Saint Whoever-the-Fuck. **un vato de atolle:** A cool dude. **y la vida dura:** And the hard life. **Sanjo:** Slang for San Jose, California. **Era de Fowler el vato:** The dude was from Fowler. **carnal del Candi y el / Ponchi:** Brother of Candi and Ponchi. **buenas garras:** Good rags (i.e., clothes). **rucas—como la Mary y / la Helen:** Women, like Mary and Helen. **siempre con . . . florero:** Always with well-tuned guitars, singing La Palma, the one that was in the vase.

Louie hit on the idea in
those days for tailor-made   30
drapes, unique idea—porque
Fowler no era nada como
Los, o'l E.P.T.° Fresno's
westside was as close as
we ever got to the big time.   35

But we had Louie, and the
Palomar, el boogie, los
mambos y cuatro suspiros
del alma y nunca faltaba°
the gut-shrinking love-   40
splitting, ass-hole-up-
tight, bad news—
        Trucha, esos! Va 'ber
        pedo!
        Abusau, ese!°   45
        Get Louie

No llores,° Carmen, we can
handle 'em.
        Ese, 'on tal Jimmy?
        Hórale, Louie   50
        Where's Primo?
        Va 'ber catos!°

En el parking lot away from
        the jura.°
        Hórale!   55
        Trais filero?
        Simón!
        Nel!
        Chale, ese!
        Oooooh, este vato!°   60

And Louie would come through—
melodramatic music, like in the

porque / Fowler . . . : Because Fowler was nothing like Los Angeles, or El Paso,
Texas. **cuatro suspiros . . . y nunca faltaba:** Four sighs from the soul—and
there was no lack of. **Trucha . . . ese!:** Watch out, dudes! There's gonna be
some shit! Be alert, dude! **No llores:** Don't cry. **Ese . . . Va 'ber catos!:**
Dude, where's Jimmy? All right, Louie, where's Primo ("Cousin")? There's gonna
be a fistfight! **jura:** Cops. **Hórale . . . este vato!:** C'mon! Got a knife?
Absolutely! Nope! No way, man! Oooooh, this dude!

mono°—tan tan tarán!°—Cruz
Diablo, El Charro Negro!° Bogart
smile (his smile as deadly as   65
his vaisas!°) He dug roles, man,
and names—like blackie, little
Louie . . .

Ese Louie . . .
Chale, call me "Diamonds," man!   70
Y en Korea fue soldado de
levita con huevos° and all the
paradoxes del soldado raso°—
heroism and the stockade!

And on leave, jump boots   75
shainadas° and ribbons, cocky
from the war, strutting to
early mass on Sunday morning.

Wow, is that el Louie

Mire, comadre, ahí va el hijo   80
de Lola!°

Afterward he and fat Richard
would hock their bronze stars
for pisto° en el Jardín Canales
y en El Trocadero.   85

At barber college he came
out with honors. Después
empeñaba su velardo de la
peluca pa' jugar pócar serrada
and lo ball en Sanjo y Alvizo.°   90

And "Legs Louie Diamond" hit
on some lean times . . .

Mono: Movies. **tan tan tarán:** Mimics the sound of melodramatic music.
Cruz / Diablo, El Charro Negro!: Characters from Mexican movies. **vaisas:**
Grips. **Y en Korea . . . :** And in Korea he was a draftee with balls. **del soldado
raso:** Of the private (i.e., an unranked soldier). **shainadas:** Chicano slang for
shined. **Mire, comadre, ahí va el hijo / de Lola!:** Look, sister (a close woman
friend), there goes Lola's son. **pisto:** An alcoholic drink. **Después . . . en
Sanjo y Alvizo:** Later he would hock his barber's briefcase to play draw poker
and low ball in San Jose.

Hoy enterraron al Louie.

Y en Fowler at Nesei's
pool parlor los baby chooks   95
se acuerdan de Louie, el carnal
del Candi y el Ponchi—la vez
que lo fileriaron en el Casa
Dome y cuando se catió con
La Chiva.°   100

Hoy enterraron al Louie.

His death was an insult
porque no murió en acción—
no lo mataron los vatos,
ni los gooks en Korea.°   105
He died alone in a rented
room—perhaps like in a
Bogart movie.

The end was a cruel hoax.
But his life had been   110
remarkable!

　　　Vato de atolle, el Louie Rodríguez.

Reading

1. What are some of the obstacles that Louie faces in his life?

2. What are some of Louie's heroic (and unheroic) characteristics?

Thinking Critically

1. What are some ways that the story of El Louie is not just about one individual but about a group?

2. What is the effect of the poet's heavy use of English and Spanish slang? What do you think the poem gains or loses because of it?

los baby chooks . . . La Chiva: The baby pachucos remember Louie, the brother of Candi and Ponchi, the time that they had a knife fight at the Casa Dome and when they beat up La Chiva ("Goat"). **Porque no murió . . . Korea:** Because he didn't die in action—the dudes didn't kill him nor did the gooks (racist term for Asians used by soldiers) in Korea.

Connecting

1. Compare Louie Rodríguez, the pachuco hero of Montoya's poem, with the character of Pachuco in Luis Valdez's play *Los Vendidos* (p. 91). What characteristics do these pachucos share? Do Montoya and Valdez use the characters for different purposes?

Writing

1. Unlike many other heroes, the protagonist of "El Louie" does not move from triumph to triumph. Instead he confronts a number of difficulties also faced by many other people. Using examples from the poem, discuss how Montoya turns Louie into a character for whom a reader or listener can feel sympathy and even admiration.

Creating

1. **Make a persuasive poster.** Poster art, which integrates text and imagery and often promotes a cause, can be as powerful and beautiful as more traditional forms of artwork. José Montoya designed posters for events and movies to help advance the goals of the Chicano Movement. Make a persuasive poster that illustrates an upcoming event (or one you wish were upcoming), or make one that promotes and makes an argument for a cause you believe in.

12

RICARDO SÁNCHEZ [1941–1995]

Soledad Was a Girl's Name • Say, Tush-Hog Convict

From Selected Poems [1985] AND Hechizospells [1976]

GENRE: POETRY

Ricardo Sánchez's poetry took him from prisoner to professor. He was born in El Paso, Texas, where he lived as a young pachuco in el barrio del Diablo *until he dropped out of high school and joined the army. Once back in the United States, Sánchez landed in jail, where he earned his GED, a credential he always proudly listed right next to his Ph.D. While there he began writing the poetry that would go into his book* Canto y grito mi liberación, *first published in 1971. In the book's preface, Sánchez called it a "response to the growing menace of a dehumanizing society that is now worldwide, for conflict and racism are rampant throughout the world,"* and its efforts to combine poetry with social protest and to find hope in the struggle of Chicanos against poverty and hatred have made it a classic text of the Chicano Movement. With its republication by Doubleday in 1973, it also made Sánchez the first Chicano poet to be published by a mainstream publisher. In 1974 he earned a doctorate from the Union Graduate School in Cincinnati, and he taught at universities for the rest of his career, culminating in a professorship at the University of Washington. Sánchez enjoyed taking his poetry on the road, performing his writing and teaching in prisons and universities all over the country and outside it. He also wrote poetry about his experiences traveling as far as Alaska and Amsterdam. Sánchez's poetic voice, as well as a powerful reading style, affirmed his pride and strength as an individual and that of all Chicanos and had a profound influence on later poets. A collection of his work titled* Selected Poems *was printed in 1985. In 1995 his life was cut short by cancer.*

The following two poems grow out of his time at Soledad Prison in California and the Ramsey Prison Farm Number One in Texas. "Say, Tush-Hog Convict" is an exploration of the dehumanizing aspects of a forced labor camp, while "Soledad Was a Girl's Name" is a search for that fragile humanity amid similarly brutal prison conditions.

As you read, try to get from each of these poems a sense of the speaker's fears and hopes, not only for himself but for society.

Soledad, June 10, 1963

SOLEDAD WAS A GIRL'S NAME

Soledad was a girl's name,
years ago
at jefferson high,

*From Luis Leal, "Introduction to the *Ricardo Sánchez Reader*."

and she was soft and brown
and beautiful.   5
i used to watch her,
and think her name
was ironic
and poetic,
for she was Soledad Guerra,   10
        solitude and war,
and she used to always smile
con ternura morena
como su piel,°
and now in this soledad   15
that i am leaving soon,
this callous nation
of bars and cement and barbarity,
it seems strange
that a name can call out to me   20
and mesmerize me,
yet repel me,
one a girl, now a woman,
and the other
a jagged prison world   25
                where hate
                is a common expletive,
                seems everyone hates,
                seems everyone is a convict,
                even the guards and counselors   30
                    do time here
                    every day trudging into
                    this abysmal human warehouse.
am leaving
and it hurts,   35
funny that it hurts;
i see the faces of my friends,
we joke about my getting out,
                and they ask pleading things,
        "DO IT ONE TIME FOR ME, ESE!°"   40
just one time, carnal,°
nomás una vez.°

con ternura morena / como su piel: With tenderness dark / like her skin.
ESE: Dude. **carnal:** Brother. **nomás una vez:** Only once.

hell, bato,° i'll go all over
and do it a million times
recalling all the sadness   45
that hides
within this place;
i'll do it a jillion times
for me, for you, for all of us,
and maybe the next soledad i see   50
is a morenita° from el chuco°
i had been too timid
to ask out . . . it's strange
that i recall her,
but then la pinta°   55
makes you think/regret.
but huáchenle, batos,°
when i'm doing it for us
i'll probably burst out laughing,
not at you or me or even at some ruca,°   60
but at all the pendejadas,°
at all the crazy lies
that say that we are savage;
i'll laugh at mean-ass convicts
who terrify the world   65
yet love to eat ice cream,
i'll laugh at convicts scurrying
from cell block to the canteen
with books of scripted money
to purchase cokes and cookies   70
and candy bars as well;
i'll laugh at contradictions
and yet within i'll hurt
remembering xmas packages
and letters full of pain,   75
recalling those sad moments
when night became the coverlet
and darkness filtered songs,
when all alone i'd die
realizing just how sordid   80
a prison life can be . . .

bato: Dude (alternate spelling of *vato*).   **morenita:** Dark girl.   **el chuco:**
Nickname for the city of El Paso, Texas.   **la pinta:** Jail.   **huáchenle, batos:**
Watch it, dudes.   **ruca:** Chick.   **pendejadas:** Fuck-ups.

yes, i'll laugh, carnales,
just like we all want to laugh,
not to mock us nor to spite you,
just to say i understand,   85

pero eso sí, compiras,
no quiero regresar.°

                                          damn cotton and furrows and rows,
                                          sun burns
                                          while bullying guards rant . . .
                                             Ramsey I Prison Farm
                                             Texas Department of Deformations
                                             sorry ass year of 1967

SAY, TUSH-HOG CONVICT

say, tush-hog convict,
pick that cotton, boy, hear?
else
ain't gonna give you a damn thing to eat,
git on, yo' sorry ass meskin,   5
pick me a nigger high hunnerd pounds,
else we'll kill
yo' meskin ass, hear?

day in, day out,
dust swirls, guts ache,   10
whipped and lashed about,
guard on horseback
with a magnum on his side,
sun drools and licks its chops,
it's beyond a bitch   15
doing this damn time
will die
before my row is picked,
    time and again,
can't hate them anymore,   20
illiterate fools,
seethe inside,

pero eso sí, compiras . . . : But, for sure, my friends, I don't want to come back.

plotting a demise
    (theirs or mine, doesn't much matter
        any goddamn more!),   25
someday, somewhere
we'll meet,
cabrones pinches guardias,°
on equal ground—
    magnum oriented grounds—   30
entonces° shall we see . . .

right now you hold the whip and gun,
i am defenseless, and though i hurt,
you'll never see my tears
nor hear my moans,   35
you better kill me while you can . . .

Reading

1. ("Soledad Was a Girl's Name") How is the prison described in the poem?
2. ("Say, Tush-Hog Convict") How do the guards treat the poem's speaker?

Thinking Critically

1. What are some examples of irony that can be found in "Soledad Was a Girl's Name"?
2. ("Soledad Was a Girl's Name") What is the speaker's attitude toward his fellow prisoners? How do you know?
3. What line do you think best captures the essence of "Say, Tush-Hog Convict"? Why?

Connecting

1. In "Say, Tush-Hog Convict," the speaker of Sánchez's poem impersonates the man giving him orders. Similarly, Luis Valdez's play *Las Dos Caras del Patroncito* (p. 83) requires a worker to impersonate his boss. To what extent do these two works share the same goals? What makes them different?

Writing

1. At first glance, these two poems present very different visions—one dark, one hopeful. After looking at them closely, how do you think they relate to each other? Do they complement one another or do they

cabrones pinches guardias: Bastards, fucking guards.   **entonces:** Then.

conflict? Using specific examples from the poems, write a brief essay about the social message of Sánchez's poetry.

Creating

1. **Write a poem about a difficult experience.** In writing some of his most enduring poetry from prison, Ricardo Sánchez joined many other artists who have produced art—including literature, music, and paintings—in spite of, or even because of, their difficult situations. Draft a poem, a song, or a piece of visual art in which you explore a difficult experience you or someone close to you has endured. What is your attitude toward the experience, and how do you convey that in your composition? How does writing about the experience affect your feelings about it?

13

ANGELA DE HOYOS [1940–2009]

Go Ahead, Ask Her • You Will Grow Old

From Woman, Woman [1985]

GENRE: POETRY

Angela de Hoyos was one of the first women poets to emerge from the Chicano Movement. Born in Mexico in the state of Coahuila, de Hoyos came to San Antonio at an early age, and while young began writing poetry and painting, encouraged by an artistically minded mother. Her education was largely informal but included classes at the De Witte Museum and the University of Texas at San Antonio. De Hoyos's poetry was published in journals in Europe and Latin America, with her poem "The Final Laugh" winning a prize from the Accademia Leonardo da Vinci in Italy in 1972, before her first book of poetry appeared in the United States. To promote the work of contemporaries in the Chicano Movement who, like her, claimed their heritage as a basis for poetic expression, she started a press in San Antonio that published a number of important poets, including Carmen Tafolla (p. 188). Her own book Arise, Chicano! and Other Poems *was published in 1975, with the agony, hope, and determination of its title poem perfectly expressing the spirit of the time: "The sadness in your eyes only reflects the mute pain of your people. Arise, Chicano!—that divine spark within you surely says—Wash your wounds and swathe your agonies. There is no one to succor you. You must be your own messiah." In her later work, including* Chicano Poems for the Barrio, Selecciones *of 1979, and* Woman, Woman *of 1985, de Hoyos expanded her focus both topically and historically, looking at the oppression and exclusion that have long existed due to poverty and racism and the relationships and struggles between men and women. Along with her poetry, her work as an editor with her own small press has also helped make San Antonio an important center of Chicano literature.*

As is evident in the following two poems from Woman, Woman, *de Hoyos is able to capture huge issues with vivid imagery and precise language. While "Go Ahead, Ask Her" hints at the potential for isolation that comes with a woman's marriage and "You Will Grow Old" points to an impossible ideal of woman held up by men, both are rebukes of male attitudes toward women and the resulting invisibility of women's real lives.*

As you read, pay attention to the way each word of "Go Ahead, Ask Her" and "You Will Grow Old" contributes to the large questions raised by the poems about the status of women in contemporary society.

GO AHEAD, ASK HER

```
      . . . . . . is it
      not true
      that when
      a woman
      cries                     5
      all the
      gentlemen
      console
      her

      but when                  10
      a wife
      cries
      she cries
      alone?
```

YOU WILL GROW OLD

forever comparing me
with your dream woman
—that goddess
    of fantasy
    of matchless perfection   5
        defying correction
    yet always
    so conspicuously absent—
while I go about
grinding my teeth   10
on the thankless endless
daily task:
        dusting your wings.

I too
will age . . .   15
        for obvious reasons.

Reading

1. ("Go Ahead, Ask Her") According to the speaker of the poem, what difference exists between the experiences of a woman and those of a wife?

2. ("You Will Grow Old") What is the main complaint expressed by the poem's speaker?

Thinking Critically

1. What explains the contrasting situations of the two kinds of women in "Go Ahead, Ask Her"?

2. Why do you think de Hoyos gave her poem the title "Go Ahead, Ask Her"?

3. Who is the speaker in "You Will Grow Old" addressing?

Connecting

1. In "Go Ahead, Ask Her," Angela de Hoyos writes of the loneliness of a married woman. Similarly, in the poems "A Marriage of Mutes" and "Saturdays," Ana Castillo (p. 260) writes about life as a married woman. What do you think is the relationship among the three poems? Are de Hoyos and Castillo addressing the same issue or different issues?

Writing

1. De Hoyos's poems can appear very simple, but they contain a lot of possible meanings. Write a brief essay in which you closely analyze one or both poems, paying attention to form, tone, word choice, and techniques employed by de Hoyos.

Creating

1. **Write a persuasive poem.** "Go Ahead, Ask Her" and "You Will Grow Old" capture issues in compact poems. Compose a poem that tackles an issue important to you. It can be about your own place in society or about a political or social issue that you feel deeply about.

14

ABELARDO "LALO" DELGADO [1931–2004]

Stupid America • The Chicano Manifesto

From Chicano: 25 Pieces of a Chicano Mind [1969]

GENRE: POETRY

Abelardo "Lalo" Delgado, the "people's poet" of the Chicano Movement, was well-known for his passionate readings of his work to audiences that were as likely to be marchers or protestors as students. Delgado was born in northern Mexico and moved with his family to El Paso, Texas, at age 11. After high school and college, he stayed in El Paso as a teacher and a social worker, helping the people from the poor barrio he'd grown up in. He went to California to work with farmworkers and to Denver to head the Colorado Migrant Council. In Denver his career as a poet was launched in 1969 with the publication of Chicano: 25 Pieces of a Chicano Mind, *in which Delgado made clear his desire for the inclusion of Chicanos in the intellectual as well as political life of the nation, a sentiment that motivated much of the artistic outpouring of Chicanos in the following decade. Delgado often composed and read his poems for special occasions, earning a reputation as an inspiring performer.* The Chicano Movement: Some Not Too Objective Observations, *written in 1973, showed that he could also be a critical observer of the Movement that he had helped start. In the following decades Delgado continued to publish his poetry, as well as the 1978 novel* Letters to Louise. *He helped develop Chicano studies programs around the country and taught for years at Metropolitan State College (now Metropolitan State University) in Denver.*

"Stupid America" and "The Chicano Manifesto" are both drawn from Delgado's first collection, Chicano: 25 Pieces of a Chicano Mind. *"Stupid America" was written in response to complaints about Chicano students. "It never occurred to them to ask whether or not the* chicanitos *were being challenged and encouraged in the schools," Delgado said. "I felt frustrated by their attitudes, and the words of the poem began to flow."* Both poems included in this anthology are motivated by more than simple political demands. They come from Delgado's desire for Chicanos to be able to express themselves fully as individuals.*

As you read these poems, think about the educational, economic, or social conditions that Delgado's vision requires.

STUPID AMERICA

stupid America, see that chicano°
with a big knife
on his steady hand
he doesn't want to knife you
he wants to sit on the bench and carve christfigures   5
but you won't let him.
stupid america, hear that chicano
shouting curses on the street
he is a poet without paper and pencil
and since he cannot write   10
he will explode.
stupid america, remember that chicanito°
flunking math and english
he is the Picasso
of your western states   15
but he will die with one thousand masterpieces
hanging only from his mind.

---

*From the *Dictionary of Literary Biography.*

chicano: Mexican American (a term used by activists).   **chicanito:** Affectionate term for a young Chicano.

THE CHICANO MANIFESTO

this is in keeping with my own physical condition
for i am tired—too tired perhaps for this rendition. . . .
but la raza° is also tired
and la raza cannot wait
until i rest   5
she wants her rest also
but there is much catching up to do.
anglos have asked (i think sincerely)
what it is that you chicanos want?
those with power to be,   10
influencing our lives, have asked. . . .
is it understanding?
is it that you want us to tolerate you?
is it admittance?
and when i heard those questions   15
like remote control my chicano anger took over
and i answered the arrogant questioning . . .
no . . . we do not want any of that
or the question "what do you want" either
you see, you can afford to sit in libraries   20
and visit mexico and in a way
learn to understand us much better than we do ourselves
but understanding a thing
and comprehending are two different matters. . . .
tolerate is a word we use   25
in reference to borrachos,°
we do not wish you strain
yourselves with toleration
of our, supposedly, intolerable ways
and . . . yes . . . question of admittance   30
is a fine one for it puts you inside and us outside
asking like cats and dogs in the rain to be let in.
the nature of your questions
assumes you have something to offer.
but there is one thing i wish   35
you would do for us,
in all your dealings with us,
in all your institutions
that affect our lives

la raza: Term used for all people of Mexican descent.   **borrachos:** Drunks.

deal with us as you openly claim you can,   40
justly. . . . with love. . . . with dignity.
correct your own abuses on la raza
for your own sake and not for ours
so you can have some peace of mind.
for. . . . you see. . . . we only lack a piece of bread   45
which comes cheaper according to your own value system
let me tell you what we want,
not from you but from ourselves and for ourselves. . . .
we want to let america know that she
belongs to us as much as we belong in turn to her   50
by now we have learned to talk
and want to be on good speaking terms
with all that is america.
from government we want to become
visible and not merely legislated   55
and supervised but included
in the design of laws and their implementation.
from education we want the most that it can offer,
a history that tells it like it is,
principals, teachers, counselors, college professors. . . .   60
scholarships, curriculum, testing
and all this from chicanos a la chicana°
and this we are not asking por favor°
but merely as an overdue payment
and we might even forget the previous score.   65
from the church we very piously ask
less sermon and more delivery
more priests to preach Christ's merciful justice,
less alms and tokens in the name of charity
and more pinpointment of the screwing going on.   70
from los chicanos del barrio y de los campos°
we also have some strong demands
(among ourselves there is much more confianza°)
we want you to plot a clean escape but very soon,
lose your habit of speaking in low voices   75
and of walking with cabezas agachadas,°

chicanos a la chicana: From Chicanos to the Chicana (implying the Chicana movement).   **por favor:** Please.   **los chicanos del barrio y de los campos:** Chicanos from the barrio (that is, urban Mexican American neighborhoods) and from the fields.   **confianza:** Trust.   **cabezas agachadas:** Heads bent down (as if in shame).

we are poor only in the material
for your heritage is very rich.
from chicanos with a little
bit of wealth and power les   80
pedimos una mano°
but to give los olvidados°
not a damn thing. . . . they are asking
for your hand. . . . but only in amistad°
as brothers that you, even if you don't want to, are.   85
and finally to the draft board
we have a few words to share with you
no la jodan. . . . metan gabachos también°
our manifesto i know is general
but we saved the specific for the end   90
for the chicano migrant is about
to become like your american buffalo. . . . extinct. . . .
those who claim that was a crime with animals
are now in good position to prevent one with humans
or will the migrant honor come as always. . . . post humous   95

Reading

1. ("Stupid America") What is Delgado's attitude toward the people in the poem?

2. ("Stupid America") What does the person "with a big knife" desire?

3. ("The Chicano Manifesto") What does the word *tolerate* mean in the context of the poem?

4. ("The Chicano Manifesto") What is the main desire expressed in the poem?

Thinking Critically

1. ("Stupid America") Why do you think the poem is titled "Stupid America"?

2. Why do you think Delgado wrote "The Chicano Manifesto" as a poem, rather than putting his ideas into an essay or into a speech?

les / pedimos una mano: We ask them for a hand.   **los olvidados:** The forgotten ones.   **amistad:** Friendship.   **no la jodan. . . . metan gabachos también:** Don't fuck (only) us . . . screw white people, too.

3. Who do you think is the intended audience for these two poems? Why do you think so?

Connecting

1. In "The Chicano Manifesto," Delgado criticizes the lack of access that Chicanos have to political and educational institutions. Read Guillermo Gómez-Peña's essay "Real-Life Border Thriller" (p. 365), which was written some three decades later. Does Gómez-Peña's essay show that Delgado's criticisms are still relevant, or does it show that things have changed in some way? Explain.

Writing

1. Both of Delgado's poems seem to indicate great disappointment in the current social conditions of the Chicano community. What do you think Delgado desires? Is he optimistic? Using examples from the poems, write briefly about what vision of the future you think Delgado holds.

Creating

1. **Compose a poetic manifesto.** Like many in the Chicano Movement, Abelardo Delgado brought together poetry and politics. Using "The Chicano Manifesto" as a model, write your own poetic manifesto. While maintaining a poetic style, give a description of a problem and your vision for its resolution.

15

ERNESTO GALARZA [1905–1984]

The Barrio

From Barrio Boy [1971]

GENRE: MEMOIR

Thousands of families fled northward from the violence of the Mexican Revolution of 1910. Among them were the six-year-old Ernesto Galarza and his parents, who arrived in Sacramento, California, in 1911. After earning a master's degree from Stanford University, Galarza moved to New York City to work on a Ph.D.

*from Columbia and to begin his wide-ranging career as a scholar,
activist, and writer. He spent a decade as a government researcher
with an expertise in labor issues, helped farmworkers in California organize labor unions, and wrote books telling the history of
migrant labor in the United States. In 1971, Galarza revisited his
earliest years in* Barrio Boy, *which tells the story of his move to
the United States and of the Mexican American neighborhood of
his childhood.* Barrio Boy, *the first widely read memoir written by
a Mexican American, has had significant influence on Chicano
literature. In addition to being a compelling story of the beginning
of an impressive career,* Barrio Boy *contains descriptions of the
distinctive culture emerging from the barrio and of the complexi-
ties of assimilation into American life. Galarza also published a
number of books for young readers.*

*In the excerpt here, Galarza describes the Sacramento barrio he
grew up in and his early experiences in school. Though Galarza's
writing shows little indication of bitterness or anger, one can easily imagine the difficulties faced by residents of the barrio, a very
poor community largely ignored by the city government.*

As you read, think about what makes Galarza's perspective
unique and why it differs from that of others who grew up in the
same environment.

We found the Americans as strange in their customs as they probably
found us. Immediately we discovered that there were no *mercados°* and
that when shopping you did not put the groceries in a *chiquihuite.°* Instead everything was in cans or in cardboard boxes or each item was put
in a brown paper bag. There were neighborhood grocery stores at the
corners and some big ones uptown, but no *mercado.* The grocers did not
give children a *pilón,°* they did not stand at the door and coax you to
come in and buy, as they did in Mazatlán. The fruits and vegetables were
displayed on counters instead of being piled up on the floor. The stores
smelled of fly spray and oiled floors, not of fresh pineapple and limes.

Neither was there a plaza,° only parks which had no bandstands, no concerts every Thursday, no Judases exploding on Holy Week, and no prome-
nades of boys going one way and girls the other. There were no parks in the
barrio;° and the ones uptown were cold and rainy in winter, and in summer

mercado: Marketplace. **chiquihuite:** A type of basket. **pilón:** A bit extra
given as a gift. **plaza:** Central square. **barrio:** Mexican American
neighborhood.

there was no place to sit except on the grass. When there were celebrations nobody set off rockets in the parks, much less on the street in front of your house to announce to the neighborhood that a wedding or a baptism was taking place. Sacramento did not have a *mercado* and a plaza with the cathedral to one side and the Palacio de Gobierno° on another to make it obvious that there and nowhere else was the center of the town.

It was just as puzzling that the Americans did not live in *vecindades*,° like our block on Leandro Valle. Even in the alleys, where people knew one another better, the houses were fenced apart, without central courts to wash clothes, talk and play with the other children. Like the city, the Sacramento *barrio* did not have a place which was the middle of things for everyone.

In more personal ways we had to get used to the Americans. They did not listen if you did not speak loudly, as they always did. In the Mexican style, people would know that you were enjoying their jokes tremendously if you merely smiled and shook a little, as if you were trying to swallow your mirth. In the American style there was little difference between a laugh and a roar, and until you got used to them you could hardly tell whether the boisterous Americans were roaring mad or roaring happy.

It was Doña Henriqueta more than Gustavo or José who talked of these   5 oddities and classified them as agreeable or deplorable. It was she also who pointed out the pleasant surprises of the American way. When a box of rolled oats with a picture of red carnations on the side was emptied, there was a plate or a bowl or a cup with blue designs. We ate the strange stuff regularly for breakfast and we soon had a set of the beautiful dishes. Rice and beans we bought in cotton bags of colored prints. The bags were unsewed, washed, ironed, and made into gaily designed towels, napkins, and handkerchiefs. The American stores also gave small green stamps which were pasted in a book to exchange for prizes. We didn't have to run to the corner with the garbage; a collector came for it.

With remarkable fairness and never-ending wonder we kept adding to our list the pleasant and the repulsive in the ways of the Americans. It was my second acculturation.

The older people of the *barrio*, except in those things which they had to do like the Americans because they had no choice, remained Mexican. Their language at home was Spanish. They were continuously taking up collections to pay somebody's funeral expenses or to help someone who had had a serious accident. Cards were sent to you to attend a burial where you would throw a handful of dirt on top of the coffin and listen

Palacio de Gobierno: Palace of Government, equivalent to a city hall.
vecindades: Group of houses with some shared facilities.

to tearful speeches at the graveside. At every baptism a new *compadre*°
and a new *comadre*° joined the family circle. New Year greeting cards
were exchanged, showing angels and cherubs in bright colors sprinkled
with grains of mica so that they glistened like gold dust. At the family
parties the huge pot of steaming tamales° was still the center of attention, the *atole*° served on the side with chunks of brown sugar for sucking
and crunching. If the party lasted long enough, someone produced a
guitar, the men took over and the singing of *corridos*° began.

In the *barrio* there were no individuals who had official titles or who
were otherwise recognized by everybody as important people. The reason must have been that there was no place in the public business of the
city of Sacramento for the Mexican immigrants. We only rented a corner
of the city and as long as we paid the rent on time everything else was
decided at City Hall or the County Court House, where Mexicans went
only when they were in trouble. Nobody from the *barrio* ever ran for
mayor or city councilman. For us the most important public officials
were the policemen who walked their beats, stopped fights, and hauled
drunks to jail in a paddy wagon we called *La Julia*.

The one institution we had that gave the *colonia*° some kind of image
was the *Comisión Honorífica*, a committee picked by the Mexican Consul
in San Francisco to organize the celebration of the *Cinco de Mayo* and
the Sixteenth of September, the anniversaries of the battle of Puebla and
the beginning of our War of Independence. These were the two events
which stirred everyone in the *barrio*, for what we were celebrating was
not only the heroes of Mexico but also the feeling that we were still Mexicans ourselves. On these occasions there was a dance preceded by
speeches and a concert. For both the *cinco* and the sixteenth queens were
elected to preside over the ceremonies.

Between celebrations neither the politicians uptown nor the *Comisión* 10
Honorífica attended to the daily needs of the *barrio*. This was done by
volunteers—the ones who knew enough English to interpret in court, on
a visit to the doctor, a call at the county hospital, and who could help
make out a postal money order. By the time I had finished the third grade
at the Lincoln School I was one of these volunteers. My services were not
professional but they were free, except for the IOU's I accumulated from
families who always thanked me with "God will pay you for it."

---

compadre, comadre: Godfather, godmother.   **tamales:** Food made of steamed
cornmeal and meat wrapped in corn husks.   **atole:** Thick, sweetened drink made
of corn, hominy, rice, or oatmeal.   **corridos:** Musical ballads sung to tell stories.
colonia: Distinctive neighborhood or "colony."

My clients were not *pochos*,° Mexicans who had grown up in California, probably had even been born in the United States. They had learned to speak English of sorts and could still speak Spanish, also of sorts. They knew much more about the Americans than we did, and much less about us. The *chicanos* and the *pochos* had certain feelings about one another. Concerning the *pochos*, the *chicanos*° suspected that they considered themselves too good for the *barrio* but were not, for some reason, good enough for the Americans. Toward the *chicanos*, the *pochos* acted superior, amused at our confusions but not especially interested in explaining them to us. In our family when I forgot my manners, my mother would ask me if I was turning *pochito*.°

Turning *pocho* was a half-step toward turning American. And America was all around us, in and out of the *barrio*. Abruptly we had to forget the ways of shopping in a *mercado* and learn those of shopping in a corner grocery or in a department store. The Americans paid no attention to the Sixteenth of September, but they made a great commotion about the Fourth of July. In Mazatlán Don Salvador had told us, saluting and marching as he talked to our class, that the *Cinco de Mayo* was the most glorious date in human history. The Americans had not even heard about it.

In Tucson, when I had asked my mother again if the Americans were having a revolution, the answer was: "No, but they have good schools, and you are going to one of them." We were by now settled at 418 L Street and the time had come for me to exchange a revolution for an American education.

The two of us walked south on Fifth Street one morning to the corner of Q Street and turned right. Half of the block was occupied by the Lincoln School. It was a three-story wooden building, with two wings that gave it the shape of a double-T connected by a central hall. It was a new building, painted yellow, with a shingled roof that was not like the red tile of the school in Mazatlán. I noticed other differences, none of them very reassuring.

We walked up the wide staircase hand in hand and through the door, which closed by itself. A mechanical contraption screwed to the top shut it behind us quietly.

Up to this point the adventure of enrolling me in the school had been carefully rehearsed. Mrs. Dodson had told us how to find it and we had circled it several times on our walks. Friends in the *barrio* explained that

15

pochos: Derisive label given by Mexicans to Americanized Mexican descendants.   **chicanos:** Here, Mexican Americans in the barrio (early, pre-Movement use of the word).   **pochito:** Dimunitive of *pocho* ("a little pocho").

the director was called a principal, and that it was a lady and not a man. They assured us that there was always a person at the school who could speak Spanish.

Exactly as we had been told, there was a sign on the door in both Spanish and English: "Principal." We crossed the hall and entered the office of Miss Nettie Hopley.

Miss Hopley was at a roll-top desk to one side, sitting in a swivel chair that moved on wheels. There was a sofa against the opposite wall, flanked by two windows and a door that opened on a small balcony. Chairs were set around a table and framed pictures hung on the walls of a man with long white hair and another with a sad face and a black beard.

The principal half turned in the swivel chair to look at us over the pinch glasses crossed on the ridge of her nose. To do this she had to duck her head slightly as if she were about to step through a low doorway.

What Miss Hopley said to us we did not know but we saw in her eyes   20 a warm welcome and when she took off her glasses and straightened up she smiled wholeheartedly, like Mrs. Dodson. We were, of course, saying nothing, only catching the friendliness of her voice and the sparkle in her eyes while she said words we did not understand. She signaled us to the table. Almost tiptoeing across the office, I maneuvered myself to keep my mother between me and the gringo lady. In a matter of seconds I had to decide whether she was a possible friend or a menace. We sat down.

Then Miss Hopley did a formidable thing. She stood up. Had she been standing when we entered she would have seemed tall. But rising from her chair she soared. And what she carried up and up with her was a buxom superstructure, firm shoulders, a straight sharp nose, full cheeks slightly molded by a curved line along the nostrils, thin lips that moved like steel springs, and a high forehead topped by hair gathered in a bun. Miss Hopley was not a giant in body but when she mobilized it to a standing position she seemed a match for giants. I decided I liked her.

She strode to a door in the far corner of the office, opened it and called a name. A boy of about ten years appeared in the doorway. He sat down at one end of the table. He was brown like us, a plump kid with shiny black hair combed straight back, neat, cool, and faintly obnoxious.

Miss Hopley joined us with a large book and some papers in her hand. She, too, sat down and the questions and answers began by way of our interpreter. My name was Ernesto. My mother's name was Henriqueta. My birth certificate was in San Blas. Here was my last report card from the Escuela Municipal Número 3 para Varones° of Mazatlán, and

Escuela Municipal Número 3 para Varones: Municipal School Number 3 for Boys.

so forth. Miss Hopley put things down in the book and my mother signed a card.

As long as the questions continued, Doña Henriqueta could stay and I was secure. Now that they were over, Miss Hopley saw her to the door, dismissed our interpreter and without further ado took me by the hand and strode down the hall to Miss Ryan's first grade.

Miss Ryan took me to a seat at the front of the room, into which I 25 shrank—the better to survey her. She was, to skinny, somewhat runty me, of a withering height when she patrolled the class. And when I least expected it, there she was, crouching by my desk, her blond radiant face level with mine, her voice patiently maneuvering me over the awful idiocies of the English language.

During the next few weeks Miss Ryan overcame my fears of tall, energetic teachers as she bent over my desk to help me with a word in the pre-primer. Step by step, she loosened me and my classmates from the safe anchorage of the desks for recitations at the blackboard and consultations at her desk. Frequently she burst into happy announcements to the whole class. "Ito can read a sentence," and small Japanese Ito, squint-eyed and shy, slowly read aloud while the class listened in wonder: "Come, Skipper, come. Come and run." The Korean, Portuguese, Italian, and Polish first graders had similar moments of glory, no less shining than mine the day I conquered "butterfly," which I had been persistently pronouncing in standard Spanish as boo-ter-flee. "Children," Miss Ryan called for attention. "Ernesto has learned how to pronounce *butterfly*!" And I proved it with a perfect imitation of Miss Ryan. From that celebrated success, I was soon able to match Ito's progress as a sentence reader with "Come, butterfly, come fly with me."

Like Ito and several other first graders who did not know English, I received private lessons from Miss Ryan in the closet, a narrow hall off the classroom with a door at each end. Next to one of these doors Miss Ryan placed a large chair for herself and a small one for me. Keeping an eye on the class through the open door she read with me about sheep in the meadow and a frightened chicken going to see the king, coaching me out of my phonetic ruts in words like *pasture, bow-wow-wow, hay*, and *pretty*, which to my Mexican ear and eye had so many unnecessary sounds and letters. She made me watch her lips and then close my eyes as she repeated words I found hard to read. When we came to know each other better, I tried interrupting to tell Miss Ryan how we said it in Spanish. It didn't work. She only said "oh" and went on with *pasture, bow-wow-wow*, and *pretty*. It was as if in that closet we were both discovering together the secrets of the English language and grieving together over the tragedies of Bo-Peep. The main reason I was graduated with honors from the first grade was that I had fallen in love with Miss Ryan. Her radiant, no-nonsense character made us either afraid not to love her or love her so we would not be afraid, I am not sure which. It was not only that we sensed she was with it, but also that she was with us.

Like the first grade, the rest of the Lincoln School was a sampling of the lower part of town where many races made their home. My pals in the second grade were Kazushi, whose parents spoke only Japanese; Matti, a skinny Italian boy; and Manuel, a fat Portuguese who would never get into a fight but wrestled you to the ground and just sat on you. Our assortment of nationalities included Koreans, Yugoslavs, Poles, Irish, and home-grown Americans.

Miss Hopley and her teachers never let us forget why we were at Lincoln: for those who were alien, to become good Americans; for those who were so born, to accept the rest of us. Off the school grounds we traded the same insults we heard from our elders. On the playground we were sure to be marched up to the principal's office for calling someone a wop, a chink, a dago, or a greaser. The school was not so much a melting pot as a griddle where Miss Hopley and her helpers warmed knowledge into us and roasted racial hatreds out of us.

At Lincoln, making us into Americans did not mean scrubbing away   30 what made us originally foreign. The teachers called us as our parents did, or as close as they could pronounce our names in Spanish or Japanese. No one was ever scolded or punished for speaking in his native tongue on the playground. Matti told the class about his mother's down quilt, which she had made in Italy with the fine feathers of a thousand geese. Encarnación acted out how boys learned to fish in the Phillipines. I astounded the third grade with the story of my travels on a stagecoach, which nobody else in the class had seen except in the museum at Sutter's Fort. After a visit to the Crocker Art Gallery and its collection of heroic paintings of the golden age of California, someone showed a silk scroll with a Chinese painting. Miss Hopley herself had a way of expressing wonder over these matters before a class, her eyes wide open until they popped slightly. It was easy for me to feel that becoming a proud American, as she said we should, did not mean feeling ashamed of being a Mexican.

The Americanization of Mexican me was no smooth matter. I had to fight one lout who made fun of my travels on the *diligencia*,° and my barbaric translation of the word into "diligence." He doubled up with laughter over the word until I straightened him out with a kick. In class I made points explaining that in Mexico roosters said "qui-qui-ri-qui" and not "cock-a-doodle-doo," but after school I had to put up with the taunts of a big Yugoslav who said Mexican roosters were crazy.

diligencia: Horse-drawn vehicle.

But it was Homer who gave me the most lasting lesson for a future American.

Homer was a chunky Irishman who dressed as if every day was Sunday. He slicked his hair between a crew cut and a pompadour. And Homer was smart, as he clearly showed when he and I ran for president of the third grade.

Everyone understood that this was to be a demonstration of how the American people vote for president. In an election, the teacher explained, the candidates could be generous and vote for each other. We cast our ballots in a shoe box and Homer won by two votes. I polled my supporters and came to the conclusion that I had voted for Homer and so had he. After class he didn't deny it, reminding me of what the teacher had said—we could vote for each other but didn't have to.

The lower part of town was a collage of nationalities in the middle of 35 which Miss Nettie Hopley kept school with discipline and compassion. She called assemblies in the upper hall to introduce celebrities like the police sergeant or the fire chief, to lay down the law of the school, to present awards to our athletic champions, and to make important announcements. One of these was that I had been proposed by my school and accepted as a member of the newly formed Sacramento Boys Band. "Now, isn't that a wonderful thing?" Miss Hopley asked the assembled school, all eyes on me. And everyone answered in a chorus, including myself, "Yes, Miss Hopley."

It was not only the parents who were summoned to her office and boys and girls who served sentences there who knew that Nettie Hopley meant business. The entire school witnessed her sizzling Americanism in its awful majesty one morning at flag salute.

All the grades, as usual, were lined up in the courtyard between the wings of the building, ready to march to classes after the opening bell. Miss Shand was on the balcony of the second floor off Miss Hopley's office, conducting us in our lusty singing of "My Country tiz-a-thee." Our principal, as always, stood there like us, at attention, her right hand over her heart, joining in the song.

Halfway through the second stanza she stepped forward, held up her arm in a sign of command, and called loud and clear: "Stop the singing." Miss Shand looked flabbergasted. We were frozen with shock.

Miss Hopley was now standing at the rail of the balcony, her eyes sparking, her voice low and resonant, the words coming down to us distinctly and loaded with indignation.

"There are two gentlemen walking on the school grounds with their 40 hats on while we are singing," she said, sweeping our ranks with her eyes. "We will remain silent until the gentlemen come to attention and remove their hats." A minute of awful silence ended when Miss Hopley, her gaze fixed on something behind us, signaled Miss Shand and we began once more the familiar hymn. That afternoon, when school was out, the word spread. The two gentlemen were the Superintendent of Schools and an important guest on an inspection.

I came back to the Lincoln School after every summer, moving up through the grades with Miss Campbell, Miss Beakey, Mrs. Wood, Miss Applegate, and Miss Delahunty. I sat in the classroom adjoining the principal's office and had my turn answering her telephone when she was about the building repeating the message to the teacher, who made a note of it. Miss Campbell read to us during the last period of the week about King Arthur, Columbus, Buffalo Bill, and Daniel Boone, who came to life in the reverie of the class through the magic of her voice. And it was Miss Campbell who introduced me to the public library on Eye Street, where I became a regular customer.

All of Lincoln School mourned together when Eddie, the blond boy everybody liked, was killed by a freight train as he crawled across the tracks going home one day. We assembled to say good-bye to Miss Applegate, who was off to Alaska to be married. Now it was my turn to be excused from class to interpret for a parent enrolling a new student fresh from Mexico. Graduates from Lincoln came back now and then to tell us about high school. A naturalist entertained us in assembly, imitating the calls of the meadow lark, the water ouzel, the oriole, and the killdeer. I decided to become a bird man after I left Lincoln.

In the years we lived in the lower part of town, La Leen-Con, as my family called it, became a benchmark in our lives, like the purple light of the Lyric Theater and the golden dome of the Palacio de Gobierno gleaming above Capitol Park.

Reading

1. What makes Galarza qualified to become one of the "volunteers" who help with the daily needs of those in the barrio?

2. What does Galarza think was the primary goal of Miss Hopley and the teachers at Lincoln School?

Thinking Critically

1. What is Galarza's attitude toward "Americanization"? What are some examples of its positive and negative effects?

2. In what ways does Galarza find the Lincoln School to be an ideal educational setting?

Connecting

1. Read "Complexion" from *Hunger of Memory* (p. 205), a memoir by Richard Rodriguez. In it, Rodriguez discusses the psychological difficulties of his own process of assimilation into American culture. In what ways is his attitude toward assimilation similar to Galarza's? What do you think is the reason for their differences?

Writing

1. The school experience Galarza writes about occurred more than seventy-five years ago. The issues he describes, though, are still relevant, as both assimilation (or "Americanization") and the promotion of cultural diversity continue to be important goals of the educational systems. Write an essay in which you discuss ways that these goals can or cannot be balanced, citing examples from Galarza's and your own experience.

Creating

1. **Photograph life in America.** Galarza writes that Mexicans found Americans "as strange in their customs as they probably found us" (par. 1), and he mentions, among many things, the fly-spray smell of grocery stores and the loudness of American speech. Take some photos that show parts of American culture that you think might appear strange to someone encountering them for the first time. For each photo, explain what in your photo could seem exotic to someone who'd never seen it, and think of how you would explain it to that person.

16

OSCAR "ZETA" ACOSTA [b. 1935, disappeared 1974]

From *The Revolt of the Cockroach People* [1973]

GENRE: FICTION

In his work, Oscar "Zeta" Acosta captures better than anyone the sheer exhilaration felt by many during the Chicano awakening of the 1960s, with its flowering of art and radical politics, antiwar demonstrations decorated with Aztec and Mayan imagery, and, of course, the acid trips and rock and roll. Acosta was born in El

Paso, Texas, and raised in California. He earned a law degree by taking night classes at San Francisco State College and then moved to Los Angeles, where he joined in the ferment of the Chicano Movement that had also brought Rubén Salazar (p. 46) to the city. His fame grew from his role as a lawyer in a series of important cases arising from demonstrations of the late 1960s, including the Chicano "Blowouts," when thousands of Chicano students had walked out of class protesting the racial inequality in Los Angeles schools. His Autobiography of a Brown Buffalo *and* The Revolt of the Cockroach People—*published in 1972 and 1973, respectively—are good, though sometimes fictionalized, accounts of an important time in the Chicano Movement and of Acosta's self-exploration and ethnic awakening. They are also exciting accounts of events and the cases that Acosta participated in, and establish Acosta, along with his good friend Hunter S. Thompson, as one of the originators of the "gonzo" style, in which reporters become part of the story instead of passive observers. Acosta's career as a writer and activist was short, ending with his mysterious disappearance in 1974.*

In this selection from The Revolt of the Cockroach People, *Buffalo Z. ("Zeta" in Spanish) Brown helps a family investigate the suspicious death of their son Robert Fernández while he was in prison. Acosta describes Buffalo Z. Brown's willingness to help others navigate the legal system, but he also describes his mad excitement at leading an autopsy.*

As you read, try to understand the connection between the two different aspects of Buffalo Z. Brown—his desire to help and his attitude toward the autopsy—and how they affect the story.

It is early one morning when the family of Robert Fernández arrives. The sign outside the basement office only announces *La Voz,*° but these strangers come in asking for me. Via the grapevine, they have heard of a lawyer who might help them. Nobody else is around. It is just them and me:

"We gotta have someone to help us, Mr. Brown. The deputies killed my brother."

A hefty woman with solid arms and thick mascara burnt into her skin is talking. She says her name is Lupe. She is the spokesman, the eldest child in a family of nine. The woman beside her is the mother, Juana, an old

La Voz: The Voice.

nurse. Juana is still in shock, sitting quietly, staring at Gilbert's paintings hung on the wall. John, Lupe's husband, sits on her other side. His arms are crossed, bright tattoos over corded muscle. He wears a white T shirt and a blue beanie, the traditional garb of the *vato loco*, the Chicano street freak who lives on a steady diet of pills, dope and wine. He does not move behind his thick mustache. He too sits quietly, as a proper brother-in-law, a cuñado who does not interfere in family business unless asked.

"Why do you say they killed your brother?" I ask.

"¡Porque son marranos!°" Juana cries out and then falls back into   5
silence, Aztec designs in black and red meet her glazed eyes.

I ask for the whole story. . . .

Robert was seventeen when the weight of his hundred and eighty pounds snapped the bones and nerves of his fat brown neck. He, too, lived in Tooner Flats, a neighborhood of shacks and clotheslines and dirty back yards. At every other corner, street lights hang high on telephone poles and cast dim yellow glows. Skinny dogs and wormy cats sniff garbage cans in the alleys. Tooner Flats is the area of gangs who spend their last dime on short dogs of T-Bird wine, where the average kid has eight years of school. Everybody there gets some kind of welfare.

You learn about life from the toughest guy in the neighborhood. You smoke your first joint in an alley at the age of ten; you take your first hit of *carga°* before you get laid; and you learn how to make your mark on the wall before you learn how to write. Your friends know you to be a *vato loco*, a crazy guy, and they call you "*ese*," or "*vato*," or "man." And when you prove you can take it, that you don't cop to nothing even if it means getting your ass whipped by some other gang or the cops, then you are allowed to put your mark, your initial, your sign, your badge, your *placa* on your turf with the name or initial of your gang: White Fence, Cuatro Flats, Barrio Nuevo, The Jokers, The Bachelors, or what have you. You write it big and fancy, scroll-like, cholo print. Grafitti on all the stores, all the garages, everywhere that you control or claim. It's like the pissing of a dog on a post. And underneath your *placa*, you always put C/S, "*Con safos*," that is: *Up yours if you don't like it, ese!*

There is no school for a *vato loco*. There is no job in sight. His only hope is for a quick score. Reds and Ripple mixed with a bennie, a white and a toke. And when your head is tight, you go down to the hangout and wait for the next score.

On the day he died, Robert had popped reds with wine and then conked   10
out for a few hours. When he awoke he was ready for more. But first he went to Cronie's on Whittier Boulevard, the Chicano Sunset Strip. Every other door is a bar, a pawn shop or a liquor store. Hustlers roam freely

¡Porque son marranos!: Because they're filthy pigs!   **carga:** Heroin.

across asphalt decorated with vomit and dogshit. If you score in East Los Angeles, you score on the Boulevard. Broads, booze and dope. Cops on every corner make no difference: the fuzz, *la placa, la chota, los marranos, la jura* or just the plain old pig, the eternal enemies of the people. The East LA Sheriff's substation is only three blocks away on Third Street, right alongside the Pomona Freeway. From the Blockhouse, deputies come out in teams of two, "To Serve and Protect!" Always with thirty-six-inch clubs, with walkie-talkies in hand; always with gray helmets, shotguns in the car and .357 Magnums in their holsters.

The *vato loco* has been fighting with the pig since the Anglos stole his land in the last century. He will continue to fight until he is exterminated.

Robert had *his* last fight in January of 1970. He met his sister, Lupe, at Cronie's. She was eating a hamburger. He was dry, he told her. Would she please go to the store across the street and get him a six-pack on credit? No, she'd pay for it. Tomorrow is his birthday so she will help him celebrate it early. Lupe left Robert with friends. They were drinking cokes and listening to the jukebox. Robert liked *mayate* music, the blues. They put in their dimes and sip on cokes, hoping some broad, a *ruka*, would come buy them a hamburger or share a joint with them.

I know Cronie's well. I live two blocks away with the three cousins. I know if you sit on the benches under the canopy long enough, *someone* comes along with *something* for the evening's action. This time the cops brought it.

By the time Lupe returned with a six-pack, two deputies were talking with Robert and his friends. It all began, he told her when she walked up, just because he shouted "Chicano Power!" and raised his fist.

"The cop told me to stay out of it, Mr. Brown. I told him Robert is my   15
brother. But they told me to get away or else they'd arrest me for interfering, you know."

Juana says, "Tell him about the dirty greaser."

"Oh, yes. . . . We know this pig. He's a Chicano. Twice he's arrested Robert," Lupe says.

"Yes, Mr. Brown!" Juana could not restrain herself. "That same man once beat up my boy. He came in one day, about a year ago, and he just pushed into the room where Robert was sleeping. He dragged him out and they held him for three days. . . . They thought he had stolen a car. . . . But the judge threw the case out of court. That pig hated my boy."

Robert had been in jail many times. He'd spent some time at the Youth Authority Camp. But he'd been off smack over a year now. He still dropped a few reds now and then. And yes, he drank wine. But he was clean now. The cops took him in from Cronie's, they said, to check him out. They wanted to see if the marks on his arms were fresh. But anyone could tell they were old.

Lupe appeals to John: 20

"That's the truth, Brown," the brother-in-law says. "Robert had cleaned up. He even got a job. He was going to start working next week."

"And we were going to have a birthday party for him that Friday," Juana says.

The deputies took Robert and told Lupe not to bother arranging bail. They told her he'd be released within a couple of hours. They thought he might just be drunk, but mainly they wanted to check out his arms. They said for her not to worry.

An hour after he was arrested, Robert called his mother. The cops had changed their minds, he said. They had booked him for Plain Drunk, a misdemeanor. The bail was set at five hundred dollars.

"He told me to call up Maldonado, his bail bondsman. Robert always   25
used him. I could get him out just like that. All I had to do was make a phone call and then go down and sign, you know? The office is just down the street. I didn't even have to put up the house or anything. Mr. Maldonado always just got him out on my word!" the mother cries.

Juana had called the bail bondsman before she received the second call. This time it was a cop. He simply wanted to tell her that Robert was dead. He'd just hung himself. And would she come down and identify the body.

"He was so cold, Mr. Brown. He didn't say he was sorry or anything like that. He just said for me to wait there and he'd send a deputy to pick me up," she says bitterly.

"I went with her," John says. "When we got there I told the man right away that they'd made some mistake. I told him Robert had just called.

"Then they brought in a picture. And I said, '*gracias a Dios*.'" I knew him. It wasn't Robert, it was somebody named Sánchez. But that lieutenant said there was no mistake. He said the picture just didn't come out too good. . . . But Juana told him, 'Well I should know, he's my son.' And I told him Robert wouldn't do a thing like that. He'd never kill himself. He was *católico, Señor Café*. He even used to be an altar boy one time. And he was going to get married, too. He was going to announce it at his party. I talked to Pattie and she told me. She said they were going to get married as soon as he got his first paycheck."

"Pattie is pregnant," Lupe says. "You might as well know, Mr. Brown."   30

"So what happened after that," I ask.

"We had the funeral and they buried him last week," Juana says.

Lupe says, "We just got the certificate last night. It says he killed himself. Suicide, it says."

"That's a goddamn lie," John says. "Excuse me. . . . But it is."

"How do you think he was killed?"   35

"I *know*," Lupe says. "At the funeral . . . you tell him, John."

"Yeah, I was there. I saw it."

gracias a Dios: Thank God.

Doris, another sister, had discovered it. At the funeral, while the others sat and cried, Doris had gone up to get her last look at the body. She bent over the casket to kiss him. Tears from her own eyes landed on the boy's face. She reached over to wipe the wetness from his cheek when she noticed purple spots on the nose. She wiped away the tears and the undertaker's white powder came off his face. It was purple underneath. She called John over and he verified it. They began to look more closely and noticed bruises on the knuckles.

"We told the doctor at the Coroner's Office," John finishes. "But he said not to worry about it. It was natural, he said."

"Anything else?"   40

"Just what Mr. de Silva told me," the mother says.

"Who's that?"

"Andy de Silva. . . . Don't you know him?"

"You mean . . . *the* Andy de Silva? The man who makes commercials? Chile Charlie?"

"Yeah, that's Mr. de Silva."   45

I know of him. He is a small-time politico in East LA. A bit actor in grade B movies who owns a bar on The Boulevard. And he considers himself something of a spokesman for the Chicano. He served on Mayor Yorty's Chicano Community Board as a rubber-stamp nigger for the establishment. He and his cronies, the small businessmen and a few hack judges, could always be counted on to endorse whatever program the Anglo laid out for the Cockroaches. He had been quoted in all the papers during our uprising against the Church. He had agreed with the Cardinal that we were all outside agitators who should be driven out on a rail.

"What did Andy say to you?" I ask.

"Well, I don't even know him. I used to go to his meetings for the old people. Anyway, he called me the next day after Robert died. He said, 'I heard about your boy and I want to help.' That's how he started out. I was so happy to get someone to help I told him to do whatever he could. He said he was very angry and he would investigate the case. He said he would have a talk with the lieutenant and even with the captain if necessary."

"What happened?"

"He called me back the next day. He said he had checked it all out and   50
that the captain had showed him everything, the files and even the cell. He said not to make any trouble. That Robert had hung himself."

"Did he say how he knew about it?"

"Yeah, I asked him that, too," John says.

"He said his nephew was the guy in the cell with Robert."

"His nephew?"

"Yeah, Mickey de Silva . . . He's just a kid like Robert. He was in there   55
for something. . . . Anyway, Andy said his nephew told him that Robert killed himself."

"But we don't believe it," Lupe says fiercely.

"Can you help us, Señor Brown?"

I pick up the phone and dial the office of Thomas Naguchi, the Coroner for the City and County of Los Angeles.

"This is Buffalo Z. Brown. I represent the family of Robert Fernández," I tell Naguchi. "And we want to talk with you about the autopsy. . . . Your doctor listed it as suicide. However, we are convinced that the boy was murdered. We have information unavailable to the pathologist conducting the autopsy. I plan to be in your office this afternoon. I'm going to bring as many people as I can and hold a press conference right outside your door."

"Mr. Brown. Please, calm yourself. I can't interfere with the findings of my staff."   60

"I'll be there around one."

I hang up and tell the family to go home, call all their friends and relatives and have them meet me in the basement of the Hall of Justice. They thank me and leave. I then call the press and announce the demonstration and press conference for that afternoon. I know my man. And since Naguchi can read the newspapers, my man knows me. The afternoon will be pure ham.

Naguchi has been in the news quite a bit. He was charged with misconduct in office by members of his own staff. They accused him of erratic behavior and incompetence. They said he took pills, that he was strung out, and hinted that perhaps he was a bit nuts. After the assassination of Robert Kennedy he allegedly said he was glad Kennedy was killed in his jurisdiction. He was a publicity hound, they contended. He was removed from his position of County Coroner. He hired a smart lawyer and challenged it. The Civil Service hearings were televised. The white liberals and his own Japanese friends came to his defense. He was completely exonerated. At least he got his job back.

A month prior to the death of Fernández, both the new City Chief of Police, Judd Davis, and the sheriff of LA County, Peter Peaches, announced they would no longer request Coroner's Inquests. The publicity served no useful purpose, the lawmen stated. Since the only time the Coroner held an inquest was when a law enforcement officer was involved in the death of a minority person, they contended that the inquest merely served to inflame the community. Naguchi made no comment at the time of this statement, although his two main clients were emasculating his office.

When we arrive at the Hall of Justice, the press is waiting. The corridor   65 is lined with Fernández' friends and relatives. The television cameras turn on their hot lights as I walk in with my red, white and green briefcase, the immediate family at my side.

"Are you making any accusations, Mr. Brown?" a CBS man asks.

"Not now, gentlemen. I plan to have a conference with Dr. Naguchi first. Then I'll speak to you."

I hurried into the Coroner's Office. The people shout "Viva Brown!" as I close the door. The blonde secretary tells me Naguchi is waiting for me. She opens the door to his office and ushers me in.

"Ah, Mr. Brown, I am so happy to make your acquaintance."

He is a skinny Jap with bug eyes. He wears a yellow sport coat and a   70
red tie and sits at a huge mahogany desk with a green dragon paper-weight. The office has black leather couches and soft chairs, a thick shag rug and inscrutable art work. It seems a nice quiet place. He points me to a fine chair.

"Now Mr. Brown, I'd like you to read this." He hands me a typed sheet of white paper.

I smile and read the paper:

The Coroner's Office announced today that it will hold a second autopsy and an inquest into the death of Robert Fernández at the request of the family through their attorney, Mr. Buffalo Z. Brown. It will be the first time in the history of the office that an inquest is being held at the request of the family.

Thomas A. Naguchi
County Coroner

I looked into the beady eyes of Mr. Moto. He is everything his men say. "I've been wanting to meet you, sir," I say.

"And I've heard about you, Mr. Brown. You get a lot of coverage in your work."

"I guess the press is interested in my cases."   75

"Would you be agreeable to holding a joint press conference?"

"Sir, I would be honored. . . . But one thing . . . If we have another autopsy, the body will have to be, uh. . . ." I am coy.

"Exhumed . . . We will take care of that, don't you worry."

"And who will perform the autopsy?"

"I assume the family will want their own pathologist."   80

I looked down at his spit-shined loafers. I shake my head and sigh.

"I just don't know. . . . The family is extremely poor."

"I understand, sir. I offer my staff, sir."

"Dr. Naguchi . . . would it be too much to ask you, *personally*, to exam-ine the boy's body? I know you are very busy. . . ." It is my trump card.

"I would be honored. But to avoid any . . . problems, why don't I call up   85
the Board of Pathologists for the county. I will request a panel. Yes, a panel of seven expert pathologists. It will be as careful and as detailed an autopsy as we had for Senator Kennedy. And it won't cost the family anything . . . I have that power."

I stand up and, walking over to him, I shake his hand.

"Dr. Naguchi, I'll be glad to let you do all the talking to the press."

"Oh no, Mr. Brown, it is your press conference."

He calls his secretary and tells her to bring in the boys. When they arrive with their pads and cameras, he greets them all by their first names. He is better than Cecil B. DeMille. His secretary has passed out copies of his statement. He tells them all where to sit and knows how many lumps of sugar they want in their coffee. Then he introduces me to them and stands by while I speak.

"Gentlemen, I'll make it short . . . We have reason to believe that Robert 90 Fernández died at the hands of another. The autopsy was inconclusive and we have since found some new evidence that was not available to Dr. Naguchi's staff. . . . The Doctor has graciously consented to exhume the body and hold a full inquest before a jury. On behalf of the family and those of us in East LA who are interested in justice, I would like to thank Dr. Naguchi."

After the press leaves, I reassure the family and all the arrangements are nailed down.

The following Tuesday, I again enter the Hall of Justice. Above me are Sirhan Sirhan, the mysterious Arab who shot Kennedy, and Charles Manson, the acid fascist. Both await their doom. I am told to go straight down the corridor, turn right and the first door to my left is where I'll find Dr. Naguchi and his seven expert pathologists. The light is dim, the hard floors waxed. Another government building with gray walls, the smell of alcohol in night air.

I open a swinging yellow door and immediately find myself inside a large dark room full of hospital carts. Naked bodies are stretched out on them. Bodies of red and purple meat; bodies of men with white skin gone yellow; bodies of black men with blood over torn faces. This one has an arm missing. The stub is tied off with plastic string. The red-headed woman with full breasts? Someone has ripped the right ear from her head. The genitals of that spade are packed with towels. Look at it! Listen! The blood is still gurgling. There, an old wino, his legs crushed, mangled, gone to mere meat. And there, young boys die too. And there, a once-beautiful chick, look at her. How many boys tried to get between those legs, now dangling pools of red-black blood?

Don't turn away from it, goddamnit! Don't be afraid of bare-ass naked death. Hold your head up, open your eyes, don't be embarrassed, boy! I walk forward, I hold my breath. My head is buzzing, my neck is taut, my hands are wet and I cannot look away from the dead cunts, the frizzled balls, the lumps of tit, the fat asses of white meat.

I have turned the wrong way. Backtracking, I find the room with 95 Dr. Naguchi and the experts.

The doctors wear white smocks. They smoke pipes. Relaxed men at
their trade. They smile and shake my hand. In front of us, the casket is
on a cart with small wheels. On a clean table we have scales and bottles
of clear liquid. There are razor-sharp tools, tweezers, clips, scissors,
hacksaws, needles and plenty of yellow gloves. The white fluorescent
light shines down upon us. It reminds me of the title of my first book: *My
Cart for My Casket.*

"Shall we begin, gentlemen?" Dr. Naguchi asks the experts.

The orderly, a giant sporting an immense mustache, takes a card and a
plastic seal from the casket. He booms it out to a gray-haired fag with
sweet eyes who sits in a corner and records on a shorthand machine.

"We shall now open the casket, Coroner's number 19444889, Robert
Fernández, deceased."

We all gather close to get the first look.   100

The body is intact, dressed in fine linen. Clearly, Robert was a bull of a
man. He had big arms and legs and a thick neck now gone purple. Two
experts lift the body and roll it on the operating table. It holds a rosary in
the hands. The orderly removes the rosary, the black suit, the white shirt,
the underwear and brown shoes. The chest has been sewn together.
Now the orderly unstitches it. Snip, snip, snip. Holding open the rib
cage, he carefully pulls out plastic packages from inside the chest cavity.
I hold my breath.

"Intestines." The meat is weighed out.

"Heart . . . Liver. . . ."

A Chinese expert is making notations of everything. So is the fruity
stenographer.

There is no blood, no gory scene. All is cold and dry. Sand and sawdust 105
spill to the table.

"Is this your first autopsy?" a doctor with a Sherlock Holmes pipe asks
me. I nod.

"You're doing pretty good."

"He'll get used to it," another one says brightly.

When the organs are all weighed out, Dr. Naguchi says, "Now, gentlemen, where do you want to begin?"

Sherlock Holmes asks, "Are we looking for anything special?"   110

"Treat this as an ordinary autopsy, Dr. Rubenstein. Just the routine,"
says Naguchi.

"Circumstances of death?"

"Well, uh . . . Mr. Brown?"

"He was found with something around his neck."

"Photographs at the scene?"   115

"No sir," a tall man from the Sheriff's Department says.

"Self-strangulation? . . . or . . ." Rubenstein lets it hang.

"That's the *issue*," I say. "The body was found in a jail cell. The Sheriff claims it was suicide. . . . We, however, believe otherwise."

"I see."

"We have reason to believe that the boy was murdered," I say.   120

"Nonsense," the man from the Sheriff's Department says.

"Now, gentlemen, please. . . ." Naguchi oils in.

Dr. Rubenstein is obviously the big cheese. He comes up to me and says, "You think there was a struggle before death?"

"It's very possible."

He ponders this and then announces: "Gentlemen, we will have to dis- 125
sect wherever hematoma appears."

"What's that?" I ask.

"Bruises."

I look at the body closely. I noticed purple spots on the face, the arms, the hands, the chest, the neck and the legs. Everywhere. I point to the face. "Could *that* be a bruise?"

"There's no way to tell without microscopic observation," Rubenstein answers.

"You can't tell from the *color*?"   130

"No . . . The body is going through decomposition and discoloration . . . purple spots . . . is normal. You find it on all dead bodies."

"Are you saying we have to cut out all those spots?"

"That's the only way to satisfy your . . . yes."

"Well, Mr. Brown?" says Naguchi. "Where do you want us to begin?"

I look around at the men in the room. Seven experts, Dr. Naguchi and a 135
Chinese doctor from his staff, the orderly and the man from the Sheriff's . . . they want *me*, a Chicano lawyer, to tell them where to begin. They want *me* to direct them. It is too fantastic to take seriously.

"How about this? Can you look there?" I point to the left cheek.

Without a word, the Chinese doctor picks up a scalpel and slices off an inch of meat. . . . He picks it up with the tweezers and plunks it into a jar of clear liquid.

"And now, Mr. Brown?" says Naguchi.

I cannot believe what is happening. I lean over the body and look at the ears. Can they get a notch from the left one?

Slit-slit-slice blut! . . . into a jar.   140

"Uh, Dr. Rubenstein? . . . Are you *sure* there's no other way?"

He nods slowly. "Usually, we only try a couple of places . . . It depends on the family." He hesitates, then says, "Is the case that important?"

"Would you please take a sample from the knuckles . . . here?"

No trouble at all, my man. Siss-sizz-sem . . . blut, into another jar.

The orderly is precisely labeling each jar. Dr. Naguchi is walking 145
around like a Hollywood mogul. He is smiling. Everything is going with-
out a hitch. He touches my shoulder.
"Just tell us what you want, Mr. Brown. . . . We're at your service."
"Would you please try the legs? . . . Those big splotches on the left."
"How about the chin?"
"Here, on the left side of the face."
"What's this on the neck?"   150
"Try this little spot here."
"We're this far into it. . . . Get a piece from the stomach there."
Cut here. Slice there. Here. There. Cut, cut, cut! Slice, slice slice! And
into a jar. Soon we have a whole row of jars with little pieces of meat.
Hrumph! Yes, men? Now we'll open up the head. See where it's
stitched? They opened it at the first autopsy. See the sand fall out from
the brain area? Yes, keeps the body together for a funeral. No blood in
here, boy. Just sand. We don't want a mess. See that little package? That,
my lad, is the brain. I mean, it was the brain. Well, actually, it *still* is the
brain . . . it just isn't working right now.
Yes, yes! Now we pull back the head. Scalp-um this lad here. Whoops, 155
the hair, the full head of hair, now it lays back, folded back like a halloween
mask so we can look *into* the head . . . inside, where the stuffings for the . . .
Jesus H. Christ, look at those little purple blotches. . . . You can tell a lot
from that, but you got to cut it out. . . . Then cut the fucking thing out, you
motherfucker! This ain't Robert no more. It's just a . . . no, not a body . . .
body is a whole . . . this is a joke. . . . Cut that piece there, doctor. *Please!*
Uh oh! Now we get really serious. If he died of strangulation . . . We'll
have to pull out the . . . uh, neck bone.
Go right ahead, *sir!* Pull out that goddamn gizzard.
Uh, we have to . . . take the face off first.
Well, Jesus Christ, go ahead!
Slit. One slice. Slit. Up goes the chin. Lift it right up over the face . . . 160
the face? The face goes up over the head. The head? The head is the face.
Huh? *There is no face!*
What do you mean?
The face is hanging down the back of the head. The face is a mask. The
mouth is where the brain . . . The nose is at the back of the neck. The hair
is the ears. The brown nose is hanging where the neck. . . . Get your god-
damn hand out of there.
My hand?
That is the doctor's hand. It is inside the fucking face.
I mean the head.   165
His hand is inside. It is pulling at something. What did he find in there.
What is it?

He's trying to pull out the . . . if we put it under a microscope, we'll be
able to make some strong findings. It's up to you. . . .
Slice, slice, slice . . . No dice.
"Give me the saw, please."
Saw, saw, saw, saw, saw . . . No luck.   170
"Give me the chisel and hammer, please."
The goddamn face is gone; the head is wide open; no mouth, nose,
eyes. They are hanging down the back of the neck. God! With hammer
and chisel in hand, the Chinese doctor goes to town. Chomp, chomp,
chomp . . . Hack, hack, chuck, chuck, chud, chomp!
Ah! Got it!
Out it comes. Long, gizzard-looking. Twelve inches of red muscle and
nerve dripping sawdust. Yes, we'll dissect this old buzzard, too.
How about those ribs? You want some bar-b-que ribs, mister?   175
Sure, *ese*. Cut those fucking ribs up. Chomp 'em up right now!
"How about the arms? Is there any question of needle marks?"
Yes, they'll claim he was geezing. Cut that arm there. Put it under your
machine and tell me later what I want to hear. Tell me they were *old*
tracks, you sonofabitch . . . And try the other one.
Why not? The body is no more.
Should we try the dick?   180
What for? What can you find in a peter?
Maybe he was raped for Christ's sake. Or maybe he raped someone.
How should I know? I just work here.
I see the tattoo on his right arm . . . God Almighty! A red heart with
blue arrows of love and the word "Mother." And I see the little black cross
between the thumb and the trigger finger. A regular *vato loco*. A real
pachuco, ese.
And when it is done, there is no more Robert. Oh, sure, they put the
head back in place. They sew it up as best they can. But there is no part
of the body that I have not ordered chopped. I, who am so good and
deserving of love. Yes, me, the big *chingón!*° I, Mr. Buffalo Z. Brown. Me,
I ordered those white men to cut up the brown body of that Chicano boy,
just another expendable Cockroach.
Forgive me, Robert, for the sake of the living brown. Forgive me, and 185
forgive me and forgive me. I am no worse off than you. For the rest of my
born days, I will suffer the knowledge of your death and your second
death and your ashes to my ashes, your dust to my dust . . . Goodbye, *ese*.
Viva la Raza!°

chingón: Big motherfucker, head honcho.   **Viva la Raza!:** Long live *la Raza!*
(*La Raza* refers to all people of Mexican descent.)

Reading

1. Why do the police arrest Robert Fernández?
2. What is the purpose of the autopsy?

Thinking Critically

1. How would you describe Buffalo Z. Brown's behavior during the autopsy?
2. Acosta ends this section of *Revolt*, and Buffalo Z. Brown's apology to Robert, with the rallying cry *Viva la Raza!* Why do you think he does this? Is the meaning of this phrase affected by its context?

Connecting

1. Read again the description of the *vato loco* at the beginning of this selection. Do you think Abelardo Delgado's poem "Stupid America" (p. 117) is about this kind of person? Why or why not?

Writing

1. Journalists often try to attain objectivity in their reporting by remaining neutral, observing events from a distance, and writing without emotion. Acosta, on the other hand, is an active participant with clear sympathies. Using examples from the text, write about what you think the advantages and disadvantages of this approach are. Do you trust his account more or less because he is involved in it? Are there parts of the story that can only be told in Acosta's way?

Creating

1. **Rewrite *The Revolt of the Cockroach People* as a news article.** In his writing, Oscar Acosta presents himself, through Buffalo Z. Brown, as a larger-than-life character, and he often exaggerates the excitement of events he participated in. Rewrite a few pages of the preceding chapter from *The Revolt of the Cockroach People* as you think a newspaper reporter would have written it, and discuss what the story gains or loses in the transformation.

17

TOMÁS RIVERA [1935–1984]

La Noche Buena

From . . . y no se lo tragó la tierra (And the Earth Did Not Part) [1971; 1977 in English]

GENRE: FICTION

Because of his pioneering achievements as a scholar and writer, Tomás Rivera is a major figure in the history of Chicano literature. Rivera was born in Crystal City, Texas, with his family often moving around the Midwest as migrant laborers. He earned a bachelor's degree from Southwest Texas State University and then worked as a high school teacher for several years, until a summer in Guadalajara under the auspices of the National Defense Education Act propelled him to go back to school. He earned his master's in English and administration from Southwest Texas State and then a doctorate from the University of Oklahoma. During this time he began to write a set of interlocking stories and vignettes about the lives of Mexican migrant workers, which would be published in 1971 as . . . y no se lo tragó la tierra. Rivera said of the subject matter of the book, "I felt that I had to document the migrant worker forever, so that their very strong spirit of endurance and will to go on under the worst of conditions should not be forgotten. A migrant worker? You owe him nothing. If he came to you, you gave him work and then just told him to leave. If he got sick, you got rid of him; you didn't have to take care of him. It was bad, labor camps and all that."* Though Rivera had not intentionally written a "Chicano book," it was awarded the inaugural Premio Quinto Sol, a prize given by the Quinto Sol, a foundational publisher of Chicano literature and of the first scholarly journal devoted to it. The book was hugely influential in its original Spanish version and in multiple English versions, first translated in 1977 as And the Earth Did Not Part. *In his lifetime, Rivera wrote poetry, stories, and several scholarly articles on the nature of Chicano literature, but the focus of his career was university administration. He moved from a professorship into administrative positions at the*

---

*From Juan Bruce-Novoa, *Chicano Authors: Inquiry by Interview.*

University of Texas at San Antonio and at El Paso, and then became
chancellor of the University of California, Riverside, the first Mexi-
can American in such a position in California. He was also a found-
ing member of the National Council of Chicanos in Higher Educa-
tion. In 1991, a few years after his death, his work was collected and
published as Tomás Rivera: The Complete Works.

  Ostensibly, the story "La Noche Buena" ("The Night before Christ-
mas"), which comes from Rivera's book . . . y no se lo tragó la
tierra, is about the agoraphobic Doña María trying to get Christ-
mas presents for her children. But, more importantly, it is also
about the distance between American consumer culture, never
more visible than at Christmastime, and migrant families like that
of Doña María and her husband.

As you read, notice the ways the story offers a description
not just of Doña María but of American culture from a new
perspective.

Christmas Eve was approaching and the barrage of commercials, music
and Christmas cheer over the radio and the blare of announcements over
the loud speakers on top of the stationwagon advertising movies at the
Teatro Ideal resounded and seemed to draw it closer. It was three days
before Christmas when Doña María decided to buy something for her
children. This was the first time she would buy them toys. Every year she
intended to do it but she always ended up facing up to the fact that, no,
they couldn't afford it. She knew that her husband would be bringing
each of the children candies and nuts anyway, and so she would rational-
ize that they didn't need to get them anything else. Nevertheless, every
Christmas the children asked for toys. She always appeased them with
the same promise. She would tell them to wait until the sixth of January,
the day of the Magi, and by the time that day arrived the children had
already forgotten all about it. But now she was noticing that each year
the children seemed less and less taken with Don Chon's visit on Christmas Eve when he came bearing a sack of oranges and nuts.

  "But why doesn't Santa Claus bring us anything?"
  "What do you mean? What about the oranges and nuts he brings you?"
  "No, that's Don Chon."
  "No, I'm talking about what you always find under the sewing machine."
  "What, Dad's the one who brings that, don't think we don't know that.
Aren't we good like the other kids?"

"Of course, you're good children. Why don't you wait until the day of the Reyes Magos. That's when toys and gifts really arrive. In Mexico, it's not Santa Claus who brings gifts, but the Three Wise Men. And they don't come until the sixth of January. That's the real date."

"Yeah, but they always forget. They've never brought us anything, not on Christmas Eve, not on the day of the Three Kings."

"Well, maybe this time they will."

"Yeah, well, I sure hope so."

That was why she made up her mind to buy them something. But they didn't have the money to spend on toys. Her husband worked almost eighteen hours a day washing dishes and cooking at a restaurant. He didn't have time to go downtown and buy toys. Besides, they had to save money every week to pay for the trip up north. Now they even charged for children too, even if they rode standing up the whole way to Iowa. So it cost them a lot to make the trip. In any case, that night when her husband arrived, tired from work, she talked to him about getting something for the children.

"Look, viejo,° the children want something for Christmas."

"What about the oranges and nuts I bring them."

"Well, they want toys. They're not content anymore with just fruits and nuts. They're a little older now and more aware of things."

"They don't need anything."

"Now, you can't tell me you didn't have toys when you were a kid."

"I used to *make* my own toys, out of clay . . . little horses and little soldiers . . ."

"Yes, but it's different here. They see so many things . . . come on, let's go get them something . . . I'll go to Kress myself."

"You?"

"Yes, me."

"Aren't you afraid to go downtown? You remember that time in Wilmar, out in Minnesota, how you got lost downtown. Are you sure you're not afraid?"

"Yes, yes, I remember, but I'll just have to get my courage up. I've thought about it all day long and I've set my mind to it. I'm sure I won't get lost here. Look, I go out to the street. From here you can see the ice house. It's only four blocks away, so Doña Regina tells me. When I get to the ice house I turn to the right and go two blocks and there's downtown. Kress is right there. Then, I come out of Kress, walk back towards the ice house and turn back on this street, and here I am."

viejo: Old man, used for *husband.*

"I guess it really won't be difficult. Yeah. Fine. I'll leave you some money on top of the table when I go to work in the morning. But be careful, vieja,° there's a lot of people downtown these days."

The fact was that Doña María very rarely left the house. The only time she did was when she visited her father and her sister who lived on the next block. And she only went to church whenever someone died and, occasionally, when there was a wedding. But she went with her husband, so she never took notice of where she was going. And her husband always brought her everything. He was the one who bought the groceries and clothing. In reality she was unfamiliar with downtown even though it was only six blocks away. The cemetery was on the other side of downtown and the church was also in that direction. The only time that they passed through downtown was whenever they were on their way to San Antonio or whenever they were returning from up north. And this would usually be during the wee hours of the morning or at night. But that day she was determined and she started making preparations.

The next day she got up early as usual, and after seeing her husband and children off, she took the money from the table and began getting ready to go downtown. This didn't take her long.

"My God, I don't know why I'm so fearful. Why, downtown is only six blocks from here. I just go straight and then after I cross the tracks turn right. Then go two blocks and there's Kress. On the way back, I walk two blocks back and then I turn to the left and keep walking until I'm home again. God willing, there won't be any dogs on the way. And I just pray that the train doesn't come while I'm crossing the tracks and catches me right in the middle . . . I just hope there's no dogs . . . I hope there's no train coming down the tracks."

She walked the distance from the house to the railroad tracks rapidly.   5
She walked down the middle of the street all the way. She was afraid to walk on the sidewalk. She feared she might get bitten by a dog or that someone might grab her. In actuality there was only one dog along the entire stretch and most of the people didn't even notice her walking toward downtown. She nevertheless kept walking down the middle of the street and, luckily, not a single car passed by, otherwise she would not have known what to do. Upon arriving at the crossing she was suddenly struck by intense fear. She could hear the sound of moving trains and their whistles blowing and this was unnerving her. She was too scared to cross. Each time she mustered enough courage to cross she heard the

vieja: Old lady, used for *wife.*

whistle of the train and, frightened, she retreated and ended up at the same place. Finally, overcoming her fear, she shut her eyes and crossed the tracks. Once she got past the tracks, her fear began to subside. She got to the corner and turned to the right.

The sidewalks were crowded with people and her ears started to fill up with a ringing sound, the kind that, once it started, it wouldn't stop. She didn't recognize any of the people around her. She wanted to turn back but she was caught in the flow of the crowd which shoved her onward toward downtown and the sound kept ringing louder and louder in her ears. She became frightened and more and more she was finding herself unable to remember why she was there amidst the crowd of people. She stopped in an alley way between two stores to regain her composure a bit. She stood there for a while watching the passing crowd.

"My God, what is happening to me? I'm starting to feel the same way I did in Wilmar. I hope I don't get worse. Let me see . . . the ice house is in that direction—no it's that way. No, my God, what's happening to me? Let me see . . . I came from over there to here. So it's in that direction. I should have just stayed home. Uh, can you tell me where Kress is, please? . . . Thank you."

She walked to where they had pointed and entered the store. The noise and pushing of the crowd was worse inside. Her anxiety soared. All she wanted was to leave the store but she couldn't find the doors anywhere, only stacks and stacks of merchandise and people crowded against one another. She even started hearing voices coming from the merchandise. For a while she stood, gazing blankly at what was in front of her. She couldn't even remember the names of the things. Some people stared at her for a few seconds, others just pushed her aside. She remained in this state for a while, then she started walking again. She finally made out some toys and put them in her bag. Then she saw a wallet and also put that in her bag. Suddenly she no longer heard the noise of the crowd. She only saw the people moving about—their legs, their arms, their mouths, their eyes. She finally asked where the door, the exit was. They told her and she started in that direction. She pressed through the crowd, pushing her way until she pushed open the door and exited.

She had been standing on the sidewalk for only a few seconds, trying to figure out where she was, when she felt someone grab her roughly by the arm. She was grabbed so tightly that she gave out a cry.

"Here she is . . . these damn people, always stealing something, stealing. I've been watching you all along. Let's have that bag."
"But . . ."

Then she heard nothing for a long time. All she saw was the pavement moving swiftly toward her face and a small pebble that bounced into her eye and was hurting a lot. She felt someone pulling her arms and when they turned her, face up, all she saw were faces far away. Then she saw a security guard with a gun in his holster and she was terrified. In that instant she thought about her children and her eyes filled with tears. She started crying. Then she lost consciousness of what was happening around her, only feeling herself drifting in a sea of people, their arms brushing against her like waves.

"It's a good thing my compadre° happened to be there. He's the one who ran to the restaurant to tell me. How do you feel?"

"I think I must be insane, viejo."

"That's why I asked you if you weren't afraid you might get sick like in Wilmar."

"What will become of my children with a mother who's insane? A crazy woman who can't even talk, can't even go downtown."

"Anyway, I went and got the notary public. He's the one who went with me to the jail. He explained everything to the official. That you got dizzy and that you get nervous attacks whenever you're in a crowd of people."

"And if they send me to the insane asylum? I don't want to leave my children. Please, viejo, don't let them take me, don't let them. I shouldn't have gone downtown."

"Just stay here inside the house and don't leave the yard. There's no need for it anyway. I'll bring you everything you need. Look, don't cry anymore, don't cry. No, go ahead and cry, it'll make you feel better. I'm gonna talk to the kids and tell them to stop bothering you about Santa Claus. I'm gonna tell them there's no Santa Claus, that way they won't trouble you with that anymore."

"No, viejo, don't be mean. Tell them that if he doesn't bring them anything on Christmas Eve, it's because the Reyes Magos will be bringing them something."

"But . . . well, all right, whatever you say. I suppose it's always best to have hope."

The children, who were hiding behind the door, heard everything, but 10 they didn't quite understand it all. They awaited the day of the Reyes Magos as they did every year. When that day came and went with no arrival of gifts, they didn't ask for explanations.

compadre: A close male friend, "brother."

Reading

1. Why does Doña María decide she needs to go downtown?

2. What happens to Doña María when she is at Kress?

Thinking Critically

1. What do you think is the reason that Doña María rarely leaves her house? Do you think she chooses to live this way? Support your answer with evidence from the text.

2. At the end of the story, we read that the children "heard everything" but "didn't quite understand it all" (par. 10). What do you think they *did* understand?

Connecting

1. Compare the life of Doña María to the life of Cleófilas in Sandra Cisneros's story "Woman Hollering Creek" (p. 264). What similarities do you find in the lives of the two characters? Do Rivera and Cisneros have different attitudes toward the characters in their stories?

Writing

1. While talking to her husband about Christmas, Doña María says, "Yes, but it's different here" (par. 2). What do you think she means by this? Using examples from the story, write an essay about the differences between Doña María's new and old lifestyles.

Creating

1. **Map out Doña María's journey.** In "La Noche Buena," Doña María walks six blocks from her home to a department store downtown and eventually ends up back home again. Sketch out a map of her travels. Refer back to the story and identify specific things she encounters along the way to Kress, in the store itself, and once she leaves. What do you think is the significance of the things you've identified? What do you think Doña María feels about them? How does visualizing her physical and emotional odyssey affect your understanding of the story?

18

ROLANDO HINOJOSA [b. 1929]

The People of Belken County

From Estampas del Valle y otras obras [1972]

GENRE: FICTION

Rolando Hinojosa was one of the first writers to emerge during the Chicano Renaissance of the 1970s. In a long career as a writer and a professor, he has remained one of the most respected names in Chicano literature. Hinojosa grew up in the Rio Grande Valley in the city of Mercedes, Texas. Too young to serve in World War II, he enlisted for two years after its close and then entered the University of Texas at Austin, only to be recalled for the Korean War. After serving in the war, he returned to Austin and finished his bachelor's degree; he then spent several years teaching high school and working various jobs before earning a master's degree from Highlands University in New Mexico and a doctorate from the University of Illinois at Urbana–Champaign. With his Ph.D. he returned to Texas to begin teaching and working on his first book, encouraged by his friend Tomás Rivera (p. 145), who was also teaching in Texas. The result was a book about the inhabitants of the imaginary Klail City, Estampas del Valle y otras obras, *which in 1972 won the Premio Quinto Sol, a recently established prize for novels written by Chicanos. Hinojosa continued the lives of his characters in several other novels written between* Klail City *in 1976 and* Becky and Her Friends *in 1990, which collectively make up the* Klail City Death Trip *series. Hinojosa joined the faculty of the University of Texas at Austin in 1981 and has remained there since. In 2014 he was awarded a Lifetime Achievement Award by the National Book Critics Circle.*

In the followings five vignettes from Hinojosa's first book, a collection of fictional narratives called Estampas del Valle, *we meet some of the characters that live in Klail City, a part of Belken County. (Note: For the purposes of this anthology, we have titled the excerpts "The People of Belken County.") We meet Rafa Buenrostro, who will become the hero of a later novel; the Leguizamón family, a powerful* *force in Klail City; and myriad other personalities, often very briefly. Hinojosa did not present these characters as specimens from an exotic culture trying to make their way through America, but as "agents and reagents for their own culture," as he once said. "The question of identity has never applied to my characters. Valley Chicanos have always known exactly who they were and who they are."**

As you read about Hinojosa's characters, try to understand them and the dynamics of the culture they live in.

To Begin with, a Dedication

In the last analysis, the world is like a drugstore: there's a little bit of everything. All kinds of people: tall, short, cry babies, fat, skinny, good, bad, sharp, dumb, some sickly and others healthy as can be. The writer, without anyone's leave, goes out into the street and takes a little bit from here and there. Don't think that there isn't a little bit of everything and don't confuse yourself thinking that there is a lot of everything—let's see, how many Napoleons have there been? or Hitlers? or Christs? But let's leave that aside for now and come back to it later.

There are people so afraid of committing a social error (showing their ears, putting their foot in their mouth, pissing their pants) that, when the time comes, they don't dare do anything. Those people, being so afraid of erring, will never taste the honest food of a Chicano wedding on a ranch where, thank God, anything goes. (Anything goes in the sense that one is among friends and acquaintances and it's better not to put on airs because, in the long run, it's insincere.)

All right. To date there has been only one Napoleon (or one Romeo and one Raskolnikov); the three, in different ways, are similar. Where does the fiction of the first begin and end and where does it begin and end for the other two? It seems useless to me to try to disguise them with other names and other clothing: a monkey in a silk shirt . . . Sketching someone who is known is like boasting about clearing a trail in a well-worn path—which is almost as bad as thinking of another woman while making love to your own.

It may be that originality, a metal as difficult to grasp as mercury, does not affect men because of "remember, man, that you are dust, etc. . . ." Once again, in the long run, we are and we are not equal as so many have realized.

---

*From Juan Bruce-Novoa, *Chicano Authors: Inquiry by Interview*.

In passing: those peculiar people who amuse themselves with scien-   5
tific data and who feel the need to explain everything have every right to
live and to say whatever they feel like saying. On the other hand, they
should stop going around pestering people—"to each his own . . ."
There's room for everyone in this world—no need to push.

What follows is dedicated to the people of Belken County and to their
mirrors who see them in good health, in sickness, in the raw, crying, etc.,
night and day.

Thus It Was Fulfilled

Not far from Bascom is the Mexican cemetery; Pioquinto Reyes was buried there on the coldest October day ever recorded. It was a simple affair
and since the weather didn't allow for much more, the people, huddled
together in little groups with their heads lowered, defending themselves
against the drizzle, scattered rapidly, abandoning that place until another
time. In the Valley, as everywhere, cold weather and death usually come
at an inconvenient time.

The deceased Pioquinto, despite his name, was a Presbyterian. In his
youth he had been overly serious and then, later on, he was already old
by the time he reached forty. There are people born that way, branded
and singled out as if someone were saying: you're going to be that way,
you this way, and you this other way; in short, as always, man proposes
and God disposes. Death took Pioquinto at the Holiday Inn on Highway
11 in front of what was, in its better days, the edge of the black ghetto.

Pioquinto didn't work in the motel: he was a guest; Pioquinto worked
as a bookkeeper for Avila Hnos.° (wholesale and retail; we deliver). When
he heard the trumpet announcing his day of judgment, Pioquinto was
mounted atop Viola Barragán, a woman who, some twenty years back,
was the best piece of ass around and who is still giving people something
to talk about. Pioquinto kicked the bucket, so to speak, in full swing, taking up the harp like anybody else.

Rafa Buenrostro says that, as a child, he went to the funeral and hap-   10
pened to meet some Buenrostro relatives from Bascom. The Buenrostro
family came to the Valley from Querétaro during the Escandón affair.
Among los Buenrostro, there are some that are poor, some rich and still
others that don't have as much, as don Víctor Peláez used to say. It happened that after the burial when everyone had left, a woman in an expensive suede coat and a little leather hat with a full veil went over to the

Avila Hnos.: Avila Brothers, the company name. (*Hnos.* is the abbreviation of
Hermanos.)

mound of earth where Pioquinto was resting. From her black patent leather purse, she took out a knotted handkerchief that she untied producing a gold ring that was neither wide nor thick. As she buried the ring at the foot of the mound, she soiled her gloves but she didn't seem to mind the mud that had formed there as a result of the recently spaded earth and the steady drizzle. There were no prayers nor sobs, but rather a resigned look, with her head held high, clear-eyed and without the slightest trace of emotion on her lips.

According to Rafa Buenrostro, Viola, widowed for the first time when she was eighteen just before the Second (so far this century) World War, played the piano poorly and sang songs no one recognized. She had married a native of Agualeguas, Nuevo León, an expatriate surgeon who came to die at the hands of a druggist who practiced without a license.

After seven months, Viola went to live with don Javier Leguizamón, owner of all that land in Edgerton which, to give him his due, he had taken from la raza° as well as the Anglos. This lasted until Viola, who was then twenty or twenty-one years old, was replaced by Gela Maldonado, but that's another story. After that separation, the little widow wised up.

After the affair with don Javier, Viola remarried; this time to a German attaché in the consulate general in Tampico, Tamaulipas, who had crossed the border to the United States on a vacation and returned arm in arm with Viola. From Tampico, the couple set sail for India where the husband had been assigned as first secretary to the German ambassador. World War II, as is well known, turned the world upside down and that's how Viola Barragán, a girl born in Ruffing, Texas, daughter of Telesforo Barragán and Felicitas Surís de Barragán, landed in an English concentration camp on the outskirts of Calcutta. They kept her in the shade alongside her husband until they were transferred to Pretoria in the Republic of South Africa. They remained there until surprised by the surrender of Colonel General Jodl in an elementary school in that somber little French town.

Viola's husband lost no time; he returned to Germany and, being neither shy nor lazy, in less than 5 years he was back in Pretoria as an official of Volkswagen Werks and with Viola at his side. Time passes, the German dies suddenly, leaving Viola well off, she returns to the United States and, just like birds returning to their nests, she lands in Belken County.

After returning to her birthplace, she discovered that Telesforo and   15
Felicitas had moved to Edgerton. Viola descended on them; she bought herself a huge house; took in her parents; didn't forget her relatives and acquaintances at all; and, apparently, gave up her nomadic and adventurous life.

la raza: Term used for all people of Mexican descent.

Being somewhat taken aback, people didn't know where to begin with her. The only thing they could say was that Viola had not forgotten her Spanish. It's more likely that she never even bothered with German; frankly, in many situations, actions speak louder than words.

As time passed, the devil, friend of the weak, presented Viola Barragán with yet another surprise in the form of Pioquinto Reyes.

Pioquinto, all serious, in a well starched striped shirt, had married Blanca Rivera; they had no children, but partly to compensate and partly following the maxim, "Nothing ventured, nothing gained," Blanca and Brother Limón managed to make Pioquinto a Presbyterian. The battle must have been short and bloodless because Pioquinto didn't enjoy putting up a fuss.

When Viola installed herself in Edgerton, Pioquinto, surely, wasn't aware of it. What happened was that one fine day, Viola, with time and money to spare, accustomed to crossing the Valley by car from Edgerton to Jonesville-on-the-River, was going through Bascom in her huge cerise colored car when she spotted Pioquinto for the first time. Seeing his serious and sanctimonious face, Viola said to herself: "This is my kind of person: I do what I do now because I feel like it and not to keep food in my belly." And that's how the devil got them together until God separated them months later in the motel.

When Pioquinto gave up the ghost in the Holiday Inn, Viola (whom   20 nothing could frighten anymore) dressed leisurely, left the room and elegantly went to Edgerton where she detached herself from the situation as if nothing had happened. Pioquinto was found by a janitor who notified the manager who etc., etc., . . .

He was buried in the Mexican cemetery in Bascom; his grieving wife and other relatives prayed to God to look after his soul and to take him into His Bosom forever and ever, Amen. The Presbyterian parishioners from the Buen Pastor Church on Ninth Street did it up brown.

Viola? Doing all right, thank you. Now, at fifty some odd years she still holds up well against time. That bit about the ring, if it need to be mentioned, was a first class gesture, one of generosity worthy of instruction to those of little heart.

A Sunday in Klail

"Let's go! Let's go! Let's have a little action out here! Let's go! He's blind as a bat! Nobody hurt, nobody hurt! Say hey!"
    The one yelling is Arturo Leyva:

Bookkeeper by profession,
Baseball's his obsession.

He had the measles at the age of four,
Cagón's° the nickname which at school he bore.

Arturo doesn't understand fully the phrase "nobody hurt" but he repeats it because it's something he's heard since he was a child. This is not to say that Arturo doesn't know English; on the contrary, he defends himself rather well in the language. Nevertheless, the phrase "nobody hurt" is still a mystery to him.

Arturo is at Leones Park watching the 30-30 team from Klail play in a   25 double-header with the Sox from Flora. It's a tough battle; Lázaro "Skinny" Peña hasn't allowed a hit (not even to his mother, should doña Estela get up to bat). The game is getting hot. Baseball is one of the few luxuries Arturo allows himself.

Even the birds know that Arturo is the husband of Yolanda Salazar, the only daughter of don Epigmenio who got a rupture before the Second World War (this rupture is strictly medical; the other, the moral rupture, he's had since he first drew breath). Arturo is allied with his father-in-law against doña Candelaria Munguía de Salazar. Perhaps Arturo doesn't know that Dr. Niccolo Machiavelli existed but he has intuited that in union there is strength.

The alliance is *de rigueur* because doña Candelaria is very despotic. In spite of all that, Arturo goes his own way, without any snags. He hasn't any problems with Yolanda; he knows how to handle her.

Among the people in Leones Park is Manzur Chajín, the confectioner. He is Lebanese, but people call him *el árabe*. Chajín lives in the barrio and is married to a Chicana (Catarina de León). By the time they'd been married two months, she knew how to make that round, red candy with peanuts; to be sure, it's not that difficult, but anything is better than nothing at all. Chajín, like most of his countrymen, pronounces p's as if they were b's and when he speaks about don Manuel, he says that he's such a good boliceman that he doesn't need his bistol. Chajín doesn't sell candy at the park; he lets the kids do it because that's what being a boss is all about.

Arturo went to piss and now he's back. In the meantime, Skinny is really making them toe the line: It's the eighth inning and he still hasn't allowed a hit (not even to his mother, doña Estela, etc. . . .).

"Say hey, 30-30! Say hey!"   30
"Arturo."
"Yea?"
"Uh, nothing. Forget it . . ."

Here comes don Manuel Guzmán: he doesn't understand very much about baseball although he realizes not everyone can get seriously involved in that sport. It's very hot (it's August) but don Manuel, as usual,

Cagón: Wimp (i.e., one who shits frequently).

has on a white shirt with sleeve garters and a black tie. And, again as usual, he's wearing his swiss watch with the gold watch chain, items he received as part of an inheritance from don Víctor Peláez.

"Arturo!"   35

"What is it, don Manuel?"

"Yolanda just left. She says to pick her up at your mother-in-law's."

"Yessir, sir."

Arturo Leyva is more at ease. He loves Yolanda, yes, and it would never occur to him to take on a mistress—perish the thought!—but baseball is baseball and—what the hell!—not every day is Sunday. Skinny hasn't allowed a hit and we're in the tenth inning: the problem is the Sox have two black brothers as their battery: Mann Moore, the pitcher, and his brother Clyde, the catcher; and to make things worse, the Klail 30-30 is what is known as "good field, no hit."

Arturo, although he's a bookkeeper, is tough: tonight, after the game,   40
he'll take Yolanda to the dance on Hidalgo Street and then, later on, to bed, because besides being tough, he's also a "fulfiller."

I believe it's already been said he knows how to handle Yolanda.

Los Leguizamón

The first Leguizamón arrived in Belken County in 1865, johnny-come-latelies, so to speak, and established themselves in what is now Bascom and part of Flora. Later on, they spread out to the North, toward Ruffing, and to the West, toward Jonesville-on-the-River. Once they arranged marriages with los Calvillo, los Surís and with los Celaya but no contracts were ever signed or anything.

The marriage proposals broke up in due time, that's how it goes. Another generation of Leguizamón came along and took over their land; another lost part of it and still another worked at keeping the land to the present time.

The first Leguizamón knew by pure instinct how to fend off the Anglos who had come to the Valley with a Bible in one hand and a club in the other.

Of the present generation, there were five offspring—all children of   45
Clemente Leguizamón who died in Freitas helping the Rangers against los Vilches and los Malacara. Clemente was twice a widower: first of Carmelita Hennington who, according to la raza, was a mulatto—anything's possible; and secondly, from Diamantina Lerdo; the five Leguizamón were therefore Leguizamón-Lerdo. Diamantina died crazy; she was bitten by a rabid dog, after Mass, during those fierce dog days of 1904, a year when it didn't rain a single day in Belken County. (That same year, seven wagons replete with people, rosaries and provisions, left Klail

City and Edgerton toward San Juan de los Lagos, Jalisco, to pray to the Virgen for rain in Belken. Julián Buenrostro, Jesús *El quieto*'s° younger brother, was born on this trip.)

The Henningtons disappeared like they came, without warning; there are some who think they went to Veracruz. Los Lerdo came to the Valley with los Buenrostro when don José de Escandón dazzled half the world in Querétaro; the blood of los Lerdo was thin, not one of them lasted more than fifty years. (It's as far as that strain could go. The mingling of blood with los Leguizamón helped the Lerdo family name, but not much.)

Los Leguizamón-Lerdo or Leguizamón, were only five, as has been said: 1) César, who died at the age of 45 in 1927, riddled with bullets by the very same Rangers he had helped during the scuffles of 1901–03, 1906–07 and lastly, 1923; 2) Alejandro, woman-chaser and gambler but not in the least bit cowardly, who also allied himself with the Anglos and in that way managed to be rewarded with those lands near Ruffing. One Sunday at dawn Alejandro was found dying in the patio of the Church of El Sagrado Corazón de Jesús;° his brains bashed in by a spatula; 3) Antonia, who married one of the rich Blanchards and whose children turned out to be Anglos; 4) Javier and Martín, twins who took over the lands in Edgerton. Martín died an alcoholic; Javier is the only male living and he's no longer as young as he thinks even though he does dye his hair.

When they were both young, don Manuel Guzmán broke Javier's nose for sticking it where it didn't belong; it happened one afternoon when they were broncobusting at the Rancho de los Tuero. In those days, Javier Leguizamón belonged to that part of la raza who played up to the Anglos. It paid off for him; he received lots of land in the west corner of the county.

He married Angelita Villalobos, daughter of don Domingo Villalobos, who succeeded in bringing peace to the Valley as much by his courage as by his ability. Don Domingo was the one who nicknamed his son-in-law, *Chinga Quedito*;° needless to say, he couldn't stand the sight of him.

As time went on, Javier also took over several clothing and grocery stores and, in one of them, Jehú Malacara worked as a jack-of-all-trades: clerk, mailman, messenger boy, janitor . . . In addition to land, Javier took over mistresses. Among them, Viola Barragán, recently widowed and all steamed up, and Gela Maldonado who squeezed quite a bit of money from him and as a result, started her own business. Naturally, she

50

El quieto: The Quiet One.   **Church of El Sagrado Corazón de Jesús:** Church of the Sacred Heart of Jesus.   **Chinga Quedito:** Mr. Screw You Over Gently.

already knew the business inside and out. This Leguizamón-Maldonado union lasted some twelve years.

The story of the older Leguizamón is perhaps of more interest but this is not the place for them. Of the five we spoke of, there are only two left, Antonia and Javier. As in every family, there's a little bit of everything. These two never see or speak to each other. I think Antonia doesn't want to remember her Chicana blood but that happens to many—what's to be done about it? Javier isn't a Chicano either, he's a Leguizamón and los Leguizamón, as is well known, never had a mother; they were the children of an aunt.

Coyotes

is the name given to those who hang around the county seat, the county court house, as some people refer to it. They aren't employees although they may seem to be: they wear a white shirt and tie or, if they happen to be women, high heels and nylons. They scurry through the hall-ways daily and live off of what they can shake from the poor who might appear at the court house on some business. They aren't lawyers either but since they speak English, they obviously have an advantage. They are always on top of any rumor at the court house and since they are shameless, they pounce on any unsuspecting soul who happens to come along. People who are ignorant of bureaucracy are frightened by any envelope bearing an official seal and for that reason are easy prey for los coyotes.

Adrián Peralta, coyote, is from Edgerton and drives from there to Klail daily. Dark, wearing a fashionable straw hat, a white shirt and a tie with a pin in the shape of a sailfish, a smile on his lips but not in his eyes, a thin mustache, with that pair of eyes which, if they haven't seen every-thing, soon will. Since his skin is so thick, neither snide remarks nor insults bother him. He presents a good appearance and an even better voice since so far no one has broken his nose. By his own report, he is very democratic and there he is, always greeting everyone, tall, short, men, women, judges, defendants, whores, queers, etc.

"And what can I do for you?"

"We-eelll, you see, I got this here paper . . . came by mail and since it sez Court House . . . Here I am." 55

"Adrián Peralta, at your service. And your name?"

"Marcial de Anda, Sir." (Don Marcial must be about 70 years old; he's a confectioner by trade. He has four children: Juan, Emerardo, Marcial Jr., and Jovita, who had to get married to Joaquín Tamez. This happened a long time ago.)

"May I see the letter?"

"Yessir."

At first, an elongated mmmmmmmmmmmmmmmmmmmmmm, reserved   60
and full of mystery. Then a quick glance at don Marcial and back at the
paper. He takes the envelope, inserts the letter in it, takes don Marcial by
the elbow and steps into an office. Nothing. Then to another office where
he also asks for so and so; no, he isn't here. Thank you. They go into a
third and the pigeon takes the bait.

"My good friend, I'm going to straighten out this matter in short order.
Speaking of being a little short, can you give me a couple of dollars to make
the machinery run? You know it can't function properly without grease."

He takes the money, returns the envelope and before saying goodbye,
points out a little window. That's the place, he says, ask for Miss Espinoza, the girl with the stylish hairdo. Since she is de la raza and not
ashamed of it, Miss Espinoza smiles at don Marcial and greets him in
Spanish. It's the County Tax Assessor's Office and don Marcial has been
asked to serve on jury duty; no, you don't have to show up now; no, they
won't meet until the end of the year; no, you don't owe me anything,
we're here to serve you . . . Miss Espinoza warns him against giving his
money to the coyotes.

Since don Marcial doesn't have to pay anything, he's overjoyed, so
much so he no longer remembers the two bucks el coyote got out of him;
nor will he recall the advice the girl gave him. Don Marcial goes home
content, until the next time.

Peralta is now having coffee in the cafeteria. He's on his feet, just in
case. Since he's finished off don Marcial, he feels at ease and ready to
pounce on the next innocent that comes to the court house with that well
known anxiety of la raza.

"Good morning, ma'am. Adrián Peralta, your most humble servant.   65
And what can I do for you?"

Reading

1. What happened to Viola Barragán's husbands?

2. How does Javier Leguizamón come to own his land?

Thinking Critically

1. How would you describe Hinojosa's attitude toward his characters?
   Support your perspective with evidence from the text.

2. Hinojosa writes that "the world is like a drugstore: there's a little bit of
   everything" (par. 1). How does he go about showing this in the excerpts
   from *Estampas del Valle*?

Connecting

1. Read "The Barrio" (p. 121) from Ernesto Galarza's memoir, *Barrio Boy*. In Galarza's work we read that the members of the barrio with a good grasp of English had to help others navigate the legal system. In the section of Hinojosa's *Estampas del Valle* above called "Coyotes," we read about the members of the community with a good grasp of English taking advantage of those who speak it less well. Why do you think Galarza and Hinojosa have such different perspectives on such similar situations?

Writing

1. In *Estampas del Valle*, Hinojosa aims to show the culture of the border region. In these selections, what do you learn about this culture? Using examples from the text, describe what makes it distinctive and analyze the way Hinojosa gives it a complex texture.

Creating

1. **Write a story about an Hinojosa character.** A great many characters pass through *Estampas del Valle*, sometimes being mentioned only in one or two lines. Choose a character, and after learning everything you can about him or her from the text, imagine the rest of his or her life. Then write a short story featuring your chosen character and, if you'd like, other characters from Belken County.

19

RUDOLFO ANAYA [b. 1937]

From *Bless Me, Ultima* [1971]

GENRE: FICTION

The 1971 novel Bless Me, Ultima *made its author, Rudolfo Anaya, one of the best-known Chicano writers in the country. Anaya also joined Tomás Rivera and Rolando Hinojosa as a winner of the annual Premio Quinto Sol award for the best work of Chicano fiction and as one of the defining names of the first generation of the Chicano Movement. Anaya identified strongly with the spirit and culture of his native state of New Mexico. He discovered a love of literature while at the University of New Mexico, where he earned a bachelor's degree and, after several years teaching high school, master's degrees in English and counseling. While earning his degrees, he had started learning, as he put it, to "write like me: a* Nuevo

Mexicano, hispano, indio, católico, *son of my mother and father, son of the earth which nurtured me, son of my community, son of my people."* The resulting novel,* Bless Me, Ultima, *was a bestseller and remains one of the most popular Chicano works; it was even made into a movie in 2013. It shows Anaya's interests in the complicated spirituality of his home region as well as his attention to contemporary issues, such as poverty and the lingering effects of war. Anaya continued writing in a variety of genres. His novels include* Alburquerque *(restoring the ancient spelling of the area's name) of 1992 and a series about the detective Sonny Baca that began with* Zia Summer *in 1995. His numerous books for children include* The Santero's Miracle: A Bilingual Story *of 2004, and his shorter fiction can be found in several collections, among them* The Man Who Could Fly and Other Stories, *published in 2006.*

In this selection from Bless Me, Ultima, *tragedy comes from a confrontation between the scars of a very modern war and a mob out to instill an old-fashioned form of justice. The young narrator, Antonio, struggles to find meaning in the violence around him and turns for understanding to Ultima, who is described by Antonio in the novel as "a woman who knew the herbs and remedies of the ancients, a miracle-worker who could heal the sick." She "could lift the curses laid by brujas, that she could exorcise the evil the witches planted in people to make them sick. And because a curandera had this power she was misunderstood and often suspected of practicing witchcraft herself."*

As you read, notice how Anaya, through his narrator, the boy Antonio, and through an appreciation of the mystery of the character Ultima, describes events vividly while also creating a sense of wonder.

It was Saturday night. My mother had laid out our clean clothes for Sunday mass, and we had gone to bed early because we always went to early mass. The house was quiet, and I was in the mist of some dream when I heard the owl cry its warning. I was up instantly, looking through the small window at the dark figure that ran madly towards the house. He hurled himself at the door and began pounding.

"¡Márez!" he shouted, "¡Márez! ¡Ándale, hombre!°"

I was frightened, but I recognized the voice. It was Jasón's father.

"¡Un momento!°" I heard my father call. He fumbled with the farol.°

*From the *Dictionary of Literary Biography*.

¡Ándale, hombre!: Hurry, man!   **¡Un momento!:** Just a moment.   **farol:** Lantern.

"¡Ándale, hombre, ándale!" Chávez cried pitifully. "Mataron a mi   5
hermano°—"

"Ya vengo°—" My father opened the door and the frightened man
burst in. In the kitchen I heard my mother moan, "Ave María Purísima,
mis hijos°—" She had not heard Chávez' last words, and so she assumed
the aviso° was one that brought bad news about her sons.

"Chávez, ¿qué pasa?" My father held the trembling man.

"¡Mi hermano, mi hermano!" Chávez sobbed. "He has killed my brother!"

"¿Pero qué dices, hombre?°" my father exclaimed. He pulled Chávez
into the hall and held up the farol. The light cast by the farol revealed the
wild, frightened eyes of Chávez.

"¡Gabriel!" my mother cried and came forward, but my father pushed   10
her back. He did not want her to see the monstrous mask of fear on the
man's face.

"It is not our sons, it is something in town—get him some water."

"Lo mató, lo mató°—" Chávez repeated.

"Get hold of yourself, hombre, tell me what has happened!" My father
shook Chávez and the man's sobbing subsided. He took the glass of water
and drank, then he could talk.

"Reynaldo has just brought the news, my brother is dead," he sighed
and slumped against the wall. Chávez' brother was the sheriff of the
town. The man would have fallen if my father had not held him up.

"¡Madre de Dios!° Who? How?"   15

"¡Lupito!" Chávez cried out. His face corded with thick veins. For the
first time his left arm came up and I saw the rifle he held.

"Jesús, María y José," my mother prayed.

My father groaned and slumped against the wall. "Ay que Lupito,°" he
shook his head, "the war made him crazy—"

Chávez regained part of his composure. "Get your rifle, we must go to
the bridge—"

"The bridge?"   20

"Reynaldo said to meet him there—The crazy bastard has taken to
the river—"

My father nodded silently. He went to the bedroom and returned with
his coat. While he loaded his rifle in the kitchen Chávez related what
he knew.

"My brother had just finished his rounds," he gasped, "he was at the
bus depot cafe, having coffee, sitting without a care in the world—and

Mataron a mi hermano: They killed my brother.   **Ya vengo:** I'm coming.
Ave María Purísima, mis hijos: Hail Virgin Mary, my children.   **aviso:** Notice.
¿Pero qué dices, hombre?: But what are you saying, man?   **Lo mató, lo mató:**
He killed him, he killed him.   **Madre de Dios:** Mother of God.   **Ay que Lupito:**
Oh that Lupito.

the bastard came up to where he sat and without warning shot him in the head—" His body shook as he retold the story.

"Perhaps it is better if you wait here, hombre," my father said with consolation.

"No!" Chávez shouted. "I must go. He was my brother!"   25

My father nodded. I saw him stand beside Chávez and put his arm around his shoulders. Now he too was armed. I had only seen him shoot the rifle when we slaughtered pigs in the fall. Now they were going armed for a man.

"Gabriel, be careful," my mother called as my father and Chávez slipped out into the dark.

"Sí," I heard him answer, then the screen door banged. "Keep the doors locked—" My mother went to the door and shut the latch. We never locked our doors, but tonight there was something strange and fearful in the air.

Perhaps this is what drew me out into the night to follow my father and Chávez down to the bridge, or perhaps it was some concern I had for my father. I do not know. I waited until my mother was in the sala° then I dressed and slipped downstairs. I glanced down the hall and saw candlelight flickering from the sala. That room was never entered unless there were Sunday visitors, or unless my mother took us in to pray novenas and rosaries for my brothers at war. I knew she was kneeling at her altar now, praying. I knew she would pray until my father returned.

I slipped out the kitchen door and into the night. It was cool. I sniffed   30
the air; there was a tinge of autumn in it. I ran up the goat path until I caught sight of two dark shadows ahead of me. Chávez and my father.

We passed Fío's dark house and then the tall juniper tree that stood where the hill sloped down to the bridge. Even from this distance I could hear the commotion on the bridge. As we neared the bridge I was afraid of being discovered as I had no reason for being there. My father would be very angry. To escape detection I cut to the right and was swallowed up by the dark brush of the river. I pushed through the dense bosque° until I came to the bank of the river. From where I stood I could look up into the flooding beams of light that were pointed down by the excited men. I could hear them giving frenzied, shouted instructions. I looked to my left where the bridge started and saw my father and Chávez running towards the excitement at the center of the bridge.

My eyes were now accustomed to the dark, but it was a glint of light that made me turn and look at a clump of bull-rushes in the sweeping water of the river just a few yards away. What I saw made my blood run cold. Crouched in the reeds and half submerged in the muddy waters lay the figure of Lupito, the man who had killed the sheriff. The glint of light was from the pistol he held in his hand.

sala: Living room.   **bosque:** Woods.

It was frightening enough to come upon him so suddenly, but as I dropped to my knees in fright I must have uttered a cry because he turned and looked directly at me. At that same moment a beam of light found him and illuminated a face twisted with madness. I do not know if he saw me, or if the light cut off his vision, but I saw his bitter, contorted grin. As long as I live I will never forget those wild eyes, like the eyes of a trapped, savage animal.

At the same time someone shouted from the bridge. "There!" Then all the lights found the crouched figure. He jumped and I saw him as clear as if it were daylight.

"Ayeeeeee!" He screamed a blood curdling cry that echoed down the 35 river. The men on the bridge didn't know what to do. They stood transfixed, looking down at the mad man waving the pistol in the air. "Ayeeeeeeee!" He cried again. It was a cry of rage and pain, and it made my soul sick. The cry of a tormented man had come to the peaceful green mystery of my river, and the great *presence* of the river watched from the shadows and deep recesses, as I watched from where I crouched at the bank.

"Japanese sol'jer, Japanese sol'jer!" he cried, "I am wounded. Come help me—" he called to the men on the bridge. The rising mist of the river swirled in the beams of spotlights. It was like a horrible nightmare.

Suddenly he leaped up and ran splashing through the water towards me. The lights followed him. He grew bigger, I heard his panting, the water his feet kicked up splashed on my face, and I thought he would run over me. Then as quickly as he had sprinted in my direction he turned and disappeared again into the dark clumps of reeds in the river. The lights moved in all directions, but they couldn't find him. Some of the lights swept over me and I trembled with fear that I would be found out, or worse, that I would be mistaken for Lupito and shot.

"The crazy bastard got away!" someone shouted on the bridge.

"Ayeeeeee!" the scream sounded again. It was a cry that I did not understand, and I am sure the men on the bridge did not either. The man they hunted had slipped away from human understanding; he had become a wild animal, and they were afraid.

"Damn!" I heard them cursing themselves. Then a car with a siren and 40 flashing red light came on the bridge. It was Vigil, the state policeman who patrolled our town.

"Chávez is dead!" I heard him shout. "He never had a chance. His brains blown out—" There was silence.

"We have to kill him!" Jasón's father shouted. His voice was full of anger, rage and desperation.

"I have to deputize you—" Vigil started to say.

"The hell with deputizing!" Chávez shouted. "He killed my brother! ¡Está loco!°"The men agreed with their silence.

¡Está loco!: He's crazy.

"Have you spotted him?" Vigil asked.   45
"Just now we saw him, but we lost him—"
"He's down there," someone added.
"He is an animal! He has to be shot!" Chávez cried out.
"¡Sí!°" the men agreed.
"Now wait a moment—" It was my father who spoke. I do not know   50
what he said because of the shouting. In the meantime I searched the
dark of the river for Lupito. I finally saw him. He was about forty feet
away, crouched in the reeds as before. The muddy waters of the river
lapped and gurgled savagely around him. Before the night had been only
cool, now it turned cold and I shivered. I was torn between a fear that
made my body tremble, and a desire to help the poor man. But I could
not move, I could only watch like a chained spectator.

"Márez is right!" I heard a booming voice on the bridge. In the lights I
could make out the figure of Narciso. There was only one man that big and
with that voice in town. I knew that Narciso was one of the old people from
Las Pasturas, and that he was a good friend to my father. I knew they often
drank together on Saturdays, and once or twice he had been to our house.

"¡Por Dios, hombres!°" he shouted. "Let us act like men! That is not an
animal down there, that is a man. Lupito. You all know Lupito. You
know that the war made him sick—" But the men would not listen to
Narciso. I guess it was because he was the town drunk, and they said he
never did anything useful.

"Go back to your drinking and leave this job to men," one of them
jeered at him.

"He killed the sheriff in cold blood," another added. I knew that the
sheriff had been greatly admired.

"I am not drinking," Narciso persisted, "it is you men who are drunk   55
for blood. You have lost your reason—"

"Reason!" Chávez countered. "What reason did he have for killing my
brother. You know," he addressed the men, "my brother did no one harm.
Tonight a mad animal crawled behind him and took his life. You call that
reason! That animal has to be destroyed!"

"¡Sí! ¡Sí!" the men shouted in unison.

"At least let us try to talk to him," Narciso begged. I knew that it was
hard for a man of the llano° to beg.

"Yes," Vigil added, "perhaps he will give himself up—"

"Do you think he'll listen to talk!" Chávez jumped forward. "He's down   60
there, and he still has the pistol that killed my brother! Go down and talk
to him!" I could see Chávez shouting in Vigil's face, and Vigil said nothing. Chávez laughed. "This is the only talk he will understand—" he
turned and fired over the railing of the bridge. His shots roared then

¡Sí!: Yes.   ¡Por Dios, hombres!: By God, men!   llano: Plain.

whined away down the river. I could hear the bullets make splashing noises in the water.

"Wait!" Narciso shouted. He took Chávez' rifle and with one hand held it up. Chávez struggled against him but Narciso was too big and strong. "I will talk to him," Narciso said. He pushed Chávez back. "I understand your sorrow Chávez," he said, "but one killing is enough for tonight—" The men must have been impressed by his sincerity because they stood back and waited.

Narciso leaned over the concrete railing and shouted down into the darkness. "Hey Lupito! It is me, Narciso. It is me, hombre, your compadre.° Listen my friend, a very bad business has happened tonight, but if we act like men we can settle it—Let me come down and talk to you, Lupito. Let me help you—"

I looked at Lupito. He had been watching the action on the bridge, but now as Narciso talked to him I saw his head slump on his chest. He seemed to be thinking. I prayed that he would listen to Narciso and that the angry and frustrated men on the bridge would not commit mortal sin. The night was very quiet. The men on the bridge awaited an answer. Only the lapping water of the river made a sound.

"¡Amigo!°" Narciso shouted, "You know I am your friend, I want to help you, hombre—" He laughed softly. "Hey, Lupito, you remember just a few years ago, before you went to the war, you remember the first time you came into the Eight Ball to gamble a little. Remember how I taught you how Juan Botas marked the aces with a little tobacco juice, and he thought you were green, but you beat him!" He laughed again. "Those were good times, Lupito, before the war came. Now we have this bad business to settle. But we are friends who will help you—"

I saw Lupito's tense body shake. A low, sad mournful cry tore itself   65
from his throat and mixed into the lapping sound of the waters of the river. His head shook slowly, and I guess he must have been thinking and fighting between surrendering or remaining free, and hunted. Then like a coiled spring he jumped up, his pistol aimed straight up. There was a flash of fire and the loud report of the pistol. But he had not fired at Narciso or at any of the men on the bridge! The spotlights found him.

"There's your answer!" Chávez shouted.

"He's firing! He's firing!" another voice shouted. "He's crazy!"

Lupito's pistol sounded again. Still he was not aiming at the men on the bridge. He was shooting to draw their fire!

"Shoot! Shoot!" someone on the bridge called.

"No, no," I whispered through clenched lips. But it was too late for   70
anything. The frightened men responded by aiming their rifles over the

compadre: Close friend.   **¡Amigo!:** Friend.

side of the bridge. One single shot sounded then a barrage followed it like the roar of a cannon, like the rumble of thunder in a summer thunderstorm.

Many shots found their mark. I saw Lupito lifted off his feet and hurled backward by the bullets. But he got up and ran limping and crying towards the bank where I lay.

"Bless me—" I thought he cried, and the second volley of shots from the bridge sounded, but this time they sounded like a great whirling of wings, like pigeons swirling to roost on the church top. He fell forward then clawed and crawled out of the holy water of the river onto the bank in front of me. I wanted to reach out and help him, but I was frozen by my fear. He looked up at me and his face was bathed in water and flowing, hot blood, but it was also dark and peaceful as it slumped into the sand of the riverbank. He made a strange gurgling sound in his throat, then he was still. Up on the bridge a great shout went up. The men were already running to the end of the bridge to come down and claim the man whose dead hands dug into the soft, wet sand in front of me.

I turned and ran. The dark shadows of the river enveloped me as I raced for the safety of home. Branches whipped at my face and cut it, and vines and tree trunks caught at my feet and tripped me. In my headlong rush I disturbed sleeping birds and their shrill cries and slapping wings hit at my face. The horror of darkness had never been so complete as it was for me that night.

I had started praying to myself from the moment I heard the first shot, and I never stopped praying until I reached home. Over and over through my mind ran the words of the Act of Contrition. I had not yet been to catechism, nor had I made my first holy communion, but my mother had taught me the Act of Contrition. It was to be said after one made his confession to the priest, and as the last prayer before death.

Did God listen? Would he hear? Had he seen my father on the bridge?   75 And where was Lupito's soul winging to, or was it washing down the river to the fertile valley of my uncles' farms?

A priest could have saved Lupito. Oh why did my mother dream for me to be a priest! How would I ever wash away the stain of blood from the sweet waters of my river! I think at that time I began to cry because as I left the river brush and headed up the hills I heard my sobs for the first time.

It was also then that I heard the owl. Between my gasps for air and my sobs I stopped and listened for its song. My heart was pounding and my lungs hurt, but a calmness had come over the moonlit night when I heard the hooting of Ultima's owl. I stood still for a long time. I realized that the owl had been with me throughout the night. It had watched over all that had happened on the bridge. Suddenly the terrible, dark fear that had possessed me was gone.

I looked at the house that my father and my brothers had built on the juniper-patched hill; it was quiet and peaceful in the blue night. The sky sparkled with a million stars and the Virgin's horned moon, the moon of my mother's people, the moon of the Lunas. My mother would be praying for the soul of Lupito.

Again the owl sang; Ultima's spirit bathed me with its strong resolution. I turned and looked across the river. Some lights shone in the town. In the moonlight I could make out the tower of the church, the school house top, and way beyond the glistening of the town's water tank. I heard the soft wail of a siren, and I knew the men would be pulling Lupito from the river.

The river's brown waters would be stained with blood, forever and ever   80 and ever . . .

In the autumn I would have to go to the school in the town, and in a few years I would go to catechism lessons in the church. I shivered. My body began to hurt from the beating it had taken from the brush of the river. But what hurt more was that I had witnessed for the first time the death of a man.

My father did not like the town or its way. When we had first moved from Las Pasturas we had lived in a rented house in the town. But every evening after work he had looked across the river to these barren, empty hills, and finally he had bought a couple of acres and began building our house. Everyone told him he was crazy, that the rocky, wild hill could sustain no life, and my mother was more than upset. She wanted to buy along the river where the land was fertile and there was water for the plants and trees. But my father won the fight to be close to his llano, because truthfully our hill was the beginning of the llano, from here it stretched away as far as the eye could see, to Las Pasturas and beyond.

The men of the town had murdered Lupito. But he had murdered the sheriff. They said the war had made him crazy. The prayers for Lupito mixed into prayers for my brothers. So many different thoughts raced through my mind that I felt dizzy, and very weary and sick. I ran the last of the way and slipped quietly into the house. I groped for the stair railing in the dark and felt a warm hand take mine. Startled, I looked up into Ultima's brown, wrinkled face.

"You knew!" I whispered. I understood that she did not want my mother to hear.

"Sí," she replied.   85

"And the owl—" I gasped. My mind searched for answers, but my body was so tired that my knees buckled and I fell forward. As small and thin as Ultima was she had the strength to lift me in her arms and carry me into her room. She placed me on her bed and then by the light of a small, flickering candle she mixed one of her herbs in a tin cup, held it over the flame to warm, then gave it to me to drink.

"They killed Lupito," I said as I gulped the medicine.

"I know," she nodded. She prepared a new potion and with this she washed the cuts on my face and feet.

"Will he go to hell?" I asked.

"That is not for us to say, Antonio. The war-sickness was not taken out   90 of him, he did not know what he was doing—"

"And the men on the bridge, my father!"

"Men will do what they must do," she answered. She sat on the bed by my side. Her voice was soothing, and the drink she had given me made me sleepy. The wild, frightening excitement in my body began to die.

"The ways of men are strange, and hard to learn," I heard her say.

"Will I learn them?" I asked. I felt the weight on my eyelids.

"You will learn much, you will see much," I heard her faraway voice. I   95 felt a blanket cover me. I felt safe in the warm sweetness of the room. Outside the owl sang its dark questioning to the night, and I slept.

Reading

1. Why is Chávez so upset at the beginning of the story?

2. At one point in the story, Narciso stops the men from shooting at Lupito. Ultimately, the men shoot Lupito. Why?

3. What vocation does Antonio's mother wish for him?

Thinking Critically

1. Márez points out about Lupito that "the war made him crazy" (par. 18). Do you think this should have changed the way that the men responded to Lupito's act? Explain.

2. Antonio is very young when the event in this story occurs. How do you think he would describe it differently if he were older?

Connecting

1. Like Rudolfo Anaya in *Bless Me, Ultima*, Gary Soto, in his poem "Where Were You When You First Heard of Air-Conditioning" (p. 199), writes about childhood. What mood or issues does the perspective of childhood enable these authors to capture?

Writing

1. Ultima tells Antonio near the end of the selection that "Men will do what they must do" (par. 92). Do you think that the men in this story had to do what they did? Using examples from the text, write a brief essay agreeing or disagreeing with Ultima's statement.

Creating

1. **Make a visual argument about traditional medicine.** As a curandera, Ultima attempts to heal body and soul using traditional practices. This may seem outdated in a time when doctors pride themselves on taking advantage of the latest scientific discoveries, but tradition continues to play a very important role in people's spiritual and even physical well-being. What is your view of traditional medicine? Make a collage of images that shows people seeking health using traditional methods.

20

RON ARIAS [b. 1941]

From *The Road to Tamazúnchale* [1975]

GENRE: FICTION

The work of novelist and journalist Ron Arias reflects the influence of the many parts of the world where he has lived and worked, connecting Mexican Americans with the burgeoning literature of Latin America. Arias was born in Los Angeles, but because his stepfather was in the army, he finished high school in Germany. His collegiate studies took him through Spain and Argentina on his way to a bachelor's degree from the University of California, Berkeley, and a master's in journalism from the University of California, Los Angeles. After college he lived in Peru as a member of the Peace Corps. He also began writing stories, and in 1975 he published his acclaimed novel The Road to Tamazúnchale, *which showed the influences of the Mexican writer Carlos Fuentes, the Argentine writer Jorge Luis Borges, and of the magical realism of the Colombian writer Gabriel García Márquez. The work was nominated for a National Book Award and made Arias one of the most highly regarded Chicano novelists. Though he continued publishing stories, Arias moved into a very successful career as a journalist, traveling the world and writing for several national publications, and eventually becoming a senior editor at* People. *His nonfiction work includes* Five Against the Sea *(1989) and a 2002 memoir called* Moving Target: A Memoir of Pursuit.*

Following are the first two chapters of the novel The Road to Tamazúnchale, *which tells the story of the last week of the life of*

Fausto Tejada, a widower and former traveling salesman who is tended to by his niece Carmela. Though he is largely confined to his bed and to short walks, he travels very far in his imagination—all the way to Peru in this section. His dying thoughts blur the lines between death and life, between fantasy and reality, and between his home and the rest of the world.

As you read, think about why Arias has chosen to emphasize the continuities described above. What do they suggest about Fausto's life?

Fausto lifted his left arm and examined the purple splotches. Liver. Liver caused them. He tugged at the largest one, near the wrist. His fingertips raised the pouch of skin as if it were a small, wrinkled tent. He tugged harder, expecting the tissue to tear. The skin drew tight at the elbow. Slowly it began to rip, peeling from the muscle. No blood. The operation would be clean, like slipping off nylon hose. He always had trouble removing chicken skins, but this, he could see, would be easier.

It bunched at the knuckles, above the fingernails. Carefully he pulled each fingertip as he would a glove. The rest was simple, and soon his body lay gleaming under the fragile light of the table lamp.

A stubborn piece of skin remained under his little toe. But what's a toe? She won't be looking at my toe.

Fausto folded his feather-light suit neatly in the meatless palm of one hand, closed his naked eyelids and waited for his niece.

"Tío,° are you awake?" Carmela leaned over the bed.   5

"Can't you see?" Fausto opened his palm to show her the wad of skin. It fell to the floor.

"You want some more Kleenex?" she asked and pushed the tissue box closer.

Fausto moved his legs over the edge of the bed, bent down and picked up the skin. She must be blind, she didn't even notice. He unfolded the dry tissue, methodically spreading it on the bedcover, stretching the legs and arms their full length. He coughed, and the skin blew off the bed. Maybe she didn't see because it's too dark. But my face? No hair . . . all bony. Next time I'll give her my heart, and she'll say, Tío, what's this? Tío, don't play games. Put it back.

Carmela waited for her uncle to slip back under the sheet and blankets. She always expected the worst, or at least him lying on the floor blacked out from a stroke or a broken bone. Twice he was in the hospital after heart attacks. She had seen him later, straining to speak, with a

Tío: Uncle.

tube in one arm and another up a nostril. Since then he took pills for chest pains. Smoking regularly.

"I'll leave your breakfast on the kitchen table."   10

"You're not staying?"

"I thought I'd do some shopping before work. All you've got in the refrigerator are those little bowls of leftovers. The barbecued veal I got you was already moldy. So was the squash."

"Mijita,° can you buy me more cigarettes? The money's on the table."

"Don't be silly. Keep your money."

At the doorway Carmela turned and noticed his feverish eyes. Wide-   15
open, they glistened in the dim light.

Fausto lay still, listening to the faint groan of freeway traffic. He heard the front door slam shut and relaxed. Slowly he stood, then shuffled to the window and peered through the rusty screen, across the river to the tracks. More smog. For six years he had shuffled to the window, to the bathroom, down to the kitchen, through gloomy rooms, resting, listening to the radio, reading, turning thin, impatient, waiting for the end. Six years ago she had convinced him to stop work.

"One of these days you'll have to stop. You can't go on forever." And that night she had watched him return home in the dark, struggling up the veranda steps, one arm dragging his briefcase.

Fausto sat in the armchair, looking dreamily at his niece. He hadn't sold a book in two weeks. Not like his best days when he would wander the Eastside, from Five Points to Bell Gardens, like a man treading gold. In one afternoon he could sell three or four dictionaries, the first volume of an eighteen-volume *Junior Book of Knowledge* set, and at least a half a dozen cookbooks in Spanish or in English.

"Fine," Fausto said.

"Fine what?"   20

"No more work."

"You'll stay home?"

"I'll stay."

Now, years later, he felt as if his muscles were finally turning to worms, his lungs to leaves and his bones to petrified stone. Suddenly the monstrous dread of dying seized his mind, his brain itched, and he trembled like a naked child in the snow. No! he shouted. It can't happen, it won't happen! As long as I breathe, it won't happen. . . .

In silence the old man listened carefully for the song of life. Curled in   25
the darkness somewhere beyond the house, it beckoned with the faint, soft sound of a flute. Then it was gone.

Mijita: My child (colloquial, contracted form of *mi hijita*).

He would leave at once. He considered strapping on his buckler but decided it would be more of a nuisance than a help. Besides, he could barely lift the sword. What would he do with the buckler? Maybe he should leave them both. But why worry now? These were details he could take care of in Peru.

Before dressing he washed himself in the bathroom. Puro indio,° he thought, looking at the hairless face in the mirror. You're more indio than a Tarahumara, his wife used to say. He wiped his face dry, wet it with cologne, then trimmed his sideburns with the cuticle scissors. The face hung in the mirror a moment longer.

He gathered his clothes in the bedroom. The drapes were open, the shade up, as Carmela had left them. Quickly he put his arms into the smoking jacket, worn to the lining at the elbows, adjusted his ascot and pulled on an uncreased pair of khaki trousers. As he hurried toward the stairs, his slippers slapped against his bare heels.

He could hardly wait. Should he send a message to the viceroy? Surely news of his coming would bolster morale of the Cuzco garrison. Cuzco, Navel of the World, the very soul of Inca greatness and power. Cuzco. Again he tasted the word and steadied himself on the banister. Perhaps he should make the climb by land instead of taking the plane. It was safer, and this way he could inspect the terrain. Yes, by land, perhaps on the bus. He was never the best of horsemen.

Excitement rose in his throat, and suddenly his fingers had sunk into 30 the carpet. In the kitchen the mute parakeet cracked a seed and almost spoke. And from outside the house came the shrill, metallic sound of freight car wheels rolling into the yard.

Fausto rushed through Lima and headed into the mountains on the first bus out. He hardly glimpsed the city, except for the smog, or the drizzle, he wasn't certain. Now and then he saw a church, a plaza, the face of food in the window, but most of the time he slept, hoping he could endure the dusty, jarring ride into the sierra.

Arriving in Huancayo, he quickly smoked his last American cigarette. Desperate, he searched the streets, approaching vendors, entering stores, combing the open market. Nothing. Finally the black market emerged in the form of a small mestizo° in a rumpled, threadbare suit. Although Fausto's Spanish wasn't the best, he noticed the man's speech was ungrammatical but to the point.

The stranger led him through a low doorway into a cavelike room. Along the whitewashed walls dark figures, mostly hunched over tables, hardly noticed him. The air reeked of stale grease and warm chicha.°

Puro indio: Pure Indian.   **mestizo:** A person of mixed Spanish and Indian blood.   **chicha:** A fermented beverage made of corn.

Fausto waited in the outdoor courtyard while the man climbed a stair-
way and disappeared in a room above the restaurant. The stranger
returned with his sale wrapped in brown paper, received his money with
a grin and left. Fausto ripped off the paper; one pack was missing. His
first setback.

Before leaving Huancayo he composed an elegant, detailed report to
the viceroy. Numerous violations of trade and customs regulations by
well-organized native elements . . . bound to undermine authority. Then
a few hints on the leader's whereabouts. Fausto made no mention of
punishment; the thought of blood sickened him.

On the way to Cuzco he suffered an attack of diarrhea, almost forcing   35
him to halt the journey. He squirmed in his seat for hours, doubling over
and clenching his fists. Once he begged the driver to stop. The narrow,
shoulderless road clung to the rock above a two-thousand-foot drop into
the Apurímac River.

The driver refused, ordering his passenger to wait a while longer. But
Fausto's patience had been drained miles back. He persisted, almost in
tears. Meanwhile the other passengers craned their necks to catch the
outcome of the argument.

"Stop!"

"No!"

"Stop or I'll report you to the authorities."

"Only God can stop this bus."   40

"And the archbishop . . . ?"

The driver halted the bus and opened the door. "One minute."

"Two!"

"One . . . I'm counting."

Fausto carefully set his feet on the ground, dropped his trousers and   45
squatted. Between his legs he could see the gleaming thread of river far
below.

As he hobbled back to his seat in the middle of the bus, several passengers smiled sympathetically. He should have taken the plane.

At last they approached Cuzco, and Fausto leaned over his neighbor's
armrest for a glimpse. No, it wasn't like the Valley of Mexico. Tenochtitlán was finer, somehow grander. Cuzco seemed a gray, hillside mass of
stone. But below the city, along the highway, he could see the green fields,
young with corn, wheat, barley and potato plants. Indian families squatted in doorways, watching the bus jog by in swirls of dust.

This time Fausto ignored the driver's refusal to stop and simply
descended from the machine of noise, odors of urine and grimy bodies.
After the dust settled, he breathed deeply and marched ahead. Leaving
the road, he struggled to push away annoying reminders of time. Telephone poles along the train tracks refused to vanish, a billboard advertising Cuzqueña beer remained in the distance.

But Fausto was determined to enter the city grandly, mounted, leading an army of foot soldiers, arquebusiers and lancers. In a loud voice he ordered the right flank brought up to spread itself across the fields. Careful with the corn, he shouted. And don't harm anyone! It has to be a peaceful entrance.

Behind a cluster of huts several farmers clutched their children and   50
ran into their homes. Chickens scattered and dogs curled their tails at the sound of pounding hooves.

But as the commander approached the new airport on the south side of the city, he winced. He should be on the *north* side. What did the map say . . . ? He had left it on the bus. The thin air had tired him, and Fausto began to breathe harder, turning his face to the rich, cloudless sky. Dizzy, he reluctantly ordered the army to continue without him.

Then he crossed the concrete runway, slowly passed through the new terminal building and called for a taxi. A good hotel, he told the driver. A clean one.

After his nap, Fausto relaxed between the starched sheets. He admired the strong, wooden ceiling beams, the burnished tile floor, the massive, iron-hinged door. Leaving his bed, he touched the smooth, white walls, the dark, hand-carved crucifix. Months of labor, of fine Iberian skill. His reverie took him to the balcony where he flung open the latticed shutters. Below him in the empty plaza a dreamy-eyed llama glanced at the odd figure in pajamas.

Later two Indian boys helped him bathe. Then they trimmed his hair, fingernails and toenails. Finally they dressed him. The silky swish of his lace cuffs reminded him of Carmela's best mantilla.° It seemed nothing had been spared the viceroy's hospitality. Perfumed and powdered, Fausto left for the noon meal. He asked for two poached eggs, a dish of cottage cheese, a veal steak and three choices of ice cream.

"And waiter," Fausto added, "tell his excellency I'm most grateful for   55
his attention."

"The best is yet to come," the young man said with a wink.

"What's that?"

"I can't tell you. . . . You'll see."

During the meal Fausto's anxiety grew. What would happen to him? Was he being fattened like a hog before slaughter? Worse, how could he explain his mission to the viceroy if he himself didn't know? A man at arms? Fausto laughed nervously and pushed away the steak. He had no army, no weapons. Who would believe him? On the other hand . . . he might be a pilgrim . . . But where was he going? What shrine? Maybe a courtier? A merchant? An emissary from Panama? No, none of these would do. But the truth was even flimsier.

mantilla: Type of woman's scarf worn over the head and shoulders.

Fausto abruptly left the table and hurried toward the elevator. He was 60
afraid this might happen. A man just doesn't wander about without a
purpose.

In his room Carmela was waiting for him. At first her beauty left him
speechless. She sat on the edge of the bed with her back to the afternoon
light, her long black hair spread over her shoulders.

"Mijita," Fausto stammered, "what are you doing here? I thought you
were at work."

"I am. I was told to come."

"I don't understand. . . . You don't work here."

"Listen, let's get started. It's much more fun than talking. Or have you 65
forgotten how?"

Fausto blushed. "Carmela!"

"My name's not Carmela. It's Ana."

"But you're my niece."

"I never saw you before. But I suppose I could be Carmela . . . for
a while."

Fausto palmed his thinning hair and shook his head. 70

"You don't want to do this, do you?" Ana said flatly.

"I don't think so, I've got a headache."

"I'll take it away, let me try."

"No, I'm tired."

Ana kicked off her sandals, unbuttoned her blouse and began to pull 75
her arms out the sleeves.

"I just want to lie down," Fausto said as her skirt dropped to the floor.
"If you want, you can rub my temples."

"Alright, old man, lie down. I'll rub your temples."

She placed his head between her legs, looked at the ceiling and sighed.
Under the steady pressure of her hands, Fausto soon fell asleep.

When he woke, Ana was sitting next to him on the wooden seat of a
train. Fausto squinted at the sudden light. Through the window he could
see a herd of dairy cows in the shade of a lone eucalyptus tree.

"What's this?" he asked. 80

"A train."

"I mean where am I? Where are we going?"

"You don't belong in Cuzco, I could see that. You even said so in your
sleep. The trip shouldn't take too long, and I think you'll like it."

"Is this the viceroy's idea?"

"No, it's mine. I'm taking you where few men have ever been." 85

"Where's that?"

"There, beyond the clouds."

In the distance above a few scattered clouds, Fausto could see the
giant white peak. He turned to Ana, and she patted his hand as if to ease

his fear. She wore many skirts, a rough cotton blouse, and the tire soles of her sandals were worn and curved up at the edge.

The narrow-gauge train wound its way down through the gorge of the Urubamba River. From Cuzco the trip had been a descent of some eight thousand feet, from the sparse grasses of the altiplano to the warm, humid lushness of the Amazon's edge. A matter of minutes at one point, and the little train entered the tropics. Fountains of tangled vines and broad, lustrous leaves pushed from both sides. Life strained from every rock. Passing quickly beneath Machu Picchu, Fausto gazed at the rock-hewn terraces and for a moment forgot the arthritic jabs in his limbs.

They left the train at a stop where the gorge widens to a warm plain of   90
coca and coffee farms. Ana helped him to the ground and they started up a narrow valley to the west.

Fausto fought exhaustion most of the afternoon. The huge greenness of nature squeezed itself upon the trail, and it was all he could do to keep his legs moving. After several hours of trudging behind Ana, he began to regret leaving home. He longed for his armchair, his bed, his dinner by the kitchen radio, his books and the quiet company of his parakeet.

"Stop, Ana."

"Again?"

"A few minutes. . . . I'll be fine."

"Maybe we shouldn't have come."   95

"I started this, I'll finish it," Fausto said, trying to sound firm.

After a short rest, the march continued. Several times he tripped and cursed his luck. The trail seemed to vanish, and he no longer could see Ana. The jungle heat tightened around his neck and chest. The air turned dark, and he glimpsed a vague, motionless figure. This was his chance. He would charge the intruder. If it were death, he would impale the monster to the hilt. But with what? Fausto asked feebly. He waved his arms weakly at the silhouette, crashed into a tree and toppled over.

Ana discovered him tangled in thick cords of vines, on his back and unable to free himself. "I thought I had lost you," she said, cutting him loose with her machete.

"I must have fainted," Fausto said, relieved at the touch of her hands.

"Not far from here is a spring. You can rest there."   100

They followed the trail for a short distance, then Ana skipped ahead toward the sound of water. When Fausto arrived, he saw her playfully splashing her feet between two puma heads that spouted small, clear streams into a rock-carved basin. A mild breeze blew flower petals over her glistening body.

She gestured with a nod toward the water. Fausto hesitated, then approached, and she gently removed his clothes, urged him in the snow-fed pool and massaged his back and shoulders. Afterward he slept in the shade of a mango tree on tiny ferns and tender blades of grass. She kept the insects away with a young palm branch, occasionally soothing his temples.

When he woke, she was sitting beside him, wild lucma fruit in her lap. She rubbed his knees a while longer, then brought him water to drink.

Now they would begin the steepest climb, several hours' journey to the barren uplands above the valley.

On the way they passed through a cloud-forest of weird, root-twisted 105 shrubs and moist, darkened hollows surrounded by spongy earth. The gnarled branches of these stunted, phantom trees seemed to reach out and block the trail. Ana explained that many travelers had been trapped here and they lived on as insects, bats, even rocks.

"Don't worry," she said. "We'll be out soon."

Fausto hobbled after her and as they emerged into the fading light of nightfall, he saw the tiny huts scattered over the wide, steep slopes. Human figures, alpacas and sheep moved beneath the glacier basins.

Ana begged him to stay on his feet. "We must hurry, something has happened . . . I can feel it."

"I can't, you go on ahead."

"Please, papacito.° It's not far." 110

"I can't . . . "

"You must!"

When the sky darkened, Ana cried out. Fausto swayed, leaned against her, and the two fell. She left him and ran to catch the long procession of torchlights winding up the mountain toward the snow.

Gasping, he clutched the knot of fire in his chest and struggled forward. Again and again he called out. Once a child, lingering behind the procession, turned and beckoned with his hand. For a long while Fausto would fall, catch his breath, then stagger on in dizzying bursts of will.

Eventually he crawled onto the hard snow, saw the group in the dis- 115 tance and pulled himself closer. In the moonlight the men danced on the eerie whiteness, their ponchos whirling in one great circle around the women who kneeled in the center, sending their wails to the rocky crags above.

On hands and knees Fausto moved into the circle and reached the crude platform where Ana helped him to lie down. Around them, the mourners tore the air with shouts and beat the ground. Fausto was too tired to refuse their grief. They mean well . . . but why me?

"Ana?" Fausto whispered.

"It's Carmela."

"Yes, Carmela. . . . Don't go."

"I'm right here," she said and wiped his forehead. 120

papacito: Daddy (a term of endearment for an older man).

Far away an unknown shepherd raised his flute and released a long, melancholy note, then another, and another. Fausto smiled.

"Hear that, mijita?"

"Yes, Tío."

"It's beautiful. . . . I can't think of anything more beautiful."

Reading

1. In Cuzco, who does Fausto believe he is on his way to see?

2. What does the sound of the flute represent?

3. What happens to Fausto in the end?

Thinking Critically

1. Why do you think Fausto dreams of travel to Peru? Why does he feel a connection to it?

2. What does Ana and Fausto's trip to Machu Picchu symbolize?

Connecting

1. In one of Lalo Alcaraz's cartoons (p. 421), Eddie and Cuco Rocha demonstrate the magical realist style by instantly, and without explanation, becoming butterflies. After reading Cuco Rocha's definition, do you think that Ron Arias's writing in *The Road to Tamazúnchale* can be called "magical realism"? Why or why not? Why do you think Arias chooses to write in the style he does?

Writing

1. Rather than describing Fausto Tejada all at once, Arias allows his character to be slowly revealed through a mix of memory and fantasy. Using examples from the text, write a brief essay about Tejada as a character. What do you learn about his past from these chapters? What do you learn about his personality?

Creating

1. **Create a photo essay about a journey and identity.** As anyone who has taken a road trip with friends or vacation with family knows, travel has a way of revealing people's personalities. Create a photo essay of a trip you've taken or of one you'd like to take. Write a brief description of the trip and explain what you think your trip, real or imaginary, reveals about your own personality.

21

TINO VILLANUEVA [b. 1941]

Scene from the Movie *GIANT* • I Too Have Walked My Barrio Streets

From Scene from the Movie *GIANT* [1993] AND Shaking Off the Dark [1984]

GENRE: POETRY

Growing up in a family of migrant farmworkers in San Marcos, Texas, Tino Villanueva knew well the tensions depicted in Giant, *the 1956 movie that inspired a book of his poetry. Villanueva made it through a racist school system while spending summers in the fields. His service in the army took him to Panama, where he developed an interest in Latin American literature. He returned to San Marcos for college and then moved to the Northeast. While working on a Ph.D. at Boston University, Villanueva published his first book of poetry,* Hay Otra Voz. *Though Villanueva was based in the Northeast, far from the centers of the Chicano Movement, the book's bilingual writing and its subject matter linked him with the Chicano literary renaissance. One poem, for instance, was entitled "Chicano is an act of defiance" and was dedicated to the recently killed Rubén Salazar (p. 46). Villanueva's academic career took him first to Wellesley and then to Boston University, and his later books include* Shaking Off the Dark, *published in 1984, and* Scene from the Movie *GIANT, published in 1993.*

In a time when Mexican Americans were rarely seen in Hollywood movies, and even more rarely seen in sympathetic roles, Giant *told the epic story of the transformation of a Texas rancher's life by the gradual acceptance of Mexican Americans into his life and even into his family. It starred some of the greats of the era: Rock Hudson, Elizabeth Taylor, and James Dean. In the film's famous climactic scene, Rock Hudson's character gets in a fistfight with a racist restaurant owner who refuses to serve a Mexican family. In good Hollywood fashion, he loses the fight but wins, finally, the respect of his beautiful wife, played by Elizabeth Taylor. "Scene from the Movie* GIANT," *written nearly four decades after the movie itself, is about the power of such a movie to last in one's memory. "I Too Have Walked My Barrio Streets" is an homage to Pablo Neruda, who is considered by many to be the greatest Latin*

*American poet of the twentieth century and whose leftist political
views and poetry were rooted in experiences with the very poor.
Like Neruda in his San Antonio (a city west of Santiago, Chile),
Villanueva sees the poverty of his barrio as fuel for a fire to come.*

As you read these poems, think about how Villanueva transforms memories of a movie and a neighborhood into powerful
experiences for his readers.

SCENE FROM THE MOVIE *GIANT*

What I have from 1956 is one instant at the Holiday
Theater, where a small dimension of a film, as in
A dream, became the feature of the whole. It
Comes toward the end . . . the café scene, which
Reels off a slow spread of light, a stark desire   5

To see itself once more, though there is, at times,
No joy in old time movies. It begins with the
Jingling of bells and the plainer truth of it:
That the front door to a roadside café opens and
Shuts as the Benedicts (Rock Hudson and Elizabeth   10

Taylor), their daughter Luz, and daughter-in-law
Juana and grandson Jordy, pass through it not
Unobserved. Nothing sweeps up into an actual act
Of kindness into the eyes of Sarge, who owns this
Joint and has it out for dark-eyed Juana, weary   15

Of too much longing that comes with rejection.
Juana, from barely inside the door, and Sarge,
Stout and unpleased from behind his counter, clash
Eye-to-eye, as time stands like heat. Silence is
Everywhere, acquiring the name of hatred and Juana   20

Cannot bear the dread—the dark-jowl gaze of Sarge
Against her skin. Suddenly: bells go off again.
By the quiet effort of walking, three Mexican-
Types step in, whom Sarge refuses to serve . . .
Those gestures of his, those looks that could kill   25

A heart you carry in memory for years. A scene from
The past has caught me in the act of living: even
To myself I cannot say except with worried phrases
Upon a paper, how I withstood arrogance in a gruff
Voice coming with the deep-dyed colors of the screen;   30

How in the beginning I experienced almost nothing to
Say and now wonder if I can ever live enough to tell
The after-tale. I remember this and I remember myself
Locked into a back-row seat—I am a thin, flickering,
Helpless light, local-looking, unthought of at fourteen.   35

I TOO HAVE WALKED MY BARRIO STREETS

> *Andando por San Antonio arriba*
> *vi la quietud de la pobreza:*
> *rechinaban los goznes quebrados,*
> *las puertas cansadas querían*
> *ir a sollozar o a dormir.*
>
> *Se preparaba para el fuego*
> *la madera de la pobreza.*
>
> "Arrabales (Canción Triste)"°
> —PABLO NERUDA

I too have walked my barrio° streets,
seen life not worth the lingering grief.

    (As a child and migrant,
    I've picked clean straight rows of cotton
    when the Summers were afire.   5
    And driven by hunger, I've come face to face
    with the uprooted fury of the West Texas wind.
    I've slept on floors of Winter's many corners,
    on linoleum-covered dirtfloors
    of the hard-sprawled Panhandle.   10
    I've taken refuge under cowsheds
    when all of driving Winter rained down a sea
    of stiff mud.)

I too have walked my barrio streets,
smelled patio flowers burning in the stabbing sun,   15
and those in grandma's flower-pots are weary flowers
that do not wilt, instead, they're crushed

Andando por San Antonio arriba . . . / "Arrabales (Canción Triste)": Walking
around San Antonio / I saw the stillness of poverty: / the broken hinges creaking, / the
tired doors wanting / to sob or to sleep. / Preparing itself for the fire / was the timber
of poverty. "Outskirts (Sad Song)."   **barrio:** Mexican American neighborhood.

by bitter dust from streets forgotten,
a corrosive dust set loose
by the official attitude of Health Department trucks: 20
I've tasted that official dust from which
official voices have appeared to thunder:

> *Yore outhouse's gotta go. It's unsanitary, and b'sides,*
> *The City of San Marcos is askin' all of y'all with*
> *out houses ta git inside plumbin.' After all, y'all've*   25
> *had a drainage system come through heah for the last*
> *three years. Ya got one month ta do it in. OK, amigo?*

> (I've printed my name at different schools
> for indifferent teachers
> who've snickered at my native surname,   30
> who've turned me in "for speaking Spanish on
>   the premises"
> long before Jamestown,
> and so I've brightly scrawled transcending obscenities
> in adolescent rage.)   35

I too have walked my barrio streets,
gone among old scars and young wounds
who, gathering at the edge of town, on nearby corners,
mend their broken history with their timely tales.

> (I've been quizzed on Texas history—   40
> history contrived in dark corridors
> by darker still textbook committees.
> I've read those tinged white pages where the ink
> went casting obscurantism across the page:
> the shadows had long dried into a fierce solid state.   45
> And Bigfoot Wallace had always been my teacher's hero,
> and what's worse, I believed it,
> oh, how we all believed it.)

I too have walked my barrio streets,
seen over-worked and hollow-eyed men   50
in the unemployment line, their wrinkled bodies worked-over
like the sharecropped furrows they once grew
under day-long mules steady as the plowing sun.

> (With many others,
> I've thrust a picket sign into the chanting Boston air: 55
> *Work's too hard,*
> *pay's too low,*
> *Farah pants have got to go!*

I've struck down
what Farah slacks   60
were hanging on the racks, and down the street,
what sold-out lettuce came to the sell-out counters
of the East:
¡Obreros unidos,
jamás serán vencidos!)   65

I too have walked my barrio streets,
heard those congenial strangers
who put up their finest drawl in yearly, murdered Spanish!

    Voutin poar mey. Yeu soay eil meijoar keindideitou
    para seyerveerleis.   70

But somewhere in the bred fever of the barrio,
Carmelita López, in a sad dress, clutches the warmth
of her raggedy doll;
Carmelita cries for milk, and so drowns out
the paid political pronouncement.   75
Carmelita, with the languid frame,
shrivels in November's fever, and her laid-off *papi*
can only wish to fix the roof that sprung a leak
a year or two ago.

Pablo, I too have walked my barrio streets.   80
And this I say: that in our barrio,
where a whole country is a parody of itself,
there's still plenty of wood to burn,
and that the winds of the people
are keeping all flames aglow,   85
until the mighty hand that holds dominion over
    Man is bent back at the finger joints;
until the swivel chairs of official leather
    are rooted out from thickly-soiled, pile carpets;
until all pain is driven out at last from the naked barrio.   90

Walking around.
So many times we've walked along
interminable streets, Pablo.
Yet one loud question keeps pounding in my ear:

    A poet's devotion, can't it reach beyond mere walking,   95
    beyond found words
    when people are stirring into the glowing wind?

Reading

1. ("Scene from the Movie *GIANT*") How does Sarge respond to the entrance of the three "Mexican-Types"?

2. ("I Too Have Walked My Barrio Streets") What does the speaker in the poem remember about his teachers?

Thinking Critically

1. What emotions do you think motivated the writing of "Scene from the Movie *GIANT*"?

2. How, if at all, does the epigraph of "I Too Have Walked My Barrio Streets" change or add to the meaning of the poem?

3. What or who does the poem's speaker suggest is the cause of the misery described in "I Too Have Walked My Barrio Streets"?

Connecting

1. In the first chapter of Denise Chávez's novel *Loving Pedro Infante* (p. 275), we find a character experiencing at the movies an emotional pull similar to that felt by the speaker in Villanueva's "Scene from the Movie *GIANT*." Are there differences between the two experiences at the movies? What are they? How do you explain the differences?

Writing

1. While both poetry and film can be used to convey a wide range of images and emotions, some things can only be communicated using the language and techniques of poetry. Write a brief essay identifying lines or sections of "I Too Have Walked My Barrio Streets" and "Scene from the Movie *GIANT*" that could not be presented in another medium. Explain why you think they could not, and discuss how Villanueva treats them in the poem.

Creating

1. **Compose a scene for a screenplay.** Villanueva's poem is about the power of film to capture and inspire complex emotions. Write a screenplay for a brief scene that you think captures an emotional tension. Include descriptions of the scenery, the actors, the camera angle—anything you think your director would need to know. After you've written your scene, briefly explain what difficulties and opportunities for communicating a message that you think movies provide.

22

CARMEN TAFOLLA [b. 1951]

Tía Sofía • Curandera

From Curandera [1983]

GENRE: POETRY

Carmen Tafolla has become an important voice in Chicano litera-
ture by synthesizing her work as a poet, an educator, and a per-
former. Tafolla spent her childhood in San Antonio, Texas, learning
to tell stories from her family and the people in her neighborhood.
"The most important literary influences in my life had to be the
elderly people in the barrios where I grew up, who told stories and
declaimed poems that represented centuries of legacy and affirma-
tion," she said of her childhood. Tafolla earned bachelor's and
master's degrees from Austin College in Sherman, Texas, and then
went to the University of Texas at Austin for a Ph.D. in bilingual
education. While earning her doctorate, Tafolla also began her lit-
erary career, joining with fellow poets Reyes Cárdenas and Cecilio
García-Camarillo to produce the collection Get Your Tortillas
Together *in 1976. Since then she has published several volumes of*
poetry, including Curandera *in 1983,* Sonnets to Human Beings
in 1995, and Rebozos *in 2012. Tafolla has taught Mexican Ameri-*
can and women's studies in California and Texas, while also be-
coming, through her work as a university administrator and
consultant, and through her numerous speeches, an important
educational advocate for Mexican Americans. A 1985 book called
To Split a Human: Mitos, Machos y La Mujer Chicana *continues*
in prose Tafolla's effort to combat stereotypes about women and
Mexican Americans in the contemporary world. Tafolla has also
written several children's books, and she has often been seen on
the stage performing her one-woman show incorporating a variety
of community voices called With Our Very Own Names. *Tafolla's*
efforts were rewarded in 2015 when she was named Poet Laureate
of Texas.

  In the poems included here, as in much of her work, Tafolla
pays tribute to women of earlier generations for their individual-
ity, strength, and wisdom. In "Tía Sofía," Tafolla writes of a quirky

aunt, whose musical tastes and habits provide an alternative model
of a woman's life. "Curandera" is a lyrical tribute to a woman who
embodies the wisdom of the past, passing it down to the speaker
of the poem through her powerful presence.

As you read, try to think of the women in these poems passing
some bit of their own history down to Tafolla, who continues to
pass it on in her poems.

TÍA SOFÍA

Mi Tía° Sofía
sang the blues
at "A" Record Shop,
on the west side of downtown,
across from Solo-Serve's   5
Thursday coupon specials
she never missed.
    — "Cuatro yardas° de floral print cottons
    por solo° eighty-nine cents—fíjate nomás,° Sara,
    you'll never get it at that price anywhere else!"   10
    she says to her younger sister.
And "A" Record Shop
grows up the walls around her like vines
like the flowers and weeds and everything in her
green-thumb garden.   15
But here—
instead of cilantro and rosas°
and Príncipe Dormid—
it's a hundred odd and only 45's
10 years too late   20
that'll never be sold
even after she dies
and a dozen hit albums that crawl up the wall,
smiling cool pachuco°-young Sonny and the Sunglos,
The Latin Breed, Flaco Jiménez, Toby Torres,   25
and the Royal Jesters.

Tía: Aunt. **Cuatro yardas:** Four yards. **por solo:** For only. **fíjate nomás:**
Just think. **rosas:** Roses. **pachuco:** Tough Mexican American street character,
known for a distinctive way of speaking and dressing.

Also: Little Stevie Wonder.
And The Supremes.
She sings to pass the time
"Ah foun' mah thr*ee*-uhl   30
own Blueberry H*ee*-uhl."
She also likes "Lavender Blue."
It seems to be her color,
but *bright* — in a big-flowered cotton print
(from Solo-Serve.)   35

Tía Sofía speaks Tex-Mex
with Black English,
and *all* the latest slang.

Not like the other aunts —
Tía Ester, always at home,   40
        haciendo caldo,
        haciendo guiso,
        haciendo tortillas,°
        she never left the house
        except to go to church,   45
        braided her hair on top of her head
        and always said,
        "Todos los gringos se parecen."
        (All Anglos look alike.)
or Tía Anita — always teaching,   50
        smart, proper, decent,
Tía Sara, Tía Eloisa, Tía Febe —
all in church, always in church.
Sofía said, "Well, I play
Tennesee Ernie Ford and Mahalia Jackson   55
on Sunday mornings."
And she *did*,
and sang along,
never learning that only singing in church
"counted."   60
        She never made it through school either.
        Instead of Polish jokes,
        the family told Sofía jokes:
        "Remember that time at the lake, con° Sofía?
        —Sophie! Come out of the water! It's raining!   65

haciendo caldo . . . tortillas: Making soup, / making stew, / making tortillas.
con: With.

—¡No, me mojo! (I'll get wet!)"
Always a little embarrassed by her lack of wisdom,
    lack of piety.
After she died, they didn't know what to say.
Didn't feel quite right saying   70
"She's always been a good Christian."
So they praised the way
"siempre se arreglaba la cara,°"
"se cuidaba,°"
and the way she never "fooled around"   75
even though she could've
after Uncle Raymond died,
When she was still young.
(Only 71).

Funeral comes every 2 years in the family now   80
—just like the births did
60 to 80 years ago.
I remember a picture of a young flapper
with large eyes—Tía Sofía.
Between the tears   85
we bump into the coffin by accident,
and get scared
and start laughing.
It seems appropriate.
I also feel like singing   90
in a Black Tex-Mex
"Blueberry Hee-uhl."

CURANDERA°

Afuera de tu casa,
    entre la hierba buena y el anís
    estoy plantada.°

siempre se arreglaba la cara: She always made up her face. **se cuidaba:** She
took care of herself. **curandera:** Medicine woman with a wealth of traditional
knowledge. **Afuera de tu casa . . . :** Outside of your house / between the mint
and the anise / I am planted.

Vine aquí a verte,°
  a preguntar tus ojos tierra-grises°   5
   a escuchar tu voz mesquite seco°
    a observar tus manos sabi-siglos°
     a llevarme alguna hierba de una de tus botellas.°

        The smell of her kitchen and the sound
           of her chanclas°   10
        are almost within my sight. Her wisdom
        the secrets that age has let grow
        slowly
        in her window
        like a wild coffee-can-seeded plant of   15
           no name
        of no dignity or fuss
        beyond that
        of its own
        presence.   20

        Those aged clouded eyes have seen the
           bodies of the dead
        sink below the crust of red-dirt sand
        and felt the swelling stomach's gift
        emerge a blood-red man.   25

        Observing, sinking in thoughts,
        I have gone no further.
        At a distance that will not stand still.
        My feet stuck, rooting

        The gnarled and earthing fingers of her mind   30
          feel the current in my veins
           and see the twilit shapes within my bodycaverns

Curandera,
   te siento arrastrando tus chanclas por los arcos-portales
     de mis venas,°   35
   bajando los botes de tu sabiduría del gabinete
     de mi cabeza.°

Vine aquí a verte: I came here to see you. **a preguntar . . . :** To ask your earth-gray eyes. **a escuchar . . . :** To listen to your voice of dried mesquite. **a observar . . . :** To observe your hands that have known centuries. **a llevarme . . . :** To take an herb from one of your bottles. **chanclas:** Slippers. **te siento arrastrando . . . :** I feel you dragging your old shoes through the arched doorways of my veins. **bajando los botes . . . :** Taking out the jars of your wisdom from the cabinet of my head.

El perro aulla, el rocío me resfría,°
mis pies cementados en sus huellas,°
mis ojos mudos preguntando la luz de tu ventana.°   40
Tiemblo aquí en tu jardín,
entre la hierba buena y el anís.°

—El horno es terremoto dormido° . . .

En tus ollitas hierben ya

　　　　　las hojas   45

　　　　　de mis sueños.°

Reading

1. ("Tía Sofía") What kinds of music does Sofía listen to?

2. ("Tía Sofía") What does Sofía do on Sunday mornings? What about the "other aunts"?

3. ("Curandera") What are some of the characteristics of the curandera that are described in the poem?

Thinking Critically

1. ("Tía Sofía") What do you think is the attitude of the poem's speaker toward Tía Sofía?

2. ("Curandera") What imagery does Tafolla use to suggest that she has absorbed the knowledge of the curandera that she is watching?

3. Do the subjects of these poems have anything in common? How are they different from each other?

Connecting

1. Ultima in Rudolfo Anaya's *Bless Me, Ultima* (p. 162) is a curandera. Though you get only a brief glimpse of her in this anthology, does she seem reminiscent of the curandera you meet in Carmen Tafolla's poem? Explain, drawing on both texts.

El perro aulla . . . : The dog howls, the dew chills me.   **mis pies cementados en sus huellas:** My feet cemented in their tracks.   **mis ojos mudos . . . :** My eyes mute, questioning the light from your window.   **Tiemblo aquí . . . :** I tremble here in your garden / between the mint and the anise.   **El orno es terremoto dormido:** The oven is a sleeping earthquake.   **En tus ollitas . . . :** In your little pots, already boiling, are / the leaves / of my dreams.

Writing

1. Using examples from both of Tafolla's poems, write a brief essay about the characteristics of Tía Sofía and the curandera that you think the poet herself finds admirable. Support your claim with evidence from the texts. Does Tafolla convince you to admire these women?

Creating

1. **Retell a story told by an elder.** Carmen Tafolla is often inspired by the stories she's heard from people of earlier generations. Talk to a grandparent or someone of similar age, record a story they tell you, and then write a short poem based on the story and its teller.

23

GARY SOTO [b. 1952]

The Elements of San Joaquin • Where Were You When You First Heard of Air-Conditioning

From The Elements of San Joaquin [1977] AND A Natural Man [1999]

GENRE: POETRY

Poet and young adult novelist Gary Soto draws much of his inspiration from his home city of Fresno, the largest city in California's San Joaquin Valley and home to a substantial Mexican American community. As a young boy, Soto worked in the fields with his parents. He struggled through high school, later attending Fresno City College before transferring to California State University, Fresno, where he worked with the poet Philip Levine. After college he quickly found success as a poet, with his work appearing in The New Yorker *and in the 1977 collection* The Elements of San Joaquin. *Soto says of his writing that he hears "lines of poetry issue from the mouths of seemingly ordinary people. And, as a writer, my duty is not to make people perfect, particularly Mexican*

*Americans. I'm not a cheerleader. I'm one who provides portraits of people in the rush of life."** He has published several other books of poetry to wide acclaim, including* Tales of Sunlight *in 1978 and* Partly Cloudy *in 2009. In 1995 his* New and Selected Poems *was a finalist for the National Book Award. Soto has also written novels and numerous books of poetry and stories for children, including* Baseball in April, *published in 1990.*

Soto's native region figures prominently in both of the poems reprinted here. "The Elements of San Joaquin" is the title poem from his 1977 book and is dedicated to César Chávez, the iconic civil rights leader who fought to improve working conditions for farmworkers in California. In it, Soto writes of people who live exposed to both the harshness and the beauty of "the elements" in the San Joaquin Valley, California's agricultural heartland. "Where Were You When You First Heard of Air-Conditioning," from Soto's 1999 collection A Natural Man, *is a humorous but poignant look at the summer heat of Fresno and the fantasies of ice and wealth that it gives rise to.*

As you read these two poems, think about the people in them and how their environment shapes their experiences.

THE ELEMENTS OF SAN JOAQUIN

for César Chávez

Field

The wind sprays pale dirt into my mouth
The small, almost invisible scars
On my hands.

The pores in my throat and elbows
Have taken in a seed of dirt of their own.   5

After a day in the grape fields near Rolinda
A fine silt, washed by sweat,
Has settled into the lines
On my wrists and palms.

Already I am becoming the valley,   10
A soil that sprouts nothing.
For any of us.

*From Soto's homepage at http://www.garysoto.com/faq.html.

Wind

A dry wind over the valley
Peeled mountains, grain by grain,
To small slopes, loose dirt   15
Where red ants tunnel.

The wind strokes
The skulls and spines of cattle
To white dust, to nothing,

Covers the spiked tracks of beetles,   20
Of tumbleweed, of sparrows
That pecked the ground for insects.

Evenings, when I am in the yard weeding,
The wind picks up the breath of my armpits

Like dust, swirls it   25
Miles away

And drops it
On the ear of a rabid dog,
And I take on another life.

Wind

When you got up this morning the sun   30
Blazed an hour in the sky,

A lizard hid
Under the curled leaves of manzanita
And winked its dark lids.

Later, the sky grayed,   35
And the cold wind you breathed
Was moving under your skin and already far
From the small hives of your lungs.

Stars

At dusk the first stars appear.
Not one eager finger points toward them.   40
A little later the stars spread with the night
And an orange moon rises
To lead them, like a shepherd, toward dawn.

Sun

In June the sun is a bonnet of light
Coming up,   45
Little by little,
From behind a skyline of pine.

The pastures sway with fiddle-neck,
Tassels of foxtail.

At Piedra   50
A couple fish on the river's edge,
Their shadows deep against the water.
Above, in the stubbled slopes,
Cows climb down
As the heat rises   55
In a mist of blond locusts,
Returning to the valley.

Rain

When autumn rains flatten sycamore leaves,
The tiny volcanos of dirt
Ants raised around their holes,   60
I should be out of work.

My silverware and stack of plates will go unused
Like the old, my two good slacks
Will smother under a growth of lint
And smell of the old dust   65
That rises
When the closet door opens or closes.

The skin of my belly will tighten like a belt
And there will be no reason for pockets.

Harvest

East of the sun's slant, in the vineyard that never failed,   70
A wind crossed my face, moving the dust
And a portion of my voice a step closer to a new year.

The sky went black in the ninth hour of rolling trays,
And in the distance ropes of rain dropped to pull me
From the thick harvest that was not mine.   75

Fog

If you go to your window
You will notice a fog drifting in.

The sun is no stronger than a flashlight.
Not all the sweaters
Hung in closets all summer   80

Could soak up this mist. The fog:
A mouth nibbling everything to its origin,
Pomegranate trees, stolen bicycles,

The string of lights at a used-car lot,
A Pontiac with scorched valves.   85

In Fresno the fog is passing
The young thief prying a window screen,
Graying my hair that falls
And goes unfound, my fingerprints
Slowly growing a fur of dust—   90

One hundred years from now
There should be no reason to believe
I lived.

Daybreak

In this moment when the light starts up
In the east and rubs   95
The horizon until it catches fire,

We enter the fields to hoe,
Row after row, among the small flags of onion,
Waving off the dragonflies
That ladder the air.   100

And tears the onions raise
Do not begin in your eyes but in ours,
In the salt blown
From one blister into another;

They begin in knowing   105
You will never waken to bear
The hour timed to a heart beat,
The wind pressing us closer to the ground.

When the season ends,
And the onions are unplugged from their sleep,   110
We won't forget what you failed to see,
And nothing will heal
Under the rain's broken fingers.

WHERE WERE YOU WHEN YOU FIRST HEARD
OF AIR-CONDITIONING

How I wanted to befriend an ice cube,
Say, "My square amigo, don't leave me!
Tell me about Grandma Glacier."

How I wanted to shrink myself to the size of a fly
And sit on the lip of an ice tea.   5
I could careen around the rim,
My toes sweet with sugar.

How I wanted to hug a shiny, olive-black dolphin,
And say, "After the ice cube, you're my best friend."
That prankster, he'd blow water in my face,   10
Then cackle.

A Fresno summer. The lawns,
Green in shade, helped, but not much.
The sun rolled over us eight-to-five sinners,
We poor people paying one more time   15
Because we were easy targets.

The heat was a bully.
He spit on us first and then got us into headlocks.
Bored with our shine, he let go at night.

And at night the police circled the blocks,   20
Looking for trouble,
Or maybe a breeze that would bring on autumn.
The stars stole only so much heat from the asphalt.
Sprinklers sighed. Dogs panted.
Snails dragged their sludge toward the moonlight.   25

And we burros of hard labor?
Adults sat in the orange glow of a porchlight,
Reading Bibles. Was it Eygpt? Israel?
Why are boils rising on our faces and arms?
Where did we go wrong?   30

And me in swim trunks but no pool?
I turned the pages of *Better Homes and Gardens*.
Nice, I thought. Cool. Air-conditioning
Even in the toilet. A breeze up
Your butt when you just sat there.   35
O Alaska! O Tundra! O greedy Greenland
With more ice than it could use.
How the rich lived, how they whistled when they flushed,
The icy belt buckles clanging around their knees
As they raised their cool, dry-to-the-touch, jockeys.   40

Reading

1. ("The Elements of San Joaquin") What "elements" are named in the poem?

2. ("The Elements of San Joaquin") In this poem, what impact do the elements have on the individuals in the fields?

3. ("Where Were You . . .") In the poem, who or what is described as a bully?

4. ("Where Were You . . .") Where is the poem's narrator when he first hears of air-conditioning?

Thinking Critically

1. What are some possible meanings of the word *elements* in the title of "The Elements of San Joaquin"?

2. Does the poem "The Elements of San Joaquin" present a positive or negative vision of life in the San Joaquin Valley? What lines in the poem indicate this?

3. What lines or phrases in "Where Were You When You First Heard of Air-Conditioning" suggest that the people in it are poor?

Connecting

1. Like Soto's poem "The Elements of San Joaquin," Luis Valdez's play *Las Dos Caras del Patroncito* (p. 83) takes as its subject matter the life of the farmworker. How do the perspectives of Soto and Valdez relate to each other? In what ways do they differ?

Writing

1. In both poems, Soto writes about natural forces, such as heat and wind. Write a brief essay, using specific examples, about the relationship between people and these natural forces that is presented in the poems. Is it harmonious? Adversarial? Something else?

Creating

1. **Compose a visual essay on human work and natural elements.** In the two poems presented here, Gary Soto creates poetic images of people responding to the forces of nature in various ways. Create a photo essay or other visual work in which you capture people interacting with some of the forces Soto writes about, such as heat, fields, wind, stars, sun, or rain.

24

JUAN FELIPE HERRERA [b. 1948]

Exiles • Inside the Jacket

From Exile of Desire [1983] AND Facegames [1987]

GENRE: POETRY

Juan Felipe Herrera speaks of his childhood spent working in the fields as a wonderful source of inspiration for his highly successful career as a poet. After years moving around California as migrant farmworkers, Herrera's family settled in San Diego when he was 8 years old. Herrera's interest in theater was sparked by the Teatro Campesino of Luis Valdez (p. 82), which he saw perform while earning a degree in anthropology at UCLA. Herrera formed his own theater group and traveled to Mexico to study theatrical expressions among indigenous groups. After college he worked in arts advocacy in California and began his career as a poet with the publication of Rebozos of love we have woven sudor de pueblos on our backs *in 1972. Herrera earned master's degrees from Stanford and from the Iowa Writers' Workshop on his way to a professorship at the University of California, Riverside. He has published numerous books of poetry, including* Facegames *in 1987,* Mayan Drifter: Chicano Poet in the Lowlands of America *in 1997, and* Cinnamon Girl *in 2005. A collection of his poems from several decades was published in 2008 as* Half of the World in Light *and was awarded the National Book Critics Circle Award, and in 2015 he became the first Mexican American to be named the nation's Poet Laureate.*

Both "Exiles" and "Inside the Jacket" highlight the tenderness and lyrical quality of Herrera's poetry. He writes of the complicated emotions of his subjects caught between worlds and filled with memories and also of the feelings that come from observation of distance and of connection. "Exiles," with its epigraph from the creator of the iconic painting The Scream, *calls attention to the mysteries behind all these emotions.*

As you read, pay attention to the ways that Herrera captures complicated emotions with a few carefully chosen words and images.

EXILES

and I heard an unending scream piercing nature.
—*from the diary of* EDVARD MUNCH, *1892*

At the greyhound bus stations, at airports, at silent wharfs
the bodies exit the crafts. Women, men, children; cast out
from the new paradise.

They are not there in the homeland, in Argentina, not there
in Santiago, Chile; never there in Montevideo, Uruguay,   5
and they are not here

in *America*

They are in exile: a slow scream across a yellow bridge
the jaws stretched, widening, the eyes multiplied into blood
orbits, torn, whirling, spilling between two slopes; the sea, black,   10
swallowing all prayers, shadeless. Only tall faceless figures
of pain flutter across the bridge. They pace in charred suits,
the hands lift, point and ache and fly at sunset as cold dark
birds. They will hover over the dead ones: a family shattered
by military, buried by hunger, asleep now with the eyes burning   15
echoes calling *Joaquín, María, Andrea, Joaquín, Joaquín, Andrea,*

en exilio

From here we see them, we the ones from here, not there or across,
only here, without the bridge, without the arms as blue liquid

quenching the secret thirst of unmarked graves, without   20
our flesh journeying refuge or pilgrimage; not passengers
on imaginary ships sailing between reef and sky, we that die
here awake on Harrison Street, on Excelsior Avenue clutching
the tenderness of chrome radios, whispering to the saints
in supermarkets, motionless in the chasms of playgrounds,   25
searching at 9 a.m. from our third floor cells, bowing mute,
shoving the curtains with trembling speckled brown hands. Alone,
we look out to the wires, the summer, to the newspapers wound
in knots as matches for tenements. We that look out from
our miniature vestibules, peering out from our old clothes,   30
the father's well-sewn plaid shirt pocket, an old woman's
oversized wool sweater peering out from the makeshift kitchen.
We peer out to the streets, to the parades, we the ones from here
not there or across, from here, only here. Where is our exile?
Who has taken it?   35

INSIDE THE JACKET

I remember, many years ago,
a mexicano working in a sweat shop
on E Street by the library.

I could see him through the window—
a tailor by trade.   5

Thought about asking him
to make me a suit for graduation.

His fingers were so thin, so dark.

Usually, he labored on a sport coat.
Could tell the owner had granted him   10
privacy.

He seemed happy and at ease.
One evening, I passed by and gazed
at his finery; his project:

venom lacing   15
a serpent feverishly winding out of the earth
wrapping around the furniture, into the ceiling,

a gold lacing, swelling,

pouring out into the night,
an iridescent skin, leaping   20
out of his scarred hands,
spreading across the city.

Reading

1. ("Exiles") Who does the poem identify as exiles?

2. ("Inside the Jacket") What kind of work is being done by the man in the poem?

Thinking Critically

1. How does the epigraph of "Exiles" affect the meaning of the poem?

2. How would you describe the mood of "Exiles"? Does Herrera do anything to lessen its darkness?

3. What emotions do you think are felt by the *mexicano* of "Inside the Jacket" as he works?

Connecting

1. In spite of the differences in their situations, the individuals that Jimmy Santiago Baca writes about in his poem "Immigrants in Our Own Land" (p. 230) seem similar to the individuals in Herrera's poem "Exiles." What do the two groups have in common? Do the poets, in their work, make similar observations about these groups? Do Herrera and Baca have similar aims in their poems?

Writing

1. In "Exiles," Juan Felipe Herrera cultivates a particular tone, just as Edvard Munch might have done in one of his impressionistic paintings. Write a brief essay analyzing how Herrera achieves this tone. What words or images contribute the most to it?

Creating

1. **Create a visual image that connects with Herrera's work.** Juan Felipe Herrera's poem "Exiles" is partly inspired by the words of Edvard Munch, a painter, and it is full of visual description. Take a photograph or make a painting that you think captures the scene or the mood of either "Exiles" or "Inside the Jacket," and briefly explain the connections between poem and image.

25

RICHARD RODRIGUEZ [b. 1944]

Complexion

From Hunger of Memory [1982]

GENRE: MEMOIR

Thanks to his appearances on national television and the broad appeal of his writing, Richard Rodriguez has become one of the best-known Mexican American intellectuals in the country. His 1981 memoir Hunger of Memory: The Education of Richard Rodriguez *was a huge success, though it also made him a controversial figure in Chicano circles, since his stances against affirmative action and bilingual education were taken as indications of hostility toward Mexican American culture. For Rodriguez, as he writes in his memoir, success in school and public life went hand in hand with a devotion to the English language. The devotion to schooling and to language that he showed as a child in California carried him to Stanford University, then into graduate work on Renaissance literature at Columbia and Berkeley.* Hunger of Memory *launched his career as a writer and public figure. He has since written for many major magazines but is perhaps best known for his video essays on* PBS NewsHour. *His other books include the memoirs* Days of Obligation: An Argument with My Mexican Father *from 1992 and* Darling: A Spiritual Autobiography *from 2013, as well as a work of journalism,* Brown: The Last Discovery of America, *published in 2002.*

Rodriguez referred to Hunger of Memory *as a set of "essays impersonating an autobiography." "Complexion," as he suggests, is best read not as one person's story but as an essay in which Rodriguez reflects on the relationships between race, class, and identity.*

As you read, think about what defines the different groups of people that Rodriguez observes and about why he sometimes wants to become a part of them.

Visiting the East Coast or the gray capitals of Europe during the long months of winter, I often meet people at deluxe hotels who comment on my complexion. (In such hotels it appears nowadays a mark of leisure and wealth to have a complexion like mine.) Have I been skiing? In the Swiss Alps? Have I just returned from a Caribbean vacation? No. I say no softly but in a firm voice that intends to explain: My complexion is dark. (My skin is brown. More exactly, terra-cotta in sunlight, tawny in shade. I do not redden in sunlight. Instead, my skin becomes progressively dark; the sun singes the flesh.)

When I was a boy the white summer sun of Sacramento would darken me so, my T-shirt would seem bleached against my slender dark arms. My mother would see me come up the front steps. She'd wait for the screen door to slam at my back. "You look like a *negrito*,°" she'd say, angry, sorry to be angry, frustrated almost to laughing, scorn. "You know how important looks are in this country. With *los gringos*° looks are all that they judge on. But you! Look at you! You're so careless!" Then she'd start in all over again. "You won't be satisfied till you end up looking like *los pobres*° who work in the fields, *los braceros*."

(*Los braceros*: Those men who work with their *brazos*, their arms; Mexican nationals who were licensed to work for American farmers in the 1950s. They worked very hard for very little money, my father would tell me. And what money they earned they sent back to Mexico to support their families, my mother would add. *Los pobres*—the poor, the pitiful, the powerless ones. But paradoxically also powerful men. They were the men with brown-muscled arms I stared at in awe on Saturday mornings when they showed up downtown like gypsies to shop at Woolworth's or Penney's. On Monday nights they would gather hours early on the steps of the Memorial Auditorium for the wrestling matches. Passing by on my bicycle in summer, I would spy them there, clustered in small groups, talking—frightening and fascinating men—some wearing Texas *sombreros* and T-shirts which shone fluorescent in the twilight. I would sit forward in the back seat of our family's '48 Chevy to see them, working alongside Valley highways: dark men on an even horizon, loading a truck amid rows of straight green. Powerful, powerless men. Their fascinating darkness—like mine—to be feared.)

"You'll end up looking just like them."

---

negrito: Somewhat condescending term for a black person.   **los gringos:** Non-Mexicans, whites.   **los pobres:** The poor.

1

Regarding my family, I see faces that do not closely resemble my own. Like   5
some other Mexican families, my family suggests Mexico's confused colo-
nial past. Gathered around a table, we appear to be from separate conti-
nents. My father's face recalls faces I have seen in France. His complexion
is white—he does not tan; he does not burn. Over the years, his dark wavy
hair has grayed handsomely. But with time his face has sagged to a perpetual sigh. My mother, whose surname is inexplicably Irish— Moran—has
an olive complexion. People have frequently wondered if, perhaps, she is
Italian or Portuguese. And, in fact, she looks as though she could be from
southern Europe. My mother's face has not aged as quickly as the rest of
her body; it remains smooth and glowing—a cool tan—which her gray
hair cleanly accentuates. My older brother has inherited her good looks.
When he was a boy people would tell him that he looked like Mario Lanza,
and hearing it he would smile with dimpled assurance. He would come
home from high school with girl friends who seemed to me glamorous
(because they were) blonds. And during those years I envied him his skin
that burned red and peeled like the skin of the *gringos*. His complexion
never darkened like mine. My youngest sister is exotically pale, almost
ashen. She is delicately featured, Near Eastern, people have said. Only my
older sister has a complexion as dark as mine, though her facial features
are much less harshly defined than my own. To many people meeting her,
she seems (they say) Polynesian. I am the only one in the family whose
face is severely cut to the line of ancient Indian ancestors. My face is
mournfully long, in the classical Indian manner; my profile suggests one
of those beak-nosed Mayan sculptures—the eaglelike face upturned,
open-mouthed, against the deserted, primitive sky.

"We are Mexicans," my mother and father would say, and taught their
four children to say whenever we (often) were asked about our ancestry.
My mother and father scorned those "white" Mexican-Americans who
tried to pass themselves off as Spanish. My parents would never have
thought of denying their ancestry. I never denied it: My ancestry is Mexican, I told strangers mechanically. But I never forgot that only my older
sister's complexion was as dark as mine.

My older sister never spoke to me about her complexion when she was a
girl. But I guessed that she found her dark skin a burden. I knew that she
suffered for being a "nigger." As she came home from grammar school, little
boys came up behind her and pushed her down to the sidewalk. In high
school, she struggled in the adolescent competition for boyfriends in a
world of football games and proms, a world where her looks were plainly
uncommon. In college, she was afraid and scornful when dark-skinned

foreign students from countries like Turkey and India found her attractive. She revealed her fear of dark skin to me only in adulthood when, regarding her own three children, she quietly admitted relief that they were all light.

That is the kind of remark women in my family have often made before. As a boy, I'd stay in the kitchen (never seeming to attract any notice), listening while my aunts spoke of their pleasure at having light children. (The men, some of whom were dark-skinned from years of working out of doors, would be in another part of the house.) It was the woman's spoken concern: the fear of having a dark-skinned son or daughter. Remedies were exchanged. One aunt prescribed to her sisters the elixir of large doses of castor oil during the last weeks of pregnancy. (The remedy risked an abortion.) Children born dark grew up to have their faces treated regularly with a mixture of egg white and lemon juice concentrate. (In my case, the solution never would take.) One Mexican-American friend of my mother's, who regarded it a special blessing that she had a measure of English blood, spoke disparagingly of her husband, a construction worker, for being so dark. "He doesn't take care of himself," she complained. But the remark, I noticed, annoyed my mother, who sat tracing an invisible design with her finger on the tablecloth.

There was affection too and a kind of humor about these matters. With daring tenderness, one of my uncles would refer to his wife as *mi negra*. An aunt regularly called her dark child *mi feito* (my little ugly one), her smile only partially hidden as she bent down to dig her mouth under his ticklish chin. And at times relatives spoke scornfully of pale, white skin. A *gringo*'s skin resembled *masa*—baker's dough—someone remarked. Everyone laughed. Voices chuckled over the fact that the *gringos* spent so many hours in summer sunning themselves. ("They need to get sun because they look like *los muertos*.°")

I heard the laughing but remembered what the women had said, with   10 unsmiling voices, concerning dark skin. Nothing I heard outside the house, regarding my skin, was so impressive to me.

In public I occasionally heard racial slurs. Complete strangers would yell out at me. A teenager drove past, shouting, "Hey, Greaser! Hey, Pancho!" Over his shoulder I saw the giggling face of his girl friend. A boy pedaled by and announced matter-of-factly, "I pee on dirty Mexicans." Such remarks would be said so casually that I wouldn't quickly realize that they were being addressed to me. When I did, I would be paralyzed with embarrassment, unable to return the insult. (Those times I happened to be with white grammar school friends, *they* shouted back. Imbued with the mysterious kindness of children, my friends would never ask later why I hadn't yelled out in my own defense.)

los muertos: The dead.

In all, there could not have been more than a dozen incidents of name-calling. That there were so few suggests that I was not a primary victim of racial abuse. But that, even today, I can clearly remember particular incidents is proof of their impact. Because of such incidents, I listened when my parents remarked that Mexicans were often mistreated in California border towns. And in Texas. I listened carefully when I heard that two of my cousins had been refused admittance to an "all-white" swimming pool. And that an uncle had been told by some man to go back to Africa. I followed the progress of the southern black civil rights movement, which was gaining prominent notice in Sacramento's afternoon newspaper. But what most intrigued me was the connection between dark skin and poverty. Because I heard my mother speak so often about the relegation of dark people to menial labor, I considered the great victims of racism to be those who were poor and forced to do menial work. People like the farmworkers whose skin was dark from the sun.

After meeting a black grammar school friend of my sister's, I remember thinking that she wasn't really "black." What interested me was the fact that she wasn't poor. (Her well-dressed parents would come by after work to pick her up in a shiny green Oldsmobile.) By contrast, the garbage men who appeared every Friday morning seemed to me unmistakably black. (I didn't bother to ask my parents why Sacramento garbage men always were black. I thought I knew.) One morning I was in the backyard when a man opened the gate. He was an ugly, square-faced black man with popping red eyes, a pail slung over his shoulder. As he approached, I stood up. And in a voice that seemed to me very weak, I piped, "Hi." But the man paid me no heed. He strode past to the can by the garage. In a single broad movement, he overturned its contents into his larger pail. Our can came crashing down as he turned and left me watching, in awe.

"*Pobres negros,*°" my mother remarked when she'd notice a headline in the paper about a civil rights demonstration in the South. "How the *gringos* mistreat them." In the same tone of voice she'd tell me about the mistreatment her brother endured years before. (After my grandfather's death, my grandmother had come to America with her son and five daughters.) "My sisters, we were still all just teenagers. And since *mi papá* was dead, my brother had to be the head of the family. He had to support us, to find work. But what skills did he have! Twenty years old. *Pobre.* He was tall, like your grandfather. And strong. He did construction work. 'Construction!' The *gringos* kept him digging all day, doing the dirtiest jobs. And they would pay him next to nothing. Sometimes they promised him one salary and paid him less when he finished. But what could he

pobres negros: Those poor blacks.

do? Report them? We weren't citizens then. He didn't even know English. And he was dark. What chances could he have? As soon as we sisters got older, he went right back to Mexico. He hated this country. He looked so tired when he left. Already with a hunchback. Still in his twenties. But old-looking. No life for him here. *Pobre.*"

Dark skin was for my mother the most important symbol of a life of oppressive labor and poverty. But both my parents recognized other symbols as well.   15

My father noticed the feel of every hand he shook. (He'd smile sometimes—marvel more than scorn—remembering a man he'd met who had soft, uncalloused hands.)

My mother would grab a towel in the kitchen and rub my oily face sore when I came in from playing outside. "Clean the *grasa* off of your face!" (*Greaser!*)

Symbols: When my older sister, then in high school, asked my mother if she could do light housework in the afternoons for a rich lady we knew, my mother was frightened by the idea. For several weeks she troubled over it before granting conditional permission: "Just remember, you're not a maid. I don't want you wearing a uniform." My father echoed the same warning. Walking with him past a hotel, I watched as he stared at a doorman dressed like a Beefeater. "How can anyone let himself be dressed up like that? Like a clown. Don't you ever get a job where you have to put on a uniform." In summertime neighbors would ask me if I wanted to earn extra money by mowing their lawns. Again and again my mother worried: "Why did they ask *you*? Can't you find anything better?" Inevitably, she'd relent. She knew I needed the money. But I was instructed to work after dinner. ("When the sun's not so hot.") Even then, I'd have to wear a hat. *Un sombrero de* baseball.

(*Sombrero.* Watching gray cowboy movies, I'd brood over the meaning of the broad-rimmed hat—that troubling symbol—which comically distinguished a Mexican cowboy from real cowboys.)

From my father came no warnings concerning the sun. His fear was of dark factory jobs. He remembered too well his first jobs when he came to this country, not intending to stay, just to earn money enough to sail on to Australia. (In Mexico he had heard too many stories of discrimination in *los Estados Unidos*.° So it was Australia, that distant island-continent, that loomed in his imagination as his "America.") The work my father found in San Francisco was work for the unskilled. A factory job. Then a cannery job. (He'd remember the noise and the heat.) Then a job at a warehouse. (He'd remember the dark stench of old urine.) At one place   20

los Estados Unidos: The United States.

there were fistfights; at another a supervisor who hated Chinese and Mexicans. Nowhere a union.

His memory of himself in those years is held by those jobs. Never making money enough for passage to Australia; slowly giving up the plan of returning to school to resume his third-grade education—to become an engineer. My memory of him in those years, however, is lifted from photographs in the family album which show him on his honeymoon with my mother—the woman who had convinced him to stay in America. I have studied their photographs often, seeking to find in those figures some clear resemblance to the man and the woman I've known as my parents. But the youthful faces in the photos remain, behind dark glasses, shadowy figures anticipating my mother and father.

They are pictured on the grounds of the Coronado Hotel near San Diego, standing in the pale light of a winter afternoon. She is wearing slacks. Her hair falls seductively over one side of her face. He appears wearing a double-breasted suit, an unneeded raincoat draped over his arm. Another shows them standing together, solemnly staring ahead. Their shoulders barely are touching. There is to their pose an aristocratic formality, an elegant Latin hauteur.

The man in those pictures is the same man who was fascinated by Italian grand opera. I have never known just what my father saw in the spectacle, but he has told me that he would take my mother to the Opera House every Friday night—if he had money enough for orchestra seats. ("Why go to sit in the balcony?") On Sundays he'd don Italian silk scarves and a camel's hair coat to take his new wife to the polo matches in Golden Gate Park. But one weekend my father stopped going to the opera and polo matches. He would blame the change in his life on one job—a warehouse job, working for a large corporation which today advertises its products with the smiling faces of children. "They made me an old man before my time," he'd say to me many years later. Afterward, jobs got easier and cleaner. Eventually, in middle age, he got a job making false teeth. But his youth was spent at the warehouse. "Everything changed," his wife remembers. The dapper young man in the old photographs yielded to the man I saw after dinner: haggard, asleep on the sofa. During 'The Ed Sullivan Show' on Sunday nights, when Roberta Peters or Licia Albanese would appear on the tiny blue screen, his head would jerk up alert. He'd sit forward while the notes of Puccini sounded before him. ("Un bel dí.")

By the time they had a family, my parents no longer dressed in very fine clothes. Those symbols of great wealth and the reality of their lives too noisily clashed. No longer did they try to fit themselves, like paperdoll figures, behind trappings so foreign to their actual lives. My father no longer wore silk scarves or expensive wool suits. He sold his tuxedo to a secondhand store for five dollars. My mother sold her rabbit fur coat to the wife of a Spanish radio station disc jockey. ("It looks better on you than it does on me," she kept telling the lady until the sale was completed.) I was six years old at the time, but I recall watching the transaction with complete understanding. The woman I knew as my mother was already physically unlike the woman in her honeymoon photos. My mother's hair was short. Her shoulders were thick from carrying children. Her fingers were swollen red, toughened by housecleaning. Already my mother would admit to foreseeing herself in her own mother, a woman grown old, bald and bowlegged, after a hard lifetime of working.

In their manner, both my parents continued to respect the symbols of 25 what they considered to be upper-class life. Very early, they taught me the *propio*° way of eating *como los ricos*.° And I was carefully taught elaborate formulas of polite greeting and parting. The dark little boy would be invited by classmates to the rich houses on Forty-fourth and Forty-fifth streets. "How do you do?" or "I am very pleased to meet you," I would say, bowing slightly to the amused mothers of classmates. "Thank you very much for the dinner; it was very delicious."

I made an impression. I intended to make an impression, to be invited back. (I soon realized that the trick was to get the mother or father to notice me.) From those early days began my association with rich people, my fascination with their secret. My mother worried. She warned me not to come home expecting to have the things my friends possessed. But she needn't have said anything. When I went to the big houses, I remembered that I was, at best, a visitor to the world I saw there. For that reason, I was an especially watchful guest. I was my parents' child. Things most middle-class children wouldn't trouble to notice, I studied. Remembered to see: the starched black and white uniform worn by the maid who opened the door; the Mexican gardeners—their complexions as dark as my own. (One gardener's face, glassed by sweat, looked up to see me going inside.)

"Take Richard upstairs and show him your electric train," the mother said. But it was really the vast polished dining room table I'd come to appraise. Those nights when I was invited to stay for dinner, I'd notice that my friend's mother rang a small silver bell to tell the black woman when to bring in the food. The father, at his end of the table, ate while wearing his tie. When I was not required to speak, I'd skate the icy cut of crystal with my eye; my gaze would follow the golden threads etched onto the rim of china. With my mother's eyes I'd see my hostess's manicured nails and judge them to be marks of her leisure. Later, when my schoolmate's father would bid me goodnight, I would feel his soft fingers

propio: Proper.   **como los ricos:** Like rich people.

and palm when we shook hands. And turning to leave, I'd see my dark self, lit by chandelier light, in a tall hallway mirror.

2

Complexion. My first conscious experience of sexual excitement concerns my complexion. One summer weekend, when I was around seven years old, I was at a public swimming pool with the whole family. I remember sitting on the damp pavement next to the pool and seeing my mother, in the spectators' bleachers, holding my younger sister on her lap. My mother, I noticed, was watching my father as he stood on a diving board, waving to her. I watched her wave back. Then saw her radiant, bashful, astonishing smile. In that second I sensed that my mother and father had a relationship I knew nothing about. A nervous excitement encircled my stomach as I saw my mother's eyes follow my father's figure curving into the water. A second or two later, he emerged. I heard him call out. Smiling, his voice sounded, buoyant, calling me to swim to him. But turning to see him, I caught my mother's eye. I heard her shout over to me. In Spanish she called through the crowd: "Put a towel on over your shoulders." In public, she didn't want to say why. I knew.

That incident anticipates the shame and sexual inferiority I was to feel in later years because of my dark complexion. I was to grow up an ugly child. Or one who thought himself ugly. (*Feo.*) One night when I was eleven or twelve years old, I locked myself in the bathroom and carefully regarded my reflection in the mirror over the sink. Without any pleasure I studied my skin. I turned on the faucet. (In my mind I heard the swirling voices of aunts, and even my mother's voice, whispering, whispering incessantly about lemon juice solutions and dark, *feo* children.) With a bar of soap, I fashioned a thick ball of lather. I began soaping my arms. I took my father's straight razor out of the medicine cabinet. Slowly, with steady deliberateness, I put the blade against my flesh, pressed it as close as I could without cutting, and moved it up and down across my skin to see if I could get out, somehow lessen, the dark. All I succeeded in doing, however, was in shaving my arms bare of their hair. For as I noted with disappointment, the dark would not come out. It remained. Trapped. Deep in the cells of my skin.

Throughout adolescence, I felt myself mysteriously marked. Nothing 30 else about my appearance would concern me so much as the fact that my complexion was dark. My mother would say how sorry she was that there was not money enough to get braces to straighten my teeth. But I never bothered about my teeth. In three-way mirrors at department stores, I'd see my profile dramatically defined by a long nose, but it was really only the color of my skin that caught my attention.

I wasn't afraid that I would become a menial laborer because of my skin. Nor did my complexion make me feel especially vulnerable to racial abuse. (I didn't really consider my dark skin to be a racial characteristic. I would have been only too happy to look as Mexican as my light-skinned older brother.) Simply, I judged myself ugly. And, since the women in my family had been the ones who discussed it in such worried tones, I felt my dark skin made me unattractive to women.

Thirteen years old. Fourteen. In a grammar school art class, when the assignment was to draw a self-portrait, I tried and I tried but could not bring myself to shade in the face on the paper to anything like my actual tone. With disgust then I would come face to face with myself in mirrors. With disappointment I located myself in class photographs—my dark face undefined by the camera which had clearly described the white faces of classmates. Or I'd see my dark wrist against my long-sleeved white shirt.

I grew divorced from my body. Insecure, overweight, listless. On hot summer days when my rubber-soled shoes soaked up the heat from the sidewalk, I kept my head down. Or walked in the shade. My mother didn't need anymore to tell me to watch out for the sun. I denied myself a sensational life. The normal, extraordinary, animal excitement of feeling my body alive—riding shirtless on a bicycle in the warm wind created by furious self-propelled motion—the sensations that first had excited in me a sense of my maleness, I denied. I was too ashamed of my body. I wanted to forget that I had a body because I had a brown body. I was grateful that none of my classmates ever mentioned the fact.

I continued to see the *braceros*, those men I resembled in one way and, in another way, didn't resemble at all. On the watery horizon of a Valley afternoon, I'd see them. And though I feared looking like them, it was with silent envy that I regarded them still. I envied them their physical lives, their freedom to violate the taboo of the sun. Closer to home I would notice the shirtless construction workers, the roofers, the sweating men tarring the street in front of the house. And I'd see the Mexican gardeners. I was unwilling to admit the attraction of their lives. I tried to deny it by looking away. But what was denied became strongly desired.

In high school physical education classes, I withdrew, in the regular   35 company of five or six classmates, to a distant corner of a football field where we smoked and talked. Our company was composed of bodies too short or too tall, all graceless and all—except mine—pale. Our conversation was usually witty. (In fact we were intelligent.) If we referred to the athletic contests around us, it was with sarcasm. With savage scorn I'd refer to the "animals" playing football or baseball. It would have been important for me to have joined them. Or for me to have taken off my shirt, to have let the sun burn dark on my skin, and to have run barefoot on the warm wet grass. It would have been very important. Too important. It would have been too telling a gesture—to admit the desire for sensation, the body, my body.

Fifteen, sixteen. I was a teenager shy in the presence of girls. Never dated. Barely could talk to a girl without stammering. In high school I went to several dances, but I never managed to ask a girl to dance. So I stopped going. I cannot remember high school years now with the parade of typical images: bright drive-ins or gliding blue shadows of a Junior Prom. At home most weekend nights, I would pass evenings reading. Like those hidden, precocious adolescents who have no real-life sexual experiences, I read a great deal of romantic fiction. "You won't find it in your books," my brother would playfully taunt me as he prepared to go to a party by freezing the crest of the wave in his hair with sticky pomade. Through my reading, however, I developed a fabulous and sophisticated sexual imagination. At seventeen, I may not have known how to engage a girl in small talk, but I had read *Lady Chatterley's Lover*.

It annoyed me to hear my father's teasing: that I would never know what "real work" is; that my hands were so soft. I think I knew it was his way of admitting pleasure and pride in my academic success. But I didn't smile. My mother said she was glad her children were getting their educations and would not be pushed around like *los pobres*. I heard the remark ironically as a reminder of my separation from *los braceros*. At such times I suspected that education was making me effeminate. The odd thing, however, was that I did not judge my classmates so harshly. Nor did I consider my male teachers in high school effeminate. It was only myself I judged against some shadowy, mythical Mexican laborer—dark like me, yet very different.

Language was crucial. I knew that I had violated the ideal of the *macho* by becoming such a dedicated student of language and literature. *Machismo* was a word never exactly defined by the persons who used it. (It was best described in the "proper" behavior of men.) Women at home, nevertheless, would repeat the old Mexican dictum that a man should be *feo, fuerte, y formal*. "The three F's," my mother called them, smiling slyly. *Feo* I took to mean not literally ugly so much as ruggedly handsome. (When my mother and her sisters spent a loud, laughing afternoon determining ideal male good looks, they finally settled on the actor Gilbert Roland, who was neither too pretty nor ugly but had looks "like a man.") *Fuerte*, "strong," seemed to mean not physical strength as much as inner strength, character. A dependable man is *fuerte*. *Fuerte* for that reason was a characteristic subsumed by the last of the three qualities, and the one I most often considered—*formal*. To be *formal* is to be steady. A man of responsibility, a good provider. Someone *formal* is also constant. A person to be relied upon in adversity. A sober man, a man of high seriousness.

I learned a great deal about being *formal* just by listening to the way my father and other male relatives of his generation spoke. A man was not silent necessarily. Nor was he limited in the tones he could sound. For example, he could tell a long, involved, humorous story and laugh at his own humor with high-pitched giggling. But a man was not talkative the way a woman could be. It was permitted a woman to be gossipy and chatty. (When one heard many voices in a room, it was usually women who were talking.) Men spoke much less rapidly. And often men spoke in monologues. (When one voice sounded in a crowded room, it was most often a man's voice one heard.) More important than any of this was the fact that a man never verbally revealed his emotions. Men did not speak about their unease in moments of crisis or danger. It was the woman who worried aloud when her husband got laid off from work. At times of illness or death in the family, a man was usually quiet, even silent. Women spoke up to voice prayers. In distress, women always sounded quick ejaculations to God or the Virgin; women prayed in clearly audible voices at a wake held in a funeral parlor. And on the subject of love, a woman was verbally expansive. She spoke of her yearning and delight. A married man, if he spoke publicly about love, usually did so with playful, mischievous irony. Younger, unmarried men more often were quiet. (The *macho* is a silent suitor. *Formal.*)

At home I was quiet, so perhaps I seemed *formal* to my relations and   40 other Spanish-speaking visitors to the house. But outside the house—my God!—I talked. Particularly in class or alone with my teachers, I chattered. (Talking seemed to make teachers think I was bright.) I often was proud of my way with words. Though, on other occasions, for example, when I would hear my mother busily speaking to women, it would occur to me that my attachment to words made me like her. Her son. Not *formal* like my father. At such times I even suspected that my nostalgia for sounds—the noisy, intimate Spanish sounds of my past—was nothing more than effeminate yearning.

High school English teachers encouraged me to describe very personal feelings in words. Poems and short stories I wrote, expressing sorrow and loneliness, were awarded high grades. In my bedroom were books by poets and novelists—books that I loved—in which male writers published feelings the men in my family never revealed or acknowledged in words. And it seemed to me that there was something unmanly about my attachment to literature. Even today, when so much about the myth of the *macho* no longer concerns me, I cannot altogether evade such notions. Writing these pages, admitting my embarrassment or my guilt, admitting my sexual anxieties and my physical insecurity, I have not been able to forget that I am not being *formal.*

So be it.

3

I went to college at Stanford, attracted partly by its academic reputation, partly because it was the school rich people went to. I found myself on a campus with golden children of western America's upper middle class. Many were students both ambitious for academic success *and* accustomed to leisured life in the sun. In the afternoon, they lay spread out, sunbathing in front of the library, reading Swift or Engels or Beckett. Others went by in convertibles, off to play tennis or ride horses or sail. Beach boys dressed in tank-tops and shorts were my classmates in undergraduate seminars. Tall tan girls wearing white strapless dresses sat directly in front of me in lecture rooms. I'd study them, their physical confidence. I was still recognizably kin to the boy I had been. Less tortured perhaps. But still kin. At Stanford, it's true, I began to have something like a conventional sexual life. I don't think, however, that I really believed that the women I knew found me physically appealing. I continued to stay out of the sun. I didn't linger in mirrors. And I was the student at Stanford who remembered to notice the Mexican-American janitors and gardeners working on campus.

It was at Stanford, one day near the end of my senior year, that a friend told me about a summer construction job he knew was available. I was quickly alert. Desire uncoiled within me. My friend said that he knew I had been looking for summer employment. He knew I needed some money. Almost apologetically he explained: It was something I probably wouldn't be interested in, but a friend of his, a contractor, needed someone for the summer to do menial jobs. There would be lots of shoveling and raking and sweeping. Nothing too hard. But nothing more interesting either. Still, the pay would be good. Did I want it? Or did I know someone who did?

I did. Yes, I said, surprised to hear myself say it.   45

In the weeks following, friends cautioned that I had no idea how hard physical labor really is. ("You only *think* you know what it is like to shovel for eight hours straight.") Their objections seemed to me challenges. They resolved the issue. I became happy with my plan. I decided, however, not to tell my parents. I wouldn't tell my mother because I could guess her worried reaction. I would tell my father only after the summer was over, when I could announce that, after all, I did know what "real work" is like.

The day I met the contractor (a Princeton graduate, it turned out), he asked me whether I had done any physical labor before. "In high school, during the summer," I lied. And although he seemed to regard me with skepticism, he decided to give me a try. Several days later, expectant, I arrived at my first construction site. I would take off my shirt to the sun. And at last grasp desired sensation. No longer afraid. At last become like a *bracero*. "We need those tree stumps out of here by tomorrow," the contractor said. I started to work.

I labored with excitement that first morning—and all the days after. The work was harder than I could have expected. But it was never as tedious as my friends had warned me it would be. There was too much physical pleasure in the labor. Especially early in the day, I would be most alert to the sensations of movement and straining. Beginning around seven each morning (when the air was still damp but the scent of weeds and dry earth anticipated the heat of the sun), I would feel my body resist the first thrusts of the shovel. My arms, tightened by sleep, would gradually loosen; after only several minutes, sweat would gather in beads on my forehead and then—a short while later—I would feel my chest silky with sweat in the breeze. I would return to my work. A nervous spark of pain would fly up my arm and settle to burn like an ember in the thick of my shoulder. An hour, two passed. Three. My whole body would assume regular movements; my shoveling would be described by identical, even movements. Even later in the day, my enthusiasm for primitive sensation would survive the heat and the dust and the insects pricking my back. I would strain wildly for sensation as the day came to a close. At three-thirty, quitting time, I would stand upright and slowly let my head fall back, luxuriating in the feeling of tightness relieved.

Some of the men working nearby would watch me and laugh. Two or three of the older men took the trouble to teach me the right way to use a pick, the correct way to shovel. "You're doing it wrong, too fucking hard," one man scolded. Then proceeded to show me—what persons who work with their bodies all their lives quickly learn—the most economical way to use one's body in labor.

"Don't make your back do so much work," he instructed. I stood impa- 50
tiently listening, half listening, vaguely watching, then noticed his work-thickened fingers clutching the shovel. I was annoyed. I wanted to tell him that I enjoyed shoveling the wrong way. And I didn't want to learn the right way. I wasn't afraid of back pain. I liked the way my body felt sore at the end of the day.

I was about to, but, as it turned out, I didn't say a thing. Rather it was at that moment I realized that I was fooling myself if I expected a few weeks of labor to gain me admission to the world of the laborer. I would not learn in three months what my father had meant by "real work." I was not bound to this job; I could imagine its rapid conclusion. For me the sensations of exertion and fatigue could be savored. For my father or uncle, working at comparable jobs when they were my age, such sensations were to be feared. Fatigue took a different toll on their bodies—and minds.

It was, I know, a simple insight. But it was with this realization that I took my first step that summer toward realizing something even more important about the "worker." In the company of carpenters, electricians, plumbers, and painters at lunch, I would often sit quietly, observant. I was not shy in such company. I felt easy, pleased by the knowledge that I was casually accepted, my presence taken for granted by men (exotics) who worked with their hands. Some days the younger men would talk and talk about sex, and they would howl at women who drove by in cars. Other days the talk at lunchtime was subdued; men gathered in separate groups. It depended on who was around. There were rough, good-natured workers. Others were quiet. The more I remember that summer, the more I realize that there was no single *type* of worker. I am embarrassed to say I had not expected such diversity. I certainly had not expected to meet, for example, a plumber who was an abstract painter in his off hours and admired the work of Mark Rothko. Nor did I expect to meet so many workers with college diplomas. (They were the ones who were not surprised that I intended to enter graduate school in the fall.) I suppose what I really want to say here is painfully obvious, but I must say it nevertheless: The men of that summer were middle-class Americans. They certainly didn't constitute an oppressed society. Carefully completing their work sheets; talking about the fortunes of local football teams; planning Las Vegas vacations; comparing the gas mileage of various makes of campers—they were not *los pobres* my mother had spoken about.

On two occasions, the contractor hired a group of Mexican aliens. They were employed to cut down some trees and haul off debris. In all, there were six men of varying age. The youngest in his late twenties; the oldest (his father?) perhaps sixty years old. They came and they left in a single old truck. Anonymous men. They were never introduced to the other men at the site. Immediately upon their arrival, they would follow the contractor's directions, start working—rarely resting—seemingly driven by a fatalistic sense that work which had to be done was best done as quickly as possible.

I watched them sometimes. Perhaps they watched me. The only time I saw them pay me much notice was one day at lunchtime when I was laughing with the other men. The Mexicans sat apart when they ate, just as they worked by themselves. Quiet. I rarely heard them say much to each other. All I could hear were their voices calling out sharply to one another, giving directions. Otherwise, when they stood briefly resting, they talked among themselves in voices too hard to overhear.

The contractor knew enough Spanish, and the Mexicans—or at least 55 the oldest of them, their spokesman—seemed to know enough English to communicate. But because I was around, the contractor decided one day to make me his translator. (He assumed I could speak Spanish.) I did what I was told. Shyly I went over to tell the Mexicans that the *patrón*° wanted them to do something else before they left for the day. As I started to speak, I was afraid with my old fear that I would be unable to pronounce the Spanish words. But it was a simple instruction I had to convey. I could say it in phrases.

The dark sweating faces turned toward me as I spoke. They stopped their work to hear me. Each nodded in response. I stood there. I wanted to say something more. But what could I say in Spanish, even if I could have pronounced the words right? Perhaps I just wanted to engage them in small talk, to be assured of their confidence, our familiarity. I thought for a moment to ask them where in Mexico they were from. Something like that. And maybe I wanted to tell them (a lie, if need be) that my parents were from the same part of Mexico.

I stood there.

Their faces watched me. The eyes of the man directly in front of me moved slowly over my shoulder, and I turned to follow his glance toward *el patrón* some distance away. For a moment I felt swept up by that glance into the Mexicans' company. But then I heard one of them returning to work. And then the others went back to work. I left them without saying anything more.

When they had finished, the contractor went over to pay them in cash. (He later told me that he paid them collectively—"for the job," though he wouldn't tell me their wages. He said something quickly about the good rate of exchange "in their own country.") I can still hear the loudly confident voice he used with the Mexicans. It was the sound of the *gringo* I had heard as a very young boy. And I can still hear the quiet, indistinct sounds of the Mexican, the oldest, who replied. At hearing that voice I was sad for the Mexicans. Depressed by their vulnerability. Angry at myself. The adventure of the summer seemed suddenly ludicrous. I would not shorten the distance I felt from *los pobres* with a few weeks of physical labor. I would not become like them. They were different from me.

After that summer, a great deal—and not very much really—changed in 60 my life. The curse of physical shame was broken by the sun; I was no longer ashamed of my body. No longer would I deny myself the pleasing sensations of my maleness. During those years when middle-class black Americans began to assert with pride, "Black is beautiful," I was able to

patrón: Boss.

regard my complexion without shame. I am today darker than I ever was as a boy. I have taken up the middle-class sport of long-distance running. Nearly every day now I run ten or fifteen miles, barely clothed, my skin exposed to the California winter rain and wind or the summer sun of late afternoon. The torso, the soccer player's calves and thighs, the arms of the twenty-year-old I never was, I possess now in my thirties. I study the youthful parody shape in the mirror: the stomach lipped tight by muscle; the shoulders rounded by chin-ups; the arms veined strong. This man. A man. I meet him. He laughs to see me, what I have become.

The dandy. I wear double-breasted Italian suits and custom-made English shoes. I resemble no one so much as my father—the man pictured in those honeymoon photos. At that point in life when he abandoned the dandy's posture, I assume it. At the point when my parents would not consider going on vacation, I register at the Hotel Carlyle in New York and the Plaza Athenée in Paris. I am as taken by the symbols of leisure and wealth as they were. For my parents, however, those symbols became taunts, reminders of all they could not achieve in one lifetime. For me those same symbols are reassuring reminders of public success. I tempt vulgarity to be reassured. I am filled with the gaudy delight, the monstrous grace of the nouveau riche.

In recent years I have had occasion to lecture in ghetto high schools. There I see students of remarkable style and physical grace. (One can see more dandies in such schools than one ever will find in middle-class high schools.) There is not the look of casual assurance I saw students at Stanford display. Ghetto girls mimic high-fashion models. Their dresses are of bold, forceful color; their figures elegant, long; the stance theatrical. Boys wear shirts that grip at their overdeveloped muscular bodies. (Against a powerless future, they engage images of strength.) Bad nutrition does not yet tell. Great disappointment, fatal to youth, awaits them still. For the moment, movements in school hallways are dancelike, a procession of postures in a sexual masque. Watching them, I feel a kind of envy. I wonder how different my adolescence would have been had I been free. . . . But no, it is my parents I see—their optimism during those years when they were entertained by Italian grand opera.

The registration clerk in London wonders if I have just been to Switzerland. And the man who carries my luggage in New York guesses the Caribbean. My complexion becomes a mark of my leisure. Yet no one would regard my complexion the same way if I entered such hotels through the service entrance. That is only to say that my complexion assumes its significance from the context of my life. My skin, in itself, means nothing. I stress the point because I know there are people who would label me "disadvantaged" because of my color. They make the same mistake I made as a boy, when I thought a disadvantaged life was cir-cumscribed by particular occupations. That summer I worked in the sun may have made me physically indistinguishable from the Mexicans working nearby. (My skin was actually darker because, unlike them, I worked without wearing a shirt. By late August my hands were probably as tough as theirs.) But I was not one of *los pobres*. What made me differ-ent from them was an attitude of *mind*, my imagination of myself.

I do not blame my mother for warning me away from the sun when I was young. In a world where her brother had become an old man in his twenties because he was dark, my complexion was something to worry about. "Don't run in the sun," she warns me today. I run. In the end, my father was right—though perhaps he did not know how right or why—to say that I would never know what real work is. I will never know what he felt at his last factory job. If tomorrow I worked at some kind of factory, it would go differently for me. My long education would favor me. I could act as a public person—able to defend my interests, to unionize, to petition, to speak up—to challenge and demand. (I will never know what real work is.) I will never know what the Mexicans knew, gathering their shovels and ladders and saws.

Their silence stays with me now. The wages those Mexicans received 65 for their labor were only a measure of their disadvantaged condition. Their silence is more telling. They lack a public identity. They remain profoundly alien. Persons apart. People lacking a union obviously, people without grounds. They depend upon the relative good will or fairness of their employers each day. For such people, lacking a better alternative, it is not such an unreasonable risk.

Their silence stays with me. I have taken these many words to describe its impact. Only: the quiet. Something uncanny about it. Its compliance. Vulnerability. Pathos. As I heard their truck rumbling away, I shuddered, my face mirrored with sweat. I had finally come face to face with *los pobres*.

Reading

1. Why do Rodriguez's parents worry about his skin getting dark?

2. According to Rodriguez's mother, what characteristics are possessed by the ideal man?

Thinking Critically

1. How would you describe Rodriguez's attitude toward his parents?

2. Do you think Rodriguez's attempt to become a laborer was doomed? Why or why not?

Connecting

1. Michele Serros writes autobiographically in her book *How to Be a Chicana Role Model* (p. 441), yet her writing is very different from that of Rodriguez. How would you describe the difference between them? Which one of them is easier for you to relate to? Why?

Writing

1. In "Complexion," Richard Rodriguez writes about the relationship between skin color and class, in particular, between dark skin and poverty. What does Rodriguez learn about this relationship? Using examples from the text, write an essay exploring Rodriguez's arguments about this relationship, paying attention to the ways in which it can be quite complicated.

Creating

1. **Write a brief memoir, focusing on a theme.** As you can see in this selection, a memoir or an autobiography is more than a recounting of the events of one's life. Using Rodriguez's writing as a model, write a memoir of a period of your life, looking, like he does, for broad themes or questions that your story presents.

26

LORNA DEE CERVANTES [b. 1954]

Poem for the Young White Man Who Asked Me How I, an Intelligent, Well-Read Person Could Believe in the War between Races • A Chicano Poem

From Emplumada [1981] AND Huizache [2012]

GENRE: POETRY

Lorna Dee Cervantes developed her love of poetry at a very early age and credits her reading of Pablo Neruda and African American poets, including Alice Walker and Maya Angelou, with awakening her to the issues of class and oppression that would become an important part of her poetry. Cervantes, of Mexican and Chumash heritage, was born in San Francisco and raised in San Jose's "Horseshoe" barrio. As a teenager she was involved with the Chicano, American Indian, and women's rights movements and put her college career temporarily on hold to create Mango Press, which published Chicano and Chicana writers. She also went on tour with a teatro group, out of which grew her first experiences reading her own poetry. Cervantes calls her identification as a Chicana writer "a strategy insofar as I take something that could be a negative thing, a stigma, and turn it into a positive so that it becomes a power, a force of self-definition." For her, "the very fact I am writing as a Chicana writer is a political act in itself."* In 1981 her first book of poetry, Emplumada, *was published and won the American Book Award the following year. Cervantes returned to San Jose State University to complete her bachelor's degree, and, following the tragic death of her mother, she began studying the roots of violence in the History of Consciousness Program at the University of California, Santa Cruz, earning her Ph.D. in 1990. Her return to poetry came with* From the Cables of Genocide *in 1991, and she has since published several more books of poetry,*

*From an interview in Karin Rosa Ikas, *Chicana Ways.*

most recently Ciento: 100 100-Word Love Poems. *Until 2007, Cervantes was the longtime director of the creative writing program at the University of Colorado, Boulder.*

The two poems presented here raise questions about the relationship between poetry and politics, suggesting that poets do not necessarily become political by choice, but become so because of a sharp awareness of reality. "Poem for the Young White Man . . ." comes from her first book and juxtaposes the poet's idealism with a feeling of being under attack. "A Chicano Poem," written decades later, connects that feeling to historical incidents of war and destruction perpetrated against Indians and Mexican Americans.

As you read, pay attention to how Cervantes carefully chooses words and images to comment on issues of race, power, and violence.

POEM FOR THE YOUNG WHITE MAN
WHO ASKED ME HOW I, AN INTELLIGENT,
WELL-READ PERSON COULD BELIEVE
IN THE WAR BETWEEN RACES

In my land there are no distinctions.
The barbed wire politics of oppression
have been torn down long ago. The only reminder
of past battles, lost or won, is a slight
rutting in the fertile fields.   5

In my land
people write poems about love,
full of nothing but contented childlike syllables.
Everyone reads Russian short stories and weeps.
There are no boundaries.   10
There is no hunger, no
complicated famine or greed.

I am not a revolutionary.
I don't even like political poems.
Do you think I can believe in a war between races?   15
I can deny it. I can forget about it
when I'm safe,
living on my own continent of harmony
and home, but I am not
there.   20

I believe in revolution
because everywhere the crosses are burning,
sharp-shooting goose-steppers round every corner,
there are snipers in the schools . . .
(I know you don't believe this.   25
You think this is nothing
but faddish exaggeration. But they
are not shooting at you.)

I'm marked by the color of my skin.
The bullets are discrete and designed to kill slowly.   30
They are aiming at my children.
These are facts.
Let me show you my wounds: my stumbling mind, my
"excuse me" tongue, and this
nagging preoccupation   35
with the feeling of not being good enough.

These bullets bury deeper than logic.
Racism is not intellectual.
I can not reason these scars away.

Outside my door   40
there is a real enemy
who hates me.

I am a poet
who yearns to dance on rooftops,
to whisper delicate lines about joy   45
and the blessings of human understanding.
I try. I go to my land, my tower of words and
bolt the door, but the typewriter doesn't fade out
the sounds of blasting and muffled outrage.
My own days bring me slaps on the face.   50
Every day I am deluged with reminders
that this is not
my land

and this is my land.

I do not believe in the war between races   55

but in this country
there is war.

A CHICANO POEM

They tried to take our words,
Steal away our hearts under
Their imaginary shawls, their laws,
Their libros,° their *Líbranos, Señor.*°
No more. They tried to take   5
Away our Spirit in the Rock, the Mountain,
The Living Waters. They tried to steal
Our languages, our grandmothers' pacts,
Our magna cartas for their own serfs.
They razed the land and raised a Constitution,   10
Declared others 3/5ths a human being,
Snapped shackles, cut off a foot,
Raped our grandmothers into near mute
Oblivion. They burned the sacred codices
And the molten goddesses rose anew   15
In their flames. They tried to silence a
Nation, tried to send The People back
To the Four Corners of the world. They drew
A line in the sand and dared us to cross it,
Tried to peel off our skins, Xipe Totec   20
Screaming through our indigenous consciousness.
They tried to brand "America" into our unread
Flesh, the skull and crossbones flying at
Half-mast. They tried to put their eggs in
Our baskets, tried to weave the Native   25
Out of us with their drink and drugs, tried to
Switch their mammy-raised offspring, beaded and
Unshaven, as the colorless pea under our mattresses
In a cultural bait and switch, hook and bait.
They tried to take our words,   30
Give us the Spanish translation for
"Pain," serve us the host of fallow fields on a
China plate, stripped us of the germ and seed,
Fed us in a steady diet of disease and famine.
Where is the word for tomorrow to the dead?   35
When is our kingdom come? They claim our
Reclamations; our reparations, a thing of our
Imaginations. I discover this truth
To be self-evident: In the beginning

libros: Books.   **Líbranos, Señor:** Free us, Lord.

We were here.   40
I declare us here today
And speaking.

Reading

1. ("Poem for the Young White Man . . .") Who does the speaker feel is the target of the "sharp-shooting goose-steppers" (line 23)?

2. ("A Chicano Poem") What are some of the terrible actions described in this poem?

Thinking Critically

1. What land does the speaker call "my land" in "Poem for the Young White Man . . ."?

2. Why does the narrator of "Poem for the Young White Man . . ." say first, "I am not a revolutionary" (line 13), and then in the next stanza, "I believe in revolution" (21)?

3. What do you think is Cervantes's purpose in writing "A Chicano Poem"? Who do you think it's addressed to?

Connecting

1. In its use of historical imagery to define an identity, Lorna Dee Cervantes's "A Chicano Poem" is highly reminiscent of Corky Gonzales's poem "I Am Joaquín" (p. 63). Do the two poets have similar goals for their poetry? In what ways are the poems different? Explain, drawing on specific lines in the poems.

Writing

1. In Cervantes's "Poem for the Young White Man . . ." the narrator declares "I don't even like political poems" (line 14). What do you think this means? Are "Poem for the Young White Man . . ." and "A Chicano Poem" themselves "political poems"? Using specific examples from the poems, write an essay in which you discuss what defines a "political poem" and whether you think your definition applies to these poems.

Creating

1. **Respond to a surprising question.** The very long title "Poem for the Young White Man Who Asked Me How I, an Intelligent, Well-Read Person Could Believe in the War between Races" accurately describes the origin of the poem. Write a poem in response to a question you've been

asked, perhaps during a debate or disagreement, that surprised and upset you in some way. In your poem—in both the title and the body of the work—make clear how different your view (or that of your poem's narrator) is from that of the inquirer.

27

JIMMY SANTIAGO BACA [b. 1952]

Immigrants in Our Own Land • I Will Remain

From Immigrants in Our Own Land [1979]

GENRE: POETRY

Jimmy Santiago Baca was born in Santa Fe, New Mexico, but his literary career began while he was in an Arizona prison. He had been abandoned by his parents while very young, and he later ran away from the orphanage he was raised in. A conviction on drug charges took him to maximum security prison, and while there he earned a GED and began writing poetry, which was initially published in Arizona in chapbook form. Denise Levertov also had his work published in Mother Jones *and helped him get a contract for his first major collection. Both* Baca *and* Immigrants in Our Own Land *were released in 1979, marking the start of his very successful career. Since earning a bachelor's degree from the University of New Mexico in 1984, Baca has written in several genres. The poetry of* Martín *and* Meditations on the South Valley, *published in 1987, was followed by* A Place to Stand: The Making of a Poet, *a memoir covering his time in prison, in 2001. His books of poetry include* Black Mesa Poems, *published in 1989, and* C-Train (Dream Boy's Story) *and* Thirteen Mexicans *from 2002, and he coproduced and cowrote the screenplay for the 1993 film* Blood In, Blood Out, *a film about gang life in Los Angeles. Baca is also an outspoken advocate for prisoners and those with drug-related problems, and he often hosts writing workshops for convicts and at-risk youths.*

"Immigrants in Our Own Land" and "I Will Remain" come from his first collection of poems and were written while he was in prison.

Though the poems show clearly the differences between prison and freedom, they also show an awareness of the continuities between life on the inside and on the outside.

As you read these examples of *pinto* poetry, look for ways that Baca sees hope in difficult surroundings. How do the poems, though they originate in prison, achieve universal relevance?

IMMIGRANTS IN OUR OWN LAND

We are born with dreams in our hearts,
looking for better days ahead.
At the gates we are given new papers,
our old clothes are taken
and we are given overalls like mechanics wear.   5
We are given shots and doctors ask questions.
Then we gather in another room
where counselors orient us to the new land
we will now live in. We take tests.
Some of us were craftsmen in the old world,   10
good with our hands and proud of our work.
Others were good with their heads.
They used common sense like scholars
use glasses and books to reach the world.
But most of us didn't finish high school.   15

The old men who have lived here stare at us,
from deep disturbed eyes, sulking, retreated.
We pass them as they stand around idle,
leaning on shovels and rakes or against walls.
Our expectations are high: in the old world,   20
they talked about rehabilitation,
about being able to finish school,
and learning an extra good trade.
But right away we are sent to work as dishwashers,
to work in fields for three cents an hour.   25
The administration says this is temporary
So we go about our business, blacks with blacks,
poor whites with poor whites,
chicanos and indians by themselves.
The administration says this is right,   30

no mixing of cultures, let them stay apart,
like in the old neighborhoods we came from.

We came here to get away from false promises,
from dictators in our neighborhoods,
who wore blue suits and broke our doors down   35
when they wanted, arrested us when they felt like,
swinging clubs and shooting guns as they pleased.
But it's no different here. It's all concentrated.
The doctors don't care, our bodies decay,
our minds deteriorate, we learn nothing of value.   40
Our lives don't get better, we go down quick.

My cell is crisscrossed with laundry lines,
my T-shirts, boxer shorts, socks and pants are drying.
Just like it used to be in my neighborhood:
from all the tenements laundry hung window to window.   45
Across the way Joey is sticking his hands
through the bars to hand Felipe a cigarette,
men are hollering back and forth cell to cell,
saying their sinks don't work,
or somebody downstairs hollers angrily   50
about a toilet overflowing,
or that the heaters don't work.

I ask Coyote next door to shoot me over
a little more soap to finish my laundry.
I look down and see new immigrants coming in,   55
mattresses rolled up and on their shoulders,
new haircuts and brogan boots,
looking around, each with a dream in their heart,
thinking they'll get a chance to change their lives.

But in the end, some will just sit around   60
talking about how good the old world was.
Some of the younger ones will become gangsters.
Some will die and others will go on living
without a soul, a future, or a reason to live.
Some will make it out of here with hate in their eyes,   65
but so very few make it out of here as human
as they came in, they leave wondering what good they are now
as they look at their hands so long away from their tools,
as they look at themselves, so long gone from their families,
so long gone from life itself, so many things have changed.   70

I WILL REMAIN

To Tello Hinojosa (xinoxosa)

I don't want to leave any more or get transferred
    to another prison because this one is too tough.
I am after a path you cannot find by looking at green fields,
    smelling high mountain air that is clear and sweetly
Odorous as when you fall in love again and again and again.   5
I am looking for a path that weaves through rock
    and swims through despair with fins of wisdom.
A wisdom to see me through this nightmare,
    not by running from it; by staying to deal blow for blow.
I will take the strength I need from me,   10
    not from fields or new friends. With my old friends
    fighting!
Bleeding! Calling me crazy! And never getting the respect I desire,
    fighting for each inch of it. . . .
I am not one of those beautiful people,   15
    but one of the old ones, a commoner of the world
You can find in taverns, seaports carrying bamboo baskets with fish,
    drinking coffee in a donut shop, weeping in the dark
In a two-for-five ramshackle hotel room,
    dreaming and walking along a city street at dawn.   20
To move about more freely, to meet and talk with new people,
    to have silence once in a while, to live in peace,
Without harassment of cops pulling you in as a suspect,
    these are very beautiful thoughts.
But I will remain here where the air is old and heavy, where life is grimy,   25
Full of hate at times, where opportunities are rare,
    anger and frustration abundant,
Here in this wretched place I most wish to leave
    I will remain.
I stay because I believe I will find something,   30
    something beautiful and astounding awaits my pleasure,
Something in the air I breathe,
    that will make all my terrors and pains seem raindrops
On a rose in summer, its head tilted in the heat
    as I do mine.   35
Here on this island of death and violence,
    I must find peace and love in myself, eventually freedom,
And if I am blessed, then perhaps a little wisdom.

I stay here searching for gold and ivory in the breast of each man.
I search for the tiny glimmering grains in smiles and words   40
    of the dying, of the young so old old, of the broken ones.

Reading

1. What is it that the speaker of these poems wants from his fellow inmates?

2. ("Immigrants in Our Own Land") What is the setting of this poem?

Thinking Critically

1. What do the words "I will remain" mean in the poem? Why does the speaker say these words?

2. In "Immigrants in Our Own Land," what similarities can be found between the speaker's life in prison and his life before? Are these similarities good or bad?

3. Based on these two poems, how would you characterize Baca's attitude toward prison?

Connecting

1. Ricardo Sánchez (p. 107) wrote the poems "Say, Tush-Hog Convict" and "Soledad Was a Girl's Name" while in prison. Do Baca's and Sánchez's prison poems express a similar attitude or style? How do they differ?

Writing

1. In the preceding poems, Baca suggests parallels between life inside and outside of prison. What are these parallels? Write an essay about what, in Baca's view, stays the same inside and outside of prison. Support your arguments with specific examples from the poems.

Creating

1. **Research and write about prison life.** Because prisons, by their nature, are closed off from the rest of society, those outside of prison often have little idea what happens in them. Write a letter to someone in prison, asking any questions you have about life inside. Alternatively, if you have been to a prison (as a visitor or otherwise), write about that experience and what struck you most about it.

28

ALBERTO ÁLVARO RÍOS [b. 1952]

True Story of the Pins • Old Man on the Hospital Porch

From Whispering to Fool the Wind [1982] AND Five
Indiscretions [1985]

GENRE: POETRY

*Arizona-based Alberto Álvaro Ríos was one of the first Chicano
poets to find success outside the traditional centers of Mexican
American power and inside the creative writing establishment. He
has found inspiration from his youth in Nogales, Arizona, where
he was raised by his Mexican father and British mother. He has
said of his childhood home: "It was a mix of very sharp and correct
Spanish and a very sharp and correct English. You start using
whatever words will get you dinner."* Ríos began writing poetry
while still in grade school. He received his bachelor's and master's
degrees from the University of Arizona and briefly attended law
school before devoting himself fully to creative writing. His first
book of poems,* Elk Heads on the Wall, *was published in 1979. His
second,* Whispering to Fool the Wind, *was written with support
from the National Endowment for the Arts and established him as
an important poet, receiving the Walt Whitman Award from the
American Academy of Poets in 1981. Ríos has been the recipient of
a Guggenheim Fellowship, and he has published numerous collections of poetry as well as a book of fiction in 1984,* The Iguana
Killer: Twelve Stories of the Heart. *His poetry includes* Teodoro
Luna's Two Kisses, *published in 1990, and* The Smallest Muscle
in the Human Body, *which was a finalist for a National Book
Award in 2002. Ríos teaches at Arizona State University and in
2013 became the inaugural Poet Laureate of Arizona.*

*Neither "True Story of the Pins" nor "Old Man on the Hospital
Porch" is particularly long, but like good stories, these poems have
strong characters, as well as elements of both levity and tragedy.
Like a good storyteller, Ríos conveys all this in a direct, conversa-
tional style.*

*Quoted from an interview found at public.asu.edu/~aarios/interviews/equinox/.

As you read, think about how Ríos suggests a complexity behind the stories he tells in these poems.

TRUE STORY OF THE PINS

Pins are always plentiful
but one day they were not
and your Uncle Humberto,
who collected all the butterflies
you see here on the walls,   5
was crazy looking for some
and he went to your cousin
Graciela the hard seamstress
who has pins it is rumored
even in hard times   10
but when she found out
why he wanted them
because the wind from the south
who was her friend
since the days of her   15
childhood on the sea
told her, she firmly refused
your poor Uncle Humberto
whose picture is here
on the wall behind you,   20
did you feel his eyes,
and he went into the most terrible
of rages, too terrible
for a butterfly collector
we all said afterward   25
and he burst the vein
that grew like a great snake
on his small forehead
and he died on the dirt
floor of Graciela's house   30
who of course felt sick
and immediately went
and put pins, this is what has
made her hard, through
the bright wings of the butterflies   35
Humberto had prepared
since he was after all

her father and she
could afford no better
light of perpetuity.   40

OLD MAN ON THE HOSPITAL PORCH

You don't know enough to die,
amusing yourself with a flyswatter,
hitting your toes, feet raised,
naked, pushing the side
of the big and colorless table   5
as if that table were a woman.
You, acting first like a young
colonel, small whip in your hands
as if your only strength
came from that stick   10
like the staff that Moses held,
and then, tired of that,
keeping time, enjoying yourself
as if that baton were the extension
of your simple smile,   15
conductor of your gray life,
encouraging first quickness
and then heaviness,
not for one moment desiring perfection.
You, who are you that you do not worry,   20
who only carries on
hour after hour, summer after summer
as if you were an animal
with only wild noises inside,
knowing nothing of death,   25
sleeping through the winter.
When I ask you, like always,
in a low voice so as not to disturb
some painful thing inside,
you give me only your eyes,   30
like two strange words
in the middle of a book,
pronounced without meaning, empty,
        like a pretty glass is empty.

Reading

1. ("True Story of the Pins") What happens to Uncle Humberto?

2. ("Old Man on the Hospital Porch") What are some of the objects that the old man holds?

Thinking Critically

1. In "True Story of the Pins," what impression do you get of the personalities of Uncle Humberto and Graciela?

2. Who do you think is speaking in "Old Man on the Hospital Porch"?

3. How would you describe the tone of the two poems? Does it differ from "True Story of the Pins" to "Old Man on the Hospital Porch"?

Connecting

1. Compare the portrayal of old age in "Old Man on the Hospital Porch" to that found in Helena María Viramontes's story "Neighbors" (p. 291). Do the works share a view on the positive or negative aspects of aging? What makes their characters different from each other?

Writing

1. Both "True Story of the Pins" and "Old Man on the Hospital Porch" are written in a poetic style that is similar to prose. What do you think makes the language poetic? Write a brief essay about what distinguishes these poems from prose. Support your argument with examples from the text.

Creating

1. **Rewrite Ríos's poem as a graphic story or cartoon.** In "True Story of the Pins," Alberto Ríos tells a story using vivid imagery. Try to retell that story in cartoon form, while keeping in mind that cartoons can be as serious or funny as you wish them to be. If you'd like, you can use the work of Lalo Alcaraz (p. 418) or The Hernandez Brothers (p. 307) as a model for your drawings.

29

GLORIA ANZALDÚA [1942–2004]

Towards a New Consciousness

From Borderlands/La Frontera: The New Mestiza [1987]

GENRE: ESSAY

*By the second half of the 1970s, writers such as Gloria Anzaldúa
began to move beyond the male-dominated political formulations
of the early Chicano Movement to create a distinctive feminist, Chicana cultural vision based on crossing sexual and cultural boundaries. Anzaldúa, like Ana Castillo (p. 260), added feminine icons to
the mythological and ancient imagery drawn on by Mexican American writers and was not afraid to point to the masculine bias they
saw in Chicano culture. "Though I'll defend my race and culture
when they are attacked by non-*mexicanos, conozco el malestar de
mi cultura," *she wrote. "I abhor some of my culture's ways, how it
cripples its women,* como burras, *our strengths used against us,
lowly* burras *bearing humility with dignity."* Anzaldúa's childhood
in Hargill, Texas, was marked by tension with her mother caused by
Anzaldúa's discovery of her own lesbianism and by the early death
of her father. She spent summers between school years in the fields,
on her way to earning a bachelor's degree at Pan American University and a master's at the University of Texas at Austin. She then
spent a number of years teaching and studying in Texas and California and developing a career as a writer. In 1981, with Cherríe Moraga (p. 250), she edited the widely read anthology of feminist writings called* This Bridge Called My Back: Writings by Radical
Women of Color, *which acted as a rebuke to a feminist movement
dominated by middle-class white women. In 1987 her own book*
Borderlands/La Frontera: The New Mestiza *was published, and it
would become Anzaldúa's best-known work. It has also become an
important part of cultural studies programs as an introduction to a
new way of looking at the mixing of cultures. Anzaldúa also wrote
several books for children, starting in 1991 with* Prietita Has a
Friend, *and she edited several other anthologies, including (with
Analouise Keating)* This Bridge We Call Home: Radical Visions
for Transformation *in 2002.*

*From *Borderlands*, Chapter 1; quoted in Ilan Stavans, ed., *The Norton Anthology
of Latino Literature.*

The word mestizo *has long been used to refer to people with a mixed Spanish and Indian ancestry. In the following essay, a chapter from* Borderlands/La Frontera: The New Mestiza, *Anzaldúa expands this meaning to envision a metaphorical* mestizaje *that includes racial and cultural mixing of all kinds, idealizing the ability to transcend prescribed boundaries, whether they be racial, cultural, national, or sexual.*

As you read this essay, think about the vision of society that Anzaldúa creates.

LA CONCIENCIA DE LA MESTIZA°

> *Por la mujer de mi raza*
> *hablará el espíritu.*°[1]

José Vasconcelos, Mexican philosopher, envisaged *una raza mestiza, una mezcla de razas afines, una raza de color—la primera raza síntesis del globo.*° He called it a cosmic race, *la raza cósmica,* a fifth race embracing the four major races of the world.[2] Opposite to the theory of the pure Aryan, and to the policy of racial purity that white America practices, his theory is one of inclusivity. At the confluence of two or more genetic streams, with chromosomes constantly "crossing over," this mixture of races, rather than resulting in an inferior being, provides hybrid progeny, a mutable, more malleable species with a rich gene pool. From this racial, ideological, cultural and biological cross-pollinization, an "alien" consciousness is presently in the making—a new *mestiza* consciousness, *una conciencia de mujer.*° It is a consciousness of the Borderlands.

Una lucha de fronteras / A Struggle of Borders

> Because I, a *mestiza,*
> continually walk out of one culture
> and into another,
> because I am in all cultures at the same time,

La conciencia de la mestiza: The consciousness of the mestiza.   **Por la mujer de mi raza . . . :** The spirit will speak for the woman of my race.   **una raza mestiza . . . :** A mestizo race, a mix of races with affinities, a race of color—the first synthesis of races on the globe.   **una conciencia de mujer:** A woman's consciousness.

alma entre dos mundos, tres, cuatro,
me zumba la cabeza con lo contradictorio.
Estoy norteada por todas las voces que me hablan
simultáneamente.°

The ambivalence from the clash of voices results in mental and emotional states of perplexity. Internal strife results in insecurity and indecisiveness. The mestiza's dual or multiple personality is plagued by psychic restlessness.

In a constant state of mental nepantilism, an Aztec word meaning torn between ways, *la mestiza* is a product of the transfer of the cultural and spiritual values of one group to another. Being tricultural, monolingual, bilingual, or multilingual, speaking a patois, and in a state of perpetual transition, the *mestiza* faces the dilemma of the mixed breed: which collectivity does the daughter of a darkskinned mother listen to?

El choque de un alma atrapado entre el mundo del espíritu y el mundo de la técnica a veces la deja entullada.° Cradled in one culture, sandwiched between two cultures, straddling all three cultures and their value systems, *la mestiza* undergoes a struggle of flesh, a struggle of borders, an inner war. Like all people, we perceive the version of reality that our culture communicates. Like others having or living in more than one culture, we get multiple, often opposing messages. The coming together of two self-consistent but habitually incompatible frames of reference[3] causes *un choque*, a cultural collision.

Within us and within *la cultura chicana,°* commonly held beliefs of the   5
white culture attack commonly held beliefs of the Mexican culture, and both attack commonly held beliefs of the indigenous culture. Subconsciously, we see an attack on ourselves and our beliefs as a threat and we attempt to block with a counterstance.

But it is not enough to stand on the opposite river bank, shouting questions, challenging patriarchal, white conventions. A counterstance locks one into a duel of oppressor and oppressed; locked in mortal combat, like the cop and the criminal, both are reduced to a common denominator of violence. The counterstance refutes the dominant culture's views and beliefs, and, for this, it is proudly defiant. All reaction is limited by, and dependent on, what it is reacting against. Because the counterstance stems from a problem with authority—outer as well as inner—it's a step towards liberation from cultural domination. But it is not a way of life.

alma entre dos mundos . . . : Soul between two worlds, three, four / my head buzzes with the contradictory. / I am confused by all the voices that speak to me / simultaneously.   **El choque de un alma . . . :** The crash of a soul trapped between the spirit world and technical world sometimes leaves her dazed. **la cultura chicana:** The culture of Chicanas and Chicanos.

At some point, on our way to a new consciousness, we will have to leave the opposite bank, the split between the two mortal combatants somehow healed so that we are on both shores at once and, at once, see through serpent and eagle eyes. Or perhaps we will decide to disengage from the dominant culture, write it off altogether as a lost cause, and cross the border into a wholly new and separate territory. Or we might go another route. The possibilities are numerous once we decide to act and not react.

A Tolerance for Ambiguity

These numerous possibilities leave *la mestiza* floundering in uncharted seas. In perceiving conflicting information and points of view, she is subjected to a swamping of her psychological borders. She has discovered that she can't hold concepts or ideas in rigid boundaries. The borders and walls that are supposed to keep the undesirable ideas out are entrenched habits and patterns of behavior; these habits and patterns are the enemy within. Rigidity means death. Only by remaining flexible is she able to stretch the psyche horizontally and vertically. *La mestiza* constantly has to shift out of habitual formations; from convergent thinking,[4] analytical reasoning that tends to use rationality to move toward a single goal (a Western mode), to divergent thinking, characterized by movement away from set patterns and goals and toward a more whole perspective, one that includes rather than excludes.

The new *mestiza* copes by developing a tolerance for contradictions, a tolerance for ambiguity. She learns to be an Indian in Mexican culture, to be Mexican from an Anglo point of view. She learns to juggle cultures. She has a plural personality, she operates in a pluralistic mode—nothing is thrust out, the good the bad and the ugly, nothing rejected, nothing abandoned. Not only does she sustain contradictions, she turns the ambivalence into something else.

She can be jarred out of ambivalence by an intense, and often painful, emotional event which inverts or resolves the ambivalence. I'm not sure exactly how. The work takes place underground—subconsciously. It is work that the soul performs. That focal point or fulcrum, that juncture where the mestiza stands, is where phenomena tend to collide. It is where the possibility of uniting all that is separate occurs. This assembly is not one where severed or separated pieces merely come together. Nor is it a balancing of opposing powers. In attempting to work out a synthesis, the self has added a third element which is greater than the sum of its severed parts. That third element is a new consciousness—a mestiza consciousness—and though it is a source of intense pain, its energy comes from continual creative motion that keeps breaking down the unitary aspect of each new paradigm.

En unas pocas centurias,° the future will belong to the mestiza. Because 10
the future depends on the breaking down of paradigms, it depends on
the straddling of two or more cultures. By creating a new mythos—that
is, a change in the way we perceive reality, the way we see ourselves, and
the ways we behave—*la mestiza* creates a new consciousness.

The work of *mestiza* consciousness is to break down the subject-object
duality that keeps her a prisoner and to show in the flesh and through the
images in her work how duality is transcended. The answer to the problem between the white race and the colored, between males and females,
lies in healing the split that originates in the very foundation of our lives,
our culture, our languages, our thoughts. A massive uprooting of dualis-
tic thinking in the individual and collective consciousness is the beginning of a long struggle, but one that could, in our best hopes, bring us to
the end of rape, of violence, of war.

La encrucijada / The Crossroads

> A chicken is being sacrificed
>   at a crossroads, a simple mound of earth
> a mud shrine for *Eshu,*
>   *Yoruba* god of indeterminacy,
> who blesses her choice of path.
> She begins her journey.

Su cuerpo es una bocacalle.° *La mestiza* has gone from being the sacrificial goat to becoming the officiating priestess at the crossroads.

As a *mestiza* I have no country, my homeland cast me out; yet all countries are mine because I am every woman's sister or potential lover. (As a
lesbian I have no race, my own people disclaim me; but I am all races
because there is the queer of me in all races.) I am cultureless because,
as a feminist, I challenge the collective cultural/religious male-derived
beliefs of Indo-Hispanics and Anglos; yet I am cultured because I am
participating in the creation of yet another culture, a new story to explain
the world and our participation in it, a new value system with images
and symbols that connect us to each other and to the planet. *Soy un ama-
samiento,* I am an act of kneading, of uniting and joining that not only
has produced both a creature of darkness and a creature of light, but also
a creature that questions the definitions of light and dark and gives them
new meanings.

En unas pocas centurias: In a few centuries.   **Su cuerpo es una bocacalle:**
Her body is a portal.

We are the people who leap in the dark, we are the people on the knees of the gods. In our very flesh, (r)evolution works out the clash of cultures. It makes us crazy constantly, but if the center holds, we've made some kind of evolutionary step forward. *Nuestra alma el trabajo,*° the opus, the great alchemical work; spiritual *mestizaje,*° a "morphogenesis,"[5] an inevitable unfolding. We have become the quickening serpent movement.

Indigenous like corn, like corn, the *mestiza* is a product of crossbreeding, designed for preservation under a variety of conditions. Like an ear of corn — a female seed-bearing organ — the *mestiza* is tenacious, tightly wrapped in the husks of her culture. Like kernels she clings to the cob; with thick stalks and strong brace roots, she holds tight to the earth — she will survive the crossroads.   15

Lavando y remojando el maíz en agua de cal, despojando el pellejo. Moliendo, mixteando, amasando, haciendo tortillas de masa.°[6] She steeps the corn in lime, it swells, softens. With stone roller on *metate,*° she grinds the corn, then grinds again. She kneads and moulds the dough, pats the round balls into *tortillas*.

> We are the porous rock in the stone *metate*
> squatting on the ground.
> We are the rolling pin, *el maíz y agua,*
> *la masa harina. Somos el amasijo.*
> *Somos lo molido en el metate.*°
> We are the *comal*° sizzling hot,
> the hot *tortilla*, the hungry mouth.
> We are the coarse rock.
> We are the grinding motion,
> the mixed potion, *somos el molcajete.*°
> We are the pestle, the *comino, ajo, pimienta,*°
> We are the *chile colorado,*°
> the green shoot that cracks the rock.
> We will abide.

Nuestra alma el trabajo: Our soul the work.   **mestizaje:** Mixture.   **Lavando y remojando el maíz . . . :** Washing and soaking the corn in lime water, stripping away the skin. Grinding, mixing, kneading, making tortillas from dough. **metate:** A flat stone for grinding corn.   **el maíz y agua, / la masa harina. Somos el amasijo. / Somos lo molido en el metate:** The corn and water, / the flour from the dough. We are the jumble. / We are what is ground on the *metate*. **comal:** A flat stone for heating tortillas.   **somos el molcajete:** We are the *molcajete* (a traditional Mexican mortar and pestle made of lava stone).   **comino, ajo, pimienta:** Cumin, garlic, pepper.   **chile colorado:** Red chile.

El camino de la mestiza / The Mestiza Way

Caught between the sudden contraction, the breath sucked in and the endless space, the brown woman stands still, looks at the sky. She decides to go down, digging her way along the roots of trees. Sifting through the bones, she shakes them to see if there is any marrow in them. Then, touching the dirt to her forehead, to her tongue, she takes a few bones, leaves the rest in their burial place.

She goes through her backpack, keeps her journal and address book, throws away the muni-bart metromaps. The coins are heavy and they go next, then the greenbacks flutter through the air. She keeps her knife, can opener and eyebrow pencil. She puts bones, pieces of bark, *hierbas,*° eagle feather, snakeskin, tape recorder, the rattle and drum in her pack and she sets out to become the complete *tolteca.*°[7]

Her first step is to take inventory. *Despojando, desgranando, quitando paja.*° Just what did she inherit from her ancestors? This weight on her back—which is the baggage from the Indian mother, which the baggage from the Spanish father, which the baggage from the Anglo?

Pero es difícil° differentiating between *lo heredado, lo adquirido, lo impuesto.*° She puts history through a sieve, winnows out the lies, looks at the forces that we as a race, as women, have been a part of. *Luego bota lo que no vale, los desmientos, los desencuentros, el embrutecimiento. Aguarda el juicio, hondo y enraízado, de la gente antigua.*° This step is a conscious rupture with all oppressive traditions of all cultures and religions. She communicates that rupture, documents the struggle. She reinterprets history and, using new symbols, she shapes new myths. She adopts new perspectives toward the darkskinned, women and queers. She strengthens her tolerance (and intolerance) for ambiguity. She is willing to share, to make herself vulnerable to foreign ways of seeing and thinking. She surrenders all notions of safety, of the familiar. Deconstruct, construct. She becomes a *nahual,*° able to transform herself into a tree, a coyote, into another person. She learns to transform the small "I" into the total Self. *Se hace moldeadora de su alma. Según la concepción que tiene de sí misma, así será.*°

hierbas: Herbs. **tolteca:** A Toltec woman. (The Toltec culture predates that of the Aztecs.) **Despojando, desgranando, quitando paja:** Stripping away, dekerneling, removing stalks. **Pero es difícil:** But it's difficult. **lo heredado, lo adquirido, lo impuesto:** What is inherited, what is acquired, what is imposed. **Luego bota lo que no vale . . . :** Then she discards what is of no value, the denials, the disagreements, the brutalization. She awaits the knowledge, deep and rooted, of the ancient people. **nahual:** Spirit. **Se hace moldeadora . . . :** She becomes the shaper of her soul. According to the conception she has of herself, so she will be.

Que no se nos olvide los hombres°

> *"Tú no sirves pa' nada°—*
> you're good for nothing.
> *Eres pura vieja.°"*

"You're nothing but a woman" means you are defective. Its opposite is to be *un macho*. The modern meaning of the word "machismo," as well as the concept, is actually an Anglo invention. For men like my father, being "macho" meant being strong enough to protect and support my mother and us, yet being able to show love. Today's macho has doubts about his ability to feed and protect his family. His "machismo" is an adaptation to oppression and poverty and low self-esteem. It is the result of hierarchical male dominance. The Anglo, feeling inadequate and inferior and powerless, displaces or transfers these feelings to the Chicano by shaming him. In the Gringo world, the Chicano suffers from excessive humility and self-effacement, shame of self and self-deprecation. Around Latinos he suffers from a sense of language inadequacy and its accompanying discomfort; with Native Americans he suffers from a racial amnesia which ignores our common blood, and from guilt because the Spanish part of him took their land and oppressed them. He has an excessive compensatory hubris when around Mexicans from the other side. It overlays a deep sense of racial shame.

The loss of a sense of dignity and respect in the macho breeds a false   20
machismo which leads him to put down women and even to brutalize them. Coexisting with his sexist behavior is a love for the mother which takes precedence over that of all others. Devoted son, macho pig. To wash down the shame of his acts, of his very being, and to handle the brute in the mirror, he takes to the bottle, the snort, the needle, and the fist.

Though we "understand" the root causes of male hatred and fear, and the subsequent wounding of women, we do not excuse, we do not condone, and we will no longer put up with it. From the men of our race, we demand the admission/acknowledgment/disclosure/testimony that they wound us, violate us, are afraid of us and of our power. We need them to say they will begin to eliminate their hurtful put-down ways. But more than the words, we demand acts. We say to them: We will develop equal power with you and those who have shamed us.

It is imperative that mestizas support each other in changing the sexist elements in the Mexican-Indian culture. As long as woman is put down, the Indian and the Black in all of us is put down. The struggle of the

---

Que no se nos olvide los hombres: Let's not forget the men.   **Tú no sirves pa' nada / Eres pura vieja:** You have no purpose / You're just a woman.

mestiza is above all a feminist one. As long as *los hombres*° think they have to *chingar mujeres*° and each other to be men, as long as men are taught that they are superior and therefore culturally favored over *la mujer*, as long as to be a *vieja* is a thing of derision, there can be no real healing of our psyches. We're halfway there—we have such love of the Mother, the good mother. The first step is to unlearn the *puta/virgen*° dichotomy and to see *Coatlapopeuh-Coatlicue* in the Mother, *Guadalupe*.

Tenderness, a sign of vulnerability, is so feared that it is showered on women with verbal abuse and blows. Men, even more than women, are fettered to gender roles. Women at least have had the guts to break out of bondage. Only gay men have had the courage to expose themselves to the woman inside them and to challenge the current masculinity. I've encountered a few scattered and isolated gentle straight men, the beginnings of a new breed, but they are confused, and entangled with sexist behaviors that they have not been able to eradicate. We need a new masculinity and the new man needs a movement.

Lumping the males who deviate from the general norm with man, the oppressor, is a gross injustice. *Asombra pensar que nos hemos quedado en ese pozo oscuro donde el mundo encierra a las lesbianas. Asombra pensar que hemos, como femenistas y lesbianas, cerrado nuestros corazones a los hombres, a nuestros hermanos los jotos, desheredados y marginales como nosotros.*° Being the supreme crossers of cultures, homosexuals have strong bonds with the queer white, Black, Asian, Native American, Latino, and with the queer in Italy, Australia and the rest of the planet. We come from all colors, all classes, all races, all time periods. Our role is to link people with each other—the Blacks with Jews with Indians with Asians with whites with extraterrestrials. It is to transfer ideas and information from one culture to another. Colored homosexuals have more knowledge of other cultures; have always been at the forefront (although sometimes in the closet) of all liberation struggles in this country; have suffered more injustices and have survived them despite all odds. Chicanos need to acknowledge the political and artistic contributions of their queer. People, listen to what your *jotería*° is saying.

The mestizo and the queer exist at this time and point on the evolutionary continuum for a purpose. We are a blending that proves that all blood is intricately woven together, and that we are spawned out of similar souls.   25

los hombres: Men.   **chingar mujeres:** Screw women.   **puta/virgen:** Whore/virgin.   **Asombra pensar que nos hemos quedado . . . :** Astonishing to think that we have come to be in this dark hole where the world encloses lesbians. Astonishing to think that we, as feminists and lesbians, have closed our hearts to the men, to our brothers the queers, disfranchised and marginalized like us. **jotería:** Queer culture, derived from *joto*, which means "queer."

Somos una gente°

> *Hay tantísimas fronteras*
> *que dividen a la gente,*
> *pero por cada frontera*
> *existe también un puente.*°
> —GINA VALDÉS[8]

Divided Loyalties. Many women and men of color do not want to have any dealings with white people. It takes too much time and energy to explain to the downwardly mobile, white middle-class women that it's okay for us to want to own "possessions," never having had any nice furniture on our dirt floors or "luxuries" like washing machines. Many feel that whites should help their own people rid themselves of race hatred and fear first. I, for one, choose to use some of my energy to serve as mediator. I think we need to allow whites to be our allies. Through our literature, art, *corridos*,° and folktales we must share our history with them so when they set up committees to help Big Mountain Navajos or the Chicano farmworkers or *los Nicaragüenses*° they won't turn people away because of their racial fears and ignorances. They will come to see that they are not helping us but following our lead.

Individually, but also as a racial entity, we need to voice our needs. We need to say to white society: We need you to accept the fact that Chicanos are different, to acknowledge your rejection and negation of us. We need you to own the fact that you looked upon us as less than human, that you stole our lands, our personhood, our self-respect. We need you to make public restitution: to say that, to compensate for your own sense of defectiveness, you strive for power over us, you erase our history and our experience because it makes you feel guilty—you'd rather forget your brutish acts. To say you've split yourself from minority groups, that you disown us, that your dual consciousness splits off parts of yourself, transferring the "negative" parts onto us. (Where there is persecution of minorities, there is shadow projection. Where there is violence and war, there is repression of shadow.) To say that you are afraid of us, that to put distance between us, you wear the mask of contempt. Admit that Mexico is your double, that she exists in the shadow of this country, that we are irrevocably tied to her. Gringo, accept the doppelganger in your psyche. By taking back your collective shadow the intracultural split will heal. And finally, tell us what you need from us.

Somos una gente: We are one people.   **Hay tantísimas fronteras: . . .** There are so many borders / that divide people, / but for every border / there also exists a bridge.   **corridos:** Musical ballads sung to tell stories.   **los Nicaragüenses:** The Nicaraguans.

By Your True Faces We Will Know You

I am visible—see this Indian face—yet I am invisible. I both blind them with my beak nose and am their blind spot. But I exist, we exist. They'd like to think I have melted in the pot. But I haven't, we haven't.

The dominant white culture is killing us slowly with its ignorance. By taking away our self-determination, it has made us weak and empty. As a people we have resisted and we have taken expedient positions, but we have never been allowed to develop unencumbered—we have never been allowed to be fully ourselves. The whites in power want us people of color to barricade ourselves behind our separate tribal walls so they can pick us off one at a time with their hidden weapons; so they can whitewash and distort history. Ignorance splits people, creates prejudices. A misinformed people is a subjugated people.

Before the Chicano and the undocumented worker and the Mexican 30 from the other side can come together, before the Chicano can have unity with Native Americans and other groups, we need to know the history of their struggle and they need to know ours. Our mothers, our sisters and brothers, the guys who hang out on street corners, the children in the playgrounds, each of us must know our Indian lineage, our afro-*mestisaje*, our history of resistance.

To the immigrant *mexicano* and the recent arrivals we must teach our history. The 80 million *mexicanos* and the Latinos from Central and South America must know of our struggles. Each one of us must know basic facts about Nicaragua, Chile and the rest of Latin America. The Latinoist movement (Chicanos, Puerto Ricans, Cubans and other Spanish-speaking people working together to combat racial discrimination in the market place) is good but it is not enough. Other than a common culture we will have nothing to hold us together. We need to meet on a broader communal ground.

The struggle is inner: Chicano, *indio*, American Indian, *mojado*,° *mexicano*, immigrant Latino, Anglo in power, working class Anglo, Black, Asian—our psyches resemble the bordertowns and are populated by the same people. The struggle has always been inner, and is played out in the outer terrains. Awareness of our situation must come before inner changes, which in turn come before changes in society. Nothing happens in the "real" world unless it first happens in the images in our heads.

---

mojado: Wetback, a derogatory word for Mexican immigrants.

NOTES

1. This is my own "take off" on José Vasconcelos' idea. José Vasconcelos, *La Raza Cósmica: Misión de la Raza Ibero-Americana* (México: Aguilar S.A. de Ediciones, 1961).

2. Vasconcelos.

3. Arthur Koestler termed this "bisociation." Albert Rothenberg, *The Creative Process in Art, Science, and Other Fields* (Chicago, IL: University of Chicago Press, 1979), 12.

4. In part, I derive my definitions for "convergent" and "divergent" thinking from Rothenberg, 12–13.

5. To borrow chemist Ilya Prigogine's theory of "dissipative structures." Prigogine discovered that substances interact not in predictable ways as it was taught in science, but in different and fluctuating ways to produce new and more complex structures, a kind of birth he called "morphogenesis," which created unpredictable innovations. Harold Gilliam, "Searching for a New World View," *This World* (January, 1981), 23.

6. *Tortillas de masa harina:* corn tortillas are of two types, the smooth uniform ones made in a tortilla press and usually bought at a tortilla factory or supermarket, and *gorditas*, made by mixing *masa* with lard or shortening or butter (my mother sometimes puts in bits of bacon or *chicharrones*).

7. Gina Valdés, *Puentes y Fronteras: Coplas Chicanas* (Los Angeles, CA: Castle Lithograph, 1982), 2.

8. Richard Wilhelm, *The I Ching or Book of Changes*, trans. Cary F. Baynes (Princeton, NJ: Princeton University Press, 1950), 98.

Reading

1. Why does Anzaldúa think the future belongs to the mestiza?

2. According to Anzaldúa, how has the meaning of the word *macho* changed?

Thinking Critically

1. What does Anzaldúa ask of individuals?

2. Do you think Anzaldúa's vision is attainable? What obstacles might stand in the way of it?

Connecting

1. Cherríe Moraga, in her essay "La Güera" (p. 250), discusses the mixing of races and cultures that she finds in her own life. What do you think is the relationship between Moraga's arguments and Anzaldúa's "new consciousness"?

Writing

1. Anzaldúa concludes this piece with the statement, "Awareness of our situation must come before inner changes, which in turn come before changes in society. Nothing happens in the 'real' world unless it first happens in the images in our heads." Using examples from your experience and from the text, write an essay agreeing or disagreeing with this statement.

Creating

1. **Write a children's story based on Anzaldúa's vision.** Gloria Anzaldúa's feminism can be found not only in her essays but also in the books she wrote for children. Write a short story for children that you think is consistent with her arguments about women and power in "Towards a New Consciousness."

30

CHERRÍE MORAGA [b. 1952]

La Güera

From This Bridge Called My Back: Writings by Radical Women of Color [1981]

GENRE: ESSAY

With the publication of the anthology This Bridge Called My Back: Writings by Radical Women of Color *in 1981, Cherríe Moraga established herself as a major Chicana voice, helping to make radical feminism and lesbianism central to discussions of Chicana/o literature. Moraga grew up in Southern California, and after college at Immaculate Heart College in Hollywood found her way north to San Francisco State University, earning a master's degree for coediting (with Gloria Anzaldúa—see p. 238) and contributing to* This Bridge Called My Back. *The book's emphasis on the centrality of sexuality, race, and class to women's lives challenged the dominance of white middle-class women in the feminist movement. She moved to New York, determined to continue her career as a writer because, as she said later, "there was nothing to read* *that affirmed my existence as a lesbian Chicana."* In 1983 she published a collection of prose and poetry called* Loving in the War Years: lo que nunca pasó por sus labios, *and she began her work as a playwright in 1984 with* Giving Up the Ghost. *She has since written numerous plays and is the longtime Artist in Residence at Stanford University.*

In the essay "La Güera," which was first published in the anthology This Bridge Called My Back, *Moraga writes of the mix of emotions that her light, güera skin gives rise to, both in herself and others. She also writes about how her lesbianism has given her insight into struggles against all kinds of oppression. In the preface to the book, Moraga wrote, "It is about physical and psychic struggle. It is about intimacy, a desire for life between all of us, not settling for less than freedom even in the most private aspects of our lives. A total vision."*

As you read this essay, ask yourself what you think is Moraga's "total vision," and notice how Moraga sees societal oppression reflected in her own attitudes.

It requires something more than personal experience to gain a philosophy or point of view from any specific event. It is the quality of our response to the event and our capacity to enter into the lives of others that help us to make their lives and experiences our own.

—EMMA GOLDMAN**

I am the very well-educated daughter of a woman who, by the standards in this country, would be considered largely illiterate. My mother was born in Santa Paula, Southern California, at a time when much of the central valley there was still farm land. Nearly thirty-five years later, in 1948, she was the only daughter of six to marry an Anglo, my father.

I remember all of my mother's stories, probably much better than she realizes. She is a fine story-teller, recalling every event of her life with the vividness of the present, noting each detail right down to the cut and

*From Frederick Luis Aldama, *Spilling the Beans in Chicanolandia.*

**Alix Kates Shulman, "Was My Life Worth Living?," *Red Emma Speaks* (New York: Random House, 1972), p. 388.

color of her dress. I remember stories of her being pulled out of school at the ages of five, seven, nine, and eleven to work in the fields, along with her brothers and sisters; stories of her father drinking away whatever small profit she was able to make for the family; of her going the long way home to avoid meeting him on the street, staggering toward the same destination. I remember stories of my mother lying about her age in order to get a job as a hat-check girl at Agua Caliente Racetrack in Tijuana. At fourteen, she was the main support of the family. I can still see her walking home alone at 3 a.m., only to turn all of her salary and tips over to her mother, who was pregnant again.

The stories continue through the war years and on: walnut-cracking factories, the Voit Rubber factory, and then the computer boom. I remember my mother doing piecework for the electronics plant in our neighborhood. In the late evening, she would sit in front of the T.V. set, wrapping copper wires into the backs of circuit boards, talking about "keeping up with the younger girls." By that time she was already in her mid-fifties.

Meanwhile, I was college-prep in school. After classes, I would go with my mother to fill out job applications for her, or write checks for her at the supermarket. We would have the scenario all worked out ahead of time. My mother would sign the check before we'd get to the store. Then, as we'd approach the checkstand, she would say—within earshot of the cashier—"oh honey, you go 'head and make out the check," as if she couldn't be bothered with such an insignificant detail. No one asked any questions.

I was educated, and wore it with a keen sense of pride and satisfaction,   5
my head propped up with the knowledge, from my mother, that my life would be easier than hers. I was educated; but more than this, I was "la güera"—fair-skinned. Born with the features of my Chicana mother, but the skin of my Anglo father, I had it made.

No one ever quite told me this (that light was right), but I knew that being light was something valued in my family (who were all Chicano, with the exception of my father). In fact, everything about my upbringing (at least what occurred on a conscious level) attempted to bleach me of what color I did have. Although my mother was fluent in it, I was never taught much Spanish at home. I picked up what I did learn from school and from over-heard snatches of conversation among my relatives and mother. She often called other lower-income Mexicans "braceros," or "wet-backs," referring to herself and family as "a different class of people." And yet, the real story was that my family, too, had been poor (some still are) and farmworkers. My mother can remember this in her blood as if it were yesterday. But this is something she would like to forget (and rightfully), for to her, on a basic economic level, being Chicana meant being "less." It was through my mother's desire to protect her children from poverty and illiteracy that we became "anglocized"; the more effectively we could pass in the white world, the better guaranteed our future.

From all of this, I experience, daily, a huge disparity between what I was born into and what I was to grow up to become. Because, (as Goldman suggests) these stories my mother told me crept under my "güera" skin. I had no choice but to enter into the life of my mother. *I had no choice.* I took her life into my heart, but managed to keep a lid on it as long as I feigned being the happy, upwardly mobile heterosexual.

When I finally lifted the lid to my lesbianism, a profound connection with my mother reawakened in me. It wasn't until I acknowledged and confronted my own lesbianism in the flesh, that my heartfelt identification with and empathy for my mother's oppression—due to being poor, uneducated, and Chicana—was realized. My lesbianism is the avenue through which I have learned the most about silence and oppression, and it continues to be the most tactile reminder to me that we are not free human beings.

You see, one follows the other. I had known for years that I was a lesbian, had felt it in my bones, had ached with the knowledge, gone crazed with the knowledge, wallowed in the silence of it. Silence *is* like starvation. Don't be fooled. It's nothing short of that, and felt most sharply when one has had a full belly most of her life. When we are not physically starving, we have the luxury to realize psychic and emotional starvation. It is from this starvation that other starvations can be recognized—if one is willing to take the risk of making the connection—if one is willing to be responsible to the result of the connection. For me, the connection is an inevitable one.

What I am saying is that the joys of looking like a white girl ain't so   10 great since I realized I could be beaten on the street for being a dyke. If my sister's being beaten because she's Black, it's pretty much the same principle. We're both getting beaten any way you look at it. The connection is blatant; and in the case of my own family, the difference in the privileges attached to looking white instead of brown are merely a generation apart.

In this country, lesbianism is a poverty—as is being brown, as is being a woman, as is being just plain poor. The danger lies in ranking the oppressions. *The danger lies in failing to acknowledge the specificity of the oppression.* The danger lies in attempting to deal with oppression purely from a theoretical base. Without an emotional, heartfelt grappling with the source of our own oppression, without naming the enemy within ourselves and outside of us, no authentic, non-hierarchical connection among oppressed groups can take place.

When the going gets rough, will we abandon our so-called comrades in a flurry of racist/heterosexist/what-have-you panic? To whose camp, then, should the lesbian of color retreat? Her very presence violates the ranking and abstraction of oppression. Do we merely live hand to mouth? Do we merely struggle with the "ism" that's sitting on top of our heads?

The answer is: yes, I think first we do; and we must do so thoroughly and deeply. But to fail to move out from there will only isolate us in our own oppression—will only insulate, rather than radicalize us.

To illustrate: a gay white male friend of mine once confided to me that he continued to feel that, on some level, I didn't trust him because he was male; that he felt, really, if it ever came down to a "battle of the sexes," I might kill him. I admitted that I might very well. He wanted to understand the source of my distrust. I responded, "You're not a woman. Be a woman for a day. Imagine being a woman." He confessed that the thought terrified him because, to him, being a woman meant being raped by men. He *had* felt raped by men; he wanted to forget what that meant. What grew from that discussion was the realization that in order for him to create an authentic alliance with me, he must deal with the primary source of his own sense of oppression. He must, first, emotionally come to terms with what it feels like to be a victim. If he—or anyone—were to truly do this, it would be impossible to discount the oppression of others, except by again forgetting how we have been hurt.

And yet, oppressed groups are forgetting all the time. There are instances of this in the rising Black middle class, and certainly an obvious trend of such "capitalist-unconsciousness" among white gay men. Because to remember may mean giving up whatever privileges we have managed to squeeze out of this society by virtue of our gender, race, class, or sexuality.

Within the women's movement, the connections among women of different backgrounds and sexual orientations have been fragile, at best. I think this phenomenon is indicative of our failure to seriously address ourselves to some very frightening questions: How have I internalized my own oppression? How have I oppressed? Instead, we have let rhetoric do the job of poetry. Even the word "oppression" has lost its power. We need a new language, better words that can more closely describe women's fear of and resistance to one another; words that will not always come out sounding like dogma.

What prompted me in the first place to work on an anthology by radical women of color was a deep sense that I had a valuable insight to contribute, by virtue of my birthright and my background. And yet, I don't really understand first-hand what it feels like being shitted on for

being brown. I understand much more about the joys of it—being Chicana and having family are synonymous for me. What I know about
loving, singing, crying, telling stories, speaking with my heart and hands,
even having a sense of my own soul comes from the love of my mother,
aunts, cousins . . .

But at the age of twenty-seven, it is frightening to acknowledge that I
have internalized a racism and classism, where the object of oppression
is not only someone *outside* my skin, but the someone *inside* my skin. In
fact, to a large degree, the real battle with such oppression, for all of us,
begins under the skin. I have had to confront the fact that much of what
I value about being Chicana, about my family, has been subverted by
anglo culture and my own cooperation with it. This realization did not
occur to me overnight. For example, it wasn't until long after my graduation from the private college I'd attended in Los Angeles, that I realized
the major reason for my total alienation from and fear of my classmates
was rooted in class and culture.

Three years after graduation, in an apple-orchard in Sonoma, a friend
of mine (who comes from an Italian Irish working-class family) says to
me, "Cherríe, no wonder you felt like such a nut in school. Most of the
people there were white and rich." It was true. All along I had felt
the difference, but not until I had put the words "class" and "race" to the
experience, did my feelings make any sense. For years, I had berated
myself for not being as "free" as my classmates. I completely bought that
they simply had more guts than I did—to rebel against their parents and
run around the country hitch-hiking, reading books and studying "art."
They had enough privilege to be atheists, for chrissake. There was no one
around filling in the disparity for me between their parents, who were
Hollywood filmmakers, and my parents, who wouldn't know the name of
a filmmaker if their lives depended on it (and precisely because their
lives didn't depend on it, they couldn't be bothered). But I knew nothing
about "privilege" then. White was right. Period. I could pass. If I got educated enough, there would never be any telling.

Three years after that, I had a similar revelation. In a letter to a friend,   20
I wrote:

> I went to a concert where Ntosake Shange was reading. There, everything
> exploded for me. She was speaking in a language that I knew—in the deep-
> est parts of me—existed, and that I ignored in my own feminist studies
> and even in my own writing. What Ntosake caught in me is the realization
> that in my development as a poet, I have, in many ways, denied the voice
> of my own brown mother—the brown in me. I have acclimated to the

sound of a white language which, as my father represents it, does not speak to the emotions in my poems—emotions which stem from the love of my mother.

The reading was agitating. Made me uncomfortable. Threw me into a week-long terror of how deeply I was affected. I felt that I had to start all over again. That I turned only to the perceptions of white middle-class women to speak for me and all women. I am shocked by my own ignorance.

Sitting in that auditorium chair was the first time I had realized to the core of me that for years I had disowned the language I knew best— ignored the words and rhythms that were the closest to me. The sounds of my mother and aunts gossiping—half in English, half in Spanish— while drinking cerveza in the kitchen. And the hands—I had cut off the hands in my poems. But not in conversation; still the hands could not be kept down. Still they insisted on moving.

The reading had forced me to remember that I knew things from my roots. But to remember puts me up against what I don't know. Shange's reading agitated me because she spoke with power about a world that is both alien and common to me: "the capacity to enter into the lives of others." But you can't just take the goods and run. I knew that then, sitting in the Oakland auditorium (as I know in my poetry), that the only thing worth writing about is what seems to be unknown and, therefore, fearful.

The "unknown" is often depicted in racist literature as the "darkness" within a person. Similarly, sexist writers will refer to fear in the form of the vagina, calling it "the orifice of death." In contrast, it is a pleasure to read works such as Maxine Hong Kingston's *Woman Warrior*, where fear and alienation are depicted as "the white ghosts." And yet, the bulk of literature in this country reinforces the myth that what is dark and female is evil. Consequently, each of us—whether dark, female, or both—has in some way *internalized* this oppressive imagery. What the oppressor often succeeds in doing is simply *externalizing* his fears, projecting them into the bodies of women, Asians, gays, disabled folks, whoever seems most "other."

call me
roach and presumptuous
nightmare on your white pillow
your itch to destroy
the indestructible
part of yourself
                    —AUDRE LORDE*

*From "The Brown Menace or Poem to the Survival of Roaches," *The New York Head Shop and Museum* (Detroit: Broadside, 1974), p. 48. [Footnote in original.]

But it is not really difference the oppressor fears so much as similarity. He fears he will discover in himself the same aches, the same longings as those of the people he has shitted on. He fears the immobilization threatened by his own incipient guilt. He fears he will have to change his life once he has seen himself in the bodies of the people he has called different. He fears the hatred, anger, and vengeance of those he has hurt.

This is the oppressor's nightmare, but it is not exclusive to him. We women have a similar nightmare, for each of us in some way has been both oppressed and the oppressor. We are afraid to look at how we have failed each other. We are afraid to see how we have taken the values of our oppressor into our hearts and turned them against ourselves and one another. We are afraid to admit how deeply "the man's" words have been ingrained in us.

To assess the damage is a dangerous act. I think of how, even as a feminist lesbian, I have so wanted to ignore my own homophobia, my own hatred of myself for being queer. I have not wanted to admit that my deepest personal sense of myself has not quite "caught up" with my "woman-identified" politics. I have been afraid to criticize lesbian writers who choose to "skip over" these issues in the name of feminism. In 1979, we talk of "old gay" and "butch and femme" roles as if they were ancient history. We toss them aside as merely patriarchal notions. And yet, the truth of the matter is that I have sometimes taken society's fear and hatred of lesbians to bed with me. I have sometimes hated my lover for loving me. I have sometimes felt "not woman enough" for her. I have sometimes felt "not man enough." For a lesbian trying to survive in a heterosexist society, there is no easy way around these emotions. Similarly, in a white-dominated world, there is little getting around racism and our own internalization of it. It's always there, embodied in someone we least expect to rub up against.

When we do rub up against this person, *there* then is the challenge. *There* then is the opportunity to look at the nightmare within us. But we usually shrink from such a challenge.

Time and time again, I have observed that the usual response among white women's groups when the "racism issue" comes up is to deny the difference. I have heard comments like, "Well, we're open to *all* women; why don't they (women of color) come? You can only do so much . . ." But there is seldom any analysis of how the very nature and structure of the group itself may be founded on racist or classist assumptions. More importantly, so often the women seem to feel no loss, no lack, no absence when women of color are not involved; therefore, there is little desire to change the situation. This has hurt me deeply. I have come to believe that the only reason women of a privileged class will dare to look at *how* it is that *they* oppress, is when they've come to know the meaning of their own oppression. And understand that the oppression of others hurts them personally.

The other side of the story is that women of color and white working-class women often shrink from challenging white middle-class women. It is much easier to rank oppressions and set up a hierarchy, rather than take responsibility for changing our own lives. We have failed to demand that white women, particularly those that claim to be speaking for all women, be accountable for their racism.

The dialogue has simply not gone deep enough.   30

In conclusion, I have had to look critically at my claim to color, at a time when, among white feminist ranks, it is a "politically correct" (and sometimes peripherally advantageous) assertion to make. I must acknowledge the fact that, physically, I have had a *choice* about making that claim, in contrast to women who have not had such a choice, and have been abused for their color. I must reckon with the fact that for most of my life, by virtue of the very fact that I am white-looking, I identified with and aspired toward white values, and that I rode the wave of that Southern California privilege as far as conscience would let me.

Well, now I feel both bleached and beached. I feel angry about this—the years when I refused to recognize privilege, both when it worked against me, and when I worked it, ignorantly, at the expense of others. These are not settled issues. This is why this work feels so risky to me. It continues to be discovery. It has brought me into contact with women who invariably know a hell of a lot more than I do about racism, as experienced in the flesh, as revealed in the flesh of their writing.

I think: what is my responsibility to my roots: both white and brown, Spanish-speaking and English? I am a woman with a foot in both worlds. I refuse the split. I feel the necessity for dialogue. Sometimes I feel it urgently.

But one voice is not enough, nor two, although this is where dialogue begins. It is essential that feminists confront their fear of and resistance to each other, because without this, there *will* be no bread on the table. Simply, we will not survive. If we could make this connection in our heart of hearts, that if we are serious about a revolution—better—if we seriously believe there should be joy in our lives (real joy, not just "good times"), then we need one another. We women need each other. Because my/your solitary, self-asserting "go-for-the-throat-of-fear" power is not enough. The real power, as you and I well know, is collective. I can't afford to be afraid of you, nor you of me. If it takes head-on collisions, let's do it. This polite timidity is killing us.

As Lorde suggests in the passage I cited earlier, it is looking to the   35 nightmare that the dream is found. There, the survivor emerges to insist on a future, a vision, yes, born out of what is dark and female. The feminist movement must be a movement of such survivors, a movement with a future.

Reading

1. What effect does Moraga's "lifting the lid" on her lesbianism have on her thinking?

2. How does Moraga hope to improve the dialogue among feminists?

Thinking Critically

1. In what ways has Moraga internalized her oppression? Why does she feel it is important to acknowledge this internalization?

2. What do the experiences of oppression that Moraga writes about have in common?

Connecting

1. Like Cherríe Moraga in "La Güera," Richard Rodriguez discusses the effects of his appearance on his life in "Complexion" (p. 205). Do they make similar points about the effects of their skin color? Does it affect their lives differently? Explain by drawing from both texts.

Writing

1. In the epigraph to Moraga's essay, Emma Goldman indicates the importance of the "capacity to enter into the lives of others." How do Moraga's ideas, as presented in "La Güera," help achieve this capacity? Drawing upon Moraga's essay and upon your own experiences, write an essay that answers this question.

Creating

1. **Write a poem in response to Moraga's essay.** In her career, Cherríe Moraga has written plays, poetry, and essays, and often has mixed them in the same books. Write a poem that expresses some of the ideas that you encounter in the essay "La Güera." It could be written from the perspective of someone she writes about, or it could be something more abstract.

31

ANA CASTILLO [b. 1953]

Saturdays • A Marriage of Mutes

From My Father Was a Toltec [1988]

GENRE: POETRY

*Ana Castillo combines work as a poet and novelist with theoreti-
cal work about the distinctive nature of Chicana literature, culture, and tradition, for which she coined the term "Xicanisma."
Along with Gloria Anzaldúa (p. 238) and Cherríe Moraga (p. 250),
she has changed the nature of feminism while strengthening its
place in any discussion of Mexican American life. Castillo was
born in Chicago and, initially inspired by the Chicano Movement
to become an art teacher, earned a bachelor's degree from North-
eastern Illinois University and a master's degree from the University of Chicago. Castillo's book* Women Are Not Roses *was published in 1984 and established her reputation as a political poet,
fighting for respect for Chicanas outside and inside the Movement.
Her first novel,* The Mixquiahuala Letters, *was first published in
1986 (later republished by Doubleday in 1992) and tells through a
series of letters the complex and intimate relationship of two
women exploring their gender and cultural identities. In 1988 she
published her second book of poetry,* My Father Was a Toltec, *and
translated Moraga and Anzaldúa's influential anthology* This
Bridge Called My Back *into Spanish. She continued her work on
feminist theory in her 1994 book,* Massacre of the Dreamers:
Essays on Xicanisma, *which she'd worked on while earning a Ph.D.
in American studies from the University of Bremen in Germany.
In the introduction to* Massacre of the Dreamers *she stated: "It is
our task as Xicanistas, to not only recall our* indigenismo—but
also to reinsert the forgotten feminine into our consciousness."
Castillo's later writings include the 1993 novel So Far from God,
a story collection of 1996 called Loverboys, *and the novel* Give It
to Me, *published in 2014.*

*The poems reprinted here, which grew out of Castillo's memo-
ries of her own family, present women who are almost invisible to
the men in their lives. "Saturdays" is about a woman spending her*

day cleaning and preparing clothing for a man oblivious to her
labor, while "A Marriage of Mutes" focuses on the lack of commu-
nication that accompanies such a relationship.

As you read, pay attention to the tone of the poems as Castillo
balances criticism with intimacy.

SATURDAYS

Because she worked all week
away from home, gone from 5 to 5,
Saturdays she did the laundry,
pulled the wringer machine
to the kitchen sink, and hung   5
the clothes out on the line.
At night, we took it down and ironed.
Mine were his handkerchiefs and
boxer shorts. She did his work
pants (never worn on the street)   10
and shirts, pressed the collars
and cuffs, just so—
as he bathed,
donned the tailor-made silk suit
bought on her credit, had her   15
adjust the tie.

"How do I look?"
"Bien,°" went on ironing.
That's why he married her, a Mexican
woman, like his mother, not like   20
they were in Chicago, not like
the one he was going out to meet.

A MARRIAGE OF MUTES

In the house
that was his house
where the woman who lived there
cut the vegetables
hacked the chicken   5

Bien: Good.

boiled on the stove
and waited across the table
as he ate, with eyes that asked,
Was it all right? Was it enough?—
the woman who slept with him   10
changed the linen
scrubbed oil from his coveralls
hung laundry on the line
never sought the face of the woman
across the yard who hung sheets,   15
coveralls and underwear—
in the house where this man lived
so at peace with himself
the air grew sparse one morning.

The hall to the bathroom narrowed   20
as his feet grew angular and
head lightened.
He startled himself to hear his first
"caw!"—beating black wings against walls,
knocking down picture frames of the woman's   25
ancestors, the offspring's bronzed shoes
off the buffet.
One could only guess what he might
have said had his beak contained teeth.
The woman who always anticipated   30
his needs opened a window.

She would have wanted the crow to sit
on the couch
to read with her,
listen to music,   35
languish in a moment of peace
before the bird who was the man
she had lived with in such gratitude flew off,
but, of course, it was too much to ask.

It had always been too much to ask.   40

Reading

1. ("Saturdays") What types of housework are being done in the poem?
2. ("Saturdays") What is the setting (place and time) of the poem?

3. ("A Marriage of Mutes") Who in the poem is the crow?

4. ("A Marriage of Mutes") What objects does the crow knock down?

Thinking Critically

1. How does Castillo indicate that the experience of the woman in "Saturdays" is typical, rather than unique?

2. Based on what the poem's speaker conveys, how would you describe the life of the woman in "A Marriage of Mutes"?

3. How does the metaphor in "A Marriage of Mutes" contribute to the poem's meaning?

Connecting

1. Though "A Marriage of Mutes" and "Saturdays" are focused on women, they also describe a male figure. How does the male figure of these poems compare to the father of the narrator of Benjamín Alire Sáenz's story "Sometimes the Rain" (p. 342)? What do you think Castillo might say about Neto's father?

Writing

1. In these poems, Castillo explores aspects of shared human experience, specifically gender roles and relationships between men and women. In a brief essay, using examples from your own life and from the poems, write about what makes the subjects of the poems meaningful and universal.

Creating

1. **Write a poem, using Castillo's work as inspiration.** In both "Saturdays" and "A Marriage of Mutes," Castillo uses imagery to show distinctive aspects of the lives of women. In a brief prose poem about your own childhood home, explore some of the questions raised by Castillo. Was work shared equally among all members of the family? Why was it divided the way it was? Do you think it was divided fairly or unfairly?

32

SANDRA CISNEROS [b. 1954]

Woman Hollering Creek

From Woman Hollering Creek [1991]

GENRE: FICTION

By combining the outlook of a Chicana feminist with her gifts as a poet and storyteller, Sandra Cisneros has become the most widely read Mexican American writer today. She is at the forefront of a generation of writers, first published in the 1980s, who are comfortable with their identity and possess an artistic and technical ability that has led to mainstream success. Cisneros grew up in Chicago and attended Loyola University, where she first started writing. She left Chicago to earn an M.F.A in creative writing from the University of Iowa Writers' Workshop. She returned to Chicago and taught high school for several years until grants from the National Endowment for the Arts enabled her to complete her most famous work, The House on Mango Street, *which was published in 1983. The book was a set of poetically written chapters about a young Mexican American who surveys the poverty and abuse around her in search of her own future.* The House on Mango Street *was enormously successful, becoming a bestseller as well as required reading in high school and college courses alike. Cisneros next returned to poems she'd written at Iowa and published her first collection,* My Wicked, Wicked Ways, *in 1987.* Woman Hollering Creek and Other Stories *appeared in 1991, followed by another book of poems,* Loose Woman, *in 1994. The following year, Cisneros received a grant from the MacArthur Foundation, which enabled her to work on her novel* Caramelo, *published in 2002.* Caramelo *is the multigenerational story of a family finding its way from Mexico to Chicago and finally, like Cisneros, to San Antonio, Texas.*

Cisneros has a great ability to tackle very serious issues with a style that is intimate and playful. "We can all communicate if we can stay really close to the speech we use when we're in our kitchens, or in our pajamas, or at Dunkin' Donuts, not trying to impress anybody, but just coming from some real heartfelt part of you,"* she has said.

---

*From Hector A. Torres, *Conversations with Contemporary Chicana and Chicano Writers*.

As you read "Woman Hollering Creek," notice how Cisneros's style draws the reader into the story of the curiously named Cleófilas and creates sympathy for her plight as a victim of physical and emotional abuse.

The day Don Serafín gave Juan Pedro Martínez Sánchez permission to take Cleófilas Enriqueta DeLeón Hernández as his bride, across her father's threshold, over several miles of dirt road and several miles of paved, over one border and beyond to a town *en el otro lado*—on the other side—already did he divine the morning his daughter would raise her hand over her eyes, look south, and dream of returning to the chores that never ended, six good-for-nothing brothers, and one old man's complaints.

He had said, after all, in the hubbub of parting: I am your father, I will never abandon you. He *had* said that, hadn't he, when he hugged and then let her go. But at the moment Cleófilas was busy looking for Chela, her maid of honor, to fulfill their bouquet conspiracy. She would not remember her father's parting words until later. *I am your father, I will never abandon you.*

Only now as a mother did she remember. Now, when she and Juan Pedrito sat by the creek's edge. How when a man and a woman love each other, sometimes that love sours. But a parent's love for a child, a child's for its parents, is another thing entirely.

This is what Cleófilas thought evenings when Juan Pedro did not come home, and she lay on her side of the bed listening to the hollow roar of the interstate, a distant dog barking, the pecan trees rustling like ladies in stiff petticoats—*shh-shh-shh, shh-shh-shh*—soothing her to sleep.

In the town where she grew up, there isn't very much to do except accompany the aunts and godmothers to the house of one or the other to play cards. Or walk to the cinema to see this week's film again, speckled and with one hair quivering annoyingly on the screen. Or to the center of town to order a milk shake that will appear in a day and a half as a pimple on her backside. Or to the girlfriend's house to watch the latest *telenovela*° episode and try to copy the way the women comb their hair, wear their makeup.   5

But what Cleófilas has been waiting for, has been whispering and sighing and giggling for, has been anticipating since she was old enough to lean against the window displays of gauze and butterflies and lace, is passion. Not the kind on the cover of the ¡*Alarma!* magazines, mind you, where the lover is photographed with the bloody fork she used to salvage

telenovela: Television soap opera.

her good name. But passion in its purest crystalline essence. The kind the books and songs and *telenovelas* describe when one finds, finally, the great love of one's life, and does whatever one can, must do, at whatever the cost.

Tú o Nadie. "You or No One." The title of the current favorite *telenovela*. The beautiful Lucía Méndez having to put up with all kinds of hardships of the heart, separation and betrayal, and loving, always loving no matter what, because *that* is the most important thing, and did you see Lucía Méndez on the Bayer aspirin commercials—wasn't she lovely? Does she dye her hair do you think? Cleófilas is going to go to the *farmacia*° and buy a hair rinse; her girlfriend Chela will apply it—it's not that difficult at all.

Because you didn't watch last night's episode when Lucía confessed she loved him more than anyone in her life. In her life! And she sings the song "You or No One" in the beginning and end of the show. *Tú o Nadie*. Somehow one ought to live one's life like that, don't you think? You or no one. Because to suffer for love is good. The pain all sweet somehow. In the end.

Seguín. She had liked the sound of it. Far away and lovely. Not like *Monclova*. *Coahuila*. Ugly.

Seguín, Tejas. A nice sterling ring to it. The tinkle of money. She would 10 get to wear outfits like the women on the *tele*, like Lucía Méndez. And have a lovely house, and wouldn't Chela be jealous.

And yes, they will drive all the way to Laredo to get her wedding dress. That's what they say. Because Juan Pedro wants to get married right away, without a long engagement since he can't take off too much time from work. He has a very important position in Seguin with, with . . . a beer company, I think. Or was it tires? Yes, he has to be back. So they will get married in the spring when he can take off work, and then they will drive off in his new pickup—did you see it?—to their new home in Seguin. Well, not exactly new, but they're going to repaint the house. You know newlyweds. New paint and new furniture. Why not? He can afford it. And later on add maybe a room or two for the children. May they be blessed with many.

Well, you'll see. Cleófilas has always been so good with her sewing machine. A little *rrrr, rrrr, rrrr* of the machine and *¡zas!* Miracles. She's always been so clever, that girl. Poor thing. And without even a mama to advise her on things like her wedding night. Well, may God help her. What with a father with a head like a burro, and those six clumsy brothers. Well, what do you think! Yes, I'm going to the wedding. Of course!

farmácia: Pharmacy.

The dress I want to wear just needs to be altered a teensy bit to bring it up to date. See, I saw a new style last night that I thought would suit me. Did you watch last night's episode of *The Rich Also Cry*? Well, did you notice the dress the mother was wearing?

La Gritona. Such a funny name for such a lovely *arroyo*.° But that's what they called the creek that ran behind the house. Though no one could say whether the woman had hollered from anger or pain. The natives only knew the *arroyo* one crossed on the way to San Antonio, and then once again on the way back, was called Woman Hollering, a name no one from these parts questioned, little less understood. *Pues, allá de los indios, quién sabe°*—who knows, the townspeople shrugged, because it was of no concern to their lives how this trickle of water received its curious name.

"What do you want to know for?" Trini the laundromat attendant asked in the same gruff Spanish she always used whenever she gave Cleófilas change or yelled at her for something. First for putting too much soap in the machines. Later, for sitting on a washer. And still later, after Juan Pedrito was born, for not understanding that in this country you cannot let your baby walk around with no diaper and his pee-pee hanging out, it wasn't nice, *¿entiendes? Pues*.°

How could Cleófilas explain to a woman like this why the name Woman 15 Hollering fascinated her. Well, there was no sense talking to Trini.

On the other hand there were the neighbor ladies, one on either side of the house they rented near the *arroyo*. The woman Soledad on the left, the woman Dolores on the right.

The neighbor lady Soledad liked to call herself a widow, though how she came to be one was a mystery. Her husband had either died, or run away with an ice-house floozie, or simply gone out for cigarettes one afternoon and never came back. It was hard to say which since Soledad, as a rule, didn't mention him.

In the other house lived *la señora°* Dolores, kind and very sweet, but her house smelled too much of incense and candles from the altars that burned continuously in memory of two sons who had died in the last war and one husband who had died shortly after from grief. The neighbor lady Dolores divided her time between the memory of these men and her garden, famous for its sunflowers—so tall they had to be supported with broom handles and old boards; red red cockscombs, fringed and bleeding a thick menstrual color; and, especially, roses whose sad scent reminded Cleófilas of the dead. Each Sunday *la señora* Dolores clipped

---

arroyo: Creek. **Pues, allá de los indios, quién sabe:** Well, it's from the Indians, who knows. **¿entiendes? Pues:** Got it? Well then. **la señora:** The lady.

the most beautiful of these flowers and arranged them on three modest headstones at the Seguin cemetery.

The neighbor ladies, Soledad, Dolores, they might've known once the name of the *arroyo* before it turned English but they did not know now. They were too busy remembering the men who had left through either choice or circumstance and would never come back.

Pain or rage, Cleófilas wondered when she drove over the bridge the   20 first time as a newlywed and Juan Pedro had pointed it out. *La Gritona*, he had said, and she had laughed. Such a funny name for a creek so pretty and full of happily ever after.

The first time she had been so surprised she didn't cry out or try to defend herself. She had always said she would strike back if a man, any man, were to strike her.

But when the moment came, and he slapped her once, and then again, and again; until the lip split and bled an orchid of blood, she didn't fight back, she didn't break into tears, she didn't run away as she imagined she might when she saw such things in the *telenovelas*.

In her own home her parents had never raised a hand to each other or to their children. Although she admitted she may have been brought up a little leniently as an only daughter—*la consentida*, the princess—there were some things she would never tolerate. Ever.

Instead, when it happened the first time, when they were barely man and wife, she had been so stunned, it left her speechless, motionless, numb. She had done nothing but reach up to the heat on her mouth and stare at the blood on her hand as if even then she didn't understand.

She could think of nothing to say, said nothing. Just stroked the dark   25 curls of the man who wept and would weep like a child, his tears of repentance and shame, this time and each.

The men at the ice house. From what she can tell, from the times during her first year when still a newlywed she is invited and accompanies her husband, sits mute beside their conversation, waits and sips a beer until it grows warm, twists a paper napkin into a knot, then another into a fan, one into a rose, nods her head, smiles, yawns, politely grins, laughs at the appropriate moments, leans against her husband's sleeve, tugs at his elbow, and finally becomes good at predicting where the talk will lead, from this Cleófilas concludes each is nightly trying to find the truth lying at the bottom of the bottle like a gold doubloon on the sea floor.

They want to tell each other what they want to tell themselves. But what is bumping like a helium balloon at the ceiling of the brain never finds its way out. It bubbles and rises, it gurgles in the throat, it rolls across the surface of the tongue, and erupts from the lips—a belch.

If they are lucky, there are tears at the end of the long night. At any given moment, the fists try to speak. They are dogs chasing their own tails before lying down to sleep, trying to find a way, a route, an out, and—finally—get some peace.

In the morning sometimes before he opens his eyes. Or after they have finished loving. Or at times when he is simply across from her at the table putting pieces of food into his mouth and chewing. Cleófilas thinks, This is the man I have waited my whole life for.

Not that he isn't a good man. She has to remind herself why she loves   30
him when she changes the baby's Pampers, or when she mops the bath-room floor, or tries to make the curtains for the doorways without doors, or whiten the linen. Or wonder a little when he kicks the refrigerator and says he hates this shitty house and is going out where he won't be both-ered with the baby's howling and her suspicious questions, and her requests to fix this and this and this because if she had any brains in her head she'd realize he's been up before the rooster earning his living to pay for the food in her belly and the roof over her head and would have to wake up again early the next day so why can't you just leave me in peace, woman.

He is not very tall, no, and he doesn't look like the men on the *telenovelas*. His face still scarred from acne. And he has a bit of a belly from all the beer he drinks. Well, he's always been husky.

This man who farts and belches and snores as well as laughs and kisses and holds her. Somehow this husband whose whiskers she finds each morning in the sink, whose shoes she must air each evening on the porch, this husband who cuts his fingernails in public, laughs loudly, curses like a man, and demands each course of dinner be served on a separate plate like at his mother's, as soon as he gets home, on time or late, and who doesn't care at all for music or *telenovelas* or romance or roses or the moon floating pearly over the *arroyo*, or through the bed-room window for that matter, shut the blinds and go back to sleep, this man, this father, this rival, this keeper, this lord, this master, this hus-band till kingdom come.

A doubt. Slender as a hair. A washed cup set back on the shelf wrong-side-up. Her lipstick, and body talc, and hairbrush all arranged in the bathroom a different way.

No. Her imagination. The house the same as always. Nothing.

Coming home from the hospital with her new son, her husband. Some-   35
thing comforting in discovering her house slippers beneath the bed, the faded housecoat where she left it on the bathroom hook. Her pillow. Their bed.

Sweet sweet homecoming. Sweet as the scent of face powder in the air, jasmine, sticky liquor.

Smudged fingerprint on the door. Crushed cigarette in a glass. Wrinkle in the brain crumpling to a crease.

Sometimes she thinks of her father's house. But how could she go back there? What a disgrace. What would the neighbors say? Coming home like that with one baby on her hip and one in the oven. Where's your husband?

The town of gossips. The town of dust and despair. Which she has traded for this town of gossips. This town of dust, despair. Houses farther apart perhaps, though no more privacy because of it. No leafy *zócalo*° in the center of the town, though the murmur of talk is clear enough all the same. No huddled whispering on the church steps each Sunday. Because here the whispering begins at sunset at the ice house instead.

This town with its silly pride for a bronze pecan the size of a baby carriage in front of the city hall. TV repair shop, drugstore, hardware, dry cleaner's, chiropractor's, liquor store, bail bonds, empty storefront, and nothing, nothing, nothing of interest. Nothing one could walk to, at any rate. Because the towns here are built so that you have to depend on husbands. Or you stay home. Or you drive. If you're rich enough to own, allowed to drive, your own car. 40

There is no place to go. Unless one counts the neighbor ladies. Soledad on one side, Dolores on the other. Or the creek.

Don't go out there after dark, *mi'jita*.° Stay near the house. *No es bueno para la salud*.° *Mala suerte*. Bad luck. *Mal aire*. You'll get sick and the baby too. You'll catch a fright wandering about in the dark, and then you'll see how right we were.

The stream sometimes only a muddy puddle in the summer, though now in the springtime, because of the rains, a good-size alive thing, a thing with a voice all its own, all day and all night calling in its high, silver voice. Is it La Llorona, the weeping woman? La Llorona, who drowned her own children. Perhaps La Llorona is the one they named the creek after, she thinks, remembering all the stories she learned as a child.

La Llorona calling to her. She is sure of it. Cleófilas sets the baby's Donald Duck blanket on the grass. Listens. The day sky turning to night. The baby pulling up fistfuls of grass and laughing. La Llorona. Wonders if something as quiet as this drives a woman to the darkness under the trees.

zócalo: A main square. **mi'jita:** My daughter. **No es bueno para la salud:** It's unhealthy.

What she needs is . . . and made a gesture as if to yank a woman's but-   45
tocks to his groin. Maximiliano, the foul-smelling fool from across the
road, said this and set the men laughing, but Cleófilas just muttered.
Grosero,° and went on washing dishes.

She knew he said it not because it was true, but more because it was
he who needed to sleep with a woman, instead of drinking each night at
the ice house and stumbling home alone.

Maximiliano who was said to have killed his wife in an ice-house
brawl when she came at him with a mop. I had to shoot, he had said—she
was armed.

Their laughter outside the kitchen window. Her husband's, his friends'.
Manolo, Beto, Efraín, el Perico. Maximiliano.

Was Cleófilas just exaggerating as her husband always said? It seemed
the newspapers were full of such stories. This woman found on the side
of the interstate. This one pushed from a moving car. This one's cadaver,
this one unconscious, this one beaten blue. Her ex-husband, her husband,
her lover, her father, her brother, her uncle, her friend, her co-worker.
Always. The same grisly news in the pages of the dailies. She dunked a
glass under the soapy water for a moment—shivered.

He had thrown a book. Hers. From across the room. A hot welt across   50
the cheek. She could forgive that. But what stung more was the fact it
was *her* book, a love story by Corín Tellado, what she loved most now
that she lived in the U.S., without a television set, without the *telenovelas*.

Except now and again when her husband was away and she could
manage it, the few episodes glimpsed at the neighbor lady Soledad's
house because Dolores didn't care for that sort of thing, though Soledad
was often kind enough to retell what had happened on what episode of
María de Nadie,° the poor Argentine country girl who had the ill fortune
of falling in love with the beautiful son of the Arrocha family, the very
family she worked for, whose roof she slept under and whose floors she
vacuumed, while in that same house, with the dust brooms and floor
cleaners as witnesses, the square-jawed Juan Carlos Arrocha had uttered
words of love, I love you, María, listen to me, *mi querida*,° but it was she
who had to say No, no, we are not of the same class, and remind him it
was not his place nor hers to fall in love, while all the while her heart was
breaking, can you imagine.

Cleófilas thought her life would have to be like that, like a *telenovela*,
only now the episodes got sadder and sadder. And there were no commercials in between for comic relief. And no happy ending in sight. She
thought this when she sat with the baby out by the creek behind the

Grosero: Rude.   **de Nadie:** Belonging to no one.   **mi querida:** My dear.

house. Cleófilas de . . . ? But somehow she would have to change her name to Topazio, or Yesenia, Cristal, Adriana, Stefania, Andrea, something more poetic than Cleófilas. Everything happened to women with names like jewels. But what happened to a Cleófilas? Nothing. But a crack in the face.

Because the doctor has said so. She has to go. To make sure the new baby is all right, so there won't be any problems when he's born, and the appointment card says next Tuesday. Could he please take her. And that's all.

No, she won't mention it. She promises. If the doctor asks she can say she fell down the front steps or slipped when she was out in the backyard, slipped out back, she could tell him that. She has to go back next Tuesday, Juan Pedro, please, for the new baby. For their child.

She could write to her father and ask maybe for money, just a loan, for 55
the new baby's medical expenses. Well then if he'd rather she didn't. All right, she won't. Please don't anymore. Please don't. She knows it's difficult saving money with all the bills they have, but how else are they going to get out of debt with the truck payments? And after the rent and the food and the electricity and the gas and the water and the who-knows-what, well, there's hardly anything left. But please, at least for the doctor visit. She won't ask for anything else. She has to. Why is she so anxious? Because.

Because she is going to make sure the baby is not turned around backward this time to split her down the center. Yes. Next Tuesday at five-thirty. I'll have Juan Pedrito dressed and ready. But those are the only shoes he has. I'll polish them, and we'll be ready. As soon as you come from work. We won't make you ashamed.

Felice? It's me, Graciela.

No, I can't talk louder. I'm at work.

Look, I need kind of a favor. There's a patient, a lady here who's got a problem.

Well, wait a minute. Are you listening to me or what?   60

I can't talk real loud 'cause her husband's in the next room.

Well, would you just listen?

I was going to do this sonogram on her — she's pregnant, right? — and she just starts crying on me. *Híjole,*° Felice! This poor lady's got black-and-blue marks all over. I'm not kidding.

From her husband. Who else? Another one of those brides from across the border. And her family's all in Mexico.

Shit. You think they're going to help her? Give me a break. This lady 65
doesn't even speak English. She hasn't been allowed to call home or write or nothing. That's why I'm calling you.

Híjole: Damn.

She needs a ride.

Not to Mexico, you goof. Just to the Greyhound. In San Anto.

No, just a ride. She's got her own money. All you'd have to do is drop her off in San Antonio on your way home. Come on, Felice. Please? If we don't help her, who will? I'd drive her myself, but she needs to be on that bus before her husband gets home from work. What do you say?

I don't know. Wait.

Right away, tomorrow even.   70

Well, if tomorrow's no good for you . . .

It's a date, Felice. Thursday. At the Cash N Carry off I-10. Noon. She'll be ready.

Oh, and her name's Cleófilas.

I don't know. One of those Mexican saints, I guess. A martyr or something.

Cleófilas. C-L-E-O-F-I-L-A-S. Cle. O. Fi. Las. Write it down.   75

Thanks, Felice. When her kid's born she'll have to name her after us, right?

Yeah, you got it. A regular soap opera sometimes. *Qué vida, comadre. Bueno°* bye.

All morning that flutter of half-fear, half-doubt. At any moment Juan Pedro might appear in the doorway. On the street. At the Cash N Carry. Like in the dreams she dreamed.

There was that to think about, yes, until the woman in the pickup drove up. Then there wasn't time to think about anything but the pickup pointed toward San Antonio. Put your bags in the back and get in.

But when they drove across the *arroyo*, the driver opened her mouth   80 and let out a yell as loud as any mariachi. Which startled not only Cleófilas, but Juan Pedrito as well.

Pues,° look how cute. I scared you two, right? Sorry. Should've warned you. Every time I cross that bridge I do that. Because of the name, you know. Woman Hollering. *Pues,* I holler. She said this in a Spanish pocked with English and laughed. Did you ever notice, Felice continued, how nothing around here is named after a woman? Really. Unless she's the Virgin. I guess you're only famous if you're a virgin. She was laughing again.

That's why I like the name of that *arroyo*. Makes you want to holler like Tarzan, right?

Everything about this woman, this Felice, amazed Cleófilas. The fact that she drove a pickup. A pickup, mind you, but when Cleófilas asked if it was her husband's, she said she didn't have a husband. The pickup was hers. She herself had chosen it. She herself was paying for it.

Qué vida, comadre. Bueno: Life is really something, sister. All right.
Pues: Well then.

I used to have a Pontiac Sunbird. But those cars are for *viejas*. Pussy cars. Now this here is a *real* car.

What kind of talk was that coming from a woman? Cleófilas thought.   85 But then again, Felice was like no woman she'd ever met. Can you imagine, when we crossed the *arroyo* she just started yelling like a crazy, she would say later to her father and brothers. Just like that. Who would've thought?

Who would've? Pain or rage, perhaps, but not a hoot like the one Felice had just let go. Makes you want to holler like Tarzan, Felice had said.

Then Felice began laughing again, but it wasn't Felice laughing. It was gurgling out of her own throat, a long ribbon of laughter, like water.

Reading

1. In what ways does Juan Pedro disappoint Cleófilas?

2. How does Cleófilas meet Felice? Where does Felice take Cleófilas?

Thinking Critically

1. Why does Cleófilas react the way she does to being hit by her husband?

2. What effect do you think the birth of Juan Pedrito has on Cleófilas?

Connecting

1. Rolando Hinojosa's *Estampas del Valle* (p. 152) presents a wide variety of characters living in South Texas. Do you think Cleófilas and Juan Pedro would fit into Hinojosa's Belken County? Why or why not?

Writing

1. Though Cleófilas thinks that life in Seguin, Texas, will be wonderful, she is quickly disappointed and finds herself terribly alone. Write an essay in which you explore the causes of Cleófilas's isolation in Seguin. Use specific examples from the story.

Creating

1. **Review a *telenovela*.** Cleófilas repeatedly compares her own situation to the romantic stories she has seen in *telenovelas*. Watch a *telenovela* or a soap opera and write a review of an episode, discussing the lifestyles of the characters in these shows.

33

DENISE CHÁVEZ [b. 1947]

¡Híjole! In the Darkness

From Loving Pedro Infante [2001]

GENRE: FICTION

*New Mexico native Denise Chávez spent many years in the theater—
as an actor, a director, and a playwright—before gaining fame as
a novelist. To all her work she brings a deep appreciation of the
culture of New Mexico and of the border region. Chávez earned a
bachelor's degree from New Mexico State University in her home-
town of Las Cruces and a master's degree in theater arts from
Trinity University in San Antonio, Texas. She then worked in theater in New Mexico for many years while also teaching and writing
fiction. Her 1984 play* Plaza *took her to New York and Edinburgh,
Scotland, and in that same year she earned a degree in creative
writing from the University of New Mexico. Speaking of the conti-
nuity between theater and writing, she said that when she began
acting, she "found that I could become someone else, get inside the
skin of another like the Mayan priests who used to dance inside
the skins of the people. I want to be able to dance within the skins
of my characters. To me there's no separation between myself the
writer and myself the actress."** *
Her first book of fiction, an interconnected set of stories called
The Last of the Menu Girls, *was published in 1986. In it and her
subsequent books, the 1993 novel* Face of an Angel *and the 2001
novel* Loving Pedro Infante, *Chávez explores the themes from
some of her plays, focusing on the lives of Mexican American
women as they develop relationships, discover identities, and find
their adult selves. Chávez, who directs a cultural center in Las
Cruces, is also the founder of the Border Books Festival, an annual
celebration of the literature and culture of the border region.*
Below we meet Teresina Ávila, the protagonist of the novel Loving Pedro Infante, *whose name is an allusion to the seventeenth-
century mystic and saint Teresa of Ávila. In this first chapter of*

*From an interview available at ir.uiowa.edu/cgi/viewcontent.cgi
?article=1161&context=ijcs.

the book, "Tere" meditates on Pedro Infante, movie star and, for Chávez, "the embodiment of Mexican machismo beauty, both in its positive and negative senses."*

As you read, think about what ideals the character Tere finds represented by Pedro Infante. Pay close attention, though, to the ways that Chávez hints that reality is doomed to fall short of such ideals. "What intrigues me in this book," Chávez has said, "is that the ideal of love is not the reality of love."**

¡HÍJOLE!° IN THE DARKNESS

In the darkness of El Colón movie theater, larger than life and superimposed on a giant screen, Pedro Infante, the Mexican movie star, stares straight at me with his dark, smoldering eyes.

It is here in the sensuous shadows that I forget all about my life as Teresina "La Tere" Ávila, teacher's aide at Cabritoville Elementary School. Maybe that's why I like Pedro's movies so much. They make me think to stop thinking or stop thinking to really think.

It is here that I prefer to dream, seated in the middle of the people I call family. To my right is my comadre,° Irma "La Wirma" Granados, and next to her is her mother, Nyvia Ester Granados.

It's dinnertime on a hot July night. I should be at home, and yet I find myself lost in the timeless transparency of El Colón watching Pedro Infante in the movie *La Vida No Vale Nada*.° Pedro plays a melancholic loner named Pablo who keeps leaving any number of possible lives behind, and all sorts of women who might have loved him. He's a good-hearted vato° who goes on these incredible life-changing borracheras° whenever he feels overwhelmed, which is pretty much most of the time. Ay, Dios mío.°   5

Pedro's lips part slightly with that naughty nene—little boy—grin of his as he breaks into a song.

¡Ay, ay, ay!

*From an interview in Karin Rosa Ikas, *Chicana Ways*.

**From the *Dictionary of Literary Biography*.

¡Híjole!: Damn!   **comadre:** Very close friend, "sister."   ***La Vida No Vale Nada:*** *Life Is Worth Nothing*.   **vato:** Guy.   **borracheras:** Drinking binges.   **Ay, Dios mío:** Oh my God.

Pedro knows me. He knows I crave his arms. His touch. His deep voice in my ear, his knowing hands on my trembling body.

Híjole.

The great flames of my dreams billow up to meet the flickering screen,   10
as a wave of intense light consumes the sweet, painful and familiar song of my untold longing.

¡Uuuuuey! The man has me going. Revved up like a swirling red, green, yellow and blue top, I can barely sit still in my seat. I sit up straight, then shiver, then melt down to hot plastic, trying to find a comfortable position. My legs are itchy, a sure sign of the troubled state of my mind, my restless body. There is no relief. I admit, years after he died tragically in a plane crash, I'm in love with Pedro.

Who isn't?

In the movie, Pedro-as-Pablo meets Cruz, the widowed owner of an antique shop in the market and he carries her groceries home for her. He offers to stay on to help and that is exactly what he does, cleaning up, fixing things, getting the shop back on its feet. And he can't help but notice how voluptuous Cruz is, despite her black widow's dress.

After exchanging glances that would have worked on any other woman, Cruz still can't admit she loves Pedro-as-Pablo. But she's thrilled to know he wants her — his lust naked, unadorned. Only when she's behind closed doors in her room can she admit the terrible truth.

What can I tell you about Pedro Infante? If you're a Mejicana or Meji-   15
cano and don't know who he is, you should be tied to a hot stove with yucca rope and beaten with sharp dry corn husks as you stand in a vat of soggy fideos.° If your racial and cultural ethnicity is Other, then it's about time you learned about the most famous of Mexican singers and actors.

Pedro was born November 18, 1917, in Mazatlán, Sinaloa, and died in 1957 in a horrible plane crash in Mérida, Yucatán, when he was forty years old and at the height of his popularity. He was the biggest movie star in the Mexican cinema of the forties and fifties, what is called La Época de Oro del Cine Mejicano.° Many know him as "El ídolo del Pueblo.°" Some people even call him the Dean Martin of Méjico, but he's more, much more than that. He was bigger than Bing Crosby or even Elvis Presley.

Pedro's real life was just as passionate as the one he played on the screen. There was his first girlfriend, Lupita Marqués, who bore him a little girl. And then there was his long-suffering wife, María Luisa. Then came Lupe Torrentera, the young dancer he met when she was fourteen

fideos: Noodles.   **La Época de Oro del Cine Mejicano:** The Golden Age of Mexican Cinema.   **El ídolo del Pueblo:** The people's idol.

and who bore him a daughter, Graciela Margarita, at age fifteen. Lupe was the mother of two of his other children. And, of course, there was Irma Dorantes, the young actress who starred in many of his movies and became the mother of his daughter, Irmita. The marriage to her was annulled the week before his death.

In between these women were many other women, some whose names we remember, many we don't. And one can never forget his mother, Doña Refugia, or Doña Cuquita, as she was known. She was really the first woman who truly loved Pedro. Pedro was the type of man who took care of the women in his life, from Doña Refugio to María Luisa to all of his mistresses. Either he had a fantastically rich and good life or a hell of a complicated one.

If I'd had a chance and been born earlier and in a different place, I might have tried to take up with Pedro as well. But I was born in Cabritoville, U.S.A., on the Tejas/Méjico border near El Paso. The closest I'll ever come to Pedro Infante is in El Colón on a Thursday night. In here time is suspended. In here I want to imagine the impossible, to leave, for an hour or two, my life behind.

Nyvia Ester sits behind a woman who keeps talking when Pedro-as-Pablo does something cute on-screen, or makes ojitos with his beautiful eyes—which makes us all sticky and hot like the popcorn with butter that we're holding even though we know he's been dead for years. 20

All I need is a little quiet and a lot of darkness. And for the man across the aisle from me to stop smacking his dry lips and murmuring under his hot breath.

When Pedro-as-Pablo suddenly takes Cruz in his arms there is a profound and sacred silence.

Then I hear a sharp intake of breath from Nyvia Ester. Irma sighs, a barely perceptible sound of pure pleasure. I slide down in my seat, my head momentarily resting on the plastic chair back, then nervously rise with dreaded anticipation of what is to come. This is the scene where Cruz gives Pablo her father's gold watch. I can't take it. I know what's going to happen.

It breaks my heart every time Pedro-as-Pablo leaves Cruz in the middle of the night after she's given him her father's watch. Later, she wakes up to find him gone and she runs down a set of dark stairs calling out his name. But he will never come back.

Pedro-as-Pablo is the type of man who will never be faithful to one woman. It's not that he doesn't want to be, he just can't. He can't stay with Silvia, the prostitute he befriends. Eventually he earns enough money as a baker to free her from the brothel owner she's indebted to, but when she finally finds him to thank him and hopefully spend the rest of her life with him, to her surprise he doesn't want her. 25

More adventures, more women, a life out of control. Pedro can't stop loving and leaving women.

Now raucous with laughter, the man across from me applauds as Pedro-as-Pablo awakes to find himself in bed again, now with Silvia.

Not even Cruz could stop Pedro-as-Pablo, make him stand still, find a life of peace. He loved her, but it wasn't meant to be. There is no rest for someone as rootless as him. Only drinking will ease his pain. Silvia is someone he pities. Marta? Ay, she's a minor distraction. How can Pedro-as-Pablo love anyone when he doesn't even like himself?

The temperature inside El Colón is ninety degrees. The main floor and the balcony are packed with people of all ages, families hovering close to each other, young lovers, older couples resting like torpid flies near the water cooler. Outside, it's hotter.

The married men wander down to the concession stand to get a Coke   30
and stare hard at the young girls, chiflando° in that soft appreciative way with their breath, a small outtake of air releasing the sexual tension, while their wives slink down in their seats, grateful for a little peace as they pull down their bunched-up panties. Someone takes out a much-used plastic bag full of tortas,° someone else a crinkly paper bag full of ripe mangos. The floor is testimony to the fierce hunger that the darkness arouses. Candy wrappers stick to it along with chewed-up stalks of sugarcane with mashed fibers that nobody wants to look at too closely. Crumpled soft drink cups and popcorn boxes are tucked between seats, wads of tired gum are glued underneath.

Voices call out incessantly to the actors on the screen, without any hesitation or embarrassment, as if the audience knows them, are friends, even family.

"Te quiero,° Pablo," Cruz tells Pedro-as-Pablo.

The woman behind us tells him as well. "Y yo te quiero a ti,° Pedro."

She's getting on my nerves. She knows all the lines to the movie and she repeats them to herself.

I know all the lines, too, but don't say them out loud.   35

In the darkness of El Colón, Pedro Infante could do it all, and he did. He sang, he rode horses, motorcycles, cars, buses, and he walked away from tragedy unlike anyone else. No one strode away from all these women, those men, their selfish attachments, all those inappropriate and terrible situations as Pedro did in *La Vida No Vale Nada*.

"Popcorn?" I whisper to Irma, who motions that the tub is with Nyvia Ester. Both of us know we may not see it for a long time. Someone is

---

chiflando: Whistling.   **torta:** A Mexican sandwich.   **Te quiero:** I love you.
Y yo te quiero a ti: And I love you.

going to have to go back for the free refill pretty soon and it's not going to be me.

The popcorn at El Colón is greasy and salty, as it should be. Irma says it smells of hot oil, of maíz,° of sweaty hands turning tortillas in small obscure villages, of present lives lived in a past tense, of ancestral struggles, of the humid breath of small children, of old, dying animals resting near crumbling adobes, of too many lives struggling for a modicum of hope. Leave it to La Wirms to try to understand the sociological and cultural meanings of different kinds of popcorn.

I say it's the way they do the butter. Gobs of it without regard to cholesterol.

Please don't ever give me a bag of day-old popcorn that isn't warm   40 enough to melt butter. There is nothing I love more than something greasy and salty unless, of course, it's something hot and greasy and salty. Or fruity and crystallized and so sweet your teeth curl in.

I've got simple tastes, ordinary needs that become extraordinary in the dark. What do I know about ancestral yearnings?

And yet this is why Irma says we're here, years after Pedro's death. "We're fulfilling the destiny set out for us, Tere, by those who came before us, the multitudes whose black-and-white dreams have allowed us to dream in color, whose misery and grief, longing and hopes have fueled our tomorrows."

"Whatever you say, comadre," I whisper to her in the dark. "I'm okay with that theory. But, mujer,° just look at the man! I don't care how many years he's been dead. I still want to taste him."

"¡Ay, tú!°" Irma says.

But I know she knows what I mean.   45

And she knows I know what she means.

When I watch Pedro's movies I'm watching the lives of my people, past, present and future, parade in front of me. Pedro Infante could have been my father; he was my father's age when I was born. He's the man we want our men to be. And he's the man we imagine ourselves to be if we are men. The man we want our daughters to have loved. Pedro's the beautiful part of our dreaming. And his looks still have the power to make my woman's blood heat up like sizzling manteca° on an old but faithful sartén.° Just watching him on the screen makes my little sopaipilla° start throbbing underneath all the folds and tucks of cloth on the old and creaky theater seat, just give me some honey.

He had a beautiful body. He lifted weights, which most Mejicanos didn't do at the time. When I think of the Mejicanos I know, I hardly

---

maíz: Corn.   **mujer:** Woman.   **¡Ay, tú!:** Oh, you!   **manteca:** Lard.
sartén: Frying pan.   **sopaipilla:** A fried pastry, often drizzled with honey.

think of them with barbells. They're not the exercising type. They're too busy working outdoors fixing the techo° or cleaning or working en los files° or running after their own or someone else's children or planting vegetables in their backyards.

When you saw Pedro boxing or riding a motorcycle, you knew he was a man ahead of his sluggish time. Physically robust, he did all his own stunts, whether it was fighting with Wolf Ruvinskis, the hunky Mexican actor who showed a lot of his chest during that era of moviemaking, or hanging on for dear life on the top of the old bus that took him down the dusty and interminable road to La Capital and into Cruz's waiting arms. Pedro loved more women than you can count, which is about the best exercise you can ever get.

He was incredibly handsome in that way only Mejicanos can be. I can't   50 explain this to you, only a Mejicana or an intuitive gringa knows what I mean. The handsomeness and sexiness come on you slowly and then hit you between the eyes. The more you contemplate a man like Pedro, observe his mannerisms, stare into his eyes, delight in his unique smile and strong arms, trim waist and good legs, and watch how gentle and yet self-assured he is with people of all ages, and see how much they love him, you will begin to understand a little of what Pedro Infante means to me, and the other members of the Pedro Infante Club de Admiradores Norteamericano° #256.

There was only one Pedro Infante, and he was a real man, and I'm very picky about men. It's a good thing. Not like Graciela Vallejos, Irma's wall-eyed cousin, who looks at men like driftwood she can just pick up whenever she wants. Nor am I like Irma, who's a little too finicky and rarely goes out on a date.

Irma never likes anyone, they're too this, too that. Too *desde*. That's the word my comadre uses for too *you know what*. For example, "Our President, Tere, he's just too *desde*. And what about his wife, she's just too, too *desde*. And not only that, but the press, why it's just been too *desde* about *desde*, if you ask me."

To Irma, most men either smell like Lavoris or pollo frito,° or they're only interested in a woman's nalgas° or her legs or her chichis° and they can't spell worth a damn, which really bothers her. She also hates a man who writes like a third grader. She rejected a CPA she met at La Tempestad Lounge, our weekend "stomping ground," after he gave her his business card, having scribbled his home phone number as a child

techo: Roof. **en los files:** In the fields. **Pedro Infante Club de Admiradores Norteamericano:** Pedro Infante American Fan Club. (*Norteamericano* is a term used in Mexico for someone from the United States.) **pollo frito:** Fried chicken. **nalgas:** Butt cheeks. **chichis:** Boobs.

would, his fingers clawed around the pen while his other hand held a cold can of Coors.

"You can imagine what he'd be like in bed," Irma said. "All fingers and none of them coordinating. And not only that, he was a Coors drinker. Hasn't he heard about the boycott?"

I never seem to think of things like that, things that can make or break   55 a romance, like if the guy has a nervous tic that will eventually become irritating, or if he smells too much of aftershave that masks sour body odor. Irma notices the way men smoke or what they say about people who smoke, or cross or don't cross their legs, the way they comb their hair, if they have hair, and if they don't have hair, what they think of themselves without hair, how they tie their shoelaces, if they have shoe-laces, or if they wear sandals, and what their toes look like in the sandals, and the way they drink their beer. She won't tolerate a smoker or a seri-ous drinker, just like me. I can understand that, what with the alcoholism in her family.

There have been a few people I know who have been drinkers, too. Tío° Santos, my mother's brother, for one. He always had a cold beer in his sweaty hands. And then there's Ubaldo Miranda, my best friend in the fan club, besides Irma. He shouldn't drink, but he does. He's been seeing a therapist in El Paso for years at Catholic Family Social Services on the sliding scale, pay as you can, and I think he's finally beginning to under-stand why he drinks. If you were molested during a Quinceañera° when everyone was in the big sala° having fun and you were in a dirty rest-room with your older cousin Mamerto Miranda's churro apestoso° forced into your mouth, you'd drink, too. Because you'd want to dull the pain for giving up hope.

But I don't want to get all philosophical on you just because it's dark here in El Colón, or because it's late. Although I have to say dark and late are my best times for thinking. I'm always carrying on this dialogue inside my head. I talk to a Tere Ávila who isn't gastada, apagada y jodida.° The other Tere, the dream Tere, still has sense and hope. I keep trying to help her out and spare her pain, but she just can't hear me. She's too busy watching the movie of her life unfold in front of her.

I turn to look at my comadre. In the flickering darkness I can see her wipe her eyes. The scene with the watch has gotten to her. Irma is a friend like no other.

My first husband, Reynaldo Ambriz, was never my friend. The only other longtime friend I've had has been Albinita, my mother. She gives

---

Tío: Uncle.   **Quinceañera:** Coming-of-age party, celebrated when a girl turns fifteen.   **sala:** Hall.   **churro apestoso:** Smelly *churro*. (A *churro* is a long, cylindrical fried pastry.)   **gastada, apagada y jodida:** Used up, burned out, and screwed.

you a hundred percent of herself when she just stands in the door looking at you, with such love and hope.

Irma's other best friend is her mother, Nyvia Ester. That's the kind of   60
person Irma is. Who would go to the movies with their mother every
Thursday night and look forward to it each week, and not only that, but
have a wonderful time? I look forward to it, too, but in a different way.

I wouldn't consider Nyvia Ester my best friend. To me, she's a little
scary, but I still respect her. Kind of how you would respect the Black
Virgin if she were standing in front of you. That's Nyvia Ester: short,
dark, tough. She's had a hard time since her husband left her. Any woman
would have to be strong, especially if you'd cleaned houses for over forty
years and sent all your kids to college on the money that you'd saved in a
world where it's impossible to save, and didn't have a man to help, and
no insurance, and you only went to the sixth grade back in Méjico.

The woman who likes to talk out loud to Pedro is starting up again.
Nyvia Ester has tried to stare her down with those dark bulldog eyes of
hers, and even made growling noises that only a pissed-off Mejicana can
make, but the woman just isn't getting it. I don't have a problem with her
loving the movie, but how can I be in the dark all anonymous when she's
in the dark all noisy?

If it weren't for her, there wouldn't be anything better than sitting in
the darkness of El Colón on a hot summer night with La Wirma. She
holds my large Dr Pepper while I dislodge a stubborn kernel of popcorn
from my back teeth.

"Pass me the popcorn, Irma," I whisper. What I really mean is wrestle
the popcorn away from your mother. Nyvia Ester always ends up with
the tub. When we get it back it's almost always empty. And not only
that, but Nyvia Ester makes us go all the way downstairs to the first floor
for refills, where you have to wait in line for about half an hour in front
of a bunch of short, horny married men in super-tight Wranglers and
Western shirts with rimmed BO circles and thick humpy necks like
Brahma bulls who stand behind you making that whistling Ssst! Ssst!
noise under their breath, which means many things, and all of them
bad. No, señor,° today it's not going to be me. I'm not going to refill the
popcorn tub.

I can tell Nyvia Ester is really getting irritated with the woman behind   65
us. She whispers, "Silencio, por favor,°" and the woman still ignores her.

"Sssh!" says Nyvia Ester.

"Sssh yourself!" answers the woman.

"Jew° got a problem?" Nyvia Ester says too loudly.

Someone yells out, "Dile que se vaya al Diablo.°"

No, señor: No, sir.   **Silencio, por favor:** Quiet, please.   **Jew:** A heavily accented
pronunciation of *you*.   **Dile que se vaya al Diablo:** Tell her to go to hell.

"¡Silencio, por Dios!° There's children in the audience, watch what you   70
say, cabrón!°"

Things are getting tense. An old man, in what was once an official-
looking white shirt and pants, slouches his way up the aisle and taps
Nyvia Ester on the shoulder. He's the only semblance of an usher I've
ever seen here. When it's really busy, he also helps out with the concession stand. Nyvia Ester stands up indignantly as a cacophony of voices
yells to her: "¡Siéntese, señora!° Down in front!"

Nyvia Ester turns around and tells the woman who started it all, "¡Vieja
testuda sin vergüenza!°" and sits down to applause.

The woman rises and everyone boos her. She sits down, momentarily
defeated. The very polite, very hard-of-hearing viejito° raises his voice,
"Señoras, por favor, ¡cálmense!°" Everyone cheers him. The movie grinds
to a halt as the projectionist yells from his booth to tell the audience
to shut up. People boo, whistle, yell and stomp on the gummy floor, flat-
tening popcorn boxes and grinding popcorn into fine chaff. Eventually,
like an old motor revving up, the movie resumes, words slurred and
thick. Pedro-as-Pablo tells Cruz he loves her and everyone cheers. The
viejito shuffles up the aisle to the back and trips over a young child in
the dark. "¡Ay, mamá!°" he calls out in pain. More noise. More shushing.
More ugliness, but now coming from the back. Two young men get in
a fight.

"¡Jóvenes infelices!°" an older woman calls out, damning all youth.
"¡Tontos!°" a man echoes her sentiments.

The old usher comes up and asks them to leave. The two disgruntled   75
young men leave, two skinny girlfriends with highly teased sprayed hair
in tow, to settle accounts in the alley behind the theater.

Things finally settle down. Pedro-as-Pablo walks on a beach near the
coast in search of his father, Leandro.

Inside El Colón you can watch el mero mero, el merito, nuestro querido,°
Pedro Infante, the world's most handsome man love the world's most
beautiful women. Like him, you can live happily ever after hasta la eternidad.° He is the man whose child we want to bear. He is the man we
wish we could be. Ay, Pedro, most fortunate and unfortunate of men.
Dead at age forty. Papi,° we miss you still.

¡Silencio, por Dios!: Quiet, for God's sake!   cabrón: Jerk.   ¡Siéntese,
señora!: Sit down, lady.   ¡Vieja testuda sin vergüenza!: Stubborn, shameless
old lady.   viejito: Little old man.   Señoras, por favor, ¡cálmense!: Ladies,
please, calm down.   ¡Ay, mamá!: Oh, dear.   ¡Jóvenes infelices!: Miserable
young people.   ¡Tontos!: Idiots!   el mero mero . . . : The top, the one and
only, our beloved.   hasta la eternidad: Until the end of time.   Papi: Daddy.

I don't care if the floor at El Colón is sticky and gummy and wet with too many spilled Cokes. I don't care if kids throw orange rinds and pieces of hard bolillo° and popcorn boxes down from the balcony or that everyone is talking or singing along with the music and it's a hot summer night and my legs stick to the torn humid theater seats. I don't even care anymore that the woman behind Nyvia Ester is making so much noise. We're all children in the darkness. In here no one watches us and tells us what to feel.

Inside El Colón I am closer to my people than I will ever be outside in the stinging sun. We are a collective here, and strong. Nothing and no one can deny us that.

Each of us yearns for Pedro, for the world he creates: a world of beauty,   80
physical perfection, song.

Just look at Pedro's expressions. No actor on the face of the earth has done more acting with his eyebrows than Pedro. Not to mention his arms, the most expressive arms I've ever seen! They're very manly, and this is played up with the type of shirts he wears, with short sleeves flaring out at the shoulder. He also sports a lot of sweaters, most of them hand-knit. In her autobiography, *Un Gran Amor,*° Lupe Torrentera, the mother of three of Pedro's children, talks about knitting Pedro the sweater he wore in the movie *Pepe el Toro.*°

Few men could get away with wearing a tight-fitting sweater or those loose suits so popular back in the fifties. You put a suit like that on one of our modern-day so-called movie stars and you have payasoville.° Most men have lost their natural grace.

Whether Pedro's arms just hang there, fisted or still, they're full of meaning. He can stride, too. Even his legs are expressive, not to mention his feet. God help us if he takes off his shirt. Who would have ever thought a man's nipples could express anger?

"Ahuumm. Ahuumm." The old man in front of us clucks like a demented rooster. He has something stuck in his throat. For a while we think he's not going to make it, but then he rallies and spits out the offending glob in the aisle near Nyvia Ester. She is not impressed.

It's hard to concentrate with so much happening around us, with the   85
noise of people laughing, crying, sighing, chewing, burping, hiccuping, applauding. Not to mention the meddling, cajoling, rebuking, interrupting, interceding and encouraging words that fly back and forth between the screen and the audience. But just looking at Pedro helps to bring me to a place of attention.

---

bolillo: Small bread roll.   ***Un Gran Amor:*** *A Great Love.*   ***Pepe el Toro:*** *Pepe the Bull.*   **payasoville:** Clown city; from payaso, which means "clown."

I admit, I've never been good at hiding my feelings in the dark. It's my undoing. I started dreaming when I was a little girl and I haven't stopped yet.

La Vida No Vale Nada is really a violent movie. Only you don't know how brutal it is until it's over.

At the end, Pedro-as-Pablo wrestles with Wolf Ruvinskis. Wolf wants sole possession of a squirrelly hussy named Marta. Go figure what Wolf Ruvinskis would want with a woman like Marta! She's been sleeping with Pablo's father, one of those aging Mejicanos who have to prove their barrel-chested manhood by either dyeing their hair jet black or taking up with a younger woman. She's been chasing Pedro-as-Pablo as well, but he doesn't want anything to do with her, even though she's always throwing herself down on the sand in front of him like a horny, beached mermaid.

Everyone gasps with fear as Wolf Ruvinskis punches Pedro-as-Pablo and then drags him into the salty water to drown him while the spurned and vindictive Marta eggs him on.

Pedro-as-Pablo seems to flounder as Wolf Ruvinskis violently pushes 90 him under the lapping waves, but then he gathers himself and flings Wolf back onto the beach with a battery of blows that leaves Wolf in a broken heap on the sandy shore.

Meanwhile, back at the pueblito,° Pablo's mother and siblings struggle in the most abject poverty. The two men, father and son, finally come to the realization that they need to get back home and take care of their kin. All is well. All is safe. All is as it should be. For the men. A 'lo Macho Bravo.°

And yet, I am left with questions. I look around El Colón. Is anyone else upset?

What about Marta? What's going to happen to her? Does anyone care?

A glowering and bitter Marta casts a long glance at Pedro-as-Pablo as he walks away arm in arm into a hopeful sunset with his now-reclaimed father, Leandro, both men the bane of her small, useless existence. Wolf Ruvinskis sputters nearby, trying to catch his breath. Marta looks at him with disgust and resignation.

Even in the darkness of El Colón I want to change my dreams, Marta's 95 dreams, but the movie credits roll.

La Vida No Vale Nada.

Pedro Infante. Rosario Granados. Lilia Prado. Domingo Soler. Magda Guzmán. Wolf Ruvinskis. Hortensia Santoveña.

Nyvia Ester picks up her purse and shimmies out of her seat with bobbing and teetering crablike movements, her bowlegs unsteady until she finds her land legs. Irma takes her mother's hand and assists her up the

pueblito: Little town.   **A 'lo Macho Bravo:** In the seriously aggressive male way.

incline toward the door that leads to the stairs and the lobby. The woman behind us smacks her lips, hoists her large body out of her seat and disappears into the uncertain night.

The sound track flares dramatically, full of reckless abandon.

I sit in the theater a little longer, my eyes full of tears, sad tears, tears 100 of hope.

My heart hurts the way it does when you can't love the man you want to. A man like Pedro.

Reading

1. What explanation does Tere give for the attractiveness of Pedro Infante?

2. What does Teresina think of the women watching the movie with her?

Thinking Critically

1. After reading this chapter, how would you characterize Teresina Ávila, its narrator?

2. What indications do you find in the chapter that the reality of Teresina's world is not as perfect as the world of the movies?

Connecting

1. Christine Granados's story "The Bride" (p. 467) also features a young woman who idealizes her love life. Compare the narrator of "The Bride" with Chávez's Teresina in *Loving Pedro Infante*. What hopes and dreams do these characters share? Is one more connected with reality than the other? Do you empathize with one or both of the characters? Explain why or why not.

Writing

1. Denise Chávez said that Pedro Infante embodied both positive and negative aspects of an idealized masculinity. Using examples from the text, discuss how the ideal he represents can be both positive and negative.

Creating

1. **Review a film that idealizes something or someone.** Denise Chávez finds in Pedro Infante's movies an idealization of love. Pick another movie that you think contains an idealization of love or another human experience, such as success, friendship, or even suffering. Write a review of the film, making sure to point out the idealization and its differences from reality.

34

PAT MORA [b. 1942]

Elena • Now and Then, America

From Chants [1984] AND Borders [1986]

GENRE: POETRY

Through her numerous books written for adults, teens, and children, Pat Mora has introduced many readers to Mexican American culture, and many young people to poetry and literature for the first time. Born and raised in El Paso, Mora earned her bachelor's and master's degrees from the University of Texas at El Paso. She then worked as a teacher and an administrator at UTEP before becoming, as a mother of three, a writer. Her first book of poetry, Chants, *was published in 1984, and since then she has published numerous collections, including* Borders *in 1986 and* Communion *in 1991. With* Nepantla: Essays from the Land in the Middle, *and* House of Houses, *published in 1993 and 1997, Mora moved into essay and autobiography. Additionally, through her writing for children and advocacy work, supported by the Kellogg Foundation and the American Library Association, Mora has helped make her own culture a part of children's education. "I often write about what I love, and what I love—Mexican heritage, Spanish and languages, the desert—is viewed by some as inferior. One of my motivations is to affirm and celebrate what I cherish."* Her books for younger readers include* A Birthday Basket for Tía, *published in 1992, and* Dizzy in Your Eyes: Poems about Love, *published in 2010.*

In "Elena" and "Now and Then, America," Mora writes of the frustrations that arise from imperfect communication between cultures. The protagonist of "Elena" watches her children from a distance, fearing that her connection to them is breaking, while the speaker of "Now and Then, America" feels a loss of connection to the culture around her.

---

*From an interview in *Journal of Children's Literature*, Vol. 32, No. 2 (Fall 2006), pp. 23–26.

As you read, think of what is lost on all sides when connections between cultures and between parents and children are damaged or destroyed, and think also about the universality of the difficulties faced by the narrators of these poems.

ELENA

My Spanish isn't enough.
I remember how I'd smile
listening to my little ones,
understanding every word they'd say,
their jokes, their songs, their plots.   5
Vamos a pedirle dulces a mamá. Vamos.°
But that was in Mexico.
Now my children go to American high schools.
They speak English. At night they sit around
the kitchen table, laugh with one another.   10
I stand by the stove and feel dumb, alone.
I bought a book to learn English.
My husband frowned, drank more beer.
My oldest said, "*Mamá*, he doesn't want you
to be smarter than he is." I'm forty,   15
embarrassed at mispronouncing words,
embarrassed at the laughter of my children,
the grocer, the mailman. Sometimes I take
my English book and lock myself in the bathroom,
say the thick words softly,   20
for if I stop trying, I will be deaf
when my children need my help.

NOW AND THEN, AMERICA

Who wants to rot
beneath dry, winter grass
in a numbered grave
in a numbered row
in a section labeled Eternal Peace   5
with neighbors plagued
by limp, plastic roses

Vamos a pedirle . . . : Let's ask mom for some candy. C'mon.

springing from their toes?
Grant me a little life now and then, America.

Who wants to rot   10
as she marches through life
in a pin-striped suit
neck chained in a soft, silk bow
in step, in style, insane.
Let me in   15
to board rooms wearing hot
colors, my hair long and free,
maybe speaking Spanish.
Risk my difference, my surprises.
Grant me a little life, America.   20

And when I die, plant *zempasúchitl,*°
flowers of the dead, and at my head
plant organ cactus, green fleshy
fingers sprouting, like in Oaxaca.
Let desert creatures hide   25
in the orange blooms.
Let birds nest in the cactus stems.
Let me go knowing life
        flower and song
will continue right above my bones.   30

Reading

1. ("Elena") Why does the speaker in the poem buy a book to learn English?

2. ("Now and Then, America") What is the speaker's critique of the grave-yard she mentions?

Thinking Critically

1. Why does the narrator of "Elena" fear losing her connection to her children?

2. When the speaker of "Now and Then, America" asks for "a little life now and then" (line 9), what do you think she means?

3. What do these poems have in common? To what extent are they held together by similar hopes or fears? Explain, drawing on lines from each work.

zempasúchitl: Marigold-like flower associated with death, used to decorate gravesites on the Day of the Dead (November 2).

Connecting

1. How do you think that the "Elena" of Pat Mora's poem might respond to Richard Rodriguez's (p. 205) belief that learning English is the key to success? Do you think her situation would be improved if her children received a bilingual education? Why or why not?

Writing

1. Pat Mora's poetry shows a concern with cultural misunderstanding. Using examples from the two poems above, write a brief essay about the consequences of such misunderstandings.

Creating

1. **Write a poem about misunderstanding.** Though "Elena" faces linguistic difficulties in communicating with her children, miscommunication between children and their parents is not unique to Mexican American families. Write a poem about problems you've had communicating across generations, whether due to differences in language, culture, or experience.

35

HELENA MARÍA VIRAMONTES [b. 1954]

Neighbors

From The Moths and Other Stories [1985]

GENRE: FICTION

Helena María Viramontes came of age during the height of the Chicano Movement and has carried its spirit into her stories and novels. Viramontes is an alumna of Garfield High School, one of the East Los Angeles schools that participated in the famous "Blowouts" of 1968, in which thousands of Mexican American students walked out of class in protest of conditions in their schools. After graduating from Immaculate Heart College in Los Angeles, she began submitting stories to competitions. Her success propelled her into the creative writing program at the University of California, Irvine. She left when her stories were criticized for being about Chicanos, returning years later to complete her *master's degree.* * *In 1985 her first book of stories,* The Moths, *was published, showing off Viramontes's careful, unsentimental style, and her attention to hardships that can come from age, from poverty, or from oppression by another culture or even by one's own.* The Moths, *like much of her later writing as well, focuses on East Los Angeles. Viramontes has written two novels,* Under the Feet of Jesus, *published in 1995, and* Their Dogs Came with Them, *from 2008. She is currently the head of the creative writing program at Cornell University.*

"Neighbors" centers on a woman and her struggle to keep the violence of her neighborhood out of her home. The story is part of Viramontes's effort to recover "the disappeared voices" of the East Los Angeles of her childhood, a place where many people were displaced by the construction of the highway system. "Where did all these people go from all these abandoned neighborhoods? Where did they all go? What happened to them?" * * *she asks, addressing her questions with her writing.*

As you read, think about how Viramontes not only tells a story but, through her detailed description, also recreates the world her characters live in.

I.

Aura Rodríguez always stayed within her perimeters, both personal and otherwise, and expected the same of her neighbors. She was quite aware that the neighborhood had slowly metamorphosed into a graveyard. People of her age died off only to leave their grandchildren with little knowledge of struggle. As a result, the children gathered near her home in small groups to drink, to lose themselves in the abyss of defeat, to find temporary solace among each other. She shared the same streets and corner stores and midnights with these tough-minded young men who threw empty beer cans into her yard; but once within her own solitude, surrounded by a tall wrought-iron fence, she belonged to a different time. Like those who barricaded themselves against an incomprehensible

*Watch a brief video where Viramontes explains: youtube.com/watch ?v=xBT8R7oHdFs.

**From Elisabeth Mermann-Jozwiak and Nancy Sullivan, *Conversations with Mexican American Writers*.

generation, Aura had resigned herself to live with the caution and silence of an apparition, as she had lived for the past seventy-three years, asking no questions, assured of no want, no deep-hearted yearning other than to live out the remainder of her years without hurting anyone, including herself.

And so it came as no surprise that when a woman appeared on a day much like every day, Aura continued sweeping her porch, oblivious to what her neighbors had stopped in mid-motion to watch.

The massive woman with a vacuous hole of a mouth entered Bixby Street, a distinct scent accompanying her. She was barefooted and her feet, which were cracked, dirty, and encrusted with dry blood, were impossible to imagine once babysmall and soft. The woman carried her belongings in two soiled brown bags. Her mouth caved into a smile as the neighbors watched her black, cotton wig flop to one side. They stared at her huge breasts sagging like sacks of sand and wobbling with every limp. Mrs. García pinched her nose as the woman passed, and Toastie, washing his candied-apple red Impala, threatened to hose her down. Aura stopped sweeping her porch and leaned on her broomstick, not to stare at the woman's badly mended dress or her wig that glistened with caked hairspray, but to watch the confident direction she took, unmoved by the taunts and stares. Aura did something she had not done in a while: she smiled. However, when the woman stopped at her gate, Aura's smile evaporated. Haphazardly, the woman placed one bag down in order to scratch beneath her wig.

"Doña° Aura Rodríguez," she said finally, her toothless mouth collapsing with each word, making it difficult for Aura to understand. "Where is Señor° Macario Fierro de Ortega? Where is he?"

Macario Fierro de Ortega? Aura repeated the name as she stepped   5
down her porch steps hesitantly, dragging the broom behind her. Fierro had lived behind her house for nearly thirty years, but she had never known his full name. Perhaps she was not referring to *her* Fierro.

"Señor Macario Fierro de Ortega?" she asked, eyeing the woman suspiciously. Aura knew of at least four ways of describing the smell of neglected flesh, but none seemed adequate to describe what stood in front of her. The woman became nervous under Aura's scrutiny. She began rummaging through her bags like one looking for proof of birth at a border crossing, and found what she had been looking for. Pinching the corner of the matchbook cover, Aura read the barely visible scribbling: 1306½ Bixby Street. It was Fierro's address, all right. She returned the matchbook and eyed the woman, all the while debating what to do. The

Doña: A title of respect used before a woman's first name.   **Señor:** Sir, used as a respectful title.

woman was indeed a massive presence, but although she overshadowed Aura's small, delicate frame, the whites of her eyes were as vague as old memories. Hard years had etched her chapped and sunburnt face. It was because of this that Aura finally said:

"In the back," and she pointed to a small weather-worn house. "But he's not home. On Tuesday's they give ten cent lunches at the center." The woman's scent made it unbearable to stand near her for long, and Aura politely stepped back.

"Who cares?" The woman laughed, crumbling the matchbook and tossing it behind her shoulder. "Waiting I know how to do!" She unhinged the gate and limped into Aura's yard, her scent following like a cloud of dust.

Aura was confused as she returned to her house. Her memory swelled with old stories which began with similar circumstances, and she began to worry about being duped. As she opened the door to a cluttered room, one thing struck her as strange, so she drew the Venetian blinds and locked the door behind her: how did the woman know her name?

II.

Dressed in his Saturday sharpest, Chuy° finished the last of his beer   10
behind the Paramount Theater before meeting Laura in the balcony, "the dark side." When he threw the *tall dog* into a huge trash bin, three men jumped the alley wall and attacked him. As they struck at him, he managed to grab a 2 by 4 which was holding the trash lid open, but it was no match for the switchblade which ripped through his chest. Chuy was nineteen when Fierro identified the body. He slowly pried the 2 by 4 from his son's almost womanly slender fingers and carried the blood-stained plank of wood home with him. Years and years later, as his legs grew as feeble as his mind, he took the 2 by 4 from his closet and sat on Aura's porch, whittling a cane for himself and murmuring to his son as she watered her beloved rose bushes, chinaberry tree, and gardenias.

The neighbors, of course, thought him crazy. Pabla from across the street insisted that talking to a dead son was an indication of senility. But others swore on their grandmother's grave that he or she saw Chuy sitting on Aura's porch, combing his hair "the way they used to comb it then." Although each aired their opinion of Fierro's son while waiting in the checkout line at the First Street Store, everyone agreed on one thing: Fierro was strangely touched. The fact that no one, not even the elderly Castillos could remember his first name, added to the mystery of the man. The butcher with the gold tooth, the priest at the Virgen de

Chuy: Nickname for Jesús.

Guadalupe Church, and the clerk who collected the money for his Tuesday ten cent lunch addressed him as Don° Fierro, but behind his back everyone shook their head with pity.

All the neighbors that is, except Aura. Throughout the years of sharing the same front gate, a silent bond between the two sprouted and grew firmer and deeper with time. As a result, he alone was allowed to sit on her porch swing as he whittled. With sad sagging eyes and whiskey breath he described for hours his mother's face and the scent of wine grapes just before harvest. He often cried afterwards and returned home in quiet shame, closing his door discreetly. Aura would continue her watering into the evening, until she saw the light in his kitchen flick on. Then she was sure that he was now sober enough to fix himself something to eat. Not until he had finished whittling the cane did he stop sitting on Aura's porch.

With the help of his cane, Fierro walked home from the Senior Citizen Center Luncheon. He coughed up some phlegm, then spit it out in disgust. Eating was no longer a pleasure for him; it was as distasteful as age. The pale, saltless vegetables, the crumbling beef and the warm milk were enough to make any man vomit. Whatever happened to the real food, the beans with cheese and onions and chile, the flour tortillas? Once again he did what he had done every Tuesday for the last five years: he cursed himself for having thrown away priceless time.

He walked with great difficulty and when he reached the freeway on-ramp crossing, he paused to catch his breath. The cars and trucks and motorcycles, in their madness to reach an unknown destination, flung past him onto the freeway causing his green unbuttoned vest to flap open. With his free hand he held the rim of his grey fedora. Fierro slowly began his trek across the on-ramp while the truckers honked impatiently.

"Cabrones!°" he yelled, waving his cane indignantly, "I hope you live to   15 be my age!" And he continued his walk, turning off his hearing aid so that the sounds in his head were not the sirens or motors or horns, but the sounds of a seashell pressed tightly against his ear. When he finally reached the freeway overpass, he stood there, listening to the absence of sound.

"Fierro, Don Fierro!" A young woman and her daughter stood in front of him. He saw the young child retreat behind her mother's skirt, frightened by the ancient face. "Don Fierro, are you all right?" The woman shouted over her grocery bag and into his ear. He remembered to turn on his hearing aid, and when he did, he heard her ask, "Are you all right?!"

"Heartaches," he said finally, shaking his head. "Incurable. It's a cancer that lays dormant only to surprise you when you least expect it."

Don: A term of respect, used before a man's first name.   **Cabrones!:** Jerks!

"What could it be?" the young woman asked as she went into her bag and busted a chip of chicharrón.° Loosening her grip on her mother's apron, the child took the chicharrón and chewed loudly, sucking the fat.

"Memories," Fierro said.

He heard the sirens again, the swift traffic whirling by beneath him. He was suddenly amazed how things had changed and how easy it would be to forget that there were once quiet hills here, hills that he roamed in until they were flattened into vacant lots where dirt paths became streets and houses became homes. Then the government letter arrived and everyone was forced to uproot, one by one, leaving behind rows and rows of wooden houses that creaked with swollen age. He remembered realizing, as he watched the carelessness with which the company men tore into the shabby homes with clawing efficiency, that it was easy for them to demolish some twenty, thirty, forty years of memories within a matter of months. As if that weren't enough, huge pits were dug up to make sure that no roots were left. The endless freeway paved over his sacred ruins, his secrets, his graves, his fertile soil in which all memories were seeded and waiting for the right time to flower, and he could do nothing.

He could stand right where he was standing now and say to himself, here was where the Paramount Theater stood, and over there I bought snow cones for the kids, here was where Chuy was stabbed, over there the citrus orchards grew. He knew it would never be the same again, never, and his greatest fear in life, greater than his fear of death or of not receiving his social security check, was that he would forget so much that he would not know whether it was like that in the first place, or whether he had made it up, or whether he had made it up so well that he began to believe it was true. He looked down at the child munching on the last of the chicharrón. I remember when you were that age, he wanted to say to the woman, but he was not sure anymore, he was not sure if he did. With his swollen, blotched hands, he tipped his grey fedora, then patted her hands softly.

"I'll be just fine," he reassured her, taking a last look at the child. "It's Tuesday," he said finally, and turning off his hearing aid once again, he prepared himself for the long walk across the ruins that still danced with Chuy's ghost.

III.

When she heard the gate open, Aura's first impulse was to warn Fierro of the woman who had been sitting on his porch for the last two hours. But since she respected him too much to meddle in his affairs, she went to

chicharrón: Fried pork rind.

the back room of her house and did something else she hadn't done in a long time: she peaked through her washroom window.

Contrary to her expectations, Fierro was not at all bewildered or surprised. He stood there, leaning on his cane while the woman rose from the porch with difficulty. They exchanged a few words. When Aura saw Fierro dig into his pocket, it infuriated her to think that the woman had come for money. But instead of producing his wallet, he brought out his keys and opened the door. The woman entered majestically while a pigeon on his porch awning cooed at her arrival.

IV.

There was a group of pigeons on Fierro's awning by morning, and it was   25
the cooing and not the knock that awoke her. Aura finally sat up, the familiar ache of her swollen feet pulsating, and with one twisted finger guided a Ben Gay–scented house slipper onto each foot. She leaned against the wall as she walked to the door, her bones, joints, and muscles of her legs and feet throbbing under the weight of her body. By the time she got to the door, no one was there. Aura retreated to her room, leaning from chair to table, from couch to wall. Her legs folded under her as she collapsed on the bed.

By the evening, she had tried almost everything to rid herself of the pain and her lips were parched with bitterness. Miserable and cornered, she began cursing her body, herself for such weakness. She slept little, rocking her head helplessly against the pillow as the pain continued to crawl up and down her body. She began to hate. She hated her body, the ticking of the hen-shaped clock which hung above the stove or the way the dogs howled at the police sirens. She hated the way her fingers distorted her hand so that she could not even grasp a glass of water. But most of all she hated the laughter and the loud music which came from the boys who stood around the candied-apple red Impala with the tape deck on full blast. They laughed and drank and threw beer cans in her yard while she burned with fever. The pain finally made her so desperate with intolerance, that she struggled to her porch steps, tears moistening her eyes, and pleaded with the boys.

"Por favor,°" she said, her feeble plea easily swallowed up by the blast of an oldie. "Don't you have homes?"

"What?" Toastie asked, not moving from where he stood.

"Go home," she pleaded, leaning against a porch pillar, her legs folding under her. "Go home. Go home."

"We *are* home!" Rubén said while opening another malt liquor. The   30

Por favor: Please.

others began to laugh. She held herself up because the laughter echoed in her head and she refused to be mocked by these little men who knew nothing of life and respect. But she slipped and fell and they continued to laugh. It was their laughter at her inability to even stand on her own two feet that made her call the police.

She raged with fever and revenge, waiting for the police to arrive. She tipped the slats of the Venetian blinds to watch the boys standing in a circle passing a joint, each savoring the sweet taste of the marijuana cigarette as they inhaled. She remembered Toastie as a child. She had even witnessed his baptism, but now he stood tall and she wondered where he had learned to laugh so cruelly. She lowered her head. The world was getting too confusing now, so that you even had to call the police in order to get some kindness from your neighbors.

Her feeling of revenge had overcome her pain momentarily, but when the police arrived, she fully realized her mistake. The five cars zeroed in on their target, halting like tanks in a cartoon. The police jumped out in military formation, ready for combat. The neighbors began emerging from behind their doors and fences to watch the red lights flashing against the policemen's batons. When the boys were lined up, spread-eagled for the search, Toastie made a run for it, leaping over Aura's wroughtiron fence and falling hard on a rose bush. His face scratched and bleeding, he ran towards her door, and for a moment Aura was sure he wanted to kill her. It was not until he lunged for the door that she was able to see the desperation and confusion, the fear in his eyes, and he screamed at the top of his lungs while pounding on her door, the *vowels* of the one word melting into a howl, he screamed to her, "Pleeeeeeease."

He pounded on the door, please. She pressed her hands against her ears until his howl was abruptly silenced by a dull thud. When the two policemen dragged him down the porch steps, she could hear the creak of their thick leather belts rubbing against their bullets. She began to cry.

It was not until way into the night, after she locked each window, each door, after her neighbors had retreated behind their T.V.s leaving her alone once again, that she remembered the last thing Rubén yelled as the patrol cars drove off, the last words he said as he struggled with the handcuffs.

"We'll get you," he said. "You'll see."   35

V.

For several days the brooding clouds began to form into animal and plant shapes until they finally burst, pelting her windows with rain. Fearful of her light bulbs attracting lightning, she turned them off and was content to sit in the dark next to the stove while the gas burners flickered blue and yellow fire upon the wall. She sat there quietly with a quilt over her shoulders, her shadow a wavering outline of a woman intimidated by natural forces. Aura sat and listened to the monotony of seconds, the thunderclaps, the pelting against her windows. It was only after the rain had subsided that a faint nasal melody playing against a rusty needle penetrated her darkness and she cocked her head to listen. Aura carried her chair to the washroom window. She seated herself, pulled up the Venetian blind slats and sought the source of the music.

The music was faint, barely an audible tune, but she recognized it just the same. She pressed her face against the coldness of the window glass and tried to remember why the song seemed so familiar. The Hallmark dance floor. She remembered the Hallmark dance floor and smiled. The toilet tank had been broken, and for a few dollars, plus tips, she was hired to fill buckets of water and pour them in the tank after every flush. She was 13 years old and the manager, a round stout man who wore a bulky gold diamond ring on his small finger, warned her against peaking out the door. She remembered sitting next to the sinks with her buckets full, tapping her feet to the rhythm of the music, as she did now, listening intently. And she imagined, as she imagined then, the prism ball encircling the couples with pieces of diamond specks. She recalled the glitter, the laughter, conversations, the thick level of cigarette smoke which hovered over the dancers so that it seemed they were dancing in clouds. It was nice to hear the laughter again, and mist collected on the window from her slow breathing. As night filtered in, Aura made out a silhouette against the shade of Fierro's room, and she recognized the massive shape immediately. The woman was dancing, slow lazy movements like those of a Sunday summer breeze teasing a field of tall grass. She held a scarf and slowly manipulated it as though it were a serpent. Fierro was laughing. The laugh was an unfamiliar sound to Aura's ears, as if a screw had loosened somewhere inside his body and began to rattle. But he continued to laugh a laugh that came from deep within and surfaced to express a genuine enjoyment of living.

Aura felt like an intruder, peering into their bedroom window and witnessing their intimacy. Although she hated herself for spying, she could not pry herself away from the window, away from the intimacies, away from the tune she had buried so far down that she had forgotten its existence. She listened way into the night, keeping the rhythm of the music with her foot, until the record finished with a scratch and Aura went to bed, cold under the bleached, white sheets.

VI.

Aura was in the mood to dance, to loosen her inhibitions from the tight confines of shoes and explore a barefoot freedom she had never experienced in her wakeful hours. But she awoke to stare at her feet, to inspect the swelling, to let reality slowly sink in, and she was thankful and quite satisfied simply to be able to walk.

She dressed slowly because she felt weak and uneasy, and at first 40 attributed the hollowness of her stomach to the medication she had taken throughout those endless nights. But when she lifted the blinds to the washroom window and saw the woman standing barefoot on the porch, tossing bread crumbs to the pigeons while her bracelets clinked with every toss, Aura knew it was not the medication. She watched the woman scratch beneath her huge breasts while she yawned, then turn towards the door, closing it with a loud slam. Aura's heart sank like an anchor into an ocean of silence. She drew the blinds quietly.

In the kitchen Aura flipped up the lid of the coffee can, spooned the grinds into the percolator, dropped in a stick of cinnamon and put the pot to boil. When the coffee was done, she poured herself a cup. It was bitter, and the more she thought about the woman, the more bitter the coffee became. She heard the children of Bixby Street, who were especially happy to see the storm pass. Having been imprisoned by the rains, they were now freed from behind their doors and allowed to run the streets under the bright sun. Aura heard their shouts, their laughter, and she yearned to feel right again.

She collected a sunbonnet, gloves and garden tools. Since the rainfall had soaked the soil, she could not pass up the opportunity to weed out her garden, and even though her movements were sluggish, she prepared herself for a day's work.

Once outside and under the bright sun, Aura was blinded for a moment. She bit her fist in disbelief. Most of the graffiti was sprayed on her front porch with black paint, but some of it was written with excrement. As she slowly stepped down, she inspected the windows, steps, walkway, pillars, all defaced with placas,° symbols, vulgarities. She rushed over the chayote vine and made a feeble attempt to replant it, but everything, her flowers, chayotes, gardenias, rose bushes, were uprooted and cast aside. Some of her bushes were twenty years old, having begun as cuttings from her mother's garden. She had spent years guiding and pruning and nurturing them until they blossomed their gratitude. She tried unsuccessfully to restore them, the thorns scratching her face, her bare hands bleeding. When she fell to her knees and began clawing away at the mud in hopes of saving some of her bushes, she failed to notice that the children had

placas: Tags (i.e., graffiti).

stopped their play and stood in front of her yard, their red, puffy faces peering from between her wrought-iron bars. It was their look of bewilderment and pity that made her realize the hopelessness of her actions.

"Leave me alone!" Aura screamed at the children, raising her arms like a menacing bird. "Leave me alone or I'll . . . ," she shouted, and the children scattered in all directions like cockroaches. She stood up, her knees trembling, and took one last look at her plants. All that remained intact was her chinaberry tree. Aura slowly returned to the house, her hands dangling uselessly at her side. "I'm so glad," she thought, fighting back the tears as the mutilated bushes began shriveling under the morning sun, "I'm so glad I'm going to die soon."

She closed the door behind her, made sure all the locks were locked, unrolled the Venetian blinds, closed the drapes. She heard Rubén's voice: "We'll get you." Picking up the phone, she decided against calling the police and making another mistake. Fierro? She was totally alone. "We'll get you, you'll see." She would have to take care of herself. She was marked, proof to other neighbors that indeed the "BIXBY BOYS RULE," as they had sprayed the neighborhood in huge bold letters. NO. She refused to be their sacrificial lamb. She shook her head as she got a candlestick out of the linen closet. She pushed the kitchen table aside, grunting under its weight, then rolled up the carpet. She lit the candlestick and opened the cellar door because she refused to be helpless.

Cupping the faint flicker of the candle, she slowly descended into the gut of the cellar, grasping at the spider webs which blocked the way to her destination. She ignored the distorted shadows of the undisturbed furniture, ignored the scent of moistened, decayed years, and moved towards the pile of boxes stacked in the corner. She opened the first box with little difficulty, the motes of dust dancing around her until they settled once again to begin a new accumulation of years. She dug her hands into the box, groping, feeling beneath the objects, kitchen utensils, books, photographs, but found nothing. She threw the box aside and opened another. And another. With each box her anger and desperation rose so that the search became frantic, almost obsessive. Finally, in the last of the boxes, her fingers froze to the cool touch. She blew the dust away and examined it like the foreign object that it was. It felt cold and clumsy in her small hand. Nonetheless, she triumphantly placed the gun in her apron pocket and blew out the last of the candlestick.

VII.

As the days passed, Fierro knew little of what went on in the neighborhood. When he heard the sirens and screams and CB radios spitting out messages, he refused to go outside for fear of finding Chuy's body limp and bloody once again. Then, this morning as he turned from his side of the bed to examine the woman's slow breathing, he couldn't imagine what had caused Aura to scream so loudly that it startled him out of a sleepy daze, though he wore no hearing aid. All that Fierro knew was that he awoke one morning to find the warm mass of a woman sleeping beside him and this was enough to silence any curiosity. He also knew never to ask a question if he wasn't prepared for the answer, and so he was content to let her stay for as long as she wanted without even asking her name.

Fierro sat up in bed, rubbed his eyes, palmed his hair back, yawned the last of his sleep away. As though in thoughtful meditation, he allowed his body to slowly return to consciousness, allowed the circulation to drive away the numbness from his limbs. Only then was he ready to make the walk across the room to the bathroom. He winced as he walked on the cold floor, and he took one last look at the woman before he closed the door.

Inside the bathroom, Fierro urinated, washed his hands and face in cool water, inspected the day's growth of beard in the mirror. He rinsed his dentures under running water, then slipped them into his mouth, clacking his jaws twice to make sure they fell securely in place. Not until he had almost finished his shave, did it occur to him that he had been humming. While he stood in front of the mirror, his raspy voice vibrated a tune. A ballroom dancing, nice-smelling women tune. He hummed louder as he shook some Wildroot into his hands and palmed his hair a second time. He combed it into a glossy ducktail, smoothed his mustache, smiled. He was about to slap on some cologne when Chuy stopped him.

"Can I do it," his young son asked eagerly. As he had done every morn- 50 ing, the boy stood on the toilet seat to watch his father's daily shave. He was small and thin, and the crotch of his underwear hung to his knees. "Can I?" Chuy repeated.

The boy had great respect for the daily shave. He would watch his father maneuver the single blade across his cheek with the same admiration he felt watching a performer swallow a sword. But Chuy knew that, unlike sword swallowing, shaving would be accessible if only he studied it with the watchful eye of an apprentice. So it was a ritual each morning to spend the time necessary to stare at the blade, apply the cologne, and touch his own cheek for hair growth.

"Ay, qué M'ijo. ¿Por qué no?°" Fierro poked his son's belly with the bottle. He handed it to Chuy, and tugged up his calzones.° While the boy shook a few drops onto his palm, Fierro noticed how dirty his son's fingernails were. He would bathe him when he returned home.

Ay, qué M'ijo. ¿Por qué no?: Oh, that's just like you, son. Why not?
calzones: Underwear.

"Ready?" Chuy asked. He kept his eyes on the palm of his hand, then when Fierro was close enough, he slapped his father's face as hard as he could. Fierro's exaggerated wince made the boy laugh. "Now your turn." The boy enjoyed this part of the ritual because his father's scent would be with him all day. Fierro shook the scented rose water onto his cement-burned hand: But time had a way of passing so that the few seconds it took to shake out some of his son's favorite cologne turned into years, and the admiration in the boy's eyes had disappeared.

"I'm 19. I think I can do it myself." Fierro felt the rose water dripping   55
through his fingers. It seemed like only yesterday . . . The bathroom seemed too small now, and they both elbowed one another. Fierro finally won over the mirror, but the defeat did not keep Chuy from trying to catch a glimpse of himself from behind his father's shoulders.

"Where do you think you're going?" Fierro asked, looking at Chuy's reflection, his face threatening a mustache. The answer was automatic: "Out."

"Don't get smart, Chuy." Fierro was becoming increasingly disturbed that Chuy was running the streets. "Hijo,° you're not a dog. You have a home to live, to sleep, to eat in."

"Listen, Jefe,°" Chuy replied, tired of the same Saturday night dialogue. "I'm old enough to know what I'm doing."

"Then why don't you act like it?"   60

"Shit, Jefe. Lay off for once."

"Qué lay off, ni qué ojo de hacha,°" Fierro replied angrily. "And don't be using that language with me, you understand?"

There was an icy silence. Chuy combed his hair back. He waited patiently for the right time to break the silence and still save face. Finally: "Listen, Apá.° I'm not going cruising, if that's what you want to know."

Fierro thought for a moment. Finally: "Good, mijito.° Good. It's just   65
that those chavalos° are a bunch of good for nothings. Thieves. Murderers and thieves."

"You forgot tecatos.°"

"That too."

"They're my friends."

"Bah! Qué friends!° Look what they did to the Reyes boy."

Chuy bent over to smooth out the creases of his khaki pants, uncon-   70
cerned by the accusation. When he looked up, he was face to face with his father. Barely whispering he said, "He had it coming to him."

Hijo: Son. **Jefe:** Boss.   **Qué lay off, ni qué ojo de hacha:** What's this "lay off," and what's this tough guy attitude?   **Apá:** Affectionate term for one's father. **mijito:** My son. **chavalos:** Guys. **tecatos:** Junkies. **Qué friends!:** What friends!

"Do you really, really believe that?" In disbelief he looked into his son's eyes and realized how little he really knew him. How could anyone deserve to be murdered? It grieved him to think that Chuy was no different than the rest. But he was; Chuy, his son, his boy, had a good heart, and that made him different. Bad ways, but a good heart. Chuy defiantly returned his father's stare, until his face broke into a smile.

"Apá," he said, slapping his father on the shoulder, "are you gonna lend me the cologne or what?" He rubbed each shoe against his pant leg. His shoulders were now stooped so that he was no longer taller than his father. "Laura and me, we're gonna go to a movie."

"Ay, qué mi'jo!" Fierro was relieved. Get him out of the neighborhood. That much he knew if he wanted to save his son's good heart. He slapped the cologne on both sides of Chuy's face. "Ay, qué mi'jo. Laura and you!"

The woman pounded on the door.

"Got your key, mi'jo? And don't forget to lock the door after . . ."   75

"Ay te watcho, Jefito,°" Chuy interrupted. Taking a last look at his reflection, he winked at his father and was gone.

The woman pounded on the door again and Fierro opened it. She handed him the hearing aid, and after a few adjustments, he was able to hear. As he followed her into the kitchen, he wanted to tell her about Chuy, but once he caught the aroma of the beans, he immediately forgot what he had wanted to say.

The woman grated some cheese, then sprinkled it on the boiling beans. After the cheese had melted, she spooned the beans onto the flour tortillas. Fierro ate the burritos as greedily as the pigeons pecked their crumbs of bread outside. As he licked his fingers, she poured some instant coffee into his tin cup, added some milk and honey. His hands trembled whenever he lifted the cup to his lips, sipping loudly.

"Good," he finally said. "It's all so good," and he reached over the table to touch her hand. As he had done for the past several days, Fierro studied her face, the crevices and creases, the moles and marks, studied those things which distinguish one person from another, in hopes of finding something which would deliver immediate recognition. But in the end, as always, his mind became exhausted, and once again he failed. Beads of perspiration formed on the temples of his forehead, and the room began to circle and circle around him.

"Macario!?" the woman asked, but before he could answer, he fainted.   80 Kneeling beside him, she looked around the room in confusion and fear hoping to find something that would revive him and make him well; but all she could do, all she could think of, was to get the dishcloth and place it on his forehead. He began to squirm. Finally, when he was semi-conscious, he whispered to her, his lips feeling heavy and swollen, "Heartaches."

Ay te watcho, Jefito: See you later, Dad.

She helped him to the bed, pulling the blankets aside, and he slipped into sleep, smelling her scent in the sheets. He slept for a while, dreaming of watermelons so cool and refreshing to his lips, until the first abdominal cramp hit and he groped around for her hand. He wanted to ask for water, but his lips were swollen and dried and he couldn't speak. He was extremely thirsty and craved melons: crenshaw melons, honeydew melons, cantaloupe melons, watermelons. The woman bathed him in cool water, but the water could not extinguish the burning in his mouth and stomach and a second spasm hit without warning, his whole body cramping into a fetal position. With the onset of the third spasm, the retching began.

The woman became frantic and she paced around and around his bed like a caged lioness. He was dying and she couldn't do anything because he had already made up his mind, and she wrung and wrung her hands in helplessness. When she finally picked up the phone, Fierro, barely able to move, motioned with his finger NO, then pointed to a chair. The hours passed as she sat next to him, rocking herself back and forth, mesmerized in deep prayer.

His lips were parched but his craving for coolness suddenly disappeared. He turned to look at the woman and finally, after some time, finally, recognized her. Before he could say her name again, he felt an avalanche crush his chest and he could no longer breathe. Fierro desperately inhaled in hopes of catching some air, but the more desperate he became, the less he could breathe. In short fits of spasms, his life snapped.

The pillow fell to her feet and she gently lifted his head to replace it. She tried to arouse him, but he lay still, his eyes yellow and dull. She pressed her ear against his chest. There was no breathing, no heart beat, just a faint buzzing sound. The woman shook her head sadly as she slowly reached into his shirt pocket and turned off the hearing aid. She began moaning. At first light and hardly audible, her moaning began to crescendo into high wails of sorrow and disbelief. Shrieking angrily at the God who convinced Fierro to die, the barefooted woman ran out, the screen door slamming behind her.

VIII.

With her heart beating in a maddening race, Aura sat facing the front 85 door, the gun on her lap. Her sunbonnet still hung limply by the side of her head, and her hands and face were smeared with dry blood and mud. The hours came and went with the ticking of the clock and she waited, cocking the gun whenever she heard car brakes, her fear swelling to her throat, then releasing the trigger and relaxing once the car had spun away.

The summer of the rattlers. The Vizcano desert was far away, yet she could almost feel the rattlers coiled up under the brittle bushes waiting for her. As a child she was frightened by their domination of the desert. If they were disturbed, they struck with such force that it was always too late to do anything. Her grandfather had taught her how to look for them, how to avoid them, and if necessary, how to kill them, but the sight of one always made her immobile because she had no protection against their menacing appearance, their slickness as they slowly slithered to a cooler location, their instinct to survive. And so she never left the house without grandfather; but he was dead and she would be soon if she didn't protect herself. Her eyes grew heavy with sleep but she refused to close them, for the rattlers were out there. Somewhere.

Aura finally dozed, her head falling forward until the loud door slam startled her into wakefulness and she groped around for the gun. She could not keep her body from trembling as she stood up from her chair to listen to the sounds coming from outside. She heard running foot-steps, panting, and she felt the sweat dripping between her breasts. Someone was on her porch and she prayed to be left alone. She held the gun high with both hands, squeezing, tightly squeezing it as she aimed at the door.

Reading

1. What is the event that has scarred Fierro so deeply?

2. What happens to Aura's garden? Why does it happen?

Thinking Critically

1. How would you describe the neighborhood where Aura and Fierro live?

2. Do you think Aura is fully responsible for the tragedy at the end of the story? What could she have done differently?

Connecting

1. Like Don Fierro in "Neighbors," Fausto Tejada in Ron Arias's novel *The Road to Tamazúnchale* (p. 172) has a rather fanciful imagination. What do you think makes the two characters different? Is one treated more sympathetically than the other? Is one crazier than the other? Explain.

Writing

1. In Viramontes's story, we read about Aura and Fierro: "Throughout the years of sharing the same front gate, a silent bond between the two

sprouted and grew firmer and deeper with time" (par. 12). What is the
nature of this bond? Are there similarities between the lives of Aura and
Fierro? In an essay, using examples from the text, discuss the bond between the two characters and why you think the author brought them
together in the story.

Creating

1. **Recover lost voices and stories.** Viramontes writes about trying to recover voices from an old neighborhood. Have there been changes to
   your neighborhood (current or past) or to one nearby? Find some evidence of the stories or voices that have disappeared because of these
   changes. Evidence could include old photographs, news articles, physical evidence of businesses and buildings, or the memories of people
   you know.

36

THE HERNANDEZ BROTHERS

[MARIO, b. 1953; GILBERT, b. 1957; JAIME, b. 1959]

Chiro el Indio

From Love and Rockets: New Stories No. 1 [2008]

GENRE: GRAPHIC FICTION

When the Hernandez Brothers started their Love and Rockets *series of comics in 1981, they helped bring a new depth and complexity to comic books. Like other creators of "underground" or
"alt" comics, they were unafraid to comment on the contemporary
world or to incorporate a wider variety of characters into their
stories. For the Hernandez Brothers this meant putting the people
they knew from an early age into their comics. They inherited a
love of comic books from their mother, and from their surroundings in Oxnard, California, they absorbed the culture of the Chicano barrio and the Southern California punk rock scene. Gilbert
and Jaime were connected to the music scene as musicians and
designers of album covers before* Love and Rockets *enabled them
to become full-time artists. Each brother contributed his own*

stories to the comic, with Jaime focusing on the "Locas" Hopey and Maggie and the Mexican American town they live in, and Gilbert focusing on a surreal South American village called "Paloma." Mario, as the eldest, had led the way in getting Love and Rockets published but his contributions (which include the selection below) became more sporadic as he became more involved with his own family life. Without setting out a clear political agenda, the Hernandez Brothers have shown that the Chicano community is varied enough to generate multiple kinds of stories—tragic, funny, fantastical, quirky, or a combination. "Our Chicano culture is so rich and has so much to offer that I've barely scratched the surface," Jaime has said. "I want the whole world to experience it. I've made it my job to make everybody understand it without watering it down and without trying to protect the reader's feelings."* Except for a hiatus in the late 1990s, the brothers have kept Love and Rockets going continuously for decades, winning acclaim and popularity not only for themselves but also for comic books as a serious genre of literature. In 2013 Gilbert received the PEN Center USA's Graphic Literature Award for Outstanding Body of Work.

In addition to Gilbert and Jaime's long-running stories, Love and Rockets also presents self-contained episodes. "Chiro el Indio," written by Mario and drawn by Gilbert, is one example. It is a quirky tale of two quirky couples, as Señor Feo and Señora Maldita enlist the Catholic Church in an effort to steal land from Chiro and his wife, Preciosa. The twists and turns of the story can be difficult to follow, but the comedy, the extreme irreverence, and the hostility toward religion and toward land theft are unmistakable.

As you read, pay attention to the portrayal of the characters Feo, Maldita, Chiro, and Preciosa. How do the writers use these characters for social commentary?

*From Frederick Luis Aldama, *Your Brain on Latino Comics: From Gus Arriola to Los Bros Hernandez*.

The Hernandez Brothers. "Chiro el Indio" from *Love and Rockets: New Stories No. 1*. Reprinted by permission of Fantagraphics Books.

Reading

1. What does Preciosa bring to Señora Maldita?
2. Why does Preciosa begin to pray and wear a veil?

Thinking Critically

1. What is the relationship between Preciosa and Maldita?
2. What attitude toward the police is reflected in the comic?
3. What is the significance of the characters' names?
4. What do you think the Hernandez Brothers were trying to communicate in this comic?

Connecting

1. Like the Hernandez Brothers, Lalo Alcaraz (p. 418) presents Mexican American culture to a wide readership by telling stories through pictures. Do you think that Alcaraz and the Hernandez Brothers reach a different audience than traditional writers? Why or why not?

Writing

1. A comic can't be summarized in words because of the importance of the drawings. Write an essay in which you discuss elements of "Chiro el Indio" that are communicated through the drawings rather than through the words. How do the images contribute to the overall tone and message?

Creating

1. **Create a comic strip.** To make a successful comic, the Hernandez Brothers must tell stories with just a few sentences and a few drawings. Using "Chiro el Indio" as a model, think of a simple story and try to tell it in three frames, complete with drawings and with dialogue or narration. Before you compose, think of the readers you want to reach, and decide what tone, message, and commentary or perspective you want to convey.

37

DAGOBERTO GILB [b. 1950]

Maria de Covina

From The New Yorker [1997] AND Woodcuts of
Women [2001]

GENRE: FICTION

*The urban, working-class sensibility of Dagoberto Gilb has helped
make him a distinctive voice among Chicano writers, and with his
national success as a writer of stories, novels, and essays, he has
helped bring attention to the Mexican American culture of the
Southwest. Gilb grew up in Los Angeles and discovered his love of
literature only after his high school years. Working full-time, he
transferred from community colleges to the University of California, Santa Barbara, for a bachelor's and a master's degree in religious studies. For the next two decades Gilb moved back and
forth between Los Angeles and El Paso, Texas, becoming a union,
high-rise carpenter and turning his experiences into stories. Several fellowships, including one from the National Endowment for
the Arts, helped him to devote more time to writing. In 1994 Gilb's
stories were collected and published as* The Magic of Blood,
*which was a PEN/Faulkner finalist and brought Gilb the PEN/
Hemingway Award, a Whiting Writer's Award, and a national reputation for well-crafted stories about family, work, and relationships.* The Last Known Residence of Mickey Acuña, *a border
novel about characters living in an El Paso YMCA, was published
in 1994, and Gilb received a Guggenheim Fellowship the following
year. Gilb's stories have been published widely in magazines, including multiple times in* The New Yorker, *and have been collected in* Woodcuts of Women *in 2003 and* Before the End, After
the Beginning *in 2011.* Gritos, *a collection of his essays, was a
finalist for a National Book Critics Circle Award in 2003, and in
2008 he wrote* The Flowers, *a novel with explosive tensions inspired by the Watts Riots. In 2010, at the University of Houston-
Victoria, Gilb founded the literary magazine* Huizache, *shining a
national spotlight onto the poetry and prose of the Latino West
and the culture of Mexican America.*

The story "Maria de Covina," first published in The New Yorker *in 1997, is a good example of Gilb's fondness for "following characters who would be minor against the headliners in novels."* The story shows Gilb's ability to fashion a story out of the rhythms and pleasures of a job that might, from the outside, seem uninteresting. The narrator works in a department store called The Broadway, and he is young, happy to be surrounded by beautiful gifts and women, and carefree perhaps to a fault.*

As you read, think about how Gilb reveals the personality of the narrator, which seems to exceed the boundaries of this particular job.

I've got two sports coats, about six ties, three dressy pants, Florsheims I polish *a la madre*,° and three weeks ago I bought a suit, with silk lining, at Lemonde for Men. It came with a matching vest. That's what made it for me. I love getting all duded up, looking fine, I really do. This is the thing: I like women. No, wait. I *love* women. I know that don't sound like anything new, nothing every guy wouldn't tell you. I mean it though, and it's that I can't say so better. It's not like I do anything different when I'm around them. I'm not like aggressive, going after them, hustling. I don't play that. I don't do anything except have a weakness for them. I don't ask anybody out. I already have my girlfriend Diana. Still, it's like I feel drunk around them. Like they make me so *pedo*° I can't move away. See what I'm saying? So yeah, of course I love working nights at The Broadway. Women's perfume is everywhere, and I'm dizzy while I'm there.

Even if what I'm about to say might not sound right, I'm saying it: It's not just me, it's them too, it's them *back*, maybe even first. Okay, I realize this sounds bad, so I won't talk about it. But why else did they put me in the Gifts department? I didn't know *ni nada*° about that stuff, and I noticed right away that most customers were women. And I'm not meaning to brag, but the truth is I sell, they buy. They're older women almost always, rich I see now, because the things we have on the racks—*cositas como*° vases and statues and baskets and bowls, from Russia, Germany, Africa, Denmark, France, Argentina, everywhere—are originals and they're expensive. These ladies, maybe they're older, but a lot really look good for being older, they come in and they ask my opinion. They're smiling when they ask me what I'd like if it was for me. I try to be honest. I smile a lot. I smile because I'm happy.

*From The Bedford Introduction to Literature.

a la madre: Like crazy.   **pedo:** Drunk.   **ni nada:** Not a thing.   **cositas como:** Little things like.

You know what? Even if I'm wrong, *no le hace*,° I don't care. Because when I go down the escalator, right at the bottom is Cindy in Cosmetics. She says, "Is your mommy coming for you tonight?" Cindy's almost blond, very pretty, and way out there. She leans over the glass to get close to me. She wears her blouses a little low-cut. She's big for being such a *flaquita*.°

"Maybe," I say. "Maybe not."

"Don't marry her yet." That bedroom voice of hers.   5

"What difference will it make?"

"None to me," she says.

"You talk big," I say, "but do you walk the walk?"

"You know where I am. What're we waiting for?"

She's not wrong. I'm the one who only talks the talk. I don't lie to   10
myself. For instance, I'm about to be nineteen, but I pretend I'm twenty. I do get away with it. I pass for older. I'm not sure why that's true—since I'm thirteen I've had a job—or why I want it to be. I feel older when I say I am. For the same reason I let them think I know so much about sex. *Ya sabes*,° pretend that I'm all experienced, like I'm all bad. Lots of girls, and that I know what they like. I feel like it's true when I'm around them. It's what Cindy thinks. And I want her to, I like it that she does, but at the same time it makes me scared of her. She's not pretending, and I'm afraid she'll find out about me: The truth is that my only experience is with Diana. I'm too embarrassed to admit it, and I don't, even to her.

It's not just Cindy though, and this isn't talk, and though it might sound like it, honest, I'm not trying to brag. Over in Women's Fashions is Ana, a *morena*° with green eyes, and strong, pretty legs. She's shy. Not that shy. She wants to be in love, wants a wedding, wants a baby. In Housewares is Brigit. Brigit is Russian, and sometimes she's hard to understand. You should see her. She's got the bones of a black girl, but her skin is snow. I think she's older than she looks. She'll go out with me, I know it. I don't know how she'd be, and I wonder. Over there, down the mall, at Lemonde for Men, is where Liz works. That's who I bought my suit from. Liz is fun. Likes to laugh. The Saturday I picked up my suit we had lunch together, and then one night, when I knew she was working, just before we closed, I called her. I told her I was hungry and would she want to go somewhere after. She said yeah. We only kissed good-bye. The next time she was letting me feel her. She likes it, and she's not embarrassed that she does. I think about her a lot. Touching her. But I don't want this to sound so *gacho*,° porno or something. I like her, that's what I mean. I like everything about her. I don't know how to say it better.

no le hace: It doesn't matter. **flaquita:** Skinny girl. **Ya sabes:** You know. **morena:** A dark-skinned girl. **gacho:** Nasty, crude.

"You're such a liar," Maria says. She's my boss. The assistant manager of Gifts and Luggage, Silverware and China. I worry that she knows how old I really am, and she's going by that. Or that she knows I'm not really going to college in the day. I don't know why I can't be honest about having that other job. I work for A-Tron Monday through Friday. A shipping clerk. It's a good job too. But it's better to say you're studying for something better. I am going to go to college next year, after I save some money.

"What're you saying?"

"You just want to get them," Maria de Covina says. "You're no different than any other man."

I have told her a lot, I'm not sure why. Probably because she catches   15
me all the time talking to them. The first times I thought she was getting mad and going around checking up on me because I'd be on a break and taking too long. But she's cool. We just seemed to run into each other a lot, and she would like shake her head at me, so now I tell her how I'm thinking. I told her about Liz after she saw us on that first Saturday, eating lunch in the mall.

"It's not true," I say.

"It's not *true*," she whines. She often repeats what I say in a mocking voice. Sometimes she gets close to me, and this time she gets real close, close enough to reach her hand around and grab one of my *nalgas*.° "It's not *true*."

"Watch it, Covina," I say. "You Italians think everything you squeeze is a soft *tomate*,° but Mexicans got *chiles* that burn."

I call her Maria de Covina because she lives in West Covina and drives in. I call her Italian because she doesn't know a word of Spanish, and Italians can be named Maria. I can't let up. She really is Mexican American, just the spoiled, *pocha*° princess type. But I don't let on. She tells me her last name over and over. What do you think Mata is? she asks. Does *Mata* sound Italian to you? I say maybe, yeah. Like a first name like Maria, I say. Like a last name like Corona. Probably it's that, I tell her, and you're messing with me. I don't understand yet what you're up to. Why is it you want everyone to think you're a Mexican when you're not? In my family, everybody always wished they weren't. So she calls me names and means them because this really upsets her. Stupid, she calls me. Buttbreath. Say those in Spanish, I suggest to her, and we'll see what you know. She says, *Estúpido*. One wrong, I tell her. What about the other? No reply. You don't know, do you? Not a clue, right? This is a game we play, and though there is part of me that can't believe she takes it seriously, another part sees how my teasing bothers her too much.

nalgas: Butt cheeks.   **tomate:** Tomato.   **pocha:** A Mexican American, born in the United States.

"Besides, no Chicanos live in West Covina."   20
"Yes they do."

It cracks me up how serious she sounds. She's too easy. "I never met any from there, ever. It's probably too rich or something."

"You've never even been there, and I bet you don't even know where it is."

"Me and nobody like me."

"My parents just never taught me any Spanish."   25
"Did they talk it at home?"
"Not really."
"You see? What'd I tell you?"

"Asshole." She whispers that in my ear because we're on the floor and customers are around.

"When they were talking something, if they did, it probably was Italian   30 and you didn't even know it."

I never tell my girlfriend Diana anything about these other girls. Though she's been mad at me anyway. We used to go out more often than we do now, but with my two jobs, and her school, it's almost only been weekends. After we go to a movie, we head back to her place because her parents go to sleep so early. I take her to the door and we kiss and then I leave. I park on the busy street around the corner and I walk back and crawl through her window. It's a big bedroom because she used to share with her sister, who went away to be a nurse. She's very sheltered in a certain way, in that Catholic way, but I'm not Diana's first boyfriend, though I am the first one she's made love to. She let me the second time we went out because she thought I expected it. Because I was so experienced. She's sixteen. She doesn't look it, but she acts it. She worries. She's scared of everything she likes. The first time she orgasmed, she told me a couple of months ago, she didn't really know what it was, and it felt too good, so she called her sister's best friend, who can talk about any subject and especially sex, and asked if she was all right. She'll let me do certain things to her, and now she'll be on top sometimes. But she worries that one of us will get too loud. She has been a couple of times. I feel her pulsate in there real hard. She worries that we'll fall asleep after and her mom or dad will be up before we know it. That happened once, and I got out of there, but she's been really worried ever since about everything, every little noise, like they're listening.

The only thing in the room that isn't just for a girl is a statue I gave her of *The Thinker*. It came from Gifts. It had a chip in the wood base and was being sold at 20 percent discount. I kept looking at it, trying to decide if I should buy it. It's big, heavy. He looks smart. I imagined having it in my own place when I got one. I guess that Maria and Joan, the manager of our department, saw how often I stared at it, and so one day they gave it to me, all gift wrapped, a ribbon and bow. I was surprised, embarrassed even, that they bought me a present, and one so expensive, and I didn't think I should accept it, until they explained how it only cost a dollar—they'd marked it down as damaged and, being the manager and assistant manager, signed off on it. This was one of those nights that Diana came to the store to pick me up after work. She was suspicious of Maria, which seemed crazy to me since she was twenty-six and my boss, and then, as we were going down the escalator, of Cindy, who made a sexy wink at me, which didn't seem crazy. So right there in the parking lot I gave *The Thinker* to Diana, and it's been on her bedstand since.

"They got these pretty glass flowers," I say, "and I keep thinking of ways to get them for you. You know, cheap."

"They're not for me," she says. "Those are gifts for grandmothers or mothers."

"Well, then I could give them to your mom."   35

"A gift from you would be a good idea."

I'm not sure I want that yet. "I could give them to my mom, too. You know, for Mother's Day."

"You better not," she says. "It's stealing."

"Joan sells marked-down things all the time."

"I think you should stop thinking like this."   40

"But it's easy," I tell her. "I'm good at it."

"How do you know if you're good at it?"

"I know what I'm good at."

"You know I don't like that kind of talk."

"You *know* I don't *like* that kind of *talk*." Lately I've been imitating   45
Maria de Covina.

"You better go," she says.

"Would you stop it," I say. "I'm playing, I'm only teasing."

"You really should go anyway," she says. She's naked, looking for her underwear in the bedsheets, in the dark. "I'm afraid. We're taking too many chances."

I don't take too many chances. One time I did sell something to a friend, for example, for a much lower price than was on the tag. But that was instead of, say, just giving it to him in the bag when he buys something else for a normal price. Which is stealing. I wouldn't do that. Another way is, a customer comes and buys an item, but instead of making a normal receipt, I ring it out on our long form, the one in three-colored triplicate, that one we use when the item has to be delivered. I wait for an expensive purchase. I give the customer the white copy, put the green copy in the register, then fill out the pink copy later—in blue pencil so it looks right, like it's from the stencil. I can stick whatever I want in a box, put that pink copy with a name and address on it, and mail it out of the store. The truth is I think of everything and do nothing. It's only a little game I play in my mind. There's nothing here I want. Well, one time I wanted a ship, a pirate ship to me, with masts and sails and rope the width of string. It was going off the floor because it never sold in over a year, and some items like this are smashed up and thrown away instead of sent back—written off as a loss. I thought I should just take it home instead of destroying it, but Maria insisted on writing me out a slip and selling it to me for three dollars. I gave it to my mom.

"If you really want the valise," I tell Mrs. Huffy, "I'll sell it to you marked   50 down as damaged." Mrs. Huffy sells the luggage. She and I often work the same shift. Sometimes she comes over and sells gifts, and sometimes I sell luggage, but mostly we keep to our separate areas. Maria takes care of the silverware and china. The valise that Mrs. Huffy likes is going to be ripped up and trashed because it's not made anymore and can't be returned to the supplier for a refund.

"It seems like such a waste to throw it away." Mrs. Huffy fidgets with her glasses all the time. She has a chain on them so she doesn't put them down and forget them. You can't tell most of the time if she sees better with them off or with them on. Sometimes the glasses go nervously onto the top of her hair, which is silver gray, the same color as the chain and the frames.

"It is a waste if you ask me."

"You'd think they'd call the Salvation Army instead." Glasses hanging like a necklace.

Mrs. Huffy makes me think of what Diana will be like when she's old. Still worried. "But they're not. They're throwing it away."

"It's terrible," she says.   55

"I could just sell it to you."

She takes the glasses up to her nose and stares at me. "You can't do that. I wouldn't. Security looks at the receipt." When we leave the building at night, guards examine our belongings, and if we've bought anything from the store, they check the receipt to make sure it matches.

"We'll get it marked down. I'll ask Maria." Everything's okay if a manager or assistant manager says so.

"It wouldn't be right." Glasses on the head.

"Okay then, but I think it's no big deal."   60

"Do you think she'd do it?"

"I'm sure she would."

"I can't." Glasses on the nose. Holding the valise, snapping it open, snapping it closed. "I can't ask."

"I told you already I'd ask. I know she won't care."

"I don't know."   65

"*Como quieras,*° whatever you decide." I'm walking back to Gifts because I see a customer.

"I don't know," Mrs. Huffy says. "Are you sure Maria would?"

Maria saw me the other night in the parking lot with Cindy, and she wouldn't stop asking me about it. So? she'd say, so? I didn't think I should talk about it. Come on, did you get some or not? I didn't think it was right to talk about it. But she kept insisting and, finally, it seemed okay. I told her how Cindy and I were parked near each other and she said something about a good-night kiss. She started pressing against me hard, and I just put my hand on a *chiche*° and then she wrapped her leg around me even harder and rubbed up against me until she put her hand on me. She was physically hot, like sweating. She put her hand down there, I put my hand down there, and then we went into her car. I didn't want to tell Covina the rest, I didn't think I should. But still she says, So? Whadaya mean, *so*? I'm delaying because I feel her close behind me, and I'm not sure. Did you or not? she says. The store's just closed, and I'm at my register, clearing it while we're talking, about to take my tray out to count money, and she's behind me very close. Why don't you want to tell me? she says. She's got her *chiches* against me, moving just a little, and, I don't know, I don't mind but I'm embarrassed too. In case someone sees. But I don't say anything. I'm also surprised. I don't know why it hadn't crossed my mind. She had her register to clear, and she left.

"I don't like it." Diana's worrying. She's in pajamas.

"It's no big deal," I say. We're whispering to each other in the dark. I'm   70 not sure why it's so dark this night but it is. I surprised her when I came to the window. I had to say her name a few times to wake her up.

"You better stop," she says. Even though I can't see them, the glass flowers I bought damaged are in a vase next to *The Thinker*. I told her I didn't want them for either her mom or mine, and once she saw them, how beautiful they were, she wanted them. "You're gonna get caught."

"You're gonna get *caught*," I say.

"Why would Maria be doing this?" she asks. "I don't trust her."

I feel like Diana is really sensing Cindy, or Liz. I told her I had to work Saturday night, and that's why we couldn't go out. I feel like it's because I'm talking too much about all this to Covina, and it's in the air, that I'm not being smart, talking *esas cosas*° out loud. "Come on, it's crazy," I tell Diana. "She's a lot older than me, and she's the assistant manager of the department. She knows what she's doing."

Suddenly she starts crying.   75

"What's the matter?" I ask.

Como quieras: Whatever you want.   **chiche:** Boob.   **esas cosas:** Those things.

She's sobbing into her pillow.

"You're making too much noise," I'm whispering. "You're gonna wake up your parents."

"You have to go," she says. She's talking in a normal voice, which is really loud at this time of night. Her face is all wet. I try to kiss her, but she pushes me away. "You have to go," she says.

"Can't we make love?" I'm being quiet at the open window, and though   80
my eyes have adjusted, it's so dark, and I can barely see her in the bed. "Don't you want to make love?"

I feel sick. I love women, but I realize I don't want to lose Diana. I love her.

Covina shakes her head as I tell her how Diana was acting. Mexican men, she says.

I do like it that she thinks of me as a man. I like being a man, even if it makes me feel too old for Diana. It's confusing. I'm not sure what to do. I wonder if she'd say the same if she didn't think I was almost twenty-one.

I go to the stockroom, and I sit on the edge of the gray desk. "Mrs. Huffy wants this valise real bad. You think you could sign this?" I've already made out a receipt. Instead of forty-five dollars, I made it for forty-five cents, damaged.

Covina gets up, and without kissing me, *ni nada*, she pushes her breast   85
into my face. She has one hand under it, and another on my neck. Pretty quick she opens her blouse and she pulls up her bra and we're both excited and she reaches over and slams the stockroom door and she gets on her knees between mine. I wouldn't tell her, but nobody's ever done that to me before. It was exciting, and I was scared—it *was* right there in our stockroom—and I guess I am a little shocked too, but I don't want her to know it. You know. I follow her to her apartment because she told me to. Before I didn't even think about whether she had her own apartment. I didn't really want to go. And I didn't do very well. She probably saw how inexperienced I am really, and then I made the mistake of telling her how I'm in love with Diana, and how bad I'm feeling.

So I'm tired when I clock in because I stayed with her. I was late in the morning getting to A-Tron, and I wouldn't have gone in if I already didn't know there were a lot of orders we had to fill. Mrs. Huffy is already in Silverware and China when I get to the floor, so worried she can't even take her glasses off when she sees me, and Joan stops me in the middle of Gifts. Joan never works at night.

When Mrs. Huffy checked out with the valise, a security guard opened her package, and asked for the receipt, and the guard said he was going to keep it and make sure it was on the up and up the next day. Instead of, like, scratching the valise when she got home so it really did look damaged, instead of waiting for Joan to deal with it so she could tell us to never do anything like this again, Mrs. Huffy panicked and brought the valise back in the morning.

"Ms. Mata told me everything," Stemp says. Stemp works for the LAPD, or used to, or something like that. I already know who he is, but I'd never talked to him before. He never talks to anybody. He might be chief of security at The Broadway. He wears cheap black slacks and a cheap white shirt and a cheap, plain blue tie. He looks like he might rock in his swivel chair, but he doesn't. He just has it tilted back, his hands folded onto his *panza*.° The office has no decorations, no photos or paintings or mirrors on the walls. On his gray desk is the cheapest lamp they sell in Furniture, which is across from Gifts, and one of those heavy black phones. He has a sheet of paper and a pen in front of him. "She told me about how you used triplicate forms and used our courtesy mailing service and how you sold goods to your friends." He stares at me for a very long time, satisfied like he just ate a big meal.

"I never did anything like that," I say. I couldn't believe Maria told him my ideas. "It's not true," I say.

"It's not true," he repeats. He shakes his head with only his eyes. "Do   90 you realize that Ms. Mata was building a career here?"

"She didn't do anything. I know she never did anything."

He really shakes his head. "I don't have time for this. I already have it all." He slides the paper over to me. "Just sign it and get outta here."

I read his form. It lists all these ways I took things from the store, and how Maria cooperated.

"No," I say. "Maria didn't cooperate, she didn't do anything. I didn't do anything either."

"I can call the police right now if you'd prefer. We can deal with this in   95 that manner."

"I guess. I have to think."

He sends me off after I sign a form admitting that I sold a forty-five-dollar valise to Mrs. Huffy for forty-five cents. I loved this job so much. I really loved being here at The Broadway, and I can't think of what I'll do now. I head to the parking lot, and I'm in my car, and I'm trying to decide whether I should go over to Diana's or to Maria's, if either of them would want to see me, when I see Liz waving at me. I get out of the car. How come you haven't called me? she wants to know. I'm wearing the suit I bought from her store. The vest is buttoned but the jacket isn't. I do always feel good in it.

panza: Belly.

Reading

1. Who is "Maria de Covina"? What does the narrator tease her about?

2. What causes the narrator to lose his job?

Thinking Critically

1. Why does Maria respond the way she does to the narrator's teasing?

2. How would you describe the character of the narrator? Do you like him or dislike him? Why?

Connecting

1. Like the narrator of "Maria de Covina," the protagonist of Tomás Rivera's story "La Noche Buena" (p. 145) gets in trouble at a department store. What do the two characters have in common? Do Gilb and Rivera have any similar themes in their stories? In what ways are the stories different?

Writing

1. The narrator of "Maria de Covina" tries to pass himself off as older and wiser than he really is. Write an essay, using examples from the story, about the narrator and the image that he is trying to project. Be sure to discuss what you think Gilb is trying to communicate through the character.

Creating

1. **Rewrite Gilb's story as a comic strip.** Pick what you think are the three or four most important moments in the story "Maria de Covina." Then make a comic strip that tells the story with a few images and words, rewriting if you feel it necessary. You can use the Hernandez Brothers' "Chiro el Indio" (p. 307) as a model for your work.

38

LUIS J. RODRÍGUEZ [b. 1954]

Tía Chucha • Always Running

From The Concrete River [1991]

GENRE: POETRY

It is no wonder that the writer Luis J. Rodríguez is best known for a memoir, as the story of his life, full of redemption and recovery, could have been invented by a filmmaker or a novelist. Rodríguez was born in El Paso, Texas, but his parents relocated to Los Angeles, and he grew up in the South San Gabriel barrio. As a teenager, he began writing poetry and was politically engaged, but he also got involved with the area's violent gang life and spent some time in jail. After his release and graduation from high school, Rodríguez spent several years working and writing in Los Angeles before turning to full-time work in journalism. In 1989, after relocating to Chicago, he published his first book of poetry, Poems Across the Pavement. *This was followed by* The Concrete River *in 1991. His 1993 memoir* Always Running: La Vida Loca: Gang Days in L.A., *with its portrayals of the brutality of gang life and its sympathetic portrayals of the people caught up in it, became his biggest success. Rodríguez started a cultural center called Tía Chucha in Los Angeles, and he has continued his involvement with community issues and his writing, publishing poetry, stories, a novel, and in 2011, a memoir called* It Calls You Back: An Odyssey Through Love, Addiction, Revolutions, and Healing. *Always close to politics, he ran for governor of California as a member of the Green Party in 2014.*

The poems presented here are from Rodríguez's 1991 book The Concrete River. *"Tía Chucha" is about a strange and perhaps halfcrazy but nonetheless inspiring relative. "Always Running" is a poem Rodríguez wrote during a time full of craziness that came after the end of his first marriage. "I eventually took that kind of craziness and decided to just run. Running was something I would always do in the neighborhood anyway. You run away from the cops. You run away from other gangs. You're running from this and that. I think that's really a metaphor for what that whole life was."*

---

*From Frederick Luis Aldama, Spilling the Beans in Chicanolandia.

As you read these poems, think about how they provide commentaries on the good and bad possibilities that come from craziness.

TÍA CHUCHA

Every few years
Tía° Chucha would visit the family
in a tornado of song
and open us up
as if we were an overripe avocado.   5
She was a dumpy, black-haired
creature of upheaval,
who often came unannounced
with a bag of presents
including home-made perfumes and colognes   10
that smelled something like
rotting fish
on a hot day at the tuna cannery.

They said she was crazy.
Oh sure, she once ran out naked   15
to catch the postman
with a letter that didn't belong to us.
I mean, she had this annoying habit
of boarding city buses
and singing at the top of her voice   20
(one bus driver even refused to go on
until she got off).
But crazy?

To me, she was the wisp
of the wind's freedom,   25
a music-maker
who once tried to teach me guitar
but ended up singing
and singing,
me listening,   30
and her singing
until I put the instrument down
and watched the clock
click the lesson time away.

Tía: Aunt.

I didn't learn guitar,   35
but I learned something
about her craving
for the new, the unbroken
. . . so she could break it.
Periodically she banished   40
herself from the family
and was the better for it.

I secretly admired Tía Chucha.
She was always quick with a story,
another *"Pepito"* joke,   45
or a hand-written lyric
that she would produce
regardless of the occasion.

She was a despot
of desire;   50
uncontainable
as a splash of water
on a varnished table.

I wanted to remove
the layers   55
of unnatural seeing
the way Tía Chucha beheld
the world, with first eyes,
like an infant
who can discern   60
the elixir
within milk.

I wanted to be
one of the prizes
she stuffed into   65
her rumpled bag.

ALWAYS RUNNING

All night vigil.
My two-and-a-half-year-old boy
and his 10-month-old sister
lay on the same bed,
facing opposite ends;   5

their feet touching.
They looked soft, peaceful,
bundled there in strands of blankets.
I brushed away roaches that meandered
across their faces,   10
but not even that could wake them.
Outside, the dark cover of night tore
as daybreak bloomed like a rose
on a stem of thorns.
I sat down on the backsteps,   15
gazing across the yellowed yard.
A 1954 Chevy Bel-Air stared back.
It was my favorite possession.
I hated it just then.
It didn't start when I tried to get it going   20
earlier that night. It had a bad solenoid.
I held a 12-gauge shotgun across my lap.
I expected trouble from the Paragons gang
of the west Lynwood *barrio*.°
Somebody said I drove the car   25
that dudes from *Colonia*° *Watts* used
to shoot up the Paragons' neighborhood.
But I got more than trouble that night.
My wife had left around 10 p.m.
to take a friend of mine home.   30
She didn't come back.
I wanted to kill somebody.
At moments, it had nothing to do
with the Paragons.
It had to do with a woman I loved.   35
But who to kill? Not her—
sweet allure wrapped in a black skirt.
I'd kill myself first.
Kill me first?
But she was the one who quit!   40
Kill her? No, think man! I was hurt, angry . . .
but to kill her? To kill a Paragon?
To kill anybody?
I went into the house
and put the gun away.   45

barrio: A poor, predominantly Mexican American neighborhood or area.
Colonia: A poor, rural neighborhood on the outskirts of town.

Later that morning, my wife came for her things:
some clothes, the babies . . . their toys.
A radio, broken TV, and some dishes remained.
I didn't stop her.
There was nothing to say that my face   50
didn't explain already.
Nothing to do . . . but run.

So I drove the long haul to Downey
and parked near an enclosed area
alongside the Los Angeles River.   55
I got out of the car,
climbed over the fence
and stumbled down the slopes.
A small line of water rippled in the middle.
On rainy days this place flooded and flowed,   60
but most of the time it was dry
with dumped garbage and dismembered furniture.
Since a child, the river and its veins of canals
were places for me to think. Places to heal.
Once on the river's bed, I began to cleanse.   65
I ran.

I ran into the mist of morning,
carrying the heat of emotion
through sun's rays;
I ran past the factories   70
that lay smack in the middle
of somebody's backyard.
I ran past alleys with overturned trashcans
and mounds of tires.
Debris lay underfoot. Overgrown weeds   75
scraped my leg as I streamed past;
recalling the song of bullets
that whirred in the wind.

I ran across bridges, beneath overhead passes,
and then back alongside the infested walls   80
of the concrete river;
splashing rainwater as I threaded,
my heels colliding against the pavement.
So much energy propelled my legs
and, just like the river,   85
it went on for miles.

When all was gone,
the concrete river
was always there
and me, always running.   90

Reading

1. ("Tía Chucha") What is Tía Chucha always doing, even while riding the bus?

2. ("Always Running") What is the narrator of the poem angry about?

Thinking Critically

1. For Rodríguez, what does Tía Chucha represent?

2. What lines or sections of "Always Running" do you think best communicate despair? Why?

3. Do you think the speaker of "Always Running" is fully recovered from his craziness at the end of the poem? Why do you think that?

Connecting

1. Carmen Tafolla's poem "Tía Sofía" (p. 189) is also about a quirky relative. Do you find any similarities in the personalities of Tía Sofía and Tía Chucha? Are they appealing (or unappealing) for similar reasons?

Writing

1. In "Tía Chucha," the narrator suggests that abnormal behavior can be a good thing, but the speaker in "Always Running" seems to suggest it can also be dangerous. From reading these two poems, what kind of behavior do you think the poems' narrators find healthy? Explore this question in a brief essay using examples from the two poems.

Creating

1. **Present one of Rodríguez's poems visually.** In "Tía Chucha" and "Always Running," the poet presents characters in situations that would fit in an action movie. Choose a scene from one of the poems, and drawing on Rodriguez's imagery, sketch it out, perhaps as a still from a movie.

39

DEMETRIA MARTÍNEZ [b. 1960]

From *Mother Tongue* [1994]

GENRE: FICTION

Demetria Martínez's work as an activist and a writer came together in a strange way when, in 1988, her work with refugees from El Salvador led to federal charges for smuggling undocumented migrants into the country. After earning a degree from Princeton University, Martínez had returned to Albuquerque, New Mexico, where she had grown up, and in 1987 had published Turning, *her first book of poetry. While working as a journalist for the* National Catholic Journal, *she participated in the Sanctuary Movement, which in the mid-1980s aimed to provide shelter for people fleeing violence in Central America in the face of the reluctance of the American government to accept them. She faced jail time and huge fines, but she won her case on constitutional grounds and later used her experience with the Movement as the basis for her first novel,* Mother Tongue, *published in 1994.*

Martínez, with an awareness of the variety of cultures that make up her own Chicano and Latino background, brings a global consciousness to her work as a storyteller and has said: "If everyone in the world can recognize that they carry within them stories, the sangre *of so many groups, then maybe people can get beyond their own understanding of nationality, religion, and race and begin to act as world citizens. That is our only hope."* She has continued both her activism, through teaching and through work with victims of domestic violence, and her poetry, with the collections* Breathing Between the Lines *and* The Devil's Workshop *appearing in 1997 and 2002, respectively. Martínez also published a book of essays called* Confessions of a Berlitz-Tape Chicana *in 2005.*

In this opening chapter from the novel Mother Tongue, *we are introduced to Mary, the novel's narrator, as she recalls the first time she met José Luis, a refugee from the extreme violence that gripped El Salvador in the 1980s. Through a mix of reflection,*

---

*From Hector A. Torres, *Conversations with Contemporary Chicana and Chicano Writers.*

recollection, and passages from letters, Mary hints at the compli-
cated love story that will continue in the rest of the novel. She also
suggests the difficulties of José Luis's journey for those involved
with the Sanctuary Movement, and especially for him.

As you read this excerpt from Martinez's novel, pay attention to
the hints provided about what is to come, and think about the
difficulties of starting over, with a new country, a new life, and a
new name.

His nation chewed him up and spat him out like a piñón° shell, and when
he emerged from an airplane one late afternoon, I knew I would one day
make love with him. He had arrived in Albuquerque to start life over, or at
least sidestep death, on this husk of red earth, this Nuevo Méjico. His was
a face I'd seen in a dream. A face with no borders: Tibetan eyelids, Spanish
hazel irises, Mayan cheekbones dovetailing delicately as matchsticks. I
don't know why I had expected Olmec: African features and a warrior's
helmet as in those sculpted basalt heads, big as boulders, strewn on their
cheeks in Mesoamerican jungles. No, he had no warrior's face. Because
the war was still inside him. Time had not yet leached its poisons to his
surfaces. And I was one of those women whose fate is to take a war out of
a man, or at least imagine she is doing so, like prostitutes once upon a time
who gave themselves in temples to returning soldiers. Before he appeared
at the airport gate, I had no clue such a place existed inside of me. But then
it opened up like an unexpected courtyard that teases dreamers with sunlight, bougainvillea, terra-cotta pots blooming marigolds.

It was Independence Day, 1982. Last off the plane, he wore jeans, shirt,
and tie, the first of many disguises. The church people in Mexico must
have told him to look for a woman with a bracelet made of turquoise
stones because he walked toward me. And as we shook hands, I saw
everything—all that was meant to be or never meant to be, but that I
would make happen by taking reality in my hands and bending it like a
willow branch. I saw myself whispering his false name by the flame of
my Guadalupe candle, the two of us in a whorl of India bedspread, Salvation Army mattresses heaped on floorboards, adobe walls painted Juárez
blue. Before his arrival the chaos of my life had no axis about which to
spin. Now I had a center. A center so far away from God that I asked
forgiveness in advance, remembering words I'd read somewhere, words
from the mouth of Ishtar: *A prostitute compassionate am I.*

. . .

piñón: Pine nut.

July 3, 1982

Dear Mary,

I've got a lot to pack, so I have to type quickly. My El Paso contact arranged for our guest to fly out on AmeriAir. He should be arriving around 4 p.m. tomorrow. As I told you last week, don't forget to take the Yale sweatshirt I gave you just in case his clothing is too suspicious looking. Send him to the nearest bathroom if this is the case. The Border Patrol looks for "un-American" clothing. I remember the time they even checked out a woman's blouse tag right there in the airport—"Hecho en El Salvador.°" It took us another year and the grace of God to get her back up after she was deported.

Anyhow, when he comes off the plane, speak to him in English. Tell him all about how "the relatives" are doing. When you're safely out of earshot of anyone remind him that if anyone asks, he should say he's from Juárez. If he should be deported, we want immigration to have no question he is from Mexico. It'll be easier to fetch him from there than from a Salvadoran graveyard. Later on it might be helpful to show him a map of Mexico. Make him memorize the capital and the names of states. And I have a tape of the national anthem. These are the kinds of crazy things la migra° asks about when they think they have a Central American. (Oh yes, and if his hair is too long, get him to Sandoval's on Second Street. The barber won't charge or ask questions.) El Paso called last night and said he should change his first name again, something different from what's on the plane ticket. Tend to this when you get home.

I've left the keys between the bottom pods of the red chile ristra° near   5
my side door. Make yourselves at home (and water my plants, please). I've lined up volunteers to get our guest to a doctor, lawyers, and so forth for as long as I'm here in Arizona. God willing, the affidavit from the San Salvador archdiocese doctor will be dropped off at the house by a member of the Guadalupe parish delegation that was just there. That is, assuming the doctor is not among those mowed down last week in La Cruz.

As I told you earlier, our guest is a classic political asylum case, assuming he decides to apply. Complete with proof of torture. Although even then he has only a two percent chance of being accepted by the United States. El Salvador's leaders may be butchers, but they're butchering on behalf of democracy so our government refuses to admit anything might be wrong. Now I know St. Paul says we're supposed to pray for our leaders and I do, but not without first fantasizing about lining them up and shooting them.

Now see, you got me going again. Anyway, we used to marry off the worst cases, for the piece of paper, so they could apply for residency and

Hecho en El Salvador: Made in El Salvador.   **la migra:** Border patrol.
red chile ristra: Red chiles strung up for drying or display.

a work permit. But nowadays, you can't apply for anything unless you've been married for several years and immigration is satisfied that the marriage is for real. Years ago, when Carlos applied, immigration interrogated us in separate rooms about the color of our bathroom tile, the dog food brand we bought, when we last did you-know-what. To see if our answers matched. Those years I was "married" I even managed to fool you. That is, until we got the divorce, the day after he got his citizenship papers. But you were too young for me to teach you about life outside the law. Which used to be so simple in the old days.

Failing everything, we'll get the underground railroad in place. Canada.

Thanks, mijita,° for agreeing to do this. The volunteers will take care of everything (they know where the key is hidden), so just make our guest feel at home. Maybe take him to Old Town. After all, it's not everyone who lives on a plaza° their great-great-etcetera-grandparents helped build. I'm glad you have some time, that you're between jobs. With your little inheritance, you can afford to take a few months off and figure out what to do with your life. But don't get yourself sick over it. I'm fifty and I still haven't figured it out for myself. Just trust the Lord, who works in mysterious ways.

I don't know how long I'll be in Phoenix. My mother's last fall was a   10
pretty hard one, and if she needs surgery, I could end up here for the summer. Don't forget to feed the cats and take out the garbage. I'm slipping this under your door so that if they ever catch me, I won't have conspiratorial use of the mails added to all the other charges I've chalked up. Rip this up! Be careful.

Love & Prayers,
Soledad

P.S.: Take it from one who survived the 60s. Assume the phone is tapped until proved otherwise.

P.S. #2: And don't go falling in love.

. . .

A clairvoyant moment doesn't make moving into the future any easier. If anything, it is a burden because one must forget what one has seen and move on, vulnerable as anyone. As we drove away from the airport in my blue pickup truck, shyness ground words to dust in my mouth. All that kept me from choking on silence was a sweet downpour of notes from a wood flute, a Cambodian wedding song on the university radio station. He was not a North American—nothing in his manner indicated awkwardness about silence. As I recall, he looked straight ahead, watched the city break in two as we cut through it, driving very fast on the

mijita: My daughter, used affectionately.   **plaza:** A central town square.

freeway. My Spanish was like an old car, parts missing or held together with clothes hanger wire, but it got me where I wanted to go. Scraping together some words at last, I asked this man who had fled his country, did the airline serve you peanuts or a meal? He said, both, but I couldn't eat. He said, the movement of the plane made me nauseated, almost as sick to my stomach as the time I breathed tear gas at the funeral of a priest that death squads shot and killed as he lifted the communion host.

I'm not sure, twenty years later, that he used the words tear gas. I didn't then know its Spanish translation and I don't know it now. But for the sake of the story, tear gas will have to do. You see, I am good at filling in blanks, at seeing meaning where there may have been none at all. In this way I get very close to the truth. Or closer still to illusion.

Soledad died many years ago, but I have her letters. He, too, is dead, but I have a tape recording of a speech he gave, the newspaper accounts of it, some love poems. El Salvador is rising from the dead, but my folder of newspaper clippings tells the story of the years when union members disappeared and nuns were ordered off buses at gunpoint, a country with its hands tied behind its back, crying, *stop, stop*. These and a few journal entries are all I have left to fasten my story to reality. Everything else is remembering. Or dismembering. Either way, I am ready to go back. To create a man out of blanks who can never wound me.

. . .

I said, we have to pick a name for you, one that you would answer to in your sleep. On the plane ticket you're identified simply as A. Romero. I said that, or something like it, in Soledad's kitchen where Zapata, Cuba, and Nicaragua libre° posters stuck to her cabinets, postage stamps mailing her house through the twentieth century. The kitchen always smelled of Guatemalan coffee beans ground with almonds. Or sometimes the air was spiked with lime, tomatillo, and cilantro that women mashed in a molcajete° made of porous volcanic rock. Nameless women who appeared at night and rose with the heaving of garbage trucks to cook, to make themselves strong before North Americans bundled them off to other houses, further north. A. Romero and I sat at an oval oak table where newspaper articles that Soledad had clipped leaked out of manila folders. All the wars that passed through her house ended in a fragile cease-fire at this table, where plates of black beans and rice

libre: Free.   **molcajete:** Mortar (as in mortar and pestle), traditionally made from lava stone.

steamed as refugees rolled corn tortillas like cigarettes. This is where
A. Romero and I lifted blue pottery mugs of hot coffee to our lips like
communion chalices.

He said, Roberto, Juan, any name will do. I said, why not Neftali, or   15
Octavio? I wondered, why not pan for gold, for something weightier than
the silt of ordinary names like Robert and John. He said, in my country
names turn up on lists. Or in the mouths of army officers at U.S. embassy
parties. A few drinks later, someone, somewhere disappears. Pick an
ordinary name.

His eyes wandered away from me and into the living room on the other
side of a white adobe arch encrusted with arabesque tiles. The house was
a forest of flea market furniture that Soledad had coaxed to a sheen with
strips of flannel nightgown. A tape player and cassettes of Gregorian
chants were set on top of a black baby grand piano, its keys shining like
the whites of eyes. A bay window of beveled glass framed the yard—elms,
fresh stubble of Bermuda grass, roses flaring like skirts of flamenco
dancers. Soledad lived in the Valley in a house made of terrones, blocks
of earth cut a century before from the banks of the Rio Grande. Shadows
of cottonwood leaves twitched on an adobe wall that marked off her
quarter acre. The house looked like it had been cut out and assembled
from pictures in architecture books Soledad piled on her coffee table—
Islamic, Pueblo revival, Territorial, things made to last, solidities refugees could only dream of.

He said, any name you pick will do. I said, it's not my place to decide. I
believe I told him a story then, a story I'd heard on the university radio
station on the way to the airport. A Spanish expedition comes upon some
Mayan Indians. The Spaniards ask, what is this place called? The Maya
answer, uic athan, we do not understand your words. The Spaniards
believe they have been told the place is Yucatán so they impose that
name on the place, inflict it. Like Adam, they think God has given them
the right to name a world. And the world never recovers.

He smiled, crescent moon, then pressed his mug to his lips as if to mold
them back into proper form. Maybe I'm imagining things, maybe more
time passed before we smiled back and forth. But everything happened
very quickly, this is the amazing thing. From day one I looked for ways to
graft a piece of myself onto him, to become indispensable. My gestures
were perfectly timed, touching his hand, twisting my hair, excusing
myself to touch up my lipstick. Ordinary actions that would reverse the
tides of my life as in the theories of physicists who say the dance of a
butterfly can cause volcanoes to erupt.

Love at first sight, this is how I explained the urgency that would later shed its skin and reveal pure desperation. Some women fall in love in advance of knowing a man because it is much easier to love a mystery. And I needed a mystery—someone outside of ordinary time who could rescue me from an ordinary life, from my name, Mary, a blessing name that had become my curse. At age nineteen, I was looking for a man to tear apart the dry rind of that name so I could see what fruit fermented inside.

This is what happened back then to women who didn't marry or have   20
babies, who quit going to Mass. They begged to differ. They questioned their own names.

He picked the name, José Luis.

. . .

Twenty years later, his name is a lens that allows me to see him as if for the first time. Five feet, five inches tall. Hair black as a pueblo pot. A scar above his right eyebrow, a seam sealing some old wound. His almond eyes were welcoming as windows open to spring, no screen, white curtain fluttering. But the rest of his face, with its hard jaw and serious mouth, was boarded up like a house whose owner knows what strangers can do when they get inside. Alert and polite, he always looked for ways to be of help. Before long he would be making coffee, taping grocery lists to the refrigerator, feeding the cats. But attention to detail was also a spiritual exercise to divert demons of exhaustion, I'm sure of this now. He had the hands of a man who had picked coffee or cut sugarcane for forty years. I'm not sure when he told me he was twenty-nine years old. By then it was too late. I had already counted the tree rings around his eyes and fallen in love with a much older man.

. . .

We must have gone down to Soledad's basement, must have heard steps creak as our soles adjusted the lower vertebrae of the house. But it is the smell I recall most clearly, the odor of damp earth, adobe walls maybe, or else just laundry swishing in the machine or hanging from a line that drooped above us like an eyelid. Red chile ristras hung from a rib cage of pipes over the door to José Luis's room. Dusty sunlight from an aboveground window touched down and lit up the objects in the room in a kind of still life: a bed with a blue Mexican blanket, chest of drawers, night table with lamp shell over a yolk of light, and a black pot blooming with dried chamisa.°

---

chamisa: Desert shrub.

He said, I don't need much space, all I have are poems and a Bible. He pulled these out of a shoulder bag, put them on the chest of drawers. His face suddenly grave, he surveyed the bed as if he feared someone might be hiding beneath it. Soledad had left running pants and a Harvard T-shirt on the pillow with a note, "For Our Guest." I translated it for him, only dimly sensing the depths of the conspiracy I was entering into, a pact to make him into someone else entirely. We were to shield him from the authorities by way of a fiction, a story that would obscure the truth rather than clarify it. It's amazing, looking back, to think that a few miles away a law library had books that were filled with words like aiding, abetting, transporting. Surely I knew the dangers. Yet surely wrongdoing was at the root of the thrill for a Catholic girl who had indulged in sex for the first time the year before, who had learned that breaking the law is a pleasure more poignant than sex itself.

Yes, from the very beginning I wanted him. In that time of my life, men   25
were mirrors that allowed me to see myself at different angles. Outside this function, they did not exist. It was a supreme selfishness, the kind that feeds on men's attentions, a void flourishing in a void. José Luis would have none of it. When desire flickered across my face, he extinguished it with talk about El Salvador, the civil war, death squads, landowners. His struggles were too large and unwieldy to be folded up and dropped into my palm like alms. In the end, I had no choice but to love him. Desire was not good enough. Love would ripen in the light of time we spent together, like an arranged marriage. Except that I was doing the arranging. And calling it fate.

Weeks or months after his arrival, he asked me, do you want to know my real name? I said no. No. I feared the authorities. But even greater than fear was my need for him to remain a stranger, his made-up name dark glasses he must never take off. Because making love with a stranger is always good. Even if you've known that stranger for a very long time.

. . .

July, 1982
Let me be
the bridge,
those troubled
waters,
his eyes,
Let me be

Reading

1. Why does Soledad instruct Mary to take a Yale sweatshirt to the airport?

2. Why does the man Mary picks up at the airport choose the name "José Luis"?

Thinking Critically

1. Why do you think Mary finds José Luis so appealing?

2. What can you tell about José Luis's personality from this chapter?

Connecting

1. Juan Felipe Herrera's poem "Exiles" (p. 202) is about immigrants, many of them from Central America, as José Luis is. Does he remind you of the people in Herrera's poem? In what ways is he similar? In what ways do you think his story is unique?

Writing

1. The opening chapter of *Mother Tongue* is told as a memory from the perspective of some twenty years later. How does this change the way that the story is told? In an essay, explore how Martínez uses hindsight in this chapter to add perspective and to hint at what is coming in the rest of the novel. Use specific examples from the text in your essay.

Creating

1. **Write a poem about a first impression.** Demetria Martínez opens her book with a poetic description of Mary's powerful first impression of José Luis, recalled many years after she met him. Write a poem about the first time that you met somebody, even if it was a great many years ago.

40

BENJAMÍN ALIRE SÁENZ [b. 1954]

Sometimes the Rain

From Everything Begins & Ends at the Kentucky Club
[2012]

GENRE: FICTION

*For poet and novelist Benjamín Alire Sáenz, the desert landscape
of southern New Mexico connects childhood memories and training for the priesthood. He grew up near Las Cruces, New Mexico,
went to seminary in Colorado, and then finished his theological
education at the University of Louvain in Belgium. Recognizing
the importance of landscape in both the Bible and his own writing, he said, "I understood the desert. It wasn't a metaphor for me.
The desert is a place of encounter. You encounter your demons
and your gods. You confront everything about yourself."* Sáenz
left the priesthood a few years after returning to the United States
and turned to writing, earning an M.F.A. from the University of
Texas at El Paso, studying at the University of Iowa and at Stanford, and publishing his first book of stories,* Calendar of Dust,
*in 1991. After a couple more books of poetry and short stories,
Sáenz's first novel,* Carry Me Like Water, *was published in 1995.
The novel introduced discussions of homosexuality, sexual abuse,
racism, and poverty along the border that his later novels and
stories would explore. Sáenz has published several more books of
poetry, including* The Book of What Remains *in 2010. While in
his fifties, Sáenz ended a long marriage and discovered a new
identity as a gay man, and in 2012, the story collection* Everything
Begins & Ends at the Kentucky Club, *his first book as an openly
gay writer, was awarded the PEN/Faulkner Prize.*

The story "Sometimes the Rain" is drawn from Everything Begins & Ends at the Kentucky Club. *The Kentucky Club is a bar a
few hundred yards from El Paso's international bridge, which
Sáenz calls "the knot that has for generations tied the two cities of*

---

*From an interview with Cecilia Ballí, found at lannan.org/events/
benjamin-alire-saenz-with-cecilia-balli/.

*Juárez and El Paso together."** In the story, it serves as a spot that helps Ernesto Zaragoza, who narrates the story, and Brian Stillman grow closer, during a time when both are finishing high school and trying to decide who they will become.*

As you read "Sometimes the Rain," think about how the club and the story tie together separate social, sexual, racial, and economic strands.

There's always a gun around—even when you can't see it.

There's always a finger that's embedded somewhere in your brain, a finger that's itching to pull the trigger of the gun that's always around.

And when the trigger is pulled, you remember all the shit that ever happened to you: that awful day in second grade when you were in a hurry and caught your foreskin in your zipper and had to be rushed to the hospital for an unplanned circumcision; that winter night when Rose slapped you again and again and again until your lip was bleeding, slapped you, yelled at you, kicked you, cussed at you—and all this for delivering the news that her husband had died in an accident; the time your father whispered that you were no good—even as he lay on his deathbed.

It could happen anytime. The finger tightens, pulls, and a bullet goes flying through the air. That's how remembering is. The gun, the trigger, the itchy finger, the bullet: a CD playing as I drove on a lonely road in New Mexico, Louie Armstrong singing a song about summer, about fish jumping and swimming holes and fishing poles—and me nodding, lipping the words, not really singing, just lipping. And then the rain pouring down. That's when the bullet went shooting right through me.

And there he was. Brian Stillman.   5

I'd never been one for having my picture taken. I always managed to skip school on picture day. I was something of a recidivist truant. The yearbook always had this dumb cartoon in place of my picture that said *Gone fishing.* When I entered high school in 1967, I was fifteen years old, looked ten, acted like I was thirteen. I hated myself because I looked like a little boy and wanted to look like a man, wanted to look like the guys who were advanced, not mentally, hell, the guys that were physically

*From Mónica Ortiz Uribe, "For Award-Winning Author, the Border Is More Than a Headline," Fronteras Desk, April 8, 2013, fronterasdesk.org/content/award-winning-author-border-more-headline.

advanced and already shaving, hell, they didn't know shit about thinking. And thinking was the last thing they were interested in. Some of those guys who looked like men in junior high school, they didn't start thinking until they were in their thirties. By then it was too late. But I still wanted to look like them.

Brian Stillman, he was one of those physically advanced guys. He must have been shaving since he was in sixth grade. And he could've been one of those guys who didn't start thinking until it was too late. But he wasn't.

I'd known him since entering high school. He was in some of my classes. And we were both on the cross-country team. I hated sports and hated guys who played them. I didn't fit in with Brian Stillman and all his buddies, didn't fit in with the coaches and their attitudes. But running wasn't a sport to me. Running was a place—the only place where I belonged.

There was no reason in the universe that I should have ever known anything about Brian Stillman. Except that something happened. I guess that about sums up living. Something always happens.

It was April of 1970 and we were weeks away from graduation. I'd   10
finally grown three or four inches and all my pimples had disappeared. I could actually bear to look at myself in the mirror. I was trying to decide if I was good looking or not. I hated that it mattered so much.

It was a Thursday and I had decided to skip school. I don't know why, not that I needed a reason. Maybe it's because I had my parents' car that day. I got to drive to school a couple of times a week—when my mom carpooled to the factory. My dad, he had a beat-up Studebaker truck. Painted it blue. Looked nice, drove like shit—and he never let me touch it. "It's a piece of shit, anyway," I told him once when he didn't let me drive it.

"That piece of shit is worth more than you are." That about summed up my father's opinion of me.

So that day, I had the car. A white Chevy Impala, twelve years old. I'd lost my wallet and my license along with it. I hadn't made the time to get a new one. My father told me I was the worst driver ever to get behind a wheel. "You're fucking gonna die in a crash. Won't live to be thirty." But my parents had bigger worries than letting me drive their car. My oldest brother was in the can—ten years for robbing a 7-Eleven with a weapon. My parents insisted he was set up. I knew better. My oldest brother was the meanest sonofabitch I'd ever met. I would never have used the word *innocent* within ten feet of him. My sister, two years younger, was pregnant and living with my grandmother. My youngest brother died of meningitis. My father's grief and disappointment turned to rage. The rage was pointed in my direction. Hell, me driving without a license didn't even register on the list of things my parents were worried about.

I lit a cigarette and sped away from the school parking lot and made good my escape. I hated fourth, fifth and sixth periods. I was acing all the classes. So why go? The rent-a-cop didn't even notice I was driving off campus without a pass. He was too busy flirting with a girl who would land him in the same place as my brother if he wasn't careful.

I didn't have a plan. Anywhere but school. School was hell. I felt like an   15
ice cube that was slowly, slowly melting. I felt if I stayed in that school one more second, I would disappear. The sad part was that nobody would notice.

I drove around town. Not much going on at one thirty in the afternoon. I always thought Las Cruces, New Mexico, took a siesta in the afternoons. On certain days, I was convinced the town didn't even bother to wake up.

I wound up at the river—which was everyone's favorite place to go, a place where you could get drunk or get stoned and put in an eight-track tape and listen to Janis Joplin sing those great songs which were angry and sad and rough and beautiful. Someone else's pain was always beautiful. And after that tape was done, you could pop it out and put in *Abbey Road* and listen to it over and over again. I memorized every word of "She Came In Through the Bathroom Window."

I parked the car and listened to Janis Joplin. I sat there on the hood of my car and smoked cigarettes and stared out at the water and the sky and I thought that this was as close as I was ever going to get to heaven.

And then I noticed Brian standing there. It was as if he just appeared. "Hey," he said, "can I bum a smoke?"

"Sure," I said. Like we were friends.   20

We sat there on the hood of my car and smoked.

"She broke up with me," he said.

I looked at him. "Bummer," I said. I don't think we'd actually ever spoken to each other. We probably said *Hi* or something like *How's it hangin'*. The thing was that I hung out with guys like me—Mexicans who went to school because they had to and who mostly had jobs after school and on weekends. Brian hung out with guys like him—gringos who belonged to the Future Farmers of America and wore blue corduroy jackets and thought they owned the school. They *did* own the school. So what? They could have it.

I think he was waiting for me to say something else besides *bummer*. "So you still like her?"

"I don't know," he said. He sort of laughed. "She's pretty, you know?   25
But her name's Beth," he said.

I don't know why I thought that was funny, but I found myself laughing. So we sat there and laughed.

We smoked. We talked, not a lot. Brian wasn't a talker. I was. I really

liked talking. Talking and sleeping, those were my two favorite things.
But I didn't have much to say, not to Brian Stillman.

I could see the guy was lost. One thing was for sure—he'd lost his ride
back into town.

"So you got dumped."   30

"Pretty much. I think I wanted her to dump me. And it's not as if I was
gonna marry her." He took a puff from his cigarette. "You still hanging
out with Rosie?" I didn't know he knew anything about my life.

"Nah. Rosie's history."

"Too bad. She's fine."

Rosie *was* fine. And she'd been right to give me the highway. What was
she doing with a guy like me? I lit another cigarette.

He looked at his watch. "School's almost out."   35

"Yeah."

"I hate school," he said.

"Brian Stillman hates school? Could have fooled me."

"Why? I'm not smart. Not like you."

"I'm not so fucking smart."   40

"How many A's you have on that report card?"

"So what?"

"You understand things, Neto."

It was funny to hear him call me Neto. Most gringos just called me
Ernie. "I'm not sure I'm getting you."

"How do you do it? The teacher calls on you and you always answer as   45
if you wrote the fucking book."

That made me laugh.

"How'd you learn how to think?"

"I don't know. I go to a lot of movies."

That really made him laugh. He flicked his cigarette. "So, you goin' to
college?"

"Yeah. Sure. Why the hell not?"   50

"Well, there's always the army."

"The army's never gonna own my ass. And that's the fucking truth."

"Well, I've kinda thought about joining."

I looked at him and shook my head. "There's a war going on, Stillman.
Anybody let you in on that dirty little secret?"

"I might get drafted."   55

"Not if you go to college."

He nodded. "Maybe I just need to get out of here."

I nodded. "I get that."

"You should leave too, Neto," he said. "You're too good for this fucking place."

Yeah, too good. Like that was true. We smoked another cigarette   60
together.

I offered him a ride home. He lived on a farm just off Highway 478. His
house was about half a mile in from the road. We didn't talk that much
as we drove along. Just listened to *Abbey Road.* He pointed. "This is my
stop. I'll walk the rest of the way."

"I can take you all the way in," I said.

"Nah. My old man—" he stopped in mid-sentence. "He's a piece of
work." He had this real sad look on his face. I wished to God I hadn't seen
that look. It made me like him. He opened the door and started to get out
of the car. But then he just sat back down on the seat. "You still run, Neto?"

"Yeah, I still run."

"So why'd you quit the team?"   65

"Cross-country wasn't my thing."

"You were the best runner. That's why they hated you. They could
never beat you."

I nodded. *Yeah, sure, they could never beat me.*

"You should have stayed on the team."

"I wasn't having a good time."   70

"Well," he said. "We sure as fuck made sure of that, didn't we?" He got
out of the car. Then he put his head through the window. "I'm sorry I was
such an asshole," he said.

"It doesn't matter," I said.

"Yeah," he said, "it *does* matter, Neto." He flipped me a peace sign, then
shut the door.

I watched him walk down the dirt road lined by pecan trees along a
ditch.

I thought about how sad he looked as I drove off. I thought of all the   75
time I'd wasted hating him.

The next night, I was going out. Friday night, on the cusp of summer and
graduation and manhood. Yeah, going out. Just some guys who wanted
to head out to a keg party at the river, maybe meet a girl and kiss her. *And*
if you were lucky, she'd kiss you back. And you might feel something
inside of you. Maybe that's why we went to the river.

School was ending and maybe, *just maybe*, life was beginning. I'd
applied to State and got accepted. That surprised me. I even got a two
thousand dollar scholarship, which was a fortune. But I'd also applied to
the University of New Mexico in Albuquerque. They'd given me the exact
same scholarship. Not that Albuquerque was worlds away, but it was far
enough. I hadn't told anyone, not even my parents. I wasn't sure what to
do, but I didn't want their advice. I wanted to make a decision that was

all mine. I kept pinching myself. Me, Ernesto Zaragoza—I was going to college. I was thinking about all those things while I waited for José and Jimmy to pick me up.

My mom and dad were sitting on the front porch, my father reading the newspaper, my mother reading (or praying) her novena.° *"No te pongas marijuano, cabrón.°"* My father shot me his favorite look. The man could scare me in two languages. Talented guy, my father.

José drove up in his father's jeep. I kissed my mom and smiled at my dad. "I'll be good, Dad." I always said that to him. It pissed him off when I said things like that. He didn't actually want me to be a good boy. He wanted me to be a man. But a man who didn't smoke marijuana. For him that was the worst.

José and Jimmy waved at my mom and dad. My mom was all smiles. 80 My dad scowled. José got a big kick out of my dad. I never really knew why. Like scowling was something amusing.

There were about five or six keg parties at the river. Five or six or seven or eight. José was looking for one in particular. His cousin Mike was hosting him and his buddies. José pointed as he drove. "That's Mike's truck." We pulled up in front of the crowd, got out of the jeep and did the shaking-hands business, the casual hugs that we learned from watching our fathers. Yeah, like we were men. But you had to hug in just the right way and always slap the other guy on the back. That's how it worked.

I got handed a beer.

The sun was setting and there was a breeze and everything was so perfect. I felt almost happy. I don't really remember much about Mike's keg party. Rosie arrived along with a group of about six girls. Then another group of girls arrived. Girls always arrived in packs. It was protection. That's how I thought about it. It made me sad to think that they needed it. Protection from guys like us.

Rosie and I talked. She was so pretty. I mean, pretty in ways that most girls envied. She was real. Sometimes, I wanted to just keep looking at her. "You should leave this town," she said.

"Are you chasing me out?" 85

She laughed. She kissed me on the cheek. "I like you, you idiot."

"Then how come you broke up with me?"

"Because we're just friends. There something wrong with that?"

"Guess not," I said. "Still, maybe I'm a little insulted."

"Don't be. I don't want boyfriends. I want to go to college and get a life. 90 A life that's mine."

"A life that's all yours, huh?"

novena: A set of prayers given over nine days, or the prayer book itself. **No te pongas marijuano, cabrón:** Don't get yourself high on marijuana, dumb ass.

She laughed. "It sounds beautiful, doesn't it, Neto?"
And then I found myself laughing my ass off. "Yeah, Rosie, it sure does sound beautiful."
She smiled. She looked like an angel. "I'm going to U.T."
"Austin? No shit?"   95
"No shit."
"Scholarship?"
"The works, Neto."
"I'm fucking impressed."
"I should thank you."   100
"For what?"
"Remember when we were in junior high?"
"What are you talking about?"
"You used to read to me."
"I almost forgot about that."   105
"It did something to me. There were other worlds out there. And you knew that. And you wanted me to know that too."
She smiled at me. It broke my heart, her smile.
I lit a cigarette. She took the cigarette away from me and took a puff. She kissed me on the cheek. "Don't forget to write." And just like that, she walked away.
I guess I didn't feel much like partying. Maybe there was something wrong with me. I had a few beers, mostly listened to people talking a lot of bullshit. Some guy tried to put his arm around Rosie. She grabbed his paw and shoved it aside. "Go wash your hands," she said.
I smiled. She noticed I was watching. She smiled back at me. Rosie 110 didn't need anybody to take care of her. That's what I liked about her.
Some guys lit a bonfire. It was getting dark and the weather was perfect and I *really was* almost happy.
I walked away and headed to another keg party. I knew some people there, not people I hung with, but you know, school friends. We shot the shit, talked about some crazy things that had happened during high school. Everyone remembered when the gym got spray-painted asking the principal to suck everyone's cock. Nice. Yeah, well, it was high school. There was a lot of laughing. I felt alone. And didn't mind it. It was one of those things, feeling alone. Sometimes it was better than being with other people.
I lit a cigarette and decided to go off and sit by the river. Think about things. I liked thinking about things. My mom called it daydreaming. My dad said I was lazy. They were both wrong. I wasn't daydreaming and the lazy thing, well, my brain didn't have a lazy cell in its body.
I don't know how long I walked, but I was pretty far from all the bonfires. I went and found a good spot by the river where I could take off my shoes. I lay down on the bank, my feet in the water, the stars in the sky. I

thought for a second that maybe my life would be a good one. And I would go through life this happy, happy guy. And then, in the middle of all that happy conversation I was having with myself, I heard something. I didn't know what it was, at first, and so I made myself perfectly still and listened. I knew the sound. Someone was having sex. I mean they were really having sex. I smiled to myself. Yeah, someone was getting lucky as hell. I knew I was being a voyeur or something but what was I supposed to do at that point? So I just sat there and listened.

Whoever they were, they were having a good time. A better time than 115 I'd ever had. And then there it was, the point of all the sex, the climax. Why did people always say, *god, god, god* when they came? I was smiling my ass off. But then I realized something. Something that really confused me. There was no girl. The voices were talking now, and both voices, well, they were both guys. I just kept listening. "I might love you," one of the voices said.

And the other voice said, "Don't love me."

"It's too late, Brian."

"Jorge, you know—I mean—I don't know what I mean."

"You're the one who started this. Now it's too late."

"It's not too late."   120

"You want to pretend that nothing's going on between us?"

"No, no, that's not what I mean."

"Then what, Brian?"

"I don't know what I mean."

They were starting to get mad at each other. My heart was beating 125 fast and I wanted to just get out of there, but I knew they'd hear me and I didn't want them to know I was there. I felt confused but I knew, I knew who they were, God, I knew them. It was Brian Stillman and Jorge Ledesma. Jorge lived on Brian's farm. His dad had come from Mexico to work with the Stillmans. Jorge was quiet and tall and had the body of an athlete. But not from working out, just from working on the Stillman farm. In grade school I'd helped him learn English. But we had never been friends. I don't know why. Maybe it was because I wasn't good at making friends. Maybe it was because I'd been an asshole and didn't want to hang around with Mexican Mexicans. I mean, maybe I wanted to be an American. Hell, I don't remember. We just weren't friends.

I kept listening even though I didn't want to listen. I tried looking up at the stars, tried concentrating on them, but I could still hear everything. And then I heard Brian say, "If I don't leave this goddamn place, I'm gonna go nuts."

"Why?" I could tell Jorge was crying. "Why are you leaving?"

"I can't stay here. I can't." And then there was this long silence. "You can come with me, Jorge."

"My mom's sick, Brian. I can't leave her."

"You need a life. *I* need a life."   130

"You hate your father."

"*He* hates me, Jorge. And I'm not fucking staying."

"And what about me?"

And then there was nothing. Nothing at all.

My heart was beating really fast. And I felt—I really don't know how I 135
felt. I just lay there, my feet in the water, unable to light a cigarette, waiting for them to leave. And then I heard them moving. And then I heard
Brian's voice. "Hey, hey, don't. Don't be sad. We'll figure something out."
I pictured Jorge leaning into Brian's shoulder. I pictured Brian's arms
around Jorge. I didn't know why I was picturing those things.

I heard them walking away.

They were talking again, saying things, but their voices were distant
now, and then their voices disappeared.

I lit a cigarette. I looked up at the stars. And suddenly the world was so
much bigger than I'd ever imagined it to be. And I couldn't get the idea of
Brian kissing Jorge out of my brain.

I had them both in my head when I masturbated that night.

I was trembling.   140

I knew something about myself that I'd never known. Just when I'd
started liking myself, I hated myself again.

The day after graduation, I decided I was going to college in Albuquerque. I told my dad. I don't know why I thought he might actually
be proud of me. "Think you're smart enough?"

"I got a scholarship, Dad."

"You'll be back after you fuck that up." That's all he had to say.

My mom cried. "Your father doesn't mean it," she said.   145

She needed my smile. "I know," I said. We both knew it wasn't true.
But we needed to lie to ourselves and to each other about the truth of
who my father was. What could a woman tell herself when she knew
what kind of man she'd married? What could a guy tell himself about a
father who'd never love him? It was easier to smile.

I worked two jobs that summer. Saved money. The scholarship gave
me two thousand dollars up front and paid my tuition for the first year.
The letter said if I kept up my grades, then the scholarship would be
renewed for another year. After that, I was on my own. That was a lot.
God, that was so much money. A fortune. But still I knew it wouldn't be
enough. And I was already thinking about the last two years and how I

would pay for that. And I kept telling myself this one thing: *I am not going to be poor*. I knew I'd have to do it on my own. So it was me and work. Hell, I knew how to do that. I was living for the future. I guess I'd always been doing that.

I didn't really hang out with anybody that summer. I was too tired. I'd work on a construction site from six in the morning till three in the afternoon. I'd come home, take a shower, eat, relax and go into work at the 7-Eleven from five till eleven. Saturdays, I'd work an eight-hour shift at the 7-Eleven. Sundays, I'd just sleep. That was my life. That, and dreaming of my new life in Albuquerque.

One Saturday afternoon in July, I decided I needed to do something besides read a book or watch television. My parents were out of town at a funeral in San Diego. They'd let me stay behind so I could work. I liked having the house to myself—not that it really felt like home. My dad had a way of making sure I knew that the house I lived in was *his*.

But being alone was really good. Really, really good.   150

I decided I'd find some beer or something. The needing-to-feel-alive thing. Yeah, that was always there. I went riding around, smoking cigarettes, felt kinda lost and kinda sad but didn't know why. I guess I hated my life. I found some homeless guy and he was asking for money. I told him to buy me a six-pack and I'd give him a couple of bucks. He was hungry to take the bait. We both got what we wanted. "God bless you, son," he said.

I shook my head. "Let's leave God out of this one."

I drove around. I don't know why, but I found myself taking the old farm road. I liked that road. I'd grown up on a farm before my father lost it. He lost it betting on a cock fight. Yeah, well, that was my father. I hated him when we had to move. But I'd never hated him as much as he hated me. I just didn't have it in me. I wondered if deep down he wanted to love me as much as I wanted to love him. But there were certain things you couldn't do anything about. Fathers were one of those certain things.

So there I was on Highway 478. Driving down the road, smoking a cigarette. And then I saw him. Brian Stillman. At first I wasn't sure if it was him, but as I drove closer I knew it *was* him. It *was*. He was all beat-up to shit. I mean, the guy's face was all bloody and he was just stumbling around, like he'd gone ten rounds. Goddamn, I thought. He'd taken off his T-shirt and was using it as a giant handkerchief for his bloody nose. I stopped the car by the side of the road and yelled his name. "Brian!" He looked at me. He was numb. He just stood there staring at me. Then he just waved me away.

"Brian?"   155

He waved me away again.

"Get in the car," I said.

He shook his head.

I got out of the car and grabbed him by the arm. "You're hurt," I said. "Get in the car."

"Don't call anyone," he said.   160

"I won't. You need help."

"Fuck you, Neto."

"Don't give me that fuck you shit. That's not gonna work on me. Just get in the car."

He was too tired and too beat-up and too sad to fight me. He got in the car and stared out the window. I handed him a beer. "Here."

He took it. He chugged down the whole thing. And then he just started 165 crying. I didn't say anything.

"Just don't tell anyone," he said. And then he was crying again.

"Who am I gonna tell?"

After a while, he stopped sobbing but the quiet tears kept running down his face.

"You need to get cleaned up," I said. "Maybe you need to see a doctor."

"No way," he said. "No fucking doctors."   170

I thought he was going to hit me. "Okay, okay," I said. I handed him a cigarette. He was trembling as he smoked. I kept watching him out of the corner of my eye.

I drove toward my house, neither one of us saying anything.

When we got to my neighborhood, Brian looked at me. "Where are we going?"

"My house," I said.

"I don't want—"   175

"My parents are out of town," I said. "It's okay."

He didn't say anything.

When we got to my house, I had to help him get out of the car. I thought he really needed to see a doctor. But I knew Brian wasn't going to go for that.

I helped him to the couch and handed him another beer. He drank this one slowly. He wasn't shaking as much. I gave him a cigarette and then went looking for a wet towel. His lip was cut but it had stopped bleeding. I could tell someone had taken a fist to his handsome face.

I handed him a wet washcloth. "Here," I said. He tried his best to clean 180 himself up. I knew he was hurting. I'd been in a couple of fights. Not a smart thing for a guy to do when he wasn't a fighter.

"Who did this to you, Brian?"

He looked at me. I guess he'd decided he could trust me. "My father," he whispered.

Great, I thought. But I didn't say anything. I just kept staring at his beat-up face. "He's a fuck," I said.

He almost smiled when I said that.

"Why?" I said. "Why did he do that to you? He's a fuck."   185
He shook his head. I knew he wasn't going to tell me.
And then I said, "Hell, it doesn't matter why. You don't deserve that."
"He hates me." He started crying again. I hated to see him like that,
like a dog that's been kicked around. God, I hated that. I almost wanted
to cry too.
"My dad hates me too," I said. "Maybe our dads went to the same
father school."
He smiled. I was glad he could still smile.   190
"Are you sure you don't want to go to a doctor?"
"I don't think anything's broken."
"You sure?"
He shrugged.
"You're gonna have a helluva shiner. Shit, Brian, *two* shiners."   195
He shrugged again.
"You don't deserve this, Brian." I wanted to shove that phrase into his
heart. But I knew he'd always believe that he did deserve what he got. I
somehow understood that.
"Maybe I do," he said.
I shook my head.
I helped him get to the shower. I could hear him groan as he washed 200
himself. I lent him some clothes. He was bigger than me but my T-shirts
fit him and I found a pair of my father's jeans that fit him.
He looked so sad and small sitting there, even though he wasn't small
at all. I gave him some aspirin and some ice to put on his shiner. We
drank a beer together. "Why are you doing this?" he asked me.
"Doing what?"
"Helping me."
"Because I'm not your father and I don't hate you."
"You should hate me," he said. "I was always an asshole around you." 205
"It didn't kill me."
"If you really knew me, I think you'd hate me."
"Maybe I do know you," I said.
He looked at me. "Nobody knows me."
I wanted to say *Jorge knows you*. But I didn't. I thought I should just 210
let it go.
He fell asleep on the couch.
I watched him sleep.
I knew what I thought as I watched him sleep even though I didn't
really want to tell myself what I thought. I thought he was beautiful. I
didn't let myself tell myself. But I did think he was beautiful.
He slept all afternoon, and then at night I let him sleep on my bed. I
slept on the couch and read a book. I couldn't sleep.

In the morning, I made breakfast. We didn't talk much.   215
He offered to wash the dishes. I let him. He wanted to do something
for me. Yeah, I let him wash the dishes.

He wasn't crying anymore. And he wasn't trembling. But his face, God,
it was swollen. We hung out that day. It was Sunday, my only day off and
I had no plans. And Brian had nowhere to go.

"Your mom won't worry about you?"

"I doubt it," he said. "She died when I was eight."

"I didn't know," I said.   220

"She loved me," he said.

I nodded. We hung out. I kept making him put ice on his face. But
since it was Sunday, we couldn't get any beer. We broke into my father's
liquor cabinet. I pulled out a nearly full bottle of Jack Daniels.

"Won't your father kill you for that?"

I smiled. I marked the bottle with a magic marker. "Tomorrow, I'll get
one of the guys on the construction site to buy me a bottle. And I'll
replace it. Easy."

"You smile a lot," he said.   225

"Do I?"

He was going to say something else—but he didn't. We drank Jack and
coke and smoked cigarettes. Brian kept feeling his face and wincing. He
looked sad and I tried to talk about stuff that didn't matter very much.
Songs we liked. Our favorite movies.

After a few Jack and cokes, we were feeling pretty good.

Brian looked at me and said, "I kinda envy you."

"First time I've ever heard that one," I said.   230

"You have a lot of friends, Neto."

"No, I don't. Not a lot."

"Everyone likes you."

That made me laugh. "That's because no one knows me."

He smiled. I was glad his father hadn't broken any of his teeth. "We're 235
the same," he said.

And then we both just laughed.

We talked about other stuff, but we didn't talk about girls. I think most
guys would have wound up talking about girls. But we didn't. And I knew
there was a reason for that. I didn't want to think about the reason.

We decided to go to a drive-in movie that night. But then, on the way
to the drive-in, I looked over at Brian and said, "Hey, let's go to Juárez."

He smiled.

I smiled back. "It'll be fun."   240

"You mean we'll get smashed."

"Yeah, I guess." I started laughing. I was thinking that maybe going to
Juárez for a night on the town would make us both feel alive. "I have

money in my wallet," I said. And just like that we were down the freeway headed for the border that was forty miles away. We didn't talk much as we drove. We smoked cigarette after cigarette and listened to the radio and both of us sang along and I noticed he had a nice voice, could carry a tune, and for a few moments nothing was wrong—nothing at all. When we got to the bridge, I parked the car at one of the parking lots and paid the attendant a couple of dollars. We paid two cents apiece to cross the Santa Fe Bridge and as we walked across, I felt my heart racing. I always felt that way when I went to Juárez. It was something that I wasn't allowed to do. And yet, all through high school, I'd always managed to make my way there with my friends. But tonight felt different. There was thunder in the summer sky and lightning in the distance and I knew the rain was coming and I wanted to reach over and touch Brian and say something to him. Something that mattered. But what could a guy like me say to a guy like Brian that would matter?

"Jorge and I used to come to the bars here sometimes."

"Yeah?" I said.

"Yeah. We got drunk one time and then ate some tacos from a street 245 vendor. Best tacos I ever had."

When we stepped out on Avenida Juárez, I looked at Brian and laughed. "So—lots of bars. Take your pick."

He didn't skip a beat. "The Kentucky Club," he said.

I was going to suggest a place called The Cave. A real dive. I liked it. But hell, I didn't care. "Sounds good," I said.

"It was my mother's favorite place," Brian whispered.

"Really?"   250

"Not that I really know. It's just that this one time, my father was drunk and he said, 'If your mother was still alive, I'd take her to the Kentucky Club. She loved that place. I'd walk over to the jukebox and play all the Frank Sinatra tunes they had. Your mother knew all the words.' That's the only time he ever said anything about my mother after she died."

I thought he was going to cry. "I'm sorry about your mother," I said.

"I'm tired of being sorry," he said. "I'm so fucking tired."

The Kentucky Club wasn't far. When we walked in, the place was half-full but there were two seats at the bar so we claimed them. We sat next to a couple of drunk gringos who were talking about the night Elizabeth Taylor sashayed in after getting a quickie divorce from Eddie Fisher. "She bought everybody in the joint a drink." They talked about that night as if they'd both been there. It's funny how people lie to themselves. But, hell, what was the harm? Brian gave me a nudge with his knee and we smiled and ordered *cuba libres*. I liked the taste of the rum and the coke and liked the feel of sitting at a bar with Brian.

"So this is what it's like," I said.   255

"What?" Brian said.

"To feel like a man."

Brian laughed. "I think it takes a little more than that."

"Yeah," I said. "I know. I'm just being an asshole."

"You're not," he said. "You're not an asshole."   260

I nodded. We had another drink. Then another. Then another.

Then Brian looked at me and said, "I could sit here forever."

And I thought, *Me too. So long as you were sitting right next to me.*

I don't know how many drinks we had, but somewhere along the line we decided to call it a night and found ourselves walking across the bridge and saying *American* when the border guard asked us to declare our citizenship. One of the border guys asked Brian if he'd gotten into a fight. Brian just nodded. "Yeah," he said. "No big deal." We made our way to the parking lot that was mostly empty.

When we were back on the freeway, Brian said, "Thanks, Neto."   265

"For what?" I said.

"For everything."

Everything. I wondered what everything meant. Maybe everything meant *not much* and a few drinks at the Kentucky Club.

I don't know how I managed to drive home that night. But I did. I remember I kept wanting to reach over and touch Brian—just touch him—but I didn't.

I went back to work the next day hungover as hell. Brian stayed at my 270
house. After work, I grabbed a shower and then we went out for a burger.
When we paid, Brian took out his wallet. I noticed that all he had was a ten dollar bill.

"I'll pay," I said.

"No," he said. "You've done enough."

I smiled. "All I did was offer you a place to stay for a few days. Big deal. It's not even my house."

"What do you mean, it's not your house?"

"I mean it's my father's house. I'm only a visitor. And if you want to 275
know the fucking truth, I don't feel that welcome."

He nodded. "I know the feeling."

"So what's your plan?" I said. God, his face was still all beat-up. But at least there wasn't any more swelling.

"I guess I'd better come up with something."

I nodded. "Why don't you drop me off at work. You can take the car. Drive around. Think about things."

"You have another job?"   280

"Yeah, two jobs. I'm saving to go to school."

"I guess I better get me a job too."

"Ever had a job, Brian?"

"I've worked my ass off on the farm my whole life. Guess that doesn't count. I mean, it's not as if I got paid."

"It counts," I said.   285

I wished to God he'd stop looking so sad.

He dropped me off at work. I was thinking he was going to try to see Jorge. That was just a hunch. When I got off work, Brian was there to pick me up. I don't know why exactly, but I drove toward the river. I parked and we got out and smoked and put our feet in the river and sat on the bank.

"I have to leave," Brian said.

"I guess so," I said. "Where?"

"Well, since I don't have a dime, I guess I'm gonna find some work, 290 save a few bucks — then take off to Denver."

"Denver?"

"I always wanted to go there. Maybe I just want to live where it snows."

"What are you gonna do in the snow?"

"Freeze my ass off. What else?"

That made me smile. "Sounds like a plan. But where are you gonna 295 stay? I mean, without money? You could stay with me — except there's this guy I call Dad."

He laughed. I'm glad he laughed. I felt bad. I hated throwing him out. But my dad, well, he wouldn't go for Brian staying with us.

"I'm sorry," I said. "Maybe you could stay with Jorge and his parents."

He shook his head. "I think my dad half expects me to show up there. So he can throw me off his land." He took a drag off his cigarette. "I don't want to cause Jorge's parents any trouble. They're nice people. They're good to me."

"Well, you have a few days to figure something out. My parents aren't coming home until Friday."

He nodded. He was looking at the water in the river. "I saw him," he 300 whispered.

"Who?" I said. But I knew who he was talking about.

"Jorge."

"So you guys good friends?" I hoped he couldn't hear anything in my voice.

"Yeah. Good friends. He's going with his parents back to Mexico."

"Why? I thought they were citizens by now."   305

"They are."

"So why are they going back?"

"His mother doesn't want to die here."

"She's that sick?"

He nodded.   310
"That's sad," I said.
"Yeah, real sad."
"Will he ever come back?"
"Some day, I guess."

So Brian went from sad to sadder. Shit. And I couldn't do anything 315
about it. I don't know what made him do it, but he leaned into me. I put
my arm around him. I could have stayed that way forever. I wanted to
whisper his name but I didn't. He started crying, so I let him sob into my
shoulder. There were so many things in his life for him to cry about. *So
let him cry*, I thought. *Let him fucking cry.*

I don't remember talking on the way home. Brian was still crying. I
think he'd held in his tears his whole life. I thought he felt safe around
me. Maybe that's why he could cry. I think it had been a long time since
he felt safe. When we got back to my house, I reached over and touched
his shoulder. "It will all work out," I said.

I got to thinking that night. And then it came to me. And I knew what
I had to do.

When I got back from work the next day, Brian was sitting on the front
porch reading a book. It was starting to thunder. A summer storm was
coming up and it smelled like rain.

"I love the rain," I said.
"Me too," he said.   320
I sat next to him and handed him an envelope.
"What's this?"
"Open it," I said.
For a long time he just stared at the money and the bus ticket to Den-
ver. "I can't take this," he said.
"Yes, you can."   325
"No, I can't."
"You can pay me back."
"This is five hundred dollars, Neto."
"I know how much it is," I said.
"I can't take it."   330
"You have to take it," I said. "This is how you start to live again."
"No, it isn't."
"Yes, it is. You start a new life by letting someone help you."
"You worked so fucking hard for this. Neto—"
"You think you can do this all by yourself?"   335
He handed the envelope back to me.
"I can join up," he said.

"Don't do that, Brian. That's fucked up. Don't do that. You don't want to do that." I shoved the envelope back in his hand. "Take it," I said. "Don't be an asshole."

He started to argue with me again.

"Shut up," I said. "Just listen." I lowered my voice. "Listen to the rain," 340 I whispered. "Sometimes the rain—"

"Sometimes the rain, what? What, Neto?"

"Just listen."

We stopped talking. It was pouring. It was beautiful and frightening, the power of a summer rain. I could feel the hot earth cooling down. I walked out from the protection of the front porch and held my hands up and smiled. "You see, Brian?"

He laughed. God, he could laugh. No one could take that away from him. He stepped out into the rain with me. And I swear that as we stood there, both of us with our hands stretched out—I swear I could hear the beating of his heart. And I thought, *Wouldn't it be sweet if he reached over and kissed me and we could pretend we were in some goddamned Hollywood movie.*

I called in sick that night at the 7-Eleven. I took Brian to a drug store so 345 he could pick up a razor and soap and toothpaste and all that other stuff he'd need. Then we went to a place called Surplus City. He bought a couple pairs of pants, a couple of shirts, underwear, some socks and a few things.

It was raining like it had never rained before. I wanted the storm to go on forever. As I drove back home, I kept smiling. I didn't love anything more than I loved the rain. Brian kept studying my face and I pretended not to notice. I gave him an old suitcase—and when he'd finished packing, he looked at me. He started to say something. But I stopped him. "Let's get you to the bus station."

"I didn't say goodbye to him," he said.

"You should call him," I said.

I went outside as he went to grab the phone. I didn't want to hear what he and Jorge were saying to each other.

After a while, Brian came outside. "He's going to meet us at the bus 350 station."

"Good," I said.

The bus station was quiet. The Greyhound bus for Denver was arriving from El Paso at nine thirty. The bus would be leaving for Denver at ten. We looked at the schedule and sat outside. The rain had stopped but there was thunder and lightning in the distance and the evening breeze was cool and carried the sweet smell of the desert. I thought I was going to cry.

"I don't know what to say," Brian whispered.

"Get yourself happy, Brian."

He nodded. "What about you?"   355

"Oh," I said, "I think I'll get myself happy too."

When Jorge showed up at the bus depot, I decided it was a good time
to make myself scarce. I waved at Jorge, then walked up to his car and
shook his hand. "I'm sorry about your mom," I said.

Maybe I said the wrong thing. He looked like he was going to cry.
Tears and rain. That's the way it was for us that night. For Jorge and
Brian. And me.

I knew the bus from El Paso was coming at any moment. Jorge and
Brian could have a little time to themselves before the bus left for Denver. I was awkward at goodbyes back then. I'm awkward even now, these
many years later. I think I looked at Brian and said, "Good luck." Or
something idiotic like that. But Brian followed me to my car. He looked
at me and said, "You're a good guy, Neto."

I nodded.   360

"You know, me and Jorge, we—"

I nodded. "I know."

"And you don't care?"

"Maybe I'm like you," I said.

We both looked at each other. I remember the way he looked at me. No 365
one had ever looked at me that way.

Me looking at him. Him looking at me. That's how we left it.

I went home. It was raining again.

I let my tears get lost among the falling drops of rain. Becoming a man
didn't feel anything like I thought it was going to feel.

About a year later, my mother forwarded me a letter from Brian Stillman.
I saw the postmark. He'd joined the Army. I didn't want to open it. I held
it for a long time. There was a money order in the envelope for five hundred dollars and a short note that said:

Dear Neto,

I'm in Da Nang. I wanted to write and tell you that I joined up. Maybe I
didn't before because I know how you feel about the whole military thing.
Maybe I wanted to feel like a real man. Maybe that's why I joined up, to
prove something to myself. I want you to understand, Neto, that I had to
do this. I know that you hate this war. I think you're the kind of guy who
would hate any war. I just couldn't find myself out there in the world. I
don't know how to put myself into words, Neto. I'm not like you.

I think about you sometimes. I should have kissed you. But I was so
afraid you wouldn't kiss me back. When I go home again, will you be there?
I promise to stop being afraid.

Love, Brian

So many things we don't do because we're afraid.   370
His note made me sad. Crazy man. Crazy, crazy man. What are you
doing in Vietnam?

I bought some serious art supplies with that five hundred dollars. I was
on my way to becoming an artist and nothing was going to stop me. Not
even all my self-doubt. I wrote to Brian and told him I might love him as
much as I loved the rain.

I don't know if he ever got the letter. He was killed trying to save one of
his buddies in a village somewhere between Da Nang and the Cambodian border.

My mother called and told me there was a picture of him in the newspaper. I couldn't bring myself to go to his funeral. Someone would hand
his father a flag and say, *From a grateful nation.* Finally, the sonofabitch
would be proud of his son.

For many days I woke with the bitter taste of regret in my mouth.   375

I was home for a few weeks the summer after I graduated. I was on my
way to art school at Columbia University. My father was dying so I came
back to spend the summer. It didn't feel like home anymore. It never had.

One evening, I walked to the 7-Eleven to buy a pack of cigarettes. As I
stood outside opening my pack of cigarettes, there he was. Just standing
there. Jorge. It's funny how people just appear in front of you sometimes.
I was buying cigarettes and he was driving around and stopped to buy a
coke. That's how it happens.

I wanted to hug him. I offered him a smile and a handshake instead.
We had a beer at the river. He asked me how I knew about him and
Brian. I told him the story of that night. He laughed. "Nothing is ever as
private as you think it is."

I asked him if he'd gone to the funeral.

"I had to."   380

"Did you see his father?"

"Yes."

"If I would have gone to the funeral, I would have taken my fists to him."

Jorge smiled. "I wanted to tell him that I had once loved his son."

"And did you tell him?"   385

"No. But he knew."

"Did you ever write to Brian?"

"No. We talked on the phone before he left for 'Nam. We decided to go
our own ways. It hurt too much to hang on—at least for me. We were boys
together. I don't think we knew how to be men together." He sipped on his
beer. "My mom died four months after we got back to Mexico. I moved to
California. My father came back here. He said it was home now."

I nodded.

He looked at me. "I think he fell in love with you."   390
"I doubt it," I said.
"Don't doubt it, Neto. I knew him." He touched my shoulder. "Someday you're going to stop beating up on yourself."
"Someday," I said.
I went home that night and thought of Brian Stillman. I dreamed about him. When I kissed his body, it tasted like the rain.
My father died a few days later. As I sat on his deathbed, he looked up 395 at me. "An artist?" he said. "You'll never be anything." He laughed. He was dying and he laughed. I suppose it's true what they say—that you die the way you lived.
I think it matters very much whether your father loves you or not. Jorge's father had loved him, had never stopped loving him. It showed. Brian's father hadn't loved him. That showed too.
And me? My father hadn't loved me either.
So why did I still cry at his funeral?

I didn't think I would ever return to the desert, but there was something of the landscape that lived in me and so I came back to live in New Mexico. It was good for my painting.
I hadn't thought of Brian Stillman for many years. It was almost as if 400 he'd disappeared from my memory.
My boyhood had been a painful country. I rarely visited that place.
But then one day there was that Louie Armstrong song on an old CD. And it was raining. The gun, the trigger, the finger.
The rain was magnificent in its rage.
I half-expected to turn and see Brian sitting next to me, inconsolable tears running down his face. I stopped the car on the side of the road and stepped out into the rain. I stuck my hands out like a thirsty boy trying to catch all the drops. I shouted out his name to the deaf and angry sky, *Brian Stillman! Brian Stillman! Brian Stillman!*
It was almost like a song.   405

Reading

1. Why does the narrator admire Brian Stillman? Why does he initially think it will be impossible for them to become friends?

2. What has happened to Brian when Ernesto sees him and drives him to his house?

Thinking Critically

1. How would you describe Ernesto, the narrator of the story? What factors contribute to the narrator feeling so out of place in school?

2. What effect do you think Brian Stillman had on Ernesto's life?

Connecting

1. The narrators of "Sometimes the Rain" and Dagoberto Gilb's story "Maria de Covina" (p. 316) are about the same age. Do you think Sáenz and Gilb had similar reasons for choosing these narrators? What do the two narrators have in common? What about their situations is similar?

Writing

1. "Sometimes the Rain" opens with the line, "There's always a gun around—even when you can't see it." The line refers to the power of memory to overtake someone at any time, but it also points to Sáenz's use of surprise throughout the story. Write a brief essay about the way that the author introduces the unexpected to advance the plot.

Creating

1. **Write a letter.** Near the end of "Sometimes the Rain," Neto receives a letter from Brian Stillman that refers to his regrets about the past. Write a letter to someone you haven't spoken to in months or years, describing what you remember and anything you might regret.

41

GUILLERMO GÓMEZ-PEÑA [b. 1955]

Real-Life Border Thriller

From The New World Border [1996]

GENRE: ESSAY

Guillermo Gómez-Peña, through writing—and the performance art for which he is best known—has tried to break down boundaries and borders between nations and cultures, adding an international dimension to the theatrical work of predecessors such as Luis Valdez (p. 82) and José Montoya (p. 102). Gómez-Peña was born and raised in Mexico City and studied at the Universidad Nacional Autónoma de México, the most prestigious school in the country, before moving to Los Angeles to earn bachelor's and master's degrees at the California Institute of the Arts. In 1988, while living in San Diego, he formed an art collective called the Border Art Workshop, and in 1993 he created La Pocha Nostra, a collaboration of artists that began in Los Angeles and later moved to its present location of San Francisco. In 1991, Gómez-Peña was awarded a grant from the MacArthur Foundation for his unique artistic work. As a performer he attempts to create a hybrid culture that transcends linguistic, cultural, and national divisions, writing in his 1996 book The New World Border, *"My America is a continent (not a country) that is not described by the outlines on any of the standard maps." Gómez-Peña also attempts to fight practices dependent on one group's belief in its own superiority or right to dominate. This includes not only the overt forms of racism visible in border politics (as in the piece below) but also the more subtle forms, such as the treatment of foreign cultures as exotic specimens to be studied, or, as American Indians are often said to be, "discovered." In one of his best-known pieces, a 1992 performance called* The Year of the White Bear and Two Undiscovered Amerindians Visit the West, *Gómez-Peña and Cuban American performer Coco Fusco traveled the world as two members of the imaginary Guatianaui tribe displayed in a cage, wearing faux-tribal clothing, staring blankly at a television while museum visitors gawked and took pictures. In addition to his performances, he has written several books, including* El Mexterminator *in 2005,* Exercises for Rebel Artists *in 2011, and, also in 2000, with visual artist Enrique Chagoya, the* Codex Espangliensis: From Columbus to the Border Patrol.

Though it is impossible to fully appreciate Gómez-Peña without seeing him perform, his writing still communicates a sense of his perspective and his goals as an artist. The essay presented here, which comes from The New World Border, *highlights Gómez-Peña's ability to show the racism of San Diego, which is unrecognized by the people he confronts, as being utterly bizarre and worthy of a bad action movie.*

As you read "Real-Life Border Thriller," pay attention to the assumptions that others make about Gómez-Peña. How do those assumptions lead to mistakes?

I am the proud father of a four-year-old boy, Guillermo Emiliano Gómez-Hicks, who happens to be half-Mexican, perfectly bilingual, and blond. I call him "el güero° de Aztlán." He has asked me several times, "Papa, how come you are brown and I am pink?" Last month, he finally learned what that means.

On April 8, 1993, I went to San Diego for my regular monthly visit with my son, but this time my visit turned into a cross-cultural nightmare. My son, my ex-wife, and I were having lunch at Chez Odette in Hillcrest, a fashionable neighborhood that prides itself on being an island of tolerance and diversity amidst the city's ultraconservatism. We talked about the plans for my weekend visit with Guillermito.° I vaguely remember two blond women staring at us intently from another table.

We left the café, and I hailed a Yellow Cab. My ex-wife opened the trunk of her car and handed me my son's little suitcases. Guillermo Jr. and I got into the cab and went to my friend, filmmaker Isaac Artenstein's house in Coronado, where we were going to spend the night. In the cab, we chatted in Spanish about going to Los Angeles to visit some friends.

After arriving in Coronado, we decided to go out for a walk in the park. At around 2 P.M. we were strolling back to the house when suddenly we were stopped by a Coronado policeman. The officer looked very nervous. He asked if I had been at a café on Fifth Avenue at around noon. I answered affirmatively. He asked if I had taken a Yellow Cab to Adela

el güero: The light-skinned one.   **Guillermito:** Affectionate form of the name Guillermo.

Lane in Coronado. I said yes, again. He then said into his radio: "I have the suspect."

He was talking to the San Diego police, telling them exactly where we were. I asked him for an explanation. He said he was "just cooperating with the San Diego police," and that all he knew was "that it had something to do with a kidnapping." I understood right away that I was being accused of kidnapping my own child.

For forty-five minutes, my son and I were held by the Coronado policeman, waiting for his San Diego colleagues to arrive. I was furious and completely devastated. I held Guillermito's hand tightly. I thought to myself, if the police try to take my son away from me, I'll fight back with all my strength. Guillermito kept asking me, "How come we can't go? What's happening, Papa?" And I answered, "It's just a movie, don't worry."

I was able to control my feelings, and politely asked the police officer to let me identify myself. He agreed. Very carefully, I pulled out my wallet and showed him my press card, an integral part of my "Mexican survival kit" in the United States. The cop turned purple. "Are you a journalist?" he inquired. "Yes," I answered, "and you and your colleagues had better give me a detailed explanation of what is happening, because I'm going to write about it!" He realized the mistake he'd made, and tried to compensate in a clumsy manner by showing my son the technological wonders of his patrol car. Guillermito was unimpressed and scared. He hugged my leg.

Finally, a sweaty and agitated San Diego policeman, officer Robert Roche arrived, ready for some action. Luckily, the Coronado cop took him aside and spoke to him in private, probably to warn him about the fact that he'd seen my press card. Officer Roche's attitude changed dramatically. I asked him to explain why I was suspected of kidnapping my own son. He told me the following story:

At 12:10 P.M., the police received a 911 call from a woman who claimed that a Latino man with a mustache and a ponytail and "a woman who also looked suspicious" were sitting at a café with an Anglo boy "who didn't look like he belonged to them." She said that the boy "was clearly being held against his will." She emphasized the fact that I was speaking to my son in Spanish and, despite the fact that she didn't speak or understand Spanish herself, concluded that I "was trying to bribe the child with presents" and "talking about taking him to Mexico." As we left the café, the woman and a friend of hers followed us and watched us take my son's suitcases out of his mother's car and get into the cab. They called the police again and told them that I "had forced the kid into the taxi." They provided the police with the license-plate numbers of both the taxi and my ex-wife's car.

The police proceeded to call the Yellow Cab company and obtained the   10
driver's radio number. They tried to contact him, but apparently the
radio was disconnected. The police concluded from this that I had not
only abducted my blond son, but "that [I] was probably holding the taxi
driver hostage with a weapon and that [we] were probably heading
toward the border."

According to Roche, the officer in charge of directing this B-movie was
Sergeant Mike Gibbs, from the SDPD's Western Division. They quickly
dispatched several helicopters and alerted units citywide to comb the
streets in search of an armed kidnapper. They even sent units to the
international line and alerted the border patrol.

I couldn't believe my ears. It sounded like a comedic thriller co-directed
by Fassbinder and Cheech Marin. I tried not to show any outrage, so as
to give officer Roche the confidence to continue telling me his version of
the story:

After the cab dropped my son and me at my friend's house, the police
finally succeeded in contacting the driver, who told them that while the
suspect didn't hold him up, "he did speak in Spanish to the kid." Led to
the residence by the cab driver, four policemen surrounded the house
with their guns drawn. Three of them broke into the empty house at
gunpoint—without a search warrant—and went through every room.

"In cases like this one, a search warrant is not necessary," officer Roche
explained. "We feared that a child's life was in danger." My son and I
were extremely lucky. Apparently, the police arrived at the house just a
few minutes after we had left. Knowing the San Diego Police Department's track record, had we been there, the possibility of a tragic outcome would have been very real.

I asked Roche what they found inside the house. He told me that they   15
saw photographs and "some letters in Spanish, which [they] couldn't
read." Again, the Spanish language was a major factor in the crescendo
of my process of criminalization.

Once they were sure the place was empty, they brought the cab driver
into the kitchen where my friends have a bulletin board, with family
photos. He mistook film producer Jude Eberhard for my ex-wife, San
Diego State University professor Emily Hicks.

The plot was becoming increasingly outrageous and racist. At one point,
Roche noted that the "cab driver was stupid," in spite of the fact that he
was Anglo, " 'cause, you know, Anglos tend to be much more intelligent . . ."
He paused. The end of the sentence was more than implied.

At this point I realized that I needed a witness. I asked officer Roche to
please take my son and me to my friends' home, in the hope that one of
them was already back from work. The house had been locked by the
police, and I didn't have a key. I asked Roche to please drive us to Isaac

and Jude's café, the popular Cafe Cinema at the corner of Front Street and Cedar, and to explain to them what had just happened.

On our way, I asked him if there had been any recent reports of missing children that encouraged the police to believe the women who phoned from the café. He said no. Then I asked him to explain to me how could there be a kidnapping without a report of a missing child. He replied that "many foreigners kidnap kids and take them across the border. Once you cross that border, you never know." He reminded me of "that famous case of this Egyptian or Iranian guy who kidnapped his son from his American ex-wife and took him to the Middle East." I told him I didn't see any connection to my case and suggested to him that perhaps racism had played an important role in the misunderstanding. Roche became visibly upset. He insisted that there had been no racial bias whatsoever and that I should be grateful because "it could have been a true kidnapping. I mean, think for a second, what if it had been true?" This, I call postmodern logic.

Once at Cafe Cinema, officer Roche repeated his version of the story to Jude. When my friend asked if they had a search warrant, he said once again that it wasn't necessary and that "if the door had been locked, we could have legally broken it." ²⁰

I phoned my ex-wife and told her to call the police department immediately to identify herself as the mother of the never-abducted child, and the owner of the other "suspicious" vehicle. An officer with a Spanish surname told her verbatim: "Don't worry, you have already been taken out of the computer. And by the way, you should be grateful. This incident proves how quickly the San Diego police can act."

When interrogated about the motivations of the manhunt by *Los Angeles Times* journalist Sebastian Rotella, San Diego police spokesman Bill Robinson denied any ethnic bias in the police actions, citing instead a recent case of the abduction of two kids who were found dead in the San Diego area as the primary motivation for their overreaction. What he didn't tell the *Times* was that in all recent kidnappings, the criminals have been Anglo. Despite the fact that officer Roche told me twice that several helicopters had been dispatched, the police spokesman downplayed the scale of the manhunt and told the *L.A. Times* that only one helicopter had been involved in the operation.

Rotella was also told that local television reporters had heard about the manhunt while it was taking place, and that they were demanding more details from the police to complete the story for the evening news. Perhaps if my son and I hadn't been detained quickly and allowed to clarify the dangerous misunderstanding, the evening news would have included a sensational case of the abduction of an Anglo child by an armed Mexican.

The following weeks were very stressful for my son, for my friends, and for me. My mind couldn't stop revising all the possible scenarios. If the police suspected, as Roche had told me, that I was armed, what would have happened if my son, or I, or anyone else had been in the house when they broke in? How would I have reacted if suddenly my son and I were surrounded by three agitated cops pointing their guns at us? What if, possessed by fear, we had tried to hide or run? And what would have happened if we didn't come back to the house until late at night? By then, the entire city would have been in a state of hysteria and the police reaction could have been far more extreme. What if, like thousands of Mexicans in San Diego, I didn't speak English or didn't have a press card with me?

When I finally came out of my shock, I realized that what had just happened to my son and me wasn't that strange or unusual. Every day, thousands of "suspicious-looking" Latinos in the United States are victims of police harassment, civilian vigilantism, racial paranoia, and cultural misunderstanding. "Mistaken identity" is nothing but a euphemism for racism. Latinos and other people of color are regularly "mistaken" for "illegal aliens," gang members, drug dealers, and rapists, and often these "mistakes" lead to far more extreme resolutions such as incarceration, beatings by patriotic civilians or policemen, and deportations.

Since "the incident" was publicized in the media, dozens of people of color have contacted me to tell me similar stories. A Mexican man in San Diego was publicly humiliated by a mob during the Persian Gulf crisis; they thought he was Iraqi. An African American man was chased by his girlfriend's concerned neighbors after he entered her building; "He looked like a rapist," they told her. A young Colombian man went to the San Francisco police department to obtain a record for immigration purposes; he was detained and interrogated for six hours because he looked like someone they were after. Perhaps the only difference in my case is that I had the capacity to respond, the connections to defend myself, and that handy press card.

I am deeply hurt. Experiences like this one cannot be forgotten that easily. I especially blame the two racist civilian vigilantes who decided that a Latino man holding a blond kid's hand had to be a criminal. If I had been blond and my kid dark, the assumption would have been quite different: "Look, how cute. He probably adopted the child." If I had been a Latina, perhaps the assumption would have been, "She's probably the nanny or the baby-sitter." But the deadly combination is a dark-skinned man with a blond child—the representations of evil and innocence in the American mythos.

And I blame the city of San Diego for breeding anti-Mexican sentiment and paranoia. A great majority of Anglo San Diegans live in constant fear of their enigmatic neighbors. For them, a Mexican walking down the wrong street, or a group of Mexicans speaking in Spanish at a public place are signs of imminent danger. I also blame the arrogant San Diego police for jeopardizing my son's life and the life of whoever could have been in the house when they broke in on the basis of pure speculation. A month has passed, and the police still haven't apologized for what they did.

Guillermito has learned a very sad lesson. His teacher told my ex-wife that since "the incident," he has been omitting his father's last name when signing his drawings. He is also falling asleep wherever he goes. His tender mind is unable to understand exactly what happened and why. All he knows is that to go out with Daddy can be a dangerous experience.

I strongly believe in the moral power of an apology to partially restore   30
our damaged dignity. I won't stop writing, talking, and lecturing about "the incident" until the San Diego police and the two women who originally invented this surreal plot decide to publicly apologize to us, in both English and Spanish. A bilingual public apology will also remind the thousands of civilian vigilantes, amateur Charles Bronsons, Texas Rangers wannabes, and racist cops roaming around the city that the next time they see a "suspicious-looking" Latino, he might be able to defend himself intelligently.

Reading

1. Why do the San Diego police detain Gómez-Peña?

2. Why are the women in the café suspicious of Gómez-Peña, his ex-wife, and their son?

3. What does Gómez-Peña keep in his "Mexican survival kit" (par. 7)?

Thinking Critically

1. Why do you think Gómez-Peña titled this essay "Real-Life Border Thriller"?

2. What is Gómez-Peña's attitude toward the police? Does he blame them for this incident?

3. What changes do you think need to be made to prevent incidents such as the one Gómez-Peña narrates?

Connecting

1. Gómez-Peña writes from San Diego, near a different border crossing than the one Rubén Martínez writes about in "The Line" (p. 372). How do you think the racism described by Gómez-Peña relates to the border issues that Rubén Martínez addresses? How does one affect the other?

Writing

1. "Guillermito has learned a very sad lesson" (par. 29), writes Gómez-Peña in his conclusion to "Real-Life Border Thriller." Write an essay in which you explore what lessons Gómez-Peña's son might have learned from the experience, using specific examples from the text.

Creating

1. **Perform a scene.** Gómez-Peña is primarily a performance artist. Try to stage a scene from "Real-Life Border Thriller" in a way that makes your audience part of the performance. You may work in groups and even use costumes if you'd like. How does performing the scene affect your experience (emotional, intellectual, etc.) of the story?

42

RUBÉN MARTÍNEZ [b. 1962]

The Line

From Crossing Over: A Mexican Family on the Migrant Trail [2001]

GENRE: JOURNALISM/ESSAY

Rubén Martínez has brought a unique history and set of skills to his journalism, enabling him to succeed as a writer, television personality, and commentator on a wide range of issues including immigration, music, and politics. Of Mexican and Salvadoran heritage, Martínez grew up in Los Angeles. After leaving the University of California, Los Angeles, in his first year, he spent several years freelancing while traveling through the American Southwest, Mexico, and El Salvador. Once back in California, he worked with the Border Art Workshop and became a staff writer for LA Weekly. *Soon he began gaining recognition as a journalist and creative writer. In 1992 his first book, a collection of poetry and essays called* The Other Side: Notes from the New L.A., Mexico City, and Beyond, *was published, and in 1995 he earned an Emmy for his work as host of KCET-TV's* Life & Times. *His 2001 book* Crossing Over: A Mexican Family on the Migrant Trail *followed a family from Mexico into the United States while offering a broad view of Mexican culture in the United States. Martínez's struggle with personal issues and his recovery in New Mexico during the following decade provided the backdrop for his 2012 book* Desert America: Boom and Bust in the New Old West. *As a journalist, Martínez has appeared on many television shows, and his print work has appeared in a wide range of publications that includes the* Nation, Spin, *and the* New York Times. *He has also collaborated with photographers on several books, produced the PBS documentary* When Worlds Collide, *and performed as a spoken word artist and musician. He now teaches creative writing at the University of Houston.*

In "The Line," a chapter from the book Crossing Over: A Mexican Family on the Migrant Trail, *Martínez examines the effects of increased American efforts to "hold the line" at the border, upping the police presence as well as the tension already existing in the border region. An underground tunnel links Nogales, Arizona, with Nogales, Sonora, its sister city across the border, and Martínez investigates and reports on the subculture that has developed around it: gangs of children who continually linger around the tunnel, social workers helping the kids, border patrol agents trying to keep the tunnel closed, even businesses catering to people who cross.*

As you read "The Line," think about what makes life in a border region unique. Also, ask yourself: How is border life affected by efforts to turn the border into a barrier?

Years ago, I wrote several dispatches from the border at Tijuana, easily the most famous crossing point along the two-thousand-mile-long line. On many occasions, I hung out at the *cancha*, a soccer field that runs along the border just a mile from downtown. All there was back then was a scraggly fence, perforated in too many places to count. On a bluff a hundred yards north, Border Patrol jeeps were perched day and night.

Through the dusty heat of day, the *cancha* was empty. But as soon as the sun set, it turned into a veritable migrant fiesta. A great crowd gathered at the fence and began organizing the evening's expeditions. The migrants came from all over Mexico and Central America and from as far away as China, Iran, Pakistan. Packs of lone men, unshaven, dusty-haired, carrying only the clothes on their backs or small, cheap vinyl bags filled with just a handful of belongings. And families, entire families, from grandmothers with crinkled faces and braided white hair to wide-eyed tots in arms.

The crowd gave rise to a mini-economy of vendors exploiting the migrants' last-minute shopping needs. Hawkers pushed everything from booze and running shoes to girlie magazines and sheets of plastic for that unforeseen thunderstorm. Matronly women stood over coal-fired stoves stirring great steaming pots of *pozole*, hominy stew, or sizzling *carne asada*, grilled beef. Prostitutes offered farewell trysts.

Music blared from boom boxes connected through a few dozen extension cords to a socket in someone's living room a couple of hundred yards away or hooked up directly to the fraying, sparking wires hanging above our heads. And there were the soccer matches, intense battles between rival regions throughout the republic: Zacatecas versus San Luis Potosí, Michoacán versus Saltillo, Durango versus Tamaulipas.

Gooooaaaallll!   5

It was a fiesta back then, like a Fourth of July barbecue; everyone was celebrating in anticipation of crossing. Back then, chances were better than fifty-fifty that you would get across on your first attempt. And even if you were nabbed by the *migra*,° you'd surely make it on your second try, probably that same night.

Later, after people had eaten, scored a few goals or a blow job in the nearby bushes, the coyotes would gather crews of twenty-five or more migrants, sometimes many more. The coyotes would huddle among themselves, drawing straws to see which route each team would take. There are hundreds of ancient footpaths in the hills above Tijuana, deep ruts carved over the decades by a million migrant footsteps.

All at once, the crews would move out, hundreds of men, women, and children streaming across the chaparral-dotted hills. The Border Patrol would spring into action, but the gringos would quickly be overwhelmed by the massive tide.

Gooooaaaallll!

Sure, it was dangerous sometimes, especially along the line in Texas,   10
where migrants had to ford the trickster currents of the muddy Bravo.° But back then migrants were more likely to get robbed or beaten by border bandits than to die of exposure in the middle of the desert.

The border wasn't a border. The line was broken. It was an idea, not a thing.

And then the idea became a reality. In the early nineties, California was in a deep recession. A lot of union jobs had been lost. The Firestone and Goodyear tire plants shut down, as did the last of the old iron and steel

---

migra: Border Patrol.   **Bravo:** Reference to the Río Bravo, as the Río Grande is called in Mexico.

works, and aerospace companies laid off tens of thousands of workers. People were angry, and then-governor Pete Wilson looked back in time for inspiration. To the Great Depression and the "repatriation" of hundreds of thousands of Mexican workers. To the postwar recession and Operation Wetback, which deported hundreds of thousands more. And then *la crisis* sent a fresh flood of refugees north. Suddenly Wilson, a Republican who'd always sold himself as friendly to Mexico and Mexicans, a man who in fact once had an undocumented woman clean his house, pointed his finger southward.

"They keep coming!" he declared.

He hated the migrants now. Narco-satanic hordes were at the gates. He swore that he would draw a line in the sand that no wetback would ever cross.

American politicos have paid lip service to "holding the line" at the southern border for the better part of the twentieth century, beginning in the days of the massive migration spawned by the Mexican Revolution of 1910–17. But in 1994, the rhetoric took the form of concrete, steel, arc lamps, infrared cameras and goggles, seismic and laser sensors, and even U.S. soldiers with M-16s offering "tactical support" to a greatly expanded Border Patrol. Operation Gatekeeper sought to block the decades-old illegal crossing at San Diego–Tijuana with a twelve-foot-high steel wall that runs inland twelve miles from the coast. At night, it is lit a harsh amber. The glow that falls from the gigantic light towers straddles the line for several hundred yards in each direction, meaning that the gringo light actually falls on Mexican territory—illegal light, as it were, but the Mexican government has never complained about it or about the constant noise pollution from the helicopters on patrol.

The migrants have complained, though. They called the governor "Pito" Wilson, *pito* for "whistle," but also, in Mexico, for "penis." During the 1994 World Cup, Wilson was on hand to inaugurate a match at the Rose Bowl in Los Angeles. Among the 100,000 people in the stands, there were at least 60,000 Mexicans, Salvadorans, Guatemalans, Nicaraguans, Hondurans, Colombians, Chileans, Uruguayans, Brazilians—migrants each and every one. Wilson stepped up to the microphone. But no one heard a single word he said over the boos, whistles, and chorus of "Pito! Pito!" in great rhythmic waves.

Gooooaaaallll!

Pete Wilson has gone, but one thing remains of his nativist legacy.

After years of being lobbied to help the Golden State beat back the illegals, the federal government obliged with a new fence at Tijuana. To cross into California today, you have to go east of the fence. You have to hike in total darkness, through mountains that block out the beacon of city light from San Diego. You take a long walk in the dark.

East of Nogales, Arizona, my Blazer clatters down the rutted dirt of   20
Duquense Road. At this point, the line consists of little more than a few
strands of barbed wire about four feet high. Somewhere close by, Rosa
Chávez crossed over with Mr. Charlie.

The sky is a deep Arizona blue, dotted with brilliant white cumuli. In
California, the pale light tends to minimize contrasts; here, shadows
stand out in stark relief. I am in the Coronado National Monument,
named for Francisco Vásquez de Coronado, a sixteenth-century Spanish
explorer who searched in vain for the fabled streets paved with gold, the
Seven Cities of Cibola. His expedition of 339 soldiers, 4 Franciscan
priests, 1,100 Indians, and 1,500 head of livestock set out from Compos-
tela, 750 miles to the south. Indians all along the route confirmed Cibola's existence. It's farther north, the expedition was told again and again.
There is some conjecture that the Indians were lying, hoping to push the
white men and their horses into a no-man's-land from which they would
never return.

Vásquez died without finding Cibola, but he did explore this brutal
land of intolerable heat and deadly cold, tracing a crucial overland trade
route to the northern territories of the Spanish Crown.

Today, Mexican migrants follow in the footsteps of a conquering Spanish explorer, seeking their own version of the Seven Cities. This is breathtaking and treacherous country, a landscape of eerie, lunarlike beauty,
the perfect backdrop for a new Western noir. Here border bandits lie in
wait for the vulnerable migrants, and of course there are the Border
Patrol, corrupt Mexican police, narcotics smugglers, and DEA agents.

The most recent additions to the tableau are the vigilantes. Dozens
of ranchers in the area whose lands are regularly trespassed by border
crossers have taken up arms—literally. Like the *migra*, whom they
consider inefficient at best, they have availed themselves of such technology as night-vision goggles, but they have also laid in heavier
weaponry—some even have assault rifles. The president of the Concerned Citizens of Cochise County has even built a twenty-foot-high
lookout station to better patrol his property.

Everywhere I look, there is evidence of migrant journeys. In the brush   25
I come across dozens of discarded bottles of Mexican purified water.
Shreds of newspaper lined with shit. A tattered Mexican comic book. A
crumpled tube of Mexican Colgate. Along the barbed-wire fence, tiny
flags of torn clothing flutter in the breeze. The Coronado National Monument has become a shrine to the migrant. The park rangers might as well
as put up exhibit placards.

There are no tourists here. As far as I can tell, I am the only moving
thing, the Blazer kicking up a cloud of yellow dust along a road that goes
ever higher into the Huachuca Mountains. I look down on the border:

a million scrub brushes dot the valley for dozens and dozens of miles southward. The fence is down there somewhere, but it's too small to see from five thousand feet.

I come around a bend and hit the brakes: there is a van stopped by the side of the road, a seventies Dodge Sportsman. I stare at the vehicle as if it were roadkill that might come back to life. There is only the sound of my car's motor idling; the Blazer's cloud of dust now flows forward over me.

The van sits off-kilter, its left rear wheel missing, the brake disc half buried in sand. I spot the tire about ten yards ahead. There is a deep rut through the dirt for over fifty yards up to where the van sits; either it took the driver that long to stop or he actually tried to keep moving forward. Probably the latter—all the van's windows have been blasted in with football-sized rocks.

I turn paranoid, wondering if the perpetrators of this violence are still close by. The incident appears to have occurred just a few hours or even a few minutes ago—no dust has settled on the van yet.

Inside the van a thousand glass shards are sprinkled amid the rocks that   30 crashed through the windows. A pair of navy blue men's bikini briefs. An embroidered Indian sash. A flyer announcing a gig by Banda la Judicial, a third-string outfit pictured in red suits with white tassels, snakeskin boots, and white Stetsons. Santa María water bottle, empty. Unopened package of Alka-Seltzer. A cheap vinyl backpack, the classic migrant's luggage, the logo a poorly stenciled map of the world. A Purépecha rebozo,° spread on the floor with a canteloupe-sized rock sitting on it.

Arizona license plates. The gas cap is missing; the driver stuck in a red rag. On the exterior right-side panel, there is a splatter that has dried a dark brown. It looks like blood.

The interior side panels have been ripped open, as has much of the floor carpet. The bandits were looking for something, probably drugs. It is impossible to tell if they found anything.

I crest the ridge at the top of the Coronado Pass, leaving the crime scene behind. To the south, the massive, craggy San Jose peak; to the east the savannalike beauty of the San Juan River Valley, promising a temperate respite from the Arizona badlands. Somewhere between the mountains and the flats stands the border, invisible and implacable.

INS agent Laura Privette is a small, sinewy woman with coarse Indian hair cut stylishly short. She is dark—*prieta*, as they say in Spanish—the descendant of immigrants. She is an Indian who's assumed the role of cowboy; tonight, she is field supervisor for Border Patrol operations in

Purépecha rebozo: The Purépecha are an indigenous people from the Mexican state of Michoacán. A *rebozo* is a shawl.

the Nogales sector. She has left her silver BMW Z3 convertible behind at the station parking lot and boarded a Ford Explorer BP cruiser to show me how the United States holds the line.

The radio crackles. The dispatcher talks in code: "Five-seventy activ- 35 ity." Marijuana. Every couple of minutes we are apprised of "hits" from the motion detectors buried in the desert along the line.

I like Privette. No woman rises through the ranks of a paramilitary agency—the most macho of environments—without proving her mettle. She grew up Mexican in southern Arizona, where there are lots of Mexicans but precious little space for them in the middle class. As a child, she saw the BP at work on the nightly news, as well as on the streets. The job struck her as heroic; just like a kid in the suburbs who dreams of being a fireman or astronaut, she dreamed of working the line, applying the righteous force of the law against unscrupulous smugglers of human and narcotic cargo. Like many other BP agents, especially Hispanics, Privette professes empathy for the migrants. She believes that there are legal ways to get into this country and illegal ones, safe passage and dangerous crossings. It is pointless to argue with her.

"Things are going pretty good right now," Privette says. With a budget that has tripled in the last five years, the INS's interdiction force has seen its ranks swell by thousands. Its logistical equipment is state of the art.

Privette guides the climate-controlled Explorer, still reeking new-car smell, toward the line—represented in Nogales by a replica of the twelve-foot-high steel wall that blocked migrants from crossing in Tijuana. After claiming success with Operation Gatekeeper in California, the INS proceeded with Operation Safeguard along the Arizona border in 1995, doubling the number of Border Patrol agents, upgrading surveillance technology, and building the wall.

It is late afternoon on a searing late-spring day. There's not much to see yet; the real action starts after dusk. We ride down the avenue that leads to the port of entry, pulling over next to a concrete-lined channel. A Church's Chicken stands nearby, along with a McDonald's, a Jack in the Box, and a taco truck advertising itself as "Parikutín," a Michoacán family enterprise named after Mexico's youngest volcano and a source of endless pride for the Michoacanos.

Back in the days before the massive BP buildup, when a handful of 40 agents battled the mighty stream of migrants who easily cut the chain-link fence, Church's was a kind of migrant drive-through. While the BP was kept busy at the fence, smugglers would bring migrants through the drainage tunnels that traverse the line, hop up to street level, grab a snack, and phone contacts to pick up the cargo. Today, only a trickle comes via the tunnels. It is, however, a popular route for migrants returning to Mexico, a way for them to avoid corrupt Mexican customs officials.

The walls of the tunnel feature generations of graffiti, most of it put there by Barrio Libre,° a gang of homeless illegal kids who call the border tunnels home. As Privette sweeps a hand over the scene in explanation, we catch sight of a group of eighteen men double-timing through the wash, headed south. When they notice us, most of them pull up their shirts to cover their faces, but there's no need to worry. The BP rarely bothers to apprehend migrants heading back to Mexico.

Despite laws and technology and the dangers of the road, the border can still be breached dozens of ways. Enterprising smugglers have concocted a scheme that allows an illegal to cross right under the nose of the *migra*. At the San Diego–Tijuana port of entry, a considerable number of crossings take the form of foot traffic through a simple turnstyle past a lone customs agent, who often doesn't press for identification from "American-looking" types. "Nationality?" the guard asks. If you say, "American," in good ole Americanese, you're in like a flint.

For up to $2,000, the smuggler serves more like an acting coach than a coyote. First off, the wardrobe. He gets rid of the invariable polyster threads of your provincial home in favor of 100 percent American cotton. Then he works on your accent and your story, which includes the city, neighborhood, streets, high school, sports teams, and so on of your supposed hometown in the States. If the customs official suspects something, you're merely herded back across the line to try again. And again. The odds, in the long run, are in your favor.

There are still other ways. It is increasingly difficult and expensive to forge the so-called green card (which actually hasn't been green in ages) that denotes legal residency in the United States. Currently, the holographic, "forgery-proof" model looks more like a credit card than a proof of residency. Therefore, there is a brisk business in buying and selling other bona fide documents, including passports, birth certificates, and Social Security cards, which can be conveniently "lost," giving smugglers a window of opportunity of weeks or months to use them until the owner reports them missing.

One day there might indeed be a truly forgery-proof method of admitting people into the country, perhaps the sci-fi scenario of a scanner that identifies on the basis of the uniqueness of the human iris. Such proposals are being seriously considered these days. But for the moment, there is a smuggler's response to every measure the INS introduces. 45

Barrio Libre: Free Barrio.

The Explorer winds into the hills east of Nogales. The border evolves—
the towering steel wall becomes a chain-link fence and, a short while
later, hip-high barbed wire, the strands cut in many places. We get out of
the truck and Agent Privette squats down on one knee, examining hoof
marks and the tire tracks that crisscross the line. This examination is
called "sign cutting."

"Horses, drugs," Privette says in law enforcement minimalese. "Car.
Probably a big old Buick or Impala. Illegals, ten, maybe fifteen."

Sunset. The long, thin fingers of ocotillo bushes stretch into the orange-
gold, reaching for the wisps of feathery, gilded cirrus in the darkening
sky. Down below, we can see the wall cutting straight across the two
Nogaleses. Streets on one side of the line continue on the other. It looks
like one huge barrio, artificially divided.

Nothing much is happening in the hills, so we head back toward town.

Suddenly, the radio comes to life. "Hits in sector 1–5." We speed 50
through the barrios on the outskirts of Nogales, past humble homes with
front doors ajar in the balmy evening, elders swaying in rockers and kids
dashing about the street. No one bats an eye at our Border Patrol truck.
In this landscape, the Explorers are as omnipresent as the ocotillos.

We pull up next to a drainage tunnel scant yards from the border,
where there is another BP truck, commanded by another Indian agent.
His bronze face shines with sweat under the amber streetlight. "I lost
sight of 'em. I think they came through here. About twenty of 'em."

Privette commands her subaltern: "I'll go above ground, you go under."
The green-suited agent, walkie-talkie tacked to his shoulder, runs off, his
black flashlight bouncing madly in the dark.

I run after him. I've purchased a flashlight myself—a rubber-coated,
impact-resistant field model—for just such an occasion. But, of course,
I've forgotten it back in the Explorer. The BP agent is about fifty yards
ahead of me in the tunnel, running east. I can see only the distant, wavering beacon of his flashlight. Around me, it is pitch-black. My footsteps
echo strangely, expanding concentric circles of sound with a metallic
ring. I kick at unseen garbage at my feet. Now puddles of dank water.
Deep puddles.

The flashlight up ahead slows its frantic dance. In a few seconds, I am
at the agent's side, at an opening in the tunnel. Above us, there is traffic,
American traffic. "Lost 'em," he says into his walkie-talkie. "Stay where
you are," Privette's voice crackles in response. We hear running steps
approaching above us. Privette looks down at us from street level. For
several moments there is only the sound of panting all around.

The two agents try more sign cutting. 55

"It doesn't look like they came this way," says the male agent. "They
might have jumped up to the road. Maybe they backtracked."

Privette: "No, they definitely came this way. I've got tennis shoes going through here. Adidas."

The migrants have disappeared into the night. The BP's billion-dollar high-tech arsenal has failed, at least on this occasion.

The border is not in a war zone, to be sure. But the battle at the line has all the trappings of a low-intensity conflict between two sides, one armed with state-of-the-art surveillance equipment and the other with the kind of ingenuity inspired only by poverty and desire.

It is a tribute to the political furor over drugs and immigration that   60 between them the two Nogaleses host one of the most impressive arrays of public safety infrastructure in the Northern Hemisphere. Consider the battery of forces amassed here, for towns whose combined population is under 200,000: the U.S. Border Patrol and Customs Police, the Arizona National Guard (which assists the Border Patrol in "intelligence gathering"), the Santa Cruz County sheriff's department and the local Nogales Police Department, mirrored on the Mexican side by the Sonora State Police (*judiciales*), the Mexican Federal Police (*federales*, akin to the American FBI), the Grupo Beta (a special force under federal control that deals with border crime), the local police, and, finally, the quixotically named Talón de Aquiles (Achilles' Heel), whose basic charge is to keep the streets of Nogales clear of unseemly characters for the important tourist industry (which includes such border mainstays as greyhound races, bookie joints, countless curios shops, and plenty of bars that won't card American teens).

Sometimes the Border Patrol can almost convince you it's winning the war. Late in the evening, Privette takes me downtown, where, she has been apprised, a large crew of illegals has been detained. When we pull up, they are seated on the benches under the shade trees of the plaza. A brazen smuggler brought them straight across the wall, maybe with a ladder, apparently convinced they would make it precisely because the BP wouldn't expect a crossing right under its nose.

Several agents, with their broken Spanish, interview the illegals, jotting information into their notebooks.

Nombre? Edad? Domicilio? Firme aquí, por favor.°

"I don't know how to write," says an elder in a cowboy hat.

"Then just put an X."   65

Eighteen men, two women. No kids. From Michoacán, from Guanajuato, from Sinaloa, from Zacatecas and Puebla. There are looks of fear, of quiet resignation, of lackadaisical boredom. A teenager with a baby mustache winks at me. *We'll be back.*

Nombre? Edad? . . . : Name? Age? Address? Sign here, please.

Privette, perhaps aware that she hasn't shown her department at its best tonight, takes me to the station, where narcotics are being registered after a bust. The agent on duty is a young, chipper African American woman named Eealey. In the evidence room, she empties two burlap sacks, each containing several plastic-wrapped bundles of marijuana. They come to 41.25 pounds on the scale, but she wasn't able to arrest the "mules," the drug runners.

Quite a scene out there, Eealey says. She and another agent arrived after receiving word from a video surveillance officer of a probable narcotics crossing. They caught sight of two kids who, with nowhere else to run, hightailed it back toward the line, hastily dumping their loads on American soil. (There'll be hell to pay on the other side.) Eealey got to one of them just as he was diving down to crawl underneath the fence. She grabbed him by the leg, and the kid actually dragged her halfway into Mexico before she realized this was an international incident in the making and let go.

In Nogales, Sonora, that night, I hang out at a dive called Palas—that's Mexican Spanish for Palace. On the stage, women from every corner of Mexico writhe, women who came to the border thinking of the States but somehow got stuck in limbo. A lot of people got stuck at the line, deferring their American dreams, because there's all kinds of underground business for provincial kids to get caught up in. Many people realized you could make more money playing the black market on the Mexican side than picking fruit on the American side. But then came the wall.

"Isis," from Puerto Vallarta, golden-skinned and Asian-eyed—Egyptian-   70
looking, come to think of it—tells me that business was good until that damn *muro*° went up a few months back. Coyotes and narcos used to party here at Palas all night, though they were often scary types with big mustaches, big paunches, big guns, and, often as not, big badges, in the true Mexican corrupt fashion.

"But it's dead now with the wall," says Isis. "Don't the Americans realize that it's bad for business?"

At night, as one looks down from the American side into Mexico, the wall is merely an amber-lit smudge in a swath of small-town light stretching across the valley to the south. Because Nogales, Arizona, is not exactly a model of American affluence and Nogales, Sonora—buoyed in recent years by the *maquiladora*° industry of giants like Sony and General Electric—is not the poorest of the Mexican border towns, the Mexican side doesn't necessarily seem Third Worldish.

muro: Wall. **maquiladora:** Factory producing low-cost goods for export.

The two Nogaleses are one, at least geographically, but also in terms of key urban infrastructure—such as the drainage canals and tunnels that traverse the cities north and south. Without this shared drainage system, the sudden summer thunderstorms that toss down a couple of inches of rain within an hour would flood both sides. If there are two cities at this border crossing, they are the Nogales aboveground and the Nogales below.

The city beneath the city is thriving, too. The drainage tunnels are home to all the characters you'd expect at a crossing as contested as this: alien smugglers and narcotics traffickers, down-and-out dope fiends and various other outlaw types. Down below, all these, along with the coyotes and illegals, face off against law enforcement from both sides of the line.

The other player in this border drama is Barrio Libre, whose members   75
range in age from five to their late teens. Barrio Libre is family to a pregnant sixteen-year-old girl, a nine-year-old boy who's been on the streets since he was four, and a few dozen others who pass the time scrounging up meals and occasionally assaulting vulnerable illegals as they cross through the tunnel. For the tunnel kids, as they're called, the battle for the border is simply one of survival.

Some are runaways escaping abusive family situations. Others were separated from their parents in the chaos of a Border Patrol bust. Still others are just plain dirt-poor, restless, and rebellious. Unable to make it aboveground—not with the *migra* and the Mexican police after them—they've descended below, just a few feet under the steps of gringo tourists, Mexican border executives, and squeaky-clean kids their age in blue and white school uniforms.

The only other place these kids call home is a drop-in center on the Mexican side called Mi Nueva Casa,° and it is here that I first meet a few members of Barrio Libre. Mi Nueva Casa, funded largely by liberal American foundations, is a humble stucco house just a hundred yards from the border wall.

A typical day begins at about nine in the morning. But Ramona Encinas, the benevolent matriarch of the center, starts brewing coffee and boiling pots of beans and rice much earlier. The kids straggle in one by one or in twos and threes, their faces pale and puffy—a telltale sign they've slept in the tunnel. They are received with a gushy "*¡Buenos días!*°" from Ramona, a counselor named Loida Molina and her twenty-something son Isaac (who's known, in the center's lingo, as the "older-brother type"), and Cecilia Guzmán, a schoolteacher. There are hugs and kisses for the girls, street handshakes for the boys, although a couple of them are in a foul mood and plop themselves down on one of the well-worn couches in the living room without uttering a word to anyone.

Mi Nueva Casa: My New House.   **¡Buenos días!:** Good morning!

Mi Nueva Casa lives up to its billing as a *casa*: besides the living room with its TV and couches, there is a dining room with fold-up tables and about a dozen chairs, which doubles as the computer room (three terminals featuring race car and ancient Pac-Man–type games); a bathroom where the kids can shower if they want (or are forced to by staffers); the small kitchen where Ramona holds court; an outdoor patio in back where washing machines are constantly sloshing the kids' clothes clean. The remaining space is taken up by a Foosball center, a dressing room (hung with dozens of donated shirts, pants, sweaters, and jackets), and a classroom.

After a light breakfast of juice or milk with cookies, some of the kids 80 join Cecilia for the day's school session. Through a screen door in the classroom, one can look straight across the street at the grounds of a local public elementary school, hear the shrieks of "regular" kids.

On this particular morning, several kids arrive late, after ten. They were detained by the *migra* on the American side of the tunnel—the place they currently call home. In comes Pablo, a thirteen-year-old wearing a T-shirt featuring Chupacabras (the blood-sucking bogeyman of northern rural Mexico), and his friend Jesús, about ten years old, in an oversize Raiders shirt. They both sport cholo buzz cuts with thin braided ponytails trailing down the backs of their necks. Their shoes are caked with mud. Within seconds of their entrance, the room begins to smell like unbathed kid.

"The *chiles verdes*° got us," says Jesús, using the kids' nickname for the *migra* officers, who wear green uniforms. He tells how Border Patrol agents confiscated the only belongings he had to his name: his flashlight and his aftershave—he doesn't have facial hair yet, but it comes in handy to cover up body odor. Now Toño, at nine the youngest in the group, walks in and promptly pulls up his shirt to show off pinkish scar tissue on his side and abdomen, the result, he says, of bites from a *migra* patrol dog.

Officials on both sides of the border agree that incidents of crime perpetrated by the tunnel kids have diminished since Mi Nueva Casa opened. What they don't say is that the law enforcement agencies on both sides have hit the kids hard—with lessons not soon to be forgotten. They are regularly run down, as this morning, by armed Border Patrol agents in four-wheel-drive vehicles. They are chased by Grupo Beta police whose shouts and threats echo terrifyingly along the concrete walls of the tunnel; several kids say they receive regular beatings from the Beta. There is also an unconfirmed report of a youngster sodomized by a Mexican agent.

But at Mi Nueva Casa the horrors of the tunnel are a world away, even though one popular entrance to the underground is barely a block and a

chiles verdes: Green chiles.

half down the street. There are also incentives to behave well. If the kids don't swear, smoke, do drugs, or carry beepers while they're here—and if they attend Cecilia's classes regularly—they can earn "benefits," all written on a sign hanging in the dining room above the computers: "love and tenderness," "food," "clothes," "respect," "bath," "computer games," "television," "videos," "guitars," and "much, much more!"

Cecilia has her hands full, even though there are only six kids in school   85 today. She dissipates a bit of her own nervous energy by chewing gum as she tries to get Jesús to concentrate on math tables. The kids are distracted by me, of course, but also plainly nervous after the morning's encounter with the *migra*. They flip pencils over and over on the desk, bounce their knees up and down.

In walks Gilberto, the coolest of the bunch, dressed all in black, his hair perfectly combed. A ceramic medallion of a classical European baby Jesus floating amid cherubs hangs on his chest. Heavy with attitude, he scoffs when Cecilia asks him if he wants milk and cookies. Says he wants coffee.

Responding to a question about drugs in the tunnel he says, "You can get crack whenever you want." And pot and pills, and if there's nothing else, well, there's always the poor kid's high—paint thinner inhaled straight from the can or spray paint sniffed from a soaked bandanna.

"If you're from Barrio Libre, you can get anything, anywhere," says Gilberto. Barrio Libre, the Free Barrio. With cliques in Phoenix, Chicago, Las Vegas, L.A., and Nogales, Gilberto claims.

Jesús talks of the war between the coyotes and the Barrio Libre kids. "They think we're bad for their business," he says. And they are. When the kids assault the migrants, word gets back quickly to the other side, causing prospective border crossers to eschew the tunnels for coyote crews that breach the line elsewhere. Jesús recounts a recent incident in which a coyote shot at him with what he says was a 9-millimeter pistol.

Gilberto justifies the assaults: he's following the adults' example. "We're   90 just asking for our *mordida* [bribe], a little something to buy a soda with," he says. But there is plenty of evidence that when some Barrio Libre kids don't get what they want from the *chúntaros* ("hayseeds," a nickname for the illegals), they are capable of viciously beating their victims.

It's nearly noon. Cecilia has done her best for the morning. As lunchtime approaches, the kids begin to drift in and out of the classroom. Some head off for a Foosball game, others to wash their clothes. Gilberto is at the chalkboard, tagging it up with BARRIO LIBRE. Jesús scratches his arms, which are covered with tiny red lumps, a rash he picked up down in the tunnel. Now Gilberto is twirling about the room, blowing up a paper bag he picked up in the trash and pantomiming the inhaling of fumes.

But one student is still intent on doing classwork, practicing his handwriting in his notebook. Cecilia tells me that up until a couple of months ago, José, one of the quieter of the group, was practically illiterate, but today his handwriting is precise. Carefully he draws the curving *o*s and *a*s in Spanish, copying down an exercise in alliteration and assonance:

Dolor, dulce dolor. Pain, sweet pain.

Mi mamá me ama. My mother loves me.

He repeats the lines over and over again, filling the entire page.   95

Homeless youth would seem to be almost an oxymoron in Mexico, where virtually every mother or grandmother is considered a saint and the family unit is by turns loving, claustrophobic, and dictatorial—all-powerful. Unmarried children typically stay at home well past their teens; many stay at home even after they marry. But something's happening to the Mexican family, and it is not just the economic crisis that's chipping away at the institution; migration has a lot to do with it as well. Hundreds of thousands of households, perhaps millions (no one knows how many) are now single-parent or parentless—Mami and Papi are working in the fields of the San Joaquin Valley or cleaning hotel rooms in Dallas; the kids remain in Mexico until there's enough money to bring them across.

Sometimes the kids themselves leave to try their luck in the north as well. Occasionally they run away; often they're encouraged by their parents. (Wense Cortéz made his first trip to the States at age thirteen; his parents did nothing to stop him.) The family separations are always thought of as temporary, but increasingly (and in proportion to the greater difficulty of crossing back and forth at will) they last for years.

Or forever. Papi, gone for two years, suddenly has a new girlfriend in Illinois or even a new family in Illinois. Or maybe Mami isn't coming back because she's sick of her small town's suffocating morality. In all the hustle and bustle and backbreaking effort to provide for the family—and amid the cultural changes that accompany the migrants' journeys—the kids are getting lost. Mexican family values, ironically, are being undone by the very effort to support family in Mexico by working in the United States.

Mi Nueva Casa does not offer a complete, twenty-four-hour shelter. It can't—funding for the program is chronically anemic. While up to twenty-two young people might hang out here during the day, the doors close at five in the afternoon Monday through Saturday and the staffers go home to their families. The kids, meanwhile, go back to their own "family" in the tunnels.

Despite the clear binational nature of homeless children accumulating 100 on the border, binational policies, free-trade agreement or no, have not made fund-raising or even donating materials easy. Mi Nueva Casa was recently awarded a major grant from the Kellogg Foundation, but the money came with the stipulation that it could be spent only for research and staff training on the American side of the border. On more than one occasion, staffers have had to sneak donated clothes into Mexico from the United States in the trunk of a car because if the items were declared before Mexican customs the red tape would be endless. (A Ping-Pong table given to Mi Nueva Casa by an American benefactor remained in a Mexican customs warehouse for over a year.)

"There've always been problems at the border," says a member of Mi Nueva Casa's board. "But the thing is, the number of people coming up, including the kids, keeps on increasing. The Mexican authorities have been overwhelmed."

But according to American law enforcement agencies, the problem has been taken care of, all because of Mi Nueva Casa. The Santa Cruz Juvenile Detention Center says there has been a dramatic decrease in youthful-offender apprehensions on the border. So does the Border Patrol. "As recently as 1994, we had our hands full," says a BP spokesperson. "But Mi Nueva Casa's made a hell of a difference. Plus, we have the tunnels effectively monitored now."

Which is not to say that the tunnels have been closed or that there aren't kids living in them. There is no way to close the tunnels. They are for drainage, after all. "Effectively monitoring" means that the Border Patrol dispatches a team down into the tunnel two or three times a week to weld shut the steel gate that serves as the barrier between the American and Mexican sides. According to Border Patrol officials, the weld can stand four hundred pounds of pressure per square inch, which means that a dozen or so kids can break it easily. And, in fact, the gate is busted open two or three times a week by the kids, or anyone else who wants to get across.

Romel is one of Barrio Libre's *veteranos*. At seventeen, he's already an old man. He's beaten others and been beaten, robbed and been robbed, known the life of the tunnel for almost four years. Now he is caught between that life and a growing desire to find a straight job. For the moment, he's leaning toward the job.

Romel sits in the living room of Mi Nueva Casa, watching the original 105 Batman and Robin dubbed in Spanish. His father was a drug dealer who was nabbed by the FBI; he lived with his stepmother in Washington State for a few years, but eventually the stepfamily sent him back to the border like a piece of unclaimed luggage. There he fell into the tunnel, into Barrio Libre. He freely admits to *tumbando*, assaulting people in the tunnel for money. But something in the back of his head has been nagging at him lately.

"I'm tired of it and . . ."—he searches for the words—"they're my own people, after all."

Romel's friend Iram shows up, a tall, lithe, good-looking teenager who still lives "down below." He teases Romel about his new life. Ultimately, he goads him into going down for a visit.

We zigzag along the tourist streets of downtown Nogales, looking out for Beta agents, who, Romel says, are after him for a tunnel rape that he swears he had nothing to do with. We head south along Avenida Obregón, Nogales's main drag. A strip joint announces "*chicas sexis.*°" A blind accordionist sits on the sidewalk playing for change. A middle-aged gringo tourist in shorts, white socks, and huaraches marvels at a wrought-iron design.

About half a mile from the border on Obregón, we veer left and drop down into a weedy abandoned lot. The kids turn left again around the corner of an apartment building, looking over their shoulders. Now we're underneath the building, in a four-foot crawl space. Knees and backs bent uncomfortably, we walk along a trickle of a river running down the middle of the tunnel. It's not so bad, I think to myself.

But the real tunnel begins only about two hundred yards later, and the 110 space there is barely over three feet high. As if someone had snapped off a switch, suddenly all light is gone. Romel flicks on the only flashlight we have—one equipped with rapidly dying batteries. The light barely cuts through the dark. Staggering along sideways, I can barely keep up with the kids.

The stench hits me: this is not supposed to be a sewage line, but there is obviously leakage from homes and businesses above. The river widens. What appear to be puddles are actually two-foot-deep mini-lakes of stagnant shit and piss. We hear the drip of more sewage coming down. The air is at once too thick and too thin. I breathe heavily and sweat profusely, although it's a few degrees cooler down here than outside.

I manage to stammer a concerned question about battery life. "Don't worry," Romel says. "Even if it goes out, I can tell you exactly where we are and how to get out of here. I can walk in and out of here without a flashlight." I wonder if he's boasting or serious; there are hundreds of yards of pitch-black tunnel left before we reach the line. *Watch out for the electrical wire—might be live or it might not, you don't want to find out. Careful of this beam. Ouch!*

Concrete dividers are encrusted with surreal collections of goo and trash—baseball caps and egg cartons, underwear and hairbrushes—that rush through here when it rains. My left leg gives way into a shit lake and I fall forward, striking my knee on something sharp. Fetid water splashes

chicas sexis: Sexy girls.

up in my face. Giggles from Iram and Romel. My jeans are torn and my knee feels like there's a knife stuck in the socket.

It's deathly quiet down here, no breeze, nothing to see, only the feeling that there are a dozen things that you could knock yourself out cold on.

We approach an ever-so-dim source of light. It's a manhole cover. Through two half-dollar-size holes, the light comes down gray-white in perfect tubes, two tiny spotlights hitting the sandy-muddy floor of the tunnel. Beyond, darkness again. I stand below the iron lid. Directly above us, I see and hear pedestrians along Obregón. A Mexican vendor is earnestly trying to get a tourist to put on a sombrero and pose with his wife next to a burro.

After a while, we come to a stop before another tunnel, running perpendicular to the first. The international line. We clamber over a three-foot-thick black sewage pipe. Iram points east with the flashlight. About twenty-five yards away is the mouth of the north-south tunnel that takes you up to Church's Chicken—where Romel once lived and where Iram and many other Barrio Libre kids still live.

Suddenly bright lights flash ahead. Unintelligible whispers ripple along the dead air, reverberating off the concrete. Iram gets nervous. "Romel—there's somebody up there!" he says. The lights disappear. A few seconds later there is a tremendous metallic bang, loud enough to be felt in the pit of your stomach. Silence again.

"That was the sound of the tunnel opening," Romel says.

But by whom? Other members of Barrio Libre? *Polleros*° eager to teach the kids a lesson? Or is it the Border Patrol on one of their strolls into the tunnel, eager to swoop up the day's quota of illegals?

Romel and Iram wait in silence. To the west, a hundred yards away, a veil of gray light—an opening to street level that is part of a construction project on the Mexican side, just a block and a half from Mi Nueva Casa.

Into the darkness or toward the light?

The kids make a run for it, scared out of their wits.

A minute later, alone, I'm climbing up through chunks of concrete and iron reinforcement rods.

The light of the sun glinting off car fenders and house windows is blinding. Above, the deep blue Sonoran sky. And then a man wearing a red beret and aviator glasses is asking me where I am going. Romel and Iram are pushed against the wall, legs spread. I have the presence of mind to show my journalist's credential and the Beta agent calls off the dogs.

"If you hadn't been there," says Romel later, "they would've beat the shit out of us."

polleros: People who lead Mexican immigrants across the border. (*Pollos* are chickens.)

The next day, another trip down into the tunnel, this time led by Toño, the nine-year-old I'd met in Mi Nueva Casa—the one with the dog bites. We take the same route, and this time there are no strangers flashing lights.

We turn toward the steel gate the Border Patrol welds shut a few times a week. As we approach, we hear whispers on the other side. Toño slows down, shines his flashlight directly at the gate. It creaks open; the BP hasn't welded it yet. Squinting into the light are a pair of glassy eyes set in a twelve-year-old's face.

"Where you from?" the kid asks.

"Barrio Libre!" Toño responds quickly, and then the door opens fully, revealing half a dozen more kids. Handshakes all around.

The boys show me the weld—it looks like nothing more than a Radio 130 Shack soldering job—that they break open whenever they want. I get a tour of the immediate surroundings, the graffiti-scarred walls. BARRIO LIBRE! on one side, BETA! on the other—the Mexican border agents, not to be outdone by the kids, do their own tagging.

We are advised by the older Barrio Libre members not to go farther into the tunnel; there is something going down deep inside. They close the door and scamper back to the Mexican side, maneuvering quickly with their dimming flashlights.

The last time I visited the tunnel, all hell broke loose. I was standing with the kids on the American side, at the mouth of the tunnel, just below Church's Chicken. There were several kids present whom I didn't know. And the ones I did know were high—very high. There was a spray can being passed around with a rag. Gold-fleck paint was everywhere, on the kids' noses and mouths, on their hands, on my tape recorder. The kids were stumbling, twirling, kicking at puddles of water, shouting themselves hoarse.

I was surprised to find Romel among the crew, although perhaps I shouldn't have been. Once you've gone underground, it's hard to stay away. I try to imagine Romel as a mature man in his thirties. I cannot.

Something was about to happen—the combination of the paint and the large number of kids, about twenty in all, was volatile. All they needed was the spark.

There was much drugged banter. Romel announced that he was going 135 to steal a TV set from someone's house on the American side.

"Yeah, we could have cable TV, and beds, and a stove ..." Jesús enthused. Romel thought there should be a library, too, with comic books and Nintendo games.

The reverie was cut short by the sudden appearance of a man in his thirties coming up from the tunnel. He was dressed in a white shirt opened several buttons down his chest, white pants, smart boots. He was definitely not *migra*, but he wasn't a typical *chúntaro*, either. The kids surrounded him instantly. It was a strange sight: a well-built, mature man mobbed by scrawny preteens and malnourished adolescents, not unlike a bear set upon by coyotes. One of the kids had noticed him stuffing something into his mouth just as he'd come within sight.

"Spit it out!" someone shouted. One kid pried the man's jaws open and took out a wadded-up ten-dollar bill.

"He's with Beta, I recognize him!" someone else yelled. The man remained quiet, amazingly calm considering the circumstances. He was fully patted down, but the kids found nothing else on him. Was he a narco? An illegal? A coyote?

"Are you alone?" a kid demanded.   140

"No, there are others behind me," he said, his voice devoid of emotion.

I was beginning to think he was bullshitting, stalling for time, but then we heard noises from deep inside the tunnel and saw the flashing of lights. The kids ran into the darkness, and the man in white slowly walked away, jumping up to street level without looking back. There were no Border Patrol agents or Nogales policemen anywhere to be seen. The kids could do what they wanted. From the tunnel I heard them shout "Barrio Libre!" and there were the sounds of scuffling. A few moments later, the kids reappeared, laughing, hoisting the spoils high: a gold necklace, a silver crucifix, diamond earrings in the shape of bunny rabbits, all the real thing. Unlucky *chúntaros*. Romel pulled me aside, breathing hard. He said the victims were about a dozen women. He suspected that the man in white was their coyote. He'd probably told them to wait inside while he checked out the scene at the mouth of the tunnel. There was nowhere for the women to run in the darkness. They sat huddled together, vulnerable as lambs, and then the kids were upon them. "There was nothing I could do to stop it," Romel told me.

As I left, the kids were still sniffing, and there was talk of a big party in the tunnel that night. When I clambered up to street level, I saw a Border Patrol Explorer pull into Church's parking lot. I looked back down. The kids were running back into the tunnel, deep into the darkness.

Naco, Arizona, is a minor port of entry some fifty miles east of Nogales. My father was stationed at the nearby army base back in the fifties. "Wasn't much in Naco," he told me. Nevertheless, I imagine him knocking back several cold ones in a cantina on the other side with his army buddies, he the Mexican in GI greens, a Mexican with papers, a Mexican with an American passport. Mexican only, in the end, for his brown skin and the memory of his parents' struggle to make it in America.

Second generation on my father's side and first on my mother's, I have 145 come back to the line, swimming against the tide, drawn by memory,

drawn by the present and by the future. I see the Mexicans pour into Los
Angeles, I see them on the banks of the Mississippi in St. Louis. I see
their brownness, I see my own. I suppose my sympathy can be summed
up simply as this: when they are denied their Americanness by U.S.
immigration policy, I feel that my own is denied as well. They are doing
exactly what my father's parents and my mother did. They are doing
exactly what all Americans' forebears did.

Here in Naco, the border is merely a few broken strands of barbed
wire. There is an obelisk marking the boundary established in 1848, in
English on the north-facing side, in Spanish on the south. I become
giddy. No wall! Just open range, and that's exactly what it is, open range
for cross-border cattle. West of here, on the O'odham Reservation, there
is no wall or fence either. The O'odham people have been caught in the
middle of a transnational caper that has nothing to do with them. They
aren't Mexican, they aren't American, they are O'odham. For most of the
last century and a half, the tribe has moved freely back and forth across
the line, along with their livestock. The Border Patrol never bothers
them; the territory is so far removed from major highways that smugglers rarely think of crossing there.

The O'odham have homes on both sides of the line. "There are no sides
here," an elder tells me. Except that in recent years the Mexican migrant
tide has begun coming across O'odham land because of the new wall in
Nogales. And so the Border Patrol has arrived on the res with its Explorers and helicopters. O'odham people have found dessicated migrant bodies in the middle of their desert.

I leap over to one side; I am Mexican!

I leap back to the other side; I am American!

I dance a jig back and forth across the line, laughing at it, damning it, 150
and recognizing the mighty power of the very idea of a line that cannot,
does not exist in nature but that exists, nevertheless, in political, that is,
human terms.

And just as I am marveling at the absurdity, an Explorer pulls up and
two BP agents, one Asian, one Caucasian, saunter over.

The Asian asks, in fairly good Spanish, "*Qué hace usted aquí?*" What
are you doing here?

I answer, of course, in English.

I am informed that I am in violation of the United States Immigration
Code. I flash my credentials, and after a bit of radio repartee between the
agents and their supervisors, all is fine and dandy. I can keep walking
along the line as much as I want, as long as I stay on this side — right
here happens to be public land so I'm free to engage in whatever lawful
activity I please. But I'm also advised that I might have many such

encounters with BP officers because I will be tripping seismic sensors all along the way, which is why I was detained by the BP outside of Naco in the first place.

"We get a lot of 'em in through here," one agent says. "Most of 'em are 155 from Mitch-oh-ah-cahn."

And so I get in the Blazer, point it east, and drive toward Douglas, Arizona, another embattled border village on the forlorn frontier. Hundreds of coyotes and tens of thousands of migrants wait on the other side in Agua Prieta, and a beefed-up Border Patrol waits on this one, not to mention mad-as-hell gringo ranchers whose land is being trampled by the migrant stampede.

In Douglas and Naco and Sonoita and El Paso and Laredo, all along the two-thousand-mile line, it's the same thing each and every day. Helicopters toss down ladders of light, and the *migra* put their night-vision goggles and laser grids and seismic sensors and video cameras to work. Mexican teenagers with slingshots target the BP trucks, so much so that the Explorers now have iron window grilles. The vigilantes patrol their properties, fingering the triggers of their assault rifles. A handful of activists protest human rights abuses on both sides of the line, and a few compassionate preachers liken the crossing to wading across the Jordan into Canaan.

It's like this all along the border, and it's a matter of politics, of money, of ideas, desire, death, life.

Reading

1. What is "Barrio Libre"? Why are its members disliked?

2. What physical obstruction does the Border Patrol use to keep the tunnel closed? What keeps happening to it?

Thinking Critically

1. What do you think a Border Patrol agent such as Laura Privette hopes to accomplish in her work?

2. After reading this chapter, how do you think the effort to close the border affects the towns and cities along it?

Connecting

1. Fifty years before Rubén Martínez wrote *Crossing Over*, Rubén Salazar was on the border in El Paso writing "La Nacha Sells Dirty Dope . . ." (p. 46). What are some similarities between the work of these two reporters? How do their writing styles differ?

Writing

1. As Martínez shows in "The Line," the border is not a solid boundary between two places, but the center of a distinctive region. In an essay, using examples from the selection, write about the places, people, and practices that characterize the border.

Creating

1. **Create a message for the border.** In "The Line," we learn that the tunnel that links the United States and Mexico is lined with graffiti. In fact, many areas along the entire U.S.-Mexico border are full of paintings and signs, some of which greet people who are crossing it, others that send messages to the other side. Paint an image or a sign that you might put along the border, including words in English or Spanish if you'd like.

43

LUIS ALBERTO URREA [b. 1954]

From *The Hummingbird's Daughter* [2005]

GENRE: FICTION

The work of Luis Alberto Urrea shows that skilled storytelling transcends the divide between fiction and nonfiction. He spent decades researching his novel The Hummingbird's Daughter, *and his journalism has the appeal of good fiction. Urrea spent his childhood and college years around San Diego, earning a bachelor's degree from the University of California, San Diego. The several years he spent with Baptist missionaries who worked with people living around Tijuana's garbage dumps became the basis for* Across the Wire: Life and Hard Times on the Mexican Border. *After moving to Boston to teach, Urrea befriended Tino Villanueva (p. 182), with whom he coedited the journal* Imagine. *While trying to establish himself as a writer, Urrea returned to school, earning a master's degree from the University of Colorado, Boulder. In 1993, after moving back to California, Urrea found a publisher for* Across the Wire *and, soon after, for his first novel and a book of poetry. Urrea continued to write in a variety of genres, achieving his greatest success with his 2004 nonfiction book* The Devil's Highway, *a finalist for the Pulitzer Prize that told the story of the deaths of a group of Mexicans attempting to enter the United States, and his 2005 novel* The Hummingbird's Daughter, *based on the life of his great-aunt Teresita Urrea, a famous healer known as the Saint of Cabora. To write it, Urrea said, "I studied with medicine men and women. I went to strange places that I wasn't quite ready for and [I] wasn't too sure how to process those experiences. If you try to enter another person's world, you can expect things to happen and they did."**

The opening chapter of The Hummingbird's Daughter *introduces "Hummingbird," the fourteen-year-old Cayetana Chávez, who is about to have a child. From this section of the book, one can find what makes Urrea's style so distinctive. With a grandiosity punctured by humor, Urrea presents cinematically rendered scenes and an environment full of wonders.*

As you read this excerpt from *The Hummingbird's Daughter,* pay close attention to Urrea's style, noticing how he uses it to create characters and to prepare his readers for an epic story.

On the cool October morning when Cayetana Chávez brought her baby to light, it was the start of that season in Sinaloa when the humid torments of summer finally gave way to breezes and falling leaves, and small red birds skittered through the corrals, and the dogs grew new coats.

On the big Santana rancho, the People had never seen paved streets, streetlamps, a trolley, or a ship. Steps were an innovation that seemed an occult work, stairways were the wicked cousins of ladders, and greatly to be avoided. Even the streets of Ocoroni, trod on certain Sundays when the People formed a long parade and left the safety of the hacienda° to attend Mass, were dirt, or cobbled, not paved. The People thought all great cities had pigs in the streets and great muddy rivers of mule piss attracting hysterical swarms of wasps, and that all places were built of dirt and straw. They called little Cayetana the Hummingbird, using the mother tongue to say it: Semalú.

*Quoted from a Bookslut interview, available for viewing at bookslut.com/features/2011_12_018440.php.

hacienda: A large estate.

On that October day, the fifteenth, the People had already begun readying for the Day of the Dead, only two weeks away. They were starting to prepare plates of the dead's favorite snacks; deceased uncles, already half-forgotten, still got their favorite green tamales,° which, due to the heat and the flies, would soon turn even greener. Small glasses held the dead's preferred brands of tequila, or rum, or rompope:° Tío° Pancho liked beer, so a clay flagon of watery Guaymas brew fizzled itself flat before his graven image on a family altar. The ranch workers set aside candied sweet potatoes, cactus and guayaba° sweets, mango jam, goat jerky, dribbly white cheeses, all food they themselves would like to eat, but they knew the restless spirits were famished, and no family could afford to assuage its own hunger and insult the dead. Jesús! Everybody knew that being dead could put you in a terrible mood.

The People were already setting out the dead's favorite corn-husk cigarettes, and if they could not afford tobacco, they filled the cigarros with machuche, which would burn just as well and only make the smokers cough a little. Grandmother's thimble, Grandfather's old bullets, pictures of Father and Mother, a baby's umbilical cord in a crocheted pouch. They saved up their centavos to buy loaves of ghost bread and sugar skulls with blue icing on their foreheads spelling out the names of the dead they wished to honor, though they could not read the skulls, and the confectioners often couldn't read them either, an alphabet falling downstairs. Tomás Urrea, the master of the rancho, along with his hired cowboys, thought it was funny to note the grammatical atrocities committed by the candy skulls: Martía, Jorse, Octablo. The vaqueros° laughed wickedly, though most of them couldn't read, either. Still, they were not about to lead Don° Tomás to think they were brutos,° or worse—pendejos.°

"A poem!" Tomás announced.   5

"Oh no," said his best friend, Don Lauro Aguirre, the great Engineer, on one of his regular visits.

"There was a young man from Guamúchil," Tomás recited, "whose name was Pinche Inútil!°"

"And?" said Don Lauro.

"I haven't worked it out yet."

Tomás rode his wicked black stallion through the frosting of starlight   10
that turned his ranch blue and pale gray, as if powdered sugar had blown off the sky and sifted over the mangos and mesquites. Most of the citizens

---

tamales: Cornmeal dough with filling, wrapped in corn husks and steamed.
rompope: A drink similar to eggnog.   **Tío:** Uncle.   **guayaba:** Small, yellow
fruit.   **vaqueros:** Cowboys.   **Don:** Title of respect, used before a man's first name.
brutos: Brutes.   **pendejos:** Assholes.   **Pinche Inútil:** Fucking Good-for-nothing.

of Sinaloa had never wandered more than 100 miles; he had traveled more than anyone else, 107 miles, an epic journey undertaken five days before, when he and his foreman, Segundo, had led a squad of armed outriders to Los Mochis, then to the Sea of Cortés beyond. All to collect Don Lauro Aguirre, arriving by ship from far Mazatlán, and with him, a shipment of goods for the ranch, which they contracted for safe delivery in a Conducta wagon train accompanied by cavalry.

In Los Mochis, Tomás had seen the legendary object called "the sea."

"More green than blue," he'd noted to his companions, already an expert on first sight. "The poets are wrong."

"Pinches° poets," said Segundo, hating all versifiers and psalmists.

They had gone on to greet the Engineer at the docks. He fairly danced off the boat, so charged with delight was he to be once again in the rustic arms of his *bon ami très enchanté!*° Under his arm, carefully wrapped in oilcloth, Aguirre clutched a leather-bound copy of Maxwell's *Treatise on Electricity and Magnetism.* In Aguirre's opinion, the Scotsman had written a classic! Don Lauro had a nagging suspicion that electricity, this occult force, and magnetism, certainly a force of spirit, could be used to locate, and even affect, the human soul. In his pocket, a greater wonder was hidden: a package of Adams's Black Jack chewing gum — the indescribable flavor of licorice! Wait until Tomás tasted that!

The ship looked to Segundo like a fat bird with gray wings floating on   15
the water after eating some fish. He was delighted with himself and pointed to the boat and told one of the buckaroos, "Fat bird. Ate some fish. Floating around." He lit a little cigar and grinned, his gums and teeth clotted with shreds of tobacco.

Segundo had the face of an Aztec carving. He had Chinese eyes, and a sloping Mayan forehead. His nose was a great curving blade that hung down over his drooping bandido mustache. He thought he was handsome. But then, Aguirre also thought himself handsome, though he seemed to have inherited the penchant for fat cheeks that was supposed to be the curse of the Urrea clan. He tried to remember to suck in his cheeks, especially when he was being compared to his friend Tomás Urrea. Where had Tomás's cheeks gone? In bright light, you could see his cheekbones casting shadows as if he were some Indian warrior. And those eyes! Urrea had a ferocious gleam in his eyes — a glare. Men found it unnerving, but women were apparently mesmerized. They were the only green eyes Aguirre had ever beheld.

"You have much work to do, you lazy bastard," said Tomás.

pinches: Fucking.   *bon ami très enchanté*: French for *very charming good friend.*

The Urrea clan paid Aguirre handsomely to exercise his education for them in elaborate hydrological and construction plans. He had designed a network of vents to carry odors from the house's revolutionary indoor toilet. He had even astounded them all by designing a system of pipes that carried water uphill.

With liquid on the mind, it was not long before they found the notorious El Farolito cantina.° There, they ate raw shellfish still gasping under tides of lime juice and hot sauce and great crystals of salt that cracked between the teeth of the men. Naked women writhed to a tuba-and-drum combo. The men regarded this display with joy, though Aguirre made the effort to feel guilty about it. Lieutenant Emilio Enríquez, in charge of the Conducta wagon train, joined them at the table.

"Teniente!°" Tomás shouted. "What do you hear?"   20

"Gentlemen," said Enríquez, arranging his sword so he could sit. "Unrest in Mexico City."

Aguirre had to admit to himself that this soldier, though an enforcer of the oppressors, was a dashing figure in his medallions and the bright brass fittings on his tunic.

"What troubles are these, sir?" he said, always ready to hear the government was being overthrown.

Enríquez twirled the ends of his upswept bigote° and nodded to the barkeep, who landed a foaming beer before him.

"Protesters," he sighed, "have dug up Santa Anna's leg again."   25

Everybody burst out laughing.

The old dictator's leg had once been blown off by a cannonball and buried with full military honors in the capital.

"Every year, somebody digs it up and kicks it around," Enríquez said.

Tomás raised his glass of beer.

"To Mexico," he said.   30

"To Santa Anna's leg!" Lieutenant Enríquez announced.

They all raised their glasses.

"The Canadians," Enríquez said, as he poured himself a fresh glass of beer, "have launched a mounted police force. They control their Indians."

"And bandits?" Tomás interjected.

Tomás Urrea's own father had been waylaid by bandits on the road to   35 Palo Cagado. The bandits, a scruffy lot said to have dropped out of the Durango hills, had been after silver. Tomás's father, Don Juan Francisco, was well known for carrying casks of coin to cover the wages of the three hundred workers on his brother's great million-acre hacienda south of Culiacán. When the outlaws discovered no silver, they stood Don Juan Francisco against an alamo tree and executed him with a volley of ninety-

El Farolito cantina: The Little Lantern bar.   **Teniente:** Lieutenant.   **bigote:** Mustache.

seven bullets. Tomás had been nine at the time. Yet his subsequent hatred of bandidos, as he grew up on the vast ranch, was so intense it transformed into a lifelong fascination. Some even said Tomás now wished he were a bandido.

"It goes without saying, caballeros.° Bandits!" said Enríquez. "Besides, we have already started the rural police program here in Mexico to accost our own outlaws."

"Gringos!° They have copied us again," Tomás announced.

"Los Rurales," Enríquez continued. "The rural mounted police force."

"To the Rurales," Tomás said.

They raised their glasses.   40

"To the bandits," said Segundo.

"And the Apaches," Enríquez said, "who keep me employed."

They drank the hot brew and pissed out the back door and tossed coins to the women to keep them dancing. Tomás suddenly grabbed a guitar and launched into a ballad about a boy who loved his schoolteacher but was too shy to tell her. Instead, he wrote her a love note every day and tucked it in a tree. One day, while he was placing his latest testimonial in the tree, it was hit by lightning, and not only did this poor boy die, but the tree with its enclosed epistles of love burned to the ground. The teacher ran to the tree in time to behold this disaster. The ballad ended with the melancholy schoolteacher, lonely and unloved, brushing the ashes of the boy's unread notes from her hair before turning out her lamp and sleeping alone for yet another night. The naked dancers covered themselves and wept.

Early the next morning, the men left the thunderously hungover barkeep and dancers behind and began their long ride inland, to where the hills started to rise and the iguanas were longer than the rattlesnakes. They began to forget the color of the sea.

Cayetana greeted that dawn with a concoction made with coffee beans   45
and burned corn kernels. As the light poured out of the eastern sea and splashed into windows from coast to coast, Mexicans rose and went to their million kitchens and cooking fires to pour their first rations of coffee. A tidal wave of coffee rushed west across the land, rising and falling from kitchen to fire ring to cave to ramada.° Some drank coffee from thick glasses. Some sipped it from colorful gourds, rough clay pots that dissolved as they drank, cones of banana leaf. Café negro.° Café with canela.° Café with goat's milk. Café with a golden-brown cone of piloncillo° melting in it like a pyramid engulfed by a black flood. Tropical café with a dollop

---

caballeros: Gentlemen.   **Gringos:** Non-Mexicans, whites.   **ramada:** Shelter made out of tree branches.   **Café negro:** Black coffee.   **Café with canela:** Coffee with cinnamon.   **piloncillo:** Dark brown sugar, usually in a cone shape.

of sugarcane rum coiling in it like a hot snake. Bitter mountaintop café that thickened the blood. In Sinaloa, café with boiled milk, its burned milk skin floating on top in a pale membrane that looked like the flesh of a peeled blister. The heavy-eyed stared into the round mirrors of their cups and regarded their own dark reflections. And Cayetana Chávez, too, lifted a cup, her coffee reboiled from yesterday's grounds and grits, sweet with spoons of sugarcane syrup, and lightened by thin blue milk stolen with a few quick squeezes from one of the patrón's° cows.

On that long westward morning, all Mexicans still dreamed the same dream. They dreamed of being Mexican. There was no greater mystery.

Only rich men, soldiers, and a few Indians had wandered far enough from home to learn the terrible truth: Mexico was too big. It had too many colors. It was noisier than anyone could have imagined, and the voice of the Atlantic was different from the voice of the Pacific. One was shrill, worried, and demanding. The other was boisterous, easy to rile into a frenzy. The rich men, soldiers, and Indians were the few who knew that the east was a swoon of green, a thick-aired smell of ripe fruit and flowers and dead pigs and salt and sweat and mud, while the west was a riot of purple. Pyramids rose between llanos° of dust and among turgid jungles. Snakes as long as country roads swam tame beside canoes. Volcanoes wore hats of snow. Cactus forests grew taller than trees. Shamans ate mushrooms and flew. In the south, some tribes still went nearly naked, their women wearing red flowers in their hair and blue skirts, and their breasts hanging free. Men outside the great Mexico City ate tacos made of live winged ants that flew away if the men did not chew quickly enough.

So what were they? Every Mexican was a diluted Indian, invaded by milk like the coffee in Cayetana's cup. Afraid, after the Conquest and the Inquisition, of their own brown wrappers, they colored their faces with powder, covered their skins in perfumes and European silks and American habits. Yet for all their beaver hats and their lace veils, the fine citizens of the great cities knew they had nothing that would ever match the ancient feathers of the quetzal.° No cacique° stood atop any temple clad in jaguar skins. Crinolines, waistcoats. Operas, High Mass, café au lait in demitasse cups in sidewalk patisseries. They attempted to choke the gods with New York pantaloons, Parisian petticoats. But still the banished spirits whispered from corners and basements. In Mexico City, the great and fallen Tenochtitlán, among streets and buildings constructed with the stones of the Pyramid of the Sun, gentlemen walked with their heads slightly tilted, cocked as if listening to this puzzling murmur of wraiths.

---

patrón: Boss.   **llanos:** Plains.   **quetzal:** Green and scarlet bird that is much revered.   **cacique:** Chief.

They still spoke a thousand languages—Spanish, too, to be sure, but also a thicket of songs and grammars. Mexico—the sound of wind in the ruins. Mexico—the waves rushing the shore. Mexico—the sand dunes, the snowfields, the steam of sleeping Popocatépetl. Mexico—across marijuana fields, tomato plants, avocado trees, the agave° in the village of Tequila.

Mexico. . . .   50

All around them, in the small woods, in the caves, in the precipitous canyons of copper country, in the swamps and at the crossroads, the harsh Old Ones gathered. Tlaloc, the rain god, lips parched because the Mexicans no longer tortured children to feed him sweet drafts of their tears. The Flayed One, Xipe Totec, shivering cold because priests no longer skinned sacrifices alive and danced in their flesh to bring forth the harvest. Tonantzin, goddess of Tepeyac, chased from her summit by the very Mother of God, the Virgen de Guadalupe. The awesome and ferocious warrior god, Hummingbird on the Left, Huitzilopochtli. Even the Mexicans' friend, Chac Mool, was lonely. Big eared and waiting to carry their hopes and dreams in his bowl as he transited to the land of the gods from the earth, he lay on his back watching forever in vain for the feathered priests to return. Other Old Ones hid behind statues in the cathedrals that the Spaniards had built with the stones of their shattered temples. The smell of sacrificial blood and copal seeped out from between the stones to mix with incense and candles. Death is alive, they whispered. Death lives inside life, as bones dance within the body. Yesterday is within today. Yesterday never dies.

Mexico. Mexico.

The pain in her belly kicked Cayetana Chávez over. She dropped her cup. She felt a cascade of fluids move down her bowels as the child awoke. Her belly!

It clenched. It jumped. It clenched.

At first, she thought it was the cherries. She had never eaten them   55
before. If she had known they would give her a case of chorro° . . .

"Ay," she said, "Dios.°"

She thought she was going to have to rush to the bushes.

They had come for her the day before. The Chávez girls were known by everybody. Although Santana Ranch was divided into two great lobes of territory—crops to the south and cattle to the north—there were only fifty workers' households, and with the children and grandparents added up, it made for fewer than 150 workers. Everybody knew better than to

agave: Also known as a maguey, succulent with thick, flat leaves.   **chorro:** Diarrhea.   **Ay . . . Dios:** Oh God.

bother Cayetana's older sister, Tía. Good Christ: the People would rather move a rattlesnake out of their babies' cribs with a stick than go to Tía's door. So when they came from the northern end of the rancho with news that one of the Chávez sisters' cousins had killed himself, they'd asked for La Semalú.

Ay, Dios. Cayetana was only fourteen, and she had already learned that life was basically a long series of troubles. So she had wrapped her rebozo° around her head and put on her flat huaraches° and begun her slow waddle through the darkness before the sun rose.

She wondered, as she walked, why the People called her Humming- 60
bird. Was it because she was small? Well, they were *all* small. Everyone knew semalús were holy birds, carrying prayers to God. She also knew she had a bad reputation, so calling her Semalú was probably some kind of joke. They loved to make jokes. Cayetana spit: she did not think anything was funny. Especially now. Her poor cousin. He had shot himself in the head. Her mother and father were dead, shot down in an army raid in Tehueco lands. Her aunt and uncle had been hanged in a grove of mango trees by soldiers that mistook them for fleeing Yaquis near El Júpare. The men were strung up with their pants around their ankles. Both men and women hung naked as fruit. Some of the Mexicans had collected scalps. She sighed. Aside from her sister, she was alone in the world. She put her hands on her belly as she walked along the north road. It was three miles to the cattle operation. The baby kicked.

Not yet, not yet.

She didn't mind being called a hummingbird.

Hours later, she pushed through the shaky gate of her cousin's jacal.° He was still lying on his back in the dirt. Someone had placed a bandana over his face. His huaraches were splayed. His toes were gray. The blood on the ground had turned black. He didn't stink yet, but the big flies had been running all over him, pausing to rub their hands. A rusty pistola lay in the dirt a few inches from his hand.

The neighbors had already raided her cousin's shack and taken all his food. Cayetana traded the pistola to a man who agreed to dig a hole. He dug it beside a maguey° plant beside the fence, and they rolled the body into it. They shoved the dirt over him and then covered the grave with rocks so the dogs wouldn't dig it up.

Inside the shack, Cayetana found a chair and a bed frame made of 65
wood and ropes. There was a machete° under the bed. A pregnant girl from distant Escuinapa was there, waiting. Cayetana didn't know her, but she let her move in, since the girl was afraid that she would lose her infant

rebozo: A shawl.   huaraches: Sandals.   jacal: Hut or shack.   maguey: Agave.   machete: Very large knife used as a tool.

to coyotes if she had it outside. Cayetana accepted the girl's blessing, then swung the machete a few times. She liked the big blade. She started to walk home.

The sun was already setting. She didn't like that. The dark frightened her. That road was also scary. It wound between black cottonwoods and gray willows. Crickets, frogs, night birds, bats, coyotes, and ranch dogs—their sounds accompanied her through the dark. When she had to pee—and since the child had sprouted inside her, she had to pee all the time—she squatted in the middle of the road and held the machete above her head, ready to kill any demon or bandit that dared leap out at her. An owl hooted in a tree behind her, and that made her hurry.

She came around a bend and saw a small campfire off to the side of the road. It was on the south side. That was a good omen—north was the direction of death. Or was it west? But south was all right.

A man stood by the fire, holding a wooden bowl. He was chewing, and he watched her approach. A horse looked over his shoulder, more interested in the bowl than in her. Her stomach growled and her mouth watered. She hadn't eaten in a day. She should have hidden in the bushes, but he had already seen her.

"Buenas noches,°" she called.

"Buenas." 70

"It's dark."

He looked up as if noticing the darkness for the first time.

"It is," he agreed. Then: "Don't hit me with that machete."

"I won't."

"Gracias.°" 75

"This is for bandidos."

"Ah!"

"Son cabrones,°" she explained. "And I'll kill the first one that tries anything."

"Excellent," he said.

"And ghosts." 80

He put food in his mouth.

"I don't think you can kill a ghost," he said.

"We'll see about that," she said, flashing her blade.

The small fire crackled.

"What are you eating?" she asked. 85

"Cherries."

"Cherries? What are cherries?"

Buenas noches: Good night.   **Gracias:** Thanks.   **Son cabrones:** They are jerks.

He held one up. In the faint fire glow, it looked like a small heart full
of blood.

"They come from trees," he said.

"Son malos?°" she asked. "They look wicked." 90

He laughed.

"They are very wicked," he said.

"I am going home," she said.

"So am I."

"Is this your horse?" 95

"It is, but I like to walk."

"You must have good shoes."

"I have good feet."

He spit out a seed and popped another cherry in his mouth. She
watched his cheeks swell as his jaw worked. Spit. Eat another cherry.

"Are they sweet?" she asked. 100

"Sí.°"

He spit a seed.

He heard her belly growl.

"You will bring a child to light soon," he said.

"Yes." 105

"A girl."

"I don't know," she replied.

"A girl."

He handed her the bowl.

"Eat," he said. 110

The cherry juice in Cayetana's mouth was dark and red, like nothing
she had ever tasted.

She spit out the seed.

"I have to go now," she said, "it is late."

"Adiós,°" he said.

Cayetana replied in the mother tongue: "Lios emak weye." God go with 115
you. She walked into the night. Funny man. But one thing she knew
from experience—all men were funny.

She'd gotten a restless night's sleep with the bellyache she blamed on
the stranger's fruit. Now the morning brought increased tumult inside
her. Cayetana thought she could make it to the row of outhouses that
Tomás had built between the workers' village and the great house where
the masters slept. But the child within her had decided it was time to
come forth, announcing the news about halfway to the outhouses when

Son malos?: Are they bad?   **Sí:** Yes.   **Adiós:** Goodbye.

the pain dropped Cayetana to her knees and the strange water broke from her and fell into the dust.

Reading

1. What distinguishes Tomás Urrea from the other characters?
2. What do you learn of Cayetana's life?

Thinking Critically

1. What picture of Mexico does the story suggest?
2. What is the significance of the nickname "Hummingbird"?

Connecting

1. Nearly five hundred years ago, Cabeza de Vaca ventured through the same region Urrea wrote about in *The Hummingbird's Daughter* and described it in his historical account of his journey, *Chronicle of the Narváez Expedition* (p. 5). What similarities or differences do you find in the two descriptions? What about in the styles of the two writers?

Writing

1. Urrea uses a style and a tone that make the landscape and culture of Sinaloa, a state in southern Mexico, seem strange and wondrous. Paying close attention to the text and using specific examples, write an essay about how Urrea's writing does this.

Creating

1. **Keep a food journal.** Luis Alberto Urrea describes a great variety of food in *The Hummingbird's Daughter*. For a week, keep a food journal. Keep an eye out for any special or new foods you encounter, perhaps at a celebration or for a holiday. Discuss what makes these foods special, trying to describe them the way a novelist might.

44

JOSEFINA LÓPEZ [b. 1969]

Act I from *Real Women Have Curves*

From Real Women Have Curves: A Full-Length Play for
Five Women [1996]

GENRE: DRAMA

With the enormous success of her play-turned-movie Real Women
Have Curves, *Josefina López has become one of the best-known
Chicana playwrights in the country. She wrote the play when she
was nineteen, basing it closely on her own life. López was born in
San Luis Potosí in Mexico and grew up in Los Angeles, undocumented until she was granted amnesty by the passage of the Immigration Control and Reform Act in 1986. After high school, she
began attending playwriting workshops, and in 1988 her first play,*
Simply María, *was produced in Los Angeles, with a shorter version of the play being created by Teatro Campesino, the theater
group led by Luis Valdez (p. 82), who was one of López's main
inspirations. López then went to Chicago to earn her bachelor's
degree at Columbia College, returning to Los Angeles for a master's
in screenwriting from the University of California. López based*
Real Women Have Curves *on a year spent working in a sewing
factory, waiting on an amnesty application before starting college.
It was fine-tuned during multiple productions over several years
and eventually became a 2002 film, cowritten by George LaVoo
and produced by HBO Films.* Real Women Have Curves *was a
hugely successful independent film, winning the Audience Award
at the Sundance Film Festival and gaining popularity for its affir-
mation of the beauty of women young and old, big and small,
Latina and not. López has also written dozens of other plays as
well as the novel* Hungry Woman in Paris *(2009), and she is the
founder of Casa 0101 in Boyle Heights, which aims to bring a new
generation of young Latinos into the theater.*

Reprinted here is the first act of the play Real Women Have
Curves, *in which the protagonist Ana is introduced to her coworkers at the sewing factory. She expects to be unhappy but finds*

*reasons to enjoy the work. López has said of the play and of her experience, "Anyone looking from the outside might say 'Ay, pobrecita, she was undocumented and working in a sewing factory.' But it was such a great eye-opening experience about the power of women, the beautiful intimacy that women have and the bond that happens when women are together."**

As you read this excerpt from *Real Women Have Curves*, notice how López captures the rhythms of work and the bond between the women.

Characters

ANA *18, plump and pretty, sister of Estela, daughter of Carmen. She is a recent high school graduate and a young feminist*

ESTELA *24, plump, plain-looking, owner of the "Garcia Sewing Factory"*

CARMEN *48, a short, large woman, mother of Ana and Estela. She has a talent for storytelling*

PANCHA *32, a huge woman who is very mellow in her ways, but quick with her tongue*

ROSALÍ *29, only a bit plump in comparison to the rest of the women. She is sweet and easygoing*

Setting: *A tiny sewing factory in East Los Angeles.*

Time: *The first week of September 1987.*

ACT ONE

Scene One

At Rise: *The stage becomes visible. The clock on the wall shows it is 6:59 a.m. Keys are heard outside the door. The door opens. ANA and CARMEN enter. ANA drags herself in, goes directly to the electricity box and switches it on. Automatically all the machines "hummmm" loudly. The lights turn on at different times. The radio also blasts on with a song in Spanish. CARMEN quickly turns off the radio. She puts her lunch on the table. ANA slumps on a machine. CARMEN then gets a broom and uses it to get a mousetrap from underneath the table. She prays that today will be the day she caught the mouse. She sees the mousetrap empty and is very disappointed.*

*From "Josefina López in her own words" on Latinopia, available at latinopia .com/latino-theater/josefina-lopez/

CARMEN. ¡Pinche rata!° I'll get you. (CARMEN *returns the broom. She takes two dollars from her purse, approaches* ANA *and presents them to her.*) Ten.° Go to the bakery.

ANA. No. I want to go back to sleep!

CARMEN. ¡Huevona!° If we don't help your sister who else is going to?   5
She already works all hours of the night trying to finish the dresses.
Por fin° she's doing something productive with her life.

ANA. I know I'm trying to be supportive, ayy! I don't want to go to the bakery. I don't want any bread.

CARMEN. That's good, at least you won't get fatter.   10

ANA. ¡Amá!°

CARMEN. I only tell you for your own good. Bueno,° I'll go get the bread myself, but you better not get any when I bring it. (CARMEN *walks to the door.*) Ana, don't forget to close the doors. This street is full of winos and drug addicts. And don't you open the door to any strangers!   15

ANA. Yeah, yeah, I know! I'm not a kid. (ANA *locks both doors with a key. She goes toward the toilet and turns on the water in the sink.* ANA *splashes water on her face to awaken. She sticks her hand behind the toilet seat and gets out a notebook and a pen. Spotlight on* ANA. *She sits and writes the following:*) Monday, September 7, 1987 . . . I don't want   20
to be here! I only come because my mother practically drags me out of bed and into the car and into the factory. She pounds on the . . . No . . . (*Scratches "pounds."*) She knocks on . . . No . . . (*She scratches "knocks."*) She pounds on the garage wall, and since I think it's an earthquake, I run out. Then she catches me and I become her pris-   25
oner . . . Is it selfish of me not to want to wake up every morning at 6:30 a.m., Saturdays included, to come work here for 67 dollars a week? Oh, but such is the life of a Chicana in the garment industry. Cheap labor . . . I've been trying to hint to my sister for a raise, but she says I don't work fast enough for her to pay me minimum   30
wage . . . The weeks get longer and I can't believe I've ended up here. I just graduated from high school . . . Most of my friends are in college . . . It's as if I'm going backwards. I'm doing the work that mostly illegal aliens do . . . (*Scratches "illegal aliens."*) No, "undocu-mented workers" . . . or else it sounds like these people come from   35
Mars . . . Soon I will have my "Temporary Residence Card," then after two years, my green card . . . I'm happy to finally be legal, but I thought things would be different . . . What I really want to do is write . . .

¡Pinche rata!: Damn rat!   **Ten:** Take it.   **Huevona:** Lazy good-for-nothing.
por fin: Finally.   **¡Amá!:** Mama!   **Bueno:** Well, good.

CARMEN (*off, interrupting*). Ana, open the door! (CARMEN *pounds on*   40
the door outside. ANA *quickly puts her writing away and goes to open
the door.*) Hurry up! There's a wino following me! (ANA *gets the
keys and unlocks both doors.*) Hurry! He's been following me from
the bakery.

(ANA *opens the first door.* CARMEN *is behind the bar door and is
impatiently waiting for* ANA *to open it.* ANA *opens the door.* CARMEN
hurries in nervously. ANA *quickly shuts the doors.* ANA *looks out the
window.*)

ANA. Amá, that's not a wino, it's an "Alelullah"!   45
CARMEN. But he was following me!
ANA. I know, those witnesses don't give up. (CARMEN *puts the bag of
bread on the table. She fills a small pot with water and puts it on the
little hot plate to boil the water for coffee.*)
CARMEN. Pos yo ya no veo.° I can't see a thing. (CARMEN *goes to her*   50
*purse and takes out her glasses. She puts them on. She looks out the
window and sees no one.*) I should retire and be an abuelita° by now,
taking care of grandchildren . . . I don't know why I work, I have
arthritis in my hands, I'm losing my sight from all this sewing, and
this arm, I can hardly move it anymore . . . (ANA *does not pay atten-*   55
tion as usual.)
ANA (*unsympathetically*). Yeah, Amá.
CARMEN. I wonder where's Estela. She should have been here by now.
ANA. I thought she left the house early.

(PANCHA *appears behind the bar door.*)

PANCHA. Buenos días,° Doña° Carmen. Can you open the door?   60
CARMEN. Buenos días, Pancha. ¿Cómo está?°
PANCHA. Not too bad.
CARMEN. Qué bien.° I brought my mole° today for all of us.
PANCHA. You're so generous, Doña Carmen.
CARMEN. It was in the 'frigerator for three days, and I thought it was   65
turning green, so I brought it. Why let it go to waste?
PANCHA. Is it still good?
CARMEN. Of course, I make great mole.

Pos yo ya no veo: I can't see a thing.   **abuelita:** Grandmother.   **Buenos días:**
Good morning.   **Doña:** A term of respect, used before a woman's first name.
¿Cómo está?: How are you?   **Qué bien:** How nice.   **mole:** A sauce made of
chocolate and chile.

(ROSALÍ *appears behind the bar door.*)

ROSALÍ. Doña Carmen, the door.

CARMEN. It's open, Rosalí. Buenos días. How are you?   70

ROSALÍ (*entering*). Okay, like always, Doña Carmen.

CARMEN. I brought my mole for all of us.

ROSALÍ. Did you? Ayy, gracias,° but remember I'm on a diet.

CARMEN. Just try a small taco, no te va hacer daño.° Try it.

ROSALÍ. I'm sure it's delicious, but I'm this close to being a size seven.   75

CARMEN. Sí. You're looking thinner now. How are you doing it?

ROSALÍ. I'm on a secret diet . . . It's from the Orient.

CARMEN. A-ha . . . It's true, those Japanese women are always skinny.
     Pues,° give me your secret, Rosalí. Maybe this way I can lose this ball
     of fat! (*She squeezes her stomach.*) Nomás mira que paresco.° You   80
     can't even see my waist anymore. But you know what it really is. It's
     just water. After having so many babies I just stopped getting rid of
     the water. It's as if I'm clogged. (ROSALÍ *and* ANA *laugh.*)

ROSALÍ. Sí, Doña Carmen.

ANA. Yeah, sure, Amá!   85

CARMEN. ¿Y tú?° Why do you laugh? You're getting there yourself.
     When I was your age I wasn't as fat as you. And look at your chichis.°

ANA. ¡Amá!

CARMEN (*grabs* ANA's *breasts as if weighing them*). They must weigh five
     pounds each.   90

ANA. Amá, don't touch me like that!

ROSALÍ. Where's Estela?

CARMEN. We don't know. Ana, I think you better call home now and
     check if she's there.

ROSALI. Because her torment is outside washing his car.   95

ALL. He is?

(*From under a large blanket on the floor* ESTELA *jumps out. The*
WOMEN *are startled and scream, but they quickly join her as she runs*
to the window to spy on her Tormento.)

ESTELA. ¡Ayy que buenote!° He's so cute.

ANA. Don't exaggerate.

ESTELA. ¡Mi Tormento! ¡O mi Tormento!

CARMEN. We thought you left home early.   100

Ayy, gracias: Ahh, thank you.   **no te va hacer daño:** It won't do you any harm.
Pues: Well.   **Nomás mira que paresco:** Just look what I look like.   **¿Y tu?:**
And you?   **chichis:** Boobs.   **¡Ayy que buenote!:** He's so fine!

ESTELA. No, I worked so late last night I decided to sleep here.

CARMEN. Then why didn't you tell us when—

ESTELA. I heard you come in, but I wanted to listen in on your chisme°
about me, Amá.

CARMEN. Me? I don't gossip!   105

ESTELA. Sure, Amá . . . I'm going to the store. (ESTELA *runs to the
mirror.*)

PANCHA. I don't know why you bother, all he cares about is his car.

CARMEN. Vénganse,° I think the water is ready. (*The* WOMEN *gather
around the table for coffee.* PANCHA *and* CARMEN *grab bread.*   110
ESTELA *goes to the bathroom and brushes her hair, puts on lipstick,
then she puts on a girdle under her skirt, which she has great trouble
getting on, but she is determined. She grabs a deodorant stick and
applies it. She also gets a bottle of perfume and sprays it accordingly.*)

ESTELA. Aquí por si me abraza. (*She sprays her wrist.*)   115

ANA (*mocks* ESTELA *in front of the* WOMEN). Here in case he
hugs me.

ESTELA. Aquí por si me besa. (*She sprays her neck.*)

ANA. Here in case he kisses me.

ESTELA. Y aquí por si se pasa. (*She sprays under her skirt.*)   120

ANA. And here in case he . . . you know what. (*The* WOMEN *are by the
door and windows looking out.* ESTELA *comes out of the bathroom.*)

ROSALI. He's gone.

CARMEN. Sí, ya se fue.°

ESTELA. No! Are you sure? (ESTELA *goes toward the door, before she*   125
reaches it CARMEN *shuts the door.*)

CARMEN (*scared*). ¡Dios mío!° (CARMEN *quickly takes a drink of her
coffee and can hardly breathe afterwards.*)

ESTELA. ¿Qué? ¿Amá, qué pasa?

CARMEN. I saw a van!   130

ROSALÍ. What van?

CARMEN. ¡La migra!° (*All the* WOMEN *scatter and hide waiting to be
discovered. Then after a few seconds* PANCHA *makes a realization.*)

PANCHA. Pero,° why are we hiding? We're all legal now.

CARMEN. ¡Ayy, de veras!° I forget! All those years of being an illegal, I   135
still can't get used to it.

PANCHA. Me too! (*She picks up a piece of bread.*) I think I just lost my
appetite.

---

chisme: Gossip.   **Vénganse:** Come you all.   **Sí, ya se fue:** Yes, he's already
left.   **¡Dios mío!:** Oh, God!   **La migra:** U.S. Immigration and Naturalization
Service officials, or border patrol.   **Pero:** But.   **¡Ayy, de veras!:** Ahh, it's true!

ROSALÍ. I'm not scared of it! I used to work in factories and whenever they did a raid, I'd always sneak out through the bathroom   140
window, y ya.°

ANA. Last night I heard on the news that la migra patrol is planning to
raid a lot of places.

PANCHA. They're going to get mean trying to enforce that Amnesty law.

ANA. Thank God, I'm legal. I will never have to lie on applications any-   145
more, except maybe about my weight . . .

ROSALÍ. ¿Saben qué?° Yesterday I got my first credit card.

CARMEN. ¿Pos cómo le hiciste?° How?

ROSALÍ. I lied on the application and I got an Americana Express.

ANA. And now you have two green cards and you never leave home   150
without them. (ANA *laughs her head off, but none of the* WOMEN *get
the joke.* ANA *slowly shuts up.*)

PANCHA. Doña Carmen, let those men in their van come! Who cares?
We're all legal now! (PANCHA *goes to the door and opens it all the way.
They all smile in relief and pride, then* ESTELA, *who has been stuffing*   155
her face, finally speaks up.)

ESTELA. I'm not. (PANCHA *slams the door shut.*)

EVERYONE. You're not?!!!

ANA. But you went with me to get the fingerprints and the medical
examination.   160

ESTELA. I didn't send them in.

ROSALÍ. But you qualify.

ESTELA. I have a criminal record.

EVERYONE. No!

ESTELA. So I won't apply until I clear it.   165

CARMEN. Estela, what did you do?

PANCHA. ¿Qué hiciste?°

ESTELA. Well, actually, I did two things.

CARMEN. Two?! ¿Y por qué no me habías dicho?° Why is the mother
always the last one to know?   170

ESTELA. Because one is very embarrassing—

CARMEN. ¡Aver dime, condenada!° What have you done?

ESTELA. I was arrested for illegal possession of—

ROSALÍ. Marijuana?!

PANCHA. A gun?!   175

ESTELA. A lobster.

y ya: And that was that.   **¿Saben qué?:** You know what?   **¿Pos cómo le
hiciste?:** Well, how did you do it?   **¿Qué hiciste?:** What did you do?   **¿Y por
qué . . . ?:** And why hadn't you told me?   **¡Aver, dime, condenada!:** Damn you,
tell me.

EVERYONE. No!

ESTELA. Out of season!

CARMEN. ¡Mentirosa!°

WOMEN. You're kidding!   180

ESTELA. A-ha! I'm not lying! I almost got handcuffed and taken to jail. Trying to "abduct" a lobster is taken very seriously in Santa Monica Beach. They wanted me to appear in court and I never did.

PANCHA. That's not a serious crime; ¿de qué te apuras?° Why worry?

CARMEN (*not amused*). That was the first crime? You mentioned two.   185

ESTELA. I'm being sued for not keeping up with my payments on the machines.

ANA. Y los° eight thousand dollars you got from your accident settlement weren't enough?

CARMEN. But I thought that everything was paid for.   190

ESTELA. I used most of it for a down-payment, but I still needed a new steam iron, the over-lock . . . I thought I could make the monthly payments if everything went as planned.

CARMEN. ¿Pos qué paso?°

PANCHA. What happened?   195

ESTELA. You know that we never finish on time. So the Glitz company doesn't pay me until we do.

ROSALÍ. Pero the orders are too big. We need at least two more seamstresses.

ESTELA. Pues sí.° But the money they pay me is not enough to hire any   200
more help. So because we get behind, they don't pay, I can't pay you, and I can't pay those pigs that sold me those machines.

CARMEN. Ayyy, Estela, how much do you owe?

ESTELA. Two thousand dollars . . .

CARMEN. ¡Hora si que estamos bien jodidas!° (*The* WOMEN *sigh*   205
hopelessly.)

ESTELA. . . . I tried. I sent some money and explained the situation to them two weeks ago, but I got a letter from their lawyer. They're taking me to court . . .

PANCHA. So you had money two weeks ago? Hey, hey, you told us you   210
couldn't pay us because you didn't have any money. You had money! Here we are bien pobres, I can't even pay for the bus sometimes, and you care more about your machines than us.

ESTELA. They're going to take everything!

ROSALÍ. ¡¿Qué?!°   215

¡Mentirosa!: Liar!   **¿de qué te apuras?:** What are you worried about?
Y los: And the   **¿Pos qué paso?:** Well then, what happened?   **Pues sí:** Well yes.
¡Hora si . . . !: Now we're really screwed!   **¡¿Qué?!:** What?!

ESTELA. They're going to repossess everything if I don't pay them. And if I appear in court they'll find out that I don't have any papers.

ANA. Then why don't you apply for Amnesty?

ESTELA. Because I won't get it if they find out about my lawsuit.

ANA. You don't know that. Estela, you should talk to this lawyer I know. 220

ESTELA. Ana, you know I can't afford a lawyer!

CARMEN. Ayy, Estela, ¡ya ni la friegas!° (ESTELA *fights the urge to cry.*)

ROSALÍ. If I had money I'd lend it to you.

PANCHA (*aside*). I wouldn't.

ROSALÍ (*kindly*). But I don't have any money because you haven't paid me. 225

ESTELA. Miren,° the Glitz company has promised to pay me for the last two weeks and this week if we get the order in by Friday.

ANA. How much of the order is left?

ESTELA. About 100 dresses.

PANCHA. N'ombre. By this Friday? What do they think we are? 230
Machines?

ESTELA. But they're not that difficult! Amá, you're so fast. This would be a cinch for you. All you have to do are the blusas° on the dresses. Rosalí, the over-lock work is simple. It's a lot, but you're the best at it. And, Pancha, all you have to do is sew the skirts. The skirts are the 235 easiest to sew. Now, Ana, with you doing all the ironing, we'll get it done by Friday. You see if we do little by little at what we do best . . . ¡Andenle!° We can do it. ¿Verá que sí,° Ana?

ANA (*uncertain*). Sure we can.

ESTELA. ¿Verá que sí, Amá? 240

CARMEN. Pos° we can try.

ROSALÍ. Estela, we can do it. (ESTELA *looks to Pancha. PANCHA remains quiet. CARMEN breaks their stare.*)

CARMEN. Wouldn't it be funny if the migra came and instead of taking the employees like they usually do, they take the patrona.° (*The* 245 WOMEN *laugh at the thought.*)

ESTELA. Don't laugh! It could happen. (*The* WOMEN *become silent.*)

CARMEN. Ayy, Estela, I'm just kidding. I'm just trying to make you feel better. (*Beat.*)

ROSALÍ. Bueno, let's try to be serious . . . I'll do the zippers. 250

ESTELA. Yes, por favor.° And, Pancha, please do the hems on the skirts.

PANCHA. The machine is not working.

ESTELA. Not again! (ESTELA *goes to the machine. She fusses around with it trying to make it work. With confidence.*) There. It should be

---

¡ya ni la friegas!: You blew it!   **Miren:** Look.   **blusas:** Blouses.   **¡Andenle!:** Come on!   **¿Verá que sí?:** Isn't it true?   **Pos:** Well.   **patrona:** Boss. **por favor:** Please.

ready. Try it. (PANCHA *sits down on a chair and tries the machine.*   255
She steps on the pedal and the machine makes an awful noise. Then it
shoots off electric sparks and explodes. PANCHA *quickly gets away*
from the machine. The WOMEN *hide under the machines.*)

WOMEN. ¡Ay, ay, ay!

ESTELA. Augghh! All this equipment is junk! (ESTELA *throws a thread*   260
spool at the machine and it explodes again.) I was so stupid to buy this
factory! (ESTELA *fights the urge to cry in frustration. The* WOMEN
stare at her helplessly.)

CARMEN. Pos no nos queda otra.° Pancha, can you do the hems by hand?

PANCHA. Bueno, I guess I have to.   265

ESTELA. Gracias . . . Ana, turn on the iron, I'm going to need you to do
the ironing all this week . . . Tell me when the iron gets hot and I'll
show you what you have to do.

CARMEN. I'll help Rosalí with the zippers.

ESTELA. No . . . I need you to do the blusas on size 7/8.   270

CARMEN. Didn't I already do them?

ESTELA. No.

CARMEN. I guess it was size 13/14 then.

ESTELA. You couldn't have, because there is no size 13/14 for this dress
style, Amá.   275

CARMEN. No? . . . Oye° did you get any more pink thread from the Glitz?

ESTELA. Oh, no. I forgot . . . Go ahead and use the over-lock machine.
That is already set up with thread.

ANA. What does the over-lock do?

ROSALÍ. It's what keeps the material from coming apart. (ROSALÍ   280
shows ANA.)

CARMEN. Why don't you give me the pink thread from the over-lock
machine, then when you get the thread you can set it up again?

ESTELA. No. I don't know how to set it up on that new machine.

CARMEN. Rosalí can do that later. She knows how to do it; qué no, Rosalí?   285

ROSALÍ. Sí, Doña Carmen.

ESTELA. Why don't you just do what I'm asking you to do?

CARMEN. Estela, no seas terca.° I know what I'm telling you.

ESTELA. So do I. I want to do things differently. I want us to work like
an assembly line.   290

CARMEN. Leave that to the big factories. I've been working long enough
to know—

ESTELA. I haven't been working long enough, but I'm intelligent
enough to—

Pos no nos queda otra: Well we have no choice.   **Oye:** Listen.   **no seas terca:**
Don't be stubborn.

CARMEN. Estela, my way is better!   295
ESTELA. Why do you think your way is better? All my life your way has
   been better. Maybe that's why my life is so screwed up!
CARMEN. ¡Desgraciada!° I'm only doing it to help you!
ESTELA. Because you know I won't be getting married any time soon so
   you want to make sure I'm doing something productive with my life   300
   so I can support myself. I don't need your help! (*Beat.*)
CARMEN. Where did all that come from? I thought we were arguing
   about the thread.
ESTELA. You know what I mean. You know I'm right!
CARMEN. All right. If you want me to do the over-lock work I'll do it . . . I   305
   have to remember I work for you now.
ESTELA. Amá, don't give me that!
CARMEN. What?
ESTELA. Guilt!
CARMEN. Well, it's true! It's not usual that a mother works for her   310
   daughter. So I have to stop being your mother and just be a regular
   employee that you can boss around and tell what to do.
ESTELA. ¡Ayy, Amá, párele!° You are my mother, but sometimes you get
   out of line. How can I tell Rosalí and Pancha to stop gossiping when
   it's you who initiates the chisme? You're a bad example!   315
CARMEN. Ay, sí. Blame me! ¡Échame la culpa!° You gossip too when it's
   convenient.
ESTELA. Look, Amá, I don't want to argue with you anymore. I'm frustrated enough by the thought that I might get deported, at the sight
   of that machine, and at the thought that I am the biggest fool for   320
   buying all this junk. So I don't need my mother to make my life any
   worse! (*Beat.*)
CARMEN. So what are we going to do about the thread?
ESTELA. ¡Oiiiii! And we're back to the same thing! (*She goes to the over-
   lock machine and angrily tears a thread spool from the machine and*   325
   throws it at CARMEN.) Here! ¡Tenga!° (*The thread spool misses*
   CARMEN *by a hair.*)
CARMEN (*dramatically*). ¡Pégame, pégame!° Go ahead! Hit me! God's
   gonna punish you for enojona!°
ANA. Estela, the iron is ready.
ESTELA. Amá, give me a finished dress from the box.
CARMEN. Where are they?
ESTELA. Right next to you by the pile.
CARMEN. Qué size?

¡**Desgraciada!:** Ungrateful!   **párele:** Stop it.   ¡**Échame la culpa!:** Blame me!
¡**Tenga!:** Take it!   ¡**Pégame!:** Hit me!   **enojona:** Grouch.

ESTELA. For the mannequin.   335

CARMEN. What size is it?

ROSALÍ. It's a size seven, Doña Carmen.

CARMEN (*sarcastically*). Thank you, Rosalí. (CARMEN *digs into the box and gets a dress. She gives it to* ESTELA *who begins to iron the dress carefully.*)   340

ESTELA (*to* ANA). Pay close attention to how I'm ironing this dress. Always, always use the steam. And don't burn the tul, por favor. On the skirt just a couple of strokes to make it look decent. It's real easy, just don't burn the tul, okay?

ANA. Okay.   345

ESTELA. Check the water, and when it gets low . . . Tell me so I can send you to buy some more water for it.

ANA. Why do you have to buy the water?

ESTELA. Because regular water is too dirty, it needs distilled water for clean steam. (ESTELA *finishes ironing the dress. She shakes it a bit*   350 *then puts it on the mannequin. All the* WOMEN *stare at the dress.*)

ROSALÍ. Que bonito.° How I would like to wear a dress like that.

PANCHA. But first you have to turn into a stick to wear something like that.

ROSALÍ. Yeah, but they're worth it.   355

ANA. How much do they pay us for making these dresses?

ROSALÍ. Estela, we get thirteen dollars for these, no?

ANA. Oh, yeah? How much do they sell them for at the stores?

ESTELA. They tell me they sell them at Bloomingdale's for about two hundred dollars.   360

WOMEN. ¡¡¿Qué?!!

ANA. Dang!! (*Lights fade.*)

Reading

1. What is Ana's attitude toward her job at the beginning of the play?

2. What problem does Estela face?

Thinking Critically

1. How would you describe Ana's character? Where do you think her expectations about the factory come from?

2. Why do you think López makes her cast of characters "plump," "large," or "huge"?

Que bonito: How pretty.

Connecting

1. Like López, Dagoberto Gilb, in his story "Maria de Covina" (p. 316), writes about a young working person. Do the protagonists of "Maria de Covina" and *Real Women Have Curves* have similar attitudes toward work or toward their coworkers? What differences are there between the two characters?

Writing

1. In *Real Women Have Curves*, López often toys with readers' expectations about the characters. Using examples from the play, write an essay about how López uses surprise, subverting expectations about Mexican Americans, about women, and about work.

Creating

1. **Write a scene or the first act of your own play.** López fashioned a play out of her experiences in what might seem to others to be a boring job. Write a scene (or the first act of a longer play) based on your own work experience. Describe the characters and include any necessary stage directions. Pay attention to the dialogue you write: it should be interesting, stay true to the characters' voices and personalities, and also move the story along.

45

LALO ALCARAZ [b. 1964]

From *La Cucaracha* [2004]

GENRE: EDITORIAL CARTOONS

Lalo Alcaraz occupies a unique position among writers as a successful editorial cartoonist. He was born and raised in San Diego, growing into a politically oriented artist while earning a bachelor's degree in art and environmental design from San Diego State University and then a master's degree in architecture from the University of California, Berkeley. While in college, he began making political cartoons, and he cofounded a humor magazine called Pocho. *After finishing and realizing he had little desire to go into*

the architecture profession, he began drawing a weekly cartoon
for LA Weekly. The subjects of the cartoon are widely varied,
though Alcaraz often tackles specific political issues; he did so in
1994 when he used the cartoon to fight California's Proposition
187, which would deny access to state resources by undocumented
immigrants. Through his work against Proposition 187, Alcaraz
also helped pull Gustavo Arellano (p. 474) into politics. Alcaraz
aims not only for political reform but also for bringing the diverse
Latino community together. "People used my images in marches
and demonstrations," Alcaraz has said. "They were a sounding
board for the Latino community. They were redefining the way the
community viewed involvement in political issues. They were
chartering a movement."* With the popularity of his strip La Cucaracha came syndication, leading to publication in hundreds of
newspapers and magazines nationwide. In 2000, he collaborated
with Ilan Stavans on the book Latino USA: A Cartoon History,
and his cartoons have been collected and published in the 2004
volumes La Cucaracha and Migra Mouse: Political Cartoons on
Immigration.

   In the twenty cartoons included here, we meet Eddie, along with
his politically minded girlfriend Veronica, and the young, apathetic Neto. But the star of La Cucaracha is undeniably Cuco
Rocha, a "human-sized anthropomorphic cucaracha" who is a
reliable—and sometimes tiresome—exponent of the radicalism
of the Chicano Movement. Alcaraz uses these characters not only
to tackle specific political issues, but also to poke fun at the blun-
dering efforts of politicians and advertisers to embrace Latino culture. He also directs a great deal of his humor toward the Chicano
community itself.

As you read the cartoons, think about the cultural roots of
the imagery and ideas in La Cucaracha. How can humor bring
people together?

---

*From Hispanic Outlook on Higher Education, available at mediabistro.com/
portfolios/samples_files/8nNHH7KxwLBtuPKiolPLV6Oip.doc.

So What's Our Story?

Lalo Alcaraz. Cartoons from *La Cucaracha*, by Lalo Alcaraz, © 2002 and © 2003 Lalo Alcaraz. Distributed by UNIVERSAL UCLICK. Reprinted with permission. All rights reserved.

Alter Ego

Slackers

English Only

Take Me to Your Leader

Taco Mart

Barriobucks Coffee and Check Cashing

Detractors

Meanwhile, in Iraq...

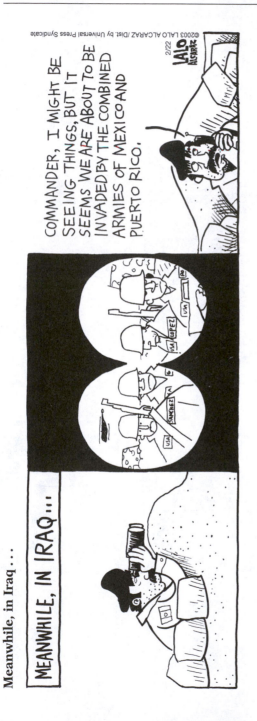

Aztec Calendar

Cinco de Mayo

Style

César Chávez Holiday

What Are You Anyway?!

Testing Time!

Not Here

Minority Student Programs

Jalapeños

Trusty Sidekick

Reading

1. ("So What's Our Story?") According to this comic, what is magical realism?

2. ("Detractors") What does Cuco Rocha think of President George W. Bush?

3. ("Meanwhile, in Iraq . . .") What does the Iraqi soldier see through his binoculars?

4. ("Toma Cerveza") According to the comic, what changes have been brought about by the "Latino marketing boom"?

5. ("César Chávez Holiday") According to this comic, when might there be a César Chávez national holiday?

6. ("What Are You Anyway?!") How does Cuco Rocha prefer to be identified?

Thinking Critically

1. What seem to be the political views of Veronica and Cuco Rocha?

2. Who are some of the people or ideas that are criticized in these cartoons?

3. How would you describe the artistic style of *La Cucaracha*?

4. How does Alcaraz challenge typical ideas about Mexican American life? About the United States?

Connecting

1. Like Alcaraz, Gustavo Arellano in his column "¡Ask a Mexican!" (p. 474) sometimes makes Mexican Americans the butt of his jokes. What do you think is the purpose of such jokes? Do you think different groups of people might have different responses to them?

Writing

1. The notorious difficulty of analyzing humor hasn't stopped people from trying. Write a brief essay about what you think makes *La Cucaracha* funny (or why you think it is not funny). Point to specific images and words in the cartoons to support your argument.

Creating

1. **Create a political cartoon.** Try your hand at drawing a political cartoon on the model of *La Cucaracha*. You can use the characters from *La Cucaracha* or invent your own if you prefer.

46

MICHELE SERROS [1966–2015]

Role Model Rule Number 1: Never Give Up an Opportunity to Eat for Free

From How to Be a Chicana Role Model [2000]

GENRE: ESSAY

As a poet, humorist, and social commentator, Michele Serros modeled how to be a Chicana while being fully conversant with American popular culture—shown, for example, by her collaborations with Flea, the bass player of the Red Hot Chili Peppers, and Billy Corgan, the leader of the Smashing Pumpkins. Serros is originally from El Rio, outside Oxnard, California. She went to Ventura College and Santa Monica City College before graduating from the University of California, Los Angeles, with a degree in Chicana/o studies, which gave her a sense of a strong tradition of art, literature, and politics. It also made her aware, however, of the distance between that tradition and her own life as a fourth-generation Californian, leading to some of the questions behind her first book, Chicana Falsa and Other Stories of Death, Identity, and Oxnard, *originally published by a small press while Serros was in college. The success of* Chicana Falsa, *which was later re-issued by a major commercial publisher, led to Serros joining the alternative music tour Lollapalooza in 1994 as a "road poet," and later to a job writing for the sitcom* The George Lopez Show. How to Be a Chicana Role Model, *a humorous book of advice based on her experiences becoming a writer, was published in 2000, and her first young adult novel,* Honey Blonde Chica, *appeared in 2006. Tragically, Michele Serros's career was cut short by cancer, and she passed away in 2015.*

Presented here is the first chapter of How to Be a Chicana Role Model, *in which Serros recounts some of her first experiences as a poet, which turn out to overlap with some of her last experiences in food service. Serros is able to find the humor in these incidents and she keeps her tone very light, but she also reminds her readers that questions about ethnic identity can enter into literary life in unexpected ways.*

As you read this excerpt from *How to Be a Chicana Role Model*, pay attention to the way that Serros cleverly mixes humor and social commentary.

I kept the poems in a Pee-Chee folder. Three poems written on college rule paper 'cause that way they looked longer. One of them I wrote in math lab, the other in the quad during my lunch hour and the third one I wrote when Paul R. broke up with me and I had nothing else to do that Friday night. Okay, so I wasn't no Jewel and my parents worked too hard to keep me from living in any ol' van, but I was pretty proud of the poems. I read them during open mike at every little bookstore and in any little coffeehouse around town and Mari and Angela were always in the audience and *they* said they were good poems. But I often wondered, did anyone else get anything out of them?

So naturally, I was excited when I got the phone call. The woman on the other end was from my college and said she got my number from a classmate. She said she was organizing a writers' conference, a Chicana writers' conference. She emphasized *Chicana*.

"We're having writers," she told me. "*Chicana* writers fly in from all over the Southwest, it'll be two days of readings, workshops, and lectures, here on campus. Can I count on your participation?"

Did she even have to ask?

Mari and Angela were happy for me, but surprised.   5

"How is it she called you?" Mari questioned. "I mean, don't take it wrong or anything and I like your poems and everything, but how did this organizer of this big ol' writers' conference connect with your work?"

"It's a *Chicana* writers' conference," I gloated. "And I guess good word gets around."

The conference was over a month away but already I was practicing. I read my poems in front of the hallway mirror. I typed them up on flat white paper and put them in a new Pee-Chee folder, one that had no scribble on it. I found a cute tank top at ClothesTime to match my lime-green skirt. I thought about shaving my legs above my knees.

A week before the event I get a call from the woman.

"I know this is last minute," she said. "But it looks like we'd like you   10 both days. Are you available?"

"Oh, of course," I assured her. Dang, three little poems and already I was in demand!

"Great," I heard her exhale, and shuffle papers. "So . . ." She spoke slowly as if she was writing while she talked. "We have Michele . . . available . . . both Saturday and Sunday . . . to serve brunch."

What? Did I hear right? Brunch? To serve food? My heart dropped.

"Oh . . ." I started. "I thought, I thought you wanted me to read, to share my poems."

"Oh, no." The woman chuckled uncomfortably, "We've had our writ-   15
ers, our *Chicana* writers, selected for months." Then her tone suddenly changed. "I'm sorry about any confusion. I thought I was clear when I first called you. I guess, I guess I'm so overwhelmed by the conference and all. Wait, let me see . . ." I could hear her shuffle more papers. "You know on Sunday, we're having an open mike. Are you familiar with those? You're more than welcome to share your poems then."

When people say, "You're more than welcome to . . ." what they really mean is "Look, not only was your name not on our original list, but we never even really thought of you. But to alleviate this feeling of guilt, the guilt for not thinking of you in the first place, we'll throw this last-minute invite your way." There's nothing more offensive than being told, "You're more than welcome to . . ." The whole gesture is really a slap in the face. So I'm sure the woman was surprised by my response.

"Sure," I told her. "I'll be there. Both days. Oh, one last question. Do I have to bring my own hair net?"

That night I complained to Angela.

"Quit being such a big baby," she said as she put up a new cleaning schedule on the fridge. "At least you'll get to eat for free and then later you can read your poems. I mean, there'll be more people at this confer-ence than at any of those ol' fake coffeehouse readings you do. So — what kind of food you think they'll have?"

On Saturday morning a week later I found myself at the conference,   20
donning a regulation name badge, meeting and greeting dozens of Chi-cana writers, essayists, and poets from all over the Southwest, and pos-ing the imperative question.

"Scone or croissant?"

"What, you don't have any pan dulce?°" A woman in a shoulder scarf looked over the pastry platter.

"No, all the kitchen help polished them off this morning with their champurrado,°" I answered. "I'm afraid you're stuck with either a scone or a croissant."

"Well . . . I'll take a croissant."

The woman behind her then asked me something in Spanish.   25

I answered her back and continued to scoop fruit salad onto her paper plate. She didn't move forward but instead looked at her friend in the

---

pan dulce: Mexican sweet pastries.   **champurrado:** Thick, sweet chocolate drink.

shoulder scarf, rolled her eyes, and remarked in Spanish, "I thought this was a *Chicana* writers' conference and this one here can't even speak Spanish!"

I looked up at her. What was *that* about? What had I said wrong? Did I use "muy" instead of "mucho"?° *R*s not rolled out long enough? Oooh, I can get so sloppy with those. Should I have asked her? A Chicana help another Chicana with her Spanish? I don't think so.

I scooped more fruit salad onto her friend's plate and my face just burned. First I was this so-called writer trying to push my poems on supposedly other fellow writers and now I was this wannabe Chicana trying to horn in on a conference, their conference. I wasn't even worthy of serving Cinnamon Crispas.*

I complained to Angela again. We were in my room watching TV that same evening.

"I'm not going back," I told her. "I ain't gonna spend my Sunday morn- 30 ing dishing out mango crepes to uppity Mexicans."

"I thought they were *Chicana*."

"Whatever."

"So you're not gonna go," she said as a statement rather than a question. "And now you're not gonna read your poems at open mike? Man, you're sure giving this woman who dissed your Spanish a lot of power."

"I ain't giving her no power." I changed the channel. "What do you mean, *power?*"

"I mean, you were so psyched about this conference and even though you 35 were just gonna serve food, you were all looking forward to meeting all these writers, your fellow *Chicana* writers and you were gonna read your poems and now, because of this woman, you're not gonna do any of it."

"But, Angela, she totally cut me down, in front of her friend. In front of other people. I don't have to take her shit."

"You know," Angela said, "why don't you write a poem or something about how you Mexicans treat other Mexicans who don't speak Spanish?"

"But I *can* speak Spanish!" I reminded her. "And I don't make fun of other people's Spanish."

"Yeah right." She changed the channel. "So anyway, how 'bout write something about Mexicans who don't speak Spanish *well*. That's something you can write about. Besides, I'm getting tired of those three old poems of yours."

muy / mucho: Very / much or many.

*Crispy flour tortilla triangles topped with sugar and cinnamon. Some people call them buñelos, but my family (and Taco Bell) tagged them Cinnamon Crispas. [Author's note]

"Nah, I don't even care," I told her. "I'm not gonna waste my Saturday   40
night worrying about that woman or this whole Woman of the Corn *Nuts*
Conference. I'm just gonna relax."

I grabbed the remote and changed the channel back. "And what do you
mean, you're tired of my three old poems?"

After Angela left my room, I worked on a new poem. A poem 'bout how
Latinos treat other Latinos who don't speak Spanish well.

> *My skin is brown,*
> *just like theirs,*
> *but now I'm unworthy of the color*
> *'cause I don't speak Spanish*
> *the way I should.*

Great idea huh? The next morning I gathered my three "old" poems
and my brand spankin' new one and stuck them in the new Pee-Chee. I
was armed. I was ready.

The open mike was held in the college's multipurpose room. I could see
the woman, in the fourth row, two aisles ahead of me. She was going
through her purse and checking her airline tickets. Man, all I could think
was that she'd better pay attention when it was my turn to read.

Thirty minutes later my name was read from the sign-up sheet and I   45
walked to the stage. From the podium I could see her more clearly. I quickly
read my three poems, saving the new one for last. Then I saw the woman
laughing with that friend of hers. Oh, she must've just heard someone
speaking Spanish and caught a grammatical error, *grammaticas wrongos*. I
cleared my throat and started reading my new poem. I looked up from my
paper and saw that she was going through her day planner with her friend.
She was checking off dates and her friend was comparing them against her
own pocket calendar. They weren't even paying attention to me! I raised my
voice and directed my voice toward her. My fingers clenched the sides of
the podium and I was balancing all my weight on the tip of my toes. She
still wasn't paying attention. I found myself not taking the time to exhale,
not swallowing my saliva, things I learned in Mr. Bower's speech class that
were very important to do when speaking in public. But all I could think
about was getting the words out, reaching this witch of a woman and
demanding she learn a lesson from me. But unfortunately, it looked hopeless. I read the last lines of my new poem and thirty short seconds later, I
was done. The woman was now offering her friend a mint.

I walked away from the podium feeling so defeated, the last thing
I wanted was idle chitchat from anyone. But then this man, in a tie

and glasses, approached me. He looked the boring business type, the kind to pull out standard business cards straight out of Kinko's from his wallet.

"Well, that was different." He clapped his hands together. "Boy, you sure have a lot of anger in your work!"

"Oh, yeah . . . thanks." Was that supposed to be a compliment? Why was I even thanking him? My poems, angry? He obviously knew nothing about poetry.

My eyes stayed on the woman as the man yakked on. She was now getting up from her seat. I needed an excuse to confront her, something direct. Obviously, my poem hadn't worked. If only I could've gotten rid of the man, but he just kept talking and talking. Men, they can be so chitchatty.

"You know, a lot of writers don't use Spanish like you do."   50

Oh great. Here we go again. And now my first critic was getting away.

"Are you working on a manuscript?"

"A what?" I wasn't really paying attention. I looked over his shoulder. The woman was leaving through a side door.

"A manuscript?" he asked again. "Do you have one?"

"No, not at all," I answered curtly. Was he making fun of me?   55

"Well, I'm a publisher." He pulled a card out from his wallet. "I have a press, it's a small one, but if you don't have a manuscript . . ."

"Oh." I took his card. It was stiff, beige, and basic with only his name and the word "Publisher" printed underneath in black block letters. I thought of my three, I mean, four poems. I thought of how I didn't even have a computer and how I used the typewriter at school to type them up. I thought about this man, a publisher, who was interested in publishing poetry. My poetry. Did people still do that anymore? If I had a book, I could sell it after my readings at the coffeehouses, I could give it to my friends as a little gift. If I had a book then maybe next year I'd be invited to read poems, rather than be asked to serve food.

"Actually," I told him, "I do have a manuscript. I mean, I thought you meant *on* me. It's actually on floppy, at home." Floppy? That was the right term, right?

He looked over his shoulder to see what I had been looking at before. "Do you need to leave? Is someone waiting for you?" he asked.

I looked after the woman. I worried that I'd never be strong enough to   60 question someone's intent or actions, no matter how much they hurt me. Would I always think about what I *should've* said and then write about it later? How could I ever get my messages across in life?

"No," I told him as I saw the woman leave with her friend. I opened my Pee-Chee folder. "So, here are a few poems. What do you think?"

Reading

1. For what reason is Serros invited to the writers' conference?

2. What is Serros's attitude toward the woman who orders a croissant from her?

Thinking Critically

1. Why does the woman who calls Serros on the telephone keep emphasizing the word *Chicana*?

2. Do you think Serros was right to be angry after her first day at the conference?

Connecting

1. Compare Michele Serros's style to that of Ernesto Galarza in "The Barrio" (p. 121). In what ways are these autobiographical writers different? Are there some subjects you think would fit better with one writer's style over the other? Explain by drawing on the texts.

Writing

1. What do you think Serros's goal in writing this piece is? Is she offering a kind of lesson? In a brief essay, using examples from the text, explore what you think Serros aims to tell her readers. Be sure to discuss the title of the chapter, "Role Model Rule Number 1: Never Give Up an Opportunity to Eat for Free."

Creating

1. **Create your own role model rules.** Michele Serros's *How to Be a Chicana Role Model* is structured as a list of rules. Make a list of rules that you think role models should follow.

47

LORRAINE LÓPEZ [b. 1956]

Soy la Avon Lady

From Soy la Avon Lady and Other Stories [2002]

GENRE: FICTION

Attention to the craft of writing and to the diversity of experience of Latinos in the United States characterizes the work of Lorraine López. She grew up moving from apartment to apartment in Los Angeles, staying in the city long enough to get her bachelor's degree from California State University, Northridge. After a few years teaching middle school, she moved east to earn master's and doctoral degrees from the University of Georgia before becoming a professor at Vanderbilt University in Nashville, Tennessee, where she still teaches. In 2002 her first book, the collection Soy la Avon Lady and Other Stories, *was published, and her first novel,* The Gifted Gabaldón Sisters, *was published in 2008. López edited the anthology* An Angle of Vision: Women Writers on Their Poor and Working-Class Roots *in 2009, and the following year she was a finalist for the PEN/Faulkner Prize for her book* Homicide Survivors Picnic and Other Stories. *Her second novel,* The Realm of Hungry Spirits, *was published in 2011. In her writing López has tried to battle against stereotypes about Chicanas and Latinas, saying, "One of the challenges that I face in my work is that I must honor the diversity within this cultural diversity. That is my challenge. If I write a work that validates assumptions, generalizations, or stereotypes, then what am I doing but endorsing lazy, unimaginative thinking? I have no desire to do that."**

The story "Soy la Avon Lady" ("I Am the Avon Lady") comes from López's first collection of stories. We read of a series of misfortunes that befall Molly, the story's narrator. The incidents each reveal something about Molly's character, even as they also reveal Molly's uncertainty about her identity.

*From David P. Wiseman and Lorraine López, "Latino Literature's Past and Future: A Conversation with Lorraine López," *Afro-Hispanic Review*, Vol. 28, No. 1 (Spring 2009), pp. 141–50.

As you read, pay close attention to the ways that the characters around Molly, the protagonist, react to her. Try to understand who they think she is, as well as who she thinks she is.

It's already dark by the time David drives me home. I was going to take the Greyhound, but my brother was coming from Barstow to L.A. anyway to get some supplies for the horse motel. Normally, I can't stand being in the same city with David, let alone the cab of the same pickup. He's one of these guys thinks there's only one way to look at a thing, and he's the only one can see it that way, so you may as well forget it because if you're not him, you won't never understand. My brother wasn't always like this. Was the horse motel made him an ass. Everyone knows he was just a sawed-off volunteer fireman and frycook at the Denny's on the business route before he married that widow, la Betty Crocker, and got her to convert her dead husband's ranch into a horse motel. Now he's Mr. David Martinez, businessman extraordinaire, though, no matter how often he showers and changes his clothes, he always smells a little like his horse motel. I talk to him about it. I even try to get him to take a little Avon for this problem.

As soon as I get in the truck I rolls down my window to let in some desert air and I says, "You know, David, we carry some very effective men's colognes."

"That's the problem with this country," he starts in, pointing out a primered Chevy loaded to the gills with Mexicans.

"Now, I know you like the Skin-So-Soft for fishing."

"Keeps the mosquitos off." He nods. "Look at that. Can't even god-damn signal. Learn to drive, *mojados*!°" he shouts out the window.   5

"Yeah, well, we have some real good aftershave and soap, too."

"Listen," he says to me, sighing. "You're what? Forty-eight? I know I got a couple years on you, and I'm hitting fifty. But a good fifty, a solid fifty. I got my business, and I got my health. But you, look at you. All that makeup. I know you're my sister an' you're a chick. I seen your twat when mama used to give us a bath together. But I have to be honest here, you're big enough to play for the 49ers. And you're running around like some overgrown campfire girl in drag for Godsake, selling cookies. Ain't no one uses Avon no more, except to keep mosquitos off. It's gutdamn irritating to hear you turn every conversation into a sales pitch. Whyn't you just settle down and stop bugging folks."

mojados: Wetbacks, a derogatory term for Mexican immigrants.

So that kind of puts me in a sour mood, even if it is coming from David, whose entire fortune and well-being comes from his settling down, marrying la Betty Crocker. Come to think of it, he's probably given me the best advice he knows. I only wish he could follow the second half of his own great advice because as soon as he made his little speech, he started in on the time Johnny Carson called him up at the horse motel.

"Now, I ain't sayin' I planned it thataway," says David, a grin cracking under his red beak of a nose. "Now, I'm not saying I arranged the call, but you gotta admit it was a pretty gutdamn strategic bit of public relations."

I just rolled my eyes, rubbing my fingers over the upsidedown "M"   10
scarred on my forehead. David calls it my "W." His way of seeing things. Anyone else'd tell you, despite all the Avon fill and foundation, the powder and whisper blush, what I got is an inverted "M" up there, for my name, for Molly. Like some kind of cockeyed monogram. I trace the path of weals through one eyebrow and up toward my hairline, rising in the middle like a reverse widow's peak. Then I stare out the window at the neon-haloed car dealerships, Kmarts, pizzerias, and dry cleaners blurring past along the highway. I have been back and forth between Barstow and L.A. at least a thousand times. There is no really scenic route, but you'd think that over time there would at least be a slightly less ugly way to go or that a person could get used to the boringness of it all.

The time Johnny Carson called David I happened to be watching the show. I was half-crocked from that wine you buy in a carton, I admit, but even I, stumbling in my negligee before the blue-gray haze of my black-and-white set, even I could see that old Johnny had just called my brother up to laugh at him. I have to jam a soup spoon between the wall and a critical place bulging out of the back of the set to get a good picture, and that night the spoon had popped out. So Johnny's smirking eyes boiled through a blizzard of static. Even so, those pebbly eyes clearly smirked, and I could even see Johnny bite back his lipless, lizard grin as he chatted on the phone with my brother.

"Johnny was pur-ty surprised to find out we have a horse motel in Barstow. Told him it was the only one in the state. Still is," David turned to nod at me in agreement with himself. "But, man, was he shocked about the elevator. 'State of the art' I says to him. 'State of the art.'"

Around that point in the famous conversation, I remember Johnny passing the phone to that big guy, the one who looks like a refrigerator wearing a suit and who laughs at everything Johnny says, that what's-his-name, on account of he, Johnny, that is, had to double over with spasms he made like he couldn't control.

"People need a horse motel, I 'splained to him," David goes on. "They's rodeos and horse shows and all kinds of reasons to take a horse somewhere overnight."

The thing is, though an idea like a horse motel sounds pure ridiculous   15
to someone like Johnny Carson, who has like a castle in Malibu and
makes jokes about how much alimony he has to shell out, and even to a
person like me, who sells Avon between temporary secretarial jobs,
plenty of people seem to truly feel the need for lodging their horses at my
brother's motel.

"You know how much business shot up after that show aired?" David
demands after he wound up the full retelling of his telephone conversation on the Tonight Show so many years ago.

I nod, closing my eyes and scrunching myself into a ball against the
car door, so David might think I'm drifting off to sleep.

"How much, then?" he persists.

"A lot," I'm yawning by now.

"Gutdamn straight."   20

We pass a batch of black-and-white cows alongside the highway, graz-
ing and staring without much curiosity at the passing cars.

"Hey, you remember when we first moved to Barstow? You were just a
little thing, black as a bullfrog. Yammered your ugly little head off in
Spanish. Scared those old folks in that diner. Remember? Musta thought
they was being invaded."

"You're nuts. I never spoke Spanish."

"Don't tell me you don't remember. You were at least four or five. Cou-
pla years later, I remember, we went back home for a visit on the train.
Was on the train. You were staring out the window and pointing a dark
little finger at a cow. You ast, 'Is thet a kay-ow?'" David does his best
Southern drawl, which is purely pathetic. "I'll never forget. You were still
as black as a bullfrog. An' I remember you had those floppy yellow shorts.
A bullfrog in a pair of yellow shorts."

I let David laugh, enjoy his little make-believe story. Pulling my jacket   25
over my shoulder, I let myself drift off. I must have slept the rest of the
ride into the city because the next thing I remember is David shaking my
shoulder and saying "end of the road." I thank him for the ride, and as
usual he doesn't wait for me to fish my key out of my handbag or find my
way to my apartment door before peeling off like some teenager playing
chicken at a stoplight. And I live in a pretty rotten building, to be honest.
If David was any kind of decent brother, he would have at least walked
me to my door.

I have to step over all the usual wadded-up disposable diapers, fast-
food wrappers and beer bottles, finally feeling my way along a mildewed
mattress propped against the wall near my door. There's a cluster of Mexicans in undershirts, jabbering at each other and drinking cans of beer
under the street lamp just across the way. Anyone might jump out with a
switchblade and rob me of my Avon case, which was all I had of any

value, as David, naturally, had forgotten to pay me for the bottles of Skin-So-Soft he ordered.

I make it to the door okay, but once inside I slam my hip on the tele-phone table, knocking the phone on the floor and scaring poor Fabian out of his little cat wits. "It's okay, Fabian, it's just me," I says in a calm voice because Fabian has pretty bad asthma, and stress can cause him to have an attack. I set my case on the floor and went to pet Fabian's thick gray fur. His breathing is already growing shallow and ragged. "Damn," I says, but quietly, and I drew him in my arms. He struggles and squeezes out of my grip, running around the house and hacking like he was trying to bring up a hair ball.

I pick the phone off the floor and dial real quick. The line rings twice, and then I hear a loud and gruff "Yah!"

"Uncle Enrique?"

"Yah!"   30

"It's me, Molly." Fabian, though heaving and retching, bounced from the couch to the coffee table like he's place-kicked by some unseen demon.

"He-e-e-ey, Mulligan! ¿Cómo estás?°" Like a lot of old guys, my uncle never quite trusts telephone wires to carry his voice over any kind of distance, so he has to holler his head off into the mouthpiece.

"Uncle Rique, it's an emergency! Can you come over and take me to the hospital right now?" I have to hold the phone at least a foot from my head and shout back.

"Of course, hita,° are you okay? Wanna ambulance?"

"NO! I just need a ride!"   35

"I'm coming right now!"

I don't mention it's Fabian that needs the hospital, and I know my uncle Enrique isn't the kind of uncle who presses too much for informa-tion, particularly personal information. He probably thinks I'm bleeding to death from a botched abortion, and if that's the case, he'd just as soon not know the particulars.

I catch up with Fabian in the bathroom where he's gagging over the plunger behind the toilet. I pull him out, wrap him in a bath towel and bring him to the kitchen, where I pour myself some handy carton chablis into a coffee cup. I stand there drinking the wine and cuddling Fabian while I wait the few minutes it takes my uncle to drive over. Fabian's plump body shudders as he gasps, struggling to breathe. This is the worst attack he has ever had, and I'm scared he's gonna die before Uncle Enrique gets here.

But still I could feel him fighting for air as I carried him to the door when I heard Uncle Enrique knocking. I'd turned on the outside light,

¿Cómo estás?: How are you?   hita: Daughter (short for mi'jita).

and Uncle blinks on the threshold. I can tell when he makes out the towel-wrapped bundle in my arms because he quickly shifts his eyes away. "It's Fabian, Uncle Rique, he's having an asthma attack!" I push out the screen door.

"Fabian?"   40

"My cat! He's gonna die if we don't hurry." Saying the words makes my voice crack, and the tears leap out of my eyes.

"A cat? Is that what you got there? A durn cat?"

"It's Fabian. You remember Fabian?"

"I remember the movie star." My uncle scratches his chin, making a raspy sound with his fingernails. "Singer, too, wasn't he?"

"C'mon, please, Uncle, hurry. Where did you park?"   45

"Just out in front," he says, leading the way past the mattress. "Can't take no cat to the hospital, though. 'S not allowed, is it?"

"The animal hospital, Uncle. It's just down Glendale Boulevard near the freeway exit. Please, we have to hurry."

When we get to the car, Uncle Enrique chuckles a little.

"What?" I says, pretty pissed. "What's so funny?"

"Nothing," he shakes his head as he unlocks the door. "Here, *hita*, get in.   50
You want me to hold that, that Fabian for you while you get the seatbelt?"

"I got it." It's tricky, but Fabian has gone even limper, and I'm able to set him on my knees while I click on the strap.

Uncle Enrique climbs in and starts the car, still laughing some. "I'm laughing at myself, *hita*. I'm laughing I got outa bed and got dressed like a fireman for a five-alarm fire to rush a cat to the hospital."

"What's funny about that?"

"C'mon, doncha cry, Mulligan. We're almost there." Uncle Enrique sighs, "I need to get myself re-married or something."

In the hospital, everything looks too bright. I feel like I should have my   55
sunglasses on. Why do they keep places so bright? When I have to squint, my scar turns so white and the skin raises so much it looks like it's ready to spring off my forehead and run around the room. I can tell it spooks the girl at the counter. She kind of jumps back a little when she sees me, and her green eyes get bigger. (Uncle Enrique has dropped me off while he hunts for a parking space. Even this late there's nowhere for him to park.) She seems to get over her surprise when she sees Fabian in my arms. "Yes?"

"My cat," I says, trying to hand her the bundle. "He has asthma, and he needs something. He had a bad attack." Since Fabian has gone limp in the car, I can't really tell if he's still breathing, and to be honest, I'm afraid to check.

"Have you been here before?"

"No, my usual vet is closed now. I just came here for the emergency hours."

"You'll have to fill out these forms, then." She hands me a clipboard.
"But Fabian needs to see the doctor now. This is an emergency," I says.   60
"My cat might die while I'm filling in these papers!"

Just then a nice-looking Middle Eastern—maybe even Lebanese—man
in a white coat steps into the waiting room from a door behind the counter.
"What is the matter here?" he asks in that choppy way foreigners have.

And I says that I think Fabian is going to die if he doesn't get help now
and that I don't have time to fill forms.

"I will look at the cat," he says, reaching over to take Fabian. "You can
fill out the paperwork while I examine your cat, Miss—"

"Martini," I says, smiling a little now and hoping there's no lipstick on   65
my teeth, "Molly Martini."

"Okay, Miss Martini, I will be back momentarily."

My heart flutters a little when he said "momentarily," and he puts his
dark eyes on mine. I feel sure he's Lebanese. My sister Gloria once dated
Lebanese twins, both butchers, and I'd hoped she'd marry one and throw
me the leftover. They were so darling in their matching bloodstained
aprons. But Gloria decided she would rather dump them both and have
a child out of wedlock with an anonymous Nordic type, who I never even
met, let alone got to ask if he had a brother. But Gloria's like that; she can
get anything. She was in the back seat when we had the accident. She
didn't go through the windshield like me and Barbara and Grandma.
And her skin is as white as the heart of a radish.

Uncle Enrique blinks his way into the glaring wait area, saying, "I had
to park clear at that filling station near the freeway." He sits beside me
and picks up a copy of *Cat Fancy* to thumb through. "Where's Fabian?"
he asks.

"The doctor's looking at him. You got a pen, Uncle?"

He leans over to reach into his side pocket and pulls out his key chain   70
with at least three million keys attached to it, a Swiss Army knife, a bottle
opener, a teensy sewing kit and a little bitty pen and pencil set. He hands
me a pen the size of a toothpick, saying, "Here you are, *hija*.°"

I take that itsy-tiny pen and start filling out the forms, while my uncle
chews on his tongue and reads an article in *Cat Fancy*.

After a while, Uncle scratches his head. "Gotta story here," he says,
"about a Siamese cat s'pose to beat up a grizzly bear to save the life of a
dog. You believe that?"

I shrug and write something unreadable under "Current Employer." I
didn't like to put Avon or "it varies" in case the doctor should look over
my form.

hija: Daughter (also, *hita, hija, mi'jita*).

"Says the cat jumped on the bear's head from a tree and scratched its eyes. Blinded him," Uncle continues. "I guess it could happen. But to save *a dog*?"

As I was signing the last sheet, the doctor appeared again. "Miss   75
Martini," he says, "I am so terribly sorry."

"Martini?" asks my uncle, looking around though we're the only ones in the waiting room.

"This is my uncle," I says, not wanting to hear the doctor say anything else.

"Yes, it's good to meet you. I have some bad news I am afraid. Your cat has died. Of course, there will be no charge. I could do nothing to help him."

I remember how my mother threw herself on Grandma's casket when they were ready to lower it in the ground, and afterwards the aunts really criticized her for that because my mother is kind of an underachiever emotionally, so when she makes a display it's usually for show. Back then at the funeral, even I, in my turban of bandages which was coming unraveled and the gauze was falling in my face, even I could see my mother was making a show, and I felt so embarrassed I wished I could shrink up like a pine nut and roll into the earth right besides Grandma. But in the animal emergency hospital that night, I thought of my mother when I fell into that doctor's strong Lebanese arms, and I realized the truth about my mother's scene at the graveside: it was only part show.

"Miss Martini, please, please," says the doctor, patting my shoulder   80
with one hand, but pushing me upright with the other.

"Name's not Martini," scoffs my uncle. He's often impatient with foreigners. "It's Mar*tinez*."

I have Uncle Enrique drop me at the VFW club. I'm way too depressed to go home and put up Fabian's little rolling toys, his catnip mouse and wash out his double-sided dish.

"Are you sure, *m'hija*?° It's pretty late."

"Yeah, I'm sure," I says, remembering I had no money. "How 'bout you come and have a drink with me?"

"No, no, no way," he says. "I gotta go to court tomorrow. Remember   85
my friend Kiko? He gotta ticket. I said I would drive him."

"Isn't Kiko the one who rides a bicycle?" I says, recalling a fat guy in a Dodger cap, teetering on a Schwinn. "He doesn't even have a car. How'd he get a ticket?"

"Riding under the influence."

m'hija: My daughter, used affectionately.

"Oh . . . You could still have one drink with me," I says.

"Oh, no. I better not." Uncle Enrique pulls along the curb in front of the VFW and leans again to reach in his back pocket. "You need some money, *hija*. I got a little extra." He hands me a twenty-dollar bill. "I'm real sorry about the cat, that Fabian," he says as I get out. "You take care of yourself, okay, Mulligan?"

"Hey, it's Molly! Molly Martini! We thought you was still in Barstow!" My   90 best friend Charlene waddles over and climbs a barstool near the door to wrap her fat, freckled little arms around my neck.

"Hi, Shorty," I says, smiling a little, but sadly, so Charlene will know right off that I'm feeling down. I call her "Shorty" because she's a dwarf, a "little people," that's what she likes to be called, anyway, and not a dwarf or a midget. She's not just one of these shorter folks that everyone exaggerates about when they call her a dwarf. She really is under three feet tall. Her mother was a dwarf, an actress who had a part in the *Wizard of Oz*, and her father was a dwarf too, but I'm not sure what he does for a living. We met one time at a funeral for another dwarf we both happened to know and got to be friends at the bar afterwards.

"What's wrong, Miss Martini?" Charlene squeaks, seeing my sad smile.

"I lost my Fabian tonight," I says, starting to sob even before Willie, the bartender, can slide me my drink.

Well, you know, I cry a lot that night, and I have to say I drink a bit, too. I go through that twenty pretty fast, even though some people buy me drinks. Turns out it's our friend Fisher Boy's birthday, and his wife Millie, an ex-school photographer from Visalia, has a cake for him and a half a case of champagne. So you know I drink my share of that, and I eat a wedge of cake the size of Charlene's ox-blood prayerbook. I know they're the same size on accounta Charlene sets her prayerbook on the pool table alongside of my paper plate.

Fisher Boy has his own bottle of champagne, and he sits at the bar   95 nursing on it like a baby. Has a bunch of friends with him, some guys I don't recognize. But old Fisher Boy won't talk to anyone 'til he's finished his drink. This heavy guy—bald on top, but with long hair, wearing a leather vest and no shirt underneath—lumbers up on the stage over past the shuffleboard table, his bootheels blasting like gunshots. He grabs the microphone, which wails in my ear painfully. Then he taps it some, causing a couple of thunder rolls. "I jes' wanna say," he mutters into the netted bulb of the mike, "we all of us here—all us veterans and friends of veterans in this club—come together to honor one of our own on his birthday. Now, don't matter if you fought in double-ewe, double-ewe one, two or three—"

I shoot a look at Charlene. I'm never good with numbers, but I'm pretty sure we'd only gotten to two with the wars. Charlene had her stubby index and middle fingers out, counting under her breath.

"Korea or Nam. Was in Nam myself, and I ain't proud of what I done. I raped. I pillaged. I even helped burn down some villages. And, in general, I ain't proud of those things, but I am proud to be a veteran of a foreign war and proud to be a member of this club and mostly proud to be a friend to this man we honor tonight on his birthday. Getcher ass up here, Fisher Boy! Willie, somebody, help him up the steps."

Fisher Boy steps up two of the stairs without help, then falls to his knees and crawls up the remaining two and over to the microphone. The rapist and pillager lifts Fisher Boy to his feet and pushes him toward the microphone stand, which Fisher Boy clings to as if it's a masthead on a ship tossed around in a storm.

"Hallo, everybody! I'm Fisher Boy, an' I'm a drunk!"

Everyone laughs, and some folks hoot back, "Hello, Fisher Boy!" It's   100
like a reverse Alcoholics Anonymous meeting. Pretty funny, really, if you consider the circumstances.

"What I want to say is, first of all, I wanna thank my good friend, Lyle, for the innerduction—"

"Lowell," hisses the rapist and pillager.

"Huh?"

"Lowell. My name's Lowell."

"Oh, yeah, right. Well, anyway, thanks a lot. An' I wanna thank every-   105
one for coming tonight, though you were probably coming here anyway and just found out it was my birthday a few minutes ago. What I got to say is, I'm seventy-eight years old, an' I'm a veteran a' World War Two. I don't think we got to Three yet, Lyle, but I ain't been payin' too much 'tention. I was a clerk typist in the army, an' I din't get any opportunities to rape an' pillage too much, but I wisht they had invented white-out then because I ruint a whole lot of forms. Man, you shoulda heard the guys cuss when I screwed up their passes. Holy Moly! Anyway, point is, we're all here, and it's my birthday. So have some cake and have a drink!"

Fisher Boy hoists his champagne bottle and pours the dregs down his chin, darkening the front of the new t-shirt his wife has given him. The front of it says, HERE COMES FISHER BOY! and the back reads, THERE GOES FISHER BOY! I think it's pretty clever, almost as funny as the baseball cap someone else has given him with a fake ponytail attached to the back.

We all clap and sing "Happy Birthday," then "For He's a Jolly Good Fellow" and clap some more. While I'm beating my hands together for old Fisher Boy, Charlene dug a sharp little elbow in my rib cage. "Guess who just come in?" she hisses.

"Who?" I says, looking around.

"Suzy Q."

"Oh, no." Now, if I feel sad about losing Fabian, I feel almost worse 110
when Charlene tells me my baby sister had just come into the VFW. Suzy
Q is good or bad, hot or cold, dark or . . . only dark, actually. But, you get
the picture. She's never in-between on anything, not ever.

When Suzy Q is good, she's at home, taking care of those three little
half-Japanese children of hers, making a super-tasty supper for her husband Dean, and keeping that house so clean you could conduct major
surgery on her bathroom floor, behind the toilet, even. But when Suzy Q
is bad, Lord, you sometimes have to scrape her off a gutter and throw her
in the drunk tank at county for at least a week, if you can find her. Last
time she was bad was around Christmas. She went missing for a week,
and poor Dean had to hire a private investigator to find her in some by-
the-hour hotel room with a skinhead junkie from Altoona, who was,
Dean says, not sorry at all to cut her loose.

"Where is she?" I ask Charlene.

"Over to the back. That tall booth she likes."

"I guess I oughta go and talk to her," I says, real slowly, so's Charlene
can interrupt and argue me out of it.

But she says, "I guess you oughta."   115

I make my way to the back of the bar, pulling off the party hat someone stuck on my head. You can't have a serious talk with someone like
Suzy Q wearing a polka dot cone spouting pink and green streamers over
your hair.

Suzy Q favors a booth near the ladies room, one of the older ones that
hasn't been reupholstered with scotch guard like most of the others. The
VFW used to be a decent kind of bar at one time, with wood floors,
stained glass windows and real near-leather booths. But they covered the
wood with parquet and sold the stained glass and only a few near-leather
booths remain. People generally don't like to sit in them, though, because
they tend to make your buttocks and backs of your legs sweat, and then
you stick, so you make bathroom sounds as you peel yourself out of
your seat.

But I doubt if my sister sweats all that much. She reminds me of a long
cool glass of ice tea. Her clear copper skin chills your finger tips when
you brush against it. And you can almost hear the ice cubes rattle when
she walks. She even smells like a sprig of mint, a wedge of lemon. With
her long brown legs, her wide eyes and Cleopatra-flat black hair, my baby
sister could be a desirable woman if she wasn't so criminally insane
when she was bad.

"Hullo, Suzy," I says, thinking how lovely she looked in a peppermint-
striped shift—ice tea in a slender barber's cup.

"Amalia," she says, putting out her frosty fingers to delicately shake 120
mine. "How good to see you." Suzy has the habit of whispering in a
breathy way when she talks. You can barely hear her, and you can't help
but hear every word at the same time. She has the kind of voice that I
imagine would be just perfect for reading stories in the tabloids out loud.
Woman Gives Birth to Baby with Dog's Head, would sound just right coming out of her mouth.

"Where's Dean?" I ask, noting the near-finished gin and tonic near her
elbow. Poor Dean doesn't like Suzy Q to drink for all the obvious reasons.

"Dean?" Suzy Q repeats like it was a foreign word. "Dean? Dean?"

"Your husband, Dean Fujimori. Where is he? And the kids? How are
the kids?"

"Bartender!" she roared right in my ear.

"Golly, Suzy, you about took my hearing out."   125

"Another, please," she says with a smile when Willie appeared at
her elbow.

Willie nods, giving me a nervous look. "Um, are you sure?"

"Perfectly sure," whispers Suzy, pulling a roll of twenties out of her
handbag. "Just keep them coming, will you?"

Willie hesitates. "How long are you staying?"

"Not long," says Suzy. "Not very long at all."   130

"You aren't going to do the ladies room like last time, are you?"

"Don't be silly," Suzy laughs.

"'Cause they said they was gonna cancel my policy, that kind of thing
happens again."

"I'm not staying long, Willie. I promise. Just bring me another, please."

Willie retreats in an undecided way, like he didn't get to say all he had 135
to say, but he brought the drink in a few minutes anyway.

"So," says Suzy Q, staring at me from head to toe. "So, Amalia, how are
you these days? My, you've grown a bit."

"Thyroid," I says. "And my metabolism's changing."

"I see."

"Heard you had some trouble around Christmas," I says, taking a
chance.

"That!" she giggles. "That was not trouble. Nothing near trouble. I'll 140
tell you what trouble is. Trouble is that people don't even know what
trouble is and what trouble can do when it wants to, and that, my sister,
is real trouble."

"Well, Dean was pretty upset."

"Dean?"

"Maybe you want to go home, Suzy, after your drink. Maybe I'll go
with you. I haven't seen the kids for a long time."

"Listen, Amalia, do you remember when we were kids? Do you

remember that skinny little tree Dad tried to get to grow in the front of the house? I keep thinking about that tree."

"What about it?" I remembered my father brought home what looked 145 like a twig one day from the nursery and said we were going to have shade for the house in a couple of years. He propped that twig with a two-by-four, watered it, fertilized it and even built a short white wire fence around the base to keep dogs off. I can still see him, coming home from work in his rumpled overalls with his lunch box and heading straight for the hose to feed his tree.

"That tree never had a chance, Amalia, the way we treated it."

"What do you mean?"

"You don't remember how we bent it and pulled the leaves, dancing around it like it was the Maypole. You don't remember that?"

"Maybe a little. But we didn't kill the tree. A tree like that can't survive in the desert."

"You were the worst one, Amalia, hanging on that tree and singing at 150 the top of your lungs at anyone driving by. You remember that song you always sang."

"You're making this up, now." I was starting to get mad. Many of my conversations with my kid sister tend to go this way: she claims to remember something stupid or shameful I did when I was drunk or when I was a senseless kid, and I get all upset about it.

"I think it was from *West Side Story*," she persists, tapping her long red fingernails on the tabletop. "What was it? Oh, I know. It went like this, 'I wanna be Americana! I wanna be Americana!' You sang that all damn day long, every day one summer. Don't you remember? It was perfectly hideous! You would wear one of Mama's floppy skirts and pearls—I remember the pearls—and pin yellow yarn to your head to give yourself long blond hair. Then you'd scream 'I wanna be Americana!' at the top of your silly lungs at any car went by. God, I was six years younger than you, but I wanted to die from embarrassment. The whole neighborhood must have thought the natives were *very* restless that summer." Suzy laughs, lighting a cigarette.

"You know what. I do remember that summer. But it was you, Suzy Q, it was you sang that stupid song over and over and over and over and—"

"Don't be ridiculous." Suzy takes a huge swallow of her drink and a drag on her cigarette. "You were the one."

"Drop it, Suzy. Drop it, please." My eyes fill, blurring my long cool ice 155 tea sister with her cigarette and her drink.

She snaps her fingers. "What does Uncle Enrique call you? What is that little nickname he gave you?"

"Mulligan."

"Just what does that mean? Mulligan?"

"I really don't know."

"Oh, I know, doesn't it mean 'do over'? Like in golf, when you make 160 some horrid error. It's so bad, they call it a 'mulligan,' and you get the chance to try again."

"I'm not sure. I don't know golf."

"Good name," says Suzy, mashing out her cigarette.

"Suzy," I hear someone say. I glance up at Dean, standing by the booth and holding out his hand toward my sister. "Suzy, let's go home. I had to leave the kids alone to come here. Let's go home. It's late."

"How did you find me?" Suzy asks, half-rising from the booth, then sinking back down.

"Willie called me."   165

"You shit!" Suzy yells across the room. From where I sit, I can see Willie give a little shrug.

"Let's go home, Suzy. I'll make you a bath and light some candles. It will be so nice." Poor Dean keeps his hand out, so Suzy can grab it and steady herself to walk out. My brother-in-law is almost as large as a sumo wrestler, and I have no doubt he could have whipped Suzy out of the booth by her hair and tucked her—hissing and spitting like a cat—under one arm to carry out to the car. But Poor Dean favors a gentle approach with my sister—soft words, tender touches, candles and warm baths.

Suzy whispered some curse words, then she takes Poor Dean's hand and lifts herself noiselessly out of the booth. "I was ready to come home anyway," she says, looking at me. "It's so goddamn boring here."

Of course, I have to dance with the rapist and pillager after a few more drinks.

"I never danced with a raper and pillagist before," I admit as we hoof 170 to some tune about Lubbock, Texas.

"Jes' call me Lowell," he says, smiling, and I notice he is either handsome in an ugly way or ugly in a handsome way. He had two full moons that stuck out on his chin, looked just like a stubbly baby's bottom and squinty green eyes hummocked in gooseflesh pouches. It sounds bad here, but if you blurred your eyes you might look at Lowell and think of Robert Mitchum. A bald Robert Mitchum with shoulder-length locks of dirty blond hair. You have to use your imagination some.

After a few more dances and a lot more drinks, I guess Lowell isn't so bad for a rapist and pillager. In between the dances, I tell him about Fabian, and he says he feels bad for me. He says he's done some time, and he can really appreciate a gal like me, then he winks. He offers to give me a lift home. So I tell him where I live, and I say good-bye to everyone. Charlene grabbed my elbow hard with her sharp little fingers as I'm on my way out. "Miss Martini," she says, "Miss Martini, you be careful. 'Sa full moon," she says. "Take care of yourself." Then she looked at Lowell and raised her eyebrows, rubbing her turned-up nose.

Turns out Lowell had a motorcycle. And, boy, am I glad I'm drunk because you can't get me on one of those things sober, I tell you. Lowell starts out a gentleman and lets me mash my big old hair under his greasy helmet, which is real good of him. Then I climb on behind Lowell, and the thing farts off down the street. Now, I don't drive. I never have, and I never want to, so I don't pay much attention to directions. I don't think it's too strange when Lowell gets on one freeway, then another. But along about the third freeway it seems like a lot of time has passed, and I know I don't live that far from the VFW.

With the rushing wind and the sounds of traffic—yes, there's traffic even in the middle of the night—it would be pretty useless to holler: "I think you're going the wrong way!" or "Where the hell are you taking me?" And anyone who's ever ridden the back of a motorcycle on a freeway knows there isn't any way of getting off or making the driver stop. So I just clutch at Lowell's lardy sides and thank God Above I'm loaded, or I would have been plenty scared.

It's one of those oily nights, when even the leaves of the oleander 175 bushes along the freeway seem slick and slimy. A fish-smelling fog from San Pedro crawls over, clouds car windows and fuzzes the street lamps. Of course, I'm about dead blind anyway without my glasses. My mother is totally blind, and I expect I'll be there, too, one day. It runs in the family. But the fog muffling the moon and my eyes tearing up from the wind in my face makes it near impossible to see where I am. Just the sensation of moving downward, descending, makes me think we're headed toward the Valley.

I recognize the In-n-Out Burger at the off-ramp that leads to my cousin Elaine's house in Sylmar, where I always went for Thanksgiving and Christmas dinner. Awhile back, In-and-Out printed up a mess of bumper-stickers for advertising. Then some brilliant jokers had the idea to scratch out the "B" and "R" from "burger," and to this day you can spot all these cars with "IN-N-OUT-URGE" pasted all over their back bumpers. Real hilarious.

I'm glad Lowell's getting off the freeway. Maybe he can drop me at Elaine's. I try to give people the benefit, you know. Maybe he's confused by my directions or too drunk to figure them out. He takes us to a little park not too far from Elaine's house. One of those small grassy jobs with the sandlot swingset near a baseball diamond and bleachers.

"My cousin Elaine lives near here," I says, climbing off the bike, my legs still atremble from the vibration of the engine. "You wanna take me to her house?"

"Let's take a walk," says Lowell. Then he grabs hold of my hand, leading me under the bleachers.

"What is that horrible stench?" I says because suddenly I smell the 180 nastiest maggotty smell, like hundred-year-old banana skins layered with fertilizer, then soaked in soured milk.

Lowell just jerks a thumb at a nearby dumpster, and before I can say another word, he jumps all over me, and we both tumble in the dirt. Then he starts grunting and dryhumping my hip like a badly behaved hound. "Jesus," I says, "get off me, will you?"

His hands are all over me, squeezing my bra padding through my blouse, stroking my hips and reaching under my skirt. "Cuss me in Spanish," he moaned. "Cuss me in Spanish."

"What?" I says, pushing his hands away from my skirt.

"C'mon, baby. Cuss me in Spanish, bad boy," he says again.

"Will you get off me!" I holler. "I don't even speak Spanish! Get off 185 before I yell 'rape'!"

One renegade hand shoots up my slip, and he froze.

"I mean it," I says, "I'll scream 'rape'!"

"My, God. What is this?" he asks, sitting up. "You *are* a chick! I thought—"

"What did you think?"

"At the bar, I thought they said . . . You look . . ."   190

"What? Tell me?"

"No offense, but chicks ain't my thing."

"Just take me to my cousin's house, and we'll forget all about this," I says, smoothing my skirt, "or you can be looking at some pretty serious trouble."

Old Lowell doesn't say anything to that. He just stands up and brushes the dirt from his Levis and starts walking back to the bike. I get up, too, and follow after him, but it's hard to keep up because I'm wearing these lamé heels that kept sinking into the soft dirt, stalling me. "She just lives a few blocks from here. I can show you how to get there," I says. But I can tell by the hunch of his back and the blank look of the hairless cap of his head that Lowell isn't listening at all. And sure enough, he pulls that smelly helmet over his own head, climbs on the bike and sputters off without me.

"Shit," I says, "shit, shit, shit." Then I take off my heels, but not my 195 pantyhose as there was a clammy feeling from the fog which leaked into the valley, and I start to walk, block by block, to Elaine's house. And I get lost and keep getting lost. The soles of my hose are shredded, only a few tough threads keep them from rolling up my ankles. I wander around looking for Elaine's place until the foothills glow like coals in the barbecue from the sun coming up. I tell you Sylmar is one hilly place, where I do not recommend tramping around in nearly bare feet. There's all these same-looking stucco houses made to look like Spanish-style adobe, some huge yards, horse property even, and at least twenty-five million loud barking dogs, snorting and throwing themselves into the chain link as I pass by.

Somewhere I take a very wrong turn, then another and another. The ranch-style houses disappear, replaced by liquor stores, dry cleaners, Mexican markets and apartments like concrete blocks scrawled with graffiti. The signs, the billboards, the street names change from English to Spanish, and the few folks I see rushing out to work are short, dark and completely uninterested in me. I might be invisible as far as they're concerned. It's almost as if they hood their eyes against me. And I feel like I'm intruding in some foreign country, like I'm in the heart of Mexico or San Salvador or some place even more dangerous.

Then I get the idea that I've died, that Lowell has snuffed me by the dumpster, and it's my soul wandering unseen in these foreign streets. I always was slow to understand things in school. Maybe I have died and am just too shocked or too stupid to realize it. That's when I see a burnt-down gas station, which has a phone booth still standing at the edge of the charred lot, so I bolt across the street to see if it would work, and I hear the shriek of brakes and feel a whalloping thud against my thigh, which sends me sprawling to my knees. A lowered Chevy breathes hotly in my face. The driver blasts the horn like an afterthought, and I stand up, waving to show I'm fine.

"*Maricón!°*" the driver, a young man in a white uniform, screams at me before speeding away. That's when I know I'm not dead; I'm only in San Fernando or maybe in Pacoima. My hip hurts. There's probably a king-size bruise forming on it, but nothing's broken, and I check both ways before continuing across the street. The phone looks to be more or less unburnt, so I lift the receiver to hear the most wonderful sound you can hear when you're lost and you've finally found a phone booth—a dial tone. I reached into my handbag, fishing for my emergency quarter, which I found straightaway for once. I push it into the coin slot, but the dial tone persisted. Thirty-five cents, a little sticker under the coin slot reads, announcing the rate change. I only had the one quarter.

I have to call someone collect. Charlene and the others will be snoring it off—deaf, unconscious even until early afternoon. Elaine will have left for work by this time. There's only one person I can think to call collect this early, so I dial the number. The operator has me give my name after the recorded message asks whether charges will be accepted. Then I hear my uncle Enrique, his voice husky with sleep, but very clear, when he says, "No, no, no, thank you," and he hung up.

Maricón: Pejorative term for a gay man.

There are some things that are beyond crying about. Now I could cry 200
and cry and cry when I lost Fabian. That's sad, but not too unbelievable.
After all, he was an old cat, and he had the asthma pretty bad. Of course,
I'll miss him, but I will get used to it. There are some things I will never
get used to like being in a foreign country not twenty minutes from where
I live, like almost being raped by a biker who mistakes me for a transves-
tite, like being hit by a car and then called *maricón*, like having the one
person who never lets you down say finally and at last, "No, no, no, thank
you," and mean, *no more, please, I don't want no more of you, Mulligan.*

I walk some more, but I don't know or care where I'm going. Then I
notice this tiny old woman, wearing a dotted jersey dress and black high-
top shoes like my grandmother used to wear, with the skinny black laces
threading all the way up to her shins. She even has a rope of silver hair
snake-coiled at the nape of her neck like Grandma's famous bun. Only
thing is, her posture isn't too straight like Grandma's. Grandma used to
walk around like she swallowed a broomstick, and it made her so straight
she could barely bend. In fact, she used to unlace those high black shoes
in the house, peel off her stockings and pick up fallen objects with her
toes, rather than stoop for them. Remembering that feels like letting a
warm breeze roll over me, a desert breeze fragrant with the smell of mesquite and piñón.° So I follow that old woman, thinking she might lead
me to a place that I would know where I was.

The aunts said I was her favorite grandchild. I used to pull a stool to
the sink to try to help her with the dishes, but she would set me down,
saying washing dishes wasn't work for me. She spoke only Spanish, and
I don't know how I understood her, never speaking the language myself.
Now I think we must have communicated through the bones. I remember brushing her long silver hair until it snapped and sparked with electricity, and I remember toying with the bottles and tubes on her dresser,
rouging my cheeks with her compact and spritzing my neck with her
atomizer of scent.

And in the car, we rode together in the front seat with Barbara, who
liked to drive. We always rode together in the front, holding hands,
Grandma and me. It made Gloria so mad, but Suzy Q was too young to
care. Grandma liked to see who was out and about and make comments
on everyone she saw. And that last day, a Sunday, we were coming from
mass, she was the one to point to the station wagon bearing down on us
like a cannonball, and she said, "*¡Ay borracho!°*" That's what she said, and
I did know that word. I got gooseflesh remembering it while I followed
that strange old woman in San Fernando or maybe in Pacoima.

I remember smiling, waiting for my grandma to make a joke about the
drunken man, but instead there was screaming, then an explosion of

piñón: Pine nut.   **¡Ay borracho!:** Oh, a drunk!

glass and metal and a red veil poured over my face. The newspaper said my grandmother had died on impact, but there weren't any reporters there; they didn't know. I was there, and I crawled all the way out the windshield, pushing the veil out of my eyes. Everyone was quiet, as though under a sleeping spell like the kingdom in that fairytale. Then I heard my grandmother's voice praying. Her vein-corded fingers groped, and I took her hand between my palms. I looked at her face, but I couldn't see her, or I don't remember. I did hear her, though. I heard what she said when I took her hand. "*¿Quién es?*" she whispered. "*¿Quién es?*"

Thinking about this, remembering all this, I've followed the old woman 205 into a small fenced yard. She notices me when the springs of the gate squeak, slapping it shut behind me. She pinches at the sides of her skirt as though ready to shoo me away in case I came too close. I smile at her and turn my palms upward to show I mean no harm. I can't know what she thought staring at the wreckage of my make up, my dusty skirt and shoeless feet. "*¿Quién es?*" she calls out. "Who are joo?"

A hurricane of words seems to funnel into that tiny fenced yard, whirling and teasing about my head. They were in all languages, and I felt as if I knew them, each one. I can reach out and grab an armful and the Chinese, the Hindustani, the Dutch, the Swahili and the French will be mine and mine forever. If I wait and if I'm quiet, the Spanish will come, too. Then I can speak the language everyone says I know. I know if I wait and I'm quiet, the Spanish will come back to me.

The old woman has asked a very good question, and we both deserve an answer.

Reading

1. Who is Fabian? How does he die?

2. How does Molly meet Lowell? How do they separate?

Thinking Critically

1. Molly mentions "the accident" while describing her sister Gloria and discusses it again later in the story. What was the accident? How does it affect Molly and the other members of her family?

2. What do you think López wants her readers to take from this story? To what extent do you relate to it? Explain.

Connecting

1. Compare the life of Molly in "Soy la Avon Lady" to that of Cleófilas in Sandra Cisneros's story "Woman Hollering Creek" (p. 264). How are

their situations related? Do Cisneros and López have different reasons for writing these stories?

Writing

1. At the end of this selection, when an old woman asks Molly to identify herself, Molly thinks to herself, "The old woman has asked a very good question, and we both deserve an answer." In what ways does the story suggest that Molly is confused about who she is? In what ways does the story tell you who she is? In an essay, discuss Molly's confusion about her identity and why you think López has written about it. Who do you think Molly is?

Creating

1. **Write a poem based on López's story.** Some of the issues raised by "Soy la Avon Lady" have been subjects of poetry. Write a poem based on a part, or the whole, of Lorraine López's story.

48

CHRISTINE GRANADOS [b. 1969]

The Bride

From Brides and Sinners in El Chuco [2006]

GENRE: FICTION

With her willingness to find the humor in the lives of her characters even as they struggle through hardship, Christine Granados represents a new style of Chicana literature. She was born and raised in El Paso, the city sometimes known as "El Chuco," and earned a bachelor's degree in journalism from the University of Texas at El Paso. She then got a master's degree in creative writing from Texas State University, and out of her work there grew her first book, the story collection Brides and Sinners in El Chuco, *published in 2006. As a journalist, Granados was the editor of* Moderna *and has written for magazines including* Hispanic, Texas Monthly, *and* The Texas Observer, *and also for the National Public Radio show* Latino USA. *In both her fiction and* *her journalism, Granados finds the unexpected quirks of the culture she writes about, the people and stories that defy outdated stereotypes, aiming to present an accurate picture of an important region. Granados has said of her work: "I am trying to write candidly about where I come from. I love the desert Southwest, and it's painful to read and watch movies that don't do the place justice. Often writers take the easy road and go with the obvious: clichéd and simple when it comes to the people, place, and environment of the Southwest and Latino community."**

In the story "The Bride," an unnamed, tomboyish narrator describes her sister Rochelle's childhood obsession with planning a perfect wedding for herself, dreaming of potential grooms and staring at bridal magazines showing the "elegance of autumn" and "tall white boys." With bemusement, the narrator notes the ironies and the impossibilities of Rochelle's plans.

As you read "The Bride," pay close attention to the difference between the images in Rochelle's magazines and the realities of her El Paso family.

When the month of June rolls around, I have to buy the five-pound bride magazine off the rack at the grocery store. The photographs of white dresses, articles with to-do lists, and advertisements for wedding planners remind me of my older sister Rochelle's wedding. She had been planning for her special day as far back as I can remember. Every year when she was a child, Rochelle dressed as a beautiful, blushing bride for Halloween. She sauntered her way down the hot, dusty streets of El Paso, accepting candy from our neighbors in her drawstring handbag. The white satin against Rochelle's olive skin made her look so pretty that I didn't mind the fact that we had to stop every three houses so she could empty the candy from her dainty bag into the ripped brown paper sack that I used for the journey. She had to drag me along with her—a reluctant Caspar—because Mom made her, and because I could hold all her candy. Her thick black hair was braided, and she wore the trenzas° in an Eva Perón–style moño.° She spent hours in the bathroom, with her friend Prissy fixing her hair just right, only to cover her head with a white tulle veil.

As Rochelle did this, Mom would prepare my costume. Spent and uninspired after a long day at work, Mom would drape a sheet over me

*From a conversation with Sheryl Luna, available at theconversant.org/?p=4091.

trenzas: Braids.   **moño:** Bun.

and cut out holes for eyes. It happened every year without fail. The fact that I couldn't make up my mind what I wanted to be for Halloween exasperated my already exhausted mother even more. In a matter of minutes, I would list the Bionic Woman, a wrestler, a linebacker, a fat man, all as potential getups before it was time to trick-or-treat.

Ro, on the other hand, had her bridal dress finished days in advance, and she'd wear it to school to show it off. When people opened their doors to us, they would say, "Ay, qué bonita la novia,° and your little brother un fantasma tan scary.°" I'd have to clear things up at every house with "I'm not a boy." They would laugh and ask Rochelle if she had a husband. She would giggle and give them a name.

When she got too old for Halloween, she started getting serious about planning her own wedding. She bought bride magazines and drew up plans, leaving absolutely no detail unattended. When it finally did happen, it was nothing like she had expected.

Rochelle was obsessed. Because all those ridiculous magazines never   5
listed mariachis° or dollar dances, she decided her wedding was going to have a string quartet, no bajo,° horns, or anything, no dollar dance, and it was going to be in October. It was going to be a bland affair, outside in a tent, like the weddings up North in the "elegance of autumn" that she read about in the thick glossy pages of the magazines. I wasn't going to tell her there is no "elegance" to autumn in El Paso. Autumn is either "scramble a huevo° on the hood of your car hot," or wind so strong the sand it blows stings your face and arms.

In the magazine pictures, all the people were white, skinny, and rich. All the women wore linen or silk slips that draped over their skeletal frames, and the men wore tuxedos or black suits and ties. She didn't take into account that in those pages, there was no tía° Trini, who we called Teeny because, at five-foot-two, she weighed at least three hundred pounds. The slip dress Rochelle wanted everyone to wear would be swallowed in Teeny's cavernous flesh. And I never saw anyone resembling tío° Lacho, who wore the burgundy tuxedo he got married in, two sizes too small, to every family wedding. The guests in the magazine weddings were polite and refined, with their long-stemmed wineglasses half full. No one ever got falling-down drunk and picked a fight, like Pilar. He would get so worked up someone would have to knock him out with a bottle of El Presidente.° He was proud of the scars on his head, too, showing them off just before the big fight started.

Ay, qué bonita la novia: Oh, how pretty the bride is.   **un fantasma tan scary:** Such a scary ghost.   **mariachis:** Musical group playing traditional Mexican music.   **bajo:** Six-string bass guitar used in mariachi music.   **huevo:** Egg.   **tía:** Aunt.   **tío:** Uncle.   **El Presidente:** A popular brandy made in Mexico.

Rochelle wanted tall white boys with jawbones that looked like they had been chiseled from stone to be her groomsmen; never mind the fact that we knew only one white boy, and he had acne so bad his face was blue. She also wanted her maid of honor to be pencil thin, although she would never admit it. Still, she was always dropping hints, telling her best friend, Prissy, that by the time they were twenty all their baby fat would be gone, and they would both look fabulous in their silk gowns. Never mind the fact that I, two years younger than Rochelle, could encircle my sister's bicep between my middle finger and thumb, and that Prissy rested her Tab colas on her huge stomach when she sat. My sister was in denial. And it wasn't just about her obese friend but about her entire life. She thought that if she planned every last detail of her wedding on paper, she could change who she was, who we were. Her lists drove me crazy.

She kept a running tally of the songs to be played by the band, adding and deleting as her musical tastes changed through the years. She carefully selected the food to be served to her guests. She resolutely decided what everyone in the family would be wearing. She even painstakingly chose what her dress would look like, down to the last sequin. But in order to marry, she needed a groom. And she was just as diligent about finding one as she was about the rest of the affair.

Every night before going to bed, she would pull out her pink wedding notebook and scratch a boy's name off her list of potential husbands. She went through two notebooks in one year. She was always on the lookout for husbands. One time, Rochelle and I spent an entire Saturday morning typing up fake raffle tickets to sell to Mike, who lived two blocks over. Ro had never met Mike, but she liked his broad shoulders—thought they'd look good in a tuxedo. So she made up a story that she was helping me sell raffle tickets for my softball team. Ro didn't let little things, like the truth, get in the way of her future. All the money raised would go into the team's travel budget. She even made up first-, second-, and third-place prizes. First place would be a color TV, second place, a dinner for two at Forti's Mexican Food Restaurant, and third, two tickets to the movies. She said Mike was going to win third place, and when she delivered his prize, she was going to suggest he take her to the movies since she was the one who sold him the winning ticket. I thought my sister was a genius, until we got to the door and knocked. When Mike answered, Ro delivered her lines like she had been selling raffle tickets all day long. When he told us he had no money, we were shocked. Ro didn't have a Plan B. Then, when his older brother came to the door and offered to buy all ten of the raffle tickets, we were speechless. All we could do was take his money, give him his stubs, and wish him luck. Ro was so upset her plan was a failure that she let me keep the ten dollars. Needless to say, Mike got scratched off her list.

Her blue notebook was where she compiled her guest list and either 10
added or deleted a name depending on what had happened in school that
day. I got scratched out six times in one month: for using all her sanitary
napkins as elbow and knee pads while skating; for wearing her real silver
concho belt and losing it at school; for telling Mom that Rochelle was
giving herself hickeys on her arms; for peeking in her diary; for feeding
her goldfish, Hughie, so much that he died; and especially, for telling her
the truth about the food she planned to serve at her wedding. That final
act kept me off the list for two months straight. She wanted finger foods
like in Anglo weddings—sandwiches with the crusts cut off.

"Those cream cheese and cucumber sandwiches aren't going to cut it,
Ro," I said through the cotton shirt I was taking off.

"My wedding is going to be classy," she yelled at me from across the
room, where she was sitting on top of her bed, smoothing lotion on her
arms. "If you don't want to eat my food, then you just won't be invited."

I laughed. Her nostrils were flaring pretty steady, and she was winding
her middle finger around her ponytail. Then she reached under the mattress for her notebook, and my name, Lily, was off the list, just like that.

"I wouldn't want to go spend hours at some dumb wedding when I
was half starving anyway. Everybody's going to faint before the dollar
dance starts."

She stopped writing, "There isn't going to be a dollar dance." Then she 15
wrinkled her wide nose, "Too gauche."

When I came back into the room after I had looked up the word, I told
her, "I'm telling Mom you think she's tacky. You're carrying your gringa
kick too far." Before shutting the bedroom door, I poked my head in and
yelled, "I'm glad I'm not invited. I don't want to go to no white wedding."

Later, I asked her how she expected to go on her Hawaii honeymoon
without a dollar dance. "You plan on selling the cucumber sandwiches at
the wedding?"

She wiped the sarcastic smile off my face when she said, "No. I'm
going to have a money tree." I told her that she was ridiculous and that
she was going to be a laughingstock, not knowing how close my words
were to the truth.

She didn't care what anyone thought. She said her wedding was hers,
and it was one thing no one could ruin.

She kept up her lists as usual, but stopped physically adding to them in 20
tenth grade—dropped and discarded as "too childish." By then, the lists
were committed to memory, and I knew that she mentally scratched ex-
friends and ex-boyfriends off of it. Lance, Rubén, Abraham, Artie, Oscar,
Henry, Joel, and who knows who else had all been potential grooms.

It turned out to be Angel. He was beautiful, too—the Mexican version
of the blond grooms in her magazines, right down to the cleft in his chin.

He was perfect as long as he didn't smile, because when he smiled, his chipped, discolored front tooth showed. Rochelle worried about it all the time. She'd pull out photographs they had taken together, and the ones he had given her, to study them, trying to figure out the right camera angle that would hide his flaw. Anytime she mentioned getting it capped, he would roll his large almond-shaped eyes and smile. They would kiss and that would be the end of the discussion.

I knew this because Rochelle always had to drag me along on her dates. It was the only way our mother would allow her out of the house with a boy. I was a walking-and-talking birth control device. When we got home, I would replay the night's events for my mother. Funny, Ro relished the details of her wedding, but she never could stand for my instant replay of her dates. She would storm out of the living room when I would begin and slam the door to our bedroom. I usually had to sleep on the couch after our dates.

On prom night, Rochelle was allowed to go out with Angel alone, and she was so excited that she let me watch her dress for the big event. Tía Trini came over and rolled her hair, Prissy was there with her Tab in hand for moral support, and Mom was making last minute altera- tions to her gown. It was a salmon-colored version of her wedding dress. After she was teased, tweezed, and tucked, she looked like a stick of cotton candy from the top of her glittered hair down to her pink sling- back heels. When Angel saw her, he licked his lips like he was going to devour her.

Because I, her birth control device, wasn't in place during this date, the two got married when she was only a junior in high school, and she was four months pregnant. Rochelle and Angel drove thirty minutes to Las Cruces to be married by the justice of peace, with Mom in the back seat bawling. Even though Rochelle didn't get her elegant autumn wedding, she stood before Judge Grijalva in her off-white linen pantsuit, which was damp on the shoulder and smeared with Mom's mascara, erect and with as much dignity as if she were under a tent at the Chamizal.° It didn't matter to her that the groom wore his blue Dickies work pants with matching shirt that had his name stitched in yellow onto the pocket. She looked at him like they were the only two people inside the closet-sized courtroom.

She didn't even blink when a baby began to wail in her ear during "Do 25 you take this man . . ."

And she never took her eyes off Angel when the woman next in line to get married, who was dressed in a skintight, leopard-print outfit, said, "Let's get this show on the road already. Kiss her, kiss her already."

Chamizal: A park located on the U.S.-Mexico border in El Paso.

And it didn't bother Rochelle that after Angel kissed her, he looked at his watch and said, "Vámonos.° I need to get back to work," because he needed to get back to Sears before the evening rush.

Reading

1. What differences does the narrator of "The Bride" find between magazine pictures and her own family?

2. Why does Rochelle get married while still in high school?

Thinking Critically

1. Do Rochelle and her sister have different attitudes toward their family? Explain.

2. How do you think Rochelle feels on her wedding day? Draw on the text to support your answer.

Connecting

1. Though Rochelle is a very different person than Doña María in Tomás Rivera's story "La Noche Buena" (p. 145), both stories offer perspectives on consumer culture. Do you think that Granados and Rivera had similar purposes in writing their stories? Do the two stories have any other similar themes? If so, what are they, and how do they function?

Writing

1. The narrator of "The Bride" has difficulty seeing her own family in the pictures in bridal magazines. Using examples from the story, write an essay about the sources of the differences between those images and the reality of life in El Paso for Rochelle and her sister.

Creating

1. **Gather images of your reality to make a collage.** Christine Granados has worked as a journalist for several magazines, trying to get the realities of her life into print. Try to find magazine pictures that represent your own family life and make a collage. Discuss what kinds of magazines and what kinds of articles your pictures came from.

Vámonos: Let's get going.

49

GUSTAVO ARELLANO [b. 1979]

From ¡Ask a Mexican! [2007]

GENRE: JOURNALISM

Before he was known to a national audience as an outrageous and funny interpreter of Mexican American culture, Gustavo Arellano was a reporter and the food editor for OC Weekly *in Orange County, California. His editor suggested the column that would become "¡Ask a Mexican!" Arellano received questions motivated by everything from ignorant racism to confused and even affectionate curiosity about Mexican culture. "I use the column to give the straight dope but also be as rude as possible to people who deserve it,"* Arellano says of his answers. Arellano himself is the son of Mexican immigrants who came to Southern California, and he attended college at Orange Coast College and Chapman University before earning a master's degree in Latin American studies at the University of California, Los Angeles. He then became a journalist in Los Angeles. His column soon gained popularity and was syndicated nationally, and in 2007, many of the questions and answers were published in book form as* ¡Ask a Mexican! *Since then, Arellano has written two other books:* Orange County: A Personal History *in 2008 and* Taco USA: How Mexican Food Conquered America *in 2012.*

The following selections from ¡Ask a Mexican! *show the ways that Arellano has responded to his readers. His style is a sometimes startling mix of combativeness and sympathy, honesty and bluster, invention and information. To those commentators who have complained about Arellano's willingness to offend readers and to use racial stereotypes in his writing, he replies that his column is "satire: outrageousness mixed in with jarring truth."*

As you read these excerpts from Arellano's satirical newspaper column, think as much about the people who are asking the questions as the answers he gives them, and think about the many different audiences Arellano is trying to bring together.

*From a *New York Times* article, available at nytimes.com/2007/06/24/fashion/24mexican.html?pagewanted=all.

1

Dear Gabachos: *Bienvenidos* to *¡Ask a Mexican!*, the world's foremost authority on America's spiciest minority! The Mexican can answer any and every question on his race, from why Mexicans stick the Virgin of Guadalupe everywhere to our obsession with tacos and green cards. In the course of his answers, the Mexican will use certain terms and phrases for better-rounded answers. Here are the most used, along with handy Spanglish sentence examples so you too can become a Mexican. Awright, *cabrones*: laugh and *comprende*!

¡: An upside-down exclamation point. Put in front of an exclamatory sentence. *¡Ohmidios, José brought his leaf blower into the living room!*

¿: An upside-down question mark. Put in front of a question. *¿Who gave María my old dress?*

~: A tilde. Put over the letter *n* from time to time to produce a sound like "nyuck." *Candelario sure has a lot of niños.*

Aztlán: The mythical birthplace of the Aztecs. Chicanos use this term to describe the southwest United States. Chicanos are idiots. *Citlali says Aztlán is somewhere in Ohio.*

Baboso: A slug or drooling person. Can also mean "asshole" or "idiot," depending on context. *Don't be a baboso to your baboso son, Josefina.*

Burrito: A flour tortilla wrapped around various goodies. Also a slur used against Mexicans. *That burrito ate a big burrito last night.*

Cabrón: Literally, a castrated goat. Mexicans understand it better as "asshole," or "badass."

Chica caliente: Hot chick. All Mexican ladies are *chicas calientes*. *¿Where can I meet some chicas calientes?*

Chicano: The poorer, stupider, more assimilated cousins of Mexicans. Otherwise known as a Mexican-American. *George López is such a Chicano with his unfunny jokes.*

Chingar: To fuck up. Its various derivatives are used for a delightful array of insults, such as *chingadera* (fucked-up situation), *chingazos* (punches thrown), and *Chinga tu madre, cabrón* (Go fuck your mother, asshole). *Chinga tu madre, cabrón—if you don't stop this chingadera, I'm going to chingar you with chingazos.*

Chino: Literally "Chinese," but the catchall phrase Mexicans use for Asians regardless of nationality. *Vietnamese food is my favorite chino cuisine.*

Chúntaro: A Mexican redneck. Term used mostly by Mexicans against each other. *Jeff Foxworthy is a white chúntaro.*

Cinco de Mayo: Holiday celebrating an obscure battle between the French and Mexicans in the 1860s that everyone in the United States uses as an excuse to get plastered. Our St. Patrick's Day.

Cochinadas: Disgusting things. Derived from the word *cochino*, which means "pig." *¡Stop seeing those* Playboy *cochinadas!*

Conquest, the: Refers to the Spanish conquest of the Americas during the 1500s. Centuries later, Mexicans still can't get over it—but having about 100 million of your ancestors slaughtered will do that to you.

¡Cu-le-ro!: The Bronx cheer of Mexico. Means "Asshole!"

Culo: Every Mexican man's obsession.

Estados Unidos, Los: "The United States" in Spanish. Come on—that one's not *that* difficult to decipher, *¿qué no?*

Familia: Guess. You're right: family! If you believe the mainstream media, the most important thing in Mexican culture after tequila.

Frontera, la: The border—specifically, the United States–Mexico border. *¿Why are there so many geezers at la frontera? Because they're Minutemen.*

Gabacho: A gringo. But Mexicans don't call gringos gringos. Only gringos call gringos gringos. Mexicans call gringos gabachos.

Gringo: Mexican slang for a white American. What gringos call gringos.

Guatemalan: The Germans had the Irish; the Irish had the Italians; the Italians had the Poles. Mexicans have the Guatemalans—our eternal punch line.

Güey: Derived from *buey*—an ox—but means "ass," as in a hoofed ass, not an ass ass. *That asshole is a güey.*

Hombre: Mexico's undisputed rulers.

Joto: Faggot. A preferred male slur.

Madre: Means "mother," but is also one of the most vulgar words in Mexican Spanish. In its various forms, can mean anything from "kick your ass" *(madrear)* to "suck my dick" *(mámamela).*

Malinche: The name of the Indian woman who served as a translator for the Spaniards as they slaughtered their way to the Aztecs during the Conquest. Mexicans turn her name into a noun, *malinchista*—that's a synonym for *traitor.* Typical Mexico—blames everything on women.

Mami: The diminutive of "mother," but also a sexual term of endearment for one's girlfriend. *Ay, mami, give me some of that sweet culo.*

MEChA: Acronym for Movimiento Estudiantil Chicano de Aztlán (Chicano Student Movement of Aztlán), a high school and college group that helps Mexican kids get to and stay in college. And that's why conservatives slur this group and all its members like no organization since the Scientologists.

Mensa: Name of an organization for people with an IQ in the upper 2 percent of the general population. Also the feminine form of "dumb" in Spanish. Mensa members can't be *that* smart given the snafu, no?

Mexicanidad: Mexican-ness. Ridiculous translation for a ridiculous concept.

Mexicano: The greatest race of people in the world—when they're in the United States. In Mexico, they're just Mexicans.

México: Country directly south of the United States with an estimated population of 105 million. America's eternal Paris Hilton.

Migra, la: Nickname for immigration agents. The brownshirts of Mexican society.

Mujer: Mexican worker whose only purpose is to make sure fresh tortillas greet the *familia* daily.

Naco: Mexico City slang for a *chúntaro*.

Norte, El: The North. The United States.

Otro lado, el: The other side. Otherwise known as the United States.

Papi: The diminutive of "father," but also a sexual term of endearment for one's boyfriend. *Ay, papi, give me your sweet green card.*

Pendejo: Literally, a pubic hair. Means "asshole" in Mexican Spanish. So many synonyms for asshole, Mexican Spanish has! *That pendejo should shave his pendejos.*

Piñata: A toy that Mexicans beat so it will spill forth its goodies. Otherwise known as the United States.

Pinche: A short-order cook. Also an adjective meaning "fucking." *Give me a pinche break.*

Pinche puto pendejo baboso: Literally means "fucking faggot pubic hair slug," but understood by Mexicans as "fucking stupid-ass asshole." The best Mexican cursing couplet of them all. *Shut up, you pinche puto pendejo baboso.*

Pocho: An Americanized Mexican.

Por favor: "Please" in Spanish. *The judge said, "Pleas, por favor."*

Puro: Pure. Put it in front of any word to come off as a braggart—a Mexican! *That chúntaro is puro mexicano.*

Puto/puta: The former means "faggot," the latter is "female whore." One of the most popular Mexican-Spanish curse words.

¿Qué no?: Ending phrase used in Mexican-Spanish to denote "right?"

Raza cósmica, la: "The cosmic race." Refers to a movement by Mexican intellectuals during the 1920s arguing Mexicans have the blood of all the world's races—white, black, Indian, and Asian—and therefore transcend the world.

Reconquista: Theory espoused by Chicano and conservative kooks insisting that Mexico is trying to take over the southwest United States, the territory the Yankees took from Mexico as spoils after the 1846 Mexican-American War.

SanTana: Santa Ana, California, from where *¡Ask a Mexican!* originates. The most Latino big city in the United States, according to the 2000 census. Please pronounce the city like the natives: "SanTana," like the famous guitarist, not "Santa Ana," like a combo of Claus and Karenina.

Señorita: A polite lady. Usually coupled with "spicy." *Salma Hayek is one spicy señorita.*

Taco: A corn tortilla stuffed with goodies. Also a slur used against Mexicans. *Tacos sure love tacos, ¿qué no?*

Tapatío: A popular hot-sauce brand featuring a man with a mustache and a sombrero. Drunk by Mexicans from cradle to crypt.

Tejana: A Stetson felt cowboy hat. Refers to Texas, where the hat supposedly originated.

Tequila: Liquor distilled from the agave plant of central Mexico. Also flows in the blood of any real Mexican.

Tortilla: A thin disk of cornmeal eaten by Mexicans since time immemorial. Also great impromptu Frisbees.

Ustedes: A fancy way of saying "y'all." *I'll be seeing ustedes tomorrow in Aztlán.*

Virgin of Guadalupe: The patron saint of Mexico. Appears everywhere in Mexican society, from churches to silk shirts to hubcaps.

Wab: The Orange County version of *wetback.* Spread our hate wide and far, *por favor.*

2

Whenever I hear people whistling at each other across the street to communicate, it always seems to be a Mexican. Is it illegal in Mexico to yell out words too loudly, and whistling is a loophole in the law? Or does the frequency of a whistle carry farther than voice frequencies across a ranch, the desert, or Mexico City traffic jams? Or is it learned behavior from living in an ambiguous environment (immigrant-friendly and -unfriendly) that whistling is somehow more discreet? Or is it cooler to whistle instead of yelling the other person's name?

WHISTLING GÜERO

Dear Gabacho: All of the above. According to *Whistled Languages*, a 1976 book by René-Guy Busnel and A. Classe, which linguists consider the definitive study on the matter, whistled tongues arose in cultures that occupied areas where daunting terrain and distance prohibited easy conversations. Many such ethnic groups influenced the formation of the Mexican nation. Before the Conquest, major indigenous languages such as Nahuatl, Zapotec, and Totonac featured a whistled-only dialect. After the Conquest, migrants from the Canary Islands, home of the world's most famous whistled language, Silbo Gomero, were among the first settlers of Texas. And since the past is ever present for Mexicans, it makes sociological sense to argue that the Mexican propensity to whistle-talk, like our obsession with death and Three Flowers brilliantine, is a (literally) breathing cultural artifact.

But don't think there's some gnostic mystery behind its use, Whistling Güero. There are really just four phrases to whistled Mexican Spanish: a sharp tweet to catch someone's attention, a longer version for showing disgust during performances, and the lecherous, drawn-out double note that plagues so many gabachas. The most infamous Mexican-Spanish whistled phrase, however, is *chinga tu madre* ("go fuck your mother"): five successive, rapid trills that roughly sound like Woody Woodpecker's infamous cackle. The last whistle is our favorite, especially because we can use it in front of unsuspecting gabachos without reproach. But don't use it around Mexicans unless you want a brown fist in your eye and a mestizo foot square upon your t'aint.

3

Why do some Mexicans who speak fluent English without an accent insist on pronouncing their names and Spanish place names with the Spanish pronunciation? Especially reporters: "This is Julio Luís Sánchez reporting from Neek-a-ra-wa." I get that the Southwest was once Spain and Mexico, that many Mexicans here can trace their roots back generations, and that many of the place names are Spanish, but I don't use an Irish brogue to pronounce my last name, we don't say Anaheim with a German accent, and it's Des Moines, not "Day Mwahn." It's fine to say words correctly—La Hoy-a and not La Jol-la—but the overly dramatic accent comes off as annoying and pretentious (same with when someone speaking Spanish comes to an English word and drops the accent as if to say, "Look, I'm bilingual!"). On a related matter, does it piss Mexicans off when non-Latinos who happen to speak Spanish do this too?

A Cunning yet Clueless Linguist

Dear Gabacho: Give me a *pinche* break. Everyone wants his last name pronounced correctly, whether you're a Jauregui ("Yah-reh-gwee"), Nguyen ("Win"), Schou ("Skow," not "Shoe"), or Limbaugh ("Run, reason!"). If you notice Mexican reporters do it more often than other ethnically surnamed scribes, it just means they're not ashamed of actively correcting decades of mispronunciations. Really, Cunning, why don't you lend a lilt to whatever your Irish moniker may be? Afraid the English might trample your potato crop?

"Why do I pronounce my name in Spanish? That's the only way it feels right," says Adolfo Guzmán López, a *chingón* reporter at KPCC-FM 89.3 in Pasadena, California. He frequently encounters strangers who can't understand his name until he Anglicizes it for them ("Uh-doll-phoe" instead of "Ah-dohl-foh"). "If you're bilingual and bicultural, you know how to navigate in those two worlds," Guzmán López told the Mexican. "But I grew up speaking Spanish, and it's never sounded right to pronounce it any other way except in Spanish. Besides, my mom would probably get mad if I did it the other way."

By the way, Mexicans love it when gabachos try to pronounce Spanish correctly. Oh, they usually butcher our rolling double *r* and *n* with the squiggly mark over it, but we respect their effort. Contrast that with my gabacho coworkers, who howl whenever I fumble words like *gamut* (I say "gah-moot," not "gah-muht") and *harpsichord* (I'll spare you the cacophony of spittle and laryngeal scratches). Gabachos can profess all the progressive ideals they want, but put them within earshot of a Mexican gamely attempting to speak the King's English and hear the snickers spread.

4

What's with the Mexican use of the word *mother*?

YO MAMA

Dear Gabacho: While the phrase *yo mama* is used as an insult worldwide, Mexican Spanish is unique in its use of the word *mother* to create some truly vicious vulgarities. Instead of concentrating on traits such as weight and sexual proclivities, Mexican-Spanish syntax uses *mother* in various grammatical forms to mean everything from the threat of physical violence to parental revulsion—the all-encompassing *aloha* of Latino cursing.

As a noun, *madre* can mean anything from "shit," as in *No vale madre* (It isn't worth shit), to "ass," in which *Te voy a partir la madre* translates into "I'm going to split for you the mother" but really means "I'm going to kick your fucking ass."

You can use *madre* as an adverb. *Te voy a dar un chingazo en la madre* translates to "I'm going to give you a fucking blow in the mother" but really means "I'm going to give you a fucking blow where it hurts the most." Or you can tell your closest kith to *Vete a la madre*, which does not mean "Go to the mother" but rather "Go to hell."

Add an *-ar* ending to *madre* and you have the verb *madrear*, which means "to fuck someone up." For example, if you tell your mom *Te voy a madrear*, you're not telling her that you're going to mother her but are letting her know "I'm going to kick your fucking ass." We advise against this.

And a mutation of *madre*, *madrazo*, denotes "harmful blow." *Te voy a dar un madrazo* is "I'm going to give you a fucking punch."

Saying how you are related to your giver of life is also fraught with swearing. *Hijo/a de tu madre* means "Son/daughter of your mother," but the phrase is uttered by parents to their irresponsible children only when they are disgusted with them. If you try telling that to your mom, she will reward your biological insight with a *madrazo* to the face.

Even the most benign form of mother, *mamá*, can be turned into a crude insult if you don't pay attention. Take off the accent, and you are left with *mama*, the present indicative from of *mamar*, which means "to suck." And when you say that, you ain't telling a baby how to get the milk out of the bottle.

5

Dear Mexican: I could've sworn I heard somewhere that the song "La Cucaracha" was originally about Pancho Villa's soldiers, and the lyrics had to do with them not being able to march without marijuana. I totally forgot where I heard it, man, but I also heard something about the U.S. cavalry tracking the troops, and how they would find joint butts strewn across the trail. Is this why gabachos from Hawaii to Ireland to Thailand refer to the end of a joint as a roach?

ALTO EN VIDA

Dear Gabacho: Next to "The Mexican Hat Dance" and "Livin' la Vida Loca," America's favorite Mexican song is "La Cucaracha." Even Carl Sandburg was a fan of the cockroach-citing ditty—the famed poet included it in his 1927 collection of folk tunes, *The American Songbag*. Sandburg wrote that he first heard it in 1916 in Chicago from two reporters who had covered the Mexican Revolution and "had eaten frijoles with Villa and slept under Pancho's poncho." Sandburg included eight stanzas of "La Cucaracha" in *The American Songbag*, but there are hundreds of variations. "'La Cucaracha' is the Spanish equivalent of 'Yankee Doodle'—a traditional satirical tune periodically fitted out with new lyrics to meet the needs of the moment," noted Cecil Adams, author of the syndicated column *The Straight Dope*, in his 2001 take on the song's meaning. Indeed, "La Cucaracha" is one of the oldest songs in Hispanic culture. There are lyrics that ridicule Pancho Villa, the French occupation of Mexico, the Carlist Wars of the mid-nineteenth century, even the Moors ("From the skin of the Moorish king / I have to make a sofa / So the Spanish captain / Can sit in it" goes one such version—and you think Europe hates Muslims today!). I'd never heard the "Cucaracha"/roach theory until you mentioned it, High on Life, but it wouldn't be the first time gabachos had appropriated Mexican culture to describe their sinful acts—"Dirty Sánchez," anyone?

6

I remember going to Metallica concerts and there being as many gaba-chos as *mexicanos*. But I thought Mexicans only liked mariachi?

I AM IRON HOMBRE

Dear Gabacho: Many gabachos get surprised when Mexicans profess to like a music form that doesn't involve accordions, tubas, or men on horseback, but one of the few places where Mexicans and gabachos exist in peace is the mosh pit. *Metaleros* boast a long history in Mexico's urban regions, especially in Mexico City, which boasts its own unique genre: *rock urbano*, a bluesy fusion of metal with stadium rock. See, gabachos? Even Mexico creates generations of young, disaffected youth whose only solace is to listen to eardrum-splitting music and crash into their neigh-bor's pancreas. If only gabachos could show the same love with our less assimilated Mexicans—or rather, something beyond the mariachi-loving music videos for Weezer's "Island in the Sun"—then this immigration debate would slide off the American consciousness as quickly as *The O.C.*

7

Why do all those Mexican cholos call us white girls *güera*? It obviously means "white girl" or something, but it's not like I go around calling them beaners or whatever. That goes for black girls too because they call them *negritas*. Why can't they just call us by our name?

MEXICAN GIRL AT HEART

Dear Gabacha: Those who throw stones shouldn't . . . look, you're whining about Mexicans calling you *güera*, and you call them Mexican cholos! Why can't you just call them wabs? Afraid they might jump you? But you can't blame Mexicans for being so obsessed with race—it's hardwired into our souls. While the United States never truly jumped into the miscegenation bed other than for the occasional slave-massa rape, Mexico owes its exis-tence to everyone fucking everyone until most of its citizens became a mes-tizo glop. To justify their place in Mexican society, the Spaniards created what's called the *casta* (caste), with *peninsulares* (natives of Spain) on the top, followed by *criollos* (full-blooded Europeans born in Mexico), mestizos (Europeans with Indians), mulattoes (Europeans with blacks), and devolving through an incredible thirty others until you reached the bottom of the bottom: a *zambo*, a mixture of Indian and black. You improved your status in society by improving your racial classification, and Mexicans have obsessed over their blood mixture since. That doesn't excuse your Mexican friends' racism, but now you know why they call you a *güera*. Be happy that the Mexicans called you a *güera*, though, and not a *puta*.

8

What's with those beautiful belts Mexican men wear?

BUCKLED UNDER

Dear Gabacho: With the decline of suspenders, Americans just don't care about what holds up their pants anymore. Not so the Mexicans. We like to use a *cinto pitiado*—a tawny leather belt embroidered with creamy white threads derived from the same plant that gives the world tequila. (It's the agave, stupid.) The *cinto pitiado* isn't some Wal-Mart castoff or the canvas strap with an initialized silver buckle that home-boys prefer for their Dickies—the *cinto pitiado* is honest-to-goodness wearable art. It's the most beautiful thing a man can wrap around his waist that doesn't have long, curly hair.

Each *cinto pitiado* features distinct ornate geometric designs spanning the length of the belt—abstract vines, geometric conundrums, elegant curves, all a legacy of the Moorish artistic influence over the Hispanic world. The carousel of shapes ends at the buckle with a singular logo—could be the wearer's initials, maybe a silhouette of a barnyard animal. With the recent rise in the narco business, some drug dealers are even adorning their belts with machine guns and marijuana leaves. Hell, I once saw a Calvin pissing on some Mexican soccer-team logo—but better you stay away from that auto fashion faux pas.

Buying a *cinto pitiado* reflects on how much pride you take in dressing splendidly. You can visit your local Mexican clothing store and come out looking sharp in a $50 imitation *cinto pitiado* produced in some Los Angeles factory. But to get the real deal, the kind that takes months to produce and costs about a month's worth of cleaning houses, talk to your neighborhood Mexican from Jalisco or Zacatecas, where the art of *cinto pitiado* reaches cubist levels. If a Mexican man visits these states, it's almost inevitable he will return with a couple of belts for his friends. Take note, Homeland Security: the *cinto pitiado* smuggling business is the best contraband since turtle soup.

9

Why do many Mexican men wear mustaches? Is there a history behind this?

BIGOTE BILL

Dear Gabacho: I am not well-endowed—not even close. I need braces, a personal trainer, and LASIK. But none of this matters—I can grow a mustache.

It sprouts almost from the instant I shave in the morning, becomes a five-o'clock shadow around noon, and transforms into a sharp, jagged line spanning my mouth within two days. After a week, the mustache is worthy of Cesar Romero; after a month, Emiliano Zapata. In a year? You can smuggle a migrant family inside it.

I don't usually grow a mustache, primarily because modern American society banishes nongoatee facial hair to the domain of the fags and Arabs. Indeed, almost all gabachas who have seen me with a mustache loudly voice their objection. "Oh my gosh!" one Hawaiian hottie once gasped after not seeing me for a couple of weeks. "The mustache makes you look like a Mexican!"

That was the point, *chula*.

Mexicans are different. They treat the initial dark hedges that spread across my upper lip like the first seedlings of spring. Murmurs of "You look good" and "You should keep it" greet me at social events. Men share their mustache envy, lamenting they can't grow something as thick and lengthy as mine. Without one, they think I look like a woman.

And the ladies? I've only had two Mexican girlfriends in my life—met them when I was clean-shaven. Both requested within days of our initial bedding that I grow a mustache.

Ladies, tongue piercings flicked toward the pudenda don't match four days' of lip growth. Imagine a mustache gliding down your neck, across your back, past your abdomen toward the sweltering Promised Land; a mustache brushing your breasts, your thighs, your everything; not quite a kiss but even more so. Like that? Let's just say there's a reason I'm known as the Mouth of the South.

But Mexican mustache love isn't just predicated on sexual sensation— it's rooted in something deeper, something more primal to the mestizo labyrinth: machismo. The mustache is power, commands respect, wins elections. Archimedes said he could move the world with a lever and a place to stand; some political observers say Vicente Fox's magnificent black *bigote* catapulted him into the Mexican presidential palace in 2000.

As with almost everything inexplicably retro in Mexican society, we can thank the Conquest for this follicle fetish. When the Spaniards arrived in the early sixteenth century, the Aztecs marveled not only at their iron armor and deer (actually horses) "as tall as the roof of a house," but also at the bizarre growths on the faces of these fair skins. One Aztec codex of the period dramatically noted the troops of Hernán Cortés wore "long and yellow [beards], and their mustaches are also yellow." This obsession wasn't trivial: the Aztecs—who could only grow pitiful wisps on their cheeks and chins—thought of the Spaniards as gods because of their facial hair. Cortés happened to arrive in Mexico in the exact year that, Aztec mythology said, the bearded god Quetzalcoatl promised to return to save his people. To the Aztecs, a full-blown mustache meant power, salvation, a chance encounter with the heavens (of course, it ultimately became genocide, but that's another story).

Nearly five hundred years later, Mexican culture still maintains the cult of the mustache. Our dads wear them; in official photos, our greatest leaders—Pancho Villa, *ranchera* legend Vicente Fernández, the Frito Bandito—brandish them like guns. Any self-respecting man grew a mustache—tellingly, the only segments of the Mexican male population that don't wear a mustache are the indigenous and the Americanized.

And so, I grow my mustache. When I told a friend about my plans, her eyes enlivened—became fearful, even. "Wow, you could look really tough—respectable, but also dangerous at the same time," she exclaimed. I know.

10

Why do Mexicans drive trucks that cost more than their homes? You drive through barrios, and Lincoln Navigators are parked outside tenement slums!

STUCK WITH MY KIA

Dear Pocha: You say it as if it were a bad thing, Kia, but rejoice: if Mexicans spend more cash on their cars than their *casas*, that's just further proof we're assimilating into American life. A telltale trait of gabachismo is conspicuous consumption, the phenomenon identified by American economist Thorstein Veblen in his 1899 classic, *The Theory of the Leisure Class*. Veblen theorized that commoners buy the most expensive and ostentatious products in the name of achieving social status—keeping up with the Gonzalezes, if you will. Conspicuous consumption, not thrift, is the true American way. Look at our government, for instance, which talks about fiscal responsibility yet spends more and more on war follies without care for the health of this nation. No one cares about ballooning federal budgets or having to rent out the garage to five perverts from Guerrero to make rent as long as you can show off the *chingo* bling.

11

Why do Mexicans traditionally like Chevys? Did Chevy once target the Mexican consumer base for some reason and it worked?

POCHO IN A PONTIAC

Dear Pocho: An urban legend suggests that Mexicans don't like Chevys (pronounced with a harsh *ch* as in *chicken* and *chupacabra, gracias*) because the auto giant named one of its 1960s-era cars the Nova—which translates to "doesn't go" in Spanish. But General Motors' stats show that the Nova did well for the company, even in Mexico. And not just the Nova. Mexicans consume Chevys like mescal and, come to think of it, sometimes together. In the 2003 report *Market Trends: Hispanic Americans and the Automobile Industry*, author Raúl Pérez found that Chevrolet ranked at or near the top of the list for Hispanic (the PC *pendejo* term for "Mexican") first-time, used-car, and general buyers. Pérez doesn't go into the *porqués*, but according to *Lowrider* magazine's book *Lowrider* (2003), the Bible of *ranflas* and *rucas* (that's hot cars and hotter chicks), the Mexican affinity for Chevys "was an economic consideration" dating back to the 1930s cruising culture. Chevys were quite simply "cheaper and more plentiful" than other brands.

Nowadays, Mexicans purchase Chevy's expensive trucks and SUVs (Chevy hasn't manufactured a *mexcellente* car since the 1964 Impala) as useful status symbols: nothing smuggles your family like a gleaming Suburban the size of a small-apartment living room. Sure, Mexicans should invest their money in better things than Chevys equipped with spinning hubcaps and built-in flat-screen televisions, but dig this, gabachos: while more and more of youse ditch Detroit in favor of jalopies pieced together by goldfish farmers, Mexicans buy American. So who's patriotic now, *cabrones*?

12

Why do Mexicans consider Charles Bronson the most fashionable gabacho ever?

DEATH WISH 1000

Dear Gabacho: Ask a group of twentysomething Mexican-Americans if they grew up watching Charles Bronson movies, and heads hang low. Eventually, someone shamefully allows that, yes, his parents rented all episodes of the *Death Wish* series, that a family night out on the town during the mid-1980s involved watching the latest Bronson bloodbath on the big screen, and that his mother thought the helmet-coiffed actor was the handsomest screen Adonis since Ricardo Montalbán. Relieved not to be alone in embarrassment, everyone soon sheepishly admits the same, and conversations shift toward the sharing of favorite Bronson bits.

The grim-faced performer maintains an earnest following throughout the world even after death because of his career-long portrayal of expressionless psychopaths. Bronson-love in Mexico and her American colonies, however, approaches the hagiographic—and not just because the actor's crumpled mug allowed him to half-believably portray Mexicans or half-Mexicans in such movies as 1960's *The Magnificent Seven* (Bernardo O'Reilly) and 1968's *Villa Rides!* (Rodolfo Fierro) and *Guns for San Sebastian* (Teclo). The Bronson canon's gallery of urban warriors enraptured the Mexican cinematic imagination like little else during the late 1970s and early 1980s and persists today despite the rise of stars even more ethnic and violent.

The Mexican cult of the man born Charles Buchinski is everywhere. Spanish-language channels broadcast such Bronsonian symphonies of mayhem as *The Valachi Papers, Mr. Majestyk,* and *The Evil That Men Do* during prime time almost weekly. Video stores in heavily Latino neighborhoods know to shore up the Bronson catalog and *still* find themselves constantly out of stock. And if there aren't any Bronson flicks around, many Mexicans will settle for the next-best approximation and rent a *narcopelícula.* This geysers-of-blood film genre that emerged during the mid-1970s—not coincidentally the same era that Bronson established himself as a major film draw throughout the world—is Mexico's most popular type of movie, consisting of little more than Mexican actors assuming Bronson's shoot-first, shoot-later wrinkled archetype. In fact, *narcopelícula's* most famous presence, eighty-four-year-old Mario Almada, has a career trajectory similar to Bronson's. Neither man hit his box-office stride until his fifties, and both made the same gleeful-vengeance film again and again even when the plot had the septuagenarians mowing down men a third their age. A bonus: both had the same fabulously sagging mustache.

So why the Mexican obsession with Bronson? One can approach the question via a psychocultural perspective and argue that Bronson embodied a sort of hypermachismo embedded in the Mexican male mind that determines an hombre's worth by how well he protects the women in his life. Mexican men are attracted to the Bronson characters, then, because his roles involve the failure and redemption of such a philosophy. Remember, Manhattan businessman Paul Kersey in the *Death Wish* films became a trigger-zealous guy only after the murder of his wife and the rape of his daughter, which stained his honor. Kersey regained his testosterone by killing man after man after man.

But let's cut the grad-student babble. When I was a child, my parents took me to the drive-in to watch Bronson flicks, their hands covering my eyes during the most violent scenes. Watching Bronson zip down opiated thugs was one of the few times my parents and their Mexican friends ventured into the English-speaking world—rains of bullets, after all, don't need subtitles.

13

Why is it that Mexicans can be put into two working classes: those who work their asses off while everyone else takes a siesta, and those who take a siesta while everyone else works their asses off? The MexiCAN and the MexiCANT?

PERSON UNDERSTANDABLY TICKED OFF

Dear Gabacho: PUTO, you have to realize it's the parents who never take the siesta—it's their children who slag off and become the stereotypical lazy Mexican gabachos so relish. In a 1993 sociological study, ethnographers Alejandro Portes and Min Zhou found that the more assimilated a Mexican-American youngster was, the worse his lot in life would be. "Seeing their parents and grandparents confined to humble menial jobs and increasingly aware of discrimination against them by the white mainstream," Portes and Zhou wrote, "U.S.-born children of earlier Mexican immigrants readily join a reactive subculture as a means of protecting their sense of self-worth." Translation: Mexican kids see their parents sweat and toil to move out of an apartment and into a dingy condo only to see gabachos dismiss them as wetbacks—and then resign from life. While the parents continue to work eighteen-hour days to make the rent, the kids leave for college, join an activist group such as MEChA, wear a Che shirt for a couple of years, and travel through Central America to "find themselves." They return as shiftless, lazy *flojos* who become vegetarians and talk of revolution while bouncing from collection job to collection job. In other words, they become Americans.

14

Why do Mexicans commit so many crimes? I've noticed police pursuits on the news, and the chase always turns up a Latino male.

LOOKING FOR A NEW JOHN WAYNE

Dear Gabacho: Look, just because Mexicans celebrate and romanticize violence and murder in film, song, art, television, popular culture, and marriage doesn't mean that Mexicans are more prone to violence than, say, Iraq-invading Americans. In fact, it's quite the opposite: a Rand Center paper, *Social Anatomy of Racial and Ethnic Disparities in Violence*, found that rates of violence for Latinos as compared with gabachos are actually 10 percent *lower*. Similar conclusions are found in 2002's *Latino Homicide: Immigration, Violence, and Community*; in it, author Ramiro Martínez examines homicide rates among Latinos in the preceding five years and finds that they're markedly lower than the national rate. I understand the misconception, since Mexicans or Hispanic-surnamed criminals usually get bragging rights on the eleven-o'clock news. Besides, crime has always been rampant among the poor—recall the similar glorification and high rates of violence in the Old West, the South, and among African-Americans.

So what's with this constant gabacho obsession with Mexicans and crime? You referenced it: the media, in a partnership with the Minuteman Project and NAFTA, have fostered a Mexican-crime conspiracy as loony as the fake moon landing. "The immigrant criminal has always projected a violent image in the public imagination, but the creation of a 'Latino bandito' formed a new caricature and gave life to a new ethnic stereotype," Martínez wrote. He dates it to the Mexican Revolution, which occurred right as silent films were revolutionizing America. "Newspapers documented the actions of Mexican revolutionaries on the battlefield, depicting bloodshed on the field between troops, translating real images of violence into fictional images of banditry, and in turn transforming the bandito into a criminal bent on violence. The stereotype of a bloodthirsty Mexican bandit became embedded in the public imagination. Mexicans were violent on the battlefield and off of it." America: you're so concerned about the 25 percent of jailed criminals who are supposedly illegal immigrants, what about the 75 percent who are not?

Reading

1. (p. 480) According to Arellano, why do Mexicans pronounce their names "in Spanish"?

2. (p. 480) What are some of the meanings that Arellano offers for the word *madre*?

3. (p. 481) Arellano compares the song "La Cucaracha" to another traditional satirical tune. What is it?

4. (p. 482) What are *gabachos*? Who are *metaleros*?

5. (p. 482) According to *¡Ask a Mexican!* why do Mexicans call white girls *güeras*?

6. (p. 485) What economist does the column refer to when explaining the purchase of expensive cars and trucks?

7. (p. 486) What does Arellano think of the term *Hispanic*?

8. (p. 486) What is one of the downsides of assimilation, according to *¡Ask a Mexican!*?

Thinking Critically

1. How would you describe the definitions Arellano gives in his welcome message? Who are they aimed at?

2. What is Arellano's attitude toward his *gabacho* questioners?

3. How does Arellano treat stereotypes about Mexicans?

4. Identify some of the passages from *¡Ask a Mexican!* that you found funniest, most memorable, and/or most irreverent. Explain why you think so, quoting from the passages.

Connecting

1. Like Arellano, Lalo Alcaraz in his cartoon *La Cucaracha* (p. 418) has an audience of both Latinos and non-Latinos. How do they attempt to appeal to both audiences? What differences do you find between their approaches?

Writing

1. What do you think Arellano's goal is as an interpreter of Mexican culture? In an essay, using specific examples from his columns, discuss what you think Arellano is trying to do with his writing. Be sure to discuss how effective you think he is in reaching his goals.

Creating

1. **Write a satirical question/answer column.** Imagine a question that someone might ask you about a group that you are part of. The group might be ethnic, cultural, or social, and the question may be a potentially offensive one. Write the question and make an attempt to answer it, using Arellano's column as a model if you'd like to.

50

DOMINGO MARTINEZ [b. 1972]

The Mimis

From The Boy Kings of Texas [2012]

GENRE: MEMOIR

Domingo Martinez's memoir The Boy Kings of Texas, *with its stories of South Texas life told with dark humor, and occasionally simply darkness, has launched him into the forefront of Mexican American writers. Martinez grew up near Brownsville, Texas, with his grandmother, his parents, and his two brothers and three sisters. After high school he briefly attended Texas A & I University–Kingsville but quit after a few unhappy and unsuccessful semesters. He stayed around for a while to work on a weekly political paper before leaving Texas, following his oldest brother to Seattle. While working on his memoir, a project that would occupy him for some fifteen years, Martinez won praise for the sections that he read on the popular National Public Radio show* This American Life. *Published in 2012,* The Boy Kings of Texas *received the National Book Award. He has followed it up with a second memoir, published in 2014, called* My Heart Is a Drunken Compass.*

In his memoir The Boy Kings of Texas, *from which "The Mimis" is drawn, Martinez revisits the most painful experiences of a childhood he describes as "an emotional concentration camp, held captive by a tyrant and his mother."* He said of the process of writing the book that he "was drawn toward the pain. If the memory felt uncomfortable, if it was something I knew our family didn't talk about, I'd attack it head-on."** Attack, for Martinez, means honest and even brutal description, even at the risk of upsetting his family members. Yet it can also mean finding the humor and the subtle ironies of his childhood, shown especially poignantly in "The Mimis." In this section of his memoir, Martinez writes of two of his sisters, who create a mirror image of their real*

*A quote from *The Boy Kings of Texas.*

**From a *New York Times* article, available at nytimes.com/2012/11/10/books/domingo-martinez-takes-a-trip-back-to-south-texas.html?_r=0.

*life. They imagine they are part of a wealthy family from an exotic
northern land rather than their poor Mexican family.*

As you read this excerpt from Martinez's memoir, note his obvious sympathy for his sisters. Think also about why the girls
develop their fantasy and why they are forced to abandon it.

Before they started junior high, my sisters Mare and Margie had preemp-
tively developed the fantasy of "the Mimis" between themselves as a
means to cope with any feelings of inferiority they might have otherwise
experienced by moving into the sinister world of teenage fashionistas,
which, in Brownsville, was always tinged with bordertown racism.

First, they dyed their brown-black hair blonde until it turned the color
and brittleness of hay, then they began dressing in Sergio Valente and
Gloria Vanderbilt fashions, and then finally, in further escalation, decided
to call each other, simply, Mimi. They had secretly reinvented themselves
for the adolescent phase of their lives, and then decided to let the rest of
us in on the secret on an "as-needed" basis.

At the time, the rest of the family had not consciously realized that our
job, as new Americans—and worse yet, as Texans—was to be as white
as possible, and we honestly didn't see their delusion as anything other
than another bewildering strata to our sisters' quest for a higher level of
superior fashion, as teenage girls do.

A typical conversation between them went like this:

"Mimi, do you like my new Jordache jeans?"   5

"Yes, Mimi, I do. Do I look rich in my new Nikes, Mimi?"

"Mimi, you look like a tennis player, Mimi."

"I know, Mimi. Maybe I should make Mom buy me a racquet."

To help reinforce this pathological delusion, Marge had enlisted the help
of Rex, a small gray terrier mix she had found rummaging in an overturned
garbage can on a street near the Matamoros Bridge. She cornered the poor
beast in an alley and caught it, lifting the matted, dreadlocked mutt by the
armpits and deciding, right there, that the dog was a poodle and that it
needed saving, naming it Rex. No one disagreed, or questioned why.

Rex was introduced to our family as the Mimis' fugue was buzzing at   10
its fever pitch, intoxicating everyone who came near and caught a whiff
of the Mimis' *Anais Anais* perfume. (We had all seen the commercials on
network television while watching *Dallas* or *Knots Landing*, and it was
a forbidden fragrance for rain-depressed English women with secret
muscular boyfriends who drove Jaguars dangerously through one-lane
unpaved Scottish roads, so the Mimis had to have it, and so they found

it at the local JC Penney, and had Mom pay for it.) Dan and Syl and me, we just kind of stank from the heat and dealt with it.

Anyhow, Rex's right hind leg had a malformed kneecap that made his leg jut stiffly at a forty-five-degree angle, so it looked as if Rex was in a constant state of micturation, even when he was walking or sprinting forward, like he had been distracted by some urgent event that demanded immediate investigation while he'd been peeing and had forgotten to lower his leg in charging forward.

The older Mimi, my sister formerly known as Marge, just overlooked this because she wasn't deathly allergic to furry animals like the younger Mimi, my sister formerly known as Mare. The older Mimi convinced our mother to adopt the dog and have his hair carved into poodle fashion, had even bought it colorful striped sweaters that made the near toothless dog pant wetly in the year-round South Texas heat.

With his fancy haircut and new powdery smell, Rex found himself terrifically misplaced on our property, about five miles outside of the Brownsville city limits. The other feral dogs that happened to be kept around didn't know what to make of him when he'd limp up to them and start barking, with his odd jutting leg, but thankfully they didn't kill him, just kind of got this look of annoyance on their dog faces and decided to avoid this new poofter that might be competing for the late afternoon dog swill Gramma would reluctantly put out at sundown.

Out there, among the outhouse and Gramma's pigsty, Rex looked as tragically displaced as his kneecap. But, in full appreciation and retrospect, perhaps that was the sort of companionship the older Mimi (Marge) had really been seeking out there, subconsciously, and had found in Rex someone as confused and dislocated as the Mimis felt in their designer jeans and trendy tennis shoes, but lacking access to an indoor toilet.

The shift to junior high had exposed the Mimis to new ideas of glam- 15 our and status, and for the first time they were really experiencing the sub- and superconscious derision that exists when cultures and races collide against one another in geopolitical reassignment, like you find in border towns, and they were smart enough to understand that which was never spoken about: None of this was ever, *ever*, pointed out. You created a polite fiction, and encouraged everyone to participate. Which is what the Mimis did.

And so the rest of us followed.

Marge and Mare, as the Mimis, had decided to align themselves with their more American—more European—genetics, even if it was through bad hair dyes and pretending not to understand Spanish.

Dad's genetic line was mostly of the Spaniard conquistador: He, like them, was tall, light skinned, and prone to fits of pork. Mom was light skinned, reddish in tint, and spoke English, so she was considered "white." We were—genetically—predominantly European. Gramma was the Indian; Gramma was the Aztec in the family. And since she had the balls in the family, we identified—culturally—as Mexican. Gramma had been made an American by Grampa, and Dad had been "naturalized" as an American when he was six years old. Mom, we would later come to understand, had a secret and very old American history.

And yet we all felt so terribly *untermensch°* that Marge and Mare had to have a psychotic episode in which we all participated to help them through junior high. We all helped in creating the Mimis.

It was really that simple: Fed up and humiliated with their circum- 20
stances, the Mimis decided to change them, retroactively.

They made a conscious decision and agreement that they would be—and act—rich and white, even if their family wasn't.

Grampa's death had plunged the barrio into a rivalry between his next younger brothers and Dad, who was seen as the illegitimate inheritor of the trucking business. They clearly felt that Gramma and Dad did not belong in the barrio and were certainly unworthy of inheriting the only viable business in that barrio, the trucking business Grampa built after he returned home from Korea. They wouldn't come right out and say it or do anything overt to draw business away from Dad, but after Grampa died the regular and paying customers who had been Grampa's were no longer Dad's and were now suspiciously doing business three houses to our west, with Grampa's brothers.

The trucking business began to disintegrate around Dad within the first few years, and he was started on his slow road toward desperation and religion.

Meanwhile, the Mimis had made their decision to be two blue-blooded, trust-funded tennis bunnies from Connecticut, accidentally living in Brownsville, Texas, with us, a poor Mexican family they had somehow befriended while undergoing some Dickensian series of misfortunes.

For those of us watching, the whole "Mimi" thing took on a momentum 25
of its own, though we seriously didn't think it would last. But at some point it took hold, and by then no one thought it peculiar, especially those in the family who didn't speak English or could not understand the Mimis when they showed up at family gatherings.

"*Yo no puedo-o hablar-o Español-o,°*" one of the Mimis would say to an uncle or cousin, who more often than not would linger lasciviously around them, at first conflicted by the idea of being turned on by so young a relative and then mentally calculating just how distantly related

untermensch: German for *subhuman*, referring to "inferior people."
Yo no puedo-o hablar-o Español-o: A play on *No puedo hablar español,* for "I can't speak Spanish."

they were and tabulating his odds at scoring with this new white chick
who just happened to show up at this barrio party.

But only after two or three beers.

"Mimi, how did you like my Spanish?"

"Oh, Mimi, it's getting really good."

"Mimi, do you think they understood me?"   30

"Oh, Mimi, who cares?"

Mom developed a fascination with the Mimis, too, like she couldn't
believe her luck, now that she was related to royalty. Feeding into their
fantasy gave her one of her own, so she was always ready for an air-
conditioned trip to the mall.

She took the little clothes budget reserved for us boys, my brother and
me, and patched it into the Mimis' wardrobe, because it was a sign of
status for the family that the Mimis look their best; it is important for
families of little wealth to have their daughters be as attractive as possible
for means of social elevation.

In this way, it became acceptable for the Mimis to take the lion's share
of the children's clothing budget, and none of the rest of us could question it, even though at the time, we didn't exactly know why.

But it still felt wrong.   35

Clothes would come in and out of fashion so quickly that I was often
left with the Mimis' recently stylish hand-me-downs. No one else in my
grade school was remotely label conscious, or capable of reading in English, really, so it passed unnoticed that most of my clothes were made
for glamorous junior high school girls. Almost every child at my school
came from recently immigrated families—kids so poor they'd save half
their free lunch to share with their younger siblings at home, their heads
shaved to rid them of lice.

My best friend, Arthur, he noticed, though. He was part black and part
Mexican and had just moved to Brownsville from some big city slum in
Michigan, where his mother's boyfriend had been employed at a GM
factory, and he read labels.

"Hey, Dom," he said in that lilting, sort of inner-urban street funk, "Yo,
man; you're wearing a girl's shirt. Or is Esprit making baggy boy's shirts
now, too?"

I loved Arthur dearly and was totally embarrassed. So to change the
subject I slugged him high in the chest and ran away crying, him in his
bald head chasing me down to punch me back in my girl's blouse.

If she had any guilt, I imagine the justification my mother probably   40
used was that my older brother and I would just ruin our clothes, working with Dad in the sandpit and under the greasy trucks. It made better
sense for the Mimis to be in high fashion than for the feral boys to ruin
their clothes.

"Mimi, you look just like Jennifer Beals in *Flashdance*. You should join the dance team at school."

"I know, Mimi, I think so, too."

"Mimi, I think you should dye your hair back to its original color, 'Ash.'"

"I know, Mimi, I'm trying."

"Mimi, is your dog OK? He just spit out another tooth."   45

During this time, Dan's eyesight was so poor, people thought he was Asian, so often did he squint. He couldn't read the blackboard in school and constantly ran into corners or short, skinny people. In every photo he took in junior high, he looked like he was trying to see into the photographer's eyes, through the camera's lens. This, of course, went entirely unnoticed, and it was the younger Mimi (Mare), with 20/20 vision, who got vanity glasses with her name etched in gold script in the corner. Dan wouldn't get glasses until he was in the military, when he was seventeen, some four years later.

"Mimi, you don't need those glasses, Mimi."

"Mimi, I do need them, Mimi. They make me look rich. They say my name in the corner, 'Mary' Mimi."

"Mimi, I think there's something wrong with Rex."

"Yes, Mimi, your dog doesn't have any teeth."   50

"No, Mimi, it's not that. He smells like pee all the time now."

Always a bit incontinent, Rex would not mind if, when he was attempting to pee, he'd just spray the underside of his own twisted leg during the larger part of the activity, because he could hardly lift it out of the way of the hot stream anyhow. Now, he didn't even attempt to move his bad leg out of the way, he just kind of let it have it where he stood, looking around like a confused Alzheimer's patient, panting breathily all the while. Our indoor plant pots, usually a collected oasis of old stinky dog urine, were now suspiciously micturation free. This had to mean he was pissing elsewhere, and freely.

Rex was definitely circling the dog drain.

After a few months of studying the toothless, stinky gray dog, I finally checked out a book on dogs from the school library. I read that people who have allergies to dogs are not allergic to poodles because poodle hair is almost identical to human hair. The younger Mimi (Mare) still could not get within a few feet of Rex without lapsing into violent sneezing fits, fits we were afraid could trigger asthma attacks. For me this clearly illustrated that the dog was not a poodle, but the older Mimi (Marge) would not hear of it. "You're just jealous of Rex," she said. And she was right.

Eventually, Dad's failure at navigating the business left to him—and   55
usurped by Gramma—crept into the Mimis' fantasy. Dad made a decision that would make his family as Mexican as his mother. He decided

that as soon as school ended, Mom would take the Mimis and Syl and drive them to California to participate in the seasonal grape harvest with the migrant workers, to meet up with Dad's cousins who did this periodically, since the Mimis were now fourteen and fifteen and Syl was sixteen, and they could all, with Mom, collect a full salary. They would be treated like adults there, paid the same as everyone else.

Mom, I remember, was horrified at the implications, at the shame of having to send her virginal and royal daughters out to the fields. Plus, Dad's extended family out in California were very different from us, wild and frightening and . . . well, Californian. (Texas Mexicans and California Mexicans are very different from each other, like the Scottish and the Irish—fundamentally the same genetic code, but completely different in accent and habits.)

The Mimis, though, were undaunted. They did not understand the implications.

"Mimi, we're going to California!"

"Oh my God, Mimi! We're going to be 'Valley Girls'!"

"Mimi, gag me with a spoon, Mimi!"   60

"Mimi, your roots are showing."

We packed up Mom, the Mimis, Rex, and Syl in the beige 1980 Pontiac Bonneville, already an antique on its second engine and failing transmission, and they drove out of Brownsville and the Rio Grande Valley, eventually took I-10 to Indio, California, and into the Coachella Valley where they would pick grapes for three months like Steinbeck's Okies, way back when. Dan and I were left seething with envy.

Although, the year after the Mimis went to California, I would take this ride as well and also ended up picking grapes for the summer, and I would realize that all my envy was utterly unfounded. That we had been "migrant workers" for that period didn't occur to me, or to anyone else. That label would never stick. Could never stick. We couldn't descend to that level. We just had to do it to help out Dad; that was all. Desperate circumstances calling for desperate measures and all that. This is actually one of the few positive lessons I learned from my father: Sometimes you need to do humiliating things for work, to get through bad times. And it actually taught me quite a bit, that summer I spent there.

When it was my turn to go to California and pick grapes, I was stuck with Dad a lot of the time, which I heavily resented, but in retrospect, I realize now that he taught me more during that summer than he had taught me in the thirteen or so years previous. In the deep early morning, when the vineyards were still damp with the morning dew, and the hordes of pickers were lining up and splitting into work groups and preparing for a difficult day, Dad held me back, had me blend in with him toward the back of whatever mob we were assigned.

"*Cálmate, cálmate,*" he'd say to me, when the whistle blew at five o'clock   65
in the morning and everyone was off to work, one person on one side of the
vine row, and his partner on the other. Every bunch was sure to get picked
this way. Dad, instead, was asking me to stay back, slow down. Keep still.

I kept still. He went to his side of the row, and I started to clip the
grapes. Slowly. Making sure not to lose a digit. I clipped the bunch, held
it up in the morning light, looking for rotten grapes, and then artistically
clipped those free. I was making a still life. This kept me preoccupied
and I didn't hear from Dad for a while, and my attention was suddenly
seized by the family clipping away next to us. They were insane: clipping
left and right, high and low, competitively throwing bunches into boxes
and having their children cart the boxes to the front, where they'd be
picked up, assessed, registered, and transported to the flatbed truck,
where strong toughs were in charge of loading the back. They were filling
up six, seven, eight boxes to my one. But mine was prettier.

Eventually, I looked through the vines on my row and saw that
Dad had found himself a nice shady spot and had cozied himself up
against a post, was taking a snooze, looking very much the picture of the
Mexican-taking-a-siesta thing, but without the sombrero. Just a baseball
cap and a mustache. So I slowed down, too.

Asking him about it later, he said, "What the hell was the point? Those
other people are going to win that bonus for the most boxes because they
had nothing else except for this, and we get paid the same anyway."

Don't get me wrong: We would eventually get to work and make a nota-
ble showing of progress by the end of the day, but not until we were good
and ready, when the sun had warmed up a little and we had had breakfast.

Anyhow, the Mimis' little excursion as migrant workers was quite differ-   70
ent. When they were at their peak, the Mimis had been capable of creating
a real sort of magic around them, enchanting both people and places, in
such a way that you could be looking at the same dreary landscape as
them, the same terrible and hopeless event, and while you might be miserable and bitter, they would be beaming, enthralled, and enthusiastically
hopeful. And then, if you got near them, or were blessed enough to maybe
talk to them, you would walk away feeling the same way they felt, too.

They were a gift to everyone who was lucky enough to get caught in
their Anais Anais, the Mimis. They made all of us Americans.

But it was too much for even them, the reality of this trip. Sadly, I
think it was childhood's end for the Mimis; the vineyards had somehow
inverted their secret garden, and the low door in the wall had closed shut
behind them.

The year previous, when they had made the first trip to California, the
Mimis had indeed become Valley Girls: the hippest, cutest, best-dressed
migrant workers of that year, and very likely for many years to come. I

would imagine those migrant workers had had every quiet, onanistic nighttime wish come true, working alongside girls with movie-star looks, picking grapes at the vineyards.

The older Mimi (Marge) continued to dress like Jennifer Beals in *Flashdance* out in the fields, where the sun would sizzle any inch of exposed skin. She wore a spaghetti-strapped, red and white–striped Esprit top, white cotton shorts, and a matching headband with her red and white leather Nike tennis shoes, and took pictures of the vineyards and the workers with her Canon AE-1. Her headband kept a white division of skin on her forehead from tanning along with the rest of her face, and as a result, she was forced to wear headbands for a few months afterward, way after headbands were out of fashion.

Eventually, though, even she started dressing like the rest of the migrant workers, or else she would have died of heat stroke. There were no photos taken of that. 75

The younger Mimi (Mare) did not fare any better. Her vanity glasses with the fake lenses were scratched well beyond recovery, even blighting out her name etched in the gold cursive. Her roots grew out eventually, except this time, her hair turned a lighter brown as a result of the heat and the pesticides of the grape fields of Southern California.

The hard work went on all summer, and eventually it became bitter enough to breach even the walls of the Mimis' perfectly constructed fantasy, which had once withstood the ugly reality that had been screaming at the door of the Mimis' magic garden: their father's failures in keeping his family together. The wolf was now breaking through, with each snip of the clippers, and each box of grapes they had to fill, Mom and the Mimis. Oh, and Syl.

And so sadly, eventually even they were humiliated, and the delusion of wealth that had kept the family's idea of itself buoyant was deflated and left buried in a Californian vineyard, because when they returned to Brownsville—the Bonneville limping in on its second transmission—no one ever mentioned the Mimis again. They had been left behind in the grape fields, and it was Marge and Mare who returned in their place.

As it happened even Rex was finally able to break out of the fantasy of the Mimis. He found his own low door in the garden, before it disappeared.

He wasn't among the returning party, though we were left with enough fleas in the carpet and the vague smell of urine to remember him for many, many years after. 80

He died unexpectedly one night, when they were still in California. Mare found him first, awoken by her allergies, and stumbled across Rex's still body on the floor on her way to the bathroom.

"Hey, Marge, wake up," she growled back to her sleeping sister. "Your dog's dead. It's four fifteen; time to go."

In his dying spasms, Rex's deformed leg had rigored stiffly into a 90-degree angle away from his body in a final salute and "thank you," I'm sure, for the hospitality of his final days. He was that kind of dog, always minding his manners. He was buried with the help of some unknown migrant in an unmarked grave out in the grape fields, but regally, in a quiet funeral fit for a dog king, a very long way from the Matamoros Bridge where he had started with the Mimis.

Reading

1. Where do the Mimis pretend to be from? Why, according to the story they tell, are they in Brownsville?
2. What causes the Mimis to end their fantasy?

Thinking Critically

1. What attitude toward their real life do you think Mare and Marge have, as indicated by the Mimis episode?
2. What reaction do you think Martinez expects this story to draw from his audience? What is your own reaction? Why do you feel this way?

Connecting

1. Rochelle, in Christine Granados's story "The Bride" (p. 467) comes from a family similar to that of the Mimis. Is her fantasy life similar? Do the girls' fantasies all come to an end for the same reason? Do Martinez and Granados have similar attitudes about the subjects of their stories?

Writing

1. In an essay, write about what you think Martinez's attitude toward his sisters is in this chapter. Does he sympathize with them? Do you think he shares their fantasy? Support your argument with quotations from the text.

Creating

1. **Write a dialogue that addresses fantasy and truth.** One of the most amusing sections of "The Mimis" is Martinez's rendering of his sisters' conversations with each other. Write a dialogue between two people who are engaged in a similar fantasy and a third person who knows the truth.

Acknowledgments

Oscar "Zeta" Acosta. "Chapter 89" from *The Revolt of the Cockroach People* by Oscar "Zeta" Acosta, copyright © 1989 by Oscar "Zeta" Acosta. Used by permission of Alfred A. Knopf, an imprint of the Knopf Doubleday Publishing Group, a division of Penguin Random House LLC. All rights reserved.

Lalo Alcaraz. Cartoons from *La Cucaracha*, by Lalo Alcaraz, © 2002 and © 2003 Lalo Alcaraz. Distributed by UNIVERSAL UCLICK. Reprinted with permission. All rights reserved.

Alurista. "What Now . . . Corn" from *Tunaluna* by Alurista. Reprinted by permission of Aztlan Libre Press. "fértil polvo" is reprinted by permission of the author.

Rudolfo Anaya. "Dos" from *Bless Me, Ultima*. Copyright © Rudolfo Anaya 1974. Published in hardcover, paperback, and ebook by Warner Books, an imprint of Hachette Book Group, in 1994; originally published by TQS Publications. By permission of Susan Bergholz Literary Services, New York and Lamy, NM. All rights reserved.

Gloria Anzaldúa. "La conciencia de la mestiza/Towards a New Consciousness" from *Borderlands/La Frontera: The New Mestiza*. Copyright © 1987, 1999, 2007, 2012 by Gloria Anzaldúa. Reprinted by permission of Aunt Lute Books. www.auntlute.com

Gustavo Arellano. Excerpt from ¡*Ask a Mexican!* Reprinted with the permission of Scribner, a Division of Simon & Schuster, Inc., from ¡*Ask a Mexican!* by Gustavo Arellano. Copyright © 2007 by Village Voice Media Holdings, L.L.C. All rights reserved.

Ron Arias. Excerpt from *The Road to Tamazúnchale* by Ron Arias. Text © 1987 by Ron Arias. Reprinted by permission of Bilingual Press/Editorial Bilingüe, Arizona State University, Tempe, AZ.

Jimmy Santiago Baca. "I Will Remain" and "Immigrants in Our Own Land" by Jimmy Santiago Baca from *Immigrants in Our Own Land*, copyright © 1979 by Jimmy Santiago Baca. Reprinted by permission of New Directions Publishing Corporation.

Álvar Núñez Cabeza de Vaca. "How the Following Day They Brought Other Sick People" from *Chronicle of the Narváez Expedition* by Álvar Núñez Cabeza de Vaca, translated by Fanny Bandelier, revised and annotated by Harold Augenbraum, revised translation and notes copyright © 2002 by Harold Augenbraum. Used by permission of Penguin Books, an imprint of Penguin Publishing Group, a division of Penguin Random House LLC.

Ana Castillo. "Saturdays" and "A Marriage of Mutes" from *My Father Was a Toltec*. Copyright © 1995 by Ana Castillo. Reprinted by permission of the author.

Lorna Dee Cervantes. "Poem for the Young White Man Who Asked Me How I, an Intelligent, Well-Read Person Could Believe in the War between Races" from *Emplumada* by Lorna Dee Cervantes, copyright © 1981. Reprinted by permission of the University of Pittsburgh Press. "A Chicano Poem" from *Huizache*, No. 2, Fall 2012. Reprinted by permission of the author.

Denise Chávez. "¡Híjole! In the Darkness" from *Loving Pedro Infante* by Denise Chávez. Copyright © 2001 by Denise Chávez. Reprinted by permission of Farrar, Straus and Giroux.

Sandra Cisneros. "Woman Hollering Creek" from *Woman Hollering Creek*. Copyright © 1991 by Sandra Cisneros. Published by Vintage Books, a division of Penguin Random House, and originally in hardcover by Random House. By permission of Susan Bergholz Literary Services, New York and Lamy, NM. All rights reserved.

Abelardo "Lalo" Delgado. "Stupid America" and "The Chicano Manifesto" are reprinted with permission from the publisher of *Here Lies Lalo* by Abelardo "Lalo" Delgado (© 2011 Arte Público Press–University of Houston).

Ernesto Galarza. Excerpt from *Barrio Boy* by Ernesto Galarza. Copyright © 2011 by the University of Notre Dame Press. Reprinted by permission of the publisher.

Dagoberto Gilb. "Maria de Covina" from *Woodcuts of Women*. Copyright © 2001 by Dagoberto Gilb. Used by permission of Grove/Atlantic, Inc. Any third party use of this material, outside of this publication, is prohibited.

Guillermo Gómez-Peña. "Real-Life Border Thriller" from *The New World Border* by Guillermo Gómez-Peña. © 2001 City Lights Books. Reprinted by permission of the publisher.

Jovita González. "The Bullet-Swallower" is reprinted with permission from the publisher of *The Woman Who Lost Her Soul and Other Stories* by Jovita González (© 2000 Arte Público Press–University of Houston).

Rodolfo "Corky" Gonzales. "I Am Joaquín" is reprinted with permission from the publisher of *Message to Aztlán* by Rodolfo "Corky" Gonzales (© 2001 Arte Público Press–University of Houston).

Christine Granados. "The Bride" from *Brides and Sinners in El Chuco* by Christine Granados © 2006. Arizona Board of Regents. Reprinted by permission of the University of Arizona Press.

The Hernandez Brothers. "Chiro el Indio" from *Love and Rockets: New Stories No. 1*. Reprinted by permission of Fantagraphics Books.

Juan Felipe Herrera. "Exiles" and "Inside the Jacket" from *Half of the World in Light: New and Selected Poems* by Juan Felipe Herrera © 2008. Arizona Board of Regents. Reprinted by permission of the University of Arizona Press.

Rolando Hinojosa. "To Begin With, a Dedication," "Thus It Was Fulfilled," "A Sunday in Klail," "Los Leguizamón," and "Coyotes" ("The People of Belken County"—editor's title) are reprinted with permission of the publisher of *Estampas del Valle y Otras Obras* by Rolando Hinojosa (© 2014 Arte Público Press–University of Houston).

Angela de Hoyos. "Go Ahead, Ask Her" and "You Will Grow Old" are reprinted with permission from the publisher of *Woman, Woman* by Angela de Hoyos (© 1995 Arte Público Press–University of Houston).

Josefina López. Act I from *Real Women Have Curves* by Josefina López is reprinted by permission of the author.

Lorraine López. "Soy la Avon Lady" from *Soy la Avon Lady and Other Stories*. Copyright © 2002 Lorraine López. All rights reserved. Published by Curbstone Press.

Demetria Martínez. Excerpt from *Mother Tongue* by Demetria Martínez, copyright © 1994 by Demetria Martínez. Used by permission of Ballantine Books, an imprint of Random House, a division of Penguin Random House LLC. All rights reserved.

Domingo Martinez. "The Mimis" from *The Boy Kings of Texas* by Domingo Martinez (Lyons Press). Reprinted by permission of The Rowman & Littlefield Publishing Group.

Gary Soto. "The Elements of San Joaquin" from *New and Selected Poems* by Gary Soto. Copyright © 1995 by Gary Soto. Excerpt from "Where Were You When You First Heard of Air-Conditioning" from pages 24–25 of *A Natural Man* by Gary Soto. Copyright © 1999 by Gary Soto. Used with permission of Chronicle Books LLC, San Francisco. Visit ChronicleBooks.com.

Mario Suárez. "Maestría" from *Chicano Sketches: Short Stories* by Mario Suárez copyright © 2004. Arizona Board of Regents. Reprinted by permission of the University of Arizona Press.

Carmen Tafolla. "Tía Sofía" and "Curandera" from *Curandera*. Copyright © 1983, 1987, 2012 by Carmen Tafolla. Reprinted by permission of Wings Press.

Sabine R. Ulibarrí. "My Grandma Smoked Cigars" (1977) from *Mi Abuela Fumaba Puros, y Otros Cuentos de Tierra Amarilla*. Ulibarrí/Anaya (Quinto Sol, 1977). Reprinted by permission of Carlos A. Ulibarrí.

Luis Alberto Urrea. Excerpt (pages 3–14) from *The Hummingbird's Daughter* by Luis Alberto Urrea. Copyright © 2005 by Luis Alberto Urrea. Reprinted by permission of Little, Brown and Company.

Luis Valdez. *Las Dos Caras del Patroncito* and *Los Vendidos* are reprinted with permission from the publisher of *Luis Valdez: Early Works* by Luis Valdez (© 1990 Arte Público Press–University of Houston).

Tino Villanueva. "I Too Have Walked My Barrio Streets" from *Shaking Off the Dark* by Tino Villanueva (1998 Bilingual Press/Editorial Bilingüe). Reprinted by permission of the publisher. Selection from *Scene from the Movie GIANT*. Copyright © 1993 by Tino Villanueva (Curbstone Press). All rights reserved. Reprinted by permission of Northwestern University Press.

Helena María Viramontes. "Neighbors" is reprinted with permission from the publisher of *The Moths and Other Stories* by Helena María Viramontes (© 1995 Arte Público Press–University of Houston).

Index of Authors and Titles

Index of First Lines